Microsoft®
Visual Basic® 5.0
ActiveX™ Controls Reference

Microsoft Press

PUBLISHED BY
Microsoft Press
A Division of Microsoft Corporation
One Microsoft Way
Redmond, Washington 98052-6399

Library of Congress Cataloging-in-Publication Data
Microsoft Visual Basic 5.0 ActiveX Controls Reference.
     p.   cm.
   ISBN 1-57231-508-3
   1. Microsoft Visual Basic.   2. Basic (Computer program language).
  3. ActiveX.   I. Microsoft Corporation.
  QA76.73.B3M556   1997
  005.2'768--dc21   97-3523
                                           CIP

Printed and bound in the United States of America.

1 2 3 4 5 6 7 8 9   QMQM   2 1 0 9 8 7

Distributed to the book trade in Canada by Macmillan of Canada, a division of Canada Publishing Corporation.

A CIP catalogue record for this book is available from the British Library.

Microsoft Press books are available through booksellers and distributors worldwide. For further information about international editions, contact your local Microsoft Corporation office. Or contact Microsoft Press International directly at fax (206) 936-7329.

Acquisitions Editor: Eric Stroo
Project Editor: Maureen Williams Zimmerman

Contents

ImageList Control   47

Internet Transfer Control 63

ListView Control 87

Masked Edit Control 181

MSComm Control 379

MSFlexGrid Control 407

Multimedia MCI Control   471

TabStrip Control   613

Toolbar Control   629

ActiveX Controls Overview

The ActiveX™ Control Reference provides an alphabetic reference for each of the controls included with the Microsoft Visual Basic programming system. Each ActiveX control is documented in its own section, providing information for the properties, events, methods, and functions for that control.

The information in this manual is the best available at the time of publication. In some cases, more up-to-date information may be available in online Help.

Contents

- What Is an ActiveX Control?
- Installing and Registering ActiveX Controls
- Upgrading VBX Controls to ActiveX controls
- Loading ActiveX Controls
- ActiveX Control Icons
- Data Bound ActiveX Controls
- The About Property
- Control Class
- Creating, Running, and Distributing Executable (.exe) Files
- Required ActiveX Control Files

What Is an ActiveX Control?

An ActiveX control is an extension to the Visual Basic Toolbox. You use ActiveX controls just as you would any of the standard built-in controls, such as the CheckBox control. When you add an ActiveX control to a program, it becomes part of the development and run-time environment and provides new functionality for your application.

ActiveX controls leverage your capabilities as a Visual Basic programmer by retaining some familiar properties, events, and methods, such as the Name property, which behave as you would expect. Then, however, the ActiveX controls feature methods and properties that greatly increase your flexibility and capability as a Visual Basic programmer.

For example, the Visual Basic Professional and Enterprise editions include the Windows Common controls that allow you to create applications with the look and feel of Windows 95 toolbars, status bars, and tree views of directory structures. Other controls allow you to create applications that take full advantage of the Internet.

Installing and Registering ActiveX Controls

At setup, the Professional and Enterprise Editions automatically install and register ActiveX controls in the \Windows\System or System32 directory. You are then able to use the ActiveX controls at design time to build your applications.

If you plan to create a setup program for your application, you'll need to include information on any ActiveX controls in the Setup.lst file. For more information, see Chapter 17, "Distributing Your Applications," in the *Visual Basic Programmer's Guide.*

Note It is a violation of your license agreement to copy and distribute any information from the "Licenses" section of the system registry.

Upgrading VBX Controls to ActiveX Controls

If you have a project with VBX custom controls that you'd like to replace with ActiveX controls, Visual Basic can do this automatically. Conversion is only possible for VBX custom controls for which replacement ActiveX controls exist on your system. For more information, see Chapter 4, "Managing Projects," in the *Visual Basic Programmer's Guide.*

The following VBX custom controls are no longer supported in Visual Basic 5.0. However, 32-bit ActiveX versions can be found as .ocx files in the \Tools\Controls directory of your Visual Basic CD-ROM:

- AniButton
- Gauge
- Graph
- KeyState
- MSGrid
- Outline
- Spin
- ThreeD

To install these controls, you will have to register the controls using the Regsvr32 application, which is also available in the Tools directory. For instructions on how to use the Regsvr32 application, consult the Controls.txt file in the \Tools\Controls directory.

Loading ActiveX Controls

ActiveX controls have the file name extension .ocx. You can use the ActiveX controls provided with Visual Basic 5.0 or obtain additional controls from third-party developers.

You can use ActiveX controls and other insertable objects to your project by adding them to the Toolbox.

Note   Visual Basic ActiveX controls are 32-bit controls. Some third-party developers offer ActiveX controls which are 16-bit controls, and these cannot be used in Visual Basic version 5.0.

▶ To add a control to a project's Toolbox

1 On the **Project** menu, click **Components** to display the **Components** dialog box, as seen in figure 1.1.

 Tip   You can also display the dialog box by right-clicking on the Toolbox.

2 Items listed in this dialog box include all registered insertable objects, designers, and ActiveX controls.

3 To add an ActiveX control to the Toolbox, select the check box to the left of the control name.

4 Click **OK** to close the **Components** dialog box. All of the ActiveX controls that you selected will now appear in the Toolbox.

Figure 1.1 The Components dialog box

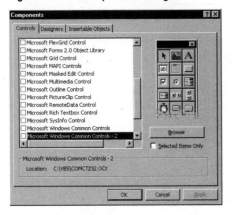

To add ActiveX controls to the Components dialog box, click the Browse button, and locate files with the .ocx file name extension. These files are commonly installed in your \Windows\System or System32 directory. When you add an ActiveX control to the list of available controls, Visual Basic automatically selects its check box in the Components dialog box.

ActiveX Control Icons

When you add an ActiveX control to your project, its icon is displayed in the Visual Basic Toolbox. You can select the ActiveX control by clicking this icon.

The icons for the ActiveX controls are listed in the following table.

Icon	Control	Allows you to
	Animation	Play .avi files soundlessly.
	Communications	Provide complete serial communications for your applications. Allows the transmission and reception of data through a serial port.
	ImageList	Contain a collection of images that can be used by other controls. This control is intended to be used as a central repository of images for an application. Windows Common Control.
	Internet Transfer	Connect to the Internet using the HTTP and FTP protocols.
	ListView	Display data in one of four different views: icons, small icons, list, and report. Windows Common Control.
	MAPI message	Develop mail-enabled applications that use MAPI functionality. This control allows the user to perform a variety of messaging system functions.

(continued)

Icon	Control	Allows you to
	MAPI session	Develop mail-enabled applications that use MAPI functionality. This control establishes a MAPI session.
	Masked edit	Restrict data input as well as display formatted data output. Can be a *bound* control. Similar to the standard text box.
	Multimedia MCI	Manage the recording and playback of multimedia files on Media Control Interface (MCI) devices.
	Picture clip	Display a portion of a source bitmap on a form or in a picture box.
	ProgressBar	Graphically show the progress of an operation by filling a rectangle with chunks from left to right as the operation proceeds. Windows Common Control.
	RichTextBox	Let the end user enter and edit text while providing more advanced formatting features than the standard TextBox control. Windows Common Control.
	Slider	Provide a graphic interface for setting values or ranges of values. Contains a slider and optional tick marks. Windows Common Control.
	Tabbed Dialog	Provide an easy way of presenting several dialog boxes or screens of information on a single form.
	StatusBar	Show a status bar as a window, usually at the bottom of a parent form, through which an application can display various kinds of status data. The StatusBar control can contain a maximum of sixteen panels. Windows Common Control.
	SysInfo	Monitor various parameters of the Windows operating system and notify your application of changes in status.
	TabStrip	Create tabbed dialog boxes. Windows Common Control.
	Toolbar	Create a toolbar with individual Button objects which can be programmed to correspond to frequently used functions of an application. Windows Common Control.
	TreeView	Display hierarchical information such as the headings in a document or the entries in an index. Windows Common Control.
	UpDown	Associate with a "buddy" control to let the user scroll through a property value of the buddy control. Windows Common Control.
	VCChart	Create pie, bar, line, and other charts.
	Winsock UDP	Send data to other computers using either the TCP or UDP protocol.

Data Bound ActiveX Controls

The RichTextBox and Masked edit controls are *bound* controls. This means that they can be linked to a data control and can display field values for the current record in the data set. These controls can also write out values to the data set.

For More Information For more on using bound controls, see Chapter 14, "Accessing Databases with the Data Control," in the *Visual Basic Programmer's Guide*.

The ActiveX Control About Property

Some ActiveX controls were developed by independent software vendors. If you would like more information about a control's vendor, click the control and press F4 to display the **Properties** window. Double-click the About property in the **Properties** window to open a dialog box that displays information about the vendor.

ActiveX Control Class

The class name for each ActiveX control is listed in the following table. (The class name for a control also appears in the Properties window.)

Control	Class name
Animation	Animation
Communications	MSComm
ImageList	ImageList
Internet Transfer	Inet
ListView	ListView
MAPI	MapiSession, MapiMessages
Masked edit	MaskEdBox
MS FlexGrid	MSFlexGrid
Multimedia MCI	MMControl
Picture clip	PictureClip
ProgressBar	ProgressBar
RichTextBox	RichTextBox
Slider	Slider
Microsoft Tabbed Dialog Control	SSTab
StatusBar	StatusBar
SysInfo	SysInfo

(continued)

Control	Class name
TabStrip	TabStrip
Toolbar	Toolbar
TreeView	TreeView
UpDown	UpDown
Visual Components Chart	VCChart
Winsock	Winsock

Creating, Running, and Distributing Executable (.exe) Files

To run your application under Microsoft Windows outside of Visual Basic, you need to create an executable (.exe) file. You create executable files for applications that use ActiveX controls the same as you would for any other application. There are a few issues to consider, however, when running such an application.

Visual Basic Executable (.exe) Files

An ActiveX control file is accessed both by Visual Basic and by applications created with Visual Basic. When you run an executable file that contains an ActiveX control, the .ocx file associated with it must be registered in the system registry. Otherwise, the application will not be able to find the code needed to create the control.

If a control cannot be found, the Visual Basic run-time DLL generates the error message "File Not Found." If you want to distribute an application that uses ActiveX controls, it is recommended that your installation procedure copy all required .ocx files into the user's \Windows\System directory. Your installation procedure should also register the required controls in the system registry.

You can freely distribute any application you create with the Visual Basic to any Microsoft Windows user. (The Setup Wizard included with Visual Basic provides tools to help you write setup programs that install your application.) Users will need copies of the following:

- The Visual Basic run-time file (Vbrun50032.dll).

- Any .ocx files.

- Additional DLLs, as required by your application or by ActiveX controls.

Required ActiveX Control Files

The files required by most ActiveX controls are listed in the following table.

Control	Required files
Animation	ComCt232.ocx
Communications	Mscomm32.ocx
ImageList	Comctl32.ocx
Internet Transfer	MSInet.ocx
ListView	Comctl32.ocx
MAPI	Msmapi32.ocx
Masked edit	Msmask32.ocx
MSFlex Grid	Msflexgrid.ocx
Multimedia MCI	Mci32.ocx
Picture clip	Picclp32.ocx
ProgressBar	Comctl32.ocx
RichTextBox	Richtx32.ocx
Slider	Comctl32.ocx
Microsoft Tabbed Dialog Control	Tabctl32.ocx
StatusBar	Comctl32.ocx
TabStrip	Comctl32.ocx
Toolbar	Comctl32.ocx
TreeView	Comctl32.ocx
UpDown	ComCt232.ocx
Visual Components Chart	VCChart.ocx
Winsock	MSWinsck.ocx

Microsoft Mail or Microsoft Exchange for Windows electronic mail system required.

Multimedia PC required.

Microsoft Windows Common Control.

Document Conventions

Visual Basic documentation uses the following typographic conventions.

Convention	Description
Sub, **If**, **ChDir**, **Print**, **True**, **Debug**	Words in bold with initial letter capitalized indicate language-specific keywords.
setup	Words you are instructed to type appear in bold.
object, *varname*, *arglist*	Italic, lowercase letters indicate placeholders for information you supply.
pathname, ***filenumber***	Bold, italic, and lowercase letters indicate placeholders for arguments where you can use either positional or named-argument syntax.
[*expressionlist*]	In syntax, items inside brackets are optional.
{**While** | **Until**}	In syntax, braces and a vertical bar indicate a mandatory choice between two or more items. You must choose one of the items unless all of the items are also enclosed in brackets. For example: [{**This** | **OrThat**}]
ESC, ENTER	Words in small capital letters indicate key names and key sequences.
ALT+F1, CTRL+R	A plus sign (+) between key names indicates a combination of keys. For example, ALT+F1 means hold down the ALT key while pressing the F1 key.

Code Conventions

The following code conventions are used:

Sample Code	Description
`MyString = "Hello, world!"`	This font is used for code, variables, and error message text.
`' This is a comment.`	An apostrophe (') introduces code comments.

`MyVar = "This is an " _`
`& "example" _`
`& " of how to continue code."`
	A space and an underscore (_) continue a line of code.

Animation Control

The **Animation** control allows you to create buttons which display animations, such as .avi files, when clicked. The control can play only AVI files that have no sound. In addition, the **Animation** control can display only uncompressed .avi files or .avi files that have been compressed using Run-Length Encoding (RLE).

Remarks

If you attempt to load an .avi file that includes sound data or that is in a format not supported by the control, an error (error 35752) is returned.

An example of this control is the file copy progress bar in Windows 95, which uses an **Animation** control. Pieces of paper "fly" from one folder to another while the copy operation executes.

See Also

Multimedia MCI Control

Properties

AutoPlay Property, **BackColor, ForeColor** Properties, **BackStyle** Property (Animation Control), **Center** Property **Container** Property, **DragIcon** Property, **DragMode** Property, **Enabled** Property, **Height, Width** Properties, **HelpContextID** Property, **hWnd** Property, **Index** Property, **Left, Top** Properties, **Name** Property, **Object** Property, **OLEDropMode** Property, **Parent** Property, **TabIndex** Property, **TabStop** Property, **Tag** Property, **ToolTipText** Property, **Visible** Property, **WhatsThisHelpID** Property

Events

Click Event, **DblClick** Event, **DragDrop** Event, **DragOver** Event, **GotFocus** Event, **LostFocus** Event, **MouseDown, MouseUp** Events, **MouseMove** Event, **OLECompleteDrag** Event, **OLEDragDrop** Event, **OLEDragOver** Event, **OLEGiveFeedback** Event, **OLESetData** Event, **OLEStartDrag** Event

Methods

Close Method (Animation Control), **Drag** Method, **Move** Method, **OLEDrag** Method, **Open** Method (Animation Control), **Play** Method, **SetFocus** Method, **ShowWhatsThis** Method, **Stop** Method (Animation Control), **Zorder** Method

Example

The following example opens an .avi file by using the Open Dialog, and begins playing it automatically. To try the example, place an **Animation** control and a **CommonDialog** control on a form, and paste the code into the form's Declarations section. Run the example, and choose an .avi file to open.

```
Private Sub Animation1_Click ()
    With CommonDialog1
        .Filter = "avi (*.avi)|*.avi"
        .ShowOpen
    End With
    With Animation1
        .Autoplay = True
        .Open CommonDialog1.Filename
    End With
End Sub
```

AutoPlay Property

Returns or sets a value which determines if the **Animation** control will begin to play an .avi file when the .avi file is loaded into the control.

Applies To

Animation Control

Syntax

object.**Autoplay** [= *boolean*]

The **AutoPlay** property syntax has these parts:

Part	Description
object	An object expression that evaluates to an **Animation** control.
boolean	A Boolean expression specifying whether the **Autoplay** Property is enabled.

Settings

The settings for *boolean* are:

Setting	Description
True	The .avi file plays automatically in a continuous loop once it is loaded into the **Animation** control.
False	An .avi file, once loaded, does not play until the **Play** method is used.

Data Type

Integer (Boolean)

Remarks

An .avi file played using the **Autoplay** property will continue to repeat until **Autoplay** is set to **False**.

See Also

Center Property

BackStyle Property (Animation Control)

Returns or sets a value that determines whether the **Animation** control draws the animation on a transparent background or on the background color specified in the animation clip. Read-only at run time.

Applies To

Animation Control

Syntax

object.**BackStyle** [= *value*]

The **BackStyle** property syntax has these parts:

Part	Description
object	An object expression that evaluates to an **Animation** control.
value	A numeric expression specifying transparency, as described in Settings.

Settings

The settings for *value* are:

Setting	Description
0	(Default) Transparent—background color of the control is visible.
1	Opaque—the background color specified in the animation clip fills the control and obscures any color behind it.

Remarks

You can use the **BackStyle** property to run an animation that shows the background color of the **Animation** control rather than the background color of the animation itself.

Data Type

Integer (Boolean)

See Also

Center Property

Close Method (Animation Control)

The **Close** method causes the **Animation** control to close the currently open AVI file. If there was no file loaded, **Close** does nothing, and no error is generated

Applies To

Animation Control

Syntax

object.**Close**

The object placeholder represents an object expression that evaluates to an **Animation** control.

Remarks

To stop a file from playing, use the **Stop** method. However, if the **Autoplay** property is set to **True**, set **Autoplay** to **False** to stop the file from playing.

See Also

AutoPlay Property, **Stop** Method (Animation Control)

Open Method (Animation Control)

Opens an .avi file to play. If the **AutoPlay** property is set to **True**, then the clip will start playing as soon as it is loaded. It will continue to repeat until the .avi file is closed or the **Autoplay** property is set to **False**.

Applies To

Animation Control

Syntax

object.**Open** *file*

Part	Description
object	Required. An object expression that evaluates to an object in the **Applies To** list.
file	Required. The name of the file to play.

Remarks

The **Animation** control cannot play .avi files that include sound data. In addition, the **Animation** control can display only uncompressed .avi files or .avi files that have been compressed using Run-Length Encoding (RLE). An error will be returned when the **Open** method is invoked with a file that includes sound data or that is in an unsupported compression format.

See Also

AutoPlay Property

Example

The following example opens an .avi file by using the Open Dialog, and begins playing it automatically. To try the example, place an **Animation** control and a **CommonDialog** control on a form, and paste the code into the form's Declarations section. Run the example, and choose an .avi file to open.

```
Private Sub Animation1_Click ()
   With CommonDialog1
      .Filter = "avi (*.avi)|*.avi"
      .ShowOpen
   End With
```

```
    With Animation1
        .Autoplay = True
        .Open CommonDialog1.Filename
    End With
End Sub
```

Play Method

Plays an .avi file in the **Animation** control.

Applies To

Animation Control

Syntax

object.**Play** [= *repeat, start, end*]

Part	Description
object	Required. An object expression that evaluates to an **Animation** control.
Repeat	Optional. Integer that specifies the number of times the clip will be repeated. The default is -1, which causes the clip to repeat indefinitely.
Start	Optional. Integer that specifies the starting frame. The default value is 0, which starts the clip on the first frame. The maximum value is 65535.
end	Optional. Integer that specifies the ending frame. The default value is -1, which indicates the last frame of the clip. The maximum value is 65535.

Data Type

Integer

Remarks

Use the **Stop** method to stop an .avi file from playing.

See Also

Stop Method (Animation Control)

Center Property

Determines whether the .avi file is centered within the **Animation** control. When set to **True** (the default), the .avi is displayed in the center of the control, based on the size of the image. When set to **False**, the .avi is positioned at 0,0 within the control.

Applies To

Animation Control

Syntax

object.**Center** [= *boolean*]

5

Part	Description
object	Required. An object expression that evaluates to an object in the **Applies To** list.
boolean	Required. A Boolean expression specifying whether the AVI file is centered within the control.

Data Type

Integer (Boolean)

Remarks

If the **Center** property is set to **True**, and the .avi frame size is larger than the control, the edges of the .avi frames will not be shown as the file plays.

See Also

AutoPlay Property, **BackStyle** Property (Animation Control), **Close** Method (Animation Control), **Open** Method (Animation Control), **Play** Method

Stop Method (Animation Control)

Stops the play of an .avi file in the **Animation** control.

Applies To

Animation Control

Syntax

object.**Stop**

The object placeholder represents an object expression that evaluates to an **Animation** control.

Remarks

The **Stop** method stops only an animation that was started with the **Play** method. Attempting to use the **Stop** method when the **Autoplay** property is set to **True** returns an error (35759).

See Also

Close Method (Animation Control), **Open** Method (Animation Control), **Play** Method

CommonDialog Control

The **CommonDialog** control provides a standard set of dialog boxes for operations such as opening and saving files, setting print options, and selecting colors and fonts. The control also has the ability to display help by running the Windows Help engine.

Syntax

CommonDialog

Remarks

The **CommonDialog** control provides an interface between Visual Basic and the routines in the Microsoft Windows dynamic-link library Commdlg.dll. To create a dialog box using this control, Commdlg.dll must be in your Microsoft Windows SYSTEM directory.

You use the **CommonDialog** control in your application by adding it to a form and setting its properties. The dialog displayed by the control is determined by the methods of the control. At run time, a dialog box is displayed or the help engine is executed, when the appropriate method is invoked; at design time, the **CommonDialog** control is displayed as an icon on a form. This icon can't be sized.

The **CommonDialog** control can display the following dialogs using the specified method.

Method	Dialog Displayed
ShowOpen	Show Open Dialog Box
ShowSave	Show Save As Dialog Box
ShowColor	Show Color Dialog Box
ShowFont	Show Font Dialog Box
ShowPrinter	Show Print or Print Options Dialog Box
ShowHelp	Invokes the Windows Help engine

The **CommonDialog** control automatically provides context sensitive help on the interface of the dialog boxes by clicking:

- The What's This help button in the title bar then clicking the item for which you want more information.
- The right mouse button over the item for which you want more information then selecting the What's This command in the displayed context menu.

The operating system provides the text shown in the Windows 95 Help popup. You can also display a Help button on the dialog boxes with the **CommonDialog** control by setting the **Flags** property, however, you must provide the help topics in this situation.

Note There is no way to specify where a dialog box is displayed.

Properties

Action Property, **CancelError** Property, **Color** Property, **Copies** Property, **DefaultExt** Property, **DialogTitle** Property, **FileName** Property, **FileTitle** Property, **Filter** Property, **FilterIndex** Property, **Flags** Property, **FontBold, FontItalic, FontStrikethru, FontUnderline** Properties, **FontName** Property, **FontSize** Property, **FromPage, ToPage** Properties, **hDC** Property, **HelpCommand** Property, **HelpContext** Property, **HelpFile** Property, **HelpKey** Property, **Index** Property, **InitDir** Property, **Left, Top** Properties, **Max,Min** Properties, **MaxFileSize** Property, **Name** Property, **Object** Property, **Parent** Property, **PrinterDefault** Property

Methods

AboutBox Method, **ShowColor** Method, **ShowFont** Method, **ShowHelp** Method, **ShowOpen** Method, **ShowPrinter** Method, **ShowSave** Method

See Also

CommonDialog Control (Color Dialog), **CommonDialog** Control (Font Dialog), **CommonDialog** Control (Open, Save As Dialogs), **CommonDialog** Control (Print Dialog), **CommonDialog** Control (Help), **Flags** Property (Color Dialog), **Flags** Property (Open, Save As Dialogs), **Flags** Property (Font Dialog), **Flags** Property (Print Dialog), **CommonDialog Control** Constants

---

Action Property (CommonDialog)

Returns or sets the type of dialog box to be displayed. Not available at design time.

Applies To

CommonDialog Control

Note The **Action** property is included for compatibility with earlier versions of Visual Basic. For additional functionality, use the following new methods: **ShowColor**, **ShowFont**, **ShowHelp**, **ShowOpen**, **ShowPrinter**, and **ShowSave**.

Syntax

object.**Action** [= *value*]

The **Action** property syntax has these parts:

Part	Description
object	An object expression that evaluates to an object in the **Applies To** list.
value	A numeric expression specifying the type of dialog box displayed, as described in Settings.

Settings

The settings for *value* are:

Setting	Description
0	No Action.
1	Displays Open dialog box.

(continued)

Setting	Description
2	Displays Save As dialog box.
3	Displays Color dialog box.
4	Displays Font dialog box.
5	Displays Printer dialog box.
6	Runs WINHLP32.EXE.

Data Type

Integer

See Also

CommonDialog Control, **ShowColor** Method, **ShowFont** Method, **ShowHelp** Method, **ShowOpen** Method, **ShowPrinter** Method, **ShowSave** Method

CancelError Property

Returns or sets a value indicating whether an error is generated when the user chooses the Cancel button.

Applies To

CommonDialog Control

Syntax

object.**CancelError** [= *boolean*]

The **CancelError** property syntax has these parts:

Part	Description
object	An object expression that evaluates to an object in the **Applies To** list.
boolean	A Boolean expression indicating whether an error is generated, as described in Settings.

Settings

The settings for *boolean* are:

Setting	Description
True	An error is generated.
False	(Default) No error is generated.

Remarks

When this property is set to **True**, error number 32755 (**cdlCancel**) occurs whenever the user chooses the Cancel button.

Data Type

Boolean

Color Property

Returns or sets the selected color.

Applies To

CommonDialog Control

Syntax

object.**Color** [= *number*]

The **Color** property syntax has these parts:

Part	Description
object	An object expression that evaluates to an object in the **Applies To** list.
number	A numeric expression that specifies the color.

Settings

The settings for *number* are:

Setting	Description
Normal RGB colors	Colors set with the **RGB** or **QBColor** functions in code.
System default colors	Colors specified with the system color constants in the Visual Basic (VB) object library in the Object Browser. The Microsoft Windows operating environment substitutes the user's choices, as specified by the user's Control Panel settings.

Remarks

For this property to return a color in a Color dialog box, the **cdlCCRGBInit** flag must be set. In the Font dialog box, the **cdlCFEffects** flag must be set.

Data Type

Long

See Also

Flags Property (Color Dialog), **Color** Constants

CommonDialog Control (Color Dialog)

The Color dialog is displayed by using the **ShowColor** method of the **CommonDialog** control. The Color dialog box allows the user to select a color from a palette or to create and select a custom color.

To use the Color dialog box, set the properties of the **CommonDialog** control relating to the Color dialog. Then use the **ShowColor** method to actually show the dialog and use the **Color** property to retrieve the selected color.

Properties

Action Property (CommonDialog), **CancelError** Property, **Color** Property, **Flags** Property (Color Dialog), **HelpCommand** Property, **HelpContext** Property

(CommonDialog), **HelpFile** Property, **HelpKey** Property, **Index** Property, **Left, To** Properties **Name** Property, **Object** Property, **Parent** Property, **Tag** Property

Methods

ShowColor Method

See Also

CommonDialog Control (Font Dialog), **CommonDialog** Control (Open, Save As Dialogs), **CommonDialog** Control (Print Dialog), **CommonDialog** Control (Help), **CommonDialog** Control, **CommonDialog Control** Constants, **CommonDialog Error** Constants

Example

The following example displays the Color dialog box and sets the BackColor of the form to the selected color:

```
Private Sub Command1_Click()
    ' Set Cancel to True
    CommonDialog1.CancelError = True
    On Error GoTo ErrHandler
    'Set the Flags property
    CommonDialog1.Flags = cdlCCRGBInit
    ' Display the Color Dialog box
    CommonDialog1.ShowColor
    ' Set the form's background color to selected color
    Form1.BackColor = CommonDialog1.Color
    Exit Sub

ErrHandler:
    ' User pressed the Cancel button
End Sub
```

CommonDialog Control (Font Dialog)

The Font dialog is displayed by using the **ShowFont** method of the **CommonDialog** control. The Font dialog box allows the user to select a font by specifying a font, size, color, and style.

To use the Font dialog box, set the properties of the **CommonDialog** control relating to the Font dialog. Then use the **ShowFont** method to actually show the dialog. Once the user makes selections in the Font dialog box, the following properties contain information about the user's selection:

Property	Determines
Color	The selected color. To use this property, you must first set the Flags property to **cdlCFEffects**.
FontBold	Whether **bold** was selected.

(continued)

(continued)

Property	Determines
FontItalic	Whether *italic* was selected.
FontStrikethru	Whether ~~strikethrough~~ was selected. To use this property, you must first set the **Flags** property to **cdlCFEffects**.
FontUnderline	Whether <u>underline</u> was selected. To use this property, you must first set the **Flags** property to **cdlCFEffects**.
FontName	The selected font name.
FontSize	The selected font size.

Properties

Action Property, **CancelError** Property, **Color** Property, **Flags** Property, **FontBold, FontItalic, FontStrikethru, FontUnderline** Properties, **FontName** Property, **FontSize** Property, **HelpCommand** Property, **HelpContext** Property, **HelpFile** Property, **HelpKey** Property, **Index** Property, **Left, Top** Properties, **Max, Min** Properties, **Name** Property, **Object** Property, **Parent** Property, **Tag** Property

Methods

ShowFont Method

See Also

CommonDialog Control (Color Dialog), **CommonDialog** Control (Open, Save As Dialogs), **CommonDialog** Control (Print Dialog), **CommonDialog** Control (Help), **CommonDialog** Control, **CommonDialog Control** Constants

Example

The following example displays the Font dialog box and sets the font attributes of a text box to the user's selections:

```
Private Sub Command1_Click()
    ' Set Cancel to True
    CommonDialog1.CancelError = True
    On Error GoTo ErrHandler
    ' Set the Flags property
    CommonDialog1.Flags = cdlCFEffects Or cdlCFBoth
    ' Display the Font dialog box
    CommonDialog1.ShowFont
    Text1.Font.Name = CommonDialog1.FontName
    Text1.Font.Size = CommonDialog1.FontSize
    Text1.Font.Bold = CommonDialog1.FontBold
    Text1.Font.Italic = CommonDialog1.FontItalic
    Text1.Font.Underline = CommonDialog1.FontUnderline
    Text1.FontStrikethru = CommonDialog1.FontStrikethru
    Text1.ForeColor = CommonDialog1.Color
    Exit Sub
ErrHandler:
    ' User pressed the Cancel button
    Exit Sub
End Sub
```

CommonDialog Control (Help)

The **ShowHelp** method of the **CommonDialog** control runs the Windows Help engine (WINHLP32.EXE) and displays a help file that is set by the **HelpFile** property.

By setting the **HelpCommand** property, you can tell the help engine what type of online help you want, such as context sensitive or help on a particular keyword, etc.

Properties

Action Property, **HelpCommand** Property, **HelpContextID** Property, **HelpFile** Property, **HelpKey** Property, **Index** Property, **Left, Top** Properties, **Name** Property, **Object** Property, **Parent** Property, **Tag** Property

Methods

ShowFont Method

See Also

CommonDialog Control (Color Dialog), **CommonDialog** Control (Font Dialog), **CommonDialog** Control (Open, Save As Dialogs), **CommonDialog** Control (Print Dialog), **CommonDialog** Control, **CommonDialog Control** Constants, **CommonDialog Error** Constants

Example

The following example displays the table of contents for the Visual Basic help file.

```
Private Sub Command1_Click()
    ' Set the name of the help file
    CommonDialog1.HelpFile = "VB5.HLP"
    CommonDialog1.HelpCommand = cdlHelpContents
    ' Display Visual Basic Help contents topic.
    CommonDialog1.ShowHelp
End Sub
```

CommonDialog Control (Open, Save As Dialogs)

The Open and Save As dialogs are displayed by using the **ShowOpen** and **ShowSave** methods of the **CommonDialog** control.

Both dialog boxes allows the user to specify a drive, directory, filename extension, and a filename. The Save As dialog is identical to the Open dialog in appearance, except for the dialog's caption.

At run time, when the user chooses a file and closes the dialog box, the **FileName** property is used to get the selected filename.

You can set the **Filter** property so the dialog displays only certain types of files, such as text files. The **Flags** property can be used to change various elements on the dialog as well as prompt the user when certain actions may occur, such as overwriting a file.

Properties

Action Property (CommonDialog), **CancelError** Property, **DefaultExt** Property, **DialogTitle** Property, **FileTitle** Property, **Filter** Property (CommonDialog), **FilterIndex** Property, **Flags** Property (Open, Save As Dialogs), **HelpCommand** Property, **HelpContext** Property (CommonDialog), **HelpFile** Property, **HelpKey** Property, **Index** Property, **InitDir** Property, **Left, Top** Properties, **MaxFileSize** Property, **Name** Property, **Object** Property, **Parent** Property, **Tag** Property

Methods

ShowOpen Method, **ShowSave** Method

See Also

CommonDialog Control (Color Dialog), **CommonDialog** Control (Font Dialog), **CommonDialog** Control (Print Dialog), **CommonDialog** Control (Help), **CommonDialog** Control, **CommonDialog Control** Constants, **CommonDialog Error** Constants

Example

The following example shows the Open dialog then displays the selected filename in a message box:

```
Private Sub Command1_Click()
    ' Set CancelError is True
    CommonDialog1.CancelError = True
    On Error GoTo ErrHandler
    ' Set flags
    CommonDialog1.Flags = cdlOFNHideReadOnly
    ' Set filters
    CommonDialog1.Filter = "All Files (*.*)|*.*|Text Files" & _
    "(*.txt)|*.txt|Batch Files (*.bat)|*.bat"
    ' Specify default filter
    CommonDialog1.FilterIndex = 2
    ' Display the Open dialog box
    CommonDialog1.ShowOpen
    ' Display name of selected file
    MsgBox CommonDialog1.filename
    Exit Sub

ErrHandler:
    'User pressed the Cancel button
    Exit Sub
End Sub
```

CommonDialog Control (Print Dialog)

The Print dialog is displayed by using the **ShowPrinter** method of the **CommonDialog** control. The Print dialog box allows the user to specify how output should be printed. The user can specify a range of pages to be printed, a print quality, a number of copies, and so on. This dialog box also contains information about the currently installed printer and allows the user to configure or reinstall a new default printer.

Note This dialog box does not send data to the printer but lets the user specify how they want data printed. If the **PrinterDefault** property is True, you can use the **Printer** object to print data in the format they select.

At run time, when the user makes selections in the Print dialog box, the following properties contain information about the user's selection.

Property	Determines
Copies	The number of copies to print.
FromPage	The page to start printing
ToPage	The page to stop printing
hDC	The device context for the selected printer.

Properties

ActiveControl Property, **CancelError** Property, **Copies** Property, **Flags** Property, **FromPage, ToPage** Properties, **hDC** Property, **HelpCommand** Property, **HelpContext** Property, **HelpFile** Property, **HelpKey** Property, **Index** Property, **Left, Top** Properties, **Max, Min** Properties, **MaxFileSize** Property, **Name** Property, **Object** Property, **Parent** Property, **PrinterDefault** Property, **Tag** Property

Methods

ShowPrinter Method

Example

The following example displays the Print dialog

```
Private Sub Command1_Click()
    Dim BeginPage, EndPage, NumCopies, i
    ' Set Cancel to True
    CommonDialog1.CancelError = True
    On Error GoTo ErrHandler
    ' Display the Print dialog box
    CommonDialog1.ShowPrinter
    ' Get user-selected values from the dialog box
    BeginPage = CommonDialog1.FromPage
    EndPage = CommonDialog1.ToPage
    NumCopies = CommonDialog1.Copies
    For i = 1 To NumCopies
        ' Put code here to send data to the printer
```

```
      Next i
      Exit Sub
ErrHandler:
      ' User pressed the Cancel button
      Exit Sub
End Sub
```

CommonDialog Control Constants

File Open/Save Dialog Box Flags

Constant	Value	Description
cdlOFNAllowMultiselect	&H200	Specifies that the File Name list box allows multiple selections.
		The user can select more than one file at run time by pressing the SHIFT key and using the UP ARROW and DOWN ARROW keys to select the desired files. When this is done, the **FileName** property returns a string containing the names of all selected files. The names in the string are delimited by spaces.
CdlOFNCreatePrompt	&H2000	Specifies that the dialog box prompts the user to create a file that doesn't currently exist. This flag automatically sets the **cdlOFNPathMustExist** and **cdlOFNFileMustExist** flags.
CdlOFNExplorer	&H80000	Use the Explorer-like Open A File dialog box template. Common dialogs that use this flag do not work under Windows NT using the Windows 95 shell.
CdlOFNExtensionDifferent	&H400	Indicates that the extension of the returned filename is different from the extension specified by the **DefaultExt** property. This flag isn't set if the **DefaultExt** property is **Null**, if the extensions match, or if the file has no extension. This flag value can be checked upon closing the dialog box.
CdlOFNFileMustExist	&H1000	Specifies that the user can enter only names of existing files in the File Name text box. If this flag is set and the user enters an invalid filename, a warning is displayed. This flag automatically sets the **cdlOFNPathMustExist** flag.
CdlOFNHelpButton	&H10	Causes the dialog box to display the Help button.
CdlOFNHideReadOnly	&H4	Hides the Read Only check box.
CdlOFNLongNames	&H200000	Use long filenames.
CdlOFNNoChangeDir	&H8	Forces the dialog box to set the current directory to what it was when the dialog box was opened.
CdlOFNNoDereferenceLinks	&H100000	Do not dereference shell links (also known as shortcuts). By default, choosing a shell link causes it to be dereferenced by the shell.
CdlOFNNoLongNames	&H40000	Do not use long file names.
CdlOFNNoReadOnlyReturn	&H8000	Specifies that the returned file won't have the Read Only attribute set and won't be in a write-protected directory.

(continued)

Constant	Value	Description
CdlOFNNoValidate	&H100	Specifies that the common dialog box allows invalid characters in the returned filename.
CdlOFNOverwritePrompt	&H2	Causes the Save As dialog box to generate a message box if the selected file already exists. The user must confirm whether to overwrite the file.
CdlOFNPathMustExist	&H800	Specifies that the user can enter only valid paths. If this flag is set and the user enters an invalid path, a warning message is displayed.
CdlOFNReadOnly	&H1	Causes the Read Only check box to be initially checked when the dialog box is created. This flag also indicates the state of the Read Only check box when the dialog box is closed.
CdlOFNShareAware	&H4000	Specifies that sharing violation errors will be ignored.

Color Dialog Box Flags

Constant	Value	Description
cdCClFullOpen	&H2	Entire dialog box is displayed, including the Define Custom Colors section
cdlCCShowHelp	&H8	Causes the dialog box to display a Help button
cdlCCPreventFullOpen	&H4	Disables the Define Custom Colors command button and prevents the user from defining custom colors
cdlCCRGBInit	&H1	Sets the initial color value for the dialog box

Fonts Dialog Box Flags

Constant	Value	Description
cdlCFANSIOnly	&H400	Specifies that the dialog box allows only a selection of the fonts that use the Windows character set. If this flag is set, the user won't be able to select a font that contains only symbols.
cdlCFApply	&H200	Enables the Apply button on the dialog box.
cdlCFBoth	&H3	Causes the dialog box to list the available printer and screen fonts. The **hDC** property identifies the device context associated with the printer.
cdlCFEffects	&H100	Specifies that the dialog box enables strikethrough, underline, and color effects.
cdlCFFixedPitchOnly	&H4000	Specifies that the dialog box selects only fixed-pitch fonts.
cdlCFForceFontExist	&H10000	Specifies that an error message box is displayed if the user attempts to select a font or style that doesn't exist.
cdlCFHelpButton	&H4	Causes the dialog box to display a Help button.
cdlCFLimitSize	&H2000	Specifies that the dialog box selects only font sizes within the range specified by the **Min** and **Max** properties.

(continued)

(continued)

Constant	Value	Description
cdlCFNoFaceSel	&H80000	No font name selected.
cdlCFNoSimulations	&H1000	Specifies that the dialog box doesn't allow graphic device interface (GDI) font simulations.
cdlCFNoSizeSel	&H200000	No font size selected.
cdlCFNoStyleSel	&H100000	
cdlCFNoVectorFonts	&H800	Specifies that the dialog box doesn't allow vector-font selections.
cdlCFPrinterFonts	&H2	Causes the dialog box to list only the fonts supported by the printer, specified by the **hDC** property.
cdlCFScalableOnly	&H20000	Specifies that the dialog box allows only the selection of fonts that can be scaled.
cdlCFScreenFonts	&H1	Causes the dialog box to list only the screen fonts supported by the system.
cdlCFTTOnly	&H40000	Specifies that the dialog box allows only the selection of TrueType fonts.
cdlCFWYSIWYG	&H8000	Specifies that the dialog box allows only the selection of fonts that are available on both the printer and on screen. If this flag is set, the **cdlCFBoth** and **cdlCFScalableOnly** flags should also be set.

Printer Dialog Box Flags

Constant	Value	Description
cdlPDAllPages	&H0	Returns or sets the state of the All Pages option button.
cdlPDCollate	&H10	Returns or sets the state of the Collate check box.
cdlPDDisablePrintToFile	&H80000	Disables the Print To File check box.
cdlPDHelpButton	&H800	Causes the dialog box to display the Help button.
cdlPDHidePrintToFile	&H100000	Hides the Print To File check box.
cdlPDNoPageNums	&H8	Disables the Pages option button and the associated edit control.
cdlPDNoSelection	&H4	Disables the Selection option button.
cdlPDNoWarning	&H80	Prevents a warning message from being displayed when there is no default printer.
cdlPDPageNums	&H2	Returns or sets the state of the Pages option button.
cdlPDPrintSetup	&H40	Causes the system to display the Print Setup dialog box rather than the Print dialog box.
cdlPDPrintToFile	&H20	Returns or sets the state of the Print To File check box.
cdlPDReturnDC	&H100	Returns a device context for the printer selection made in the dialog box. The device context is returned in the dialog box's **hDC** property.

(continued)

Constant	Value	Description
cdlPDReturnDefault	&H400	Returns default printer name.
cdlPDReturnIC	&H200	Returns an information context for the printer selection made in the dialog box. An information context provides a fast way to get information about the device without creating a device context. The information context is returned in the dialog box's **hDC** property.
cdlPDSelection	&H1	Returns or sets the state of the Selection option button. If neither **cdlPDPageNums** nor **cdlPDSelection** is specified, the All option button is in the selected state.
cdlPDUseDevModeCopies	&H40000	If a printer driver doesn't support multiple copies, setting this flag disables the copies edit control. If a driver does support multiple copies, setting this flag indicates that the dialog box stores the requested number of copies in the **Copies** property.

Help Constants

Constant	Value	Description
cdlHelpCommandHelp	&H102	Displays Help for a particular command
cdlHelpContents	&H3	Displays the contents topic in the current Help file
cdlHelpContext	&H1	Displays Help for a particular topic
cdlHelpContextPopup	&H8	Displays a topic identified by a context number
cdlHelpForceFile	&H9	Creates a Help file that displays text in only one font
cdlHelpHelpOnHelp	&H4	Displays Help for using the Help application itself
cdlHelpIndex	&H3	Displays the index of the specified Help file
cdlHelpKey	&H101	Displays Help for a particular keyword
cdlHelpPartialKey	&H105	Calls the search engine in Windows Help
cdlHelpQuit	&H2	Notifies the Help application that the specified Help file is no longer in use
cdlHelpSetContents	&H5	Designates a specific topic as the contents topic
cdlHelpSetIndex	&H5	Sets the current index for multi-index Help

See Also

CommonDialog Error Constants, **Alignment** Constants, **BorderStyle** Property Constants, **Clipboard Object** Constants, **Color** Constants, **Control** Constants, **DDE** Constants, **Drag-and-Drop** Constants, **Drawing** Constants, **Form** Constants, **Graphics** Constants, **Help** Constants, **Key Code** Constants, **Menu Control** Constants, **Mouse Pointer** Constants, **OLE Container Control** Constants, **Picture Object** Constants, **Printer Object** Constants, **RasterOp** Constants, **Variant Type** Constants, **Visual Basic** Constants

CommonDialog Error Constants

Constant	Value	Description
cdlAlloc	&H&H7FF0 &	Couldn't allocate memory for **FileName** or **Filter** property
cdlCancel	&H&H7FF3 &	Cancel was selected
cdlDialogFailure	&H&H8000 &	The function failed to load the dialog box
cdlFindResFailure	&H&H7FF9 &	The function failed to load a specified resource
cdlHelp	&H&H7FEF &	Call to Windows Help failed
cdlInitialization	&H&H7FFD &	The function failed during initialization
cdlLoadResFailure	&H&H7FF8 &	The function failed to load a specified string
cdlLockResFailure	&H&H7FF7 &	The function failed to lock a specified resource
cdlMemAllocFailure	&H&H7FF6 &	The function was unable to allocate memory for internal data structures
cdlMemLockFailure	&H&H7FF5 &	The function was unable to lock the memory associated with a handle
cdlNoFonts	&H&H5FFE &	No fonts exist
cdlBufferTooSmall	&H&H4FFC &	The buffer at which the member lpstrFile points is too small
cdlInvalidFileName	&H4&H4FFD &	Filename is invalid
cdlSubclassFailure	&H&H4FFE &	An attempt to subclass a list box failed due to insufficient memory
cdlCreateICFailure	&H&H6FF5 &	The **PrintDlg** function failed when it attempted to create an information context
cdlDndmMismatch	&H&H6FF6 &	Data in the DevMode and DevNames data structures describe two different printers
cdlGetDevModeFail	&H&H6FFA &	The printer device driver failed to initialize a DevMode data structure
cdlInitFailure	&H&H6FF9 &	The **PrintDlg** function failed during initialization
cdlLoadDrvFailure	&H&H6FFB &	The **PrintDlg** function failed to load the specified printer's device driver
cdlLoadStrFailure	&H7FFA	The function failed to load a specified string.
cdlNoDefaultPrn	&H&H6FF7 &	A default printer doesn't exist
cdlNoDevices	&H&H6FF8 &	No printer device drivers were found
cdlParseFailure	&H&H6FFD &	The **CommonDialog** function failed to parse the strings in the [devices] section of Win.ini

(continued)

Constant	Value	Description
cdlPrinterCodes	&H&H6FFF &	The PDReturnDefault flag was set, but either the hDevMode or hDevNames field was nonzero
cdlPrinterNotFound	&H&H6FF4 &	The [devices] section of Win.ini doesn't contain an entry for the requested printer
cdlRetDefFailure	&H&H6FFC &	The PDReturnDefault flag was set, but either the hDevMode or hDevNames field was nonzero
cdlSetupFailure	&H&H6FFE &	Failed to load required resources

See Also

CommonDialog Control Constants, **Alignment** Constants, **BorderStyle** Property Constants, **Clipboard Object** Constants, **Color** Constants, **CommonDialog Control** Constants, **Control** Constants, **DDE** Constants, **Drag-and-Drop** Constants, **Drawing** Constants, **Form** Constants, **Graphics** Constants, **Help** Constants, **Key Code** Constants, **Menu Control** Constants, **Mouse Pointer** Constants, **OLE Container Control** Constants, **Picture Object** Constants, **Printer Object** Constants, **RasterOp** Constants, **Variant Type** Constants, **Visual Basic** Constants

---

DefaultExt Property

Applies To

CommonDialog Control (Open, Save As Dialogs)

Returns or sets the default filename extension for the dialog box.

Syntax

object.**DefaultExt** [= *string*]

The **DefaultExt** property syntax has these parts:

Part	Description
object	An object expression that evaluates to an object in the **Applies To** list.
string	A string expression specifying the file extension.

Remarks

Use this property to specify a default filename extension, such as .txt or .doc.

When a file with no extension is saved, the extension specified by this property is automatically appended to the filename.

Data Type

String

DialogTitle Property

Returns or sets the string displayed in the title bar of the dialog box.

Applies To

CommonDialog Control (Open, Save As Dialogs)

Syntax

object.**DialogTitle** [= *title*]

The **DialogTitle** property syntax has these parts:

Part	Description
object	An object expression that evaluates to an object in the **Applies To** list.
title	A string expression specifying the name of the dialog box.

Remarks

Use this property to display the name of the dialog box in the title bar.

Note   The **CommonDialog** control ignores the setting of the **DialogTitle** property when displaying the Color, Font, or Print dialog boxes.

The default title for an Open dialog box is Open; the default title for a Save As dialog box is Save As.

Data Type

String

FileTitle Property

Returns the name (without the path) of the file to open or save.

Applies To

CommonDialog Control (Open, Save As Dialogs)

Syntax

object.**FileTitle**

The *object* placeholder is an object expression that evaluates to an object in the **Applies To** list.

Remarks

When the user selects a file and clicks OK in the File dialog box, the **FileTitle** property takes a value that can then be used to open or save the selected file.

Note   If the **cdlOFNNoValidate** flag is set, the **FileTitle** property won't return a value.

Data Type

> **String**

See Also

> **CommonDialog Control** Constants

Filter Property (CommonDialog)

Returns or sets the filters that are displayed in the Type list box of a dialog box.

Applies To

> **CommonDialog** Control (Open, Save As Dialogs)

Syntax

> *object*.**Filter** [= *description1* |*filter1* |*description2* |*filter2*...]

The **Filter** property syntax has these parts:

Part	Description
object	An object expression that evaluates to an object in the **Applies To** list.
description	A string expression describing the type of file.
filter	A string expression specifying the filename extension.

Remarks

A filter specifies the type of files that are displayed in the dialog box's file list box. For example, selecting the filter *.txt displays all text files.

Use this property to provide the user with a list of filters that can be selected when the dialog box is displayed.

Use the pipe (|) symbol (ASCII 124) to separate the *description* and *filter* values. Don't include spaces before or after the pipe symbol, because these spaces will be displayed with the *description* and *filter* values.

The following code shows an example of a filter that enables the user to select text files or graphic files that include bitmaps and icons:

```
Text (*.txt)|*.txt|Pictures (*.bmp;*.ico)|*.bmp;*.ico
```

When you specify more than one filter for a dialog box, use the **FilterIndex** property to determine which filter is displayed as the default.

Data Type

> **String**

See Also

> **FilterIndex** Property

FilterIndex Property

Returns or sets a default filter for an Open or Save As dialog box.

Applies To

CommonDialog Control (Open, Save As Dialogs)

Syntax

object.**FilterIndex** [= *number*]

The **FilterIndex** property syntax has these parts:

Part	Description
object	An object expression that evaluates to an object in the **Applies To** list.
number	A numeric expression specifying a default filter.

Remarks

This property specifies the default filter when you use the **Filter** property to specify filters for an Open or Save As dialog box.

The index for the first defined filter is 1.

Data Type

Integer

See Also

Filter Property (CommonDialog)

Flags Property (All Common Dialogs)

Flags Property (Color Dialog)

Flags Property (Font Dialog)

Flags Property (Open, Save As Dialogs)

Flags Property (Print Dialog)

Flags Property (Color Dialog)

Returns or sets the options for a Color dialog box.

Applies To

CommonDialog Control

Syntax

object.**Flags** [= *value*]

The **Flags** property syntax has these parts:

Part	Description
object	An object expression that evaluates to an object in the **Applies To** list.
value	A constant or value specifying the options for a Color dialog box, as described in Settings.

Settings

The settings for *value* are:

Constant	Value	Description
cdCClFullOpen	&H2	Entire dialog box is displayed, including the Define Custom Colors section.
cdlCCHelpButton	&H8	Causes the dialog box to display a Help button.
cdlCCPreventFullOpen	&H4	Disables the Define Custom Colors command button and prevents the user from defining custom colors.
cdlCCRGBInit	&H1	Sets the initial color value for the dialog box.

Remarks

These constants are listed in the Microsoft **CommonDialog** Control (MSComDlg) object library in the Object Browser.

You can also define selected flags. Use the **Const** keyword in the Declarations section of the startup form to define the flags you want to use.

You can set more than one flag for a dialog box using the **Or** operator. For example:

```
CommonDialog1.Flags = &H10& Or &H200&
```

Adding the desired constant values produces the same results. The following is equivalent to the preceding example:

```
CommonDialog1.Flags = &H210&
```

Data Type

Long

Flags Property (Font Dialog)

Returns or sets the options for the Font dialog box.

Applies To

CommonDialog Control

Syntax

object.**Flags** [= *value*]

The **Flags** property syntax has these parts:

Part	Description
object	An object expression that evaluates to an object in the **Applies To** list.
value	A constant or value specifying the options for a Font dialog box, as described in Settings.

Settings

The settings for *value* are:

Constant	Value	Description
cdlCFANSIOnly	&H400	Specifies that the dialog box allows only a selection of the fonts that use the Windows character set. If this flag is set, the user won't be able to select a font that contains only symbols.
cdlCFApply	&H200	Enables the Apply button on the dialog box.
cdlCFBoth	&H3	Causes the dialog box to list the available printer and screen fonts. The **hDC** property identifies the device context associated with the printer.
cdlCFEffects	&H100	Specifies that the dialog box enables strikethrough, underline, and color effects.
cdlCFFixedPitchOnly	&H4000	Specifies that the dialog box selects only fixed-pitch fonts.
cdlCFForceFontExist	&H10000	Specifies that an error message box is displayed if the user attempts to select a font or style that doesn't exist.
cdlCFHelpButton	&H4	Causes the dialog box to display a Help button.
cdlCFLimitSize	&H2000	Specifies that the dialog box selects only font sizes within the range specified by the **Min** and **Max** properties.
cdlCFNoFaceSel	&H80000	No font name selected.
cdlCFNoSimulations	&H1000	Specifies that the dialog box doesn't allow graphic device interface (GDI) font simulations.
cdlCFNoSizeSel	&H200000	No font size selected.
cdlCFNoStyleSel	&H100000	No style was selected.
cdlCFNoVectorFonts	&H800	Specifies that the dialog box doesn't allow vector-font selections.
cdlCFPrinterFonts	&H2	Causes the dialog box to list only the fonts supported by the printer, specified by the **hDC** property.
cdlCFScalableOnly	&H20000	Specifies that the dialog box allows only the selection of fonts that can be scaled.
cdlCFScreenFonts	&H1	Causes the dialog box to list only the screen fonts supported by the system.

(continued)

Constant	Value	Description
cdlCFTTOnly	&H40000	Specifies that the dialog box allows only the selection of TrueType fonts.
cdlCFWYSIWYG	&H8000	Specifies that the dialog box allows only the selection of fonts that are available on both the printer and on screen. If this flag is set, the **cdlCFBoth** and **cdlCFScalableOnly** flags should also be set.

Remarks

These constants are listed in the Microsoft **CommonDialog** Control (MSComDlg) object library in the Object Browser.

You can also define selected flags. Use the **Const** keyword in the Declarations section of the startup form to define the flags you want to use. For example:

```
Const ReadOnly  = &H00000001&
Const Effects   = &H00000100&
```

You can set more than one flag for a dialog box using the **Or** operator. For example:

```
CommonDialog1.Flags = &H10& Or &H200&
```

Adding the desired constant values produces the same results. The following is equivalent to the preceding example:

```
CommonDialog1.Flags = &H210&
```

Note   You must set the **Flags** property to **cdlCFScreenFonts**, **cdlCFPrinterFonts**, or **cdlCFBoth** before displaying the Fonts dialog box. Otherwise, the error `No Fonts Exist` occurs.

Data Type

Long

Flags Property (Open, Save As Dialogs)

Returns or sets the options for the Open and Save As dialog boxes.

Applies To

CommonDialog Control

Syntax

object.**Flags** [= *value*]

The **Flags** property syntax has these parts:

Part	Description
object	An object expression that evaluates to an object in the **Applies To** list.
value	A constant or value specifying the options for the Open and Save As dialog boxes, as described in Settings.

Settings

The settings for *value* are:

Constant	Value	Description
cdlOFNAllowMultiselect	&H200	Specifies that the File Name list box allows multiple selections.
		The user can select more than one file at run time by pressing the SHIFT key and using the UP ARROW and DOWN ARROW keys to select the desired files. When this is done, the **FileName** property returns a string containing the names of all selected files. The names in the string are delimited by spaces.
cdlOFNCreatePrompt	&H2000	Specifies that the dialog box prompts the user to create a file that doesn't currently exist. This flag automatically sets the **cdlOFNPathMustExist** and **cdlOFNFileMustExist** flags.
cdlOFNExplorer	&H80000	Use the Explorer-like Open A File dialog box template. Works with Windows 95 and Windows NT 4.0.
cdlOFNExtensionDifferent	&H400	Indicates that the extension of the returned filename is different from the extension specified by the **DefaultExt** property. This flag isn't set if the **DefaultExt** property is **Null**, if the extensions match, or if the file has no extension. This flag value can be checked upon closing the dialog box.
cdlOFNFileMustExist	&H1000	Specifies that the user can enter only names of existing files in the File Name text box. If this flag is set and the user enters an invalid filename, a warning is displayed. This flag automatically sets the **cdlOFNPathMustExist** flag.
cdlOFNHelpButton	&H10	Causes the dialog box to display the Help button.
cdlOFNHideReadOnly	&H4	Hides the Read Only check box.
cdlOFNLongNames	&H200000	Use long filenames.

(continued)

Constant	Value	Description
cdlOFNNoChangeDir	&H8	Forces the dialog box to set the current directory to what it was when the dialog box was opened.
cdlOFNNoDereferenceLinks	&H100000	Do not dereference shell links (also known as shortcuts). By default, choosing a shell link causes it to be dereferenced by the shell.
cdlOFNNoLongNames	&H40000	No long file names.
cdlOFNNoReadOnlyReturn	&H8000	Specifies that the returned file won't have the Read Only attribute set and won't be in a write-protected directory.
cdlOFNNoValidate	&H100	Specifies that the common dialog box allows invalid characters in the returned filename.
cdlOFNOverwritePrompt	&H2	Causes the Save As dialog box to generate a message box if the selected file already exists. The user must confirm whether to overwrite the file.
cdlOFNPathMustExist	&H800	Specifies that the user can enter only valid paths. If this flag is set and the user enters an invalid path, a warning message is displayed.
cdlOFNReadOnly	&H1	Causes the Read Only check box to be initially checked when the dialog box is created. This flag also indicates the state of the Read Only check box when the dialog box is closed.
cdlOFNShareAware	&H4000	Specifies that sharing violation errors will be ignored.

Remarks

The **cdlOFNExplorer** and **cdlOFNNoDereferenceLinks** flags work only under Windows 95 and Windows NT 4.0. Multiselect common dialogs under Windows 95 using **cdlOFNExplorer** use null characters for delimiters, but under previous versions of Windows NT without the Windows 95 shell, the multiselect uses spaces for delimiters (thus no support for long filenames).

Under both Windows NT 4.0 and Windows 95 if you do not choose the **cdlOFNAllowMultiselect** flag, then both the **cdlOFNExplorer** and **cdlOFNLongNames** flags have no effect and are essentially the default.

If you use the **cdlOFNAllowMultiselect** flag by itself under both Windows NT 4.0 and Windows 95, you will not have support for long filenames. This is because the multiple filenames come back space delimited and long filenames could include spaces. You cannot avoid this behavior if you have Windows NT 3.5. If you use **cdlOFNAllowMultiselect**, you cannot see long filenames. If you add the **cdlOFNExplorer** flag under Windows 95, you will be able to both multiselect and see long filenames. But the filenames come back null character delimited and not space delimited. Thus, using **cdlOFNAllowMultiselect** with **cdlOFNExplorer** will require different parsing of the filename result under Windows 95 and Windows NT 4.0.

These constants are listed in the Microsoft **CommonDialog** Control (MSComDlg) object library in the Object Browser.

You can also define selected flags. Use the **Const** keyword in the Declarations section of the startup form to define the flags you want to use. For example:

```
Const ReadOnly  = &H00000001&
Const Effects   = &H00000100&
CommonDialog1.Flags = &H10& Or &H200&
```

Adding the desired constant values produces the same results. The following is equivalent to the preceding example:

```
CommonDialog1.Flags = &H210&
```

Data Type

Long

Flags Property (Print Dialog)

Returns or sets the options for the Print dialog box.

Applies To

CommonDialog Control

Syntax

object.**Flags** [= *value*]

The **Flags** property syntax has these parts:

Part	Description
object	An object expression that evaluates to an object in the **Applies To** list.
value	A constant or value specifying the options for the Print dialog box, as described in Settings.

Settings

The settings for *value* are:

Constant	Value	Description
cdlPDAllPages	&H0	Returns or sets the state of the All Pages option button.
cdlPDCollate	&H10	Returns or sets the state of the Collate check box.
cdlPDDisablePrintToFile	&H80000	Disables the Print To File check box.
cdlPDHelpButton	&H800	Causes the dialog box to display the Help button.

(continued)

Constant	Value	Description
cdlPDHidePrintToFile	&H100000	Hides the Print To File check box.
cdlPDNoPageNums	&H8	Disables the Pages option button and the associated edit control.
cdlPDNoSelection	&H4	Disables the Selection option button.
cdlPDNoWarning	&H80	Prevents a warning message from being displayed when there is no default printer.
cdlPDPageNums	&H2	Returns or sets the state of the Pages option button.
cdlPDPrintSetup	&H40	Causes the system to display the Print Setup dialog box rather than the Print dialog box.
cdlPDPrintToFile	&H20	Returns or sets the state of the Print To File check box.
cdlPDReturnDC	&H100	Returns a device context for the printer selection made in the dialog box. The device context is returned in the dialog box's **hDC** property.
cdlPDReturnDefault	&H400	Returns default printer name.
cdlPDReturnIC	&H200	Returns an information context for the printer selection made in the dialog box. An information context provides a fast way to get information about the device without creating a device context. The information context is returned in the dialog box's **hDC** property.
cdlPDSelection	&H1	Returns or sets the state of the Selection option button. If neither **cdlPDPageNums** nor **cdlPDSelection** is specified, the All option button is in the selected state.
cdlPDUseDevModeCopies	&H40000	If a printer driver doesn't support multiple copies, setting this flag disables the Number of copies spinner control in the Print dialog. If a driver does support multiple copies, setting this flag indicates that the dialog box stores the requested number of copies in the **Copies** property.

Remarks

These constants are listed in the Microsoft **CommonDialog** Control (MSComDlg) object library in the Object Browser.

You can also define selected flags. Use the **Const** keyword in the Declarations section of the startup form to define the flags you want to use. For example:

```
Const ReadOnly = &H00000001&
Const Effects  = &H00000100&
```

You can set more than one flag for a dialog box using the **Or** operator. For example:

```
CommonDialog1.Flags = &H10& Or &H200&
```

Adding the desired constant values produces the same results. The following is equivalent to the preceding example:

```
CommonDialog1.Flags = &H210&
```

Data Type

> **Long**

FromPage, ToPage Properties

Return or set the values for the From and To text boxes of the Print dialog.

Applies To

> **CommonDialog** Control (Print Dialog)

Syntax

> *object*.**FromPage** [= *number*]
> *object*.**ToPage** [= *number*]

The **FromPage** and **ToPage** property syntax has these parts:

Part	Description
object	An object expression that evaluates to an object in the **Applies To** list.
number	A numeric expression that specifies the first and last pages to be printed.

Remarks

These properties are valid only when the **cdlPDPageNums** flag has been set.

Data Type

> **Integer**

See Also

> **CommonDialog Control** Constants

---

hDC Property (CommonDialogDummy Topicl)

Applies To

> **CommonDialog** Control, **FormObject**, **Forms** Collection, **PictureBox** Control, **PrinterObject**, **Printers** Collection **PropertyPage** Object, **UserControl** Object, **UserDocument** Object

HelpCommand Property

Returns or sets the type of online Help requested.

Applies To

CommonDialog Control

Syntax

object.**HelpCommand** [= *value*]

The **HelpCommand** property syntax has these parts:

Part	Description
object	An object expression that evaluates to an object in the **Applies To** list.
value	A constant or value specifying the type of Help, as described in Settings.

Settings

The settings for *value* are:

Constant	Value	Description
cdlHelpCommand	&H102&	Executes a Help macro.
cdlHelpContents	&H3&	Displays the Help contents topic as defined by the Contents option in the [OPTION] section of the .hpj file.
cdlHelpContext	&H1&	Displays Help for a particular context. When using this setting, you must also specify a context using the **HelpContext** property.
cdlHelpContextPopup	&H8&	Displays in a pop-up window a particular Help topic identified by a context number defined in the [MAP] section of the .hpj file.
cdlHelpForceFile	&H9&	Ensures WinHelp displays the correct Help file. If the correct Help file is currently displayed, no action occurs. If the incorrect Help file is displayed, WinHelp opens the correct file.
cdlHelpHelpOnHelp	&H4&	Displays Help for using the Help application itself.
cdlHelpIndex	&H3&	Displays the index of the specified Help file. An application should use this value only for a Help file with a single index.
cdlHelpKey	&H101&	Displays Help for a particular keyword. When using this setting, you must also specify a keyword using the **HelpKey** property.

(continued)

(continued)

Constant	Value	Description
cdlHelpPartialKey	&H105&	Displays the topic found in the keyword list that matches the keyword passed in the dwData parameter if there is one exact match. If more than one match exists, the Search dialog box with the topics found listed in the Go To list box is displayed. If no match exists, the Search dialog box is displayed. To bring up the Search dialog box without passing a keyword, use a long pointer to an empty string.
cdlHelpQuit	&H2&	Notifies the Help application that the specified Help file is no longer in use.
cdlHelpSetContents	&H5&	Determines which contents topic is displayed when a user presses the F1 key.
cdlHelpSetIndex	&H5&	Sets the context specified by the **HelpContext** property as the current index for the Help file specified by the **HelpFile** property. This index remains current until the user accesses a different Help file. Use this value only for Help files with more than one index.

Remarks

The values for the **HelpCommand** property constants are listed in the Microsoft **CommonDialog** Control (MSComDlg) object library in the Object Browser.

Data Type

Integer

See Also

HelpContext Property (CommonDialog), **HelpKey** Property, **CommonDialog Control** Constants, **HelpFile** Property (App, CommonDialog, MenuLine)

HelpContext Property (CommonDialog)

Returns or sets the context ID of the requested Help topic.

Applies To

CommonDialog Control

Syntax

object.**HelpContext** [= *value*]

The **HelpContext** property syntax has these parts:

Part	Description
object	An object expression that evaluates to an object in the **Applies To** list.
value	A string expression specifying the context ID of the requested Help topic.

Remarks

Use this property with the **HelpCommand** property (set **HelpCommand = cdlHelpContext**) to specify the Help topic to be displayed.

Data Type

String

See Also

HelpCommand Property

HelpKey Property

Returns or sets the keyword that identifies the requested Help topic.

Applies To

CommonDialog Control

Syntax

object.**HelpKey** [= *string*]

The **HelpKey** property syntax has these parts:

Part	Description
object	An object expression that evaluates to an object in the **Applies To** list.
string	A string expression specifying the keyword that identifies the Help topic.

Remarks

Use this property with the **HelpCommand** property (set **HelpCommand = cdlHelpKey**) to specify the Help topic to be displayed.

Data Type

String

See Also

HelpCommand Property

InitDir Property

Returns or sets the initial file directory.

Applies To

CommonDialog Control (Open, Save As Dialogs)

Syntax

object.**InitDir** [= *string*]

The **InitDir** property syntax has these parts:

Part	Description
object	An object expression that evaluates to an object in the **Applies To** list.
string	A string expression specifying the initial file directory.

Remarks

This property is used to specify the initial directory for an Open or Save As dialog. If this property isn't specified, the current directory is used.

Data Type

String

Max, Min Properties (CommonDialog)

You can set the **Max** and **Min** properties for the following:

- Font dialog boxreturn or set the smallest and largest font sizes displayed in the Size list box.

- Print dialog boxreturn or set the minimum and maximum allowed values for the print range.

Applies To

CommonDialog Control

Syntax

object.**Min** [= *points*]
object.**Max** [= *points*]
object.**Min** [= *number*]
object.**Max** [= *number*]

The **Max** and **Min** property syntaxes have these parts:

Part	Description
object	An object expression that evaluates to an object in the **Applies To** list.
points	A numeric expression specifying the smallest and largest font sizes.
number	A numeric expression specifying the minimum and maximum page numbers.

Remarks

- With the Font dialog box, the **cdlCFLimitSize** flag must be set before using these properties.

- With the Print dialog box, the **Min** property determines the smallest number the user can specify in the From text box. The **Max** property determines the largest number the user can specify in the To text box.

Data Type

Integer

MaxFileSize Property

Returns or sets the maximum size of the filename opened using the **CommonDialog** control.

Applies To

CommonDialog Control

Syntax

object.**MaxFileSize** [= *value*]

The **MaxFileSize** property syntax has these parts:

Part	Description
object	An object expression that evaluates to an object in the **Applies To** list.
value	An integer specifying the maximum size of the filename in bytes. The range for this property is 132K. The default is 256.

Remarks

The **MaxFileSize** property allocates memory to store the actual names of the selected file or files. When using the **cdlOFNAllowMultiselect** flag, you may want to increase the size of the **MaxFileSize** property to allow enough memory for the selected file names.

Data Type

Integer

PrinterDefault Property

Returns or sets an option that determines if the user's selections in the Print dialog box are used to change the system's default printer settings.

Applies To

CommonDialog Control

Syntax

object.**PrinterDefault** [= *value*]

The **PrinterDefault** property syntax has these parts:

Part	Description
object	An object expression that evaluates to an object in the **Applies To** list.
value	A Boolean expression specifying whether the user's selections are used to change the system's default printer settings, as described in Settings.

Settings

The settings for *value* are:

Setting	Description
True	Any selections the user makes in the Setup portion of the Print dialog box (printer selection, orientation, and so on) are used to change the printer settings in the user's WIN.INI file. (On the Windows NT operating system, this information is stored in the Registry.)
False	User's selections can't be used to change the system's default printer settings.

Remarks

When **PrinterDefault** is **True**, you can write code to print directly to the Visual Basic **Printer** object. Otherwise, you must use the graphic device interface (GDI) calls to print to the printer specified by the control's **hDC** property.

Note If you've previously printed to the **Printer** object, make sure you've ended that print job using `Printer.EndDoc`. This releases the hDC associated with that printer. You will get a new hDC for the default printer the next time you print to the **Printer** object. If you don't do this, it's possible for the user to select a new printer while the **Printer** object contains a handle to the old printer.

Data Type

Boolean

ShowColor Method

Displays the **CommonDialog** control's Color dialog box.

Applies To

CommonDialog Control

Syntax

object.**ShowColor**

The *object* placeholder represents an object expression that evaluates to an object in the **Applies To** list.

See Also

ShowFont Method, **ShowHelp** Method, **ShowOpen** Method, **ShowPrinter** Method, **ShowSave** Method

Example

This example uses the **CommonDialog** control and the **ShowColor**, **ShowFont**, **ShowHelp**, **ShowOpen**, **ShowPrinter**, and **ShowSave** methods to display the common dialog boxes. To try this example, paste the code into the Declarations section of a form with **CommandButton**, **OptionButton** (set the option button's **Index** property to 0), and **CommonDialog** controls. Press F5 and select the option button for the common dialog box you want and choose the command button.

```
Private Sub Form_Paint ()
    Static FlagFormPainted As Integer
    ' When form is painting for first time,
    If FlagFormPainted <> True Then
        For i = 1 To 5
            Load Option1(i)                 ' Add five option buttons to array.
            Option1(i).Top = Option1(i - 1).Top + 350
            Option1(i).Visible = True
        Next i
        Option1(0).Caption = "Open"         ' Put caption on each option button.
        Option1(1).Caption = "Save"
        Option1(2).Caption = "Color"
        Option1(3).Caption = "Font"

        Option1(4).Caption = "Printer"
        Option1(5).Caption = "Help"
        Command1.Caption = "Show Dlg"       ' Label command button.
        FlagFormPainted = True              ' Form is done painting.
    End If
End Sub

Private Sub Command1_Click ()
    If Option1(0).Value Then                ' If Open option button selected,
        CommonDialog1.ShowOpen              ' display Open common dialog box.
    ElseIf Option1(1).Value Then            ' Or,
        CommonDialog1.ShowSave              ' display Save common dialog box.

ElseIf Option1(2).Value Then               ' Or,
        CommonDialog1.ShowColor             ' display Color common dialog box.
    ElseIf Option1(3).Value Then            ' Or,
        CommonDialog1.Flags = cdlCFBoth     ' Flags property must be set
                                            ' to cdlCFBoth,
                                            ' cdlCFPrinterFonts,
                                            ' or cdlCFScreenFonts before
                                            ' using ShowFont method.
        CommonDialog1.ShowFont              ' Display Font common dialog box.
    ElseIf Option1(4).Value Then            ' Or,
        CommonDialog1.ShowPrinter           ' display Printer common dialog box.

ElseIf Option1(5).Value Then               ' Or,
        CommonDialog1.HelpFile = "VB5.HLP"
        CommonDialog1.HelpCommand = cdlHelpContents
        CommonDialog1.ShowHelp              ' Display Visual Basic Help
                                            ' contents topic.
    End If
End Sub
```

ShowFont Method

Displays the **CommonDialog** control's Font dialog box.

Applies To

CommonDialog Control

Syntax

object.**ShowFont**

The *object* placeholder represents an object expression that evaluates to an object in the **Applies To** list.

Remarks

Before you use the **ShowFont** method, you must set the **Flags** property of the **CommonDialog** control to one of three constants or values: **cdlCFBoth** or &H3, **cdlCFPrinterFonts** or &H2, or **cdlCFScreenFonts** or &H1. If you don't set **Flags**, a message box is displayed advising you that "There are no fonts installed.", and a run-time error occurs.

See Also

Flags Property (Font Dialog), **ShowColor** Method, **ShowHelp** Method, **ShowOpen** Method, **ShowPrinter** Method, **ShowSave** Method, **CommonDialog Control** Constants, **Font** Object

Example

This example uses the **CommonDialog** control and the **ShowColor**, **ShowFont**, **ShowHelp**, **ShowOpen**, **ShowPrinter**, and **ShowSave** methods to display the common dialog boxes. To try this example, paste the code into the Declarations section of a form with **CommandButton**, **OptionButton** (set the option button's **Index** property to 0), and **CommonDialog** controls. Press F5 and select the option button for the common dialog box you want and choose the command button.

```
Private Sub Form_Paint ()
   Static FlagFormPainted As Integer
   ' When form is painting for first time,
   If FlagFormPainted <> True Then
      For i = 1 To 5
         Load Option1(i)               ' Add five option buttons to array.
         Option1(i).Top = Option1(i - 1).Top + 350
         Option1(i).Visible = True
      Next i
      Option1(0).Caption = "Open"      ' Put caption on each option button.
      Option1(1).Caption = "Save"
      Option1(2).Caption = "Color"
      Option1(3).Caption = "Font"

      Option1(4).Caption = "Printer"
      Option1(5).Caption = "Help"
      Command1.Caption = "Show Dlg"    ' Label command button.
```

```
            FlagFormPainted = True              ' Form is done painting.
        End If
    End Sub

    Private Sub Command1_Click ()
        If Option1(0).Value Then               ' If Open option button selected,
            CommonDialog1.ShowOpen             ' display Open common dialog box.
        ElseIf Option1(1).Value Then           ' Or,
            CommonDialog1.ShowSave             ' display Save common dialog box.

    ElseIf Option1(2).Value Then               ' Or,
        CommonDialog1.ShowColor                ' display Color common dialog box.
        ElseIf Option1(3).Value Then           ' Or,
            CommonDialog1.Flags = cdlCFBoth    ' Flags property must be set
                                               ' to cdlCFBoth,
                                               ' cdlCFPrinterFonts,
                                               ' or cdlCFScreenFonts before
                                               ' using ShowFont method.
            CommonDialog1.ShowFont             ' Display Font common dialog box.
        ElseIf Option1(4).Value Then           ' Or,
            CommonDialog1.ShowPrinter          ' display Printer common dialog box.

    ElseIf Option1(5).Value Then               ' Or,
        CommonDialog1.HelpFile = "VB5.HLP"
        CommonDialog1.HelpCommand = cdlHelpContents
        CommonDialog1.ShowHelp    ' Display Visual Basic Help contents topic.
        End If
    End Sub
```

ShowHelp Method

Runs Winhlp32.exe and displays the Help file you specify.

Applies To

CommonDialog Control

Syntax

object.**ShowHelp**

The *object* placeholder represents an object expression that evaluates to an object in the **Applies To** list.

Remarks

Before you use the **ShowHelp** method, you must set the **HelpFile** and **HelpCommand** properties of the **CommonDialog** control to one of their appropriate constants or values. Otherwise, Winhlp32.exe doesn't display the Help file.

See Also

HelpCommand Property, **ShowColor** Method, **ShowFont** Method, **ShowOpen** Method, **ShowPrinter** Method, **ShowSave** Method, **HelpFile** Property (App, CommonDialog, MenuLine)

Example

This example uses the **CommonDialog** control and the **ShowColor**, **ShowFont**, **ShowHelp**, **ShowOpen**, **ShowPrinter**, and **ShowSave** methods to display the common dialog boxes. To try this example, paste the code into the Declarations section of a form with **CommandButton**, **OptionButton** (set the option button's **Index** property to 0), and **CommonDialog** controls. Press F5 and select the option button for the common dialog box you want and choose the command button.

```
Private Sub Form_Paint ()
    Static FlagFormPainted As Integer
    ' When form is painting for first time,
    If FlagFormPainted <> True Then
        For i = 1 To 5
            Load Option1(i)              ' Add five option buttons to array.
            Option1(i).Top = Option1(i - 1).Top + 350
            Option1(i).Visible = True
        Next i
        Option1(0).Caption = "Open"      ' Put caption on each option button.
        Option1(1).Caption = "Save"
        Option1(2).Caption = "Color"
        Option1(3).Caption = "Font"

        Option1(4).Caption = "Printer"
        Option1(5).Caption = "Help"
        Command1.Caption = "Show Dlg"    ' Label command button.
        FlagFormPainted = True           ' Form is done painting.
    End If
End Sub

Private Sub Command1_Click ()
    If Option1(0).Value Then             ' If Open option button selected,
        CommonDialog1.ShowOpen           ' display Open common dialog box.
    ElseIf Option1(1).Value Then         ' Or,
        CommonDialog1.ShowSave           ' display Save common dialog box.

ElseIf Option1(2).Value Then             ' Or,
        CommonDialog1.ShowColor          ' display Color common dialog box.
    ElseIf Option1(3).Value Then         ' Or,
        CommonDialog1.Flags = cdlCFBoth  ' Flags property must be set
                                         ' to cdlCFBoth,
                                         ' cdlCFPrinterFonts,
                                         ' or cdlCFScreenFonts before
                                         ' using ShowFont method.
        CommonDialog1.ShowFont           ' Display Font common dialog box.
    ElseIf Option1(4).Value Then         ' Or,
        CommonDialog1.ShowPrinter        ' display Printer common dialog box.

ElseIf Option1(5).Value Then             ' Or,
        CommonDialog1.HelpFile = "VB5.HLP"
        CommonDialog1.HelpCommand = cdlHelpContents
        CommonDialog1.ShowHelp  ' Display Visual Basic Help contents topic.
    End If
End Sub
```

ShowOpen Method

Displays the **CommonDialog** control's Open dialog box.

Applies To

CommonDialog Control

Syntax

object.**ShowOpen**

The *object* placeholder represents an object expression that evaluates to an object in the **Applies To** list.

See Also

ShowColor Method, **ShowFont** Method, **ShowHelp** Method, **ShowPrinter** Method, **ShowSave** Method

Example

This example uses the **CommonDialog** control and the **ShowColor**, **ShowFont**, **ShowHelp**, **ShowOpen**, **ShowPrinter**, and **ShowSave** methods to display the common dialog boxes. To try this example, paste the code into the Declarations section of a form with **CommandButton**, **OptionButton** (set the option button's **Index** property to 0), and **CommonDialog** controls. Press F5 and select the option button for the common dialog box you want and choose the command button.

```
Private Sub Form_Paint ()
   Static FlagFormPainted As Integer
   ' When form is painting for first time,
   If FlagFormPainted <> True Then
      For i = 1 To 5
         Load Option1(i)               ' Add five option buttons to array.
         Option1(i).Top = Option1(i - 1).Top + 350
         Option1(i).Visible = True
      Next i
      Option1(0).Caption = "Open"      ' Put caption on each option button.
      Option1(1).Caption = "Save"
      Option1(2).Caption = "Color"
      Option1(3).Caption = "Font"

      Option1(4).Caption = "Printer"
      Option1(5).Caption = "Help"
      Command1.Caption = "Show Dlg"     ' Label command button.
      FlagFormPainted = True            ' Form is done painting.
   End If
End Sub

Private Sub Command1_Click ()
   If Option1(0).Value Then            ' If Open option button selected,
      CommonDialog1.ShowOpen           ' display Open common dialog box.
   ElseIf Option1(1).Value Then        ' Or,
      CommonDialog1.ShowSave           ' display Save common dialog box.
```

```
    ElseIf Option1(2).Value Then          ' Or,
        CommonDialog1.ShowColor           ' display Color common dialog box.
      ElseIf Option1(3).Value Then        ' Or,
        CommonDialog1.Flags = cdlCFBoth   ' Flags property must be set
                                          ' to cdlCFBoth,
                                          ' cdlCFPrinterFonts,
                                          ' or cdlCFScreenFonts before
                                          ' using ShowFont method.
        CommonDialog1.ShowFont            ' Display Font common dialog box.
      ElseIf Option1(4).Value Then        ' Or,
        CommonDialog1.ShowPrinter         ' display Printer common dialog box.

    ElseIf Option1(5).Value Then          ' Or,
        CommonDialog1.HelpFile = "VB5.HLP"
        CommonDialog1.HelpCommand = cdlHelpContents
        CommonDialog1.ShowHelp            ' Display Visual Basic Help contents topic.
        End If
    End Sub
```

ShowPrinter Method

Displays the **CommonDialog** control's Printer dialog box.

Applies To

CommonDialog Control

Syntax

object.**ShowPrinter**

The *object* placeholder represents an object expression that evaluates to an object in the **Applies To** list.

See Also

ShowColor Method, **ShowFont** Method, **ShowHelp** Method, **ShowOpen** Method, **ShowSave** Method, **Printer** Object, **Printers** Collection

Example

This example uses the **CommonDialog** control and the **ShowColor**, **ShowFont**, **ShowHelp**, **ShowOpen**, **ShowPrinter**, and **ShowSave** methods to display the common dialog boxes. To try this example, paste the code into the Declarations section of a form with **CommandButton**, **OptionButton** (set the option button's **Index** property to 0), and **CommonDialog** controls. Press F5 and select the option button for the common dialog box you want and choose the command button.

```
Private Sub Form_Paint ()
    Static FlagFormPainted As Integer
    ' When form is painting for first time,
    If FlagFormPainted <> True Then
        For i = 1 To 5
            Load Option1(i)               ' Add five option buttons to array.
            Option1(i).Top = Option1(i - 1).Top + 350
```

```
            Option1(i).Visible = True
        Next i
        Option1(0).Caption = "Open"        ' Put caption on each option button.
        Option1(1).Caption = "Save"
        Option1(2).Caption = "Color"
        Option1(3).Caption = "Font"

        Option1(4).Caption = "Printer"
        Option1(5).Caption = "Help"
        Command1.Caption = "Show Dlg"      ' Label command button.
        FlagFormPainted = True             ' Form is done painting.
    End If
End Sub

Private Sub Command1_Click ()
    If Option1(0).Value Then               ' If Open option button selected,
        CommonDialog1.ShowOpen             ' display Open common dialog box.
    ElseIf Option1(1).Value Then           ' Or,
        CommonDialog1.ShowSave             ' display Save common dialog box.

ElseIf Option1(2).Value Then               ' Or,
        CommonDialog1.ShowColor            ' display Color common dialog box.
    ElseIf Option1(3).Value Then           ' Or,
        CommonDialog1.Flags = cdlCFBoth    ' Flags property must be set
                                           ' to cdlCFBoth,
                                           ' cdlCFPrinterFonts,
                                           ' or cdlCFScreenFonts before
                                           ' using ShowFont method.
        CommonDialog1.ShowFont             ' Display Font common dialog box.
    ElseIf Option1(4).Value Then           ' Or,
        CommonDialog1.ShowPrinter          ' display Printer common dialog box.

ElseIf Option1(5).Value Then               ' Or,
        CommonDialog1.HelpFile = "VB5.HLP"
        CommonDialog1.HelpCommand = cdlHelpContents
        CommonDialog1.ShowHelp             ' Display Visual Basic Help contents topic.
    End If
End Sub
```

ShowSave Method

Displays the **CommonDialog** control's Save As dialog box.

Applies To

CommonDialog Control

Syntax

object.**ShowSave**

The *object* placeholder represents an object expression that evaluates to an object in the **Applies To** list.

See Also

ShowColor Method, **ShowFont** Method, **ShowHelp** Method, **ShowOpen** Method, **ShowPrinter** Method

Example

This example uses the **CommonDialog** control and the **ShowColor**, **ShowFont**, **ShowHelp**, **ShowOpen**, **ShowPrinter**, and **ShowSave** methods to display the common dialog boxes. To try this example, paste the code into the Declarations section of a form with **CommandButton**, **OptionButton** (set the option button's **Index** property to 0), and **CommonDialog** controls. Press F5 and select the option button for the common dialog box you want and choose the command button.

```
Private Sub Form_Paint ()
    Static FlagFormPainted As Integer
    ' When form is painting for first time,
    If FlagFormPainted <> True Then
        For i = 1 To 5
            Load Option1(i)                 ' Add five option buttons to array.
            Option1(i).Top = Option1(i - 1).Top + 350
            Option1(i).Visible = True
        Next i
        Option1(0).Caption = "Open"         ' Put caption on each option button.
        Option1(1).Caption = "Save"
        Option1(2).Caption = "Color"
        Option1(3).Caption = "Font"
        Option1(4).Caption = "Printer"
        Option1(5).Caption = "Help"
        Command1.Caption = "Show Dlg"       ' Label command button.
        FlagFormPainted = True              ' Form is done painting.
    End If
End Sub

Private Sub Command1_Click ()
    If Option1(0).Value Then               ' If Open option button selected,
        CommonDialog1.ShowOpen             ' display Open common dialog box.
    ElseIf Option1(1).Value Then           ' Or,
        CommonDialog1.ShowSave             ' display Save common dialog box.
    ElseIf Option1(2).Value Then           ' Or,
        CommonDialog1.ShowColor            ' display Color common dialog box.
    ElseIf Option1(3).Value Then           ' Or,
        CommonDialog1.Flags = cdlCFBoth    ' Flags property must be set
                                           ' to cdlCFBoth, cdlCFPrinterFonts,
                                           ' or cdlCFScreenFonts before
                                           ' using ShowFont method.
        CommonDialog1.ShowFont             ' Display Font common dialog box.
    ElseIf Option1(4).Value Then           ' Or,
        CommonDialog1.ShowPrinter          ' display Printer common dialog box.
    ElseIf Option1(5).Value Then           ' Or,
        CommonDialog1.HelpFile = "VB5.HLP"
        CommonDialog1.HelpCommand = cdlHelpContents
        CommonDialog1.ShowHelp   ' Display Visual Basic Help contents topic.
    End If
End Sub
```

ImageList Control

An **ImageList** control contains a collection of **ListImage** objects, each of which can be referred to by its index or key. The **ImageList** control is not meant to be used alone, but as a central repository to conveniently supply other controls with images.

Syntax

ImageList

Remarks

You can use the **ImageList** control with any control that assigns a **Picture** object to a **Picture** property. For example, the following code assigns the first **ListImage** object in a **ListImages** collection to the **Picture** property of a newly created **StatusBar** panel:

```
Dim pnlX As Panel
Set pnlX = StatusBar1.Panels.Add()    ' Add a new Panel object.
Set pnlX.Picture = ImageList1.ListImages(1).Picture    ' Set Picture.
```

Note You must use the **Set** statement when assigning an image to a **Picture** object.

Images of different sizes can be added to an **ImageList** control, but it constrains them all to be the same size. The size of the **ListImage** objects is determined by one of the following:

- The setting of **ImageWidth** and **ImageHeight** properties before any images are added.

- The dimensions of the first image added.

You are not limited to any particular image size, but the total number of images that can be loaded is limited by the amount of available memory.

At design time, you can add images using the General tab of the ImageList Control Properties dialog box. At run time, you can add images using the **Add** method for the **ListImages** collection.

Besides storing **Picture** objects, the **ImageList** control can also perform graphical operations on images before assigning them to other controls. For example, the **Overlay** method creates a composite image from two different images.

Additionally, you can bind one or more **ImageList** controls to certain other Windows 95 common controls to conserve system resources. These include the **ListView**, **ToolBar**, **TabStrip**, and **TreeView** controls. In order to use an **ImageList** with one of these controls, you must associate a particular **ImageList** with the control through an appropriate property. For the **ListView** control, you must set the **Icons** and **SmallIcons** properties to **ImageList** controls. For the **TreeView**, **TabStrip**, and **Toolbar** controls, you must set the **ImageList** property to an **ImageList** control.

For these controls, you can specify an **ImageList** at design time using the Custom Properties dialog box. At run time, you can also specify an **ImageList** which sets a **TreeView** control's **ImageList** property, as in the following example:

```
TreeView1.ImageList = ImageList1   ' Specify ImageList
```

Once you associate an **ImageList** with a control, you can use the value of either the **Index** or **Key** property to refer to a **ListImage** object in a procedure. The following example sets the **Image** property of a **TreeView** control's third **Node** object to the first **ListImage** object in an **ImageList** control:

```
' Use the value of the Index property of ImageList1.
TreeView1.Nodes(3).Image = 1
' Or use the value of the Key property.
TreeView1.Nodes(3).Image = "image 1"   ' Assuming Key is "image 1."
```

Distribution Note   The **ImageList** control is part of a group of **ActiveX** controls that are found in the COMCTL32.OCX file. To use the **ImageList** control in your application, you must add the COMCTL32.OCX file to the project. When distributing your application, install the COMCTL32.OCX file in the user's Microsoft Windows System or System32 directory. For more information on how to add an **ActiveX** control to a project, see the *Programmer's Guide*.

Properties

BackColor, ForeColor Properties, **hImageList** Property, **ImageHeight, ImageWidth** Properties, **Index** Property, **ListImages** Property, **MaskColor** Property, **Name** Property, **Object** Property, **Parent** Property, **Tag** Property, **UseMaskColor** Property

Methods

Overlay Method

See Also

ListImage Object, **ListImages** Collection, **ImageList** Control Constants, **ListView** Control, **Icons, SmallIcons** Properties, **TabStrip** Control, **Toolbar** Control, **TreeView** Control, **Node** Object, **Nodes** Collection, **Add** Method, **Picture** Object, **ImageList** Property (ActiveX Controls), **Picture** Property (ActiveX Controls)

Add Method (ListImages Collection)

Adds a **ListImage** object to a **ListImages** collection.

Applies To

ListImage Object, **ListImages** Collection

Syntax

object.**Add**(*index*, *key*, *picture*)

The **Add** method syntax has these parts:

Part	Description
object	Required. An object expression that evaluates to an object in the **Applies To** list.
index	Optional. An integer specifying the position where you want to insert the **ListImage**. If no *index* is specified, the **ListImage** is added to the end of the **ListImages** collection.
key	Optional. A unique string that identifies the **ListImage** object. Use this value to retrieve a specific **ListImage** object. An error occurs if the key is not unique.
picture	Required. Specifies the picture to be added to the collection.

Remarks

The **ListImages** collection is a 1-based collection.

You can load either bitmaps or icons into a **ListImage** object. To load a bitmap or icon, you can use the **LoadPicture** function, as follows:

```
Set imgX = ImageList1.ListImages.Add(,,LoadPicture("file name"))
```

You can also load a **Picture** object directly into the **ListImage** object. For example, this example loads a **PictureBox** control's picture into the **ListImage** object:

```
Set imgX = ImageList1.ListImages.Add(,,Picture1.Picture)
```

If no **ListImage** objects have been added to a **ListImages** collection, you can set the **ImageHeight** and **ImageWidth** properties before adding the first **ListImage** object. The first **ListImage** object you add to a collection can be any size. However, all subsequent **ListImage** objects will be forced to be the same size as the first **ListImage** object. Once a **ListImage** object has been added to the collection, the **ImageHeight** and **ImageWidth** properties become read-only properties, and any image added to the collection must have the same **ImageHeight** and **ImageWidth** values.

You should use the **Key** property to reference a **ListImage** object if you expect the value of the **Index** property to change. For example, if you allow users to add and delete their own images to the collection, the value of the **Index** property may change.

When a **ListImage** object is added to the collection, a reference to the newly created object is returned. You can use the reference to set other properties of the **ListImage**, as follows:

```
Dim imgX As ListImage
Dim I As Integer
    Set imgX = ImageList1.ListImages. _
    Add(,,LoadPicture("icons\comm\net01.ico"))
    imgX.Key = "net connect" ' Use the new reference to assign Key.
```

See Also

Clear Method (ActiveX Controls), **Clear** Method (ActiveX Common Help), **ImageList** Control, **ImageHeight, ImageWidth** Properties, **hDC** Property, **Index** Property (ActiveX Controls), **Index** Property (Control Array), **Key** Property (ActiveX Controls), **LoadPicture** Function, **Picture** Object, **PictureBox** Control, **Remove** Method (ActiveX Controls)

Example

This example adds several images to a **ListImages** collection, and then uses the images in a **TreeView** control. To try the example, place **ImageList** and **TreeView** controls on a form, and paste the code into the form's Declarations section. Run the example to see the **TreeView** populated with pictures from the **ImageList**.

```
Private Sub Form_Load()
    Dim imgX As ListImage
    ' Load three icons into the ImageList control's collection.
    Set imgX = ImageList1.ListImages. _
    Add(,"rocket", LoadPicture("icons\industry\rocket.ico"))
    Set imgX = ImageList1.ListImages. _
    Add(,"plane",LoadPicture("icons\industry\plane.ico"))
    Set imgX = ImageList1.ListImages. _
    Add(,"car",LoadPicture("icons\industry\cars.ico"))

    ' Set TreeView control's ImageList property.
    Set TreeView1.ImageList = ImageList1

    ' Create a Treeview, and use ListImage objects for its images.
    Dim nodX As Node
    Set nodX = TreeView1.Nodes.Add(,,,"Rocket")
    nodX.Image = 1 ' Use the Index property of image 1.
    Set nodX = TreeView1.Nodes.Add(,,,"Plane")
    nodX.Image = "plane" ' Use the Key property of image 2.
    Set nodX = TreeView1.Nodes.Add(,,,"Car")
    nodX.Image = "car"' Use the Key property of image 3.
End Sub
```

Draw Method

Draws an image into a destination device context, such as a **PictureBox** control, after performing a graphical operation on the image.

Applies To

ImageList Control

Syntax

object.**Draw** (*hDC*, *x*,*y*, *style*)

The **Draw** method syntax has these parts:

Part	Description
object	Required. An object expression that evaluates to an object in the **Applies To** list.
hDC	Required. A value set to the target object's **hDC** property.
x,*y*	Optional. The coordinates used to specify the location within the device context where the image will be drawn. If you don't specify these, the image is drawn at the origin of the device context.
style	Optional. Specifies the operation performed on the image, as described in **Settings**.

Settings

The settings for *style* are:

Constant	Value	Description
imlNormal	0	(Default) Normal. Draws the image with no change.
imlTransparent	1	Transparent. Draws the image using the **MaskColor** property to determine which color of the image will be transparent.
imlSelected	2	Selected. Draws the image dithered with the system highlight color.
imlFocus	3	Focus. Draws the image dithered and striped with the highlight color creating a hatched effect to indicate the image has the focus.

Remarks

The **hDC** property is a handle (a number) that the Windows operating system uses for internal reference to an object. You can paint in the internal area of any control that has an **hDC** property. In Visual Basic, these include the **Form** object, **PictureBox** control, and **Printer** object.

Because an object's **hDC** can change while an application is running, it is better to specify the **hDC** property rather than an actual value. For example, the following code ensures that the correct **hDC** value is always supplied to the **ImageList** control:

```
ImageList1.ListImages(1).Draw Form1.hDC
```

See Also

ExtractIcon Method, **Overlay** Method, **ImageList** Control Constants, **Form** Object, **Forms** Collection, **hDC** Property, **MaskColor** Property, **PictureBox** Control, **Printer** Object, **Printers** Collection

Example

This example loads an image into an **ImageList** control. When you click the form, the image is drawn on the form in four different styles. To try the example, place an **ImageList** control on a form and paste the code into the form's Declarations section. Run the example and click the form.

```
Private Sub Form_Load()
   Dim X As ListImage
   'Load one image into the ImageList.
   Set X = ImageList1.ListImages. _
   Add(, , LoadPicture("bitmaps\assorted\intl_no.bmp"))
End Sub

Private Sub Form_Click()
   Dim space, intW As Integer ' Create spacing variables.

   ' Use the ImageWidth property for spacing.
   intW = ImageList1.ImageWidth
   space = Form1.Font.Size * 2 ' Use the Font.Size for height spacing.

   ScaleMode = vbPoints ' Set ScaleMode to points.
   Cls ' Clear the form.
```

```
' Draw the image with Normal style.
ImageList1.ListImages(1).Draw Form1.hDC, , space,imlNormal
' Set MaskColor to red, which will become transparent.
ImageList1.MaskColor = vbRed
' Draw the image with red (MaskColor) the transparent color.
ImageList1.ListImages(1).Draw Form1.hDC, intW, space,imlTransparent
' Draw image with the Selected style.
ImageList1.ListImages(1).Draw Form1.hDC, intW * 2,space,imlSelected
' Draw image with Focus style.
ImageList1.ListImages(1).Draw Form1.hDC, intW * 3, space,imlFocus

' Print a caption for the images.
Print _
"Normal             Transparent          Selected          Focus"

End Sub
```

ExtractIcon Method

Creates an icon from a bitmap in a **ListImage** object of an **ImageList** control and returns a reference to the newly created icon.

Applies To

ImageList Control

Syntax

object.**ExtractIcon**

The *object* placeholder represents an object expression that evaluates to an object in the **Applies To** list.

Remarks

You can use the icon created with the **ExtractIcon** method like any other icon. For example, you can use it as a setting for the **MouseIcon** property, as the following code illustrates:

```
Set Command1.MouseIcon = ImageList1.ListImages(1).ExtractIcon
```

See Also

ListImage Object, **ListImages** Collection, **Add** Method (ListImages Collection), **MouseIcon** Property

Example

This example loads a bitmap into an **ImageList** control. When the user clicks the form, the **ExtractIcon** method is used to create an icon from the bitmap, and that icon is used as a setting in the **Form** object's **MouseIcon** property. To try the example, place an **ImageList** control on a form and paste the code into the form's Declarations section. Run the example and click the form.

```
Private Sub Form_Load()
    Dim imgX As ListImage
    Set imgX = ImageList1.ListImages. _
    Add(, , LoadPicture("bitmaps\assorted\balloon.bmp"))
End Sub

Private Sub Form_Click()
    Dim picX As Picture
    Set picX = ImageList1.ListImages(1).ExtractIcon  ' Make an icon.

    With Form1
    .MouseIcon =  picX' Set new icon.
    .MousePointer = vbCustom   ' Set to custom icon.
    End With
End Sub
```

hImageList Property (ImageList Control)

Returns a handle to an **ImageList** control.

Applies To

ImageList Control

Syntax

object.**hImageList**

The *object* placeholder represents an object expression that evaluates to an **ImageList** control.

Remarks

The Microsoft Windows operating environment identifies an **ImageList** control in an application by assigning it a handle, or **hImageList**. The **hImageList** property is used with Windows API calls. Many **ImageList**-related API functions require the **hImageList** of the active window as an argument.

Note   Because the value of this property can change while a program is running, never store the **hImageList** value in a variable.

ImageHeight, ImageWidth Properties

- The **ImageHeight** property returns or sets the height of **ListImage** objects in an **ImageList** control.

- The **ImageWidth** property returns or sets the width of **ListImage** objects in an **ImageList** control.

Applies To

ImageList Control

Syntax

object.**ImageHeight**
object.**ImageWidth**

The *object* placeholder represents an object expression that evaluates to an object in the **Applies To** list.

Remarks

Both height and width are measured in pixels. All images in a **ListImages** collection have the same height and width properties.

When an **ImageList** contains no **ListImage** objects, you can set both **ImageHeight** and **ImageWidth** properties. However, once a **ListImage** object has been added, all subsequent images must be of the same height and width as the first object. If you try to add an image of a different size, an error is returned.

See Also

Add Method (ListImages Collection)

Example

This example loads an icon into an **ImageList** control, and uses the image in a **ListView** control. When the user clicks the form, the code uses the **ImageHeight** property to adjust the height of the **ListView** control to accommodate the **ListImage** object. To try the example, place **ImageList** and **ListView** controls on a form and paste the code into the form's Declarations section. Run the example and click the form.

```
Private Sub Form_Load()
    ' Create variables for ImageList and ListView objects.
    Dim imgX As ListImage
    Dim itmX As ListItem

    Form1.ScaleMode = vbPixels ' Make sure ScaleMode is set to pixels.

    ListView1.BorderStyle = FixedSingle ' Show border.
    ' Shorten ListView control so later contrast is more obvious.
    ListView1.Height = 50

    ' Put a large bitmap into the ImageList.
    Set imgX = ImageList1.ListImages. _
    Add(,, LoadPicture("bitmaps\gauge\vert.bmp"))

    ListView1.Icons = ImageList1 ' Set Icons property.

    ' Add an item to the ListView control.
    Set itmX = ListView1.ListItems.Add()
    itmX.Icon = 1   ' Set Icon property to ListImage 1 of ImageList.
    itmX.Text = "Thermometer"  ' Set text of ListView ListItem object.
End Sub

Private Sub Form_Click()
    Dim strHW As String
```

```
strHW = "Height: " & ImageList1.ImageHeight & _
"   Width: " & ImageList1.ImageWidth
caption = strHW' Show dimensions.
' Enlarge ListView to accommodate the tallest image.
ListView1.Height = ImageList1.ImageHeight + 50
End Sub
```

ImageList Control Constants

Constant	Value	Description
imlNormal	0	Image is drawn with no change.
imlTransparent	1	Image is drawn transparently.
imlSelected	2	Image is drawn selected.
imlFocus	3	Image is drawn with focus.

See Also

ImageList Control, **Draw** Method, **Visual Basic** Constants, **ActiveX** Control Constants

ListImage Object, ListImages Collection

- A **ListImage** object is a bitmap of any size that can be used in other controls.
- A **ListImages** collection is a collection of **ListImage** objects.

Syntax

imagelist.**ListImages**
imagelist.**ListImages**(*index*)

The syntax lines above refer to the collection and to individual elements in the collection, respectively, according to standard collection syntax.

The **ListImage** Object, **ListImages** Collection syntaxes have these parts:

Part	Description
imagelist	Required. An object expression that evaluates to an object in the **Applies To** list.
index	An integer or string that uniquely identifies the object in the collection. The integer is the value of the **Index** property; the string is the value of the **Key** property.

Remarks

The **ListImages** collection is a 1-based collection.

You can add and remove a **ListImage** at design time using the General tab of the **ImageList** Control Properties page, or at run time using the **Add** method for **ListImage** objects.

Each item in the collection can be accessed by its index or unique key. For example, to get a reference to the third **ListImage** object in a collection, use the following syntax:

```
Dim imgX As ListImage
    ' Reference by index number.
Set imgX = ImageList.ListImages(3)
    ' Or reference by unique key.
Set imgX = ImageList1.ListImages("third") ' Assuming Key is "third."
    ' Or use Item method.
Set imgX = ImageList1.ListImages.Item(3)
```

Each **ListImage** object has a corresponding mask that is generated automatically using the **MaskColor** property. This mask is not used directly, but is applied to the original bitmap in graphical operations such as the **Overlay** and **Draw** methods.

Properties

Count Property, **Index** Property, **Item** Property, **Key** Property, **Picture** Property, **Tag** Property

Methods

Add Method (ListImages Collection), **Draw** Method, **ExtractIcon** Method, **Clear** Method, **Remove** Method

See Also

MaskColor Property, **Overlay** Method, **hImageList** Property (ImageList Control), **PictureBox** Control, **Stretch** Property

---

ListImages Property

Returns a reference to a collection of **ListImage** objects in an **ImageList** control.

Applies To

ImageList Control

Syntax

object.**ListImages**

The *object* placeholder represents an object expression that evaluates to an object in the **Applies To** list.

Remarks

You can manipulate **ListImage** objects using standard collection methods (for example, the **Add** and **Clear** methods). Each member of the collection can be accessed by its index or unique key. These are stored in the **Index** and **Key** properties, respectively, when **ListImage** is added to a collection.

See Also

ListImage Object, **ListImages** Collection, **Add** Method (ListImages Collection), **Clear** Method (ActiveX Controls), **Remove** Method (Visual Basic Extensibility)

Example

This example adds three **ListImage** objects to a **ListImages** collection and uses them in a **ListView** control. The code refers to the **ListImage** objects using both their **Key** and **Item** properties. To try the example, place **ImageList** and **ListView** controls on a form and paste the code into the form's Declarations section. Run the example.

```
Private Sub Form_Load()
    Dim imgX As ListImage
    ' Add images to ListImages collection.
    Set imgX = ImageList1. _
    ListImages.Add(,"rocket",LoadPicture("icons\industry\rocket.ico"))
    Set imgX = ImageList1. _
    ListImages.Add(,"jet",LoadPicture("icons\industry\plane.ico"))
    Set imgX = ImageList1. _
    ListImages.Add(,"car",LoadPicture("icons\industry\cars.ico"))

    ListView1.Icons = ImageList1 ' Set Icons property.

    ' Add Item objects to the ListView control.
    Dim itmX as ListItem
    Set itmX = ListView1.ListItems.Add()
    ' Reference by index.
    itmX.Icon = 1
    itmX.Text = "Rocket" ' Set Text string.
    Set itmX = ListView1.ListItems.Add()
    ' Reference by key ("jet").
    itmX.Icon = "jet"
    itmX.Text = "Jet" ' Set Text string.
    Set itmX = ListView1.ListItems.Add()
    itmX.Icon = "car"
    itmX.Text = "Car" ' Set Text string.
End Sub
```

MaskColor Property

Returns or sets the color used to create masks for an **ImageList** control.

Applies To

ImageList Control

Syntax

object.**MaskColor** [= *color*]

The **MaskColor** property syntax has these parts:

Part	Description
object	Required. An object expression that evaluates to an object in the **Applies To** list.
color	A value or constant that determines the color used to create masks. You can specify colors using either Visual Basic intrinsic constants, the **QBColor** function, or the **RGB** function.

Remarks

Every image in a **ListImages** collection has a corresponding mask associated with it. The mask is a monochrome image derived from the image itself, automatically generated using the **MaskColor** property as the specific color of the mask. This mask is not used directly, but is applied to the original bitmap in graphical operations such as the **Overlay** and **Draw** methods. For example, the **MaskColor** property determines which color of an image will be transparent in the **Overlay** method.

If the system colors change, then the color which is transparent will change, making the look of your picture unpredictable. It is good programming practice to use non-system colors.

See Also

Draw Method, **ListImage** Object, **ListImages** Collection, **Overlay** Method, **QBColor** Function, **RGB** Function

Example

This example loads several bitmaps into an **ImageList** control. As you click the form, one **ListImage** object is overlaid on one of the other **ListImage** objects. To try the example, place an **ImageList** control and a **Picture** control on a form and paste the code into the form's Declarations section. Run the program and click the form.

```
Private Sub Form_Load()
   Dim imgX As ListImage

   ' Load bitmaps.
   Set imgX = ImageList1.ListImages. _
   Add(, "No", LoadPicture("bitmaps\assorted\Intl_No.bmp"))
   Set imgX = ImageList1.ListImages. _
   Add(, , LoadPicture("bitmaps\assorted\smokes.bmp"))
   Set imgX = ImageList1.ListImages. _
   Add(, , LoadPicture("bitmaps\assorted\beany.bmp"))

   ScaleMode = vbPixels
   ' Set MaskColor property.
   ImageList1.MaskColor = vbGreen
   ' Set the form's BackColor to white.
   Form1.BackColor = vbWhite
End Sub

Private Sub Form_Click()
   Static intCount As Integer ' Static variable to count images.

   ' Reset variable to 2 if it is over the ListImages.Count value.
   If intCount > ImageList1.ListImages.Count Or intCount < 1 Then
      intCount = 2 ' Reset to second image
   End If
```

```
' Overlay ListImage(1) over ListImages 2-3.
Picture1.Picture = ImageList1.Overlay(intCount, 1)
' Increment count.
intCount = intCount + 1

' Create variable to hold ImageList.ImageWidth value.
Dim intW
intW = ImageList1.ImageWidth

' Draw images onto the form for reference. Use the ImageWidth
' value to space the images.
ImageList1.ListImages(1).Draw Form1.hDC, 0, 0, imlNormal
ImageList1.ListImages(2).Draw Form1.hDC, 0, intW, imlNormal
ImageList1.ListImages(3).Draw Form1.hDC, 0, intW * 2, imlNormal
End Sub
```

Overlay Method

Draws one image from a **ListImages** collection over another, and returns the result.

Applies To

ImageList Control

Syntax

object.**Overlay** (*index1*, *index2*)

The **Overlay** method syntax has these parts:

Part	Description
object	Required. An object expression that evaluates to an object in the **Applies To** list.
index1	Required. An integer (**Index** property) or unique string (**Key** property) that specifies the image to be overlaid.
index2	Required. An integer (**Index** property) or unique string (**Key** property) that specifies the image to be drawn over the object specified in *index1*. The color of the image that matches the **MaskColor** property is made transparent. If no color matches, the image is drawn opaquely over the other image.

Remarks

Use the **Overlay** method in conjunction with the **MaskColor** property to create a single image from two disparate images. The **Overlay** method imposes one bitmap over another to create a third, composite image. The **MaskColor** property determines which color of the overlaying image is transparent.

The *index* can be either an index or a key. For example, to overlay the first picture in the collection with the second:

```
Set Picture1.Picture = ImageList1.Overlay(1,2) ' Reference by Index.
   'Or reference by Key property.
Set Picture1.Picture = ImageList1.Overlay("First", "Second")
```

See Also

ListImage Object, **ListImages** Collection, **Draw** Method, **Index** Property (ActiveX Controls), **Item** Method (Add-In), **Key** Property (ActiveX Controls), **MaskColor** Property

Example

This example loads five **ListImage** objects into an **ImageList** control and displays any two images in two **PictureBox** controls. For each **PictureBox**, select an image to display from one of the two **ComboBox** controls. When you click the form, the code uses the **Overlay** method to create a third image that is displayed in a third **PictureBox** control. To try the example, place an **ImageList** control, two **ComboBox** controls, and three **PictureBox** controls on a form and paste the code into the form's Declarations section. Run the example and click the form.

```
Private Sub Form_Load()
   Dim X As ListImage
   ' Add 5 images to a ListImages collection.
   Set X = ImageList1.ListImages. _
    Add(, , LoadPicture("icons\elements\moon05.ico"))
   Set X = ImageList1.ListImages. _
    Add(, , LoadPicture("icons\elements\snow.ico"))
   Set X = ImageList1.ListImages. _
    Add(, , LoadPicture("icons\writing\erase02.ico"))
   Set X = ImageList1.ListImages. _
    Add(, , LoadPicture("icons\writing\note06.ico"))
   Set X = ImageList1.ListImages. _
    Add(, , LoadPicture("icons\flags\flgfran.ico"))

   With combo1                       ' Populate the first ComboBox.
      .AddItem "Moon"
      .AddItem "Snowflake"
      .AddItem "Pencil"
      .AddItem "Note"
      .AddItem "Flag"
      .ListIndex = 0
   End With

   With combo2                       ' Populate the second ComboBox.
      .AddItem "Moon"
      .AddItem "Snowflake"
      .AddItem "Pencil"
      .AddItem "Note"
      .AddItem "Flag"
      .ListIndex = 2
   End With
```

```
   Picture1.BackColor = vbWhite        ' Make BackColor white.
   Picture2.BackColor = vbWhite
   Picture3.BackColor = vbWhite
End Sub

Private Sub Form_Click()
   ' Overlay the two images, and display in PictureBox3.
   Set Picture3.Picture = ImageList1. _
   Overlay(combo1.ListIndex + 1, combo2.ListIndex + 1)
End Sub

Private Sub combo1_Click()
   ' Change PictureBox to reflect ComboBox selection.
   Set Picture1.Picture = ImageList1. _
   ListImages(combo1.ListIndex + 1).ExtractIcon
End Sub

Private Sub combo2_Click()
   ' Change PictureBox to reflect ComboBox selection.
   Set Picture2.Picture = ImageList1. _
   ListImages(combo2.ListIndex + 1).ExtractIcon
End Sub
```

UseMaskColor Property (ImageList Controls)

Returns or sets a value that determines whether the color assigned in the **MaskColor** property is used as a mask.

Applies To

ImageList Control

Syntax

object.**UseMaskColor** [= *value*]

The **UseMaskColor** property syntax has these parts:

Part	Description
object	An object expression that evaluates to an object in the **Applies To** list.
value	A Boolean value that determines whether the **MaskColor** property is used, as described in **Settings**.

Settings

The settings for *value* are:

Value	Description
True	The **MaskColor** is used to create transparent regions.
False	(Default) The **MaskColor** is not used.

Remarks

The **MaskColor** and **UseMaskColor** properties are used only when the **Style** property is set to 1—Graphical.

See Also

Overlay Method, **MaskColor** Property

Internet Transfer Control

The **Internet Transfer** control provides implementation of two of the most widely used protocols on the Internet, HyperText Transfer Protocol (HTTP) and File Transfer Protocol (FTP).

Using the HTTP protocol, you can connect to World Wide Web servers to retrieve HTML documents. With the FTP protocol, you can log on to FTP servers to download and upload files. The **UserName** and **Password** properties allow you to log on to private servers that require authentication. Otherwise, you can connect to public FTP servers and download files. Common FTP commands, such as **CD** and **GET**, are supported through the **Execute** method.

Properties

AccessType Property, **Document** Property, **hInternet** Property, **Index** Property, **Name** Property, **Object** Property, **Parent** Property, **Password** Property, **Protocol** Property, **Proxy** Property, **RemoteHost** Property, **RemotePort** Property, **RequestTimeout** Property, **ResponseCode** Property, **ResponseInfo** Property, **StillExecuting** Property, **Tag** Property, **URL** Property, **UserName** Property

Events

StateChanged Event

Methods

Cancel Method, **Execute** Method, **GetChunk** Method (Internet Transfer Control), **GetHeader** Method, **OpenURL** Method

See Also

Trappable Errors for the Internet Transfer Control

AccessType Property

Sets or returns a value that determines the type of access (through a proxy or directly) that the control will use to communicate with the Internet. This value can be changed while an asynchronous request is being processed, but will not take effect until the next connection is established.

Applies To

Microsoft Internet Transfer Control

Syntax

object.**AccessType** = *type*

The **AccessType** property syntax has these parts:

Part	Description
object	An object expression that evaluates to an object in the **Applies To** list.
type	Integer (enumerated). A numeric expression that determines the type of access used, as described in **Settings**.

Settings

Valid settings for *type* are:

Constant	Value	Description
icUseDefault	0	Default. Use Defaults. The control uses default settings found in the registry to access the Internet.
icDirect	1	Direct to Internet. The control has a direct connection to the Internet.
icNamedProxy	2	Named Proxy. Instructs the control to use the proxy server specified in the **Proxy** property.

See Also

Proxy Property

Cancel Method

Cancels the current request and closes any connections currently established.

Applies To

Microsoft Internet Transfer Control

Syntax

object.**Cancel**

The *object* placeholder represents an object expression that evaluates to an object in the **Applies To** list.

Return Value

None

Document Property

Returns or sets the file or document that will be used with the **Execute** method. If this property is not specified, the default document from the server will be returned; for write operations, an error occurs if no document is specified.

Applies To

Microsoft Internet Transfer Control

Syntax

> *object.***Document** = *string*

The **Document** property syntax has these parts:

Part	Description
object	An object expression that evaluates to an object in the **Applies To** list.
string	The name of the file or document to be used with the **Execute** method.

See Also

Execute Method

Execute Method (Internet Control)

Executes a request to a remote server. You can only send requests which are valid for the particular protocol.

Applies To

Microsoft Internet Transfer Control

Syntax

> *object.***Execute** *url, operation, data, requestHeaders*

The **Execute** property syntax has these parts:

Part	Description
object	An object expression that evaluates to an object in the **Applies To** list.
url	Optional. String that specifies the URL to which the control should connect. If no URL is specified here, the URL specified in the **URL** property will be used.
operation	Optional. String that specifies the type of operation to be executed. See **Settings** below for a list of supported operations.
data	Optional. String that specifies the data for operations (See **Settings** below.)
requestHeaders	Optional. String that specifies additional headers to be sent from the remote server. The format for these is: `header name: header value vbCrLf`

Settings

Note Valid settings for *operation* are determined by the protocol being used. The tables below are organized by protocol.

Supported HTTP commands

Valid settings for *operation* are:

Operation	Description
GET	Retrieve data from the URL specified in the **URL** property.
HEAD	Sends the Request headers.
POST	Posts data to the server. The data is located in the *data* argument. This is an alternate method to **GET**, for which additional instructions are specified in the *data* argument.
PUT	Put operation. The name of the page to be replaced is located in the *data* argument.

Supported FTP commands

Important   The FTP protocol uses a single string that includes the operation name and any other parameters needed by the operation. In other words, the *data* and *requestHeaders* arguments are not used; all of the operations and their parameters are passed as a single string in the *operation* argument. Parameters are separated by a space. In the descriptions below, do not confuse the terms "file1" and "file2" with the *data* and *requestHeaders* arguments.

The syntax for FTP operations is:

operationName file1 file2.

For example, to get a file, the following code invokes the **Execute** method, which includes the operation name ("GET"), and the two file names required by the operation:

```
Inet1.Execute "FTP://ftp.microsoft.com", _
"GET Disclaimer.txt C:\Temp\Disclaimer.txt"
```

Note   File names that include embedded spaces are not supported.

Valid FTP settings for *operation* are:

Operation	Description
CD *file1*	Change Directory. Changes to the directory specified in *file1*.
CDUP	Change to parent directory. Equivalent to "CD..".
CLOSE	Closes the current FTP connection.
DELETE *file1*	Deletes the file specified in *file1*.
DIR *file1*	Directory. Searches the directory specified in *file1*. (Wildcards are permitted but the remote host dictates the syntax.) If no file1 is specified, a full directory of the current working directory is returned. Use the **GetChunk** method to return the directory data.
GET *file1 file2*	Retrieves the remote file specified in *file1*, and creates a new local file specified in *file2*.
LS *file1*	List. Searches the directory specified in *file1*. (Wildcards are permitted but the remote host dictates the syntax.) Use the **GetChunk** method to return the file directory data.

(continued)

Operation	Description
MKDIR *file1*	Make Directory. Creates a directory as specified in *file1*. Success is dependent on user privileges on the remote host.
PUT *file1 file2*	Copies a local file specified in *file1* to the remote host specified in *file2*.
PWD	Print Working Directory. Returns the current directory name. Use the **GetChunk** method to return the data.
QUIT	Terminates the current user.
RECV *file1 file2*	Retrieves the remote file specified in *file1*, and creates a new local file specified in *file2*. Equivalent to **GET**.
RENAME *file1 file2*	Renames the remote file named in *file1* to the new name specified in *file2*. Success is dependent on user privileges on the remote host.
RMDIR *file1*	Remove Directory. Removes the remote directory specified in *file1*. Success is dependent on user privileges on the remote host.
SEND *file1 file2*	Copies a local file, specified in *file1*, to the remote host, specified in *file2*. Equivalent to **PUT**.
SIZE *file1*	Returns the size of the directory specified in *file1*.

Return Type

None

Remarks

Many commands listed above can be carried out only if the user has privileges on the host server. For example, anonymous FTP sites will not allow anyone to delete files or directories.

See Also

Document Property, **Protocol** Property (Internet Transfer Control), **URL** Property

Example

The example shows a series of common FTP operations using the **Execute** method. The example assumes that three **TextBox** controls exist on the form. The first, **txtURL** contains the URL of the FTP server. The second, **txtRemotePath**, contains additional information needed by the particular command. The third, **txtResponse**, contains the response of the server.

```
Private Sub cmdChangeDirectory_Click()
    ' Change directory to txtRemotePath.
    Inet1.Execute txtURL.Text, "CD " & _
    txtRemotePath.Text
End Sub

Private Sub cmdDELETE_Click()
    ' Delete the directory in txtRemotePath.
    Inet1.Execute txtURL.Text, "DELETE " & _
    txtRemotePath.Text
End Sub
```

```
Private Sub cmdDIR_Click()
   Inet1.Execute txtURL.Text, "DIR FindThis.txt"
End Sub

Private Sub cmdGET_Click()
   Inet1.Execute txtURL.Text, _
   "GET GetThis.txt C:\MyDocuments\GotThis.txt"
End Sub

Private Sub cmdSEND_Click()
   Inet1.Execute txtURL.Text, _
   "SEND C:\MyDocuments\Send.txt SentDocs\Sent.txt"
End Sub

Private Sub Inet1_StateChanged(ByVal State As Integer)
   ' Retrieve server response using the GetChunk
   ' method when State = 12.

   Dim vtData As Variant ' Data variable.
   Select Case State
   ' ... Other cases not shown.
   Case icError ' 11
      ' In case of error, return ResponseCode and
      ' ResponseInfo.
      vtData = Inet1.ResponseCode & ":" & _
      Inet1.ResponseInfo
   Case icResponseCompleted ' 12
      vtData = Inet1.GetChunk(1024)
   End Select
   txtResponse.Text = vtData
End Sub
```

GetChunk Method (Internet Transfer Control)

Retrieves data from in the **StateChanged** event. Use this method after invoking the **Execute** method as a **GET** operation.

Applies To

Microsoft Internet Transfer Control

Syntax

*object.***GetChunk**(*size [,datatype]*)

The **Get** property syntax has these parts:

Part	Description
object	An object expression that evaluates to an object in the **Applies To** list.
size	Required. A long numeric expression that determines the size of the chunk to be retrieved.
datatype	Optional. An integer that specifies the data type of the retrieved chunk, as shown in **Settings** below.

Settings

The settings for *datatype* are:

Constant	Value	Description
icString	0	Default. Retrieves data as string.
icByteArray	1	Retrieves data as a byte array.

Return Type

Variant

Remarks

Use the **GetChunk** method in the **StateChanged** event. When the **State** property is **icResponseCompleted** (12), then use the **GetChunk** method to retrieve the buffer's contents.

Specifics

Execute Method, **StateChanged** Event

See Also

Execute Method, **StateChanged** Event

Example

The example uses the **GetChunk** method in the **StateChanged** event to retrieve a chunk of data. The example uses a **Select Case** statement to determine what to do with every possible state. The example assumes a **TextBox** control named **txtData** exists on the form.

```
Private Sub Inet1_StateChanged(ByVal State As Integer)
    ' Retrieve server response using the GetChunk
    ' method when State = 12. This example assumes the
    ' data is text.

    Select Case State
    ' ... Other cases not shown.

    Case icResponseReceived ' 12
        Dim vtData As Variant ' Data variable.
        Dim strData As String: strData = ""
        Dim bDone As Boolean: bDone = False

        ' Get first chunk.
        vtData = Inet1.GetChunk(1024, icString)
```

```
                   Do While Not bDone
                      strData = Data & vtData
                      ' Get next chunk.
                      vtData = Inet1.GetChunk(1024, icString)
                      If Len(vtData) = 0 Then
                         bDone = True
                      End If
                   Loop

                   txtData.Text = strData
                End Select

            End Sub
```

GetHeader Method

The **GetHeader** method is used to retrieve header text from an HTTP file.

Applies To

Microsoft Internet Transfer Control

Syntax

*object***.GetHeader** (*hdrName*)

The **GetHeader** method syntax has these parts:

Part	Description
object	An object expression that evaluates to an object in the **Applies To** list.
hdrName	Optional. A string that specifies the header to be retrieved.

Return Type

String

Remarks

If no header is named, all of the headers will be returned.

The table below shows some of the typical headers available.

Header	Description
Date	Returns the time and date of the document's transmission. The format of the returned data is Wednesday, 27-April-96 19:34:15 GMT.
MIME-version	Returns the MIME protocol version, which is currently 1.00.
Server	Returns the name of the server.
Content-length	Returns the length in bytes of the data.
Content-type	Returns the MIME Content-type of the data.
Last-modified	Returns the date and time of the document's last modification. The format of the returned data is Wednesday, 27-April-96 19:34:15 GMT.

hInternet Property

Returns the Internet handle from the underlying Wininet.dll API. This handle can then be used in direct calls into the API. This property is not used when accessing the control from Visual Basic.

Applies To

Microsoft Internet Transfer Control

Syntax

object.**hInternet**

The *object* placeholder represents an object expression that evaluates to an object in the **Applies To** list.

Data Type

Long

OpenURL Method

Opens and returns the document at the specified URL. The document is returned as a variant. When the method has completed, the URL properties (and portions of the URL such as the protocol) are updated to reflect the current URL.

Applies To

Microsoft Internet Transfer Control

Syntax

object.**OpenUrl** *url [,datatype]*

The **OpenURL** property syntax has these parts:

Part	Description
object	An object expression that evaluates to an object in the **Applies To** list.
url	Required. The URL of the document to be retrieved.
datatype	Optional. Integer that specifies the type of the data, as shown in **Settings**.

Settings

The settings for *datatype* are:

Constant	Value	Description
icString	0	Default. Retrieves data as string.
icByteArray	1	Retrieves data as a byte array.

Return Type

Variant

Remarks

The **OpenURL** method's return value depends on the target of the URL. For example, if the target URL is the directory of an FTP server, the directory will be returned. On the other hand, if the target is a file, the file will be retrieved.

The **OpenURL** method is equivalent to invoking the **Execute** method with a GET operation, followed by a **GetChunk** method invoked in the **StateChanged** event. The **OpenURL** method, however, results in a synchronous stream of data being returned from the site.

If you are retrieving a binary file, be sure to use a byte array as a temporary variable before writing it to disk, as shown below:

```
Dim b() As Byte
Dim strURL As String
' Set the strURL to a valid address.
strURL = "FTP://ftp.GreatSite.com/China.exe"
b() = Inet1.OpenURL(strURL, icByteArray)

Open "C:\Temp\China.exe" For Binary Access _
Write As #1
Put #1, , b()
Close #1
```

See Also

Protocol Property (Internet Transfer Control)

Examples

The example uses the **OpenURL** method to retrieve the directory of an FTP server. To try the example, place an **Internet Transfer** control and a **RichTextBox** control on a form. Paste the code into the Declarations section. Press F5 to run the example, and double-click on the form.

```
Private Sub Form_DblClick()
    Inet1.AccessType = icUseDefault
    RichTextBox1.Text = Inet1.OpenURL _
    (InputBox("URL", , "ftp://ftp.microsoft.com"))
End Sub
```

This example presumes the data is a binary file. Using a byte array, the file is retrieved and written to the disk using the **Open**, **Put**, and **Close** statements. To try the example, place an **Internet Transfer** control on a form and paste the code into the Declarations section. Press F5 and double-click on the form.

```
Private Sub Form_DblClick()
    Inet1.AccessType = icUseDefault
    Dim b() As Byte
    Dim strURL As String

    ' Presuming this is still a valid URL.
    strURL = "ftp://ftp.microsoft.com/" & _
    "developr/drg/Win32/Autorun.zip"
```

```
' Retrieve the file as a byte array.
b() = Inet1.OpenURL(strURL, icByteArray)

Open "C:\Temp\Autorun.zip" For Binary Access _
Write As #1
Put #1, , b()
Close #1
MsgBox "Done"
End Sub
```

Password Property (Internet Transfer Control)

Returns or sets the password that will be sent with the request to log on to remote computers. If this property is left blank, the control will send a default password.

Applies To

Microsoft Internet Transfer Control

Syntax

*object.***Password** = *string*

The **Password** property syntax has these parts:

Part	Description
object	An object expression that evaluates to an object in the **Applies To** list.
string	The password to be sent when logging on to a remote computer.

Remarks

The default password the control sends will depend on the exact scenario, as shown in the table below:

UserName Property	Password Property	UserName sent to FTP Server	Password sent to FTP server
Null or ""	Null or ""	"anonymous"	User's email name
Non-null string	Null or ""	**UserName** property	""
Null	Non-null string	Error	Error
Non-null string	Non-null string	**UserName** property	**Password** property

See Also

UserName Property

Protocol Property (Internet Transfer Control)

Returns or sets a value that specifies the protocol that will be used with the **Execute** method.

Applies To

Microsoft Internet Transfer Control

Syntax

*object.***Protocol** = *integer*

The **Protocol** property syntax has these parts:

Part	Description
object	An object expression that evaluates to an object in the **Applies To** list.
integer	Integer. A numeric expression that determines the protocol used, as described in **Settings**.

Settings

Valid settings for **Protocol** are:

Constant	Value	Description
icUnknown	0	Unknown.
icDefault	1	Default protocol.
icFTP	2	FTP. File Transfer Protocol.
icReserved	3	Reserved for future use.
icHTTP	4	HTTP. HyperText Transfer Protocol.
icHTTPS	5	Secure HTTP.

Remarks

When this property is specified, the **URL** property is updated to show the new value. Also, if the protocol portion of the **URL** is updated, the **Protocol** property is updated to reflect the new value. The **OpenURL** and **Execute** methods may both modify the value of this property.

Changing the value of this property will have no effect until the next **Execute** or **OpenURL** method is called.

See Also

Execute Method, **OpenURL** Method

Proxy Property

Returns or sets the name of the proxy server used to communicate with the Internet. This property is only used when the **AccessType** property is set to **icNamedProxy** (3).

Applies To

Microsoft Internet Transfer Control

Syntax

*object.***Proxy** = *proxy*

The **Proxy** property syntax has these parts:

Part	Description
object	An object expression that evaluates to an object in the **Applies To** list.
proxy	The name of the proxy server to be used.

Data Type

String

Remarks

Changing the value of this property will have no effect until the next **Execute** or **OpenURL** method is called.

See Also

AccessType Property

RemoteHost Property (ActiveX Controls)

Returns or sets the remote machine to which a control sends or receives data. You can either provide a host name, for example, "FTP://ftp.microsoft.com," or an IP address string in dotted format, such as "100.0.1.1".

Applies To

Microsoft Internet Transfer Control, **Winsock** Control

Syntax

*object.***RemoteHost** = *string*

The **RemoteHost** property syntax has these parts:

Part	Description
object	An object expression that evaluates to an object in the **Applies To** list.
string	The name or address of the remote computer.

Remarks

When this property is specified, the **URL** property is updated to show the new value. Also, if the host portion of the **URL** is updated, this property is also updated to reflect the new value.

The **RemoteHost** property can also be changed when invoking the **OpenURL** or **Execute** methods.

At run time, changing this value has no effect until the next connection.

Data Type

String

See Also

Bind Method

RemotePort Property (ActiveX Controls)

Returns or sets the remote port number to connect to.

Applies To

Microsoft Internet Transfer Control, **Winsock** Control

Syntax

object.**RemotePort** = *port*

The **RemotePort** property syntax has these parts:

Part	Description
object	An object expression that evaluates to an object in the **Applies To** list.
port	The port to connect to. The default value of this property is 80.

Remarks

When you set the **Protocol** property, the **RemotePort** property is set automatically to the appropriate default port for each protocol. Default port numbers are shown in the table below:

Port	Description
80	HTTP, commonly used for WorldWideWeb connections.
21	FTP.

Data Type

Long

See Also

Bind Method

RequestTimeout Property

Returns or sets the length, in seconds, to wait before a time-out expires. If a request doesn't respond within the specified time, and if the request was made with the **OpenURL** method (synchronous), an error is generated; if the request was made with the **Execute** method, the **StateChanged** event will occur with an error code. Setting this property to 0 means infinity.

Applies To

Microsoft Internet Transfer Control

Syntax

*object.***RequestTimeout** = *time*

The **RequestTimeout** property syntax has these parts:

Part	Description
object	An object expression that evaluates to an object in the **Applies To** list.
time	The length of time, in seconds, to wait before an error occurs.

Data Type

Long

ResponseCode Property

Returns the error code from the connection when the **icError** (11) state occurs in the **StateChanged** event. For a description of the error, check the **ResponseInfo** property.

Applies To

Microsoft Internet Transfer Control

Syntax

*object.***ResponseCode**= *code*

The **ResponseCode** property syntax has these parts:

Part	Description
object	An object expression that evaluates to an object in the **Applies To** list.
code	The number returned by the remote server.

Remarks

Use the **StateChanged** event to receive notification of an error, as shown below:

```
Private Sub Inet1_StateChanged(ByVal State As Integer)
   Dim strMess As String ' Message variable.
   Select Case State
   ' ... Other cases not shown.
   Case icError  ' 11
```

```
                  ' Get the Text of the error.
                  strMess = "ErrorCode: " & Inet1.ResponseCode & _
                  " : " & Inet1.ResponseInfo
            End Select

            Debug.Print strMess
      End Sub
```

Data Type

Long

See Also

ResponseInfo Property, **StateChanged** Event

ResponseInfo Property

Returns the text of the last error that occurred. Check the **ResponseCode** property for the error code.

Applies To

Microsoft Internet Transfer Control

Syntax

*object.***ResponseInfo**

The **ResponseInfo** property syntax has these parts:

Part	Description
object	An object expression that evaluates to an object in the **Applies To** list.
info	The response returned by the connection.

Return Type

String

Remarks

Use the **StateChanged** event to receive notification of an error, as shown below:

```
Private Sub Inet1_StateChanged(ByVal State As Integer)
   Dim strMess As String ' Message variable.
   Select Case State
   ' ... Other cases not shown.
   Case icError  ' 11
      ' Get the Text of the error.
      strMess = "ErrorCode: " & Inet1.ResponseCode & _
      " : " & Inet1.ResponseInfo
   End Select

   Debug.Print strMess
End Sub
```

See Also

ResponseCode Property, **StateChanged** Event

StateChanged Event

Occurs whenever there is a state change in the connection.

Applies To

Microsoft Internet Transfer Control

Syntax

*object*_**StateChanged(ByVal** *State* **As Integer)**

The **StateChanged** event syntax has these parts:

Part	Description
object	An object expression that evaluates to an object in the **Applies To** list.
State	Integer. Specifies the state, as shown in **Settings** below.

Settings

The settings for *State* are:

Constant	Value	Description
icNone	0	No state to report.
icHostResolvingHost	1	The control is looking up the IP address of the specified host computer.
icHostResolved	2	The control successfully found the IP address of the specified host computer.
icConnecting	3	The control is connecting to the host computer.
icConnected	4	The control successfully connected to the host computer.
icRequesting	5	The control is sending a request to the host computer.
icRequestSent	6	The control successfully sent the request.
icReceivingResponse	7	The control is receiving a response from the host computer.
icResponseReceived	8	The control successfully received a response from the host computer.
icDisconnecting	9	The control is disconnecting from the host computer.
icDisconnected	10	The control successfully disconnected from the host computer.
icError	11	An error occurred in communicating with the host computer.
icResponseCompleted	12	The request has completed and all data has been received.

Remarks

In general, you will use the **StateChanged** event to determine when to retrieve data using the **GetChunk** method. To do this, use a **Select Case** statement and test for **icResponseReceived** (8) or **icResponseCompleted** (12).

Note, however, that the **icResponseReceived** state may occur when the control has completed an operation that hasn't resulted in any data in the buffer. For example, when connecting to an FTP site, the control will perform a "handshake" with the site that doesn't result in any data transfer, yet the **icResponseReceived** state will occur.

On the other hand, the **icResponseCompleted** state occurs after an operation has completed in its entirety. For example, if you are using the **Execute** method with the **GET** operation to retrieve a file, the **icResponseCompleted** event will occur only once—after the file has been totally retrieved.

In practice, using the **icResponseReceived** state allows you to parse the data until you have retrieved only the information you need (for example, when retrieving an HTML file, retrieving only the headers). Once you have the information, you can cancel the retrieval. On the other hand, if you are intent on retrieving the whole file, the **icResponseCompleted** state will notify you that the transfer is completed, allowing you to proceed.

See Also

Execute Method, **GetChunk** Method (Internet Transfer Control), **GetHeader** Method, **OpenURL** Method, **ResponseCode** Property, **ResponseInfo** Property

Example

The example uses the **GetChunk** method in the **StateChanged** event to retrieve a chunk of data. The example uses a **Select Case** statement to determine what to do with every possible state. The example assumes a **TextBox** control named **txtData** exists on the form.

```
Private Sub Inet1_StateChanged(ByVal State As Integer)
   ' Retrieve server response using the GetChunk
   ' method when State = 12. This example assumes the
   ' data is text.

   Select Case State
   ' ... Other cases not shown.

   Case icResponseReceived ' 12
      Dim vtData As Variant ' Data variable.
      Dim strData As String: strData = ""
      Dim bDone As Boolean: bDone = False

      ' Get first chunk.
      vtData = Inet1.GetChunk(1024, icString)

      Do While Not bDone

strData = Data & vtData
         ' Get next chunk.
         vtData = Inet1.GetChunk(1024, icString)
         If Len(vtData) = 0 Then
            bDone = True
         End If
      Loop

      txtData.Text = strData
   End Select

End Sub
```

StillExecuting Property

Returns a value that specifies if the **Internet Transfer** control is busy. The control will return **True** when it is engaged in an operation such as retrieving a file from the Internet. The control will not respond to other requests when it is busy.

Applies To

Microsoft Internet Transfer Control

Syntax

object.**StillExecuting** = *boolean*

The **StillExecuting** property syntax has these parts:

Part	Description
object	An object expression that evaluates to an object in the **Applies To** list.
boolean	A Boolean expression specifying whether the control is busy or not.

Data Type

Boolean

Settings

The settings for *boolean* are:

Constant	Value	Description
True	-1	The control is busy.
False	0	The control is not busy.

Trappable Errors for the Internet Transfer Control

The following tables list the trappable errors and constants for the **Internet Transfer** control.

Constant	Value	Description
icOutOfMemory	7	"Out of memory"
icTypeMismatch	13	"Type mismatch"
icInvalidPropertyValue	380	Invalid property value
icInetOpenFailed	35750	Unable to open Internet handle.
icOpenFailed	35751	"Unable to open URL"
icBadUrlL	35752	"URL is malformed"

(continued)

(continued)

Constant	Value	Description
icProtMismatch	35753	"Protocol not supported for this method"
icConnectFailed	35754	"Unable to connect to remote host"
icNoRemoteHost	35755	"No remote computer is specified"
icRequestFailed	35756	"Unable to complete request"
icNoExecute	35757	"You must execute an operation before retrieving data"
icBlewChunk	35758	"Unable to retrieve data"
icFtpCommandFailed	35759	"FTP command failed"
icUnsupportedType	35760	"Cannot coerce type"
icTimeOut	35761	"Request timed out"
icUnsupportedCommand	35762	"Not a valid or supported command"
icInvalidOperation	35763	"Invalid operation argument"
icExecuting	35764	"Still executing last request"
icInvalidForFtp	35765	"This call is not valid for an FTP connection"
icOutOfHandles	35767	"Out of handles"
icinetTimeout	35768	"Timeout"
icInetTimeout	35768	Timeout
icExtendedError	35769	Extended error.
icIntervalError	35770	Internal error.
icInvalidURL	35771	Invalid URL.
icUnrecognizedScheme	35772	Unrecognized scheme
icNameNotResolved	35773	Name not resolved.
icProtocolNotFound	35774	Protocol not found.
icInvalidOption	35775	Invalid option.
icBadOptionLength	35776	Bad option length.
icOptionNotSettable	35777	Option not settable
icShutDown	35778	Shutdown
icIncorrectUserName	35779	Incorrect User name.
icLoginFailure	35781	Login failure.
icInetIvalidOpertation	35782	Invalid operaion.
icOperationCancelled	35783	Operation cancelled.
icIncorrectHandleType	35784	incorrect handle type.
icIncorrectHandleState	35785	incorrect handle state.
icNotProxyRequest	35786	Not a proxy.
icRegistryValueNotFound	35787	Registry value not found.
icbadRegistryParameter	35788	bad registry parameter.

(continued)

Constant	Value	Description
icNoDirectAccess	35789	No direct access.
icIncorrect Password	35779	Incorrect password.
icNoContext	35790	No context.
icNoCallback	35791	No callback.
icRequestPending	35792	Request pending.
icIncorrectFormat	35793	Incorrect format.
icItemNotFound	35794	Item not found.
icCannotConnect	35795	Cannot connect.
icConnectionAborted	35796	Connection aborted.
icConnectionReset	35797	Connection reset.
icForceEntry	35798	Force entry.
icInvalidProxyRequest	35799	Invalid proxy reques
icWouldBlock	35800	Would block.
icHandleExists	35802	Handle exists.
icSecCertDateInvalid	35803	Security certificate date invalid.
icSecCertCnInvalid	35804	Security certificate number invalid.
icHttpsToHttpOnRedir	35806	HTTPS to HTTP on redirect.
icMixedSecurity	35807	Mixed security
icChgPostIsNotSecure	35808	Change post is not secure
icHttpToHttpsOnRedir	35808	HTTPS to HTTP on redirect.
icPostIsNonSecure	35809	Post is non-secure.
icClientAuthCertNeeded	35810	Client authorization certificate needed.
icInvalidCa	35811	Invalid client authorization.
icClientAuthNotSetup	35812	Client Authorization not set up.
icAsyncThreadFailed	35813	Async thread failed.
icRedirectSchemeChange	35814	Redirect scheme change.
icFtpTransferInProgress	35876	FTP: transfer in progress.
icFtpDropped	35877	Connection dropped.
icGopherProtocolError	35896	Gopher: protocol error.
icGopherNotFile	35897	Gopher: not a file.
icGopherDataError	35898	Gopher: data error.
icGopherEndOfData	35899	Gopher: end of data.
icGopherInvalidLocator	35900	Gopher: invalid locator.
icGopherIncorrectLocatorType	35901	Gopher: incorrect locator type.
icGopherNotGopherPlus	35902	Gopher: not Gopher plus.

(continued)

(continued)

Constant	Value	Description
icGopherAttributeNotFound	35903	Gopher: attribute not found.
icGopherUnknownLocator	35904	Gopher:unknown locator.
icHeaderNotFound	35916	HTTP: header not found.
icHttpDownlevelServer	35917	HTTP: downlevel server.
icHttpInvalidServerResponse	35918	HTTP: invalid server response.
icHttpInvalidHeader	35919	HTTP: invalid header.
icHttpInvalidQueryRequest	35920	HTTP: invalid query request.
icHttpHeaderAlreadyExists	35921	HTTP:Header already exists.
IcHttpRedirectFailed	35922	HTTP: redirect failed.
IcSecurityChannelError	35923	Security channel error.
IcUnableToCacheFile	35924	Unable to cache file.

See Also

Microsoft Internet Transfer Control

URL Property

Returns or sets the URL that is used by the **Execute** or **OpenURL** methods.

Applies To

Microsoft Internet Transfer Control

Syntax

*object.***URL** [= *url*]

The **URL** property syntax has these parts:

Part	Description
object	An object expression that evaluates to an object in the **Applies To** list.
url	String that specifies the URL to be used in the **Execute** method.

Remarks

Invoking the **OpenURL** or **Execute** method changes the value of this property.

Changing this property will have no effect until the next **OpenURL** or **Execute** method is called.

The **URL** property must contain at least a protocol and remote host name.

The **URL** property can be either a directory or a file. For example, both of the URLs below are valid:

```
' Setting this URL will return only the file directory:
Inet1.URL = "HTTP://www.microsoft.com"
' However, this URL will return the text of the file:
Inet1.URL = "HTTP://www.microsoft.com/disclaimer.txt"
```

Data Type

String

See Also

Execute Method

UserName Property

Returns or sets the name that will be sent with requests to remote computers. If this property is left blank, the control will send "anonymous" as the user name when requests are made.

Applies To

Microsoft Internet Transfer Control

Syntax

*object.***UserName**[= *name*]

The **UserName** property syntax has these parts:

Part	Description
object	An object expression that evaluates to an object in the **Applies To** list.
name	String that specifies the **UserName** to be used in the **Execute** method.

Remarks

Invoking the **OpenURL** or **Execute** method changes the value of this property.

Changing this property will have no effect until the next **OpenURL** or **Execute** method is called.

Data Type

String

See Also

Password Property (Internet Transfer Control)

ListView Control

The **ListView** control displays items using one of four different views. You can arrange items into columns with or without column headings as well as display accompanying icons and text.

Syntax

ListView

Remarks

With a **ListView** control, you can organize list entries, called **ListItem** objects, into one of four different views:

- Large (standard) Icons
- Small Icons
- List
- Report

The **View** property determines which view the control uses to display the items in the list. You can also control whether the labels associated with items in the list wrap to more than one line using the **LabelWrap** property. In addition, you can manage how items in the list are sorted and how selected items appear.

The **ListView** control contains **ListItem** and **ColumnHeader** objects. A **ListItem** object defines the various characteristics of items in the **ListView** control, such as:

- A brief description of the item.
- Icons that may appear with the item, supplied by an **ImageList** control.
- Additional pieces of text, called subitems, associated with a **ListItem** object that you can display in Report view.

You can choose to display column headings in the **ListView** control using the **HideColumnHeaders** property. They can be added at both design and run time. At design time, you can use the Column Headers tab of the **ListView** Control Properties dialog box. At run time, use the **Add** method to add a **ColumnHeader** object to the **ColumnHeaders** collection.

Distribution Note   The **ListView** control is part of a group of **ActiveX** controls that are found in the COMCTL32.OCX file. To use the **ListView** control in your application, you must add the COMCTL32.OCX file to the project. When distributing your application, install the COMCTL32.OCX file in the user's Microsoft Windows System or System32 directory. For more information on how to add an **ActiveX** control to a Visual Basic project, see the Visual Basic *Programmer's Guide*.

Properties

Appearance Property, **Arrange** Property, **BackColor, ForeColor** Properties, **BorderStyle** Property, **ColumnHeaders** Property, **Container** Property, **Drag Icon** Property, **DragMode** Property, **DropHighlight** Property, **Enabled** Property, **Font** Property, **Height, Width** Properties, **HelpContextID** Property, **HideColumnHeaders** Property, **HideSelection** Property, **hWnd** Property, **Icons, SmallIcons** Property, **Index** Property, **LabelEdit** Property, **LabelWrap** Property, **Left, Top** Properties, **ListItems** Property, **MouseIcon** Property, **MousePointer** Property, **MultiSelect** Property, **Name** Property, **Object** Property, **OLEDrag Mode** Property, **OLEDropMode** Property, **Parent** Property, **SelectedItem** Property, **Sorted** Property, **SortKey** Property, **SortOrder** Property, **TabIndex** Property, **TabStop** Property, **Tag** Property, **ToolTipText** Property, **View** Property, **WhatsThisHelpID** Property

Events

AfterLabelEdit Event, **BeforeLabelEdit** Event, **Click** Event, **ColumnClick** Event, **DblClick** Event, **DragDrop** Event, **DragOver** Event, **GotFocus** Event, **Item Click** Event, **KeyDown, KeyUp** Events, **KeyPress** Event, **LostFocus** Event, **MouseDown, MouseUp** Events, **MouseMove** Event, **OLECompleteDrag** Event, **OLEDragDrop** Event, **OLEDragOver** Event, **OLEGiveFeedback** Event, **OLESetData** Event, **OLEStartDrag** Event

Methods

Drag Method, **FindItem** Method, **GetFirstVisible** Method, **Hit Test** Method, **Move** Method, **OLEDrag** Method, **Refresh** Method, **SetFocus** Method, **ShowWhatsThis** Method, **StartLabelEdit** Method, **ZOrder** Method

See Also

ImageList Control, **ColumnHeader** Object, **ColumnHeaders** Collection, **Add** Method (ColumnHeaders Collection), **ListItem** Object, **ListItems** Collection, **HideColumnHeaders** Property, (ListView Control), **LabelWrap** Property, (ListView Control), **ListView** Control Constants, **TreeView** Control

---

Add Method (ColumnHeaders Collection)

Adds a **ColumnHeader** object to a **ColumnHeaders** collection in a **ListView** control.

Applies To

ColumnHeader Object, **ColumnHeaders** Collect

Syntax

object.**Add**(*index, key, text, width, alignment*)

The **Add** method syntax has these parts:

Part	Description
object	Required. An object expression that evaluates to a **ColumnHeaders** collection.
index	Optional. An integer that uniquely identifies a member of an object collection.
key	Optional. A unique string expression that can be used to access a member of the collection.
text	Optional. A string that appears in the **ColumnHeader** object.
width	Optional. A numeric expression specifying the width of the object using the scale units of the control's container.
alignment	Optional. An integer that determines the alignment of text in the **ColumnHeader** object. For settings, choose the **Alignment** property from the See Also list.

Remarks

The **Add** method returns a reference to the newly inserted **ColumnHeader** object.

Use the *index* argument to insert a column header in a specific position in the **ColumnHeaders** collection.

When the members of a **ColumnHeaders** collection can change dynamically, you may want to reference them using the **Key** property, because the **Index** property for any **ColumnHeader** object may be changing.

See Also

Alignment Property (ColumnHeader Object), **Clear** Method, **Index** Property, **Key** Property, **Remove** Method, **SubItemIndex** Property, **SubItems** Property (ListView Control)

Example

The following example uses the Biblio.mdb database as a source to populate a **ListView** control with **ListItem** objects. To try this example, place a **ListView** control on a form and paste the code into the Declarations section. You must also be sure that the Biblio.mdb has been installed on your machine. In the code below, check the path in the **OpenDatabase** function and change it to reflect the actual path to Biblio.mdb on your machine.

Note The example will not run unless you add a reference to the Microsoft DAO 3.5 Object Library. To do this, on the **Project** menu click **References**. Search for Microsoft DAO 3.5 Object Library and click the checkbox to select it.

```
Private Sub Form_Load()
    ' Add ColumnHeaders. The width of the columns is
    ' the width of the control divided by the number of
    ' ColumnHeader objects.
    ListView1.ColumnHeaders. _
    Add , , "Author", ListView1.Width / 3
```

```
        ListView1.ColumnHeaders. _
        Add , , "Author ID", ListView1.Width / 3, _
        lvwColumnCenter
        ListView1.ColumnHeaders. _
        Add , , "Birthdate", ListView1.Width / 3
        ' Set View property to Report.
        ListView1.View = lvwReport

    ' Declare object variables for the
        ' Data Access objects.
        Dim myDb As Database, myRs As Recordset
        ' Set the Database to the BIBLIO.MDB database.
        ' IMPORTANT: the Biblio.mdb must be on your
        ' machine, and you must set the correct path to
        ' the file in the OpenDatabase function below.
        Set myDb =  DBEngine.Workspaces(0) _
            .OpenDatabase("c:\Program Files\VB\BIBLIO.MDB")
        ' Set the recordset to the "Authors" table.
        Set myRs = _
        myDb.OpenRecordset("Authors", dbOpenDynaset)

    ' Declare a variable to add ListItem objects.
        Dim itmX As ListItem

        ' While the record is not the last record,
        ' add a ListItem object. Use the author field for
        ' the ListItem object's text. Use the AuthorID
        ' field for the ListItem object's SubItem(1).
        ' Use the "Year of Birth" field for the ListItem
        ' object's SubItem(2).

        While Not myRs.EOF
            Set itmX = ListView1.ListItems. _
            Add(, , CStr(myRs!Author))        ' Author.


    ' If the AuthorID field is not null, then set
            ' SubItem 1 to it.
            If Not IsNull(myRs!Au_id) Then
                itmX.SubItems(1) = CStr(myRs!Au_id)
            End If

            ' If the birth field is not Null, set
            ' SubItem 2 to it.
            If Not IsNull(myRs![Year Born]) Then
                itmX.SubItems(2) = myRs![Year Born]
            End If
            myRs.MoveNext   ' Move to next record.
        Wend
    End Sub
```

Add Method (ListItems Collection)

Adds a **ListItem** object to a **ListItems** collection in a **ListView** control and returns a reference to the newly created object.

Applies To

ListItem Object, **ListItems** Collection

Syntax

object.**Add**(*index, key, text, icon, smallIcon*)

The **Add** method syntax has these parts:

Part	Description
object	Required. An object expression that evaluates to a **ListItems** collection.
index	Optional. An integer specifying the position where you want to insert the **ListItem**. If no index is specified, the **ListItem** is added to the end of the **ListItems** collection.
key	Optional. A unique string expression that can be used to access a member of the collection.
text	Optional. A string that is associated with the **ListItem** object control.
icon	Optional. An integer that sets the icon to be displayed from an **ImageList** control, when the **ListView** control is set to **Icon** view.
smallIcon	Optional. An integer that sets the icon to be displayed from an **ImageList** control, when the **ListView** control is set to **SmallIcon** view.

Remarks

Before setting either the **Icons** or **SmallIcons** properties, you must first initialize them. You can do this at design time by specifying an **ImageList** object with the General tab of the **ListView** Control Properties dialog box, or at run time with the following code:

```
ListView1.Icons = ImageList1   'Assuming the Imagelist is ImageList1.
ListView1.SmallIcons = ImageList2
```

If the list is not currently sorted, a **ListItem** object can be inserted in any position by using the *index* argument. If the list is sorted, the *index* argument is ignored and the **ListItem** object is inserted in the appropriate position based upon the sort order.

If *index* is not supplied, the **ListItem** object is added with an index that is equal to the number of **ListItem** objects in the collection + 1.

Use the **Key** property to reference a member of the **ListItems** collection if you expect the value of an object's **Index** property to change, such as by dynamically adding objects to or removing objects from the collection.

See Also

ListView Control, **Ghosted** Property, **Icons, SmallIcons** Properties, **Index** Property, **Key** Property, **SubItems** Property (ListView Control), **Sorted** Property (ListView Control), **Selected** Property (ActiveX Controls)

Example

The following example uses the Biblio.mdb database as a source to populate a **ListView** control with **ListItem** objects. To try this example, place a **ListView** control on a form and paste the code into the Declarations section. You must also be sure that the Biblio.mdb has been installed on your machine. In the code below, check the path in the **OpenDatabase** function and change it to reflect the actual path to Biblio.mdb on your machine.

Note The example will not run unless you add a reference to the Microsoft DAO 3.5 Object Library. To do this, on the **Project** menu click **References**. Search for Microsoft DAO 3.5 Object Library and click the checkbox to select it.

```
Private Sub Form_Load()
    ' Add ColumnHeaders. The width of the columns is
    ' the width of the control divided by the number of
    ' ColumnHeader objects.
    ListView1.ColumnHeaders. _
    Add , , "Author", ListView1.Width / 3
    ListView1.ColumnHeaders. _
    Add , , "Author ID", ListView1.Width / 3, _
    lvwColumnCenter
    ListView1.ColumnHeaders. _
    Add , , "Birthdate", ListView1.Width / 3
    ' Set View property to Report.
    ListView1.View = lvwReport

    ' Declare object variables for the
    ' Data Access objects.
    Dim myDb As Database, myRs As Recordset
    ' Set the Database to the BIBLIO.MDB database.
    ' IMPORTANT: the Biblio.mdb must be on your
    ' machine, and you must set the correct path to
    ' the file in the OpenDatabase function below.
    Set myDb = DBEngine.Workspaces(0) _
        .OpenDatabase("c:\Program Files\VB\BIBLIO.MDB")
    ' Set the recordset to the "Authors" table.
    Set myRs = _
    myDb.OpenRecordset("Authors", dbOpenDynaset)

    ' Declare a variable to add ListItem objects.
    Dim itmX As ListItem

    ' While the record is not the last record,
    ' add a ListItem object. Use the author field for
    ' the ListItem object's text. Use the AuthorID
    ' field for the ListItem object's SubItem(1).
    ' Use the "Year of Birth" field for the ListItem
    ' object's SubItem(2).
```

```
    While Not myRs.EOF
        Set itmX = ListView1.ListItems. _
        Add(, , CStr(myRs!Author))      ' Author.

        ' If the AuthorID field is not null, then set
        ' SubItem 1 to it.
        If Not IsNull(myRs!Au_id) Then
            itmX.SubItems(1) = CStr(myRs!Au_id)
        End If

        ' If the birth field is not Null, set
        ' SubItem 2 to it.
        If Not IsNull(myRs![Year Born]) Then
            itmX.SubItems(2) = myRs![Year Born]
        End If
        myRs.MoveNext  ' Move to next record.
    Wend
End Sub
```

Alignment Property (ColumnHeader Object)

Returns or sets the alignment of text in a **ColumnHeader** object.

Applies To

ListView Control, **ColumnHeader** Object, **ColumnHeaders** Collection

Syntax

object.**Alignment** [= *integer*]

The **Alignment** Property syntax has these parts:

Part	Description
object	An object expression that evaluates to a **ColumnHeader** object.
integer	An integer that determines the alignment, as described in **Settings**.

Settings

The settings for *integer* are:

Constant	Value	Description
lvwColumnLeft	0	(Default) Left. Text is aligned left.
lvwColumnRight	1	Right. Text is aligned right.
lvwColumnCenter	2	Center. Text is centered.

See Also

ColumnHeader Object, **ColumnHeaders** Collection, **Add** Method (ColumnHeaders Collection), **Align** Property

Arrange Property (ListView Control)

Returns or sets a value that determines how the icons in a **ListView** control's **Icon** or **SmallIcon** view are arranged.

Applies To

ListView Control

Syntax

object.**Arrange** [= *value*]

The **Arrange** property syntax has these parts:

Part	Description
object	An object expression that evaluates to a **ListView** control.
value	An integer or constant that determines how the icons or small icons are arranged, as described in **Settings**.

Settings

The settings for *value* are:

Constant	Value	Description
lvwNone	0	(Default) None.
lvwAutoLeft	1	Left. Items are aligned automatically along the left side of the control.
lvwAutoTop	2	Top. Items are aligned automatically along the top of the control.

See Also

Icons, SmallIcons Properties, **SortKey** Property (ListView Control), **SortOrder** Property (ListView Control), **View** Property (ListView Control), **ListView** Control Constants, **Sorted** Property (ListView Control)

Example

This example adds several **ListItem** objects and subitems to a **ListView** control. When you click on an **OptionButton** control, the **Arrange** property is set with the **Index** value of the **OptionButton**. To try the example, place a control array of three **OptionButton** controls, a **ListView** control, and two **ImageList** controls on a form and paste the code into the form's Declarations section. Run the example and click on an **OptionButton** to change the **Arrange** property.

```
Private Sub Option1_Click(Index as Integer)
    ' Set Arrange property to Option1.Index.
    ListView1.Arrange = Index
End Sub

Private Sub Form_Load()
    ' Label OptionButton controls with Arrange choices.
    Option1(0).Caption = "No Arrange"
```

```
        Option1(1).Caption = "Align Auto Left"
        Option1(2).Caption = "Align Auto Top"

    ' Declare variables for creating ListView and ImageList objects.
    Dim i As Integer
    Dim itmX As ListItem              ' Object variable for ListItems.
    Dim imgX As ListImage             ' Object variable for ListImages.

    ' Add a ListImage object to an ImageList control.
    Set imgX = ImageList1.ListImages. _
    Add(,,LoadPicture("icons\mail\mail01a.ico"))

    ListView1.Icons = ImageList1       ' Associate an ImageList control.

    ' Add ten ListItem objects, each with an Icon.
    For i = 1 To 10
        Set itmX = ListView1.ListItems.Add()
        itmX.Icon = 1                  ' Icon.
        itmX.Text = "ListItem " & i
    Next i
End Sub
```

ColumnClick Event

Occurs when a **ColumnHeader** object in a **ListView** control is clicked. Only available in Report view.

Applies To

ListView Control

Syntax

Private Sub *object*_**ColumnClick(ByVal** *columnheader* **As ColumnHeader)**

The **ColumnClick** event syntax has these parts:

Part	Description
object	An object expression that evaluates to a **ListView** control.
columnheader	A reference to the **ColumnHeader** object that was clicked.

Remarks

The **Sorted**, **SortKey**, and **SortOrder** properties are commonly used in code to sort the **ListItem** objects in the clicked column.

See Also

ColumnHeader Object, **ColumnHeaders** Collection, **SortKey** Property (ListView Control), **SortOrder** Property (ListView Control), **Sorted** Property (ListView Control)

Example

This example adds three **ColumnHeader** objects to a **ListView** control and populates the control with the Publishers records of the BIBLIO.MDB database. An array of two **OptionButton** controls offers the two choices for sorting records. When you click on a **ColumnHeader**, the **ListView** control is sorted according to the **SortOrder** property, as determined by the **OptionButtons**. To try the example, place a **ListView** and a control array of two **OptionButton** controls on a form and paste the code into the form's Declarations section. Run the example and click on the **ColumnHeaders** to sort, and click on the **OptionButton** to switch the **SortOrder** property.

Note   The example will not run unless you add a reference to the Microsoft DAO 3.0 Object Library by using the References command on the Tools menu.

```
Private Sub Option1_Click(Index as Integer)
    ' These OptionButtons offer two choices: Ascending (Index 0),
    ' and Descending (Index 1). Clicking on one of these
    ' sets the SortOrder for the ListView control.
    ListView1.SortOrder = Index
    ListView1.Sorted = True ' Sort the List.
End Sub

Private Sub Form_Load()
    ' Create an object variable for the ColumnHeader object.
    Dim clmX As ColumnHeader
    ' Add ColumnHeaders. The width of the columns is the width

' of the control divided by the number of ColumnHeader objects.
    Set clmX = ListView1.ColumnHeaders. _
    Add(, , "Company", ListView1.Width / 3)
    Set clmX = ListView1.ColumnHeaders. _
    Add(, , "Address", ListView1.Width / 3)
    Set clmX = ListView1.ColumnHeaders. _
    Add(, , "Phone", ListView1.Width / 3)

    ListView1.BorderStyle = ccFixedSingle ' Set BorderStyle property.
    ListView1.View = lvwReport ' Set View property to Report.

    ' Label OptionButton controls with SortOrder options.

Option1(0).Caption = "Ascending (A-Z)"
        Option1(1).Caption = "Descending (Z-A)"
        ListView1.SortOrder = 0 ' Set to Icon view

    ' Create object variables for the Data Access objects.
    Dim myDb As Database, myRs As Recordset
    ' Set the Database to the BIBLIO.MDB database.
    Set myDb = DBEngine.Workspaces(0).OpenDatabase("BIBLIO.MDB")
    ' Set the recordset to the Publishers table.
    Set myRs = myDb.OpenRecordset("Publishers", dbOpenDynaset)

    ' Create a variable to add ListItem objects.
```

```
        Dim itmX As ListItem

        ' While the record is not the last record, add a ListItem object.
        ' Use the Name field for the ListItem object's text.
        ' Use the Address field for the ListItem object's subitem(1).
        ' Use the Phone field for the ListItem object's subitem(2).

        While Not myRs.EOF
            Set itmX = ListView1.ListItems.Add(, , CStr(myRs!Name))

            ' If the Address field is not Null, set subitem 1 to the field.
            If Not IsNull(myRs!Address) Then
                itmX.SubItems(1) = CStr(myRs!Address)  ' Address field.

    End If

            ' If the Phone field is not Null, set subitem 2 to the field.
            If Not IsNull(myRs!Telephone) Then
                itmX.SubItems(2) = myRs!Telephone  ' Phone field.
            End If

            myRs.MoveNext  ' Move to next record.
        Wend
    End Sub

    Private Sub ListView1_ColumnClick(ByVal ColumnHeader As ColumnHeader)
        ' When a ColumnHeader object is clicked, the ListView control is
        ' sorted by the subitems of that column.
        ' Set the SortKey to the Index of the ColumnHeader - 1

    ListView1.SortKey = ColumnHeader.Index - 1
        ' Set Sorted to True to sort the list.
        ListView1.Sorted = True
    End Sub
```

ColumnHeader Object, ColumnHeaders Collection

- A **ColumnHeader** object is an item in a **ListView** control that contains heading text.
- A **ColumnHeaders** collection contains one or more **ColumnHeader** objects.

Syntax

*listview.***ColumnHeaders**
*listview.***ColumnHeaders**(*index*)

The syntax lines above refer to the collection and to individual elements in the collection, respectively, according to the standard collection syntax.

The **ColumnHeader** object, **ColumnHeaders** collection syntax has these parts:

Part	Description
listview	An object expression that evaluates to a **ListView** control.
index	Either an integer or string that uniquely identifies a member of an object collection. An integer would be the value of the **Index** property; a string would be the value of the **Key** property.

Remarks

You can view **ColumnHeader** objects in Report view only.

You can add **ColumnHeader** objects to a **ListView** control at both design time and run time.

With a **ColumnHeader** object, a user can:

- Click it to trigger the **ColumnClick** event and sort the items based on that data item.

- Grab the object's right border and drag it to adjust the width of the column.

- Hide **ColumnHeader** objects in Report view.

There is always one column in the **ListView** control, which is Column 1. This column contains the actual **ListItem** objects; not their subitems. The second column (Column 2) contains subitems. Therefore, you always have one more **ColumnHeader** object than subitems and the **ListItem** object's **SubItems** property is a 1-based array of size `ColumnHeaders.Count—1`.

The number of **ColumnHeader** objects determines the number of subitems each **ListItem** object in the control can have. When you delete a **ColumnHeader** object, all of the subitems associated with the column are also deleted, and each **ListItem** object's subitem array shifts to update the indices of the **ColumnHeader**, causing the remaining column headers' **SubItemIndex** properties to change.

Properties

Alignment Property, **Count** Property, **Index** Property, **Item** Property, **Key** Property, **Left, Top** Properties, **SubItemIndex** Property, **Tag** Property, **Text** Property

Methods

Add Method, **Clear** Method, **Remove** Method

See Also

Add Method (ColumnHeaders Collection), **Clear** Method, **ListItem** Object, **ListItems** Collection, **ColumnClick** Event, **ColumnHeaders** Property (ListView Control), **HideColumnHeaders** Property (ListView Control), **Remove** Method, **SortKey** Property (ListView Control), **SortOrder** Property (ListView Control), **SubItemIndex** Property, **SubItems** Property (ListView Control), **Sorted** Property (ListView Control)

ColumnHeaders Property (ListView Control)

Returns a reference to a collection of **ColumnHeader** objects.

Applies To

ListView Control, **ColumnHeader** Object, **ColumnHeaders** Collection

Syntax

object.**ColumnHeaders**

The *object* placeholder represents an object expression that evaluates to a **ListView** control.

Remarks

You can manipulate **ColumnHeader** objects using standard collection methods (for example, the **Remove** method). Each **ColumnHeader** in the collection can be accessed either by its index or by a unique key, stored in the **Key** property.

See Also

Add Method (ColumnHeaders Collection), **Remove** Method

FindItem Method (ListView Control)

Finds and returns a reference to a **ListItem** object in a **ListView** control.

Applies To

ListView Control, **ListItem** Object, **ListItems** Collection

Syntax

object.**FindItem** (*string*, *value*, *index*, *match*)

The **FindItem** method syntax has these parts:

Part	Description
object	Required. An object expression that evaluates to a **ListView** control.
String	Required. A string expression indicating the **ListItem** object to be found.
Value	Optional. An integer or constant specifying whether the string will be matched to the **ListItem** object's **Text**, **Subitems**, or **Tag** property, as described in **Settings**.
Index	Optional. An integer or string that uniquely identifies a member of an object collection and specifies the location from which to begin the search. The integer is the value of the **Index** property; the string is the value of the **Key** property. If no index is specified, the default is 1.
Match	Optional. An integer or constant specifying that a match will occur if the item's **Text** property is the same as the string, as described in **Settings**.

Settings

The settings for *value* are:

Constant	Value	Description
lvwText	0	(Default) Matches the string with a **ListItem** object's **Text** property.
lvwSubitem	1	Matches the string with any string in a **ListItem** object's **SubItems** property.
lvwTag	2	Matches the string with any **ListItem** object's **Tag** property.

The settings for *match* are:

Constant	Value	Description
lvwWholeWord	0	(Default) An integer or constant specifying that a match will occur if the item's **Text** property begins with the whole word being searched. Ignored if the criteria is not text.
lvwPartial	1	An integer or constant specifying that a match will occur if the item's **Text** property begins with the string being searched. Ignored if the criteria is not text.

Remarks

If you specify Text as the search criteria, you can use **lvwPartial** so that a match occurs when the **ListItem** object's **Text** property begins with the string you are searching for. For example, to find the **ListItem** whose text is "Autoexec.bat", use:

```
' Create a ListItem variable.
Dim itmX As ListItem
' Set the variable to the found item.
Set itmX = ListView1.FindItem("Auto",,,lvwpartial)
```

See Also

SubItems Property (ListView Control), **ListView** Control Constants, **Tag** Property, **Index** Property, **Key** Property, **Text** Property

Example

This example populates a **ListView** control with the contents of the Publishers table of the BIBLIO.MDB database. A **ComboBox** control is also populated with three options for the **FindItem** method. A **CommandButton** contains the code for the **FindItem** method; when you click on the button, you are prompted to enter the string to search for, and the **FindItem** method searches the **ListView** control for the string. If the string is found, the control is scrolled using the **EnsureVisible** method to show the found **ListItem** object. To try the example, place a **ListView**, **ComboBox**, and a **CommandButton** control on a form and paste the code into the form's Declarations section. Run the example and click on the command button.

Note The example will not run unless you add a reference to the Microsoft DAO 3.0 Object Library by using the References command from the Tools menu.

```
Private Sub Form_Load()
    ' Create an object variable for the ColumnHeader object.
    Dim clmX As ColumnHeader
    ' Add ColumnHeaders. The width of the columns is the width
    ' of the control divided by the number of ColumnHeader objects.
    Set clmX = ListView1.ColumnHeaders. _
    Add(, , "Company", ListView1.Width / 3)
    Set clmX = ListView1.ColumnHeaders. _
    Add(, , "Address", ListView1.Width / 3)
    Set clmX = ListView1.ColumnHeaders. _
    Add(, , "Phone", ListView1.Width / 3)

    ListView1.BorderStyle = ccFixedSingle   ' Set BorderStyle property.
    ListView1.View = lvwReport   ' Set View property to Report.
    Command1.Caption = "&FindItem"

    ' Label OptionButton controls with FindItem options.
        Option1(0).Caption = "Text"
        Option1(1).Caption = "SubItem"
        Option1(2).Caption = "Tag"
        ListView1.FindItem = 0 ' Set the ListView FindItem property to Text.
    End With

    ' Populate the ListView control with database records.
    ' Create object variables for the Data Access objects.
    Dim myDb As Database, myRs As Recordset
    ' Set the Database to the BIBLIO.MDB database.
    Set myDb = DBEngine.Workspaces(0).OpenDatabase("BIBLIO.MDB")
    ' Set the recordset to the Publishers table.
    Set myRs = myDb.OpenRecordset("Publishers", dbOpenDynaset)

    ' While the record is not the last record, add a ListItem object.
    ' Use the reference to the new object to set properties.
    ' Set the Text property to the Name field (myRS!Name).
    ' Set SubItem(1) to the Address field (myRS!Address).
    ' Set SubItem(7) to the Phone field (myRS!Telephone).

    While Not myRs.EOF
        Dim itmX As ListItem                    ' A ListItem variable.
        Dim intCount As Integer                 ' A counter variable.
        ' Use the Add method to add a new ListItem and set an object
        ' variable to the new reference. Use the reference to set
        ' properties.
        Set itmX = ListView1.ListItems.Add(, , CStr(myRs!Name))
        intCount = intCount + 1                 ' Increment counter
    for the Tag property.
        itmX.Tag = "ListItem " & intCount       ' Set Tag with counter.

        ' If the Address field is not Null, set SubItem 1 to Address.
        If Not IsNull(myRs!Address) Then
            itmX.SubItems(1) = CStr(myRs!Address) ' Address field.
        End If
```

```
            ' If the Phone field is not Null, set SubItem 2 to Phone.
            If Not IsNull(myRs!Telephone) Then
                itmX.SubItems(2) = myRs!Telephone      ' Phone field.
            End If

            myRs.MoveNext                              ' Move to next record.
        Wend
    End Sub

Private Sub Command1_Click()
    ' FindItem method.
    ' Create an integer variable called intSelectedOption
    ' to store the index of the selected button
    ' Create a string variable called strFindMe. Use the InputBox
    ' to store the string to be found in the variable. Use the
    ' FindItem method to find the string. Option1 is used to
    ' switch the FindItem argument that determines where to look.

    Dim intSelectedOption as Integer
    Dim strFindMe As String
    If Option1(0).Value = True then
        strFindMe = InputBox("Find in " & Option1(0).Caption)
        intSelectedOption = lvwText
    End If
    If Option1(1).Value = True then
        strFindMe = InputBox("Find in " & Option1(1).Caption)
        intSelectedOption = lvwSubItem
    End If
    If Option1(2).Value = True then
        strFindMe = InputBox("Find in " & Option1(2).Caption)
        intSelectedOption = lvwTag
    End If

    ' FindItem method returns a reference to the found item, so
    ' you must create an object variable and set the found item
    ' to it.
    Dim itmFound As ListItem        ' FoundItem variable.

    Set itmFound = ListView1. _
    FindItem(strFindMe, intSelectedOption, , lvwPartial)

    ' If no ListItem is found, then inform user and exit. If a
    ' ListItem is found, scroll the control using the EnsureVisible
    ' method, and select the ListItem.
    If itmFound Is Nothing Then    ' If no match, inform user and exit.
        MsgBox "No match found"
        Exit Sub
    Else
        itmFound.EnsureVisible     ' Scroll ListView to show found ListItem.
        itmFound.Selected = True   ' Select the ListItem.
        ' Return focus to the control to see selection.
        ListView1.SetFocus
    End If
End Sub
```

```
Private Sub ListView1_LostFocus()
   ' After the control loses focus, reset the Selected property
   ' of each ListItem to False.
   Dim i As Integer
   For i = 1 to ListView1.ListItems.Count
      ListView1.ListItems.Item(i).Selected = False
   Next i
End Sub
```

GetFirstVisible Method (ListView Control)

Returns a reference to the first **ListItem** object visible in the internal area of a **ListView** control.

Applies To

ListView Control, **ListItem** Object, **ListItems** Collection

Syntax

object.**GetFirstVisible()**

The *object* placeholder represents an object expression that evaluates to a **ListView** control.

Remarks

A **ListView** control can contain more **ListItem** objects than can be seen in the internal area of the **ListView** control. You can use the reference returned by the **GetFirstVisible** method to determine the first visible **ListItem** object in **List** or **Report** view.

See Also

EnsureVisible Method, **Index** Property, **Key** Property

Example

This example populates a **ListView** control with the contents of the Publishers table in the BIBLIO.MDB database. When you click on the **CommandButton** control, the text of the first visible item is displayed. Click on the column headers to change the **SortKey** property and click the **CommandButton** again. To try the example, place a **ListView** and a **CommandButton** control on a form and paste the code into the form's Declarations section.

Note The example will not run unless you add a reference to the Microsoft DAO 3.0 Object Library using the References command from the Tools menu. Run the example.

```
Private Sub Command1_Click()
   ' Create a ListItem variable and set the variable to the object
   ' returned by the GetFirstVisible method. Use the reference to
   ' display the text of the ListItem.
   Dim itmX As ListItem
   Set itmX = ListView1.GetFirstVisible
   MsgBox itmX.Text
End Sub
```

```
Private Sub Form_Load()
    ' Create an object variable for the ColumnHeader object.
    Dim clmX As ColumnHeader
    ' Add ColumnHeaders. The width of the columns is the width
    ' of the control divided by the number of ColumnHeader objects.
    Set clmX = ListView1.ColumnHeaders. _
    Add(, , "Company", ListView1.Width / 3)
    Set clmX = ListView1.ColumnHeaders. _
    Add(, , "Address", ListView1.Width / 3)
    Set clmX = ListView1.ColumnHeaders. _
    Add(, , "Phone", ListView1.Width / 3)

    ListView1.BorderStyle = ccFixedSingle    ' Set BorderStyle property.

    ' Create object variables for the Data Access objects.
    Dim myDb As Database, myRs As Recordset
    ' Set the Database to the BIBLIO.MDB database.
    Set myDb = DBEngine.Workspaces(0).OpenDatabase("BIBLIO.MDB")
    ' Set the recordset to the Publishers table.
    Set myRs = myDb.OpenRecordset("Publishers", dbOpenDynaset)

    ' Create a variable to add ListItem objects.
    Dim itmX As ListItem

    ' While the record is not the last record, add a ListItem object.
    ' Use the Name field for the ListItem object's text.
    ' Use the Address field for the ListItem object's subitem(1).
    ' Use the Phone field for the ListItem object's subitem(2).

    While Not myRs.EOF

        Set itmX = ListView1.ListItems.Add(, , CStr(myRs!Name))

        ' If the Address field is not Null, set SubItem 1 to the field.
        If Not IsNull(myRs!Address) Then
            itmX.SubItems(1) = CStr(myRs!Address)  ' Address field.
        End If

        ' If the Phone field is not Null, set the SubItem 2 to the field.
        If Not IsNull(myRs!Telephone) Then
            itmX.SubItems(2) = myRs!Telephone      ' Phone field.
        End If

        myRs.MoveNext                              ' Move to next record.
    Wend
    ListView1.View = lvwReport                     ' Set view to Report.
End Sub

Private Sub ListView1_ColumnClick(ByVal ColumnHeader As ColumnHeader)
    ListView1.SortKey = ColumnHeader.Index - 1
    ListView1.Sorted = True
End Sub
```

Ghosted Property

Returns or sets a value that determines whether a **ListItem** object in a **ListView** control is unavailable (it appears dimmed).

Applies To

ListView Control, **ListItem** Object, **ListItems** Collection

Syntax

*object.***Ghosted** [= *boolean*]

The **Ghosted** property syntax has these parts:

Part	Description
object	An object expression that evaluates to a **ListItem** object.
boolean	A Boolean expression specifying if the icon or small icon is ghosted, as described in **Settings**.

Settings

The settings for *boolean* are:

Setting	Description
True	The **ListItem** object is unavailable to the user.
False	(Default) The **ListItem** is available.

Remarks

The **Ghosted** property is typically used to show when a **ListItem** is cut, or disabled for some reason.

When a ghosted **ListItem** is selected, the label is highlighted but its image is not.

See Also

SelectedItem Property (ActiveX Controls)

Example

This example populates a **ListView** control with the contents of the Authors table from the BIBLIO.MDB database, and lets you use **OptionButton** controls to set **MultiSelect** property options. You can select any item, or hold down the SHIFT Key and select multiple items. Clicking on the **CommandButton** sets the **Ghosted** property of the selected items to **True**. To try the example, place a control array of two **OptionButton** controls, a **ListView** control, an **ImageList** control, and a **CommandButton** control on a form and paste the code into the form's Declarations section.

Note The example will not run unless you add a reference to the Microsoft DAO 3.0 Object Library by using the References command on the Tools menu. Run the example, select a **MultiSelect** option by clicking an **OptionButton**, click on items to select them and click the **CommandButton** to ghost them.

```
Private Sub Command1_Click()
    Dim x As Object
    Dim i As Integer
    ' Ghost selected ListItem.
If ListView1.SelectedItem Is Nothing Then Exit Sub
    For i = 1 To ListView1.ListItems.Count
        If ListView1.ListItems(i).Selected = True Then
            ListView1.ListItems(i).Ghosted = True
        End If
    Next i
End Sub

Private Sub Form_Load()
    ' Create an object variable for the ColumnHeader object.
    Dim clmX As ColumnHeader
    ' Add ColumnHeaders. The width of the columns is the width
    ' of the control divided by the number of ColumnHeader objects.
    Set clmX = ListView1.ColumnHeaders. _
    Add(, , "Company", ListView1.Width / 3)
    Set clmX = ListView1.ColumnHeaders. _
    Add(, , "Address", ListView1.Width / 3)
    Set clmX = ListView1.ColumnHeaders. _
    Add(, , "Phone", ListView1.Width / 3)

    ' Label OptionButton controls with MultiSelect options.
        Option1(0).Caption = "No MultiSelect"
        Option1(1).Caption = "MultiSelect"
        ListView1.MultiSelect = 1 ' Set MultiSelect to True

    ListView1.BorderStyle = ccFixedSingle ' Set BorderStyle property.
    ListView1.View = lvwReport ' Set View property to Report.
    ' Add one image to ImageList control.
    Dim imgX As ListImage
    Set imgX = ImageList1.ListImages. _
    Add(, , LoadPicture("icons\mail\mail01a.ico"))
    ListView1.Icons = ImageList1

    ' Create object variables for the Data Access objects.
    Dim myDb As Database, myRs As Recordset
    ' Set the Database to the BIBLIO.MDB database.
    Set myDb = DBEngine.Workspaces(0).OpenDatabase("BIBLIO.MDB")
    ' Set the recordset to the Publishers table.
    Set myRs = myDb.OpenRecordset("Publishers", dbOpenDynaset)

    ' Create a variable to add ListItem objects.
    Dim itmX As ListItem

    ' While the record is not the last record, add a ListItem object.
    ' Use the Name field for the ListItem object's text.
    ' Use the Address field for the ListItem object's SubItem(1).
    ' Use the Phone field for the ListItem object's SubItem(2).
```

```
While Not myRs.EOF
    Set itmX = ListView1.ListItems.Add(, , CStr(myRs!Name))
    itmX.Icon = 1  ' Set icon to the ImageList icon.

    ' If the Address field is not Null, set SubItem 1 to the field.
    If Not IsNull(myRs!Address) Then
        itmX.SubItems(1) = CStr(myRs!Address)  ' Address field.
    End If

    ' If the Phone field is not Null, set SubItem 2 to the field.
    If Not IsNull(myRs!Telephone) Then
        itmX.SubItems(2) = myRs!Telephone  ' Phone field.
    End If

    myRs.MoveNext  ' Move to next record.
Wend

ListView1.View = lvwIcon  ' Show Icons view.
Command1.Caption = "Cut"  ' Set caption of the CommandButton.
' Add a caption to the form.
Me.Caption = "Select any item(s) and click 'Cut'."
End Sub

Private Sub Option1_Click(Index as Integer)
    ListView1.MultiSelect = Index
End Sub
```

HideColumnHeaders Property (ListView Control)

Returns or sets whether **ColumnHeader** objects in a **ListView** control are hidden in Report view.

Applies To

ListView Control, **ColumnHeader** Object, **ColumnHeaders** Collection

Syntax

object.**HideColumnHeaders** [= *boolean*]

The **HideColumnHeaders** property syntax has these parts:

Part	Description
object	An object expression that evaluates to a **ListView** control.
Boolean	A Boolean expression that specifies if the column headers are visible in **Report** view, as described in **Settings**.

Settings

The settings for *boolean* are:

Setting	Description
True	The column headers are not visible.
False	(Default) The column headers are visible.

Remarks

The **ListItem** objects and any related subitems remain visible even if the **HideColumnHeaders** property is set to **True**.

See Also

ColumnHeaders Property (ListView Control)

Example

This example adds several **ListItem** objects with subitems to a **ListView** control. When you click on the **CommandButton**, the **HideColumnHeaders** property toggles between **True** (-1) and **False** (0). To try the example, place **ListView** and **CommandButton** controls on a form and paste the code into the form's Declarations section. Run the example and click the **CommandButton** to toggle the **HideColumnHeaders** property.

```
Private Sub Command1_Click()
    ' Toggle HideColumnHeaders property off and on.
    ListView1.HideColumnHeaders = Abs(ListView1.HideColumnHeaders) - 1
End Sub

Private Sub Form_Load()
    Dim clmX As ColumnHeader
    Dim itmX As ListItem
    Dim i As Integer
    Command1.Caption = "HideColumnHeaders"

    ' Add 3 ColumnHeader objects to the control.
    For i = 1 To 3
        Set clmX = ListView1.ColumnHeaders.Add()
        clmX.Text = "Col" & i
    Next I

    ' Set View to Report.
    ListView1.View = lvwReport

    ' Add 10 ListItems to the control.
    For i = 1 To 10
        Set itmX = ListView1.ListItems.Add()
        itmX.Text = "ListItem " & i
        itmX.SubItems(1) = "Subitem 1"
        itmX.SubItems(2) = "Subitem 2"
    Next i
End Sub
```

Icon, SmallIcon Properties (ListItem Object)

Returns or sets the index or key value of an icon or small icon associated with a **ListItem** object in an **ImageList** control.

Applies To

ListView Control

Syntax

object.**Icon** [= *index*]
object.**SmallIcon** [= *index*]

The **Icon, SmallIcon** properties syntax has the following parts:

Part	Description
object	An object expression that evaluates to a **ListItem** object.
index	An integer or unique string that identifies an icon or small icon in an associated **ImageList** control. The integer is the value of the **ListItem** object's **Index** property; the string is the value of the **Key** property.

Remarks

Before you can use an icon in a **ListItem** object, you must associate an **ImageList** control with the **ListView** control containing the object. See the **Icons, SmallIcons** Properties (ListView Control) for more information. The example below shows the proper syntax:

```
ListView1.ListItems(1).SmallIcons=1
```

The images will appear when the **ListView** control is in **SmallIcons** view.

Specifics

Icons, SmallIcons Properties

See Also

ImageList Control, **ListItem** Object**, ListItems** Collection, **Icons, SmallIcons** Properties

Example

This example populates a **ListView** control with the contents of the Publishers table in the BIBLIO.MDB database. Four **OptionButton** controls are labeled with View property choices. You must place two **ImageList** controls on the form, one to contain images for the Icon property, and a second to contain images for the **SmallIcon** property of each **ListItem** object. To try the example, place a **ListView**, a control array of four **OptionButton** controls, and two **ImageList** controls on a form and paste the code into the form's Declarations section.

Note The example will not run unless you add a reference to the Microsoft DAO 3.0 Object Library by using the References command on the Tools menu. Run the example and click on the **ComboBox** control to switch views.

```
Private Sub Option1_Click(Index as Integer)
    ' Set the ListView control's View property to the
    ' Index of Option1
    ListView1.View = Index
End Sub

Private Sub Form_Load()
    ' Create an object variable for the ColumnHeader object.
    Dim clmX As ColumnHeader
    ' Add ColumnHeaders. The width of the columns is the width
    ' of the control divided by the number of ColumnHeader objects.
    Set clmX = ListView1.ColumnHeaders. _
    Add(, , "Company", ListView1.Width / 3)

Set clmX = ListView1.ColumnHeaders. _
    Add(, , "Address", ListView1.Width / 3)
    Set clmX = ListView1.ColumnHeaders. _
    Add(, , "Phone", ListView1.Width / 3)

    ListView1.BorderStyle = ccFixedSingle ' Set BorderStyle property.
    ListView1.View = lvwReport ' Set View property to Report.

    ' Add one image to ImageList1--the Icons ImageList.
    Dim imgX As ListImage
    Set imgX = ImageList1.ListImages. _
    Add(, , LoadPicture("icons\mail\mail01a.ico"))

' Add an image to ImageList2--the SmallIcons ImageList.
    Set imgX = ImageList2.ListImages. _
    Add(, , LoadPicture("bitmaps\assorted\w.bmp"))

    ' To use ImageList controls with the ListView control, you must
    ' associate a particular ImageList control with the Icons and
    ' SmallIcons properties.
    ListView1.Icons = ImageList1
    ListView1.SmallIcons = ImageList2
    ' Label OptionButton controls with View options.
      Option1(0).Caption = "Icon"
      Option1(1).Caption = "SmallIcon"

Option1(2).Caption = "List"
      Option1(3).Caption = "Report"
      ListView1.View = lvwIcon ' Set to Icon view

    ' Create object variables for the Data Access objects.
    Dim myDb As Database, myRs As Recordset
    ' Set the Database to the BIBLIO.MDB database.
    Set myDb = DBEngine.Workspaces(0).OpenDatabase("BIBLIO.MDB")
    ' Set the recordset to the Publishers table.
    Set myRs = myDb.OpenRecordset("Publishers", dbOpenDynaset)
```

```
        ' Create a variable to add ListItem objects.

Dim itmX As ListItem

        ' While the record is not the last record, add a ListItem object.
        ' Use the Name field for the ListItem object's text.
        ' Use the Address field for the ListItem object's SubItem(1)
        ' Use the Phone field for the ListItem object's SubItem(2)

        While Not myRs.EOF

            Set itmX = ListView1.ListItems.Add(, , CStr(myRs!Name))
            itmX.Icon = 1   ' Set an icon from ImageList1.
            itmX.SmallIcon = 1' Set an icon from ImageList2.

' If the Address field is not Null, set SubItem 1 to the field.
        If Not IsNull(myRs!Address) Then
            itmX.SubItems(1) = CStr(myRs!Address) ' Address field.
        End If

            ' If the Phone field is not Null, set SubItem 2 to the field.
        If Not IsNull(myRs!Telephone) Then
            itmX.SubItems(2) = myRs!Telephone   ' Phone field.
        End If

        myRs.MoveNext   ' Move to next record.
    Wend
End Sub
```

Icons, SmallIcons Properties

Returns or sets the **ImageList** controls associated with the **Icon** and **SmallIcon** views in a **ListView** control.

Syntax

object.**Icons** [= *imagelist*]
object.**SmallIcons** [= *imagelist*]

The **Icons, SmallIcons** properties syntax has the following parts:

Part	Description
object	An object expression that evaluates to the **ListView** control.
imagelist	An object expression that evaluates to an **ImageList** control.

Remarks

To associate an **ImageList** control with a **ListView** control at run time, set these properties to the desired **ImageList** control.

Each **ListItem** object in the **ListView** control also has **Icon** and **SmallIcon** properties, which index the **ListImage** objects and determine which image is displayed.

Once you associate an **ImageList** with the **ListView** control, you can use the value of either the **Index** or **Key** property to refer to a **ListImage** object in a procedure.

See Also

ImageList Control, **ListImage** Object, **ListImages** Collection, **ListItem** Object, **ListItems** Collection, **Icon**, **SmallIcon** Properties (ListItem Object)

Example

This example populates a **ListView** control with the contents of the Publishers table in the BIBLIO.MDB database. Four **OptionButton** controls are labeled with **View** property choices. You must place two **ImageList** controls on the form, one to contain images for the **Icon** property, and a second to contain images for the **SmallIcon** property of each **ListItem** object. To try the example, place a **ListView**, a control array of four **OptionButton** controls, and two **ImageList** controls on a form and paste the code into the form's Declarations section.

Note The example will not run unless you add a reference to the Microsoft DAO 3.0 Object Library by using the References command on the Tools menu. Run the example and click on the **ComboBox** control to switch views.

```
Private Sub Option1_Click(Index as Integer)
    ' Set the ListView control's View property to the
    ' Index of Option1
    ListView1.View = Index
End Sub

Private Sub Form_Load()
    ' Create an object variable for the ColumnHeader object.
    Dim clmX As ColumnHeader
    ' Add ColumnHeaders. The width of the columns is the width
    ' of the control divided by the number of ColumnHeader objects.
    Set clmX = ListView1.ColumnHeaders. _
    Add(, , "Company", ListView1.Width / 3)
    Set clmX = ListView1.ColumnHeaders. _
    Add(, , "Address", ListView1.Width / 3)
    Set clmX = ListView1.ColumnHeaders. _
    Add(, , "Phone", ListView1.Width / 3)

    ListView1.BorderStyle = ccFixedSingle    ' Set BorderStyle property.
    ListView1.View = lvwReport               ' Set View property to Report.

    ' Add one image to ImageList1--the Icons ImageList.
    Dim imgX As ListImage
    Set imgX = ImageList1.ListImages. _
    Add(, , LoadPicture("icons\mail\mail01a.ico"))
    ' Add an image to ImageList2--the SmallIcons ImageList.
    Set imgX = ImageList2.ListImages. _
    Add(, , LoadPicture("bitmaps\assorted\w.bmp"))

    ' To use ImageList controls with the ListView control, you must
    ' associate a particular ImageList control with the Icons and
    ' SmallIcons properties.
    ListView1.Icons = ImageList1
```

```
    ListView1.SmallIcons = ImageList2
' Label OptionButton controls with View options.
    Option1(0).Caption = "Icon"
    Option1(1).Caption = "SmallIcon"
    Option1(2).Caption = "List"
    Option1(3).Caption = "Report"
    ListView1.View = lvwIcon                    ' Set to Icon view

' Create object variables for the Data Access objects.
Dim myDb As Database, myRs As Recordset
' Set the Database to the BIBLIO.MDB database.
Set myDb = DBEngine.Workspaces(0).OpenDatabase("BIBLIO.MDB")
' Set the recordset to the Publishers table.
Set myRs = myDb.OpenRecordset("Publishers", dbOpenDynaset)

' Create a variable to add ListItem objects.
Dim itmX As ListItem

' While the record is not the last record, add a ListItem object.
' Use the Name field for the ListItem object's text.
' Use the Address field for the ListItem object's SubItem(1)
' Use the Phone field for the ListItem object's SubItem(2)

While Not myRs.EOF

    Set itmX = ListView1.ListItems.Add(, , CStr(myRs!Name))
    itmX.Icon = 1                ' Set an icon from ImageList1.
    itmX.SmallIcon = 1           ' Set an icon from ImageList2.

    ' If the Address field is not Null, set SubItem 1 to the field.
    If Not IsNull(myRs!Address) Then
       itmX.SubItems(1) = CStr(myRs!Address)  ' Address field.
    End If

    ' If the Phone field is not Null, set SubItem 2 to the field.
    If Not IsNull(myRs!Telephone) Then
       itmX.SubItems(2) = myRs!Telephone      ' Phone field.
    End If

    myRs.MoveNext                            ' Move to next record.
    Wend
End Sub
```

ItemClick Event

Occurs when a **ListItem** object in a **ListView** control is clicked

Applies To

ListView Control, **ListItem** Object, **ListItems** Collection

Syntax

Private Sub *object*_**ItemClick(ByVal** *Item* **As ListItem)**

The **ItemClick** event syntax has these parts:

Part	Description
object	An object expression that evaluates to a **ListView** control.
listitem	The **ListItem** object that was clicked.

Remarks

Use this event to determine which **ListItem** was clicked. This event is triggered before the **Click** event. The standard **Click** event is generated if the mouse is clicked on any part of the **ListView** control. The **ItemClick** event is generated only when the mouse is clicked on the text or image of a **ListItem** object.

See Also

Click Event

Example

This example populates a **ListView** control with contents of the Publishers table in the BIBLIO.MDB database. When a **ListItem** object is clicked, the code checks the value of the **Index** property. If the value is less than 15, nothing occurs. If the value is greater than 15, the **ListItem** object is ghosted. To try the example, place a **ListView** control on a form and paste the code into the form's Declarations section. Run the example and click on one of the items.

```
Private ListView1_ItemClick(ByVal Item As ListItem)
   Select Case Item.Index
   Case Is = <15
      Exit Sub
   Case Is => 15
      ' Toggle Ghosted property.
      Item.Ghosted = Abs(Item.Ghosted) - 1
   End Select
End Sub

Private Sub Form_Load()
   ' Create an object variable for the ColumnHeader object.
   Dim clmX As ColumnHeader
   ' Add ColumnHeaders. The width of the columns is the width
   ' of the control divided by the number of ColumnHeader objects.
   Set clmX = ListView1.ColumnHeaders. _
   Add(, , "Company", ListView1.Width / 3)
   Set clmX = ListView1.ColumnHeaders. _
   Add(, , "Address", ListView1.Width / 3)
   Set clmX = ListView1.ColumnHeaders. _
   Add(, , "Phone", ListView1.Width / 3)

   ListView1.BorderStyle = ccFixedSingle   ' Set BorderStyle property.

   ' Create object variables for the Data Access objects.
   Dim myDb As Database, myRs As Recordset
   ' Set the Database to the BIBLIO.MDB database.
   Set myDb = DBEngine.Workspaces(0).OpenDatabase("BIBLIO.MDB")
   ' Set the recordset to the Publishers table.
   Set myRs = myDb.OpenRecordset("Publishers", dbOpenDynaset)
```

```
' Create a variable to add ListItem objects.
Dim itmX As ListItem

' While the record is not the last record, add a ListItem object.
' Use the Name field for the ListItem object's text.
' Use the Address field for the ListItem object's SubItem(1).
' Use the Phone field for the ListItem object's SubItem(2).

While Not myRs.EOF

    Set itmX = ListView1.ListItems.Add(, , CStr(myRs!Name))

    ' If the Address field is not Null, set SubItem 1 to the field.
    If Not IsNull(myRs!Address) Then
       itmX.SubItems(1) = CStr(myRs!Address)  ' Address field.
    End If

    ' If the Phone field is not Null, set the SubItem 2 to the field.
    If Not IsNull(myRs!Telephone) Then
       itmX.SubItems(2) = myRs!Telephone      ' Phone field.
    End If

    myRs.MoveNext                             ' Move to next record.
  Wend
  ListView1.View = lvwReport                  ' Set View to Report.
End Sub

Private Sub ListView1_ColumnClick(ByVal ColumnHeader As ColumnHeader)
    ListView1.SortKey = ColumnHeader.Index - 1
    ListView1.Sorted = True
End Sub
```

LabelWrap Property (ListView Control)

Returns or sets a value that determines whether or not labels are wrapped when a **ListView** control is in **Icon** view.

Applies To

ListView Control

Syntax

object.**LabelWrap** [= *boolean*]

The **LabelWrap** property syntax has these parts:

Part	Description
object	An object expression that evaluates to a **ListView** control.
boolean	A Boolean expression specifying if the labels wrap, as described in **Settings**.

Settings

The settings for *boolean* are:

Setting	Description
True	(Default) The labels wrap.
False	The labels don't wrap.

Remarks

The length of the label is determined by setting the icon spacing in the Control Panel, Desktop option, in Windows NT. In Windows 95, use the Appearance tab in the Display control panel.

See Also

View Property (ListView Control)

ListItem Object, ListItems Collection

- A **ListItem** consists of text, the index of an associated icon (ListImage object), and, in Report view, an array of strings representing subitems.
- A **ListItems** collection contains one or more **ListItem** objects.

Syntax

listview.**ListItems**
listview.**ListItems**(*index*)

The syntax lines above refer to the collection and to individual elements in the collection, respectively, according to the standard collection syntax.

The **ListItem** object, **ListItems** collection syntax has these parts:

Part	Description
listview	An object expression that evaluates to a **ListView** control.
Index	Either an integer or string that uniquely identifies a member of a **ListItem** collection. The integer is the value of the **Index** property; the string is the value of the **Key** property.

Remarks

ListItem objects can contain both text and pictures. However, to use pictures, you must reference an **ImageList** control using the **Icons** and **SmallIcons** properties.

You can also change the image by using the **Icon** or **SmallIcon** property.

The following example shows how to add **ColumnHeaders** and several **ListItem** objects with **subitems** to a **ListView** control.

```
Private Sub Form_Load()
    Dim clmX As ColumnHeader
    Dim itmX As ListItem
    Dim i As Integer
```

```
      For i = 1 To 3
         Set clmX = ListView1.ColumnHeaders.Add()
         clmX.Text = "Col" & i
      Next i

      ' Add 10 items to list, all with the same icon

      For i = 1 To 10
         Set itmX = ListView1.ListItems.Add()
         itmX.SmallIcon = 1
         itmX.Text = "ListItem " & i
         itmX.SubItems(1) = "Subitem 1"
         itmX.SubItems(2) = "Subitem 2"
      Next i
   End Sub
```

Properties

Count Property, **Ghosted** Property, **Icon, SmallIcon** Properties, **Index** Property, **Item** Property, **Key** Property, **Selected** Property, **SubItems** Property, **Tag** Property, **Text** Property

Methods

Add Method (**ListItems** Collection), **CreateDragImage** Method, **EnsureVisible** Method, **Clear** Method, **Remove** Method

See Also

ImageList Control, **ListImage** Object, **ListImages** Collection, **ColumnHeader** Object, **ColumnHeaders** Collection, **Icon, SmallIcon** Properties (ListItem Object), **Icons, SmallIcons** Properties, **Left, Top** Properties

Example

The following example uses the Biblio.mdb database as a source to populate a **ListView** control with **ListItem** objects. To try this example, place a **ListView** control on a form and paste the code into the Declarations section. You must also be sure that the Biblio.mdb has been installed on your machine. In the code below, check the path in the **OpenDatabase** function and change it to reflect the actual path to Biblio.mdb on your machine.

Note   The example will not run unless you add a reference to the Microsoft DAO 3.5 Object Library. To do this, on the **Project** menu click **References**. Search for Microsoft DAO 3.5 Object Library and click the checkbox to select it.

```
Private Sub Form_Load()
   ' Add ColumnHeaders. The width of the columns is
   ' the width of the control divided by the number of
   ' ColumnHeader objects.
   ListView1.ColumnHeaders. _
   Add , , "Author", ListView1.Width / 3
   ListView1.ColumnHeaders. _
   Add , , "Author ID", ListView1.Width / 3, _
   lvwColumnCenter
   ListView1.ColumnHeaders. _
   Add , , "Birthdate", ListView1.Width / 3
```

```
              ' Set View property to Report.
              ListView1.View = lvwReport

      ' Declare object variables for the
              ' Data Access objects.
              Dim myDb As Database, myRs As Recordset
              ' Set the Database to the BIBLIO.MDB database.
              ' IMPORTANT: the Biblio.mdb must be on your
              ' machine, and you must set the correct path to
              ' the file in the OpenDatabase function below.
              Set myDb = DBEngine.Workspaces(0) _
                  .OpenDatabase("c:\Program Files\VB\BIBLIO.MDB")
              ' Set the recordset to the "Authors" table.
              Set myRs = _
              myDb.OpenRecordset("Authors", dbOpenDynaset)

      ' Declare a variable to add ListItem objects.
              Dim itmX As ListItem

              ' While the record is not the last record,
              ' add a ListItem object. Use the author field for
              ' the ListItem object's text. Use the AuthorID
              ' field for the ListItem object's SubItem(1).
              ' Use the "Year of Birth" field for the ListItem
              ' object's SubItem(2).

              While Not myRs.EOF
                  Set itmX = ListView1.ListItems. _
                  Add(, , CStr(myRs!Author))        ' Author.

      ' If the AuthorID field is not null, then set
                  ' SubItem 1 to it.
                  If Not IsNull(myRs!Au_id) Then
                     itmX.SubItems(1) = CStr(myRs!Au_id)
                  End If

                  ' If the birth field is not Null, set
                  ' SubItem 2 to it.
                  If Not IsNull(myRs![Year Born]) Then
                     itmX.SubItems(2) = myRs![Year Born]
                  End If
                  myRs.MoveNext   ' Move to next record.
              Wend
      End Sub
```

ListItems Property (ListView Control)

Returns a reference to a collection of **ListItem** objects in a **ListView** control.

Applies To

ListView Control

Syntax

object.**ListItems**

The *object* placeholder represents an object expression that evaluates to a **ListView** control.

Remarks

ListItem obects can be manipulated using the standard collection methods. Each **ListItem** in the collection can be accessed by its unique key, which you create and store in the **Key** property.

You can also retrieve **ListItem** objects by their display position using the **Index** property.

See Also

ListItem Object, **ListItems** Collection, **Icons, SmallIcons** Properties

Example

The following example uses the Biblio.mdb database as a source to populate a **ListView** control with **ListItem** objects. To try this example, place a **ListView** control on a form and paste the code into the Declarations section. You must also be sure that the Biblio.mdb has been installed on your machine. In the code below, check the path in the **OpenDatabase** function and change it to reflect the actual path to Biblio.mdb on your machine.

Note The example will not run unless you add a reference to the Microsoft DAO 3.5 Object Library. To do this, on the **Project** menu click **References**. Search for Microsoft DAO 3.5 Object Library and click the checkbox to select it.

```
Private Sub Form_Load()
    ' Add ColumnHeaders. The width of the columns is
    ' the width of the control divided by the number of
    ' ColumnHeader objects.
    ListView1.ColumnHeaders. _
    Add , , "Author", ListView1.Width / 3
    ListView1.ColumnHeaders. _
    Add , , "Author ID", ListView1.Width / 3, _
    lvwColumnCenter
    ListView1.ColumnHeaders. _
    Add , , "Birthdate", ListView1.Width / 3
    ' Set View property to Report.
    ListView1.View = lvwReport

' Declare object variables for the
    ' Data Access objects.
    Dim myDb As Database, myRs As Recordset
    ' Set the Database to the BIBLIO.MDB database.
    ' IMPORTANT: the Biblio.mdb must be on your
    ' machine, and you must set the correct path to
    ' the file in the OpenDatabase function below.
    Set myDb =  DBEngine.Workspaces(0) _
       .OpenDatabase("c:\Program Files\VB\BIBLIO.MDB")
    ' Set the recordset to the "Authors" table.
    Set myRs = _
    myDb.OpenRecordset("Authors", dbOpenDynaset)
```

```
' Declare a variable to add ListItem objects.
  Dim itmX As ListItem

   ' While the record is not the last record,
   ' add a ListItem object. Use the author field for
   ' the ListItem object's text. Use the AuthorID
   ' field for the ListItem object's SubItem(1).
   ' Use the "Year of Birth" field for the ListItem
   ' object's SubItem(2).

   While Not myRs.EOF
      Set itmX = ListView1.ListItems. _
      Add(, , CStr(myRs!Author))      ' Author.


' If the AuthorID field is not null, then set
      ' SubItem 1 to it.
      If Not IsNull(myRs!Au_id) Then
         itmX.SubItems(1) = CStr(myRs!Au_id)
      End If

      ' If the birth field is not Null, set
      ' SubItem 2 to it.
      If Not IsNull(myRs![Year Born]) Then
         itmX.SubItems(2) = myRs![Year Born]
      End If
      myRs.MoveNext   ' Move to next record.
   Wend
End Sub
```

ListView Control Constants

Listview Control Constants

Constant	Value	Description
lvwIcon	0	(Default) Icon. Each **ListItem** object is represented by a full-sized (standard) icon and a text label.
lvwSmallIcon	1	SmallIcon. Each **ListItem** is represented by a small icon and a text label that appears to the right of the icon. The items appear horizontally.
LvwList	2	List. Each **ListItem** is represented by a small icon and a text label that appears to the right of the icon. Each **ListItem** appears vertically and on its own line with information arranged in columns.
lvwReport	3	Report. Each **ListItem** is displayed with its small icons and text labels. You can provide additional information about each **ListItem**. The icons, text labels, and information appear in columns with the leftmost column containing the small icon, followed by the text label. Additional columns display the text for each of the item's subitems.

ListArrange Constants

Constant	Value	Description
lvwNone	0	(Default) None.
lvwAutoLeft	1	Left. **ListItem** objects are aligned along the left side of the control.
lvwAutoTop	2	Top. **ListItem** objects are aligned along the top of the control.

ListColumnAlignment Constants

Constant	Value	Description
lvwColumnLeft	0	(Default) Left. Text is aligned left.
lvwColumnRight	1	Right. Text is aligned right.
lvwColumnCenter	2	Center. Text is centered.

ListLabelEdit Constants

Constant	Value	Description
lvwAutomatic	0	(Default) Automatic. The **BeforeLabelEdit** event is generated when the user clicks the label of a selected node.
lvwManual	1	Manual. The **BeforeLabelEdit** event will be generated only when the **StartLabelEdit** method is invoked.

ListSortOrder Constants

Constant	Value	Description
lvwAscending	0	(Default) Ascending order. Sorts from the beginning of the alphabet (A-Z), the earliest date, or the lowest number.
lvwDescending	1	Descending order. Sorts from the end of the alphabet (Z-A), the latest date, or the highest number.

ListFindItemWhere Constants

Constant	Value	Description
lvwText	0	(Default) Text. Matches the string with a **ListItem** object's **Text** property.
lvwSubItem	1	SubItem. Matches the string with any string in a **ListItem** object's **SubItems** property.
lvwTag	2	Tag. Matches the string with any **ListItem** object's **Tag** property.

ListFindItemHow Constants

Constant	Value	Description
lvwWholeWord	0	(Default) Whole word. Sets the search so that a match occurs if the item's **Text** property begins with the whole word being searched for. Ignored if the criteria is not text.
lvwPartial	1	Partial. Sets the search so that a match occurs if the item's **Text** property begins with the string being searched for. Ignored if the criteria is not text.

See Also

Alignment Property (ColumnHeader Object), **Arrange** Property (ListView Control),
SortOrder Property (ListView Control), **View** Property (ListView Control),
FindItem Method (ListView Control), **LabelEdit** Property, **Visual Basic** Constants

MultiSelect Property (ListView Control)

Returns or sets a value indicating whether a user can select multiple **ListItems** in the
ListView control.

Applies To

ListView Control, **ListItem** Object, **ListItems** Collection

Syntax

object.**MultiSelect** [= *boolean*]

The **MultiSelect** property syntax has these parts:

Part	Description
object	An object expression that evaluates to a **ListView** control.
boolean	A value specifying the type of selection, as described in **Settings**.

Settings

The settings for *boolean* are:

Constant	Description
False	(Default) Selecting multiple **ListItems** isn't allowed.
True	Multiple selection. Pressing SHIFT and clicking the mouse or pressing SHIFT and one of the arrow keys (UP ARROW, DOWN ARROW, LEFT ARROW, and RIGHT ARROW) extends the selection from the previously selected **ListItem** to the current **ListItem**. Pressing CTRL and clicking the mouse selects or deselects a **ListItem** in the list.

See Also

ListView Control, **ColumnHeader** Object, **ColumnHeaders** Collection, **ListItem**
Object, **ListItems** Collection, **Ghosted** Property

Example

This example populates a **ListView** control with the contents of the Authors table
from the BIBLIO.MDB database, and lets you use **OptionButton** controls to set
MultiSelect property options. You can select any item, or hold down the SHIFT
Key and select multiple items. Clicking on the **CommandButton** sets the **Ghosted**
property of the selected items to **True**. To try the example, place a control array
of two **OptionButton** controls, a **ListView** control, an **ImageList** control, and a
CommandButton control on a form and paste the code into the form's Declarations
section.

Note The example will not run unless you add a reference to the Microsoft DAO 3.0 Object Library by using the References command on the Tools menu. Run the example, select a **MultiSelect** option by clicking an **OptionButton**, click on items to select them and click the **CommandButton** to ghost them.

```
Private Sub Command1_Click()
    Dim x As Object
    Dim i As Integer
    ' Ghost selected ListItem.
If ListView1.SelectedItem Is Nothing Then Exit Sub
    For i = 1 To ListView1.ListItems.Count
        If ListView1.ListItems(i).Selected = True Then
            ListView1.ListItems(i).Ghosted = True
        End If
    Next i
End Sub

Private Sub Form_Load()
    ' Create an object variable for the ColumnHeader object.
    Dim clmX As ColumnHeader
    ' Add ColumnHeaders. The width of the columns is the width

' of the control divided by the number of ColumnHeader objects.
    Set clmX = ListView1.ColumnHeaders. _
    Add(, , "Company", ListView1.Width / 3)
    Set clmX = ListView1.ColumnHeaders. _
    Add(, , "Address", ListView1.Width / 3)
    Set clmX = ListView1.ColumnHeaders. _
    Add(, , "Phone", ListView1.Width / 3)

    ' Label OptionButton controls with MultiSelect options.
    Option1(0).Caption = "No MultiSelect"
    Option1(1).Caption = "MultiSelect"
    ListView1.MultiSelect = 1          ' Set MultiSelect to True

ListView1.BorderStyle = ccFixedSingle  ' Set BorderStyle property.
    ListView1.View = lvwReport          ' Set View property to Report.
    ' Add one image to ImageList control.
    Dim imgX As ListImage
    Set imgX = ImageList1.ListImages. _
    Add(, , LoadPicture("icons\mail\mail01a.ico"))
    ListView1.Icons = ImageList1

    ' Create object variables for the Data Access objects.
    Dim myDb As Database, myRs As Recordset
    ' Set the Database to the BIBLIO.MDB database.
    Set myDb = DBEngine.Workspaces(0).OpenDatabase("BIBLIO.MDB")

' Set the recordset to the Publishers table.
    Set myRs = myDb.OpenRecordset("Publishers", dbOpenDynaset)

    ' Create a variable to add ListItem objects.
    Dim itmX As ListItem
```

```
           ' While the record is not the last record, add a ListItem object.
           ' Use the Name field for the ListItem object's text.
           ' Use the Address field for the ListItem object's SubItem(1).
           ' Use the Phone field for the ListItem object's SubItem(2).

           While Not myRs.EOF
               Set itmX = ListView1.ListItems.Add(, , CStr(myRs!Name))

       itmX.Icon = 1   ' Set icon to the ImageList icon.

               ' If the Address field is not Null, set SubItem 1 to the field.
               If Not IsNull(myRs!Address) Then
                  itmX.SubItems(1) = CStr(myRs!Address)   ' Address field.
               End If

               ' If the Phone field is not Null, set SubItem 2 to the field.
               If Not IsNull(myRs!Telephone) Then
                  itmX.SubItems(2) = myRs!Telephone   ' Phone field.
               End If

               myRs.MoveNext   ' Move to next record.
           Wend

           ListView1.View = lvwIcon   ' Show Icons view.

       Command1.Caption = "Cut"   ' Set caption of the CommandButton.
           ' Add a caption to the form.
           Me.Caption = "Select any item(s) and click 'Cut'."
       End Sub

       Private Sub Option1_Click(Index as Integer)
           ListView1.MultiSelect = Index
       End Sub
```

Sorted Property (ListView Control)

Returns or sets a value that determines whether the **ListItem** objects in a **ListView** control are sorted.

Applies To

ListView Control, **ListItem Object, ListItems** Collection

Syntax

object.**Sorted** [= *boolean*]

The **Sorted** property syntax has these parts:

Part	Description
object	An object expression that evaluates to a **ListView** control.
Boolean	A Boolean expression specifying whether the **ListItem** objects are sorted, as described in **Settings**.

Settings

The settings for *boolean* are:

Setting	Description
True	The list items are sorted alphabetically, according to the **SortOrder** property.
False	The list items are not sorted.

Remarks

The **Sorted** property must be set to **True** for the settings in the **SortOrder** and **SortKey** properties to take effect.

Each time the coordinates of a **ListItem** change, the **Sorted** property becomes **False**.

See Also

SortKey Property (ListView Control), **SortOrder** Property (ListView Control)

Example

This example adds three **ColumnHeader** objects to a **ListView** control and populates the control with the Publishers records of the BIBLIO.MDB database. An array of two **OptionButton** controls offers the two choices for sorting records. When you click on a **ColumnHeader**, the **ListView** control is sorted according to the **SortOrder** property, as determined by the **OptionButtons**. To try the example, place a **ListView** and a control array of two **OptionButton** controls on a form and paste the code into the form's Declarations section. Run the example and click on the **ColumnHeaders** to sort, and click on the **OptionButton** to switch the **SortOrder** property.

Note The example will not run unless you add a reference to the Microsoft DAO 3.0 Object Library by using the References command on the Tools menu.

```
Private Sub Option1_Click(Index as Integer)
    ' These OptionButtons offer two choices: Ascending (Index 0),
    ' and Descending (Index 1). Clicking on one of these
    ' sets the SortOrder for the ListView control.
    ListView1.SortOrder = Index
    ListView1.Sorted = True ' Sort the List.
End Sub

Private Sub Form_Load()
    ' Create an object variable for the ColumnHeader object.
    Dim clmX As ColumnHeader
    ' Add ColumnHeaders. The width of the columns is the width

' of the control divided by the number of ColumnHeader objects.
    Set clmX = ListView1.ColumnHeaders. _
    Add(, , "Company", ListView1.Width / 3)
    Set clmX = ListView1.ColumnHeaders. _
    Add(, , "Address", ListView1.Width / 3)
    Set clmX = ListView1.ColumnHeaders. _
    Add(, , "Phone", ListView1.Width / 3)
```

```
       ListView1.BorderStyle = ccFixedSingle ' Set BorderStyle property.
       ListView1.View = lvwReport ' Set View property to Report.

    ' Label OptionButton controls with SortOrder options.

Option1(0).Caption = "Ascending (A-Z)"
      Option1(1).Caption = "Descending (Z-A)"
      ListView1.SortOrder = 0 ' Set to Icon view

    ' Create object variables for the Data Access objects.
    Dim myDb As Database, myRs As Recordset
    ' Set the Database to the BIBLIO.MDB database.
    Set myDb = DBEngine.Workspaces(0).OpenDatabase("BIBLIO.MDB")
    ' Set the recordset to the Publishers table.
    Set myRs = myDb.OpenRecordset("Publishers", dbOpenDynaset)

    ' Create a variable to add ListItem objects.

Dim itmX As ListItem

    ' While the record is not the last record, add a ListItem object.
    ' Use the Name field for the ListItem object's text.
    ' Use the Address field for the ListItem object's subitem(1).
    ' Use the Phone field for the ListItem object's subitem(2).

    While Not myRs.EOF
        Set itmX = ListView1.ListItems.Add(, , CStr(myRs!Name))

        ' If the Address field is not Null, set subitem 1 to the field.
        If Not IsNull(myRs!Address) Then
           itmX.SubItems(1) = CStr(myRs!Address)  ' Address field.

End If

        ' If the Phone field is not Null, set subitem 2 to the field.
        If Not IsNull(myRs!Telephone) Then
           itmX.SubItems(2) = myRs!Telephone  ' Phone field.
        End If

        myRs.MoveNext  ' Move to next record.
    Wend
End Sub

Private Sub ListView1_ColumnClick(ByVal ColumnHeader As ColumnHeader)
    ' When a ColumnHeader object is clicked, the ListView control is
    ' sorted by the subitems of that column.
    ' Set the SortKey to the Index of the ColumnHeader - 1

ListView1.SortKey = ColumnHeader.Index - 1
    ' Set Sorted to True to sort the list.
    ListView1.Sorted = True
End Sub
```

SortKey Property (ListView Control)

Returns or sets a value that determines how the **ListItem** objects in a **ListView** control are sorted.

Applies To

ListView Control, **ListItem** Object, **ListItems** Collection

Syntax

object.**SortKey** [= *integer*]

The **SortKey** property syntax has these parts:

Part	Description
object	An object expression that evaluates to a **ListView** control.
integer	An integer specifying the sort key, as described in **Settings**.

Settings

The settings for *integer* are:

Setting	Description
0	Sort using the **ListItem** object's **Text** property.
> 1	Sort using the subitem whose collection index is specified here.

Remarks

The **Sorted** property must be set to **True** before the change takes place.

It is common to sort a list when the column header is clicked. For this reason, the **SortKey** property is commonly included in the **ColumnClick** event to sort the list using the clicked column, as determined by the sort key, and demonstrated in the following example:

```
Private Sub ListView1_ColumnClick (ByVal ColumnHeader as ColumnHeader)
   ListView1.SortKey=ColumnHeader.Index-1
End Sub
```

See Also

ColumnClick Event, **SortOrder** Property (ListView Control), **Sorted** Property (ListView Control), **Text** Property

Example

This example adds three **ColumnHeader** objects to a **ListView** control and populates the control with the Publishers records of the BIBLIO.MDB database. An array of two **OptionButton** controls offers the two choices for sorting records. When you click on a **ColumnHeader**, the **ListView** control is sorted according to the **SortOrder** property, as determined by the **OptionButtons**. To try the example, place a **ListView** and a control array of two **OptionButton** controls on a form and paste the code into the form's Declarations section. Run the example and click on the **ColumnHeaders** to sort, and click on the **OptionButton** to switch the **SortOrder** property.

Note The example will not run unless you add a reference to the Microsoft DAO 3.0 Object Library by using the References command on the Tools menu.

```vb
Private Sub Option1_Click(Index as Integer)
    ' These OptionButtons offer two choices: Ascending (Index 0),
    ' and Descending (Index 1). Clicking on one of these
    ' sets the SortOrder for the ListView control.
    ListView1.SortOrder = Index
    ListView1.Sorted = True ' Sort the List.
End Sub

Private Sub Form_Load()
    ' Create an object variable for the ColumnHeader object.
    Dim clmX As ColumnHeader
    ' Add ColumnHeaders. The width of the columns is the width

' of the control divided by the number of ColumnHeader objects.
    Set clmX = ListView1.ColumnHeaders. _
    Add(, , "Company", ListView1.Width / 3)
    Set clmX = ListView1.ColumnHeaders. _
    Add(, , "Address", ListView1.Width / 3)
    Set clmX = ListView1.ColumnHeaders. _
    Add(, , "Phone", ListView1.Width / 3)

    ListView1.BorderStyle = ccFixedSingle ' Set BorderStyle property.
    ListView1.View = lvwReport ' Set View property to Report.

    ' Label OptionButton controls with SortOrder options.

Option1(0).Caption = "Ascending (A-Z)"
      Option1(1).Caption = "Descending (Z-A)"
      ListView1.SortOrder = 0 ' Set to Icon view

    ' Create object variables for the Data Access objects.
    Dim myDb As Database, myRs As Recordset
    ' Set the Database to the BIBLIO.MDB database.
    Set myDb = DBEngine.Workspaces(0).OpenDatabase("BIBLIO.MDB")
    ' Set the recordset to the Publishers table.
    Set myRs = myDb.OpenRecordset("Publishers", dbOpenDynaset)

    ' Create a variable to add ListItem objects.

Dim itmX As ListItem

    ' While the record is not the last record, add a ListItem object.
    ' Use the Name field for the ListItem object's text.
    ' Use the Address field for the ListItem object's subitem(1).
    ' Use the Phone field for the ListItem object's subitem(2).

    While Not myRs.EOF
        Set itmX = ListView1.ListItems.Add(, , CStr(myRs!Name))

        ' If the Address field is not Null, set subitem 1 to the field.
        If Not IsNull(myRs!Address) Then
            itmX.SubItems(1) = CStr(myRs!Address)  ' Address field.

    End If
```

```
        ' If the Phone field is not Null, set subitem 2 to the field.
        If Not IsNull(myRs!Telephone) Then
            itmX.SubItems(2) = myRs!Telephone   ' Phone field.
        End If

        myRs.MoveNext   ' Move to next record.
    Wend
End Sub

Private Sub ListView1_ColumnClick(ByVal ColumnHeader As ColumnHeader)
    ' When a ColumnHeader object is clicked, the ListView control is
    ' sorted by the subitems of that column.
    ' Set the SortKey to the Index of the ColumnHeader - 1

ListView1.SortKey = ColumnHeader.Index - 1
    ' Set Sorted to True to sort the list.
    ListView1.Sorted = True
End Sub
```

SortOrder Property (ListView Control)

Returns or sets a value that determines whether **ListItem** objects in a **ListView** control are sorted in ascending or descending order.

Applies To

ListView Control, **ListItem** Object, **ListItems** Collection

Syntax

object.**SortOrder** [= *integer*]

The **SortOrder** property syntax has these parts:

Part	Description
object	An object expression that evaluates to a **ListView** control.
integer	An integer specifying the type of sort order, as described in **Settings**.

Settings

The settings for *integer* are:

Constant	Value	Description
lvwAscending	0	(Default) Ascending order. Sorts from the beginning of the alphabet (A-Z) or the earliest date. Numbers are sorted as strings, with the first digit determining the initial position in the sort, and subsequent digits determining sub-sorting.
lvwDescending	1	Descending order. Sorts from the end of the alphabet (Z-A) or the latest date. Numbers are sorted as strings, with the first digit determining the initial position in the sort, and subsequent digits determining sub-sorting.

Remarks

The **Sorted** property must be set to **True** before a list will be sorted in the order specified by **SortOrder**.

See Also

SortKey Property (ListView Control), **ListView** Control Constants, **Sorted** Property (ListView Control), **Text** Property

Example

This example adds three **ColumnHeader** objects to a **ListView** control and populates the control with the Publishers records of the BIBLIO.MDB database. An array of two **OptionButton** controls offers the two choices for sorting records. When you click on a **ColumnHeader**, the **ListView** control is sorted according to the **SortOrder** property, as determined by the **OptionButtons**. To try the example, place a **ListView** and a control array of two **OptionButton** controls on a form and paste the code into the form's Declarations section. Run the example and click on the **ColumnHeaders** to sort, and click on the **OptionButton** to switch the **SortOrder** property.

Note   The example will not run unless you add a reference to the Microsoft DAO 3.0 Object Library by using the References command on the Tools menu.

```
Private Sub Option1_Click(Index as Integer)
    ' These OptionButtons offer two choices: Ascending (Index 0),
    ' and Descending (Index 1). Clicking on one of these
    ' sets the SortOrder for the ListView control.
    ListView1.SortOrder = Index
    ListView1.Sorted = True              ' Sort the List.
End Sub

Private Sub Form_Load()
    ' Create an object variable for the ColumnHeader object.
    Dim clmX As ColumnHeader
    ' Add ColumnHeaders. The width of the columns is the width
    ' of the control divided by the number of ColumnHeader objects.
    Set clmX = ListView1.ColumnHeaders. _
    Add(, , "Company", ListView1.Width / 3)
    Set clmX = ListView1.ColumnHeaders. _
    Add(, , "Address", ListView1.Width / 3)
    Set clmX = ListView1.ColumnHeaders. _
    Add(, , "Phone", ListView1.Width / 3)

    ListView1.BorderStyle = ccFixedSingle  ' Set BorderStyle property.
    ListView1.View = lvwReport             ' Set View property to Report.

    ' Label OptionButton controls with SortOrder options.
       Option1(0).Caption = "Ascending (A-Z)"
       Option1(1).Caption = "Descending (Z-A)"
       ListView1.SortOrder = 0             ' Set to Icon view

    ' Create object variables for the Data Access objects.
    Dim myDb As Database, myRs As Recordset
```

```
' Set the Database to the BIBLIO.MDB database.
Set myDb = DBEngine.Workspaces(0).OpenDatabase("BIBLIO.MDB")
' Set the recordset to the Publishers table.
Set myRs = myDb.OpenRecordset("Publishers", dbOpenDynaset)

' Create a variable to add ListItem objects.
Dim itmX As ListItem

' While the record is not the last record, add a ListItem object.
' Use the Name field for the ListItem object's text.
' Use the Address field for the ListItem object's subitem(1).
' Use the Phone field for the ListItem object's subitem(2).

While Not myRs.EOF
    Set itmX = ListView1.ListItems.Add(, , CStr(myRs!Name))

    ' If the Address field is not Null, set subitem 1 to the field.
    If Not IsNull(myRs!Address) Then
       itmX.SubItems(1) = CStr(myRs!Address) ' Address field.
    End If

    ' If the Phone field is not Null, set subitem 2 to the field.
    If Not IsNull(myRs!Telephone) Then
       itmX.SubItems(2) = myRs!Telephone      ' Phone field.
    End If

    myRs.MoveNext                            ' Move to next record.
  Wend
End Sub

Private Sub ListView1_ColumnClick(ByVal ColumnHeader As ColumnHeader)
   ' When a ColumnHeader object is clicked, the ListView control is
   ' sorted by the subitems of that column.
   ' Set the SortKey to the Index of the ColumnHeader - 1
   ListView1.SortKey = ColumnHeader.Index - 1
   ' Set Sorted to True to sort the list.
   ListView1.Sorted = True
End Sub
```

SubItemIndex Property

Returns the index of the subitem associated with a **ColumnHeader** object in a
ListView control.

Applies To

ListView Control, **ColumnHeader** Object, **ColumnHeaders** Collection

Syntax

object.**SubItemIndex** [= *integer*]

The **SubItemIndex** property syntax has these parts:

Part	Description
object	An object expression that evaluates to a **ColumnHeader** object.
integer	An integer specifying the index of the subitem associated with the **ColumnHeader** object.

Remarks

Subitems are arrays of strings representing the **ListItem** object's data when displayed in Report view.

The first column header always has a **SubItemIndex** property set to 0 because the small icon and the **ListItem** object's text always appear in the first column and are considered **ListItem** objects rather than subitems.

The number of column headers dictates the number of subitems. There is always exactly one more column header than there are subitems.

See Also

ListItem Object, **ListItems** Collection, **SubItems** Property (ListView Control)

Example

This example adds three **ColumnHeader** objects to a **ListView** control. The code then adds several **ListItem** and **Subitems** using the **SubItemIndex** to associate the **SubItems** string with the correct **ColumnHeader** object. To try the example, place a **ListView** control on a form and paste the code into the form's Declarations section. Run the example.

```
' Make sure ListView control is in report view.
ListView1.View = lvwReport

' Add three columns.
ListView1.ColumnHeaders.Add , "Name", "Name"
ListView1.ColumnHeaders.Add , "Address", "Address"
ListView1.ColumnHeaders.Add , "Phone", "Phone"

' Add ListItem objects to the control.
Dim itmX As ListItem
' Add names to column 1.
Set itmX= ListView1.ListItems.Add(1, "Mary", "Mary")
' Use the SubItemIndex to associate the SubItem with the correct
' ColumnHeader. Use the key ("Address") to specify the right
' ColumnHeader.
itmX.SubItems(ListView1.ColumnHeaders("Address").SubItemIndex) _
= "212 Grunge Street"
' Use the ColumnHeader key to associate the SubItems string
' with the correct ColumnHeader.
itmX.SubItems(ListView1.ColumnHeaders("Phone").SubItemIndex) _
= "555-1212"
```

```
Set itmX = ListView1.ListItems.Add(2, "Bill", "Bill")
itmX.SubItems(ListView1.ColumnHeaders("Address").SubItemIndex) _
= "101 Pacific Way"
itmX.SubItems(ListView1.ColumnHeaders("Phone").SubItemIndex) _
= "555-7879"

Set itmX= ListView1.ListItems.Add(3, "Susan", "Susan")
itmX.SubItems(ListView1.ColumnHeaders("Address").SubItemIndex) = _
"800 Chicago Street"
itmX.SubItems(ListView1.ColumnHeaders("Phone").SubItemIndex) = _
"555-4537"

Set itmX= ListView1.ListItems.Add(4, "Tom", "Tom")
itmX.SubItems(ListView1.ColumnHeaders("Address").SubItemIndex) _
= "200 Ocean City"
itmX.SubItems(ListView1.ColumnHeaders("Phone").SubItemIndex) = _
"555-0348"
```

SubItems Property (ListView Control)

Returns or sets an array of strings (a subitem) representing the **ListItem** object's data in a **ListView** control.

Applies To

ListView Control, **ListItem** Object, **ListItems** Collection

Syntax

object.**SubItems**(*index*) [= *string*]

The **SubItems** property syntax has these parts:

Part	Description
object	An object expression that evaluates to a **ListItem** object.
index	An integer that identifies a subitem for the specified **ListItem**.
string	Text that describes the subitem.

Remarks

Subitems are arrays of strings representing the **ListItem** object's data that are displayed in Report view. For example, you could show the file size and the date last modified for a file.

A **ListItem** object can have any number of associated item data strings (subitems) but each **ListItem** object must have the same number of subitems.

There are corresponding column headers defined for each subitem.

You cannot add elements directly to the subitems array. Use the **Add** method of the **ColumnHeaders** collection to add subitems.

See Also

ColumnHeader Object, ColumnHeaders Collection, Add Method (ColumnHeaders Collection)

Example

The following example uses the Biblio.mdb database as a source to populate a ListView control with ListItem objects. To try this example, place a ListView control on a form and paste the code into the Declarations section. You must also be sure that the Biblio.mdb has been installed on your machine. In the code below, check the path in the OpenDatabase function and change it to reflect the actual path to Biblio.mdb on your machine.

Note The example will not run unless you add a reference to the Microsoft DAO 3.5 Object Library. To do this, on the **Project** menu click **References**. Search for Microsoft DAO 3.5 Object Library and click the checkbox to select it.

```
Private Sub Form_Load()
    ' Add ColumnHeaders. The width of the columns is
    ' the width of the control divided by the number of
    ' ColumnHeader objects.
    ListView1.ColumnHeaders. _
    Add , , "Author", ListView1.Width / 3
    ListView1.ColumnHeaders. _
    Add , , "Author ID", ListView1.Width / 3, _
    lvwColumnCenter
    ListView1.ColumnHeaders. _
    Add , , "Birthdate", ListView1.Width / 3
    ' Set View property to Report.
    ListView1.View = lvwReport

    ' Declare object variables for the
    ' Data Access objects.
    Dim myDb As Database, myRs As Recordset
    ' Set the Database to the BIBLIO.MDB database.
    ' IMPORTANT: the Biblio.mdb must be on your
    ' machine, and you must set the correct path to
    ' the file in the OpenDatabase function below.
    Set myDb =  DBEngine.Workspaces(0) _
        .OpenDatabase("c:\Program Files\VB\BIBLIO.MDB")
    ' Set the recordset to the "Authors" table.
    Set myRs = _
    myDb.OpenRecordset("Authors", dbOpenDynaset)

    ' Declare a variable to add ListItem objects.
    Dim itmX As ListItem

    ' While the record is not the last record,
    ' add a ListItem object. Use the author field for
    ' the ListItem object's text. Use the AuthorID
    ' field for the ListItem object's SubItem(1).
    ' Use the "Year of Birth" field for the ListItem
    ' object's SubItem(2).
```

```
    While Not myRs.EOF
        Set itmX = ListView1.ListItems. _
        Add(, , CStr(myRs!Author))        ' Author.


        ' If the AuthorID field is not null, then set
        ' SubItem 1 to it.
        If Not IsNull(myRs!Au_id) Then
            itmX.SubItems(1) = CStr(myRs!Au_id)
        End If


        ' If the birth field is not Null, set
        ' SubItem 2 to it.
        If Not IsNull(myRs![Year Born]) Then
            itmX.SubItems(2) = myRs![Year Born]
        End If
        myRs.MoveNext  ' Move to next record.
    Wend
End Sub
```

View Property (ListView Control)

Returns or sets the appearance of the **ListItem** objects in a **ListView** control.

Applies To

ListView Control, **ListItem** Object, **ListItems** Collection

Syntax

object.**View** [= *value*]

The **View** property syntax has these parts:

Part	Description
object	The object expression that evaluates to a **ListView** control.
value	An integer or constant specifying the control's appearance, as described in **Settings**.

Settings

The settings for *value* are:

Constant	Value	Description
lvwIcon	0	(Default) **Icon**. Each **ListItem** object is represented by a full-sized (standard) icon and a text label.
lvwSmallIcon	1	**SmallIcon**. Each **ListItem** object is represented by a small icon and a text label that appears to the right of the icon. The items appear horizontally.

(continued)

(continued)

Constant	Value	Description
lvwList	2	**List**. Each **ListItem** object is represented by a small icon and a text label that appears to the right of the icon. The **ListItem** objects are arranged vertically, each on its own line with information arranged in columns.
lvwReport	3	**Report**. Each **ListItem** object is displayed with its small icon and text labels. You can provide additional information about each **ListItem** object in a subitem. The icons, text labels, and information appear in columns with the leftmost column containing the small icon, followed by the text label. Additional columns display the text for each of the item's subitems.

Remarks

In **Icon** view only, use the **LabelWrap** property to specify if the **ListItem** object's labels are wrapped or not.

In **Report** view, you can hide the column headers by setting the **HideColumnHeaders** property to **True**. You can also use the **ColumnClick** event and the **Sorted**, **SortOrder**, and **SortKey** properties to sort the **ListItem** objects or subitems when a user clicks a column header. The user can change the size of the column by grabbing the right border of a column header and dragging it to the desired size.

See Also

ColumnClick Event, **HideColumnHeaders** Property (ListView Control), **LabelWrap** Property (ListView Control), **SortKey** Property (ListView Control), **SortOrder** Property (ListView Control), **ListView** Control Constants, **Sorted** Property (ListView Control)

Example

This example populates a **ListView** control with the contents of the Publishers table in the BIBLIO.MDB database. Four **OptionButton** controls are labeled with View property choices. You must place two **ImageList** controls on the form, one to contain images for the Icon property, and a second to contain images for the **SmallIcon** property of each **ListItem** object. To try the example, place a **ListView**, a control array of four **OptionButton** controls, and two **ImageList** controls on a form and paste the code into the form's Declarations section.

Note The example will not run unless you add a reference to the Microsoft DAO 3.0 Object Library by using the References command on the Tools menu. Run the example and click on the **ComboBox** control to switch views.

```
Private Sub Option1_Click(Index as Integer)
    ' Set the ListView control's View property to the
    ' Index of Option1
    ListView1.View = Index
End Sub
```

```
Private Sub Form_Load()
    ' Create an object variable for the ColumnHeader object.
    Dim clmX As ColumnHeader
    ' Add ColumnHeaders. The width of the columns is the width
    ' of the control divided by the number of ColumnHeader objects.
    Set clmX = ListView1.ColumnHeaders. _
    Add(, , "Company", ListView1.Width / 3)

Set clmX = ListView1.ColumnHeaders. _
    Add(, , "Address", ListView1.Width / 3)
    Set clmX = ListView1.ColumnHeaders. _
    Add(, , "Phone", ListView1.Width / 3)

    ListView1.BorderStyle = ccFixedSingle  ' Set BorderStyle property.
    ListView1.View = lvwReport  ' Set View property to Report.

    ' Add one image to ImageList1--the Icons ImageList.
    Dim imgX As ListImage
    Set imgX = ImageList1.ListImages. _
    Add(, , LoadPicture("icons\mail\mail01a.ico"))

' Add an image to ImageList2--the SmallIcons ImageList.
    Set imgX = ImageList2.ListImages. _
    Add(, , LoadPicture("bitmaps\assorted\w.bmp"))

    ' To use ImageList controls with the ListView control, you must
    ' associate a particular ImageList control with the Icons and
    ' SmallIcons properties.
    ListView1.Icons = ImageList1
    ListView1.SmallIcons = ImageList2
    ' Label OptionButton controls with View options.
        Option1(0).Caption = "Icon"
        Option1(1).Caption = "SmallIcon"

Option1(2).Caption = "List"
        Option1(3).Caption = "Report"
        ListView1.View = lvwIcon  ' Set to Icon view

    ' Create object variables for the Data Access objects.
    Dim myDb As Database, myRs As Recordset
    ' Set the Database to the BIBLIO.MDB database.
    Set myDb = DBEngine.Workspaces(0).OpenDatabase("BIBLIO.MDB")
    ' Set the recordset to the Publishers table.
    Set myRs = myDb.OpenRecordset("Publishers", dbOpenDynaset)

    ' Create a variable to add ListItem objects.

Dim itmX As ListItem

    ' While the record is not the last record, add a ListItem object.
    ' Use the Name field for the ListItem object's text.
    ' Use the Address field for the ListItem object's SubItem(1)
    ' Use the Phone field for the ListItem object's SubItem(2)
```

```
    While Not myRs.EOF

        Set itmX = ListView1.ListItems.Add(, , CStr(myRs!Name))
        itmX.Icon = 1        ' Set an icon from ImageList1.
        itmX.SmallIcon = 1   ' Set an icon from ImageList2.

' If the Address field is not Null, set SubItem 1 to the field.
        If Not IsNull(myRs!Address) Then
            itmX.SubItems(1) = CStr(myRs!Address)   ' Address field.
        End If

        ' If the Phone field is not Null, set SubItem 2 to the field.
        If Not IsNull(myRs!Telephone) Then
            itmX.SubItems(2) = myRs!Telephone   ' Phone field.
        End If

        myRs.MoveNext   ' Move to next record.
    Wend
End Sub
```

MAPIMessages Control

The messaging application program interface (MAPI) controls allow you to create mail-enabled Visual Basic MAPI applications. There are two MAPI controls:

- **MAPISession**
- **MAPIMessages**

The **MAPISession** control signs on and establishes a MAPI session. It is also used to sign off from a MAPI session. The **MAPIMessages** control allows the user to perform a variety of messaging system functions.

The MAPI controls are invisible at run time. In addition, there are no events for the controls. To use them, you must specify the appropriate methods.

The **MAPIMessages** control performs a variety of messaging system functions after a messaging session is established with the **MAPISession** control.

For these controls to work, MAPI services must be present. MAPI services are provided in MAPI compliant electronic mail systems.

Note If you attempt to run a program that uses the MAPI controls, make sure that you have the 32-bit MAPI DLLs installed properly or you may not be able to perform simple MAPI functions such as SignOn. For example, on Windows 95, you must install Mail during the operating system setup, or install it separately from the control panel to correctly use MAPI functions or MAPI custom controls from Visual Basic.

Syntax

MAPIMessages

Remarks

With the **MAPIMessages** control, you can:

- Access messages currently in the Inbox.
- Compose a new message.
- Add and delete message recipients and attachments.
- Send messages (with or without a supporting user interface).
- Save, copy, and delete messages.
- Display the Address Book dialog box.
- Display the Details dialog box.
- Access attachments, including Object Linking and Embedding (OLE) attachments.
- Resolve a recipient name during addressing.
- Perform reply, reply-all, and forward actions on messages.

Most of the properties of the **MAPIMessages** control can be categorized into four functional areas: address book, file attachment, message, and recipient properties. The file attachment, message, and recipient properties are controlled by the **AttachmentIndex**, **MsgIndex**, and **RecipIndex** properties, respectively.

Message Buffers

When using the **MAPIMessages** control, you need to keep track of two buffers, the *compose buffer* and the *read buffer*. The read buffer is made up of an indexed set of messages fetched from a user's Inbox. The **MsgIndex** property is used to access individual messages within this set, starting with a value of 0 for the first message and incrementing by one for each message through the end of the set.

The message set is built using the **Fetch** method. The set includes all messages of type **FetchMsgType** and is sorted as specified by the **FetchSorted** property. Previously read messages can be included or left out of the message set with the **FetchUnreadOnly** property. Messages in the read buffer can't be altered by the user, but can be copied to the compose buffer for alteration.

Messages can be created or edited in the compose buffer. The compose buffer is the active buffer when the **MsgIndex** property is set to −1. Many of the messaging actions are valid only within the compose buffer, such as sending messages, sending messages with a dialog box, saving messages, or deleting recipients and attachments.

Refer to the object library in the Object Browser for property and error constants for the control.

Properties

Action Property (MAPIMessages Control), **AddressCaption** Property, **AddressEditFieldCount** Property, **AddressLabel** Property, **AddressModifiable** Property, **AddressResolveUI** Property, **AttachmentCount** Property, **AttachmentIndex** Property, **AttachmentName** Property, **AttachmentPathName** Property, **AttachmentPosition** Property, **AttachmentType** Property, **FetchMsgType** Property, **FetchSorted** Property, **FetchUnreadOnly** Property, **Index** Property, **MsgConversationID** Property, **MsgCount** Property, **MsgDateReceived** Property, **MsgID** Property, **MsgIndex** Property, **MsgNoteText** Property, **MsgOrigAddress** Property, **MsgOrigDisplayName** Property, **MsgRead** Property, **MsgReceiptRequested** Property, **MsgSent** Property, **MsgSubject** Property, **MsgType** Property, **Name** Property, **Object** Property, **Parent** Property, **RecipAddress** Property, **RecipCount** Property, **RecipDisplayName** Property, **RecipIndex** Property, **RecipType** Property, **SessionID** Property (MAPIMessages Control), **Tag** Property

Methods

Compose Method, **Copy** Method (**MAPIMessages** Control), **Delete** Method (MAPIMessages Control), **Fetch** Method, **Forward** Method, **Reply** Method, **ReplyAll** Method, **ResolveName** Method, **Save** Method, **Send** Method, **Show** Method (MAPIMessages Control)

See Also

MAPISession Control, MAPI Control Constants, Error Messages, MAPI Controls

MAPISession Control

The messaging application program interface (MAPI) controls allow you to create mail-enabled Visual Basic MAPI applications. There are two MAPI controls:

- **MAPISession**
- **MAPIMessages**

The **MAPISession** control signs on and establishes a MAPI session. It is also used to sign off from a MAPI session. The **MAPIMessages** control allows the user to perform a variety of messaging system functions.

Syntax

MAPISession

Remarks

After sign-on is successful, the **SessionID** property contains the handle to the MAPI session. The session handle must then be passed to the **MAPIMessages** control or an error results when using the **MAPIMessages** control.

The **MAPISession** control is invisible at run time. In addition, there are no events for the control. To use it, you must specify the appropriate properties and methods.

For these controls to work, MAPI services must be present. MAPI services are provided in MAPI compliant electronic mail systems.

Note If you attempt to run a program that uses the MAPI controls, make sure that you have the 32-bit MAPI DLLs installed properly or you may not be able to perform simple MAPI functions such as SignOn. For example, on Windows 95, you must install Exchange during the operating system setup, or install it separately from the control panel to correctly use MAPI functions or MAPI custom controls from Visual Basic.

Properties

Action Property (MAPISession Control), **DownloadMail** Property, **Index** Property, **LogonUI** Property, **Name** Property, **NewSession** Property, **Object** Property, **Parent** Property, **Password** Property (MAPISession Control), **SessionID** Property (MAPISession Control), **Tag** Property, **UserName** Property

Methods

SignOff Method, **SignOn** Method

See Also

MAPIMessages Control, MAPI Control Constants, Error Messages, MAPI Controls

Action Property (MAPIMessages Control)

Determines what action is performed when the **MAPIMessages** control is invoked. This property is not available at design time. Setting the **Action** property at run time invokes the control. This property is write-only at run time.

Note The **Action** property is included for compatibility with earlier versions of Visual Basic. For additional functionality, use the new methods listed in the Methods table for the **MAPIMessages** control.

Applies To

MAPIMessages Control

Syntax

*object.***Action** [= *value*]

The **Action** property syntax has these parts:

Part	Description
object	An object expression that evaluates to an object in the **Applies To** list.
value	An integer expression specifying the action to perform.

Remarks

The following table lists the **Action** property settings used for backwards compatibility and the corresponding new methods.

Action property setting	Corresponding method
MESSAGE_FETCH	**Fetch** method
MESSAGE_SENDDLG	**Send** method
MESSAGE_SEND	**Send** method
MESSAGE_SAVEMSG	**Save** method
MESSAGE_COPY	**Copy** method
MESSAGE_COMPOSE	**Compose** method
MESSAGE_REPLY	**Reply** method
MESSAGE_REPLYALL	**ReplyAll** method
MESSAGE_FORWARD	**Forward** method
MESSAGE_DELETE	**Delete** method
MESSAGE_SHOWADBOOK	**Show** method
MESSAGE_SHOWDETAILS	**Show** method
MESSAGE_RESOLVENAME	**ResolveName** method
RECIPIENT_DELETE	**Delete** method
ATTACHMENT_DELETE	**Delete** method

Data Type

Integer

See Also

MAPISession Control, **MAPIMessages** Control, **MAPI** Control Constants, **Error Messages**, **MAPI** Controls

---

Action Property (MAPISession Control)

Determines what action is performed when the **MAPISession** control is invoked. This property is not available at design time. Setting the **Action** property at run time invokes the control. The **Action** property is write-only at run time.

Note The **Action** property is included for compatibility with earlier versions of Visual Basic. For additional functionality, use the new methods listed in the Methods list for the **MAPISession** control.

Applies To

MAPISession Control

Syntax

object.**Action** [= *value*]

The **Action** property syntax has these parts:

Part	Description
object	An object expression that evaluates to an object in the **Applies To** list.
value	An integer expression specifying the action to perform, as described in Settings.

Settings

The settings for *value* are:

Constant	Value	Description
mapSignOn	1	Logs user into the account specified by the **UserName** and **Password** properties and provides a session handle to the underlying message subsystem. The session handle is stored in the **SessionID** property.
		Depending on the value of the **NewSession** property, the session handle may refer to a newly created session or an existing session.
mapSignOff	2	Ends the messaging session and signs the user off the specified account.

Remarks

This property is used to select between signing on and signing off from a messaging session. When signing on, a session handle is returned in the **SessionID** property.

Data Type

Integer

See Also

MAPISession Control, **NewSession** Property, **Password** Property (MAPISession Control), **SessionID** Property (**MAPISession** Control), **UserName** Property, **MAPI** Control Constants

AddressCaption Property

Specifies the caption appearing at the top of the Address Book dialog box when the **Show** method is specified with the *value* argument missing or set to **False**.

Applies To

MAPIMessages Control

Syntax

object.**AddressCaption** [= *value*]

The **AddressCaption** property syntax has these parts:

Part	Description
object	An object expression that evaluates to an object in the **Applies To** list.
value	A string expression specifying the address book dialog box caption.

Remarks

If this property is a null or empty string, the default value of the Address Book is used.

Data Type

String

See Also

MAPISession Control, **MAPIMessages** Control, **Show** Method (MAPIMessages Control), **MAPI** Control Constants, **Error Messages**, **MAPI** Controls

AddressEditFieldCount Property

Specifies which edit controls to display to the user in the Address Book dialog box when the **Show** method is specified with the *value* argument missing or set to **False**.

Applies To

MAPIMessages Control

Syntax

object.**AddressEditFieldCount** [= *value*]

The **AddressEditFieldCount** property syntax has these parts:

Part	Description
object	An object expression that evaluates to an object in the **Applies To** list.
value	An integer expression specifying which edit controls to display, as described in Settings.

Settings

The settings for *value* are:

Setting	Description
0	No edit controls; only browsing is allowed.
1	(Default) Only the To edit control should be present in the dialog box.
2	The To and CC (copy) edit controls should be present in the dialog box.
3	The To, CC (copy), and BCC (blind copy) edit controls should be present in the dialog box.
4	Only those edit controls supported by the messaging system should be present in the dialog box.

Remarks

For example, if **AddressEditFieldCount** is 3, the user can select from the To, CC, and BCC edit controls in the Address Book dialog box. The **AddressEditFieldCount** is adjusted so that it is equal to at least the minimum number of edit controls required by the recipient set.

Data Type

Integer

See Also

MAPISession Control, **MAPIMessages** Control, **AddressLabel** Property, **Show** Method (MAPIMessages Control), **MAPI** Control Constants, **Error Messages**, **MAPI** Controls

---

AddressLabel Property

Specifies the appearance of the To edit control in the Address Book when the **Show** method is specified with the *value* argument missing or set to **False**.

Applies To

MAPIMessages Control

Syntax

object.**AddressLabel** [= *value*]

The **AddressLabel** property syntax has these parts:

Part	Description
object	An object expression that evaluates to an object in the **Applies To** list.
value	A string expression specifying an address label.

Remarks

This property is normally ignored and should contain an empty string to use the default label "To." However, when the **AddressEditFieldCount** property is set to 1, the user has the option of explicitly specifying another label (providing the number of editing controls required by the recipient set equals 1).

Data Type

String

See Also

MAPISession Control, **MAPIMessages** Control, **AddressEditFieldCount** Property, **Show** Method (MAPIMessages Control), **MAPI** Control Constants, **Error Messages**, **MAPI** Controls

AddressModifiable Property

Specifies whether the Address Book can be modified.

Applies To

MAPIMessages Control

Syntax

object.**AddressModifiable** [= *value*]

The **AddressModifiable** property syntax has these parts:

Part	Description
object	An object expression that evaluates to an object in the **Applies To** list.
value	A Boolean expression specifying whether the Address Book can be modified, as described in Settings.

Settings

The settings for *value* are:

Setting	Description
True	The user is allowed to modify their personal address book.
False	(Default) The user is not allowed to modify their personal address book.

Data Type

Boolean

See Also

MAPISession Control, **MAPIMessages** Control, **MAPI** Control Constants, **Error Messages**, **MAPI** Controls

AddressResolveUI Property

Specifies whether a dialog box is displayed for recipient name resolution during addressing when the **ResolveName** method is specified.

Applies To

MAPIMessages Control

Syntax

object.**AddressResolveUI** [= *value*]

The **AddressResolveUI** property syntax has these parts:

Part	Description
object	An object expression that evaluates to an object in the **Applies To** list.
value	A Boolean expression specifying whether a dialog box is displayed, as described in Settings.

Settings

The settings for *value* are:

Setting	Description
True	A dialog box is displayed with names that closely match the intended recipient's name.
False	(Default) No dialog box is displayed for ambiguous names. An error occurs if no potential matches are found (no matches is not an ambiguous situation).

Data Type

Boolean

See Also

MAPISession Control, **MAPIMessages** Control, **ResolveName** Method, **MAPI** Control Constants, **Error Messages**, **MAPI** Controls

---

AttachmentCount Property

Returns the total number of attachments associated with the currently indexed message. This property is not available at design time, and is read-only at run time.

Applies To

MAPIMessages Control

Syntax

object.**AttachmentCount**

The *object* placeholder represents an object expression that evaluates to an object in the **Applies To** list.

Remarks

The default value is 0. The value of **AttachmentCount** depends on the number of attachments in the current indexed message.

Data Type

Long

See Also

MAPISession Control, **MAPIMessages** Control, **MAPI** Control Constants, **Error Messages**, **MAPI** Controls

---

AttachmentIndex Property

Sets the currently indexed attachment. This property is not available at design time.

Applies To

MAPIMessages Control

Syntax

object.**AttachmentIndex** [= *value*]

The **AttachmentIndex** property syntax has these parts:

Part	Description
object	An object expression that evaluates to an object in the **Applies To** list.
value	A long expression specifying the currently indexed attachment.

Remarks

Specifies an index number to identify a particular message attachment. The index number in this property determines the values in the **AttachmentName**, **AttachmentPathName**, **AttachmentPosition**, and **AttachmentType** properties. The attachment identified by the **AttachmentIndex** property is called the *currently indexed* attachment. The value of **AttachmentIndex** can range from 0 (the default) to **AttachmentCount – 1**.

To add a new attachment, set the **AttachmentIndex** to a value greater than or equal to the current attachment count while in the compose buffer (**MsgIndex** =–1). The **AttachmentCount** property is updated automatically to reflect the implied new number of attachments.

For example, if the current **AttachmentCount** property has the value 3, setting the **AttachmentIndex** property to 4 adds 2 new attachments and increases the **AttachmentCount** property to 5.

To delete an existing attachment, specify the **Delete** method with the *value* parameter set to 2. Attachments can be added or deleted only when the **MsgIndex** property is set to–1.

Data Type

Long

See Also

MAPISession Control, **MAPIMessages** Control, **AttachmentCount** Property, **AttachmentName** Property, **AttachmentPathName** Property, **AttachmentPosition** Property, **AttachmentType** Property, **MAPI** Control Constants, **Error Messages**, **MAPI** Controls

AttachmentName Property

Specifies the name of the currently indexed attachment file. This property is not available at design time. It is read-only unless **MsgIndex** is set to–1.

Applies To

MAPIMessages Control

Syntax

object.**AttachmentName** [= *value*]

The **AttachmentName** property syntax has these parts:

Part	Description
object	An object expression that evaluates to an object in the **Applies To** list.
value	A string expression specifying the name of the currently indexed attachment file.

Remarks

The file name specified is the file name seen by the recipients of the currently indexed message. If **AttachmentName** is an empty string, the file name from the **AttachmentPathName** property is used.

If the attachment is an OLE object, **AttachmentName** contains the class name of the object, for example, "Microsoft Excel Worksheet."

Attachments in the read buffer are deleted when a subsequent fetch occurs. The value of **AttachmentName** depends on the currently indexed message as selected by the **AttachmentIndex** property.

Data Type

String

See Also

MAPISession Control, **MAPIMessages** Control, **AttachmentIndex** Property, **AttachmentPathName** Property, **MsgIndex** Property, **MAPI** Control Constants, **Error Messages**, **MAPI** Controls

AttachmentPathName Property

Specifies the full path name of the currently indexed attachment. This property is not available at design time. It is read-only unless **MsgIndex** is set to –1.

Applies To

MAPIMessages Control

Syntax

object.**AttachmentPathName** [= *value*]

The **AttachmentPathName** property syntax has these parts:

Part	Description
object	An object expression that evaluates to an object in the **Applies To** list.
value	A string expression specifying the full path name of the currently indexed attachment.

Remarks

If you attempt to send a message with an empty string for a path name, an error results. Attachments in the read buffer are deleted when a subsequent fetch occurs. Attachments in the compose buffer need to be manually deleted. The value of **AttachmentPathName** depends on the currently indexed message, as selected by the **AttachmentIndex** property.

Data Type

String

See Also

MAPISession Control, **MAPIMessages** Control, **AttachmentIndex** Property, **MsgIndex** Property, **MAPI** Control Constants, **Error Messages**, **MAPI** Controls

---

AttachmentPosition Property

Specifies the position of the currently indexed attachment within the message body. This property is not available at design time. It is read-only unless **MsgIndex** is set to –1.

Applies To

MAPIMessages Control

Syntax

object.**AttachmentPosition** [= *value*]

The **AttachmentPosition** property syntax these parts:

Part	Description
object	An object expression that evaluates to an object in the **Applies To** list.
value	A long expression specifying the position of the currently indexed attachment.

Remarks

To determine where an attachment is placed, count the characters in the message body and decide which character position you wish to replace with the attachment. The character count at that position should be used for the **AttachmentPosition** value.

For example, in a message body that is five-characters long, you could place an attachment at the end of the message by setting **AttachmentPosition** equal to 4. (The message body occupies character positions 0 to 4.)

You can't place two attachments in the same position within the same message. In addition, you can't place an attachment beyond the end of the message body.

The value of **AttachmentPosition** depends on the currently indexed attachment, as selected by the **AttachmentIndex** property.

Data Type

Long

See Also

MAPISession Control, **MAPIMessages** Control, **AttachmentIndex** Property, **MsgIndex** Property, **MAPI** Control Constants, **Error Messages**, **MAPI** Controls

---

AttachmentType Property

Specifies the type of the currently indexed file attachment. This property is not available at design time. It is read-only unless **MsgIndex** is set to -1.

Applies To

MAPIMessages Control

Syntax

object.**AttachmentType** [= *value*]

The **AttachmentType** property syntax has these parts:

Part	Description
object	An object expression that evaluates to an object in the **Applies To** list.
value	An integer expression specifying the type of the currently indexed file attachment, as described in Settings.

Settings

The settings for *value* are:

Constant	Value	Description
mapData	0	The attachment is a data file.
mapEOLE	1	The attachment is an embedded OLE object.
mapSOLE	2	The attachment is a static OLE object.

Remarks

The value of **AttachmentType** depends on the currently indexed attachment, as selected by the **AttachmentIndex** property.

Data Type

Integer

See Also

MAPISession Control, **MAPIMessages** Control, **AttachmentIndex** Property, **MsgIndex** Property, **MAPI** Control Constants, **Error Messages**, **MAPI** Controls

Compose Method

Composes a message.

Applies To

MAPIMessages Control

Syntax

object.**Compose**

The *object* placeholder represents an object expression that evaluates to an object in the **Applies To** list.

Remarks

This method clears all the components of the compose buffer, and sets the **MsgIndex** property to−1.

See Also

MAPISession Control, **MAPIMessages** Control, **MsgIndex** Property, **MAPI** Control Constants, **Error Messages**, **MAPI** Controls

Copy Method (MAPIMessages Control)

Copies the currently indexed message to the compose buffer.

Applies To

MAPIMessages Control

Syntax

object.**Copy**

The *object* placeholder represents an object expression that evaluates to an object in the **Applies To** list.

Remarks

This method sets the **MsgIndex** property to−1.

See Also

MAPISession Control, **MAPIMessages** Control, **MsgIndex** Property, **MAPI** Control Constants, **Error Messages**, **MAPI** Controls

Delete Method (MAPIMessages Control)

Deletes a message, recipient, or attachment.

Applies To

MAPIMessages Control

Syntax

object.**Delete** [*value*]

The **Delete** method syntax has these parts:

Part	Description
object	An object expression that evaluates to an object in the **Applies To** list.
value	An integer expression specifying the item to delete, as described in settings.

Settings

The settings for *value* are:

Constant	Value	Description
mapMessageDelete	0	Deletes all components of the currently indexed message, reduces the **MsgCount** property by 1, and decrements the index number by 1 for each message that follows the deleted message.
		If the deleted message was the last message in the set, this method decrements the **MsgIndex** property by 1.
mapRecipientDelete	1	Deletes the currently indexed recipient. Automatically reduces the **RecipCount** property by 1, and decrements the index number by 1 for each recipient that follows the deleted recipient.
		If the deleted recipient was the last recipient in the set, this method decrements the **RecipIndex** property by 1.
mapAttachmentDelete	2	Deletes the currently indexed attachment. Automatically reduces the **AttachmentCount** property by 1, and decrements the index by 1 for each attachment that follows the deleted attachment.
		If the deleted attachment was the last attachment in the set, this method decrements the **AttachmentIndex** by 1.

See Also

MAPISession Control, **MAPIMessages** Control, **AttachmentCount** Property, **AttachmentIndex** Property, **MsgCount** Property, **MsgIndex** Property, **RecipCount** Property, **RecipIndex** Property, **MAPI** Control Constants, **Error Messages**, **MAPI** Controls

DownloadMail Property

Specifies when new messages are downloaded from the mail server for the designated user.

Applies To

MAPISession Control

Syntax

object.**DownloadMail** [= *value*]

The **DownloadMail** property syntax has these parts:

Part	Description
object	An object expression that evaluates to an object in the **Applies To** list.
value	A Boolean expression specifying when new mail is downloaded, as described in Settings.

Settings

The settings for *value* are:

Setting	Description
True	(Default) All new messages from the mail server are forced to the user's Inbox during the sign-on process.
False	New messages on the server are *not* forced to the user's Inbox immediately, but are downloaded at the time interval set by the user.

Remarks

This property can be set to **True** when you want to access the user's complete set of messages when signing on. However, processing time may increase as a result.

Data Type

Boolean

See Also

MAPISession Control, **MAPIMessages** Control, **MAPI** Control Constants, **Error Messages**, **MAPI** Controls

---

Fetch Method

Creates a message set from selected messages in the Inbox.

Applies To

MAPIMessages Control

Syntax

object.**Fetch**

The *object* placeholder represents an object expression that evaluates to an object in the **Applies To** list.

Remarks

The message set includes all messages in the Inbox which are of the types specified by the **FetchMsgType** property. They are sorted as specified by the **FetchSorted** property. If the **FetchUnreadOnly** property is set to **True**, only unread messages are included in the message set.

Any attachment files in the read buffer are deleted when a subsequent fetch action occurs.

See Also

MAPISession Control, **MAPIMessages** Control, **FetchMsgType** Property, **FetchSorted** Property, **FetchUnreadOnly** Property, **MAPI** Control Constants, **Error Messages**, **MAPI** Controls

FetchMsgType Property

Specifies the message type to populate the message set.

Applies To

MAPIMessages Control

Syntax

object.**FetchMsgType** [= *value*]

The **FetchMsgType** property syntax has these parts:

Part	Description
object	An object expression that evaluates to an object in the **Applies To** list.
value	A string expression specifying the message type.

Remarks

This property determines which message types are added to the message set when the **Fetch** method is specified. A null or empty string in this property specifies an interpersonal message type (IPM), which is the default.

Note The availability of message types other than IPM is dependent on your mail system. Refer to its documentation for more details.

Data Type

String

See Also

MAPISession Control, **MAPIMessages** Control, **Fetch** Method, **MAPI** Control Constants, **Error Messages**, **MAPI** Controls

FetchSorted Property

Specifies the message order when populating the message set with messages from the Inbox.

Applies To

MAPIMessages Control

Syntax

object.**FetchSorted** [= *value*]

The **FetchSorted** property syntax has these parts:

Part	Description
object	An object expression that evaluates to an object in the **Applies To** list.
value	A Boolean expression specifying the message order, as described in Settings.

Settings

The settings for *value* are:

Setting	Description
True	Messages are added to the message set in the order they were received (first in, first out).
False	(Default) Messages are added in the sort order as specified by the user's Inbox.

Data Type

Boolean

See Also

MAPISession Control, **MAPIMessages** Control, **Fetch** Method, **MAPI** Control Constants, **Error Messages**, **MAPI** Controls

---

FetchUnreadOnly Property

Determines whether to restrict the messages in the message set to unread messages only.

Applies To

MAPIMessages Control

Syntax

object.**FetchUnreadOnly** [= *value*]

The **FetchUnreadOnly** property syntax has these parts:

Part	Description
object	An object expression that evaluates to an object in the **Applies To** list.
value	A Boolean expression specifying whether to restrict messages in the message set, as described in Settings.

Settings

The settings for *value* are:

Setting	Description
True	(Default) Only unread messages of the type specified in the **FetchMsgType** property are added to the message set.
False	All messages of the proper type in the Inbox are added.

Data Type

Boolean

See Also

MAPISession Control, **MAPIMessages** Control, **FetchMsgType** Property, **Fetch** Method, **MAPI** Control Constants, **Error Messages**, **MAPI** Controls

---

Forward Method

Forwards a message.

Applies To

MAPIMessages Control

Syntax

object.**Forward**

The *object* placeholder represents an object expression that evaluates to an object in the **Applies To** list.

Remarks

This method copies the currently indexed message to the compose buffer as a forwarded message and adds **FW:** to the beginning of the Subject line. It also sets the **MsgIndex** property to−1.

See Also

MsgIndex Property

LogonUI Property

Specifies whether or not a dialog box is provided for sign-on.

Applies To

MAPISession Control

Syntax

object.**LogonUI** [= *value*]

The **LogonUI** property syntax has these parts:

Part	Description
object	An object expression that evaluates to an object in the **Applies To** list.
value	A Boolean expression specifying whether a logon dialog box is displayed, as described in Settings.

Settings

The settings for *value* are:

Setting	Description
True	(Default) A dialog box prompts new users for their user name and password (unless a valid messaging session already exists. See the **NewSession** property for more information).
False	No dialog box is displayed.

Remarks

The **False** setting is useful when you want to begin a mail session without user intervention, and you already have the account name and password for the user. If insufficient or incorrect values are provided, however, an error is generated.

Data Type

Boolean

See Also

MAPISession Control, **NewSession** Property, **MAPIMessages** Control, **MAPI** Control Constants, **Error Messages**, **MAPI** Controls

MAPI Control Constants

MAPISession Action Constants

Constant	Value	Description
mapSignOn	1	Log user into account
mapSignOff	2	End messaging session

MAPIMessages Delete Constants

Constant	Value	Description
mapMessageDelete	0	Delete current message
mapRecipientDelete	1	Delete the currently indexed recipient
mapAttachmentDelete	2	Delete the currently indexed attachment

MAPI Controls Error Constants

Constant	Value	Description
mapSuccessSuccess	32000	Action returned successfully
mapUserAbort	32001	User canceled process
mapFailure	32002	Unspecified failure
mapLoginFail	32003	Login failure
mapDiskFull	32004	Disk full
mapInsufficientMem	32005	Insufficient memory
mapAccessDenied	32006	Access denied
mapGeneralFailure	32007	General failure
mapTooManySessions	32008	Too many sessions
mapTooManyFiles	32009	Too many files
mapTooManyRecipients	32010	Too many recipients
mapAttachmentNotFound	32011	Attachment not found
mapAttachmentOpenFailure	32012	Attachment open failure
mapAttachmentWriteFailure	32013	Attachment write failure
mapUnknownRecipient	32014	Unknown recipient
mapBadRecipType	32015	Invalid recipient type
mapNoMessages	32016	No message
mapInvalidMessage	32017	Invalid message
mapTextTooLarge	32018	Text too large
mapInvalidSession	32019	Invalid session
mapTypeNotSupported	32020	Type not supported
mapAmbiguousRecipient	32021	Ambiguous recipient
mapMessageInUse	32022	Message in use
mapNetworkFailure	32023	Network failure
mapInvalidEditFields	32024	Invalid editfields
mapInvalidRecips	32025	Invalid Recipients
mapNotSupported	32026	Current action not supported
mapSessionExist	32050	Session ID already exists
mapInvalidBuffer	32051	Read-only in read buffer
mapInvalidReadBufferAction	32052	Valid in compose buffer only
mapNoSession	32053	No valid session ID
mapInvalidRecipient	32054	Originator information not available
mapInvalidComposeBufferAction	32055	Action not valid for Compose Buffer
mapControlFailure	32056	No messages in list
mapNoRecipients	32057	No recipients
mapNoAttachment	32058	No attachments

MAPIMessages Reciptype Constants

Constant	Value	Description
mapOrigList	0	Message originator
mapToList	1	Recipient is a primary recipient
mapCcList	2	Recipient is a copy recipient
mapBccList	3	Recipient is a blind copy recipient

MAPIMessages Attachtype Constants

Constant	Value	Description
mapData	0	Attachment is a data file
mapEOLE	1	Attachment is an embedded OLE object
mapSOLE	2	Attachment is a static OLE object

See Also

MAPISession Control, **Action** Property (MAPISession Control), **MAPIMessages** Control, **AttachmentType** Property, **RecipType** Property, **Delete** Method (MAPIMessages Control), **Error Messages**, **MAPI** Controls, **Visual Basic** Constants

MsgConversationID Property

Specifies the conversation thread identification value for the currently indexed message. It is read-only unless **MsgIndex** is set to –1.

Applies To

MAPIMessages Control

Syntax

object.**MsgConversationID** [= *value*]

The **MsgConversationID** property syntax has these parts:

Part	Description
object	An object expression that evaluates to an object in the **Applies To** list.
value	A string expression specifying the conversation identification value.

Remarks

A conversation thread is used to identify a set of messages beginning with the original message and including all the subsequent replies. Identical conversation IDs indicate that the messages are part of the same thread. New messages are assigned an ID by the message system. The value of **MsgConversationID** depends on the currently indexed message, as selected by the **MsgIndex** property.

Data Type

String

See Also

MAPISession Control, MAPIMessages Control, MsgIndex Property, MAPI Control Constants, Error Messages, MAPI Controls

MsgCount Property

Returns the total number of messages present in the message set during the current messaging session. This property is not available at design time, and is read-only at run time.

Applies To

MAPIMessages Control

Syntax

object.MsgCount

The MsgCount property syntax has these parts:

Part	Description
object	An object expression that evaluates to an object in the **Applies To** list.

Remarks

This property is used to get a current count of the messages in the message set. The default value is 0. This property is reset each time a fetch is performed.

Data Type

Long

See Also

MAPISession Control, MAPIMessages Control, MsgIndex Property, MAPI Control Constants, Error Messages, MAPI Controls

MsgDateReceived Property

Returns the date on which the currently indexed message was received. This property is not available at design time and is read-only at run time.

Applies To

MAPIMessages Control

Syntax

object.MsgDateReceived

The MsgDateReceived property syntax has these parts:

Part	Description
object	An object expression that evaluates to an object in the **Applies To** list.

Remarks

The format for this property is YYYY/MM/DD HH:MM. Hours are measured on a standard 24-hour base. The value of **MsgDateReceived** is set by the message system and depends on the currently indexed message, as selected by the **MsgIndex** property.

Data Type

String

See Also

MAPISession Control, **MAPIMessages** Control, **MsgIndex** Property, **MAPI** Control Constants, **Error Messages**, **MAPI** Controls

---

MsgID Property

Returns the string identifier of the currently indexed message. This property is not available at design time and is read-only at run time.

Applies To

MAPIMessages Control

Syntax

object.**MsgID**

The **MsgID** property syntax has these parts:

Part	Description
object	An object expression that evaluates to an object in the **Applies To** list.

Remarks

The message-identifier string is a system-specific, 64-character string used to uniquely identify a message. The value of **MsgID** depends on the currently indexed message, as selected by the **MsgIndex** property.

Data Type

String

See Also

MAPISession Control, **MAPIMessages** Control, **MsgIndex** Property, **MAPI** Control Constants, **Error Messages**, **MAPI** Controls

---

MsgIndex Property

Specifies the index number of the currently indexed message. This property is not available at design time.

Applies To

MAPIMessages Control

Syntax

object.**MsgIndex** [= *value*]

The **MsgIndex** property syntax these parts:

Part	Description
object	An object expression that evaluates to an object in the **Applies To** list.
value	A long expression specifying the index number of the currently indexed message.

Remarks

The **MsgIndex** property determines the values of all the other message-related properties of the **MAPI Messages** control. The index number can range from–1 to **MsgCount** – 1.

Note Changing the **MsgIndex** property also changes the entire set of attachments and recipients.

The message identified by the **MsgIndex** property is called the *currently indexed* message. When this index is changed, all of the other message properties change to reflect the characteristics of the indexed message. A value of–1 signifies a message being built in the compose buffer—in other words, an outgoing message.

Data Type

Long

See Also

MAPISession Control, **MAPIMessages** Control, **MsgCount** Property, **MAPI** Control Constants, **Error Messages**, **MAPI** Controls

---

MsgNoteText Property

Specifies the text body of the message. This property is not available at design time. It is read-only unless **MsgIndex** is set to–1.

Applies To

MAPIMessages Control

Syntax

object.**MsgNoteText** [= *value*]

The **MsgNoteText** property syntax has these parts:

Part	Description
object	An object expression that evaluates to an object in the **Applies To** list.
value	A string expression specifying message text.

Remarks

This property consists of the entire textual portion of the message body (minus any attachments). An empty string indicates no text.

For inbound messages, each paragraph is terminated with a carriage return-line feed pair (0x0d0a). For outbound messages, paragraphs can be delimited with a carriage return (0x0d), line feed (0x0a), or a carriage return-line feed pair (0x0d0a). The value of **MsgNoteText** depends on the currently indexed message, as selected by the **MsgIndex** property.

Data Type

String

See Also

MAPISession Control, **MAPIMessages** Control, **MsgIndex** Property, **MAPI** Control Constants, **Error Messages**, **MAPI** Controls

---

MsgOrigAddress Property

Returns the mail address of the originator of the currently indexed message. This property is not available at design time and is read-only at run time. The messaging system sets this property for you when sending a message.

Applies To

MAPIMessages Control

Syntax

object.**MsgOrigAddress**

The **MsgOrigAddress** property syntax has these parts:

Part	Description
object	An object expression that evaluates to an object in the **Applies To** list.

Remarks

The value of **MsgOrigAddress** depends on the currently indexed message as selected by the **MsgIndex** property. The value is null in the compose buffer.

Data Type

String

See Also

MAPISession Control, **MAPIMessages** Control, **MsgIndex** Property, **MAPI** Control Constants, **Error Messages**, **MAPI** Controls

MsgOrigDisplayName Property

Returns the originator's name for the currently indexed message. This property is not available at design time and is read-only at run time. The messaging system sets this property for you.

Applies To

MAPIMessages Control

Syntax

object.**MsgOrigDisplayName**

The **MsgOrigDisplayName** property syntax has these parts:

Part	Description
object	An object expression that evaluates to an object in the **Applies To** list.

Remarks

The name in this property is the originator's name, as displayed in the message header. The value of **MsgOrigDisplayName** depends on the currently indexed message, as selected by the **MsgIndex** property. The value is null in the compose buffer.

Data Type

String

See Also

MAPISession Control, **MAPIMessages** Control, **MsgIndex** Property, **MAPI** Control Constants, **Error Messages**, **MAPI** Controls

---

MsgRead Property

Returns a Boolean expression indicating whether the message has already been read. This property is not available at design time and is read-only at run time.

Applies To

MAPIMessages Control

Syntax

object.**MsgRead**

The **MsgRead** property syntax has these parts:

Part	Description
object	An object expression that evaluates to an object in the **Applies To** list.

Settings

The settings for the **MsgRead** property are:

Setting	Description
True	The currently indexed message has already been read by the user.
False	(Default) The message remains unread.

Remarks

The value of **MsgRead** depends on the currently indexed message, as selected by the **MsgIndex** property. The message is marked as read when the note text or any of the attachment information is accessed. However, accessing header information does not mark the message as read.

Data Type

Boolean

See Also

MAPISession Control, **MAPIMessages** Control, **MsgIndex** Property, **MAPI** Control Constants, **Error Messages**, **MAPI** Controls

---

MsgReceiptRequested Property

Specifies whether a return receipt is requested for the currently indexed message. This property is not available at design time.

Applies To

MAPIMessages Control

Syntax

object.**MsgReceiptRequested** [= *value*]

The **MsgReceiptRequested** property syntax has these parts:

Part	Description
object	An object expression that evaluates to an object in the **Applies To** list.
value	A Boolean expression specifying whether a return receipt is requested, as described in Settings.

Settings

The settings for *value* are:

Setting	Description
True	A receipt notification is returned to the sender when the recipient opens the message.
False	(Default) No return receipt is generated.

Remarks

The value of **MsgReceiptRequested** depends on the currently indexed message, as selected by the **MsgIndex** property.

Data Type

Boolean

See Also

MAPISession Control, **MAPIMessages** Control, **MsgIndex** Property, **MAPI** Control Constants, **Error Messages**, **MAPI** Controls

---

MsgSent Property

Specifies whether the currently indexed message has already been sent to the mail server for distribution. This property is not available at design time and is read-only at run time. The messaging system sets this property for you when sending a message.

Applies To

MAPIMessages Control

Syntax

object.**MsgSent**

The **MsgSent** property syntax has these parts:

Part	Description
object	An object expression that evaluates to an object in the **Applies To** list.

Settings

The settings for the **MsgSent** property are:

Setting	Description
True	The currently indexed message has already been submitted to the mail server as an outgoing message.
False	The currently indexed message has not yet been delivered to the server.

Remarks

The value of **MsgSent** depends on the currently indexed message, as selected by the **MsgIndex** property.

Data Type

Boolean

See Also

MAPISession Control, **MAPIMessages** Control, **MsgIndex** Property, **MAPI** Control Constants, **Error Messages**, **MAPI** Controls

MsgSubject Property

Specifies the subject line for the currently indexed message as displayed in the message header. This property is not available at design time. It is read-only unless **MsgIndex** is set to−1.

Applies To

MAPIMessages Control

Syntax

object.**MsgSubject** [= *value*]

The **MsgSubject** property syntax has these parts:

Part	Description
object	An object expression that evaluates to an object in the **Applies To** list.
value	A string expression specifying the subject line.

Remarks

The value of **MsgSubject** depends on the currently indexed message, as selected by the **MsgIndex** property. **MsgSubject** is limited to 64 characters, including the Null character.

Data Type

String

See Also

MAPISession Control, **MAPIMessages** Control, **MsgIndex** Property, **MAPI** Control Constants, **Error Messages**, **MAPI** Controls

---

MsgType Property

Specifies the type of the currently indexed message. This property is not available at design time. It is read-only unless **MsgIndex** is set to−1.

Applies To

MAPIMessages Control

Syntax

object.**MsgType** [= *value*]

The **MsgType** property syntax has these parts:

Part	Description
object	An object expression that evaluates to an object in the **Applies To** list.
value	A string expression specifying the type of message.

Remarks

The **MsgType** property is for use by applications other than interpersonal mail (IPM message type). Not all mail systems support message types that are not IPM and may not provide (or may ignore) this parameter.

A null or empty string indicates an IPM message type. The value of **MsgType** depends on the currently indexed message, as selected by the **MsgIndex** property. This property is not meant for use as a filter to isolate messages by sender, receipt time, and other categories.

Data Type

String

See Also

MAPISession Control, **MAPIMessages** Control, **MsgIndex** Property, **MAPI** Control Constants, **Error Messages**, **MAPI** Controls

NewSession Property

Specifies whether a new mail session should be established, even if a valid session currently exists.

Applies To

MAPISession Control

Syntax

object.**NewSession**[= *value*]

The **NewSession** property syntax has these parts:

Part	Description
object	An object expression that evaluates to an object in the **Applies To** list.
value	A Boolean expression specifying whether a new mail session should be established, as described in Settings.

Settings

The settings for *value* are:

Setting	Description
True	A new messaging session is established, regardless of whether a valid session already exists.
False	(Default) Use the existing session established by the user.

Data Type

Boolean

See Also

MAPISession Control, **MAPIMessages** Control, **MAPI** Control Constants, **Error Messages**, **MAPI** Controls

Password Property (MAPISession Control)

Specifies the account password associated with the **UserName** property.

Applies To

MAPISession Control

Syntax

object.**Password**[= *value*]

The **Password** property syntax has these parts:

Part	Description
object	An object expression that evaluates to an object in the **Applies To** list.
value	A string expression specifying the account password

Remarks

An empty string in this property indicates that a sign-on dialog box with an empty password field should be generated. The default is an empty string.

Data Type

String

See Also

MAPISession Control, **UserName** Property, **MAPIMessages** Control, **MAPI** Control Constants, **Error Messages**, **MAPI** Controls

RecipAddress Property

Specifies the electronic mail address of the currently indexed recipient. This property is not available at design time. It is read-only unless **MsgIndex** is set to−1.

Applies To

MAPIMessages Control

Syntax

object.**RecipAddress** [= *value*]

The **RecipAddress** property syntax has these parts:

Part	Description
object	An object expression that evaluates to an object in the **Applies To** list.
value	A string expression specifying mail address.

Remarks

The value of **RecipAddress** depends on the currently indexed recipient, as selected by the **RecipIndex** property.

Data Type

String

See Also

MAPISession Control, **MAPIMessages** Control, **MsgIndex** Property, **RecipIndex** Property, **MAPI** Control Constants, **Error Messages**, **MAPI** Controls

---

RecipCount Property

Returns the total number of recipients for the currently indexed message in a long integer. This property is not available at design time, and is read-only at run time.

Applies To

MAPIMessages Control

Syntax

object.**RecipCount**

The **RecipCount** property syntax has these parts:

Part	Description
object	An object expression that evaluates to an object in the **Applies To** list.

Remarks

The default value is 0. The value of **RecipCount** depends on the currently indexed message, as selected by the **MsgIndex** property.

Data Type

Long

See Also

MAPISession Control, **MAPIMessages** Control, **MsgIndex** Property, **RecipIndex** Property, **MAPI** Control Constants, **Error Messages**, **MAPI** Controls

---

RecipDisplayName Property

Specifies the name of the currently indexed recipient. This property is not available at design time. It is read-only unless **MsgIndex** is set to–1.

Applies To

MAPIMessages Control

Syntax

object.**RecipDisplayName** [= *value*]

The **RecipDisplayName** property syntax has these parts:

Part	Description
object	An object expression that evaluates to an object in the **Applies To** list.
value	A string expression specifying the name of the recipient.

Remarks

The name in this property is the recipient's name, as displayed in the message header. The value of **RecipDisplayName** depends on the currently indexed message, as selected by the **RecipIndex** property. The **ResolveName** method uses the recipient name as it is stored here.

Data Type

String

See Also

MAPISession Control, **MAPIMessages** Control, **RecipIndex** Property, **MAPI Control** Constants, **Error Messages**, **MAPI** Controls

---

RecipIndex Property

Sets the currently indexed recipient. This property is not available at design time.

Applies To

MAPIMessages Control

Syntax

object.**RecipIndex** [= *value*]

The **RecipIndex** property syntax these parts:

Part	Description
object	An object expression that evaluates to an object in the **Applies To** list.
value	A long expression specifying the currently indexed recipient.

Remarks

Specifies an index number to identify a particular message recipient. The index number in this property determines the values in the **RecipAddress**, **RecipCount**, **RecipDisplayName**, and **RecipType** properties.

The recipient identified by the **RecipIndex** property is called the *currently indexed* recipient. The value of **RecipIndex** can range from 0 (the default) to **RecipCount** − 1. When in the read buffer with **RecipIndex** set to −1, values of the other recipient properties show message originator information. The default setting is 0.

To add a new recipient, set the **RecipIndex** to a value greater than or equal to the current recipient count while in the compose buffer. The **RecipCount** property is updated automatically to reflect the implied new number of recipients. For example, if the current **RecipCount** property has the value 3, setting the **RecipIndex** property to 4 adds 2 new recipients and increases the **RecipCount** property to 5.

To delete an existing recipient, specify the **Delete** method with the *value* parameter set to 1. Recipients can be added or deleted only when the **MsgIndex** property is set to−1.

Data Type

Long

See Also

MAPISession Control, **MAPIMessages** Control, **MsgIndex** Property, **RecipAddress** Property, **RecipCount** Property, **RecipDisplayName** Property, **RecipType** Property, **Delete** Method (MAPIMessages Control), **MAPI** Control Constants, **Error Messages**, **MAPI** Controls

---

RecipType Property

Specifies the type of the currently indexed recipient. This property is not available at design time. It is read-only unless **MsgIndex** is set to−1.

Applies To

MAPIMessages Control

Syntax

object.**RecipType** [= *value*]

The **RecipType** property syntax has these parts:

Part	Description
object	An object expression that evaluates to an object in the **Applies To** list.
value	An integer expression specifying the type of recipient, as described in Settings.

Settings

The settings for *value* are:

Constant	Value	Description
mapOrigList	0	The message originator.
mapToList	1	The recipient is a primary recipient.
mapCcList	2	The recipient is a copy recipient.
map BccList	3	The recipient is a blind copy recipient.

Remarks

The value of **RecipType** depends on the currently indexed message, as selected by the **RecipIndex** property. You cannot set the recipient type to 0 (the message system uses a value of 0 to indicate the message originator.)

Data Type

Integer

See Also

MAPISession Control, **MAPIMessages** Control, **MsgIndex** Property, **RecipIndex** Property, **MAPI** Control Constants, **Error Messages**, **MAPI** Controls

Reply Method

Replies to a message.

Applies To

MAPIMessages Control

Syntax

object.**Reply**

The *object* placeholder represents an object expression that evaluates to an object in the **Applies To** list.

Remarks

This method copies the currently indexed message to the compose buffer and adds **RE:** to the beginning of the Subject line. It also sets the **MsgIndex** property to−1.

The currently indexed message originator becomes the outgoing message recipient.

See Also

MAPISession Control, **MAPIMessages** Control, **MsgIndex** Property, **MAPI** Control Constants, **Error Messages**, **MAPI** Controls

ReplyAll Method

Replies to all message recipients.

Applies To

MAPIMessages Control

Syntax

object.**ReplyAll**

The *object* placeholder represents an object expression that evaluates to an object in the **Applies To** list.

Remarks

This method copies the currently indexed message to the compose buffer and adds **RE:** to the beginning of the Subject line. It also sets the **MsgIndex** property to−1.

The message is sent to the currently indexed message originator and to all **To:** and **CC:** recipients.

See Also

MAPISession Control, **MAPIMessages** Control, **MsgIndex** Property, **MAPI** Control Constants, **Error Messages**, **MAPI** Controls

ResolveName Method

Resolves the name of the currently indexed recipient.

Applies To

MAPIMessages Control

Syntax

object.**ResolveName**

The *object* placeholder represents an object expression that evaluates to an object in the **Applies To** list.

Remarks

This method searches the address book for a match on the currently indexed recipient name. If no match is found, an error is returned. It does not provide additional resolution of the message originator's name or address.

The **AddressResolveUI** property determines whether to display a dialog box to resolve ambiguous names.

This method may cause the **RecipType** property to change.

See Also

MAPISession Control, **MAPIMessages** Control, **AddressResolveUI** Property, **RecipType** Property, **MAPI** Control Constants, **Error Messages**, **MAPI** Controls

Save Method

Saves the message currently in the compose buffer (with **MsgIndex** $=-1$).

Applies To

MAPIMessages Control

Syntax

object.**Save**

The *object* placeholder represents an object expression that evaluates to an object in the **Applies To** list.

See Also

MAPISession Control, **MAPIMessages** Control, **MsgIndex** Property, **MAPI** Control Constants, **Error Messages**, **MAPI** Controls

Send Method

Sends a message.

Applies To

MAPIMessages Control

Syntax

object.**Send** [*value*]

The **Send** method syntax has these parts:

Part	Description
object	An object expression that evaluates to an object in the **Applies To** list.
value	A Boolean expression specifying whether to show a dialog box, as described in settings.

Settings

The settings for *value* are:

Setting	Description
True	Sends a message inside a dialog box. Prompts the user for the various components of the message and submits the message to the mail server for delivery.
	All message properties associated with the message being built in the compose buffer form the basis for the message dialog box. However, changes made in the dialog box do not alter information in the compose buffer.
False	(Default) Submits the outgoing message to the mail server without displaying a dialog box. An error occurs if you attempt to send a message with no recipients or with missing attachment path names.

See Also

MAPISession Control, **MAPIMessages** Control, **MAPI** Control Constants, **Error Messages**, **MAPI** Controls

SessionID Property (MAPIMessages Control)

Stores the current messaging session handle. This property is not available at design time.

Applies To

MAPIMessages Control

Syntax

object.**SessionID** [= *value*]

The **SessionID** property syntax these parts:

Part	Description
object	An object expression that evaluates to an object in the **Applies To** list.
value	A long expression specifying the current session handle.

Remarks

This property contains the messaging session handle returned by the **SessionID** property of the **MAPISession** control. To associate the **MAPIMessages** control with a valid messaging session, set this property to the **SessionID** of a **MAPISession** control that was successfully signed on.

See Also

MAPISession Control, **MAPIMessages** Control, **MAPI** Control Constants, **Error Messages**, **MAPI** Controls

---

SessionID Property (MAPISession Control)

Returns the current messaging session handle. This property is not available at design time, and is read only at run time.

Applies To

MAPISession Control

Syntax

object.**SessionID**

The **SessionID** property syntax has these parts:

Part	Description
object	An object expression that evaluates to an object in the **Applies To** list.

Remarks

This property is set when you specify the **SignOn** method. The **SessionID** property contains the unique messaging session handle. The default is 0.

Use this property to set the **SessionID** property of the **MAPIMessages** control.

Data Type

Long

See Also

MAPISession Control, **SignOn** Method, **MAPIMessages** Control, **MAPI** Control Constants, **Error Messages**, **MAPI** Controls

Show Method (MAPIMessages Control)

Displays the mail Address Book dialog box or the details of the currently indexed recipient.

Applies To

MAPIMessages Control

Syntax

object.**Show** [*value*]

The **Show** method syntax has these parts:

Part	Description
object	An object expression that evaluates to an object in the **Applies To** list.
value	A Boolean expression specifying the type of dialog box to show, as described in Settings.

Settings

The settings for *value* are:

Setting	Description
True	Displays a dialog box that shows the details of the currently indexed recipient. The amount of information presented in the dialog box is determined by the message system. At a minimum, it contains the display name and address of the recipient.
False	(Default) Displays the mail **Address Book** dialog box. You can use the address book to create or modify a recipient set. Any changes to the address book outside of the compose buffer are not saved.

See Also

MAPISession Control, **MAPIMessages** Control, **MAPI** Control Constants, **Error Messages**, **MAPI** Controls

---

SignOff Method

Ends the messaging session and signs the user off from the account specified by the **UserName** and **Password** properties.

Applies To

MAPISession Control

Syntax

object.**SignOff**

The *object* placeholder represents an object expression that evaluates to an object in the **Applies To** list.

See Also

> **MAPISession** Control, **Password** Property (MAPISession Control), **UserName** Property, **MAPIMessages** Control, **MAPI** Control Constants, **Error Messages**, **MAPI** Controls

---

SignOn Method

> Logs the user into the account specified by the **UserName** and **Password** properties, and provides a session handle to the underlying message subsystem.

Applies To

> **MAPISession** Control

Syntax

> *object*.**SignOn**
>
> The *object* placeholder represents an object expression that evaluates to an object in the **Applies To** list.

Remarks

> The session handle is stored in the **SessionID** property. Depending on the value of the **NewSession** property, the session handle may refer to a newly created session or an existing session.

See Also

> **MAPISession** Control, **NewSession** Property, **Password** Property (MAPISession Control), **SessionID** Property (MAPISession Control), **UserName** Property, **MAPIMessages** Control, **MAPI** Control Constants, **Error Messages**, **MAPI** Controls

---

UserName Property

> Specifies the account user name.

Applies To

> **MAPISession** Control

Syntax

> *object*.**UserName** [= *value*]
>
> The **UserName** property syntax has these parts:

Part	Description
object	An object expression that evaluates to an object in the **Applies To** list.
value	A string expression specifying the user account.

Remarks

This property contains the name of the user account desired for sign-on or sign-off. If the **LogonUI** property is **True**, an empty string in the **UserName** property indicates that a sign-on dialog box with an empty name field should be generated. The default is an empty string.

Data Type

String

See Also

MAPISession Control, **LogonUI** Property, **MAPIMessages** Control, **MAPI** Control Constants, **Error Messages**, **MAPI** Controls

Masked Edit Control

The **Masked Edit** control provides restricted data input as well as formatted data output. This control supplies visual cues about the type of data being entered or displayed. This is what the control looks like as an icon in the Toolbox:

File Name

MSMASK32.OCX

Class Name

MaskEdBox

Remarks

The **Masked Edit** control generally behaves as a standard text box control with enhancements for optional masked input and formatted output. If you don't use an input mask, the **Masked Edit** control behaves much like a standard text box, except for its dynamic data exchange (DDE) capability.

If you define an input mask using the **Mask** property, each character position in the **Masked Edit** control maps to either a placeholder of a specified type or a literal character. Literal characters, or *literals*, can give visual cues about the type of data being used. For example, the parentheses surrounding the area code of a telephone number are literals: (206).

If you attempt to enter a character that conflicts with the input mask, the control generates a **ValidationError** event. The input mask prevents you from entering invalid characters into the control.

The **Masked Edit** control has three bound properties: **DataChanged**, **DataField**, and **DataSource**. This means that it can be linked to a data control and display field values for the current record in the recordset. The **Masked Edit** control can also write out values to the recordset.

When the value of the field referenced by the **DataField** property is read, it is converted to a **Text** property string, if possible. If the recordset is updatable, the string is converted to the data type of the field.

To clear the **Text** property when you have a mask defined, you first need to set the **Mask** property to an empty string, and then the **Text** property to an empty string:

```
MaskedEdit1.Mask = ""
MaskedEdit1.Text = ""
```

When you define an input mask, the **Masked Edit** control behaves differently from the standard text box. The insertion point automatically skips over literals as you enter data or move the insertion point.

When you insert or delete a character, all nonliteral characters to the right of the insertion point are shifted, as necessary. If shifting these characters leads to a validation error, the insertion or deletion is prevented, and a **ValidationError** event is triggered.

Suppose the **Mask** property is defined as "?###", and the current value of the **Text** property is "A12." If you attempt to insert the letter "B" to the left of the letter "A," the "A" would shift to the right. Since the second value of the input mask requires a number, the letter "A" would cause the control to generate a **ValidationError** event.

The **Masked Edit** control also validates the values of the **Text** property at run time. If you set the **Text** property so that it conflicts with the input mask, the control generates a run-time error.

You may select text in the same way as for a standard text box control. When selected text is deleted, the control attempts to shift the remaining characters to the right of the selection. However, any remaining character that might cause a validation error during this shift is deleted, and no **ValidationError** event is generated.

Normally, when a selection in the **Masked Edit** control is copied onto the Clipboard, the entire selection, including literals, is transferred onto the Clipboard. You can use the **ClipMode** property to transfer only user-entered data onto the Clipboard—literal characters that are part of the input mask are not copied.

See Also

Masked Edit Control, **ClipMode** Property, **Appearance** Property, **BorderStyle** Property, **DragOver** Event, **Visual Basic** Constants

Properties

AllowPrompt Property, **Appearance** Property, **AutoTab** Property, **BackColor, ForeColor** Properties, **BorderStyle** Property, **ClipMode** Property, **ClipText** Property, **Container** Property, **DataBinding** Object, **DataChanged** Property, **DataField** Property, **DragIcon** Property, **DragMode** Property, **Enabled** Property, **Font** Property, **Format** Property, **FormattedText** Property, **Height, Width** Properties, **HelpContextID** Property, **HideSelection** Property, **hWnd** Property, **Index** Property, **Left, Top** Properties, **Mask** Property, **MaxLength** Property, **MouseIcon** Property, **MousePointer** Property, **Name** Property, **Object** Property, **OLEDragMode** Property, **OLEDropMode** Property, **Parent** Property, **PromptChar** Property, **PromptInclude** Property, **SelLength, SelStart, SelText** Properties, **SelText** Property (Masked Edit Control), **TabIndex** Property, **TabStop** Property, **Tag** Property, **Text** Property (MaskedEdit Control), **ToolTipText** Property, **Visible** Property, **WhatsThisHelpId** Property

Methods

DataBindings Property, **Drag** Method, **Move** Method, **OLEDrag** Method, **Refresh** Method, **SetFocus** Method, **ShowWhatsThis** Method, **Zorder** Method

Events

> **Change** Event, **DragDrop** Event, **DragOver** Event, **GotFocus** Event, **KeyDown, KeyUp** Events, **KeyPress** Event, **LostFocus** Event, **OLECompleteDrag** Event, **OLEDragDrop** Event, **OLEDragOver** Event, **OLEGiveFeedback** Event, **OLESetData** Event, **OLEStartDrag** Event, **ValidationError** Event

AllowPrompt Property

> Determines whether or not the prompt character is a valid input character.

Applies To

> **Masked Edit** Control

Syntax

> [*form.*]**MaskedEdit.AllowPrompt** [= {**True** | **False**}]

Remarks

> The **AllowPrompt** property settings are as follows:

Setting	Description
False	(Default) The prompt character is not a valid input character. A **ValidationError** event is triggered if you enter the prompt character.
True	The prompt character is a valid input character.

> For example, suppose you have defined a prompt character of 0, and you want the **Masked Edit** control to accept five digits between 0 and 9. You specify a mask of #####. If the **AllowPrompt** property is **False** and you enter 0, a **ValidationError** event occurs. If **AllowPrompt** is set to **True**, you can enter 0 as a valid input character.

Data Type

> **Integer** (Boolean)

See Also

> **Masked Edit** Control, **PromptChar** Property, **ValidationError** Event, **Masked Edit** Control Constants

AutoTab Property

> Determines whether or not the next control in the tab order receives the focus as soon as the **Text** property of the **Masked Edit** control is filled with valid data. The **Mask** property determines whether the values in the **Text** property are valid.

Applies To

> **Masked Edit** Control

Syntax

> [*form.*]**MaskedEdit.AutoTab**[= {**True** | **False**}]

Remarks

Automatic tabbing occurs only if all the characters defined by the **Mask** property are entered into the control, the characters are valid, and the **AutoTab** property is set to **True.**

Setting	Description
False	(Default) **AutoTab** is not on. A **ValidationError** event occurs when you enter more characters than are defined by the input mask.
True	**AutoTab** is on. When you enter all the characters defined by the input mask, focus goes to the next control in the tab sequence, and all subsequent characters entered are handled by the next control.

The **Masked Edit** control is considered filled when you enter the last valid character in the control, regardless of where the character is in the input mask. This property has no effect if the **Mask** property is set to the empty string (" ").

Data Type

Integer (Boolean)

See Also

Masked Edit Control, **Text** Property (**Masked Edit** Control), **ValidationError** Event

ClipMode Property

Determines whether to include or exclude the literal characters in the input mask when doing a cut or copy command.

Applies To

Masked Edit Control

Syntax

[*form.*]**MaskedEdit.ClipMode** [= *setting%*]

Remarks

The following table lists the **ClipMode** property settings for the **Masked Edit** control.

Setting	Description
mskIncludeLiterals (0)	(Default) Include literals on a cut or copy command.
mskExcludeLiterals (1)	Exclude literals on a cut or copy command.

This property has no effect if the **Mask** property is set to the empty string (" ").

Data Type

Integer (Enumerated)

See Also

Masked Edit Control, **Masked Edit Control** Constants, **Cut, Copy, and Paste** Commands (Class Builder Edit Menu)

ClipText Property

Returns the text in the **Masked Edit** control, excluding literal characters of the input mask. This property is not available at design time and is read-only at run time.

Applies To

Masked Edit Control

Syntax

[*form.*]**MaskedEdit.ClipText**

Remarks

This property acts the same as the **SelText** property when the **Mask** property is set to the empty string (" ").

Data Type

String

See Also

Masked Edit Control, **SelText** Property (**Masked Edit** Control)

Format Property

Specifies the format for displaying and printing numbers, dates, times, and text.

Applies To

Masked Edit Control

Syntax

[*form.*]**MaskedEdit.Format** [= *posformat$; negformat$; zeroformat$; nullformat$*]

Parameter	Description
posformat$	Expression used to display positive values.
negformat$	Expression used to display negative values.
zeroformat$	Expression used to display zero values.
nullformat$	Expression used to display null or empty values.

Remarks

The **Format** property defines the format expressions used to display the contents of the control. You can use the same format expressions as defined by the Visual Basic **Format** function, with the exception that named formats ("On/Off") can't be used.

This property can have from one to four parameters separated by semicolons. If one of the parameters is not specified, the format specified by the first parameter is used. If multiple parameters appear, the appropriate number of separators must be used. For example, to specify *posformat$* and *nullformat$*, use the syntax

[*form.*]*MaskedEdit.***Format** = *posformat$;;; nullformat$*

The following table shows examples of standard formats that you may wish to use.

Data type	Value	Description
Number	(Default) Empty string	General Numeric format. Displays as entered.
Number	$#,##0.00;($#,##0.00)	Currency format. Uses thousands separator; displays negative numbers enclosed in parentheses.
Number	0	Fixed number format. Displays at least one digit.
Number	#,##0	Commas format. Uses commas as thousands separator.
Number	0%	Percent format. Multiplies value by 100 and appends a percent sign.
Number	0.00E+00	Scientific format. Uses standard scientific notation.
Date/Time	(Default) c	General Date and Time format. Displays date, time, or both.
Date/Time	dddddd	Long Date format. Same as the Long Date setting in the International section of the Microsoft Windows Control Panel. Example: Tuesday, May 26, 1992.
Date/Time	dd-mmm-yy	Medium Date format. Example: 26-May-92.
Date/Time	ddddd	Short Date format. Same as the Short Date setting in the International section of the Microsoft Windows Control Panel. Example: 5/26/92.
Date/Time	ttttt	Long Time format. Same as the Time setting in the International section of the Microsoft Windows Control Panel. Example: 05:36:17 A.M.
Date/Time	hh:mm AM/PM	Medium Time format. Example: 05:36 A.M.
Date/Time	hh:mm	Short Time format. Example: 05:36.

Data Type

String

FormattedText Property

The **FormattedText** property returns the string displayed in the **Masked Edit** control when the control doesn't have the focus. This property is not available at design time, and is read-only at run time.

Applies To

Masked Edit Control

Syntax

[*form.*]**MaskedEdit. FormattedText**

Remarks

If the **Format** property is equal to the empty string (""), this property is identical to the **Text** property, except that it is read-only. If the **HideSelection** property is set to **False**, the control doesn't display the formatted text when it doesn't have the focus. However, the formatted text is still available through this property.

Data Type

> **String**

See Also

> **Masked Edit** Control, **Text** Property (**Masked Edit** Control), **HideSelection** Property

---

Mask Property

Determines the input mask for the control.

Applies To

> **Masked Edit** Control

Syntax

> [*form.*]**MaskedEdit.Mask** [= *string$*]

Remarks

You can define input masks at both design time and run time. However, the following are examples of standard input masks that you may want to use at design time. The control can distinguish between numeric and alphabetic characters for validation, but cannot check for valid content, such as the correct month or time of day.

Mask	Description
Null String	(Default) No mask. Acts like a standard text box.
##-???-##	Medium date (US). Example: 20-May-92
##-##-##	Short date (US). Example: 05-20-92
##:## ??	Medium time. Example: 05:36 AM
##:##	Short time. Example: 17:23

The input mask can consist of the following characters.

Mask character	Description
#	Digit placeholder.
.	Decimal placeholder. The actual character used is the one specified as the decimal placeholder in your international settings. This character is treated as a literal for masking purposes.
,	Thousands separator. The actual character used is the one specified as the thousands separator in your international settings. This character is treated as a literal for masking purposes.
:	Time separator. The actual character used is the one specified as the time separator in your international settings. This character is treated as a literal for masking purposes.
/	Date separator. The actual character used is the one specified as the date separator in your international settings. This character is treated as a literal for masking purposes.

(continued)

(continued)

Mask character	Description
\	Treat the next character in the mask string as a literal. This allows you to include the '#', '&', 'A', and '?' characters in the mask. This character is treated as a literal for masking purposes.
&	Character placeholder. Valid values for this placeholder are ANSI characters in the following ranges: 32-126 and 128-255.
>	Convert all the characters that follow to uppercase.
<	Convert all the characters that follow to lowercase.
A	Alphanumeric character placeholder (entry required). For example: a–z, A–Z, or 0–9.
a	Alphanumeric character placeholder (entry optional).
9	Digit placeholder (entry optional). For example: 0–9.
C	Character or space placeholder (entry optional). This operates exactly like the & placeholder, and ensures compatibility with Microsoft Access.
?	Letter placeholder. For example: a–z or A–Z.
Literal	All other symbols are displayed as literals; that is, as themselves.

When the value of the **Mask** property is an empty string (" "), the control behaves like a standard text box control. When an input mask is defined, underscores appear beneath every placeholder in the mask. You can only replace a placeholder with a character that is of the same type as the one specified in the input mask. If you enter an invalid character, the masked edit control rejects the character and generates a **ValidationError** event.

Note When you define an input mask for the **Masked Edit** control and you tab to another control, the **ValidationError** event is generated if there are any invalid characters in the **Masked Edit** control.

Data Type
String

See Also
Masked Edit Control, **Text** Property (**Masked Edit** Control), **ValidationError** Event

Masked Edit Control Constants

Appearance Constants

Constant	Value	Description
mskFlat	0	Flat. Paints controls and forms without visual effects.
mskThreeD	1	(Default) 3D. Paints controls with three-dimensional effects.

BorderStyle Constants

Constant	Value	Description
vbBSNone	0	No border
vbFixedSingle	1	Fixed single

ClipBoard Constants

Constant	Value	Description
mskCFRTF	&HFFFFBF01	Rich Text Format (.rtf file)
mskCFText	1	Text (.txt file)
mskCFBitmap	2	Bitmap (.bmp file)
mskCFMetafile	3	Metafile (.wmf file)
mskCFDIB	8	Device-independent bitmap
mskCFPalette	9	Color palette
mskCFEMetafile	14	Extended Metafile (.emf file)
mskCFFiles	15	Filename list

ClipMode Constants

Constant	Value	Description
mskIncludeLiterals	0	Include literals on cut or copy.
mskExcludeLiterals	1	Exclude literals on cut or copy.

DragOver Constants

Constant	Value	Description
mskEnter	0	Source control dragged into target.
mskLeave	1	Source control dragged out of target.
mskOver	2	Source control dragged from one position in target to another.

Error Constants

Constant	Value	Description
mskDataObjectLocked	672	DataObject formats list may not be cleared or expanded outside of the OLEStartDrag event.
mskExpectedAnArgument	673	Expected at least one argument.
mskFormatNotByteArray	675	Non-intrinsic OLE drag and drop formats used with SetData require Byte array data. GetData may return more bytes than were given to SetData.
mskGetNotSupported	394	Property is write-only.
mskInvalidObjectUse	425	Invalid object use.

(continued)

(continued)

Constant	Value	Description
mskInvalidProcedureCall	5	Invalid procedure call.
mskInvalidPropertyValue	380	Invalid property value.
mskRecursiveOleDrag	674	Illegal recursive invocation of OLE drag and drop.
mskSetNotSupported	383	Property is read-only.
mskWrongClipboardFormat	461	Specified format doesn't match format of data.

MousePointer Constants

Constant	Value	Description
mskDefault	0	Default
mskArrow	1	Arrow
mskCross	2	Crosshair
mskIbeam	3	I beam
mskIcon	4	Icon
mskSize	5	Size
mskSizeNESW	6	Size NE, SW mouse pointer
mskSizeNS	7	Size N, S mouse pointer
mskSizeNWSE	8	Size NW, SE mouse pointer
mskSizeEW	9	Size W, E mouse pointer
mskUpArrow	10	Up arrow
mskHourglass	11	Hourglass
mskNoDrop	12	No drop
mskArrowHourglass	13	Arrow and hourglass
mskArrowQuestion	14	Arrow and question mark
mskSizeAll	15	Size all
mskCustom	99	Custom icon specified by the **MouseIcon** property

OLEDrag Constants

Constant	Value	Description
mskOLEDragManual	0	OLE drag/drop is initialized only under programmatic control.
mskOLEDragAutomatic	1	OLE drag/drop is initialized when the user drags 'out' of the control, or under programmatic control.

OLEDrop Constants

Constant	Value	Description
mskOLEDropNone	0	Accepts no OLE drag/drop operations.
mskOLEDropManual	1	Accepts an OLE drag/drop under programmatic control only.
mskOLEDropAutomatic	2	Accepts an OLE drag/drop without programmatic control.

OLEDropEffect Constants

Constant	Value	Description
mskOLEDropEffectNone	0	No OLE drag/drop operation has taken place/would take place.
mskOLEDropEffectCopy	1	A mask to indicate that a copy has taken place/would take place.
mskOLEDropEffectMove	2	A mask to indicate that a move has take place/would take place.
mskOLEDropEffectScroll	&H80000000	A mask to indicate that the drop target window has scrolled/would scroll.

See Also

Masked Edit Control, **ClipMode** Property, **Appearance** Property, **BorderStyle** Property, **DragOver** Event, **Visual Basic** Constants

---

MaxLength Property

Sets or returns the maximum length of the **Masked Edit** control.

Applies To

Masked Edit Control

Syntax

[*form.*]**MaskedEdit.MaxLength** [= *setting%*]

Remarks

The **Masked Edit** control can have a maximum of 64 characters (the valid range for this property is 1 to 64). The default value is set to 64 characters, including literal characters in the input mask.

If the user enters characters beyond the specified maximum length, the control generates a beep.

Data Type

Integer

See Also

Masked Edit Control

PromptChar Property

Sets or returns the character used to prompt a user for input.

Applies To

Masked Edit Control

Syntax

[*form.*]**MaskedEdit.PromptChar** [= *char$*]

Remarks

The underscore character "_" is the default character value for the property. The **PromptChar** property can only be set to exactly one character.

Use the **PromptInclude** property to specify whether prompt characters are contained in the **Text** property.

Use the **AllowPrompt** property to test whether a prompt character is entered by a user.

Data Type

String

See Also

Masked Edit Control, **AllowPrompt** Property, **PromptInclude** Property

---

PromptInclude Property

Specifies whether prompt characters are contained in the **Text** property value. Use the **PromptChar** property to change the value of the prompt character.

Applies To

Masked Edit Control

Syntax

[*form.*]**MaskedEdit.PromptInclude** [= { **True** | **False** }]

Remarks

The following table lists the **PromptInclude** property settings for the **Masked Edit** control.

Setting	Description
False	The value of the **Text** property does not contain any prompt character.
True	(Default) The value of the **Text** property contains prompt characters, if any.

If the **Masked Edit** control is bound to a data control, the **PromptInclude** property affects how the data control reads the bound **Text** property. If **PromptInclude** is **False**, the data control ignores any literals or prompt characters in the **Text** property.

In this mode, the value that the data control retrieves from the **Masked Edit** control is equivalent to the value of the **ClipText** property.

If **PromptInclude** is **True**, the data control uses the value of the **Text** property as the data value to store.

Data Type

Integer (Boolean)

See Also

Masked Edit Control, **Text** Property (**Masked Edit** Control), **DataBinding** Object, **DataField** Property

SelText Property (Masked Edit Control)

Sets or returns the text contained in the control.

Applies To

Masked Edit Control

Syntax

[*form.*]**MaskedEdit.SelText**[= *string$*]

Remarks

If an input mask is not defined for the **Masked Edit** control, the **SelText** property behaves like the standard **SelText** property for the **Text Box** control.

If an input mask is defined and there is selected text in the **Masked Edit** control, the **SelText** property returns a text string. Depending on the value of the **ClipMode** property, not all the characters in the selected text are returned. If **ClipMode** is on, literal characters don't appear in the returned string.

When the **SelText** property is set, the **Masked Edit** control behaves as if text was pasted from the Clipboard. This means that each character in *string$* is entered into the control as if the user typed it in.

Data Type

String

See Also

Masked Edit Control, **ClipMode** Property, **SelLength**, **SelStart**, **SelText** Properties

Text Property (MaskedEdit Control)

Sets or returns the text contained in the control. This property is not available at design time.

Applies To

Masked Edit Control

Syntax

[*form.*]**MaskedEdit.Text**[= *string$*]

Remarks

This property sets and retrieves the text in the **Masked Edit** control, including literal characters and underscores that are part of the input mask. When setting the **Text** property, the *string$* value must match the characters in the input mask exactly, including literal characters and underscores.

Note   The **ClipMode** property setting has no effect on the value of the **Text** property.

The **SelText** property provides an easier way of setting the text in the **Masked Edit** control.

Data Type

Variant

See Also

Masked Edit Control, **ClipMode** Property, **FormattedText** Property, **SelText** Property (**Masked Edit** Control)

ValidationError Event

Occurs when the **Masked Edit** control receives invalid input, as determined by the input mask.

Applies To

Masked Edit Control

Syntax

Private Sub *ctlname_***ValidationError**(*InvalidText* **As String**; *StartPosition* **As Integer**)

Remarks

InvalidText is the value of the **Text** property, including the invalid character. This means that any placeholders and literal characters used in the input mask are included in *InvalidText*.

StartPosition is the position in *InvalidText* where the error occurred (the first invalid character).

See Also

MaskedEdit Control, **AllowPrompt** Property, **AutoTab** Property, **Mask** Property, **Text** Property (**MaskedEdit** Control)

Microsoft Tabbed Dialog Control

The **SSTab** control provides a group of tabs, each of which acts as a container for other controls. Only one tab is active in the control at a time, displaying the controls it contains to the user while hiding the controls in the other tabs.

Syntax

SSTab

Remarks

An **SSTab** control is like the dividers in a notebook or the labels on a group of file folders. Using an **SSTab** control, you can define multiple pages for the same area of a window or dialog box in your application. Using the properties of this control, you can:

- Determine the number of tabs.
- Organize the tabs into more than one row.
- Set the text for each tab.
- Display a graphic on each tab.
- Determine the style of tabs used.
- Set the size of each tab.

To use this control, you must first decide how you want to organize the controls you will place into various tabs. Set the **Tabs** and **TabsPerRow** properties to create the tabs and organize them into rows. Then select each tab at design time by clicking the tab. For each tab, draw the controls you want displayed when the user selects that tab. Set the **Caption**, **Picture**, **TabHeight**, and **TabMaxWidth** properties as needed to customize the top part of the tab.

At run time, users can navigate between tabs by either pressing CTRL+TAB or by using accelerator keys defined in the caption of each tab.

You can also customize the entire **SSTab** control using the **Style**, **ShowFocusRect**, **TabOrientation**, and **WordWrap** properties.

Distribution Note   The **SSTab** control is found in the TABCTL32.OCX file. To use the **SSTab** control in your application, you must add the control's .OCX file to the project. When distributing your application, install the appropriate .OCX file in the user's Microsoft Windows System or System32 directory. For more information on how to add an additional control to a project, see the Visual Basic *Programmer's Guide*.

Properties

BackColor, ForeColor Properties**, Caption** Property, **Container** Property, **DataBindings** Property, **DragIcon** Property, **DragMode** Property, **Enabled** Property, **Font** Property, **Height, Width** Properties **HelpContextID** Property, **hWnd** Property, **Index** Property, **Left, Top** Properties**, MouseIcon** Property, **MousePointer** Property,

Name Property, **Object** Property, **OLEDropMode** Property, **Parent** Property, **Picture** Property, **Rows** Property, **ShowFocusRect** Property, **Style** Property, **Tab** Property, **TabCaption** Property, **TabEnabled** Property, **TabHeight** Property, **TabMaxWidth** Property, **Tab Orientation** Property, **TabPicture** Property, **Tabs** Property, **TabsPerRow** Property, **TabStop** Property, **TabVisible** Property, **Tag** Property, **ToolTipText** Property, **Visible** Property, **WordWrap** Property

Events

Click Event, **DblClick** Event, **DragDrop** Event, **DragOver** Event, **GotFocus** Event, **KeyDown, KeyUp** Events, **KeyPress** Event, **LostFocus** Event, **MouseDown, MouseUp** Events, **MouseMove** Event, **OLECompleteDrag** Event, **OLEDragDrop** Event, **OLEDragOver** Event, **OLEGiveFeedback** Event, **OLESetData** Event, **OLEStartDrag** Event

Methods

Drag Method, **Move** Method, **OLEDrag** Method, **SetFocus** Method, **ShowWhatsThis** Method, **ZOrder** Method

See Also

SSTab Control Constants, **Style** Property (SSTab Control), **TabOrientation** Property (SSTab Control), **Caption** Property, **Picture** Property (SSTab Control), **ShowFocusRect** Property (MSTab Control), **TabHeight** Property (SSTab Control), **TabMaxWidth** Property (SSTab Control), **Tabs** Property (SSTab Control), **TabsPerRow** Property (SSTab Control), **WordWrap** Property (SSTab Control)

Click Event (SSTab Control)

The **Click** event occurs when the user selects one of the tabs on an **SSTab** control.

Applies To

SSTab Control

Syntax

Private **Sub** *object_***Click** ([*index* **As Integer**], *previoustab* **As Integer**)

The **Click** event syntax has these parts:

Part	Description
object	An object expression that evaluates to an **SSTab** control.
Index	An integer that uniquely identifies a control if it is in a control array.
previoustab	A numeric expression that identifies the tab that was previously active.

Remarks

Use the **Click** event to determine when a user clicks a tab to make it the active tab. When a tab receives a **Click** event, that tab becomes the active tab and the controls placed on it at design time appear.

With the *previoustab* argument, you can check for changes made when the user clicks another tab.

Use the **Tab** property to determine the current tab.

See Also

Tab Property (SSTab Control), **DblClick** Event

Example

This example saves preferences information from two tabs of an **SSTab** control as soon as the user selects a different tab.

```
Private Sub sstbPrefs_Click(PreviousTab As Integer)
    Dim ThisSetting As String
    Select Case PreviousTab
        Case 0
            If optLoanLen(0) = True Then
                ThisSetting = "Months"
            Else
                ThisSetting = "Years"
            End If
            SaveSetting("LoanSheet", "LoanLength", _
                    "Period", ThisSetting)
        Case 1
            Dim X As Integer
            For X = 0 To 3
                If optPctsShown(X) = True Then
                    SaveSetting("LoanSheet", "InterestRate", _
                    "Precision", optPctsShown(X).Tag)
                    Exit For
                End If
            Next X
    End Select
End Sub
```

Picture Property (SSTab Control)

Returns or sets a graphic to be displayed in the current tab of an **SSTab** control.

Applies To

SSTab Control

Syntax

object.**Picture** [= *picture*]

The **Picture** property syntax has these parts:

Part	Description
object	An object expression that evaluates to an **SSTab** control.
Picture	A string expression that designates a bitmap or icon to display on the current tab, as described in **Settings**.

Settings

The settings for *picture* are:

Setting	Description
(None)	An object expression that evaluates to an **SSTab** control.
(Bitmap, icon, metafile)	A string expression that designates a bitmap or icon to display on the current tab.

Remarks

At design time, you set the **Picture** property for a tab by clicking that tab and then setting the property in the Properties window. At run time, you can set the **Picture** property using the **LoadPicture** function or the **Picture** property of another control or of a **Form** object. You can make any tab the current tab by setting the **Tab** property.

When setting the **Picture** property at design time, the graphic is saved and loaded with the **Form** object containing the **SSTab** control. If you create an executable file, the file contains the image. When you load a graphic at run time, the graphic isn't saved with the application.

Setting the **Picture** property affects the value of the **TabPicture** property for the current tab as well as displays the picture in the active tab.

See Also

Tab Property (SSTab Control), **TabPicture** Property (SSTab Control), **Form** Object, **Forms** Collection, **LoadPicture** Function

Example

This example loads a bitmap from a file and places that bitmap on the active tab. To try this example, put the **SSTab** and **CommandButton** controls on the **Form**. Then run the example.

```
Private Sub Command1_Click()
    SSTab1.Picture = LoadPicture("c:\windows\cars.bmp")
End Sub
```

Rows Property (SSTab Control)

Returns the total number of rows of tabs in an **SSTab** control.

Applies To

SSTab Control

Syntax

object.**Rows**

The *object* placeholder represents an object expression that evaluates to an **SSTab** control.

Remarks

You specify the number of rows in the **SSTab** control at design time by setting the **Tabs** and **TabsPerRow** properties.

Tabs Property (SSTab Control), **TabsPerRow** Property (SSTab Control)

ShowFocusRect Property

Returns or sets a value that determines if the focus rectangle is visible on a tab on an **SSTab** control when the tab gets the focus.

Applies To

SSTab Control

Syntax

object.**ShowFocusRect** [= *boolean*]

The **ShowFocusRect** property syntax has these parts:

Part	Description
object	An object expression that evaluates to an **SSTab** control.
boolean	A Boolean expression that specifies how the focus rectangle behaves, as described in **Settings**.

Settings

The settings for *boolean* are:

Setting	Description
True	(Default) The control shows the focus rectangle on the tab that has the focus.
False	The control does not show the focus rectangle on the tab that has the focus.

See Also

GotFocus Event, **LostFocus** Event

SSTab Control Constants

Clipboard constants

Constant	Value	Description
ssCFText	1	Text (.TXT) file
ssCFBitmap	2	Bitmap (.BMP) file
ssCFMetafile	3	Metafile (.WMF) file
ssCFDIB	8	Device-independent bitmap
ssCFPallette	9	Color palette
ssCFEMetafile	14	Enhanced metafile (.EMF) file
ssCFFiles	15	Filename list (Microsoft Windows Explorer)
ssCFRTF	-16639	Rich Text format (.RTF) file

DragOver constants

Constant	Value	Description
ssEnter	0	Source control dragged into target.
ssLeave	1	Source control dragged out of target.
ssOver	2	Source control dragged from one position in target to another.

Error constants

Constant	Value	Description
ssInvalidProcedureCall	5	Invalid procedure call.
ssOutOfMemory	7	Out of memory.
ssInvalidPropertyValue	380	Invalid property value.
ssBadIndex	381	Invalid property array index.
ssSetNotSupported	383	Property is read-only.
ssGetNotSupported	394	Property is write-only.
ssInvalidObjectUse	425	Invalid use of object.
ssWrongClipBoardFormat	461	Specified format doesn't match format of data.
ssInvalidPicture	481	Invalid picture.
ssDataObjectLocked	672	DataObject formats list may not be cleared or expanded outside of the OLEStartDrag event.
ssExpectedAnArgument	673	Expected at least one argument.
ssRecursiveOLEDrag	674	Illegal recursive invocation of OLE drag and drop.
ssFormatNotByteArray	675	Non-intrinsic OLE drag and drop formats used with SetData require Byte array data. GetData may return more bytes than were given to SetData.
ssDataNotSetForFormat	676	Requested data was not supplied to the DataObject during the OLESetData event.

MousePointer constants

Constant	Value	Description
ssDefault	0	Default.
ssArrow	1	Arrow mouse pointer.
ssCross	2	Cross mouse pointer.
ssIBeam	3	I-Beam mouse pointer.
ssIcon	4	Icon mouse pointer.
ssSize	5	Size mouse pointer.
ssSizeNESW	6	Size NE SW mouse pointer.
ssSizeNS	7	Size N S mouse pointer.
ssSizeNWSE	8	Size NW SE mouse pointer.
ssSizeEW	9	Up arrow mouse pointer.

(continued)

Constant	Value	Description
ssUpArrow	10	Up arrow mouse pointer.
ssHourglass	11	Hourglass mouse pointer.
ssNoDrop	12	No drop mouse pointer.
ssArrowHourglass	13	Arrow and hourglass mouse pointer.
ssArrowQuestion	14	Arrow and question mark mouse pointer.
ssSizeAll	15	Size all mouse pointer.
ssCustom	99	Custom mouse pointer icon specified by the **MouseIcon** property.

OLEDrop constants

Constant	Value	Description
ssOLEDropNone	0	Accepts no OLE drag/drop operations.
ssOLEDropManual	1	Accepts an OLE drag/drop under programmatic control only.

OLEDropEffect constants

Constant	Value	Description
ssOLEDropEffectNone	0	No OLE drag/drop operation has taken, or would take place.
ssOLEDropEffectCopy	1	A mask to indicate that a copy has taken, or would take place.
ssOLEDropEffectMove	2	A mask to indicate that a move has taken, or would take place.
ssOLEDropEffectScroll	&H80000000	A mask to indicate that the drop target window has scrolled, or would scroll.

Style constants

Constant	Value	Description
ssStyleTabbedDialog	0	The tabs look like those in the tabbed dialogs in Microsoft Office for Microsoft Windows 3.1 applications.
ssStylePropertyPage	1	The tabs look like the tabs in Microsoft Windows 95.

Tab Orientation constants

Constant	Value	Description
ssTabOrientationTop	0	The tabs appear at the top of the control.
ssTabOrientationBottom	1	The tabs appear at the bottom of the control.
ssTabOrientationLeft	2	The tabs appear on the left side of the control.
ssTabOrientationRight	3	The tabs appear on the right side of the control.

See Also

SSTab Control, **Style** Property (SSTab Control), **TabOrientation** Property (SSTab Control), **Visual Basic** Constants

Style Property (SSTab Control)

Returns or sets the style of the tabs on an **SSTab** control.

Applies To

SSTab Control

Syntax

object.**Style** [= *value*]

The **Style** property syntax has these parts:

Part	Description
object	An object expression that evaluates to an **SSTab** control.
value	A constant or integer that specifies the style of the tabs, as described in **Settings**.

Settings

The settings for *value* are:

Constant	Value	Description
ssStyleTabbedDialog	0	(Default) The tabs that appear in the tabbed dialogs look like those in Microsoft Office for Microsoft Windows 3.1 applications. If you select this style, the active tab's font is bold.
ssStylePropertyPage	1	The tabs that appear in the tabbed dialogs look like those in Microsoft Windows 95. When you select this setting, the **TabMaxWidth** property is ignored and the width of each tab adjusts to the length of the text in its caption. The font used to display text in the tab is not bold.

See Also

TabMaxWidth Property (SSTab Control), **SSTab** Control Constants

Tab Property (SSTab Control)

Returns or sets the current tab for an **SSTab** control.

Applies To

SSTab Control

Syntax

object.**Tab** [= *tabnumber*]

The **Tab** property syntax has these parts:

Part	Description
object	An object expression that evaluates to an **SSTab** control.
tabnumber	A numeric expression that indicates a specific tab. The first tab is always 0.

Remarks

The current tab moves to the front and becomes the active tab.

Typically, the user of your application clicks a tab to make it the current tab. However, you may need to select the current tab in code. For example, you may want the same tab to be the current tab each time you display a certain dialog box in your application. If you dismiss the dialog box by using the **Hide** method of the **Form**, the last tab to be the active tab when the **Form** was hidden will be the active tab the next time the dialog box appears. You can set the **Tab** property of the **SSTab** control so the same tab is active every time the dialog box appears.

See Also

Form Object, **Forms** Collection, **Hide** Method

Example

This example always makes the first tab in the **SSTab** control the active tab just before showing the form which contains the control. To try this example, create two **Form** objects. Place a **CommandButton** control on Form1 and an **SSTab** control on Form2. Paste the code into the **Click** event of the **CommandButton** on Form1, and then run the example.

```
Private Sub Command1_Click()
   Form2.SSTab1.Tab = 1
   Form2.Show
End Sub
```

TabCaption Property (SSTab Control)

Returns or sets the caption for each tab for an **SSTab** control.

Applies To

SSTab Control

Syntax

object.**TabCaption**(*tab*) [= *text*]

The **TabCaption** property syntax has these parts:

Part	Description
object	An object expression that evaluates to an **SSTab** control.
tab	A numeric expression that specifies the tab you want the caption to appear on.
text	A string expression that evaluates to the text displayed as the caption for the specified tab.

Remarks

At design time, you can set the **TabCaption** property by clicking a tab and then setting the **Caption** property in the Properties window. Or you can select (Custom) in the Properties window and set the **TabCaption** property in the General tab of the Properties dialog box.

At run time, you can read or change the caption of any tab using the **TabCaption** property. You can also use the **Caption** property to change the **TabCaption** property for just the active tab.

You can use the **TabCaption** property to assign an access key to a tab. In the **TabCaption** setting, include an ampersand (&) immediately preceding the character you want to designate as an access key. The character is underlined. Press the ALT key plus the underlined character to make that tab the active tab. To include an ampersand in a caption without creating an access key, include two ampersands (&&). A single ampersand is displayed in the caption and no characters are underlined.

See Also

Tab Property (SSTab Control), **TabMaxWidth** Property (SSTab Control), **Caption** Property

Example

This example adds or removes an extra word from the tabs of an **SSTab** control that lists the defensive players of a sport on one tab and the offensive players on another tab. By clicking the **CheckBox** control on the **Form**, the user can toggle between longer captions or shorter ones.

```
Private Sub Check1_Click()
   Dim X As Integer
   For X = 0 To SSTab1.Tabs - 1
      Select Case Check1.Value
         Case 0  ' Toggle to short captions.
            SSTab1.TabCaption(X) = Left(SSTab1.TabCaption(X), 7)
         Case 1  ' Toggle to long captions.
            SSTab1.TabCaption(X) = SSTab1.TabCaption(X) & " Players"
      End Select
   Next X
End Sub
```

TabEnabled Property (SSTab Control)

Returns or sets a value that determines whether a tab in an **SSTab** control is available when clicked.

Applies To

SSTab Control

Syntax

*object.***TabEnabled**(*tab*)[= *boolean*]

The **TabEnabled** property syntax has these parts:

Part	Description
object	An object expression that evaluates to an **SSTab** control.
tab	A numeric expression that specifies the tab.
boolean	A Boolean expression that specifies if the tab will respond to being clicked, as described in **Settings**.

Settings

The settings for *boolean* are:

Setting	Description
True	(Default) The tab responds when clicked.
False	The tab doesn't respond when clicked.

Remarks

When a tab is disabled, the text on the tab appears dimmed and the user cannot select that tab.

The **TabEnabled** property enables or disables a single tab. Use the **Enabled** property to enable or disable the entire **SSTab** control.

See Also

Tab Property (SSTab Control), **Enabled** Property

TabHeight Property (SSTab Control)

Returns or sets the height of all tabs on an **SSTab** control.

Applies To

SSTab Control

Syntax

object.**TabHeight** [= *height*]

The **TabHeight** property syntax has these parts:

Part	Description
object	An object expression that evaluates to an **SSTab** control.
height	A numeric expression that specifies the height of the tab, based on the scale mode of its container.

See Also

TabMaxWidth Property (SSTab Control)

TabMaxWidth Property (SSTab Control)

Returns or sets the maximum width of each tab on an **SSTab** control.

Applies To

SSTab Control

Syntax

object.**TabMaxWidth** [= *width*]

The **TabMaxWidth** property syntax has these parts:

Part	Description
object	An object expression that evaluates to an **SSTab** control.
width	A numeric expression that determines the maximum width of each tab in the scale mode of its container.

Remarks

When the **Style** property setting is **ssStyleTabbedDialog** and the **TabMaxWidth** property is set to zero (0), the **SSTab** control automatically sizes the tabs, based on the **TabsPerRow** property, to fit evenly across the control.

If you select the **ssStylePropertyPage** setting in the **Style** property, the **TabMaxWidth** property is ignored. The width of each tab adjusts automatically to the length of the text in the **TabCaption** property.

See Also

Style Property (SSTab Control), **TabCaption** Property (SSTab Control), **TabHeight** Property (SSTab Control), **TabsPerRow** Property (SSTab Control), **SSTab** Control Constants

---

TabOrientation Property (SSTab Control)

Returns or sets the location of the tabs on the **SSTab** control.

Applies To

SSTab Control

Syntax

object.**TabOrientation** [= *number*]

The **TabOrientation** property syntax has these parts:

Part	Description
object	An object expression that evaluates to an **SSTab** control.
number	A numeric expression that specifies the location of the tabs, as described in **Settings**.

Settings

The settings for *number* are:

Constant	Value	Description
ssTabOrientationTop	**0**	The tabs appear at the top of the control.
ssTabOrientationBottom	**1**	The tabs appear at the bottom of the control.
ssTabOrientationLeft	**2**	The tabs appear on the left side of the control.
ssTabOrientationRight	**3**	The tabs appear on the right side of the control.

Remarks

If you are using TrueType fonts, the text is rotated when the **TabOrientation** property is set to **ssTabOrientationLeft** or **ssTabOrientationRight**.

See Also

TabHeight Property (SSTab Control), **TabMaxWidth** Property (SSTab Control), **SSTab** Control Constants

TabPicture Property (SSTab Control)

Returns or sets the bitmap or icon to display on the specified tab of an **SSTab** control.

Applies To

SSTab Control

Syntax

object.**TabPicture**(*tab*) [= *picture*]

The **TabPicture** property syntax has these parts:

Part	Description
object	An object expression that evaluates to an **SSTab** control.
tab	A numeric expression that specifies the tab on which to display the picture.
picture	A string expression that specifies a graphic, as described in **Settings**.

Settings

The settings for *picture* are:

Setting	Description
(None)	(Default) No picture.
(Bitmap, icon, metafile)	Specifies a graphic. At run time, you can set this property using the **LoadPicture** function or the **Picture** property of another control or **Form** object.

Remarks

At design time, you can set the **TabPicture** property by clicking a tab then setting the **Picture** property in the Properties window. Or you can select (Custom) in the

Properties window and set the **Picture** property in the Pictures tab of the Properties dialog box.

At run time, you can refer to or change the graphic on any tab using the **TabPicture** property or use the **Picture** property to work with the active tab.

See Also

Form Object, **Forms** Collection, **LoadPicture** Function, **Picture** Property (ActiveX Controls), **Tab** Property (SSTab Control)

Tabs Property (SSTab Control)

Returns or sets the total number of tabs on an **SSTab** control.

Applies To

SSTab Control

Syntax

object.**Tabs** [= *tabnumber*]

The **Tabs** property syntax has these parts:

Part	Description
object	An object expression that evaluates to an **SSTab** control.
tabnumber	A numeric expression that specifies the number of tabs you want on the control. The tabs are automatically given the captions Tab x where x is 0, 1, 2, 3, and so on.

Remarks

You can change the **Tabs** property at run time to add new tabs or remove tabs.

At design time, use the **Tabs** property in conjunction with the **TabsPerRow** property to determine the number of rows of tabs displayed by the control. At run time, use the **Rows** property.

See Also

Rows Property (SSTab Control), **TabsPerRow** Property (SSTab Control)

TabsPerRow Property (SSTab Control)

Returns or sets the number of tabs for each row of an **SSTab** control.

Applies To

SSTab Control

Syntax

object.**TabsPerRow** [= *tabnumber*]

Part	Description
object	An object expression that evaluates to an **SSTab** control.
tabnumber	A numeric expression that specifies the number of tabs you want on each row.

Remarks

Use this property at design time in conjunction with the **Tabs** property to determine the number of rows displayed by the control. At run time, use the **Rows** property.

See Also

Rows Property (SSTab Control), **Tabs** Property (SSTab Control)

TabVisible Property (SSTab Control)

Returns or sets a value indicating if a tab in an **SSTab** control is visible or hidden. Not available at design time.

Applies To

SSTab Control

Syntax

object.**TabVisible**(*tab*) [= *boolean*]

The **TabVisible** property syntax has these parts:

Part	Description
object	An object expression that evaluates to an **SSTab** control.
tab	A numeric expression that specifies the tab you want to be visible or hidden.
boolean	A Boolean expression that specifies if the tab is visible or hidden, as described in **Settings**.

Settings

The settings for *boolean* are:

Setting	Description
True	(Default) Tab is visible.
False	Tab is hidden. Other tabs adjust their position so there are no gaps between tabs.

Remarks

The **TabVisible** property hides or displays a single tab. Use the **Visible** property to hide or display the entire **SSTab** control.

See Also

Rows Property (SSTab Control), **Tabs** Property (SSTab Control), **Visible** Property (ActiveX Controls)

WordWrap Property (SSTab Control)

Returns or sets a value indicating whether the text on each tab is wrapped to the next line if it is too long to fit horizontally on the tab on an **SSTab** control.

Applies To

SSTab Control

Syntax

object.**WordWrap** [= *boolean*]

The **WordWrap** property syntax has these parts:

Part	Description
object	An object expression that evaluates to an **SSTab** control.
boolean	A Boolean expression that specifies whether the text on each tab will wrap to the next line if it does not fit horizontally, as described in **Settings**.

Settings

The settings for *boolean* are:

Setting	Description
True	The text wraps if it is too long to fit within the width of each tab.
False	(Default) The text doesn't wrap and will be truncated if it is too long.

Remarks

Use the **WordWrap** property to determine how an **SSTab** control displays the text on each tab. For example, a tabbed dialog that changes dynamically might have text that also changes. To make sure that text will not be truncated if it is too long, set the **WordWrap** property to **True,** the **TabMaxWidth** property to 0, and the **TabHeight** property to a height that allows you to view the longest piece of text.

See Also

TabCaption Property (SSTab Control), **TabHeight** Property (SSTab Control), **TabMaxWidth** Property (SSTab Control), **Tabs** Property (SSTab Control), **Caption** Property

MSChart Control

A chart that graphically displays data.

Syntax

MSChart

Remarks

The **MSChart** control supports the following features:

- True three-dimensional representation.

- Support for all major chart types.

- Data grid population via random data and data arrays.

The **MSChart** control is associated with a data grid (**DataGrid** object). This data grid is a table that holds the data being charted. The data grid can also include labels used to identify series and categories on the chart. The person who designs your chart application fills the data grid with information by inserting data or by importing data from a spreadsheet or array.

Properties

ActiveSeriesCount Property, **AllowDithering** Property, **AllowDynamicRotation** Property, **AllowSelections** Property, **AllowSeriesSelection** Property, **AutoIncrement** Property, **Backdrop** Property, **BorderStyle** Property, **Chart3d** Property, **ChartData** Property, **ChartType** Property, **Column** Property, **ColumnCount** Property, **ColumnLabel** Property, **ColumnLabelCount** Property, **ColumnLabelIndex** Property, **Container** Property, **Data** Property, **DataBindings** Property, **DataGrid** Property, **DoSetCursor** Property, **Drag** Property, **DragIcon** Property, **DragMode** Property, **Enabled** Property, **Footnote** Property, **FootnoteText** Property, **Height, Width** Properties, **HelpContextID** Property, **hWnd** Property, **Index** Property, **LabelLevelCount** Property, **Left, Top** Properties, **Legend** Property, **MousePointer** Property, **Name** Property, **Object** Property, **Parent** Property, **Plot** Property, **RandomFill** Property, **Repaint** Property, **RowProperty** Property, **RowCount** Property, **RowLabel** Property, **RowLabelCount** Property, **RowLabelIndex** Property, **SerieColumn** Property, **SeriesType** Property, **ShowLegend** Property, **Stacking** Property, **TabIndex** Property, **Tag** Property, **TextLengthType** Property, **Title** Property, **TitleText** Property, **ToolTipText** Property, **Visible** Property (MSChart), **WhatsThisHelpID** Property

Events

AxisActivated Event, **AxisLabelActivated** Event, **AxisLabelSelected** Event, **AxisLabelUpdated** Event, **AxisSelected** Event, **AxisTitleActivated** Event, **AxisTitleSelected** Event, **AxisTitleUpdated** Event, **AxisUpdated** Event, **ChartActivated** Event, **ChartSelected** Event, **ChartUpdated** Event, **Click** Event, **DataUpdated** Event, **DblClick** Event, **DonePainting** Event, **DragDrop** Event, **DragOver** Event, **FootnoteActivated** Event, **FootnoteSelected** Event,

FootnoteUpdated Event, **GotFocus** Event, **KeyDown, KeyUp** Events, **KeyPress** Event, **LegendActivated** Event, **LegendSelected** Event, **LegendUpdated** Event, **LostFocus** Event, **MouseDown, MouseUp** Events, **MouseMove** Event, **PlotActivated** Event, **PlotSelected** Event, **PlotUpdated** Event, **PointActivated** Event, **PointLabelActivated** Event, **PointLabelSelected** Event, **PointLabelUpdated** Event, **PointSelected** Event, **PointUpdated** Event, **SeriesActivated** Event, **SeriesSelected** Event, **SeriesUpdated** Event, **TitleActivated** Event, **TitleSelected** Event, **TitleUpdated** Event

Methods

Drag Method, **EditCopy** Method, **EditPaste** Method, **GetSelectedPart** Method, **Layout** Method, **Move** Method, **Refresh** Method, **SelectPart** Method, **SetFocus** Method, **SetFocus** Method, **ShowWhatsThis** Method, **ToDefaults** Method, **TwipsToChartPart** Method, **Zorder** Method

See Also

AngleUnits Constants, **Axis** Object, **AxisGrid** Object, **AxisScale** Object, **AxisTitle** Object, **Backdrop** Object, **Brush** Object, **CategoryScale** Object, **Coor** Object, **DataGrid** Object, **DataPoint** Object, **DataPointLabel** Object, **Error Messages** (MSChart Control), **Fill** Object, **Footnote** Object, **Frame** Object, **Intersection** Object, **Label** Object (Item), **LCoor** Object, **Legend** Object, **Light** Object, **LightSource** Object, **Location** Object, **Marker** Object, **Pen** Object, **Plot** Object, **PlotBase** Object, **Rect** Object, **Series** Object, **SeriesMarker** Object, **SeriesPosition** Object, **Shadow** Object, **StatLine** Object, **TextLayout** Object, **Tick** Object, **Title** Object, **ValueScale** Object, **View3D** Object, **VtColor** Object, **VtFont** Object, **Wall** Object, **Weighting** Object

Example

The following example displays a three-dimensional chart with eight columns and rows of data and sets the legend parameters.

```
Private Sub Command1_Click()
   With Form1.MSChart1
      ' Displays a 3d chart with 8 columns and 8 rows
      ' data.
      .ChartType = VtChChartType3dBar
      .ColumnCount = 8
      .RowCount = 8
      For column = 1 To 8
         For row = 1 To 8
            .Column = column
            .Row = row
            .Data = row * 10
         Next row
      Next column
      ' Use the chart as the backdrop of the legend.
      .ShowLegend = True
```

```
        .SelectPart VtChPartTypePlot, index1, index2, _
        index3, index4
        .EditCopy
        .SelectPart VtChPartTypeLegend, index1, _
        index2, index3, index4
        .EditPaste
    End With
End Sub
```

ActiveSeriesCount Property

Returns the number of series that appear on a chart based on the number of columns in the **DataGrid** object and the type of chart being drawn.

Applies To

MSChart Control

Syntax

*object.***ActiveSeriesCount**

The object placeholder represents an object expression that evaluates to an object in the **Applies To** list.

See Also

DataGrid Object

Add Method (MSChart)

Adds a **LightSource** object to the **LightSources** collection.

Applies To

LightSources Collection

Syntax

*object.***Add** (*x,y,z,intensity*)

The **Add** method syntax has these parts:

Part	Description
collection	A object expression that evaluates to an object in the **Applies To** list.
x, y, z	Integers. Indicate the light source location.
intensity	Single. Indicates the light source intensity.

Remarks

Setting *x*, *y*, and *z* to zero generates a **VtChInvalidArgument** error.

AllowDithering Property

Returns or sets a value that determines whether to disable color dithering for charts on 8-bit color monitors in order to enable use of **MSChart** control's own color palette and enhance the chart display.

Applies To

MSChart Control

Syntax

object.**AllowDithering** [=*boolean*]

The **AllowDithering** property syntax has these parts:

Part	Description
object	An object expression that evaluates to an object in the **Applies To** list.
boolean	A Boolean expression that specifies whether a color dithering is allowed, as described in **Settings**.

Settings

The settings for *boolean* are:

Setting	Description
True	Color dithering is allowed.
False	**MSChart** control's color palette is used for enhanced color matching and display.

AllowDynamicRotation Property

Returns or sets a value that indicates whether users can interactively rotate three-dimensional charts by holding down the control key to display the rotation cursor.

Applies To

MSChart Control

Syntax

object.**AllowDynamicRotation** [= *boolean*]

The **AllowDynamicRotation** property syntax has these parts:

Part	Description
object	An object expression that evaluates to an object in the **Applies To** list.
boolean	A Boolean expression that specifies whether a dynamic rotation is allowed, as described in **Settings**.

Settings

The settings for *boolean* are:

Setting	Description
True	The user can interactively rotate the chart with the cursor.
False	The user cannot interactively rotate the chart with the cursor.

AllowSelections Property

Returns or sets a value that indicates whether or not users can select chart objects.

Applies To

MSChart Control

Syntax

*object.***AllowSelections** [= *boolean*]

The **AllowSelections** property syntax has these parts:

Part	Description
object	An object expression that evaluates to an object in the **Applies To** list.
boolean	A Boolean expression that specifies whether selections can be made, as described in **Settings**.

Settings

The settings for *boolean* are:

Setting	Description
True	The user can interactively select chart objects.
False	The user cannot select chart objects.

AllowSeriesSelection Property

Returns or sets a value that indicates whether a series is selected when a user clicks on an individual chart data point.

Applies To

MSChart Control

Syntax

*object.***AllowSeriesSelection** [= *boolean*]

The **AllowSeriesSelection** property syntax has these parts:

Part	Description
object	An object expression that evaluates to an object in the **Applies To** list.
boolean	A Boolean expression that specifies whether series are selected, as described in **Settings**.

Settings

The settings for *boolean* are:

Setting	Description
True	Users can select a series by clicking a data point.
False	Clicking a data point selects just that data point, not the entire series.

AmbientIntensity Property

Returns or sets the percentage of ambient light illuminating a three-dimensional chart.

Applies To

Light Object

Syntax

*object.***AmbientIntensity** [= *intensity*]

The **AmbientIntensity** property syntax has these parts:

Part	Description
object	An object expression that evaluates to an object in the **Applies To** list.
intensity	Single. The chart light intensity. Valid values are 0 to 1. If set to 1, all sides of the chart elements are fully illuminated no matter what light sources are turned on. If set at 0, there is no contribution from ambient light; only the sides of the chart elements facing active light sources are illuminated.

AngleUnit Property

Returns or sets the unit of measure used for all chart angles.

Applies To

Plot Object

Syntax

*object.***AngleUnit** [= *unit*]

The **AngleUnit** property syntax has these parts:

Part	Description
object	An object expression that evaluates to an object in the **Applies To** list.
unit	Integer. A **VtAngleUnits** constant describing the unit of measure. The angles can be measured in degrees, radians, or grads.

See Also

AngleUnits Constants

AngleUnits Constants

VtAngleUnits provides the valid units for measuring chart angles.

Constants	Description
VtAngleUnitsDegrees	Chart angles are measured in degrees.
VtAngleUnitsRadians	Chart angles are measured in radians.
VtAngleUnitsGrads	Chart angles are measured in grads.

See Also

AngleUnit Property, **Visual Basic** Constants

Auto Property (CategoryScale)

Returns or sets a value that indicates whether the axis is automatically scaled.

Applies To

CategoryScale Object

Syntax

*object.***Auto** [= *boolean*]

The **Auto** property syntax has these parts:

Part	Description
object	An object expression that evaluates to an object in the **Applies To** list.
boolean	A Boolean expression that specifies whether the item is displayed, as described in **Settings**.

Settings

The settings for *boolean* are:

Setting	Description
True	The axis is automatically scaled based on the data being charted.
False	The axis is not automatically scaled. Values in **DivisionsPerLabel** and **DivisionsPerTick** are used to determine the scale.

See Also

DivisionsPerLabel Property, **DivisionsPerTick** Property, **LabelTick** Property, **Auto** Property (Intersection), **Auto** Property (Label), **Auto** Property (SeriesMarker), **Auto** Property (ValueScale)

Auto Property (Intersection)

Returns or sets a value that determines whether or not the **Intersection** object uses the value of the **Point** property to position the axis.

Applies To

Intersection Object

Syntax

*object.***Auto** [= *boolean*]

The **Auto** property syntax has these parts:

Part	Description
object	An object expression that evaluates to an object in the **Applies To** list.
boolean	A Boolean expression that specifies whether the item is displayed, as described in **Settings**.

Settings

The settings for *boolean* are:

Setting	Description
True	The axis is positioned in its standard location.
False	The intersecting axis is positioned at the value indicated by **Point.**

See Also

Auto Property (CategoryScale), **Auto** Property (Label), **Auto** Property (SeriesMarker), **Auto** Property (ValueScale)

Auto Property (Label)

Returns or sets a value that determines whether axis labels are automatically rotated to improve the chart layout.

Applies To

Label Object (Item)

Syntax

*object.***Auto** [= *boolean*]

The **Auto** property syntax has these parts:

Part	Description
object	An object expression that evaluates to an object in the **Applies To** list.
boolean	A Boolean expression that specifies where to display the axis labels, as described in **Settings**.

Settings

The settings for *boolean* are:

Setting	Description
True	The labels may be rotated.
False	The labels are not rotated. Long labels may not display properly.

See Also

Auto Property (CategoryScale), **Auto** Property (Intersection), **Auto** Property (SeriesMarker), **Auto** Property (ValueScale)

Auto Property (SeriesMarker)

Returns or sets a value that determines if the **SeriesMarker** object assigns the next available marker to all data points in the series.

Applies To

SeriesMarker Object

Syntax

*object.***Auto** [= *boolean*]

The **Auto** property syntax has these parts:

Part	Description
object	An object expression that evaluates to an object in the **Applies To** list.
boolean	A Boolean expression that controls how markers are assigned, as described in **Settings**.

Settings

The settings for *boolean* are:

Setting	Description
True	The **SeriesMarker** object assigns the marker.
False	You can assign a custom marker.

Remarks

Set this property to **False** if you wish to change the series marker type.

This property is automatically set to **False** if the **Marker** property of the **DataPoint** object is set.

See Also

Auto Property (CategoryScale), **Auto** Property (Intersection), **Auto** Property (Label), **Auto** Property (ValueScale)

Auto Property (ValueScale)

Returns or sets a value that determines whether automatic scaling is used to draw the value axis.

Applies To

ValueScale Object

Syntax

object.**Auto** [= *boolean*]

The **Auto** property syntax has these parts:

Part	Description
object	An object expression that evaluates to an object in the **Applies To** list.
boolean	A Boolean expression that determines whether automatic scaling is used, as described in **Settings**.

Settings

The settings for *boolean* are:

Setting	Description
True	The scale is automatically set based on the data being charted.
False	The values in the **Minimum, Maximum, MajorDivisions** and **MinorDivisions** properties are used to scale the axis.

See Also

Auto Property (CategoryScale), **Auto** Property (Intersection), **Auto** Property (Label), **Auto** Property (SeriesMarker)

AutoIncrement Property

Returns or sets a value that determines if the properties that set the current data point are incremented during data entry without manually setting the **Column** and **Row** properties.

Applies To

MSChart Control

Syntax

object.**AutoIncrement** [= *boolean*]

The **AutoIncrement** property syntax has these parts:

Part	Description
object	An object expression that evaluates to an object in the **Applies To** list.
boolean	A Boolean expression that specifies whether the current data point is incremented, as described in **Settings**.

Settings

The settings for *boolean* are:

Setting	Description
True	When the **Data** property is changed, the **Row** property updates to the next row in the column. If you are at the end of a column, the **Column** property increments to the next column.
False	The current data point is not incremented.

AutoLayout Property

Returns or sets a value that determines whether or not a **Plot** object is in manual or automatic layout mode.

Applies To

Plot Object

Syntax

*object.***AutoLayout** [= *boolean*]

The **AutoLayout** property syntax has these parts:

Part	Description
object	An object expression that evaluates to an object in the **Applies To** list.
boolean	A Boolean expression that specifies the layout mode, as described in **Settings**.

Settings

The settings for *boolean* are:

Setting	Description
True	The **Plot** object automatically determines the proper size and position of the plot based on the size and position of other elements.
False	The coordinates specified by **Plot** object's **LocationRect** property are used to position the plot.

Automatic Property

Returns or sets a value that determines whether the color is calculated automatically. This is only used for edge pens on chart elements.

Applies To

VtColor Object

Syntax

*object.***Automatic** [= *boolean*]

The **Automatic** property syntax has these parts:

Part	Description
object	An object expression that evaluates to an object in the **Applies To** list.
boolean	A Boolean expression that determines whether the color is calculated automatically, as described in **Settings**.

Settings

The settings for *boolean* are:

Setting	Description
True	Color automatically picks up the brush color used on the chart series.
False	The color is determined based on the settings of **Value.**

Axis Object

An axis on a chart.

Syntax

Axis (*axisID, index*)

The **Axis** object syntax has these parts:

Part	Description
axisID	A **VtChAxisId** constant that identifies a specific axis.
index	Reserved for future use. Identifies the specific axis when there is more than one axis with the same *axisID*.

Properties

AxisGrid Property, **AxisScale** Property, **AxisTitle** Property, **CategoryScale** Property, **Intersection** Property, **LabelLevelCount** Property, **Labels** Property, **Pen** Property, **Tick** Property, **ValueScale** Property

See Also

AxisGrid Object, **AxisScale** Object, **AxisTitle** Object, **CategoryScale** Object, **Intersection** Object, **Labels** Collection

Example

The following example reads the number of label levels present on the x axis using the x Axis object.

```
Private Sub Command1_Click()
    Dim XAxis As Object
    Dim NumberOfLevels As Integer
    ' Read the number of label level present on the X
    ' Axis.
    Set XAxis = MSChart1.Plot.Axis(VtChAxisIdX, 1)
    NumberOfLevels = XAxis.LabelLevelCount
    MsgBox "Number of Label Levels = " _
    & Str(NumberOfLevels)
End Sub
```

Axis Property

Returns a reference to an **Axis** object that describes an axis on a chart.

Applies To

Plot Object

Syntax

object.**Axis**

The **Axis** property syntax has these parts:

Part	Description
object	An object expression that evaluates to an object in the **Applies To** list.
axisID	A **VtChAxisId** constant that identifies a specific axis.
index	Reserved for future use. Identifies the specific axis when there is more than one axis with the same *axisID*.

See Also

AxisId Constants

AxisActivated Event

Occurs when the user double clicks on a chart axis.

Applies To

MSChart Control

Syntax

Private Sub *object*_**AxisActivated** (*axisId* **As Integer**, *axisIndex* **As Integer**
↳ *mouseFlag* **As Integer**, *cancel* **As Integer**)

The **AxisActivated** event syntax has these parts:

Part	Description
object	An object expression that evaluates to an object in the **Applies To** list.
axisId	Integer. An integer that identifies a specific axis, as described in **Settings**.
axisIndex	Integer. An integer reserved for future use. For this version of **MSChart** control, 1 is the only valid value for this argument.
mouseFlag	Integer. An integer that indicates whether a key is held down when the mouse button is clicked, as described in **Settings**.
cancel	Integer. An integer that is not used at this time.

Settings

The event handler determines which axis is activated and sets *axisId* to:

Constants	Description
VtChAxisIdX	If the x axis is affected.
VtChAxisIdY	If the y axis is affected.
VtChAxisIdY2	If the secondary y axis is affected.
VtChAxisIdZ	If the z axis is affected.

The event handler determines if a key is held down when the mouse button is clicked and sets *mouseFlag* to:

Constants	Description
VtChMouseFlagShiftKeyDown	If the SHIFT key is held down.
VtChMouseFlagControlKeyDown	If the CONTROL key is held down.

AxisGrid Object

The planar area surrounding a chart axis.

Syntax

AxisGrid

Properties

MajorPen Property, **MinorPen** Property

Example

The following example changes the x AxisGrid line style to dashed.

```
Private Sub Command1_Click()
   ' Changes Grid line style to dashed.
   With MSChart1.Plot.Axis(VtChAxisIdX).AxisGrid
      .MajorPen.Style = VtPenStyleDashed
      .MajorPen.VtColor.Set 255, 0, 0
   End With
End Sub
```

AxisGrid Property

Returns a reference to an **AxisGrid** object that describes the planar area surrounding a chart axis.

Applies To

Axis Object

Syntax

object.**AxisGrid**

The object placeholder represents an object expression that evaluates to an object in the **Applies To** list.

AxisId Constants

The **VtChAxisId** constants provide options for identifying a chart axis.

Constants	Description
VtChAxisIdX	Identifies the x axis.
VtChAxisIdY	Identifies the y axis.
VtChAxisIdY2	Identifies the secondary y axis.
VtChAxisIdZ	Identifies the z axis.

See Also

Axis Property, **GetSelectedPart** Method, **AxisId** Property, **SelectPart** Method, **ShowGuideLines** Property, **TwipsToChartPart** Method, **Visual Basic** Constants

AxisId Property

Returns a specific axis that intersects with the current axis.

Applies To

Intersection Object

Syntax

object.**AxisId**

The object placeholder represents an object expression that evaluates to an object in the **Applies To** list.

Return Value

The return value is an integer that identifies the intersecting axis.

See Also

AxisId Constants

AxisLabelActivated Event

Occurs when the user double clicks on an axis label.

Applies To

MSChart Control

Syntax

Private Sub *object_***AxisLabelActivated** (*axisId* **As Integer**, *axisIndex* **As Integer**,
↪ *labelSetIndex* **As Integer**, *labelIndex* **As Integer**, *mouseFlag* **As Integer**,
↪ *cancel* **As Integer**)

The **AxisLabelActivated** event syntax has these parts:

Part	Description
object	An object expression that evaluates to an object in the **Applies To** list.
axisId	Integer. An integer that identifies a specific axis, as described in **Settings**.
axisIndex	Integer. An integer reserved for future use. For this version of **MSChart** control, 1 is the only valid value for this argument.
labelSetIndex	Integer. An integer that identifies the level of labels you are double clicking on. Levels of labels are numbered from the axis out, beginning with 1.
labelIndex	Integer. An integer that is currently unused.
mouseFlag	Integer. An integer that indicates if a key is held down when the mouse button is clicked.
cancel	Integer. An integer that is not used at this time.

Settings

The event handler determines which axis label is activated and sets *axisId* to:

Constants	Description
VtChAxisIdX	If the x axis is affected.
VtChAxisIdY	If the y axis is affected.
VtChAxisIdY2	If the secondary y axis is affected.
VtChAxisIdZ	If the z axis is affected.

The event handler determines if a key is held down when the mouse button is clicked and sets *mouseFlag* to:

Constants	Description
VtChMouseFlagShiftKeyDown	If the SHIFT key is held down.
VtChMouseFlagControlKeyDown	If the CONTROL key is held down.

See Also

AxisLabelSelected Event, **AxisLabelUpdated** Event

AxisLabelSelected Event

Occurs when the user clicks an axis label.

Applies To

MSChart Control

Syntax

Private Sub *object*_**AxisLabelSelected** (*axisId* **As Integer**, *axisIndex* **As Integer**,
↳ *labelSetIndex* **As Integer**, *labelIndex* **As Integer**, *mouseFlag* **As Integer**,
↳ *cancel* **As Integer**)

The **AxisLabelSelected** event syntax has these parts.

Part	Description
object	An object expression that evaluates to an object in the **Applies To** list.
axisId	Integer. An integer that identifies a specific axis, as described in **Settings**.
axisIndex	Integer. An integer reserved for future use. For this version of **MSChart** control, 1 is the only valid value for this argument.
labelSetIndex	Integer. An integer that identifies the level of labels you are double clicking on. Levels of labels are numbered from the axis out, beginning with 1.
labelIndex	Integer. An integer that is currently unused.
mouseFlag	Integer. An integer that indicates if a key is held down when the mouse button is clicked, as described in **Settings**.
cancel	Integer. An integer that is not used at this time.

Settings

The event handler determines which axis label is selected and sets *axisId* to:

Constants	Description
VtChAxisIdX	If the x axis is affected.
VtChAxisIdY	If the y axis is affected.
VtChAxisIdY2	If the secondary y axis is affected.
VtChAxisIdZ	If the z axis is affected.

The event handler determines if a key is held down when the mouse button is clicked and sets *mouseFlag* to:

Constants	Description
VtChMouseFlagShiftKeyDown	If the SHIFT key is held down.
VtChMouseFlagControlKeyDown	If the CONTROL key is held down.

See Also

AxisLabelActivated Event, **AxisLabelUpdated** Event

AxisLabelUpdated Event

Occurs when an axis label has changed.

Applies To

MSChart Control

Syntax

Private Sub *object*_**AxisLabelUpdated** (*axisId* **As Integer**, *axisIndex* **As Integer**,
↪ *labelSetIndex* **As Integer**, *labelIndex* **As Integer**, *updateFlags* **As Integer**)

The **AxisLabelUpdated** event syntax has these parts:

Part	Description
object	An object expression that evaluates to an object in the **Applies To** list.
axisId	Integer. An integer that identifies a specific axis, as described in **Settings**.
axisIndex	Integer. An integer reserved for future use. For this version of **MSChart** control, 1 is the only valid value for this argument.
labelSetIndex	Integer. An integer that identifies the level of labels you are double clicking on. Levels of labels are numbered from the axis out, beginning with 1.
labelIndex	Integer. An integer that is currently unused.
updateFlags	Integer. An integer provides information about the update of the label, as described in **Settings**.

Settings

The event handler determines which axis label is updated and sets *axisId* to:

Constants	Description
VtChAxisIdX	If the x axis is affected.
VtChAxisIdY	If the y axis is affected.
VtChAxisIdY2	If the secondary y axis is affected.
VtChAxisIdZ	If the z axis is affected.

The event handler determines the affect of the update, and sets *updateFlag* to:

Constants	Description
VtChNoDisplay	Absence of update flags; the chart display is not affected. (Defined as 0.)
VtChDisplayPlot	Update will cause the plot to repaint.
VtChLayoutPlot	Update will cause the plot to lay out.
VtChDisplayLegend	Update will cause the legend to repaint.
VtChLayoutLegend	Update will cause the legend to lay out.
VtChLayoutSeries	Update will cause the series to lay out.
VtChPositionSection	A chart section has been moved or resized.

AxisLabelActivated Event, **AxisLabelSelected** Event

AxisScale Object

Controls how chart values are plotted on an axis.

Syntax

AxisScale

Properties

Hide Property, **LogBase** Property, **PercentBasis** Property, **Type** Property (MSChart)

See Also

Axis Object, **AxisScale** Property

Example

The following example sets the x and y axes to percent scale for a two-dimensional line chart.

```
Private Sub Command1_Click()
    ' Change both x and y axes to Percent scale for 2D
    ' Line chart.
    Form1.MSChart1.ChartType = VtChChartType2dLine
    For AxisId = VtChAxisIdX To VtChAxisIdY
        With Form1.MSChart1.Plot.Axis(AxisId).AxisScale
            .Type = VtChScaleTypePercent
            .PercentBasis = VtChPercentAxisBasisSumChart
        End With
    Next
End Sub
```

AxisScale Property

Returns a reference to an **AxisScale** object that describes how chart values are plotted on an axis.

Applies To

Axis Object

Syntax

object.**AxisScale**

See Also

AxisScale Object

AxisSelected Event

Occurs when the user clicks on a chart axis.

Applies To

MSChart Control

Syntax

Private Sub *object*_**AxisSelected** (*axisId* **As Integer**, *axisIndex* **As Integer**,
↳ *mouseFlag* **As Integer**, *cancel* **As Integer**)

The **AxisSelected** event syntax has these parts:

Part	Description
object	An object expression that evaluates to an object in the **Applies To** list.
axisId	Integer. An integer that identifies a specific axis, as described in **Settings**.
AxisIndex	Integer. An integer reserved for future use. For this version of **MSChart** control, 1 is the only valid value for this argument.
mouseFlag	Integer. An integer that indicates whether key is held down when the mouse button is clicked, as described in **Settings**.
cancel	Integer. An integer that is not used at this time.

Settings

The event handler determines which axis is selected and sets *axisId* to:

Constants	Description
VtChAxisIdX	If the x axis is affected.
VtChAxisIdY	If the y axis is affected.
VtChAxisIdY2	If the secondary y axis is affected.
VtChAxisIdZ	If the z axis is affected.

The event handler determines if a key is held down when the mouse button is clicked and sets *mouseFlag* to:

Constants	Description
VtChMouseFlagShiftKeyDown	If the SHIFT key is held down.
VtChMouseFlagControlKeyDown	If the CONTROL key is held down.

AxisTickStyle Constants

The **VtChAxisTickStyle** constants provide options for indicating axis tick mark location.

Constants	Description
VtChAxisTickStyleNone	No tick marks are displayed on the axis.
VtChAxisTickStyleCenter	Tick marks are centered across the axis.

(continued)

Constants	Description
VtChAxisTickStyleInside	Tick marks are displayed inside the axis.
VtChAxisTickStyleOutside	Tick marks are displayed outside the axis.

See Also

Style Property (MSChart), **Visual Basic** Constants

AxisTitle Object

An axis title on a chart.

Syntax

AxisTitle

Properties

Text Property (MSChart), **TextLength** Property, **Visible** Property (MSChart), **Backdrop** Property, **Font** Property (MSChart), **TextLayout** Property, **VtFont** Property

See Also

Axis Object, **Backdrop** Object

Example

The following example makes the axis title visible for all axes of a three-dimensional chart.

```
Private Sub Command1_Click()
    ' Makes Axis title visible for all axes of a
    ' 3D chart.
    MSChart1.chartType = VtChChartType3dBar
    For axisId = VtChAxisIdX To VtChAxisIdZ
        With MSChart1.Plot.axis(axisId, 1).AxisTitle
            .Visible = True
            Select Case axisId
                Case 0
                    .text = "X Axis Title"
                Case 1
                    .text = "Y Axis Title"
                Case 2
                    .text = "2nd Y Axis Title"
                Case 3
                    .text = "Z Axis Title"

End Select
        End With
    Next
End Sub
```

AxisTitle Property

Returns a reference to an **AxisTitle** object associated with the axis of a chart.

Applies To

Axis Object

Syntax

*object.***AxisTitle**

The object placeholder represents an object expression that evaluates to an object in the **Applies To** list.

AxisTitleActivated Event

Occurs when the user double clicks on an axis title.

Applies To

MSChart Control

Syntax

Private Sub *object_***AxisTitleActivated** (*axisId* **As Integer**, *axisIndex* **As Integer**,
  ↪ *mouseFlag* **As Integer**, *cancel* **As Integer**)

The **AxisTitleActivated** event syntax has these parts:

Part	Description
object	An object expression that evaluates to an object in the **Applies To** list.
axisId	Integer. An integer that identifies a specific axis.
AxisIndex	Integer. An integer reserved for future use. For this version of **MSChart** control, 1 is the only valid value for this argument.
mouseFlag	Integer. An integer that indicates whether a key is held down when the mouse button is clicked.
cancel	Integer. This argument is not used at this time.

Settings

The event handler determines which axis title is activated and sets *axisId* to:

Constants	Description
VtChAxisIdX	If the x axis is affected.
VtChAxisIdY	If the y axis is affected.
VtChAxisIdY2	If the secondary y axis is affected.
VtChAxisIdZ	If the z axis is affected.

The event handler determines if a key is held down when the mouse button is clicked and sets *mouseFlag* to:

Constants	Description
VtChMouseFlagShiftKeyDown	If the SHIFT key is held down.
VtChMouseFlagControlKeyDown	If the CONTROL key is held down.

See Also

AxisTitleSelected Event, **AxisTitleUpdated** Event

AxisTitleSelected Event

Occurs when the user clicks on an axis title.

Applies To

MSChart Control

Syntax

Private Sub *object*_**AxisTitleSelected** (*axisId* **As Integer**, *axisIndex* **As Integer**,
↳ *mouseFlag* **As Integer**, *cancel* **As Integer**)

The **AxisTitleSelected** event syntax has these parts:

Part	Description
object	An object expression that evaluates to an object in the **Applies To** list.
axisId	Integer. An integer that identifies a specific axis.
AxisIndex	Integer. An integer reserved for future use. For this version of **MSChart** control, 1 is the only valid value for this argument.
mouseFlag	Integer. An integer that indicates whether a key is held down when the mouse button is clicked.
cancel	Integer. This argument is not used at this time.

Settings

The event handler determines which axis title is selected and sets *axisId* to:

Constants	Description
VtChAxisIdX	If the x axis is affected.
VtChAxisIdY	If the y axis is affected.
VtChAxisIdY2	If the secondary y axis is affected.
VtChAxisIdZ	If the z axis is affected.

The event handler determines if a key is held down when the mouse button is clicked
and sets *mouseFlag* to:

Constants	Description
VtChMouseFlagShiftKeyDown	If the SHIFT key is held down.
VtChMouseFlagControlKeyDown	If the CONTROL key is held down.

See Also

    AxisTitleActivated Event, **AxisTitleUpdated** Event

AxisTitleUpdated Event

Occurs when an axis title has changed.

Applies To

    MSChart Control

Syntax

    Private Sub *object*_**AxisTitleUpdated** (*axisId* **As Integer**, *axisIndex* **As Integer**,
      ↳ *updateFlags* **As Integer**)

The **AxisTitleUpdated** event syntax has these parts:

Part	Description
object	An object expression that evaluates to an object in the **Applies To** list.
axisId	Integer. An integer that identifies a specific axis.
AxisIndex	Integer. An integer reserved for future use. For this version of **MSChart** control, 1 is the only valid value for this argument.
updateFlag	Integer. An integer that provides information about the update of the title.

Settings

The event handler determines which axis title is updated and sets *axisId* to:

Constants	Description
VtChAxisIdX	If the x axis is affected.
VtChAxisIdY	If the y axis is affected.
VtChAxisIdY2	If the secondary y axis is affected.
VtChAxisIdZ	If the z axis is affected.

The following table lists the constants for *updateFlag*.

Constants	Description
VtChNoDisplay	Absence of update flags; the chart display is not affected. (Defined as 0.)
VtChDisplayPlot	Update will cause the plot to repaint.
VtChLayoutPlot	Update will cause the plot to lay out.
VtChDisplayLegend	Update will cause the legend to repaint.
VtChLayoutLegend	Update will cause the legend to lay out.
VtChLayoutSeries	Update will cause the series to lay out.
VtChPositionSection	A chart section has been moved or resized.

See Also

AxisTitleActivated Event, **AxisTitleSelected** Event

AxisUpdatedEvent

Occurs when an axis has changed.

Applies To

MSChart Control

Syntax

Private Sub *object*_**AxisUpdated** (*axisId* **As Integer**, *axisIndex* **As Integer**,
↪ *updateFlags* **As Integer**)

The **AxisUpdated** event syntax has these parts:

Part	Description
object	An object expression that evaluates to an object in the **Applies To** list.
axisId	Integer. An integer that identifies a specific axis.
axisIndex	Integer. An integer reserved for future use. For this version of **MSChart** control, 1 is the only valid value for this argument.
updateFlag	Integer. An integer that provides information about the update of the axis.

Settings

The event handler determines which axis is updated and sets *axisId* to:

Constants	Description
VtChAxisIdX	If the x axis is affected.
VtChAxisIdY	If the y axis is affected.
VtChAxisIdY2	If the secondary y axis is affected.
VtChAxisIdZ	If the z axis is affected.

The following table lists the constants for *updateFlag*.

Constants	Description
VtChNoDisplay	Absence of update flags; the chart display is not affected. (Defined as 0.)
VtChDisplayPlot	Update will cause the plot to repaint.
VtChLayoutPlot	Update will cause the plot to lay out.
VtChDisplayLegend	Update will cause the legend to repaint.
VtChLayoutLegend	Update will cause the legend to lay out.
VtChLayoutSeries	Update will cause the series to lay out.
VtChPositionSection	A chart section has been moved or resized.

Backdrop Object

A shadow or pattern behind a chart element.

Syntax

Backdrop

Properties

Fill Property, **Frame** Property, **Shadow** Property

See Also

Backdrop Property, **Fill** Object, **Frame** Object

Backdrop Property

Returns a reference to a **Backdrop** object that describes the shadow, pattern, or picture behind a chart or chart element.

Applies To

MSChart Control, **AxisTitle** Object, **DataPointLabel** Object, **Footnote** Object, **Label** Object (Item), **Legend** Object, **Plot** Object, **Title** Object

Syntax

object.**Backdrop**

The object placeholder represents an object expression that evaluates to an object in the **Applies To** list.

BarGap Property

Returns or sets the spacing of two-dimensional bars or clustered three-dimensional bars within a category.

Applies To

Plot Object

Syntax

object.**BarGap** [= *value*]

The **BarGap** property syntax has these parts:

Part	Description
object	An object expression that evaluates to an object in the **Applies To** list.
value	Single. The bar spacing value. This is measured as a percentage of the bar width. A value of 0 results in the bars touching. A value of 100 means the gap between the bars is as wide as the bars.

BaseHeight Property

Returns or sets the height of the three-dimensional chart base in points.

Applies To

PlotBase Object

Syntax

*object.***BaseHeight** [= *height*]

The **BaseHeight** property syntax has these parts:

Part	Description
object	An object expression that evaluates to an object in the **Applies To** list.
height	Single. The base height.

Basis Property

Returns or sets the type of weighting used to determine pie size on a chart.

Applies To

Weighting Object

Syntax

*object.***Basis** [= *type*]

The **Basis** property syntax has these parts:

Part	Description
object	An object expression that evaluates to an object in the **Applies To** list.
type	A **VtChPieWeightBasis** constant that identifies the weighting type.

See Also

PieWeightBasis Constants

Blue Property

Returns or sets the blue component of the RGB value in a chart.

Applies To

VtColor Object

Syntax

*object.***Blue** [=*b*]

The **Blue** property syntax has these parts:

Part	Description
object	An object expression that evaluates to an object in the **Applies To** list.
b	Integer. The blue value.

Remarks

RGB specifies the relative intensity of red, green, and blue to cause a specific color to be displayed. The valid range for a normal RGB color is 0 to 16,777,215. The value for any argument to RGB that exceeds 255 is assumed to be 255.

BorderStyle Constants (MSChart)

The **VtBorderStyle** constants provide options for the type of border to be placed around the chart control.

Constant	Description
VtBorderStyleFixedSingle	A single border is placed around the chart control.
VtBorderStyleNone	No border is placed around the chart control.

BorderStyle Property (ActiveX Controls)

Returns or sets the border style for an object.

Syntax

object.**BorderStyle** [= *value*]

The **BorderStyle** property syntax has these parts:

Part	Description
object	An object expression that evaluates to an object in the **Applies To** list.
value	A value or constant that determines the border style, as described in **Settings**.

Settings

The settings for *value* are:

Constant	Value	Description
ccNone	0	(Default) No border or border-related elements.
ccFixedSingle	1	Fixed single.

Note The cc prefix refers to the Windows 95 controls. For the other controls, prefixes for the settings change with the specific control or group of controls. However, the description remains the same unless indicated.

Remarks

Setting **BorderStyle** for a **ProgressBar** control decreases the size of the chunks the control displays.

Brush Object

The fill type used to display a chart element.

Syntax

Brush

Properties

FillColor Property, **Index** Property (Brush), **PatternColor** Property, **Style** Property (MSChart)

See Also

Brush Property

Example

The following example sets a bold vertical line pattern for the chart backdrop using the Brush object.

```
Private Sub Command1_Click()
    ' Sets Backdrop to Fill - Brush Style.
    MSChart1.Backdrop.Fill.Style = VtFillStyleBrush
    ' Sets a pattern for the chart backdrop using the
    ' Brush object.
    With MSChart1.Backdrop.Fill.Brush
        .Style = VtBrushStylePattern
        .Index = VtBrushPatternBoldVertical
    ' Sets Pattern to Bold Vertical lines.
        .FillColor.Set 255, 0, 0          ' Fill Color = Red.
        .PatternColor.Set 0, 0, 255       ' Pattern Color =
                                          ' Blue.

    End With
End Sub
```

Brush Property

Returns a reference to a **Brush** Object that describes the fill type used to display a chart element.

Applies To

DataPoint Object, **Fill** Object, **PlotBase** Object, **Shadow** Object, **Wall** Object

Syntax

object.**Brush**

The object placeholder represents an object expression that evaluates to an object in the **Applies To** list.

See Also

Brush Object

BrushHatch Constants

VtBrushHatch provides valid brush types if **VtBrushStyle** is set to **VtBrushStyleHatch**.

Constant	Description
VtBrushHatchHorizontal	Horizontal hatch lines
VtBrushHatchVertical	Vertical hatch lines
VtBrushHatchDownDiagonal	Down diagonal hatch lines
VtBrushHatchUpDiagonal	Up diagonal hatch lines
VtBrushHatchCross	Cross hatch lines
VtBrushHatchDiagonalCross	Diagonal cross hatch lines

See Also

Index Property (Brush), **Visual Basic** Constants

BrushPattern Constants

VtBrushPattern provides valid brush types if **VtBrushStyle** is set to **VtBrushStylePattern**.

Constant	Description
VtBrushPattern94percent	94 percent pattern color
VtBrushPattern88percent	88 percent pattern color
VtBrushPattern75percent	75 percent pattern color
VtBrushPattern50percent	50 percent pattern color
VtBrushPattern25percent	25 percent pattern color
VtBrushPatternBoldHorizontal	Bold horizontal lines
VtBrushPatternBoldVertical	Bold vertical lines
VtBrushPatternBoldDownDiagonal	Bold down diagonal lines
VtBrushPatternBoldUpDiagonal	Bold up diagonal lines
VtBrushPatternChecks	Checks pattern
VtBrushPatternWeave	Weave pattern
VtBrushPatternHorizontal	Horizontal lines
VtBrushPatternVertical	Vertical lines

(continued)

Constant	Description
VtBrushPatternDownDiagonal	Down diagonal lines
VtBrushPatternUpDiagonal	Up diagonal lines
VtBrushPatternGrid	Grid pattern
VtBrushPatternTrellis	Trellis pattern
VtBrushPatternInvertedTrellis	Inverted trellis pattern

See Also

Index Property (Brush), **Visual Basic** Constants

BrushStyle Constants

VtBrushStyle provides valid brush types.

Constant	Description
VtBrushStyleNull	No brush (background shows through)
VtBrushStyleSolid	Solid color brush
VtBrushStylePattern	Bitmap patterned brush
VtBrushStyleHatched	Hatched brush

See Also

Style Property (MSChart)

Cap Property

Returns or sets a value that determines how line ends are capped.

Applies To

Pen Object

Syntax

object.**Cap** [= *type*]

The **Cap** property syntax has these parts:

Part	Description
object	An object expression that evaluates to an object in the **Applies To** list.
type	Integer. A **VtPenCap** constant that describes the line pen cap style.

See Also

PenCap Constants

CategoryScale Object

The scale for a category axis.

Syntax

CategoryScale

See Also

CategoryScale Property

Properties

Auto Property (CategoryScale), **DivisionsPerLabel** Property, **DivisionsPerTick** Property, **LabelTick** Property

Example

The following example sets the scaling attributes for a category axis.

```
Private Sub Command1_Click()
    ' Sets scaling attributes for a category axis.
    MSChart1.ChartType = VtChChartType2dLine
    With MSChart1.Plot.Axis(VtChAxisIdX, _
    1).CategoryScale
        .Auto = False          ' Sets manual scaling.
        .DivisionsPerLabel = 2 ' Label appears every two
                               ' divisions.
        .DivisionsPerTick = 2  ' Ticks appear every two
                               ' divisions.
        .LabelTick = True      ' Labels displayed on top of
                               ' Tick marks.

End With
End Sub
```

CategoryScale Property

Returns a reference to a **CategoryScale** object that describes the scale information for a category axis.

Applies To

Axis Object

Syntax

object.**CategoryScale**

The object placeholder represents an object expression that evaluates to an object in the **Applies To** list.

See Also

ValueScale Property

Chart3d Property

Returns a value that determines whether or not a chart is three dimensional.

Applies To

MSChart Control

Syntax

object.**Chart3D**

The object placeholder represents an object expression that evaluates to an object in the **Applies To** list.

Return Values

Setting	Description
True	The chart is a three-dimensional chart.
False	The chart is not a three-dimensional chart.

ChartActivated Event

Occurs when the user double clicks the Microsoft Chart control, but not on a specific element in the chart.

Applies To

MSChart Control

Syntax

Private Sub *object*_**ChartActivated** (*mouseFlag* **As Integer**, *cancel* **As Integer**)

The **ChartActivated** event syntax has these parts:

Part	Description
object	An object expression that evaluates to an object in the **Applies To** list.
mouseFlag	Integer. Indicates whether a key is held down when the mouse button is clicked, as described in **Settings**.
cancel	Integer. This argument is not used at this time.

Settings

The event handler determines if a key is held down when the mouse button is clicked and sets *mouseFlag* to:

Constants	Description
VtChMouseFlagShiftKeyDown	If the SHIFT key is held down.
VtChMouseFlagControlKeyDown	If the CONTROL key is held down.

See Also

ChartSelected Event, **ChartUpdated** Event

ChartData Property

Returns or sets a value that determines if the contents of an array are loaded directly into a chart data grid or if a chart is queried for data and returns an array.

Applies To

MSChart Control

Syntax

object.**ChartData** [= *data*]

The **ChartData** property syntax has these parts:

Part	Description
object	An object expression that evaluates to an object in the **Applies To** list.
data	Variant. A two-dimensional array that holds the data used to draw the chart.

Remarks

ChartData is the default property for the **MSChart** control.

Example

The following example uses a Visual Basic array to load the chart data grid directly:

```
' Declare the variant array.
Dim X(1 To 3, 1 To 3) as Variant
' Set the data.
For i = 1 To Ubound3
   For j = 1 To 3
      X(i,j) = i*j
   Next
Next
' Set the row labels.
X(1,2) = "Wheat"
X(1,3) = "Corn"
' Set the column labels.
X(2,1) = "January"
X(3,1) = "February"
' Set the chart data.
MSChart1.ChartData = X
```

In this example, the lower subscript bound was declared as 1, rather than the default of 0. We used a **Variant** array where the top row and left column are set to string variables and the lower right 2x2 submatrix is set to numeric values. This allows both the chart's labels and data to be set simultaneously. Note that declaring the array as type **String** works too, as long as the lower right submatrix contains text representations of numeric values. If you wish only to set the charts data, the array may be of the numeric types **Integer**, **Long**, **Single** or **Double**. Note that doing this will replace the existing chart labels with default row/column labels. Note, a one-dimensional array will work as well as a two-dimensional one as long as the last values are either numeric or text representations of numeric values.

The following example queries data from the chart. In this example, it is not necessary to declare the variable first. The example contains a loop to print out the array returned from the chart. Note the use of the **Lbound** and **Ubound** functions to determine the array bounds from the chart.

```
' Set the variant from the chart data.
Y = MSChart1.ChartData
    ' Print out the variant.
  For i = LBound(Y,1) To Ubound(Y,1)
    For j = Lbound(Y,2) To UBound(Y,2)
        MsgBox Y(i,j)
    Next
  Next
```

The returned array lower bound values are equal to 0. The returned array will always be a two-dimensional array of type Variant. Since **ChartData** is the default property for the chart, the object name alone, such as MSChart1, may be substituted for MSChart1.ChartData. So you could use MSChart1 = data or data = MSChart1.

ChartSelected Event

Occurs when the user clicks the Microsoft Chart control, but not on a specific element in the chart.

Applies To

MSChart Control

Syntax

Private Sub *object*_**ChartSelected** (*mouseFlag* **As Integer**, *cancel* **As Integer**)

The **ChartSelected** event syntax has these parts:

Part	Description
object	An object expression that evaluates to an object in the **Applies To** list.
mouseFlag	Integer. Indicates whether a key is held down when the mouse button is clicked, as described in **Settings**.
cancel	Integer. This argument is not used at this time.

Settings

The event handler determines if a key is held down when the mouse button is clicked and sets *mouseFlag* to:

Constants	Description
VtChMouseFlagShiftKeyDown	If the SHIFT key is held down.
VtChMouseFlagControlKeyDown	If the CONTROL key is held down.

See Also

ChartActivated Event, **ChartUpdated** Event

ChartType Constants

VtChChartType provides chart type options.

Constant	Description
VtChChartType3dBar	3D Bar
VtChChartType2dBar	2D Bar
VtChChartType3dLine	3D Line
VtChChartType2dLine	2D Line
VtChChartType3dArea	3D Area
VtChChartType2dArea	2D Area
VtChChartType3dStep	3D Step
VtChChartType2dStep	2D Step
VtChChartType3dCombination	3D Combination
VtChChartType2dCombination	2D Combination
VtChChartType2dPie	2D Pie
VtChChartType2dXY	2D XY

See Also

ChartType Property, **TypeByChartType** Method, **Visual Basic** Constants

ChartType Property

Returns or sets the chart type being used to display a chart.

Applies To

MSChart Control

Syntax

*object.***ChartType** [= *type*]

The **ChartType** property syntax has these parts:

Part	Description
object	An object expression that evaluates to an object in the **Applies To** list.
type	Integer. A **VtChChartType** constant that describes the chart type.

See Also

ChartType Constants

ChartUpdated Event

Occurs when the chart has changed.

Applies To

MSChart Control

Syntax

Private Sub *object*_**ChartUpdated** (*updateFlags* **As Integer**)

Part	Description
object	An object expression that evaluates to an object in the **Applies To** list.
updateFlag	Integer. Provides information about the update of the chart, as described in **Settings**.

Settings

The following table lists the constants for *updateFlag*.

Constant	Description
VtChNoDisplay	Absence of update flags; the chart display is not affected. (Defined as 0.)
VtChDisplayPlot	Update will cause the plot to repaint.
VtChLayoutPlot	Update will cause the plot to lay out.
VtChDisplayLegend	Update will cause the legend to repaint.
VtChLayoutLegend	Update will cause the legend to lay out.
VtChLayoutSeries	Update will cause the series to lay out.
VtChPositionSection	A chart section has been moved or resized.

See Also

ChartActivated Event, **ChartSelected** Event

Clockwise Property

Returns or sets a value that specifies whether pie charts are drawn in a clockwise direction.

Applies To

Plot Object

Syntax

object.**Clockwise** [= *boolean*]

The **Clockwise** property syntax has these parts:

Part	Description
object	An object expression that evaluates to an object in the **Applies To** list.
boolean	A Boolean expression that controls the direction used to draw pie charts, as described in **Settings**.

Settings

The settings for *boolean* are:

Setting	Description
True	Pie charts are drawn in a clockwise direction.
False	The charts are drawn in a counterclockwise direction.

Column Property

Returns or sets the current data column in the data grid.

Applies To

MSChart Control

Syntax

*object.***Column** [= *col*]

The **Column** property syntax has these parts:

Part	Description
object	An object expression that evaluates to an object in the **Applies To** list.
col	Integer. The current data column.

Remarks

You must select a column before you can use other properties to change the column's corresponding chart series or any data point within the series.

ColumnCount Property

Returns or sets the number of columns in the current data grid associated with a chart.

Applies To

MSChart Control, **DataGrid** Object

Syntax

*object.***ColumnCount** [= *count*]

The **ColumnCount** property syntax has these parts:

Part	Description
object	An object expression that evaluates to an object in the **Applies To** list.
count	The number of data columns.

See Also
   SetSize Method

ColumnLabel Property (DataGrid)

Returns or sets the label on a data column in the grid associated with a chart.

Applies To

DataGrid Object

Syntax

object.**ColumnLabel**(*column, labelIndex*) [= *text*]

The **ColumnLabel** property syntax has these parts:

Part	Description
object	An object expression that evaluates to an object in the **Applies To** list.
column	Integer. Identifies a specific data column. Columns are numbered from left to right beginning with 1. Any columns containing labels are not counted as data columns.
labelIndex	Integer. Identifies a specific label. If more than one level of column labels exist for the column, you must identify one of them. Column labels are numbered from bottom to top beginning at 1.
text	String. The column label text.

See Also

   ColumnLabel Property (MSChart), **RowLabel** Property (DataGrid)

ColumnLabel Property (MSChart)

Returns or sets the label text associated with a column in the data grid of a chart.

Applies To

MSChart Control

Syntax

object.**ColumnLabel** [= *text*]

The **ColumnLabel** property syntax has these parts:

Part	Description
object	An object expression that evaluates to an object in the **Applies To** list.
text	String. Label text associated with a column in the data grid.

Remarks

This property sets the label for the column currently identified by the **Column** property.

See Also

ColumnLabel Property (DataGrid), **RowLabel** Property (MSChart)

ColumnLabelCount Property

Returns or sets the number of levels of labels on the columns in the data grid associated with a chart.

Applies To

MSChart Control, **DataGrid** Object

Syntax

*object.***ColumnLabelCount** [= *count*]

The **ColumnLabelCount** property syntax has these parts:

Part	Description
object	An object expression that evaluates to an object in the **Applies To** list.
count	Integer. The number of column label levels. Set this property to add or delete levels of labels on data grid columns.

Remarks

Column label levels are numbered from bottom to top, beginning at 1. Levels are added or subtracted from the top.

See Also

SetSize Method

ColumnLabelIndex Property

Returns or sets a specific level of column labels associated with a chart.

Applies To

MSChart Control

Syntax

*object.***ColumnLabelIndex** [= *index*]

The **ColumnLabelIndex** property syntax has these parts:

Part	Description
object	An object expression that evaluates to an object in the **Applies To** list.
index	Integer. Identifies a column label level.

Remarks

To set a label on a column with more than one level of labels, or to return the current value for a label, you must first identify which level you want to affect. Column label levels are numbered from bottom to top, beginning at 1.

Component Property

Returns or sets the type of label to be used to identify the data point.

Applies To

DataPointLabel Object

Syntax

*object.***Component** [= *type*]

The **Component** property syntax has these parts:

Part	Description
object	An object expression that evaluates to an object in the **Applies To** list.
type	Integer. A **VtChLabelComponent** constant that identifies the label type.

See Also

LabelComponent Constants

CompositeColumnLabel Property

Returns the multilevel label string that identifies a column in the data grid associated with a chart.

Applies To

DataGrid Object

Syntax

*object.***CompositeColumnLabel**(*column*)

The **CompositeColumnLabel** property syntax has these parts:

Part	Description
object	An object expression that evaluates to an object in the **Applies To** list.
column	Integer. Identifies a specific data column. Columns are numbered from left to right beginning with 1. Any columns containing labels are not counted as data columns.

See Also

CompositeRowLabel Property

CompositeRowLabel Property

Returns the multilevel label string that identifies a row in the data grid associated with a chart.

Applies To

DataGrid Object

Syntax

*object.***CompositeRowLabel** (*row*)

The **CompositeRowLabel** property syntax has these parts:

Part	Description
object	An object expression that evaluates to an object in the **Applies To** list.
row	Integer. Identifies a specific data row. Rows are numbered from top to bottom beginning with 1. Any rows containing labels are not counted as data rows.

See Also

CompositeColumnLabel Property

Coor Object

Describes a floating x and y coordinate pair for a chart.

Syntax

Coor

Properties

X Property, **Y** Property

Methods

Set Method (MSChart)

See Also

LCoor Object

Count Method

Returns the number of objects in a collection.

Applies To

SeriesCollection Collection

Syntax

*object.***Count**

The object placeholder represents an object expression that evaluates to an object in the **Applies To** list.

Custom Property

Returns or sets a value that determines if custom text is used to label a data point on a chart.

Applies To

DataPointLabel Object

Syntax

object.**Custom** [= *boolean*]

The **Custom** property syntax has these parts:

Part	Description
object	An object expression that evaluates to an object in the **Applies To** list.
boolean	A Boolean expression that specifies whether custom text is used, as described in **Settings**.

Settings

The settings for *boolean* are:

Setting	Description
True	The label contains custom text.
False	Information specified by the **DataPointLabel** object's **Components** property is used to label the data point.

Data Property (MSChart)

Returns or sets a value that is inserted into the current data point in the data grid of a chart.

Applies To

MSChart Control

Syntax

object.**Data** [= *value*]

The **Data** property syntax has these parts:

Part	Description
object	An object expression that evaluates to an object in the **Applies To** list.
value	Integer. The data point value.

Remarks

If the current data point already contains a value, it is replaced by the new value. The chart is redrawn to reflect the new value for the current data point.

DataGrid Object

A chart data grid.

Syntax

DataGrid

Properties

ColumnCount Property, **ColumnLabelCount** Property, **ColumnLabel** Property
(DataGrid), **CompositeColumnLabel** Property, **CompositeRowLabel** Property,
RowLabel Property (DataGrid), **RowCount** Property (MSChart), **RowLabelCount**
Property

Methods

DeleteColumns Method, **DeleteColumnLabels** Method, **DeleteRows** Method,
DeleteRowLabels Method, **GetData** Method (MSChart), **InitializeLabels** Method,
InsertColumns Method, **InsertColumnLabels** Method, **InsertRows** Method,
InsertRowLabels Method, **MoveData** Method, **RandomDataFill** Method,
RandomFillColumns Method, **RandomFillRows** Method, **SetData** Method
(MSChart), **SetSize** Method

See Also

DataGrid Property

Example

The following example sets the chart parameters for a three-dimensional bar chart,
fills the chart with random data and labels the data grid columns.

```
Private Sub Command1_Click()
   Dim rowLabelCount As Integer
   Dim columnLabelCount As Integer
   Dim rowCount As Integer
   Dim columnCount As Integer
   Set DataGrid = MSChart1.DataGrid
   MSChart1.ChartType = VtChChartType3dBar
   With MSChart1.DataGrid
   ' Set Chart parameters using methods.
      rowLabelCount = 2
      columnLabelCount = 2
      rowCount = 6
      columnCount = 6
      .SetSize RowLabelCount, RolumnLabelCount, _
      RowCount, ColumnCount

' Randomly fill in the data.
      .RandomDataFill
      ' Then assign labels to second Level.
      labelIndex = 2
      column = 1
      .ColumnLabel(column, labelIndex) = "Product 1"
      column = 4
      .ColumnLabel(column, labelIndex) = "Product 2"
```

```
      row = 1
      .RowLabel(row, labelIndex) = "1994"
      row = 4
      .RowLabel(row, labelIndex) = "1995"
   End With
End Sub
```

DataGrid Property

Returns a reference to a **DataGrid** object that describes the data grid associated with a chart.

Applies To

MSChart Control

Syntax

object.**DataGrid**

The object placeholder represents an object expression that evaluates to an object in the **Applies To** list.

DataPoint Object

One item within a **DataPoints** collection that describes the attributes of an individual data point on a chart.

Syntax

DataPoint

Properties

Brush Object, **DataPoints** Property, **DataPoints** Collection, **DataPointLabel** Object

Methods

ResetCustom Method**, Select** Method

See Also

Brush Object, **DataPoints** Property, **DataPoints** Collection, **DataPointLabel** Object

Example

The following example assigns a variable to a data point and sets the data point color and marker.

```
Private Sub Command1_Click()
   ' Change the color and marker of First DataPoint in
   ' the First Series.
   With MSChart1.Plot.SeriesCollection._
   Item(1).DataPoint
      ' Change Data Point color to blue.
      .Brush.Style = VtBrushStyleSolid
```

```
                ' Set Color=Blue.
                .Brush.FillColor.Set 0, 255, 255
                ' Set DataPoint marker visible.
                .Marker.Visible = True
        End With
End Sub
```

DataPointLabel Object

The label for a data point on a chart.

Syntax

DataPointLabel

Properties

Backdrop Property, **Component** Property, **Custom** Property, **Font** Property, **LineStyle** Property, **LocationType** Property, **Offset** Property, **PercentFormat** Property, **Text** Property, **TextLayout** Property, **TextLength** Property, **ValueFormat** Property, **VtFont** Property

Methods

ResetCustomLabel Method**, Select** Method

See Also

Coor Object, **DataPointLabel** Property

DataPointLabel Property

Returns a reference to a **DataPointLabel** object that describes a label on an individual chart data point.

Applies To

DataPoint Object

Syntax

object.**DataPointLabel**

The object placeholder represents an object expression that evaluates to an object in the **Applies To** list.

DataPoints Collection

A group of chart data points.

Syntax

DataPoints.Item(*index*)

The **DataPoints** collection syntax has these parts:

Part	Description
index	Identifies a specific data point within the current series. For this version of the chart, −1 is the only valid value for this argument. This allows you two make changes to the default settings for all data points in the series. **Settings** cannot be changed for individual data points within the series.

Properties

Item Property (MSChart), **Count** Property

See Also

DataPoint Object, **DataPoints** Property

Example

The following example sets the markers for each data point in a chart.

```
Private Sub Command1_Click()
    Dim DataPoint As Object
    Dim Index As Integer
    For Each DataPoint In _
    MSChart1.plot.SeriesCollection.Item(1).DataPoints
    ' Set DataPoint marker visible.
    DataPoint.Marker.visible = True
    DataPoint.Marker.width = 12
    Next
End Sub
```

The **Datapoints** collection **Item** method takes a special −1 argument to designate default properties for all data points of the series. The **Datapoint** object returned by **Item**(−1) can be manipulated just like a normal **Datapoint** object. A property set on this default data point affects every data point in the series, except those data points that have had that property set individually. In the example below, data point 2 of series 1 has its data point label location set to the base of the bar (assuming a bar chart). The rest of the data point labels for series 1 are set to appear above the data point. It makes no difference whether individual data point settings come before or after default settings; the individual settings always override the default settings. The **ResetCustom** method can be used to remove any individual settings for a data point and cause it to use the default settings for the series.

```
With MSChart1.Plot.SeriesCollection.Item(1)
    .DataPoints.Item(2).DataPointLabel._
    LocationType = VtChLabelLocationTypeBase
    .Item(-1).DataPointLabel.LocationType = _
    VtChLabelLocationTypeAbovePoint
End With
```

DataPoints Property

Returns a reference to a **DataPoint** Collection that describes the data points within a chart series.

Applies To

Series Object

Syntax

object.**DataPoints**

The object placeholder represents an object expression that evaluates to an object in the **Applies To** list.

DataSeriesInRow Property

Returns or sets a value that indicates whether series data is being read from a row or a column in a data grid associated with a chart.

Applies To

Plot Object

Syntax

object.**DataSeriesInRow** [= *boolean*]

The **DataSeriesInRow** property syntax has these parts:

Part	Description
object	An object expression that evaluates to an object in the **Applies To** list.
boolean	A Boolean expression that controls how series data is read, as described in **Settings**.

Settings

The settings for *boolean* are:

Setting	Description
True	Series data is being read from a row in a data grid.
False	Series data is being read from a column.

DataUpdated Event

Occurs when the chart data grid has changed.

Applies To

MSChart Control

Syntax

Private Sub *object*_**DataUpdated** (*row* **As Integer**, *column* **As Integer**, *labelRow*
↳ **As Integer**, *labelColumn* **As Integer**, *labelSetIndex* **As Integer**,
↳ *updateFlags* **As Integer**)

The **DataUpdated** event syntax has these parts:

Part	Description
object	An object expression that evaluates to an object in the **Applies To** list.
row	Integer. Indicates the row in the data grid.
column	Integer. Indicates the column in the datagrid.
labelRow	Integer. Indicates the row label.
labelColumn	Integer. Indicates the column label.
labelSetIndex	Integer. Identifies the level of labels. Levels of labels are numbered from the axis out, beginning with 1.
updateFlag	Integer. Provides information about the update of the data, as described in **Settings**.

Settings

The following table lists the constants for *updateFlag*.

Constant	Description
VtChNoDisplay	Absence of update flags; the chart display is not affected. (Defined as 0.)
VtChDisplayPlot	Update will cause the plot to repaint.
VtChLayoutPlot	Update will cause the plot to lay out.
VtChDisplayLegend	Update will cause the legend to repaint.
VtChLayoutLegend	Update will cause the legend to lay out.
VtChLayoutSeries	Update will cause the series to lay out.
VtChPositionSection	A chart section has been moved or resized.

Remarks

If row and column are nonzero, the change occurs to the indicated data cell.
If *labelRow* or *labelColumn*, along with *labelSetIndex*, are nonzero, the indicated
row or column label changes. If none of these are nonzero, no specific information
about the change is available.

DefaultPercentBasis Property

Returns the default axis percentage basis for the chart.

Applies To

Plot Object

Syntax

object.**DefaultPercentBasis**

The object placeholder represents an object expression that evaluates to an object in the **Applies To** list.

Return Value

The return value is an integer that specifies the default axis percentage basis.

DeleteColumnLabels Method

Deletes levels of labels from the data columns in a data grid associated with a chart.

Applies To

DataGrid Object

Syntax

object.**DeleteColumnLabels** (*labelIndex*, *count*)

The **DeleteColumnLabels** method syntax has these parts:

Part	Description
object	An object expression that evaluates to an object in the **Applies To** list.
LabelIndex	Integer. Identifies the number of the first level of labels you want to delete. Column label levels are numbered bottom to top, beginning with 1.
Count	Integer. Specifies the number of label levels you want to delete. The number of columns being deleted is calculated from the column identified in *labelIndex* up.

See Also

DeleteColumns Method, **DeleteRows** Method, **DeleteRowLabels** Method

DeleteColumns Method

Deletes columns of data and their associated labels from the data grid associated with a chart.

Applies To

DataGrid Object

Syntax

*object.***DeleteColumns** (*column, count*)

The **DeleteColumns** method syntax has these parts:

Part	Description
object	An object expression that evaluates to an object in the **Applies To** list.
column	Integer. Identifies a specific data column. Columns are numbered from left to right beginning with 1.
count	Integer. Specifies the number of columns you want to delete.

See Also

DeleteColumnLabels Method, **DeleteRows** Method, **DeleteRowLabels** Method

---

DeleteRowLabels Method

Deletes levels of labels from the data rows in a data grid associated with a chart.

Applies To

DataGrid Object

Syntax

*object.***DeleteRowLabels** (*labelIndex, count*)

The **DeleteRowLabels** method syntax has these parts:

Part	Description
object	An object expression that evaluates to an object in the **Applies To** list.
labelIndex	Integer. Identifies the number of the first level of labels you want to delete. Row labels are numbered right to left, beginning with 1.
count	Integer. Specifies the number of label levels you want to delete. Row labels are deleted from the row identified by *labelIndex* to the left.

See Also

DeleteColumns Method, **DeleteColumnLabels** Method, **DeleteRows** Method

DeleteRows Method

Deletes rows of data and their associated labels from the data grid associated with a chart.

Applies To

DataGrid Object

Syntax

*object.***DeleteRows** (*row*, *count*)

The **DeleteRows** method syntax has these parts:

Part	Description
object	An object expression that evaluates to an object in the **Applies To** list.
row	Integer. Identifies a specific data row. Rows are numbered from top to bottom beginning with 1.
count	Integer. Specifies the number of rows you want to delete.

See Also

DeleteColumns Method, **DeleteColumnLabels** Method, **DeleteRowLabels** Method

DepthToHeightRatio Property

Returns or sets the percentage of the chart height to be used as the chart depth.

Applies To

Plot Object

Syntax

*object.***DepthToHeightRatio** [= *pctg*]

The **DepthToHeightRatio** property syntax has these parts:

Part	Description
object	An object expression that evaluates to an object in the **Applies To** list.
pctg	Single. The chart height percentage.

DivisionsPerLabel Property

Returns or sets the number of divisions to skip between labels.

Applies To

CategoryScale Object

Syntax

*object.***DivisionsPerLabel** [= *num*]

The **DivisionsPerLabel** property syntax has these parts:

Part	Description
object	An object expression that evaluates to an object in the **Applies To** list.
num	Integer. An integer representing the number of divisions.

Remarks

If this property is set, the object's **Auto** property is automatically set to **False**.

See Also

Auto Property (CategoryScale), **DivisionsPerTick** Property

DivisionsPerTick Property

Returns or sets the number of divisions to skip between tick marks.

Applies To

CategoryScale Object

Syntax

*object.***DivisionsPerTick** [= *num*]

The **DivisionsPerTick** property syntax has these parts:

Part	Description
object	An object expression that evaluates to an object in the **Applies To** list.
num	Integer. An integer representing the number of divisions.

Remarks

If this property is set, the object's **Auto** property is automatically set to **False**.

See Also

Auto Property (CategoryScale), **DivisionsPerLabel** Property

DonePainting Event

Occurs immediately after the chart repaints or redraws.

Applies To

MSChart Control

Syntax

Private Sub *object_***DonePainting** ( )

The object placeholder represents an object expression that evaluates to an object in the **Applies To** list.

DoSetCursor Property

Returns or sets a value that indicates whether or not the cursor can be set by a chart. The **DoSetCursor** property determines whether or not the application can control what the mouse pointer looks like.

Applies To

MSChart Control

Syntax

*object.***DoSetCursor** [= *boolean*]

The **DoSetCursor** property syntax has these parts:

Part	Description
object	An object expression that evaluates to an object in the **Applies To** list.
boolean	A Boolean expression that specifies whether custom text is used, as described in **Settings**.

Settings

The settings for *boolean* are:

Setting	Description
True	The application can control the mouse pointer appearance.
False	The application cannot control the mouse pointer appearance.

DrawMode Constants

The **VtChDrawMode** constants provide options for redisplaying a chart after it has been altered.

Constants	Description
VtChDrawModeDraw	Draw mode. The chart is redrawn on the screen every time you change a setting.
VtChDrawModeBlit	Blit mode. The chart is redrawn off the screen and displayed after the redraw is complete.

Blit mode stores a bitmap copy of the chart in memory when the chart is laid out. Repainting the chart uses the bitmap and draws very quickly. It requires more memory than Draw mode, but can save time waiting for the chart to redraw on screen. Blit mode is particularly useful when working with charts that contain many elements.

DrawMode Property (MSChart)

Returns or sets a value that determines when and how a chart is repainted.

Applies To

MSChart Control

Syntax

*object.***DrawMode** [= *mode*]

The **DrawMode** property syntax has these parts:

Part	Description
object	An object expression that evaluates to an object in the **Applies To** list.
mode	Integer. A value that determines how and when the chart will be redrawn, as shown in **Settings**.

Settings

The settings for *mode* are:

Constant	Value	Description
VtChDrawModeDraw	0	Draws directly to the display device.
VtChDrawModeBlit	1	Blits an offscreen drawing to the display device.

EdgeIntensity Property

Returns or sets the intensity of light used to draw the edges of objects in a three-dimensional chart.

Applies To

Light Object

Syntax

*object.***EdgeIntensity** [= *edgeint*]

The **EdgeIntensity** property syntax has these parts:

Part	Description
object	An object expression that evaluates to an object in the **Applies To** list.
edgeint	Single. The edge light intensity. Valid values are 0 to 1.0. An intensity of 0 turns edges off, drawing the edges as black lines; and an intensity of 1 fully illuminates the edges using the element's pen color.

Remarks

If this property is set, then the **Light** object's **EdgeVisible** property is automatically set to **True**.

EdgePen Property

Returns the **Pen** object used to draw the edge of the data point on a chart.

Applies To

DataPoint Object

Syntax

object.**EdgePen**

The object placeholder represents an object expression that evaluates to an object in the **Applies To** list.

EdgeVisible Property

Returns or sets a value that determines whether edges are displayed on the elements in a three-dimensional chart.

Applies To

Light Object

Syntax

object.**EdgeVisible** [= *boolean*]

The **EdgeVisible** property syntax has these parts:

Part	Description
object	An object expression that evaluates to an object in the **Applies To** list.
boolean	A Boolean expression that specifies edges are displayed, as described in **Settings**.

Settings

The settings for *boolean* are:

Setting	Description
True	Edges are visible.
False	Edges are not displayed on elements in the three-dimensional chart.

EditCopy Method

Copies a picture of the current chart to the clipboard in Windows metafile format. It also copies the data being used to create the chart to the clipboard.

Applies To

MSChart Control

Syntax

object.**EditCopy**

The object placeholder represents an object expression that evaluates to an object in the **Applies To** list.

Remarks

This method allows you to paste the chart's data or a picture of the chart itself into another application. Since both the data and the picture of the chart are stored on the clipboard, what gets pasted into the new application varies depending on the type of application. For example, if you execute the chart's **EditCopy** method in your code and then go to an Excel spreadsheet and select **Edit Paste**, the chart data set is placed in the spreadsheet. To insert the picture of the chart into the spreadsheet, select **Edit Paste Special** and select the **Picture** type.

See Also

EditPaste Method

EditPaste Method

Pastes a Windows metafile graphic or tab-delimited text from the clipboard into the current selection on a chart.

Applies To

MSChart Control

Syntax

object.**EditPaste**

The object placeholder represents an object expression that evaluates to an object in the **Applies To** list.

Remarks

The chart can accept several types of information from the clipboard, depending on the currently selected chart element when **EditPaste** is called. If the entire chart is selected, the chart looks for data on the clipboard and attempts to use this new data to redraw the chart. If an item that can accept a picture, such as a bar or chart backdrop is selected, the chart looks for a metafile on the clipboard. If it finds a metafile, it uses that metafile to fill the selected object.

See Also

EditCopy Method

Effect Property

Returns or sets the font effects in a chart.

Applies To

VtFont Object

Syntax

object.**Effect** [= *effects*]

The **Effect** property syntax has these parts:

Part	Description
object	An object expression that evaluates to an object in the **Applies To** list.
effects	Integer. A **VtFontEffect** constant describing the font effect.

See Also

FontEffect Constants

Elevation Property

Returns or sets a value that describes the degree of elevation from which a three-dimensional chart is viewed.

Applies To

View3D Object

Syntax

object.**Elevation** [= *degree*]

The **Elevation** property syntax has these parts:

Part	Description
object	An object expression that evaluates to an object in the **Applies To** list.
degree	Single. The degree of elevation.
	Elevation can be any number from 0 to 90 degrees. If you set the elevation to 90 degrees, you look directly down onto the top of the chart. If you set the elevation to 0, you look directly at the side of the chart. The default elevation is 30 degrees. By default, degrees are used to measure elevation. However, these settings use the current settings for the **AngleUnits** property. The other options are: Grads and Radians.

Excluded Property

Returns or sets a value that determines whether a series is included on the chart.

Applies To

SeriesPosition Object

Syntax

*object.*__Excluded__ [= *boolean*]

The **Excluded** property syntax has these parts:

Part	Description
object	An object expression that evaluates to an object in the **Applies To** list.
boolean	A Boolean expression that controls whether a series is included on the chart, as described in **Settings**.

Settings

The settings for *boolean* are:

Setting	Description
True	The chart is drawn without including the series.
False	The series is included when the chart is drawn. A series may be included in a chart, but still not display because it is **Hidden.**

See Also

Hidden Property (MSChart)

Fill Object

Describes the type and appearance of an object's backdrop in a chart.

Syntax

Fill

Properties

Brush Property, **Style** Property (MSChart)

See Also

Brush Object, **Fill** Property

Example

The following example sets a gradient backdrop for a chart using the **Fill** object.

```
Private Sub Command1_Click()
   With MSChart1.backdrop.Fill
      ' Set a brush pattern backdrop.
      .Style = VtFillStyleBrush
      .Brush.Style. = VtBrushPattern50Percent
   End With
End Sub
```

Fill Property

Returns a reference to a **Fill** object that describes the type and appearance of a chart object's backdrop.

Applies To

Backdrop Object

Syntax

object.**Fill**

The object placeholder represents an object expression that evaluates to an object in the **Applies To** list.

FillColor Property

Returns a reference to a **VtColor** object that describes the color used to fill a chart element.

Applies To

Brush Object, **Marker** Object

Syntax

object.**FillColor**

The object placeholder represents an object expression that evaluates to an object in the **Applies To** list.

Remarks

If the **FillColor** property of the **Marker** object is set, then the **Marker** object's **Visible** property is automatically set to **True**.

Example

The following example sets the fill color for a chart backdrop brush. The FillColor property returns a reference to the VtColor object.

```
Private Sub Command1_Click()
' Sets Backdrop to Fill - Brush Style.
   MSChart1.Backdrop.Fill.Style = VtFillStyleBrush
   ' Sets chart fill color to red.
   With MSChart1.Backdrop.Fill.Brush.FillColor
      .Red = 255   ' Use properties to set color.
      .Green = 0
      .Blue = 0
   End With
End Sub
```

FillStyle Constants

The **VtFillStyle** constants provide options for indicating the type of fill used to paint a backdrop.

Constant	Description
VtFillStyleNull	No fill (background shows through)
VtFillStyleBrush	A solid color or pattern fill

See Also

Style Property (MSChart), **Visual Basic** Constants

Flag Property

Returns or sets which statistic lines are being displayed for a series.

Applies To

StatLine Object

Syntax

object.**Flag** [= *lines*]

The **Flag** property syntax has these parts:

Part	Description
object	An object expression that evaluates to an object in the **Applies To** list.
lines	Integer. A **VtChStats** constant used to describe the stat line. If more than one statistics line is displayed, the constants are combined with an OR operator.

See Also

StatsType Constants

Font Property (MSChart)

Returns a reference to a standard **Font** object that describes the font used to display text on the chart.

Applies To

AxisTitle Object, **DataPointLabel** Object, **Footnote** Object, **Label** Object (Item), **Legend** Object, **Title** Object

Syntax

object.**Font**

The object placeholder represents an object expression that evaluates to an object in the **Applies To** list.

FontEffect Constants

VtFontEffect provides methods of altering fonts for the desired effect.

Constant	Description
VtFontEffectStrikeThrough	Applies the strike-through attribute to the font.
VtFontEffectUnderline	Applies the underscore attribute to the font.

See Also

Effect Property), **Visual Basic** Constants

FontStyle Constants

VtFontStyle provides valid font attribute options.

Constant	Description
VtFontStyleBold	Applies the bold attribute to the font.
VtFontStyleItalic	Applies the italic attribute to the font.
VtFontStyleOutline	Applies the outline attribute to the font.

See Also

Style Property (MSChart), **Visual Basic** Constants

Footnote Object

Descriptive text that appears beneath a chart.

Syntax

Footnote

Properties

Text Property (MSChart), **TextLength** Property, **Backdrop** Property, **Font** Property (MSChart), **Location** Property, **TextLayout** Property, **VtFont** Property

Methods

Select Method

See Also

Backdrop Object, **Footnote** Property

Example

The following example sets the footnote location, text and color for a chart.

```
Private Sub Command1_Click()
```

```
With MSChart1.Footnote
    ' Make Footnote Visible.
    .Location.Visible = True
    .Location.LocationType = _
    VtChLocationTypeBottomLeft

    ' Set Footnote properties.
    .text = "Chart Footnote"
    .VtFont.VtColor.Set 255, 0, 0
End With

End Sub
```

Footnote Property

Returns a reference to a **Footnote** object that provides information about the descriptive text used to annotate a chart.

Applies To

MSChart Control

Syntax

object.**Footnote**

The object placeholder represents an object expression that evaluates to an object in the **Applies To** list.

See Also

Footnote Object

FootnoteActivated Event

Occurs when the user double clicks the chart footnote.

Applies To

MSChart Control

Syntax

Private Sub *object*_**FootnoteActivated** (*mouseFlag* **As Integer**, *cancel* **As Integer**)

The **FootnoteActivated** event syntax has these parts:

Part	Description
object	An object expression that evaluates to an object in the **Applies To** list.
mouseFlag	Integer. Indicates whether a key is held down when the mouse button is clicked, as described in **Settings**.
cancel	This argument is not used at this time.

Settings

The event handler determines if a key is held down when the mouse button is clicked and sets *mouseFlag* to:

Constants	Description
VtChMouseFlagShiftKeyDown	If the SHIFT key is held down.
VtChMouseFlagControlKeyDown	If the CONTROL key is held down.

See Also

FootnoteSelected Event, **FootnoteUpdated** Event

FootnoteSelected Event

Occurs when the user clicks the chart footnote.

Applies To

MSChart Control

Syntax

Private Sub *object*_**FootnoteSelected** (*mouseFlag* **As Integer**, *cancel* **As Integer**)

The **FootnoteSelected** event syntax has these parts:

Part	Description
object	An object expression that evaluates to an object in the **Applies To** list.
mouseFlag	Integer. Indicates whether a key is held down when the mouse button is clicked, as described in **Settings**.
cancel	This argument is not used at this time.

Settings

The event handler determines if a key is held down when the mouse button is clicked and sets *mouseFlag* to:

Constants	Description
VtChMouseFlagShiftKeyDown	If the SHIFT key is held down.
VtChMouseFlagControlKeyDown	If the CONTROL key is held down.

See Also

FootnoteActivated Event, **FootnoteUpdated** Event

FootnoteText Property

Returns or sets the text used as the footnote.

Applies To

MSChart Control

Syntax

object.**FootnoteText** [= *text*]

The **FootnoteText** property syntax has these parts:

Part	Description
object	An object expression that evaluates to an object in the **Applies To** list.
text	String. The footnote text.

Remarks

The same results can be achieved by using the **Text** property of the **Footnote** object.

FootnoteUpdated Event

Occurs when the chart footnote changes.

Applies To

MSChart Control

Syntax

Private Sub *object*_**FootnoteUpdated** (*updateFlags* **As Integer**)

The **FootnoteUpdated** event syntax has these parts:

Part	Description
object	An object expression that evaluates to an object in the **Applies To** list.
updateFlag	Integer. Provides information about the update of the footnote, as described in **Settings**.

Settings

The following table lists the constants for *updateFlag*.

Constant	Description
VtChNoDisplay	Absence of update flags; the chart display is not affected. (Defined as 0.)
VtChDisplayPlot	Update will cause the plot to repaint.
VtChLayoutPlot	Update will cause the plot to lay out.
VtChDisplayLegend	Update will cause the legend to repaint.
VtChLayoutLegend	Update will cause the legend to lay out.
VtChLayoutSeries	Update will cause the series to lay out.
VtChPositionSection	A chart section has been moved or resized.

See Also

FootnoteActivated Event, **FootnoteSelected** Event

Format Property (MSChart)

Returns or sets the characters that define the format used to display the axis label.

Applies To

Label Object (Item)

Syntax

object.**Format** [= *format*]

The **Format** property syntax has these parts:

Part	Description
object	An object expression that evaluates to an object in the **Applies To** list.
format	String. Defines the format used to display the axis label.

FormatLength Property

Returns the length of the format string.

Applies To

Label Object (Item)

Syntax

object.**FormatLength**

The object placeholder represents an object expression that evaluates to an object in the **Applies To** list.

Return Value

The return value is a string that specifies the axis label text string length.

Frame Object

Holds information about the appearance of the frame around a chart element.

Syntax

Frame

Properties

Style Property (MSChart), **Width** Property (MSChart), **FrameColor** Property, **SpaceColor** Property

See Also

Frame Property

Example

The following example sets a blue, double-line frame on a chart backdrop.

```
Private Sub Command1_Click()
    With MSChart1.backdrop.Frame
        .Style = VtFrameStyleDoubleLine
        .Width = 2
        .FrameColor.Set 0, 0, 255        ' Blue frame.
        .SpaceColor.Set 255, 0, 0        ' Red spacing.
    End With
End Sub
```

Frame Property

Returns a reference to a **Frame** object that describes the appearance of the frame around a chart element.

Applies To

Backdrop Object

Syntax

object.**Frame**

The object placeholder represents an object expression that evaluates to an object in the **Applies To** list.

See Also

Frame Object

FrameColor Property

Returns a reference to a **VtColor** object that specifies the color used to frame a chart element.

Applies To

Frame Object

Syntax

object.**FrameColor**

The object placeholder represents an object expression that evaluates to an object in the **Applies To** list.

See Also

SpaceColor Property

Example

The following example sets a blue, double-line frame on a chart backdrop.

```
Private Sub Command1_Click()
    With MSChart1.backdrop.Frame
        .Style = VtFrameStyleDoubleLine
        .Width = 2
        .FrameColor.Set 0, 0, 255        ' Blue frame.
        .SpaceColor.Set 255, 0, 0        ' Red spacing.
    End With
End Sub
```

FrameStyle Constants

The **VtFrameStyle** constants provide options for displaying backdrop frames.

Constant	Description
VtFrameStyleNull	No frame.
VtFrameStyleSingleLine	A single line encloses the backdrop.
VtFrameStyleDoubleLine	Two equal width lines enclose the backdrop.
VtFrameStyleThickInner	A thick inner line and a thin outer line enclose the backdrop.
VtFrameStyleThickOuter	A thin inner line and a thick outer line enclose the backdrop.

See Also

Style Property (MSChart), **Frame** Property, **Frame** Object, **FrameColor** Property, **Visual Basic** Constants

GetData Method (MSChart)

Returns the value currently stored in a specific data point in the data grid associated with a chart.

Applies To

DataGrid Object

Syntax

object.**GetData** (*row, column, dataPoint, nullFlag*)

The **GetData** method syntax has these parts:

Part	Description
object	An object expression that evaluates to an object in the **Applies To** list.
row	Integer. Identifies the row containing the data point value.
column	Integer. Identifies the column containing the data point value.
dataPoint	Double. The data point value.
nullFlag	Integer. Indicates whether or not the data point value is a null.

GetSelectedPart Method

Identifies the currently selected chart element.

Applies To

MSChart Control

Syntax

object.**GetSelectedPart** (*part*, *index1*, *index2*, *index3*, *index4*)

The **GetSelectedPart** method syntax has these parts:

Part	Description
object	An object expression that evaluates to an object in the **Applies To** list.
part	Integer. Specifies the chart element. Valid constants are **VtChPartType**.
index1	Integer. If element refers to a series or a data point, this argument specifies which series. Series are numbered in the order their corresponding columns appear in the data grid from left to right, beginning with 1. If element refers to an axis or axis label, this argument identifies the axis type with a **VtChAxisId** constant.
Index2	Integer. If element refers to a data point, this argument specifies which data point in the series identified by index1.
index3	Integer. If element refers to an axis label, this argument refers to the level of the label. Axis label levels are numbered from the axis out, beginning with 1. If element is not an axis label, the argument is unused.
index4	Integer. This argument is unused at this time.

See Also

AxisId Constants, **PartType** Constants

Green Property

Returns or sets the green component of the RGB value in a chart.

Applies To

VtColor Object

Syntax

object.**Green** [=*g*]

The **Green** property syntax has these parts:

Part	Description
object	An object expression that evaluates to an object in the **Applies To** list.
g	Integer. The green value.

Remarks

RGB specifies the relative intensity of red, green, and blue to cause a specific color to be displayed. The valid range for a normal RGB color is 0 to 16,777,215. The value for any argument to RGB that exceeds 255 is assumed to be 255.

GuidelinePen Property

Returns a reference to a **Pen** object that describes the pattern of line and color used to display guidelines.

Applies To

Series Object

Syntax

object.**GuidelinePen**

The object placeholder represents an object expression that evaluates to an object in the **Applies To** list.

Remarks

Setting this property automatically sets the **ShowGuideLines** property to **True**.

Example

The following example sets the pen attributes for a two-dimensional xy chart series. The GuideLinePen property returns a reference to a Pen object.

```
Private Sub Command1_Click()
   ' Set Guide Lines for 2D XY chart Series 1.
   MSChart1.ChartType = VtChChartType2dXY
   MSChart1.Plot.SeriesCollection.Item(1) _
   .ShowGuideLine(VtChAxisIdX) = True
   With _
   MSChart1.Plot.SeriesCollection.Item(1).GuideLinePen
      ' Set Pen attributes.
      .VtColor.Set 255, 255, 0
      .Width = 10
      .Style = VtPenStyleDashDot
      .Join = VtPenRound
      .Cap = VtPenCapRound
   End With
End Sub
```

Hidden Property (MSChart)

Returns or sets a value that determines whether a series is displayed on the chart.

Applies To

SeriesPosition Object

Syntax

object.**Hidden** [= *boolean*]

The **Hidden** property syntax has these parts:

Part	Description
object	An object expression that evaluates to an object in the **Applies To** list.
boolean	A Boolean expression that controls whether a series is displayed on the chart, as described in **Settings**.

Settings

The settings for *boolean* are:

Setting	Description
True	The chart is drawn without displaying the series. However, any space allocated for the series still exists.
False	The series is displayed.

Hide Property

Returns or sets a value that determines whether the axis on a chart is hidden.

Applies To

AxisScale Object

Syntax

object.**Hide** [= *boolean*]

The **Hide** property syntax has these parts:

Part	Description
object	An object expression that evaluates to an object in the **Applies To** list.
boolean	A Boolean expression that specifies whether the axis is hidden, as described in **Settings**.

Settings

The settings for *boolean* are:

Setting	Description
True	The axis scale, line, ticks and title are hidden.
False	The axis appears on the chart.

HorizontalAlignment Constants

The **VtHorizontalAlignment** constants provide options for text alignment.

Constant	Description
VtHorizontalAlignmentLeft	All lines of text are aligned on the left margin.
VtHorizontalAlignmentRight	All lines of text are aligned on the right margin.
VtHorizontalAlignmentCenter	All lines of text are centered horizontally.

See Also

HorzAlignment Property, **Visual Basic** Constants

HorzAlignment Property

Returns or sets the method of horizontal alignment of text.

Applies To

TextLayout Object

Syntax

*object.***HorzAlignment** [= *type*]

The **HorzAlignment** property syntax has these parts:

Part	Description
object	An object expression that evaluates to an object in the **Applies To** list.
type	Integer. A **VtHorizontalAlignment** constant used to describe the horizontal alignment method of text.

See Also

HorizontalAlignment Constants

Index Property (Brush)

Returns or sets the pattern or hatch used in the brush if its **Style** property is set to **VtBrushStylePattern** or **VtBrushStyleHatch**.

Applies To

Brush Object

Syntax

*object.***Index** [= *num*]

The **Index** property syntax has these parts:

Part	Description
object	An object expression that evaluates to an object in the **Applies To** list.
num	A **VtBrushPattern** constant or **VtBrushHatch** constant describing the brush pattern.

See Also

BrushPattern Constants, **BrushHatch** Constants, **Index** Property (Intersection)

Index Property (Intersection)

Returns which axis intersects another axis when there is more than one axis with the same index.

Applies To

Intersection Object

Syntax

object.**Index**

The object placeholder represents an object expression that evaluates to an object in the **Applies To** list.

Return Value

The return value is an integer that specifies the index of the intersecting axis. Currently, 1 is the only valid value for this argument.

See Also

Index Property (Brush)

InitializeLabels Method

Assigns each label in the first level of data grid labels a unique identifier.

Applies To

DataGrid Object

Syntax

object.**InitializeLabels**

The *object* placeholder represents an object expression that evaluates to an object in the **Applies To** list.

InsertColumnLabels Method

Inserts levels of labels for the data columns in a data grid associated with a chart.

Applies To

DataGrid Object

Syntax

object.**InsertColumnLabels** (*labelIndex, count*)

The **InsertColumnLabels** method syntax has these parts:

Part	Description
object	An object expression that evaluates to an object in the **Applies To** list.
labelIndex	Integer. Identifies the number of the first level of labels you want to insert. Column label levels are numbered bottom to top, beginning with 1.
count	Integer. Specifies the number of label levels you want to insert. The number of columns being inserted is calculated from the column identified in *labelIndex* up.

See Also

InsertColumns Method, **InsertRows** Method, **InsertRowLabels** Method

---

InsertColumns Method

Adds one or more data columns to the data grid associated with a chart.

Applies To

DataGrid Object

Syntax

object.**InsertColumns** (*column, count*)

The **InsertColumns** method syntax has these parts:

Part	Description
object	An object expression that evaluates to an object in the **Applies To** list.
column	Integer. Identifies a specific data column. Columns are numbered from left to right beginning with 1.
count	Integer. Specifies the number of columns you want to insert.

See Also

InsertColumnLabels Method, **InsertRows** Method, **InsertRowLabels** Method

InsertRowLabels Method

Inserts levels of labels from the data rows in a data grid associated with a chart.

Applies To

DataGrid Object

Syntax

object.**InsertRowLabels** (*labelIndex, count*)

The **InsertRowLabels** method syntax has these parts:

Part	Description
object	An object expression that evaluates to an object in the **Applies To** list.
labelIndex	Integer. Identifies the number of the first level of labels you want to insert. Row labels are numbered right to left, beginning with 1.
count	Integer. Specifies the number of label levels you want to insert. Row labels are inserted from the row identified by *labelIndex* to the left.

See Also

InsertColumns Method, **InsertColumnLabels** Method, **InsertRows** Method

---

InsertRows Method

Adds one or more data rows to the data grid associated with a chart.

Applies To

DataGrid Object

Syntax

object.**InsertRows** (*row, count*)

The **InsertRows** method syntax has these parts:

Part	Description
object	An object expression that evaluates to an object in the **Applies To** list.
row	Integer. Identifies a specific data row. Rows are numbered from top to bottom beginning with 1.
count	Integer. Specifies the number of rows you want to insert. Rows contain null data until you fill them with data.

See Also

InsertColumns Method, **InsertColumnLabels** Method, **InsertRowLabels** Method

Intensity Property

Returns or sets the strength of the light coming from the light source.

Applies To

LightSource Object

Syntax

*object.***Intensity** [= *strength*]

The **Intensity** property syntax has these parts:

Part	Description
object	An object expression that evaluates to an object in the **Applies To** list.
strength	Single. The light strength. If the intensity is set to 100 percent (1), chart surfaces facing the light source are fully illuminated. If the light is set at 50 percent (.5), these surfaces receive 50 percent illumination from this light. Valid range is 0 to 1.

Remarks

Intensity is the default property of the **LightSource** object.

Intersection Object

The point at which an axis intersects an intersecting axis on a chart.

Syntax

Intersection

Properties

Auto Property (Intersection), **AxisId** Property, **Index** Property (Intersection), **LabelsInsidePlot** Property, **Point** Property

See Also

Intersection Property

Example

The following example sets manual intersection position properties and displays labels with the axis.

```
Private Sub Command1_Click()
   ' Change chart type to 3D Line.
   MSChart1.ChartType = VtChChartType3dLine
   With MSChart1.Plot.Axis(VtChAxisIdX).Intersection
      ' Set Intersection Properties.
      .Auto = False                  ' Set positioning to manual.
      .Point = 20                    ' Set intersection with the Y
                                     ' Axis to 20.
      .LabelsInsidePlot = True       ' Display Labels with
                                     ' Axis not at the base.
   End With
End Sub
```

Intersection Property

Returns a reference to an **Intersection** object that describes the point at which an axis intersects another axis on a chart.

Applies To

Axis Object

Syntax

object.**Intersection**

The object placeholder represents an object expression that evaluates to an object in the **Applies To** list.

See Also

Intersection Object

Item Property (MSChart)

Returns a reference to an object within a collection that describes a chart element.

Applies To

DataPoints Collection, **Labels** Collection, **LightSources** Collection, **SeriesCollection** Collection

Syntax

object.**Item** (*index*)

Join Property

Returns or sets a value that determines how line segments are formed.

Applies To

Pen Object

Syntax

object.**Join** [= *type*]

The **Join** property syntax has these parts:

Part	Description
object	An object expression that evaluates to an object in the **Applies To** list.
type	Integer. A **VtPenJoin** constant that describes the style of pen join.

See Also

PenJoin Constants

Label Object (Item)

An item within a **Labels** collection that describes a specific chart axis label.

Syntax

axis.**Label**

Properties

Backdrop Property, **Font** Property (MSChart), **Auto** Property (Label), **Format** Property (MSChart), **FormatLength** Property, **Standing** Property, **TextLayout** Property, **VtFont** Property

See Also

Labels Property, **Labels** Collection

LabelComponent Constants

The **VtChLabelComponent** constants provide options for displaying chart labels.

Constant	Description
VtChLabelComponentValue	The value of the data point appears in the label. Data points in XY, Polar, and Bubble charts actually have two or three values. The default label for these chart types display all values in a standard format. You can customize this format to highlight an individual data value.
VtChLabelComponentPercent	The value of the data point is displayed in the label as a percentage of the total value of the series.
VtChLabelComponentSeriesName	The series name is used to label the data point. This name is taken from the label associated with the column in the data grid.
VtChLabelComponentPointName	The data point name is used to label the data point.

See Also

Component Property, **Visual Basic** Constants

LabelLevelCount Property

Returns or sets the number of levels of labels for a given axis.

Applies To

MSChart Control, **Axis** Object

Syntax

object.**LabelLevelCount** [= *count*]

The **LabelLevelCount** property syntax has these parts:

Part	Description
object	An object expression that evaluates to an object in the **Applies To** list.
count	Integer. An integer that describes the number of labels.

LabelLineStyle Constants

The **VtChLabelLineStyle** constants provide options for displaying lines connecting a label and series.

The following table lists the valid constants for **VtChLabelLineStyle:**

Constants	Description
VtChLabelLineStyleNone	No line connects the label and series.
VtChLabelLineStyleStraight	A straight line connects the label and series.
VtChLabelLineStyleBent	A bent line connects the label and series.

See Also

LineStyle Property, **Visual Basic** Constants

LabelLocationType Constants

The **VtChLabelLocationType** constants provide options for determining series label location.

The following table lists the valid constants for **VtChLabelLocationType:**

Constants	Description
VtChLabelLocationTypeNone	No label displayed.
VtChLabelLocationTypeAbovePoint	The label is displayed above the data point.
VtChLabelLocationTypeBelowPoint	The label is displayed below the data point.
VtChLabelLocationTypeCenter	The label is displayed centered on the data point.
VtChLabelLocationTypeBase	The label is displayed at the base along the category axis, directly beneath the data point.
VtChLabelLocationTypeInside	The label is displayed inside a pie slice.
VtChLabelLocationTypeOutside	The label is displayed outside a pie slice.
VtChLabelLocationTypeLeft	The label is displayed to the left of the data point.
VtChLabelLocationTypeRight	The label is displayed to the right of the data point.

Labels Collection

A group of chart axis labels.

Syntax

axis.**Labels**(*index*)

The **Labels** collection syntax has these parts:

Part	Description
axis	An **Axis** object.
index	Identifies a specific axis label (**Label** object) within the current collection.

Properties

Item Property (MSChart), **Count** Property

See Also

Labels Property, **Label** Object (Item)

Labels Property

Returns a reference to a **Labels** collection that describes the labels on a chart axis.

Applies To

Axis Object

Syntax

object.**Labels**

The object placeholder represents an object expression that evaluates to an object in the **Applies To** list.

See Also

Labels Collection, **Label** Object (Item)

LabelsInsidePlot Property

Returns or sets a value that determines whether to leave the axis labels at the normal location or move them with the axis to the new intersection point.

Applies To

Intersection Object

Syntax

object.**LabelsInsidePlot** [= *boolean*]

The **LabelsInsidePlot** property syntax has these parts:

Part	Description
object	An object expression that evaluates to an object in the **Applies To** list.
boolean	A Boolean expression that specifies where to display the axis labels, as described in **Settings**.

Settings

The settings for *boolean* are:

Setting	Description
True	The axis labels remain at the normal location.
False	The labels move inside the plot to the new intersection point.

Remarks

If this property is set, then the **Intersection** object's **Auto** property is automatically set to **False**.

LabelTick Property

Returns or sets a value that indicates whether category axis labels are centered on an axis tick mark.

Applies To

CategoryScale Object

Syntax

object.**LabelTicks** [= *boolean*]

The **LabelTicks** property syntax has these parts:

Part	Description
object	An object expression that evaluates to an object in the **Applies To** list.
boolean	A Boolean expression that specifies whether the item is displayed, as described in **Settings**.

Settings

The settings for *boolean* are:

Setting	Description
True	The labels are centered on a tick mark.
False	The labels are centered between two tick marks.

Remarks

If this property is set, the object's **Auto** property is automatically set to **False**.

See Also

Auto Property (CategoryScale)

Layout Method

Lays out a chart, forcing recalculation of automatic values.

Applies To

MSChart Control

Syntax

object.**Layout**

The object placeholder represents an object expression that evaluates to an object in the **Applies To** list.

Remarks

A chart is laid out the first time it is drawn. When any chart settings change, the chart is again laid out at the next draw. There are a number of settings the chart calculates, such as the axis minimum and maximum values, based on the chart type or some other setting. These values are not determined until the chart is laid out. If you attempt to "get" these automatic values before the chart is properly laid out, they will not reflect the new values.

LCoor Object

Describes a long integer x and y coordinate pair.

Syntax

Lcoor

Properties

X Property, **Y** Property

Methods

Set Method (MSChart)

See Also

Coor Object

Legend Object

Represents the graphical key and accompanying text that describes a chart series.

Syntax

Legend

Properties

Backdrop Property, **Font** Property (MSChart), **Location** Property, **TextLayout** Property, **VtFont** Property

Methods

Select Method

See Also

Backdrop Object, **Legend** Property

Example

The following example sets the text and backdrop parameters for a chart legend.

```
Private Sub Command1_Click()
    With MSChart1.Legend
        ' Make Legend Visible.
        .Location.Visible = True
        .Location.LocationType = VtChLocationTypeRight
        ' Set Legend properties.
        .TextLayout.HorzAlignment = _
        VtHorizontalAlignmentRight      ' Right justify.
        ' Use Yellow text.
        .VtFont.VtColor.Set 255, 255, 0
        .Backdrop.Fill.Style = VtFillStyleBrush
        .Backdrop.Fill.Brush.Style = VtBrushStyleSolid
        .Backdrop.Fill.Brush.FillColor.Set 255, 0, 255
    End With
End Sub
```

Legend Property

Returns a reference to a **Legend** object that contains information about the appearance and behavior of the graphical key and accompanying text that describes the chart series.

Applies To

MSChart Control

Syntax

object.**Legend**

The object placeholder represents an object expression that evaluates to an object in the **Applies To** list.

LegendActivated Event

Occurs when the user double clicks on the chart legend.

Applies To

MSChart Control

Syntax

Private Sub *object*_**LegendActivated** (*mouseFlag* **As Integer**, *cancel* **As Integer**)

The **LegendActivated** event syntax has these parts:

Part	Description
object	An object expression that evaluates to an object in the **Applies To** list.
mouseFlag	Integer. Indicates whether a key is held down when the mouse button is clicked, as described in **Settings**.
cancel	Integer. This argument is not used at this time.

Settings

The event handler determines if a key is held down when the mouse button is clicked and sets *mouseFlag* to:

Constants	Description
VtChMouseFlagShiftKeyDown	If the SHIFT key is held down.
VtChMouseFlagControlKeyDown	If the CONTROL key is held down.

LegendSelected Event

Occurs when the user clicks on the chart legend.

Applies To

MSChart Control

Syntax

Private Sub *object*_**LegendSelected** (*mouseFlag* **As Integer**, *cancel* **As Integer**)

The **LegendSelected** event syntax has these parts:

Part	Description
object	An object expression that evaluates to an object in the **Applies To** list.
mouseFlag	Integer. Indicates whether a key is held down when the mouse button is clicked.
cancel	Integer. This argument is not used at this time.

Settings

The event handler determines if a key is held down when the mouse button is clicked and sets *mouseFlag* to:

Constants	Description
VtChMouseFlagShiftKeyDown	If the SHIFT key is held down.
VtChMouseFlagControlKeyDown	If the CONTROL key is held down.

LegendText Property

Returns or sets the text that identifies the series in the legend of a chart.

Applies To

Series Object

Syntax

object.**LegendText** [= *text*]

The **LegendText** property syntax has these parts:

Part	Description
object	An object expression that evaluates to an object in the **Applies To** list.
text	String. The text that identifies the current series in the legend.

Remarks

By default, this text is the same as the **Text** property of the **ColumnLabel** object.

LegendUpdated Event

Occurs when the chart legend has changed.

Applies To

MSChart Control

Syntax

Private Sub *object*_**LegendUpdated** (*updateFlags* **As Integer**)

The **LegendUpdated** event syntax has these parts:

Part	Description
object	An object expression that evaluates to an object in the **Applies To** list.
updateFlag	Integer. Provides information about the update of the legend, as described in **Settings**.

Settings

The following table lists the constants for *updateFlag*.

Constant	Description
VtChNoDisplay	Absence of update flags; the chart display is not affected. (Defined as 0.)
VtChDisplayPlot	Update will cause the plot to repaint.
VtChLayoutPlot	Update will cause the plot to lay out.
VtChDisplayLegend	Update will cause the legend to repaint.
VtChLayoutLegend	Update will cause the legend to lay out.
VtChLayoutSeries	Update will cause the series to lay out.
VtChPositionSection	A chart section has been moved or resized.

Length Property (MSChart)

Returns or sets the length of axis tick marks, measured in points.

Applies To

Tick Object

Syntax

object.**Length** [= *length*]

The **Length** property syntax has these parts:

Part	Description
object	An object expression that evaluates to an object in the **Applies To** list.
length	Integer. The axis tick mark length.

Light Object

Represents the light source illuminating a three-dimensional chart.

Syntax

Light

Properties

AmbientIntensity Property, **EdgeIntensity** Property, **EdgeVisible** Property, **LightSources** Property

Methods

Set Method (MSChart)

See Also

LightSources Collection, **LightSource** Object, **Z** Property

Example

The following example sets the ambient light and edge lighting intensity for a chart.

```
Private Sub Command1_Click()
    ' Changes the Lighting for 3D Chart.
    MSChart1.ChartType = VtChChartType3dBar
    With MSChart1.Plot.Light
        .AmbientIntensity = 1    ' 100 % Intensity.
        .EdgeIntensity = 0.5     ' 50 % Intensity.
        .EdgeVisible = True
    End With
End Sub
```

Light Property

Returns a reference to a **Light** object that provides information about the light illuminating a three-dimensional chart.

Applies To

Plot Object

Syntax

object.**Light**

The object placeholder represents an object expression that evaluates to an object in the **Applies To** list.

LightSource Object

Represents the light source used to illuminate elements in a three-dimensional chart.

Syntax

LightSource

Properties

X Property, **Y** Property, **Z** Property, **Intensity** Property

Methods

Set Method (MSChart)

LightSources Collection

A group of **LightSource** objects in a chart.

Syntax

LightSources(*index*)

The **LightSources** collection syntax has the following parts:

Part	Description
index	Integer. A number that uniquely identifies a member of the collection.

Properties

Item Property (MSChart)

Methods

Add Method (MSChart), **Remove** Method (MSChart)

Example

The following example sets the coordinates and intensity for a light source, then adds and removes a light source from a chart.

```
Private Sub Command1_Click()
    Dim LightSource As Object
    Dim Index As Integer
    ' Set variable to Light Source 1.
    Set LightSource = _
    MSChart1.Plot.Light.LightSources.Item(1)
    ' Set coordinates for Light Source 1 as well as its
    ' intensity.
    LightSource.X = 1
    LightSource.Y = 0.5
    LightSource.Z = 1
    LightSource.Intensity = 1
    ' Add a new light source.
    MSChart1.Plot.Light.LightSources.Add 0.5, 1, 1, 1
    ' Remove Light Source 1.

MSChart1.Plot.Light.LightSources.Remove (1)
End Sub
```

LightSources Property

Returns a reference to a **LightSources** collection that describe all light sources used to illuminate a three-dimensional chart.

Applies To

Light Object

Syntax

object.**LightSources**

The object placeholder represents an object expression that evaluates to an object in the **Applies To** list.

See Also

LightSources Collection

Limit Property

Returns or sets the joint limit, in points, of the line.

Applies To

Pen Object

Syntax

object.**Limit** [= *joint*]

The **Limit** property syntax has these parts:

Part	Description
object	An object expression that evaluates to an object in the **Applies To** list.
joint	Single. A joint limit as a multiple of the line width. If two lines meet at a sharp angle, a mitered join results in a corner point that extends beyond the actual corner. If the distance from the inner join point to the outer join point exceeds the value in this variable, the join automatically changes to a bevel.

LineStyle Property

Returns or sets the type of line used to connect a data point to a label on a chart.

Applies To

DataPointLabel Object

Syntax

object.**LineStyle** [= *type*]

The **LineStyle** property syntax has these parts:

Part	Description
object	An object expression that evaluates to an object in the **Applies To** list.
type	Integer. A **VtChLabelLineStyle** constant identifying the connecting line.

See Also

LabelLineStyle Constants

Location Object

Represents the current position of a textual chart element such as the title, legend, or footnote.

Syntax

Location

The object placeholder represents an object expression that evaluates to an object in the **Applies To** list.

Properties

Visible Property (MSChart), **LocationType** Property, **Rect** Property

See Also

Footnote Object, **Legend** Object, **Title** Object

Example

The following example sets the title location for a chart using the **TitleLocation** object.

```
Private Sub Command1_Click()
    ' Set Title Text.
    MSChart1.TitleText = "Test Title Location"
    With MSChart1.Title.Location
        ' Make Title Visible.
        .Visible = True
        ' Use Top Left locaiton to display the title.
        .LocationType = VtChLocationTypeTopLeft
    End With
End Sub
```

Location Property

Returns a reference to a **Location** object that describes the position of textual chart elements.

Applies To

Footnote Object, **Legend** Object, **Title** Object

Syntax

object.**Location**

The object placeholder represents an object expression that evaluates to an object in the **Applies To** list.

See Also

Location Object

LocationRect Property

Returns a reference to a **Rect** object that specifies the location of the chart plot using x and y coordinates.

Applies To

Plot Object

Syntax

object.**LocationRect**

The object placeholder represents an object expression that evaluates to an object in the **Applies To** list.

Remarks

The values of this property are used to position the plot if **AutoLayout** is **False.**

If this property is set, then the **AutoLayout** property is automatically set to **False**.

Example

The following example sets the location of the chart plot using the **LocationRect** property that returns the **Rect** object.

```
Private Sub Command1_Click()
    ' Sets the location of the chart plot.
    MSChart1.Plot.AutoLayout = False
    With MSChart1.Plot.LocationRect
        .Min.X = 0.4
        .Min.Y = 0.4
        .Max.X = 0.5
        .Max.Y = 0.5
    End With
End Sub
```

LocationType Constants

VtChLocationType provides location options for chart elements.

Constant	Example
VtChLocationTypeTop	Top
VtChLocationTypeTopLeft	Top Left
VtChLocationTypeTopRight	Top Right
VtChLocationTypeLeft	Left
VtChLocationTypeRight	Right
VtChLocationTypeBottom	Bottom
VtChLocationTypeBottomLeft	Bottom Left
VtChLocationTypeBottomRight	Bottom Right
VtChLocationTypeCustom	Custom

See Also

LocationType Property, **Visual Basic** Constants

LocationType Property

Returns or sets the standard position used to display a chart element.

Applies To

DataPointLabel Object, **Location** Object

Syntax

object.**LocationType** [*=type*]

The **LocationType** property syntax has these parts:

Part	Description
object	An object expression that evaluates to an object in the **Applies To** list.
type	Integer. For the **DataPointLabel** object, A **VtChLabelLocationType** constant identifying label position.
	For a **Location** object, A **VtChLocationType** constant describing the location of text.

See Also

LocationType Constants

LogBase Property

Returns or sets the logarithm base used to plot chart values on a logarithmic axis.

Applies To

AxisScale Object

Syntax

object.**LogBase** [= *base*]

The **LogBase** property syntax has these parts:

Part	Description
object	An object expression that evaluates to an object in the **Applies To** list.
base	Integer. An integer that identifies the logarithm base. The default base is 10. The valid range is 2 to 100.

Remarks

The axis type is controlled by the **Type** property.

MajorDivision Property

Returns or sets the number of major divisions displayed on the axis.

Applies To

ValueScale Object

Syntax

object.**MajorDivision** [= *num*]

The **MajorDivision** property syntax has these parts:

Part	Description
object	An object expression that evaluates to an object in the **Applies To** list.
num	Integer. Number of divisions.

Remarks

If this property is set, then the **ValueScale** object's **Auto** property is automatically set to **False**.

See Also

MinorDivision Property

MajorPen Property

Returns a reference to a **Pen** object that describes the appearance of the major axis grid lines.

Applies To

AxisGrid Object

Syntax

object.**MajorPen**

The object placeholder represents an object expression that evaluates to an object in the **Applies To** list.

See Also

MinorPen Property

Marker Object

A marker that identifies a data point on a chart.

Syntax

Marker

Properties

Visible Property (MSChart), **FillColor** Property, **Style** Property (MSChart), **Size** Property (MSChart), **Pen** Property

See Also

DataPoint Object

Example

The following example sets a blue X marker style for a chart series.

```
Private Sub Command1_Click()
    ' Display Markers for Series 1.
    For Index = 1 To MSChart1.rowCount
        With MSChart1.Plot.SeriesCollection _
        .Item(1).DataPoints.Item(Index).Marker
            .Visible = True
            .Size = 20
```

```
            .Style = VtMarkerStyleX
            .FillColor.automatic = False
            .FillColor.Set 0, 0, 255
        End With
    Next Index
End Sub
```

Marker Property

Returns a reference to a **Marker** object that describes the icon used to identify a data point on a chart.

Applies To

DataPoint Object

Syntax

object.**Marker**

The object placeholder represents an object expression that evaluates to an object in the **Applies To** list.

MarkerStyle Constants

The **VtMarkerStyle** constants provide options for displaying data point markers.

Constant	Description
VtMarkerStyleNull	Supressed
VtMarkerStyleDash	Dash marker
VtMarkerStylePlus	Plus marker
VtMarkerStyleX	X marker
VtMarkerStyleStar	Star marker
VtMarkerStyleCircle	Circle marker
VtMarkerStyleSquare	Square marker
VtMarkerStyleDiamond	Diamond marker
VtMarkerStyleUpTriangle	Triangle marker
VtMarkerStyleDownTriangle	Down triangle marker
VtMarkerStyleFilledCircle	Filled circle marker
VtMarkerStyleFilledSquare	Filled square marker
VtMarkerStyleFilledDiamond	Filled diamond marker
VtMarkerStyleFilledUpTriangle	Filled triangle marker
VtMarkerStyleFilledDownTriangle	Filled down triangle marker
VtMarkerStyle3dBall	Three-dimensional ball marker

Style Property (MSChart), **Visual Basic** Constants

Max Property (MSChart)

Returns a reference to a **Coor** object that specifies the ending corner of a rectangle.

Applies To

Rect Object

Syntax

*object.***Max**

The object placeholder represents an object expression that evaluates to an object in the **Applies To** list.

See Also

Min Property (MSChart)

Maximum Property

Returns or sets the highest or ending value on the chart value axis.

Applies To

ValueScale Object

Syntax

*object.***Maximum** [= *value*]

The **Maximum** property syntax has these parts:

Part	Description
object	An object expression that evaluates to an object in the **Applies To** list.
value	Double. The highest axis value.

Remarks

If this property is set, then the **ValueScale** object's **Auto** property is automatically set to **False**.

The **Maximum** property should be set before the **Minimum** property to avoid a chart display error.

See Also

Minimum Property

Min Property (MSChart)

Returns a reference to a **Coor** object that specifies the starting corner of a rectangle.

Applies To

Rect Object

Syntax

object.**Min**

The object placeholder represents an object expression that evaluates to an object in the **Applies To** list.

See Also

Max Property (MSChart)

Minimum Property

Returns or sets the lowest or beginning value on the chart value axis.

Applies To

ValueScale Object

Syntax

object.**Minimum** [= *value*]

The **Minimum** property syntax has these parts:

Part	Description
object	An object expression that evaluates to an object in the **Applies To** list.
value	Double. The lowest axis value.

Remarks

If this property is set, then the **ValueScale** object's **Auto** property is automatically set to **False**.

The **Maximum** property should be set before the **Minimum** property to avoid a chart display error.

See Also

MajorDivision Property

MinorDivision Property

Returns or sets the number of minor divisions displayed on the axis.

Applies To

ValueScale Object

Syntax

object.**MinorDivision** [= *num*]

The **MinorDivision** property syntax has these parts:

Part	Description
object	An object expression that evaluates to an object in the **Applies To** list.
num	Integer. Number of minor divisions.

Remarks

If this property is set, then the **ValueScale** object's **Auto** property is automatically set to **False**.

MinorPen Property

Returns a reference to a **Pen** object that describes the appearance of the minor axis grid lines.

Applies To

AxisGrid Object

Syntax

object.**MinorPen**

The object placeholder represents an object expression that evaluates to an object in the **Applies To** list.

See Also

MajorPen Property

MouseFlag Constants

VtChMouseFlag indicates which keyboard key is being held down while the mouse button is clicked.

Constant	Description
VtChMouseFlagShiftKeyDown	The SHIFT key is held down when the mouse button is clicked.
VtChMouseFlagControlKeyDown	The CONTROL key is held down when the mouse button is clicked.

MousePointer Constants

The **VtMousePointer** constants provide the following types of pointers.

Constant	Description
VtMousePointerArrow	Arrow pointer
VtMousePointerArrowHourGlass	Arrow and hourglass
VtMousePointerArrowQuestion	Arrow and question mark
VtMousePointerCross	Crosshair pointer
VtMousePointerDefault	Default chart pointer
VtMousePointerHourGlass	Hourglass pointer
VtMousePointerIbeam	Ibeam pointer
VtMousePointerIcon	Small square within a square pointer
VtMousePointerNoDrop	No drop pointer
VtMousePointerSize	Sizing arrows
VtMousePointerSizeAll	Sizing in all directions arrows
VtMousePointerSizeNESW	Double arrow pointing northeast and southwest
VtMousePointerNS	Double arrow pointing north and south
VtMousePointerNWSE	Double arrow pointing northwest and southeast
VtMousePointerWE	Double arrow pointing east and west
VtMousePointerUpArrow	Arrow pointing up

See Also

MousePointer Property (MSChart), **Visual Basic** Constants)

MousePointer Property (MSChart)

Returns or sets a *value* indicating the type of mouse pointer displayed when the mouse is over a particular part of an object at run time.

Applies To

MSChart Control

Syntax

object.**MousePointer** [= *value*]

The **MousePointer** property syntax has these parts:

Part	Description
object	An object expression that evaluates to an object in the **Applies To** list.
value	Integer. A **VtMousePointerConstants** type constant that specifies the type of mouse pointer displayed.

See Also

MousePointer Constants

MoveData Method

Moves a range of data within a data grid associated with a chart.

Applies To

DataGrid Object

Syntax

object.**MoveData** (*top*, *left*, *bottom*, *right*, *overOffset*, *downOffset*)

The **MoveData** method syntax has these parts:

Part	Description
object	An object expression that evaluates to an object in the **Applies To** list.
top	Integer. Identifies the first row in the range to move.
left	Integer. Identifies the first column in the range to move.
bottom	Integer. Identifies the last row in the range to move.
right	Integer. Identifies the last column in the range to move.
overOffset	Integer. Identifies the horizontal direction data should be moved. A positive value moves data to the right; a negative value moves data to the left.
downOffset	Integer. Identifies the vertical direction data should be moved. A positive value moves data down, a negative value moves data up.

Name Property (VtFont)

Returns or sets the name of the font. This is the default property of the **VtFont** object.

Applies To

MSChart Control, **VtFont** Object

Syntax

object.**Name** [= *text*]

The **Name** property syntax has these parts:

Part	Description
object	An object expression that evaluates to an object in the **Applies To** list.
text	Integer. The text containing the font name.

Offset Property

Returns or sets the distance that a chart element is offset or pulled away from its default location.

Applies To

DataPoint Object, **DataPointLabel** Object, **Shadow** Object

Syntax

*object.***Offset** [= *offset*]

The **Offset** property syntax has these parts:

Part	Description
object	An object expression that evaluates to an object in the **Applies To** list.
offset	For the **DataPoint** object, this is an integer describing the offset distance. Offset is measured in inches or centimeters depending upon your default Windows settings.
	For the **DataPointLabel** and **Shadow** objects, this is a reference to a **Coor** object that describe the x and y values of the offset.

Remarks

For the **DataPointLabel** object, this property indicates the distance that a data point label is offset or pulled away from one of the predefined (standard) label positions. The offset is added to the position calculated for the point based on the **DataPointLabel** object's **LocationType** setting.

Order Property

Returns or sets the position of the series in the chart. If the position in order matches another series, the series are stacked.

Applies To

SeriesPosition Object

Syntax

*object.***Order** [= *order*]

The **Order** property syntax has these parts:

Part	Description
object	An object expression that evaluates to an object in the **Applies To** list.
order	Integer. The position order.

Orientation Constants

The **VtOrientation** constants provide options for positioning text.

Constant	Description
VtOrientationHorizontal	The text is displayed horizontally.
VtOrientationVertical	The letters of the text are drawn one on top of each other from the top down.
VtOrientationUp	The text is rotated to read from bottom to top.
VtOrientationDown	The text is rotated to read from top to bottom.

See Also

Orientation Property (MSChart), **Visual Basic** Constants

Orientation Property (MSChart)

Returns or sets the method of orientation for text.

Applies To

TextLayout Object

Syntax

object.**Orientation** [= *type*]

The **Orientation** property syntax has these parts:

Part	Description
object	An object expression that evaluates to an object in the **Applies To** list.
type	Integer. A **VtOrientation** constant used to describe the orientation method.

See Also

Orientation Constants

PartType Constants

The **VtChPartType** constants provide options for chart elements.

Constant	Description
VtChPartTypeChart	Identifies the chart control.
VtChPartTypeTitle	Identifies the chart title.
VtChPartTypeFootnote	Identifies the chart footnote.
VtChPartTypeLegend	Identifies the chart legend.

(continued)

(continued)

Constant	Description
VtChPartTypePlot	Identifies the chart plot.
VtChPartTypeSeries	Identifies a chart series.
VtChPartTypePoint	Identifies an individual data point.
VtChPartTypePointLabel	Identifies a data point label.
VtChPartTypeAxis	Identifies an axis.
VtChPartTypeAxisLabel	Identifies an axis label.
VtChPartTypeAxisTitle	Identifies an axis title.

See Also

GetSelectedPart Method, **SelectPart** Method, **TwipsToChartPart** Method, **Visual Basic** Constants

PatternColor Property

Returns a reference to a **VtColor** object that describes the pattern color used to fill a chart element.

Applies To

Brush Object

Syntax

object.**PatternColor**

The *object* placeholder represents an object expression that evaluates to an object in the **Applies To** list.

Pen Object

Describes the color and pattern of lines or edges on a chart.

Syntax

Pen

Properties

Style Property (MSChart), **Width** Property (MSChart), **Cap** Property, **Join** Property, **Limit** Property, **VtColor** Property

See Also

Axis Object, **Marker** Object, **PlotBase** Object, **Series** Object, **Wall** Object

Example

The following example sets the pen attributes for a two-dimensional xy chart series. The GuideLinePen property returns a reference to a Pen object.

```
Private Sub Command1_Click()
    ' Set Guide Lines for 2D XY chart Series 1.
    MSChart1.ChartType = VtChChartType2dXY
    MSChart1.Plot.SeriesCollection.Item(1) _
    .ShowGuideLine(VtChAxisIdX) = True
    With _
    MSChart1.Plot.SeriesCollection.Item(1).GuideLinePen
        ' Set Pen attributes.
        .VtColor.Set 255, 255, 0
        .Width = 10
        .Style = VtPenStyleDashDot
        .Join = VtPenRound
        .Cap = VtPenCapRound
    End With
End Sub
```

Pen Property

Returns or sets a reference to a **Pen** object that describes the color and pattern of lines or edges on chart elements.

Applies To

Axis Object, **Marker** Object, **PlotBase** Object, **Series** Object, **Wall** Object

Syntax

object.**Pen**

The object placeholder represents an object expression that evaluates to an object in the **Applies To** list.

See Also

Pen Object

PenCap Constants

VtPenCap provides methods for displaying line endings.

Constant	Description
VtPenCapButt	The line is squared off at the endpoint.
VtPenCapRound	A semicircle with the diameter of the line thickness is drawn at the end of the line.
VtPenCapSquare	The line continues beyond the endpoint for a distance equal to half the line thickness and is squared off.

See Also

Cap Property, **Visual Basic** Constants

PenJoin Constants

The **VtPenJoin** constants provide options for joining line segments in a series.

Constant	Description
VtPenJoinMiter	The outer edges of the two lines are extended until they meet.
VtPenJoinRound	A circular arc is drawn around the point where the two lines meet.
VtPenJoinBevel	The notch between the ends of two joining lines is filled.

See Also

Join Property, **Visual Basic** Constants

PenStyle Constants

The **VtPenStyle** constants provide options for the pen used to draw chart lines.

Constant	Description
VtPenStyleNull	No pen is applied
VtPenStyleSolid	Solid line pen
VtPenStyleDashed	Dashed line pen
VtPenStyleDotted	Dotted line pen
VtPenStyleDashDot	Dash-dot line pen
VtPenStyleDashDotDot	Dash-dot-dot line pen
VtPenStyleDitted	Ditted line pen
VtPenStyleDashDit	Dash-ditted line pen
VtPenStyleDashDitDit	Dash-dit-dit line pen

See Also

Style Property (MSChart), **Style** Property (StatLine)

PercentAxisBasis Constants

VtChPercentAxisBasis provides methods of displaying percentage axes.

Constant	Description
VtChPercentAxisBasisMaxChart	The largest value in the chart is considered 100 percent and all other values on the chart are displayed as percentages of that value.
VtChPercentAxisBasisMaxRow	The largest value in each row is considered 100 percent and all other values in that row are displayed as percentages of that value.

(continued)

Constant	Description
VtChPercentAxisBasisMaxColumn	The largest value in each series is considered 100 percent and all other values in that series are displayed as percentages of that value.
VtChPercentAxisBasisSumChart	All values in the chart are added together, and that value is considered 100 percent. All other values are displayed as percentages of that value.
VtChPercentAxisBasisSumRow	All values in each row are added together and the total value for each row is considered 100 percent. All other values in that same row are displayed as percentages of that value. This is the basis for 100 percent stacked charts.
VtChPercentAxisBasisSumColumn	All values in each series are added together to give a total value for each series. All values are displayed as a percentage of their series total value.

See Also

PercentBasis Property, **Visual Basic** Constants

PercentBasis Property

Returns or sets the type of percentage used to plot chart values on a percent axis.

Applies To

AxisScale Object

Syntax

object.**PercentBasis** [= *type*]

The **PercentBasis** property syntax has these parts:

Part	Description
object	An object expression that evaluates to an object in the **Applies To** list.
type	A **VtChPercentAxisBasis** constant used to describe the percentage used to plot percent axis values.

Remarks

The axis type is controlled by the **Type** property.

See Also

Type Property (MSChart), **PercentAxisBasis** Constants

PercentFormat Property

Returns or sets a string that describes the format used to display the label as a percent.

Applies To

DataPointLabel Object

Syntax

object.**PercentFormat** [= *format*]

The **PercentFormat** property syntax has these parts:

Part	Description
object	An object expression that evaluates to an object in the **Applies To** list.
format	String. Describes the format used to display a label as a percent.

Remarks

Use the **DataPointLabel** object's **Component** property to change the label type.

The following table lists several examples of percentage format strings. The values listed at left are the valid formats.

	3	-3	.3
0%	300%	-300%	30%
0.0%	300.0%	-300.0%	30.0%
0.00%	300.00%	-300.00%	30.00%

PieWeightBasis Constants

The **VtChPieWeightBasis** constants provide options for displaying pie chart slices.

Constant	Description
VtChPieWeightBasisNone	All pies are drawn the same size.
VtChPieWeightBasisTotal	The slice values in each pie are totaled and the pie with the highest total identified. The size of each pie in the chart is determined by the ratio of its total value compared to the largest pie.
VtChPieWeightBasisSeries	The first column of data in the data grid holds the relative size index. In other words, if you have 5 categories, you can control the size of the pies representing each category by using the first column of the data grid to number the rows 1 through 5. The size of the pie is determined by the ratio of its first column value and the largest value in the first column. The pie containing the 1 is the largest pie; the one containing the 5 the smallest. It is most common to exclude this first column of data so that the values are not drawn as a pie slice.

See Also

Basis Property, Set Method (Weighting), **Visual Basic** Constants

PieWeightStyle Constants

The **VtChPieWeightStyle** constants provide options for displaying individual pies within a single chart.

Constant	Description
VtChPieWeightStyleArea	The area of the individual pies changes, based on their weighting.
VtChPieWeightStyleDiameter	The diameter of the individual pies changes, based on their weighting.

See Also

Style Property (MSChart), **Set** Method (Weighting), **Visual Basic** Constants

Plot Object

The area upon which a chart is displayed.

Syntax

Plot

Properties

AngleUnit Property, **AutoLayout** Property, **Axis** Property, **Backdrop** Property, **BarGap** Property, **Clockwise** Property, **DataSeriesInRow** Property, **DefaultPercentBasis** Property, **DepthToHeightRatio** Property, **Light** Property, **LocationRect** Property, **PlotBase** Property, **Projection** Property, **SeriesCollection** Property, **Sort** Property, **StartingAngle** Property, **SubPlotLabelPosition** Property, **UniformAxis** Property, **View3D** Property, **Wall** Property, **Weighting** Property, **WidthToHeightRatio** Property, **Xgap** Property, **Zgap** Property

See Also

Light Object

Example

The following example sets the chart viewing distance and axis division spacing.

```
Private Sub Command1_Click()
   ' Change the chart type to 3D Bar.
   Form1.MSChart1.ChartType = VtChChartType3dBar
   With Form1.MSChart1.Plot
      ' Changes 3d bar chart's viewing.
      .DepthToHeightRatio = 2
      .WidthToHeightRatio = 2
      ' Changes the spacing between divisions on the
      ' X-Axis.
```

```
          .xGap = 0
          ' Changes the spacing between divisions on the
          ' Z-Axis.
          .zGap = 0.8
      End With
End Sub
```

Plot Property

Returns a reference to a **Plot** object that describes the area upon which a chart is displayed.

Applies To

MSChart Control

Syntax

object.**Plot**

The object placeholder represents an object expression that evaluates to an object in the **Applies To** list.

PlotActivated Event

Occurs when the user double clicks the chart plot.

Applies To

MSChart Control

Syntax

Private Sub *object*_**PlotActivated** (*mouseFlag* **As Integer**, *cancel* **As Integer**)

The **PlotActivated** event syntax has these parts:

Part	Description
object	An object expression that evaluates to an object in the **Applies To** list.
mouseFlag	Integer. Indicates whether a key is held down when the mouse button is clicked, as described in **Settings**.
cancel	Integer. This argument is not used at this time.

Settings

The event handler determines if a key is held down when the mouse button is clicked and sets *mouseFlag* to:

Constants	Description
VtChMouseFlagShiftKeyDown	If the SHIFT key is held down.
VtChMouseFlagControlKeyDown	If the CONTROL key is held down.

PlotBase Object

The area beneath a chart.

Syntax

PlotBase

Properties

Brush Property, **Pen** Property, **BaseHeight** Property

See Also

Backdrop Object, **Brush** Object, **Plot** Object

Example

The following example sets the chart base parameters on a three-dimensional bar chart.

```
Private Sub Command1_Click()
    ' Change the chart type to 3D.
    MSChart1.ChartType = VtChChartType3dBar
    With Form1.MSChart1.Plot.PlotBase
        ' Change the base height.
        .BaseHeight = 20
        ' Use the pattern style for base.
        .Brush.Style = VtBrushStylePattern
        .Brush.Index = VtBrushPatternHorizontal
        .Brush.FillColor.Set 255, 160, 160
        .Brush.PatternColor.Set 180, 180, 255
        .Pen.Style = VtPenStyleSolid
        .Pen.VtColor.Set 72, 72, 255

    End With
End Sub
```

PlotBase Property

Returns a reference to a **PlotBase** object that describes the appearance of the area beneath a chart.

Applies To

Plot Object

Syntax

object.**PlotBase**

The object placeholder represents an object expression that evaluates to an object in the **Applies To** list.

PlotSelected Event

Occurs when the user clicks the chart plot.

Applies To

MSChart Control

Syntax

Private Sub *object*_**PlotSelected** (*mouseFlag* **As Integer**, *cancel* **As Integer**)

The **PlotSelected** event syntax has these parts:

Part	Description
object	An object expression that evaluates to an object in the **Applies To** list.
mouseFlag	Integer. Indicates whether a key is held down when the mouse button is clicked, as described in **Settings**.
cancel	Integer. This argument is not used at this time.

Settings

The event handler determines if a key is held down when the mouse button is clicked and sets *mouseFlag* to:

Constants	Description
VtChMouseFlagShiftKeyDown	If the SHIFT key is held down.
VtChMouseFlagControlKeyDown	If the CONTROL key is held down.

PlotUpdated Event

Occurs when the chart plot has changed.

Applies To

MSChart Control

Syntax

Private Sub *object*_**PlotUpdated** (*updateFlags* **As Integer**)

The **PlotUpdated** event syntax has these parts:

Part	Description
object	An object expression that evaluates to an object in the **Applies To** list.
updateFlag	Integer. Provides information about the update of the plot, as described in **Settings**.

Settings

The following table lists the constants for *updateFlag*.

Constant	Description
VtChNoDisplay	Absence of update flags; the chart display is not affected. (Defined as 0.)
VtChDisplayPlot	Update will cause the plot to repaint.
VtChLayoutPlot	Update will cause the plot to lay out.
VtChDisplayLegend	Update will cause the legend to repaint.
VtChLayoutLegend	Update will cause the legend to lay out.
VtChLayoutSeries	Update will cause the series to lay out.
VtChPositionSection	A chart section has been moved or resized.

Point Property

Returns or sets the point where the current axis intersects with another axis.

Applies To

Intersection Object

Syntax

*object.***Point** [= *point*]

The **Point** property syntax has these parts:

Part	Description
object	An object expression that evaluates to an object in the **Applies To** list.
point	Double. The point on an axis where the current axis intersects.

Remarks

If this property is set, then the **Intersection** object's **Auto** property is automatically set to **False**.

PointActivated Event

Occurs when the user double clicks on a data point.

Applies To

MSChart Control

Syntax

Private Sub *object_***PointActivated** (*series* **As Integer**, *dataPoint* **As Integer**,
➥ *mouseFlag* **As Integer**, *cancel* **As Integer**)

The **PointActivated** event syntax has these parts:

Part	Description
object	An object expression that evaluates to an object in the **Applies To** list.
series	Integer. Identifies the series containing the data point. Series are numbered in the order that their columns appear in the data grid, beginning with 1.
dataPoint	Integer. Identifies the data point's position in the series. Points are numbered in the order that their rows appear in the data grid, beginning with 1.
mouseFlag	Integer. Indicates whether a key is held down when the mouse button is clicked, as described in **Settings**.
cancel	Integer. This argument is not used at this time.

Settings

The event handler determines if a key is held down when the mouse button is clicked and sets *mouseFlag* to:

Constants	Description
VtChMouseFlagShiftKeyDown	If the SHIFT key is held down.
VtChMouseFlagControlKeyDown	If the CONTROL key is held down.

PointLabelActivated Event

Occurs when the user double clicks a data point label.

Applies To

MSChart Control

Syntax

Private Sub *object*_**PointLabelActivated** (*series* **As Integer**, *dataPoint* **As Integer**,
↪ *mouseFlag* **As Integer**, *cancel* **As Integer**)

The **PointLabelActivated** event syntax has these parts:

Part	Description
object	An object expression that evaluates to an object in the **Applies To** list.
series	Integer. Identifies the series containing the data point. Series are numbered in the order that their columns appear in the data grid, beginning with 1.
dataPoint	Integer. Identifies the data point's position in the series. Points are numbered in the order that their rows appear in the data grid, beginning with 1.
mouseFlag	Integer. Indicates whether a key is held down when the mouse button is clicked, as described in **Settings**.
cancel	Integer. This argument is not used at this time.

Settings

The event handler determines if a key is held down when the mouse button is clicked and sets *mouseFlag* to:

Constants	Description
VtChMouseFlagShiftKeyDown	If the SHIFT key is held down.
VtChMouseFlagControlKeyDown	If the CONTROL key is held down.

PointLabelSelected Event

Occurs when the user clicks a data point label.

Applies To

MSChart Control

Syntax

Private Sub *object*_**PointLabelSelected** (*series* **As Integer**, *dataPoint* **As Integer**,
↳ *mouseFlag* **As Integer**, *cancel* **As Integer**)

The **PointLabelSelected** event syntax has these parts:

Part	Description
object	An object expression that evaluates to an object in the **Applies To** list.
series	Integer. Identifies the series containing the data point. Series are numbered in the order that their columns appear in the data grid, beginning with 1.
dataPoint	Integer. Identifies the data point's position in the series. Points are numbered in the order that their rows appear in the data grid, beginning with 1.
mouseFlag	Integer. Indicates whether a key is held down when the mouse button is clicked, as described in **Settings**.
cancel	This argument is not used at this time.

Settings

The event handler determines if a key is held down when the mouse button is clicked and sets *mouseFlag* to:

Constants	Description
VtChMouseFlagShiftKeyDown	If the SHIFT key is held down.
VtChMouseFlagControlKeyDown	If the CONTROL key is held down.

PointLabelUpdated Event

Occurs when a data point label has changed.

Applies To

MSChart Control

Syntax

Private Sub *object*_**PointLabelUpdated** (*series* **As Integer**, *dataPoint* **As Integer**,
↪ *updateFlags* **As Integer**)

The **PointLabelUpdated** event syntax has these parts:

Part	Description
object	An object expression that evaluates to an object in the **Applies To** list.
series	Integer. Identifies the series containing the data point. Series are numbered in the order that their columns appear in the data grid, beginning with 1.
dataPoint	Integer. Identifies the data point's position in the series. Points are numbered in the order that their rows appear in the data grid, beginning with 1.
updateFlag	Integer. Provides information about the update of the data point label, as described in **Settings**.

Settings

The following table lists the constants for *updateFlag*.

Constant	Description
VtChNoDisplay	Absence of update flags; the chart display is not affected. (Defined as 0.)
VtChDisplayPlot	Update will cause the plot to repaint.
VtChLayoutPlot	Update will cause the plot to lay out.
VtChDisplayLegend	Update will cause the legend to repaint.
VtChLayoutLegend	Update will cause the legend to lay out.
VtChLayoutSeries	Update will cause the series to lay out.
VtChPositionSection	A chart section has been moved or resized.

PointSelected Event

Occurs when the user clicks a data point.

Applies To

MSChart Control

Syntax

Private Sub *object*_**PointSelected** (*series* **As Integer**, *dataPoint* **As Integer**,
↪ *mouseFlag* **As Integer**, *cancel* **As Integer**)

The **PointSelected** event syntax has these parts:

Part	Description
object	An object expression that evaluates to an object in the **Applies To** list.
series	Integer. Identifies the series containing the data point. Series are numbered in the order that their columns appear in the data grid, beginning with 1.
dataPoint	Integer. Identifies the data point's position in the series. Points are numbered in the order that their rows appear in the data grid, beginning with 1.
mouseFlag	Integer. Indicates whether a key is held down when the mouse button is clicked, as described in **Settings**.
cancel	Integer. This argument is not used at this time.

Settings

The event handler determines if a key is held down when the mouse button is clicked and sets *mouseFlag* to:

Constants	Description
VtChMouseFlagShiftKeyDown	If the SHIFT key is held down.
VtChMouseFlagControlKeyDown	If the CONTROL key is held down.

PointUpdated Event

Occurs when a data point has changed.

Applies To

MSChart Control

Syntax

Private Sub *object*_**PointUpdated** (*series* **As Integer**, *dataPoint* **As Integer**,
↪ *updateFlags* **As Integer**)

The **PointUpdated** event syntax has these parts:

Part	Description
object	An object expression that evaluates to an object in the **Applies To** list.
series	Integer. Identifies the series containing the data point. Series are numbered in the order that their columns appear in the data grid, beginning with 1.
dataPoint	Integer. Identifies the data point's position in the series. Points are numbered in the order that their rows appear in the data grid, beginning with 1.
updateFlag	Integer. Provides information about the update of the data point, as described in **Settings**.

Settings

The following table lists the constants for *updateFlag*.

Constant	Description
VtChNoDisplay	Absence of update flags; the chart display is not affected. (Defined as 0.)
VtChDisplayPlot	Update will cause the plot to repaint.
VtChLayoutPlot	Update will cause the plot to lay out.
VtChDisplayLegend	Update will cause the legend to repaint.
VtChLayoutLegend	Update will cause the legend to lay out.
VtChLayoutSeries	Update will cause the series to lay out.
VtChPositionSection	A chart section has been moved or resized.

Position Property (MSChart)

Returns a reference to a **SeriesPosition** object that describes the location of one series in relation to other chart series.

Applies To

Series Object

Syntax

object.**Position**

The object placeholder represents an object expression that evaluates to an object in the **Applies To** list.

See Also

SeriesPosition Object

Projection Property

Returns or sets the type of projection used to display the chart.

Applies To

Plot Object

Syntax

object.**Projection** [= *type*]

The **Projection** property syntax has these parts:

Part	Description
object	An object expression that evaluates to an object in the **Applies To** list.
type	Integer. A **VtProjectionType** constant used to describe the type of chart projection.

See Also

      ProjectionType Constants

ProjectionType Constants

      VtProjectionType provides viewpoint and perspective options for displaying and viewing a chart.

Constants	Description
VtProjectionTypePerspective	This provides the most realistic three-dimensional appearance. Objects farther away from you converge toward a vanishing point. This is the default projection.
VtProjectionTypeOblique	This is sometimes referred to as 2.5 dimensional. The chart does have depth, but the xy plane does not change when the chart is rotated or elevated.
VtProjectionTypeOrthogonal	Perspective is not applied in this three-dimensional view. The major advantage of using this type of projection is that vertical lines remain vertical, making some charts easier to read.

See Also

      Projection Property

RandomDataFill Method

      Fills the data grid associated with a specific chart with randomly generated data.

Applies To

      DataGrid Object

Syntax

      *object.***RandomDataFill**

      The object placeholder represents an object expression that evaluates to an object in the **Applies To** list.

See Also

      MoveData Method, **RandomFillColumns** Method, **RandomFillRows** Method, **RandomFill** Property

RandomFill Property

Indicates whether the data for a chart data grid was randomly generated.

Applies To

MSChart Control

Syntax

object.**RandomFill** [= *boolean*]

The **RandomFill** property syntax has these parts:

Part	Description
object	An object expression that evaluates to an object in the **Applies To** list.
boolean	A Boolean expression that controls how data is generated, as described in **Settings**.

Settings

The settings for *boolean* are:

Setting	Description
True	Random data is used to draw the chart.
False	No random data is generated. The user provides the data for the chart.

See Also

RandomDataFill Method, **RandomFillColumns** Method, **RandomFillRows** Method

RandomFillColumns Method

Fills a number of data grid columns associated with a chart with random values.

Applies To

DataGrid Object

Syntax

object.**RandomFillColumns** (*column, count*)

The **RandomFillColumns** method syntax has these parts:

Part	Description
object	An object expression that evaluates to an object in the **Applies To** list.
column	Integer. Identifies the first column you wish to fill. Columns are numbered from left to right beginning with 1.
count	Integer. Specifies the number of columns you want to fill with random data.

See Also

RandomDataFill Method, **RandomFillRows** Method, **RandomFill** Property

RandomFillRows Method

Fills a number of data grid rows associated with a chart with random values.

Applies To

DataGrid Object

Syntax

*object.***RandomFillRows** (*row, count*)

The **RandomFillRows** method syntax has these parts:

Part	Description
object	An object expression that evaluates to an object in the **Applies To** list.
row	Integer. Identifies the first row you wish to fill. Rows are numbered from top to bottom beginning with 1.
count	Integer. Specifies the number of rows you want to fill with random data.

See Also

MoveData Method, **RandomDataFill** Method, **RandomFillColumns** Method, **RandomFill** Property

---

Rect Object

Defines a coordinate location.

Syntax

Rect

Properties

Min Property (MSChart), **Max** Property (MSChart)

See Also

Coor Object

Example

The following example sets the location of the chart plot using the LocationRect property that returns the Rect object.

```
Private Sub Command1_Click()
    ' Sets the location of the chart plot.
    MSChart1.Plot.AutoLayout = False
    With MSChart1.Plot.LocationRect
        .Min.X = 0.4
        .Min.Y = 0.4
        .Max.X = 0.5
        .Max.Y = 0.5
    End With
End Sub
```

Rect Property

Returns a reference to a **Rect** object that defines a coordinate location.

Applies To

Location Object

Syntax

object.**Rect**

The object placeholder represents an object expression that evaluates to an object in the **Applies To** list.

See Also

Rect Object

Red Property

Returns or sets the red component of the RGB value in a chart.

Applies To

VtColor Object

Syntax

object.**Red** [=*r*]

The **Red** property syntax has these parts:

Part	Description
object	An object expression that evaluates to an object in the **Applies To** list.
r	Integer. The red value.

Remarks

RGB specifies the relative intensity of red, green, and blue to cause a specific color to be displayed. The valid range for a normal RGB color is 0 to 16,777,215. The value for any argument to RGB that exceeds 255 is assumed to be 255.

Remove Method (MSChart)

Removes a **LightSource** from the **LightSources** collection.

Applies To

LightSources Collection

Syntax

object.**Remove** (*index*)

The **Remove** method syntax has these parts:

Part	Description
collection	A object expression that evaluates to an object in the **Applies To** list.
index	Integer. A specific light source by position in the list of light sources.

Repaint Property

Returns or sets a value that determines if the **MSChart** control is repainted after a change is made to the chart.

Applies To

MSChart Control

Syntax

object.**Repaint** [= *boolean*]

The **Repaint** property syntax has these parts:

Part	Description
object	An object expression that evaluates to an object in the **Applies To** list.
boolean	A Boolean expression that controls whether the chart is repainted, as described in **Settings**.

Settings

The settings for *boolean* are:

Setting	Description
True	Refreshes the control.
False	Does not allow the control to repaint when a change is made to the chart. This is useful when several operations are performed on the chart and you do not want the chart to continually repaint during the process.

ResetCustom Method

Resets any custom attributes placed on a data point to the series default.

Applies To

DataPoint Object

Syntax

object.**ResetCustom**

The object placeholder represents an object expression that evaluates to an object in the **Applies To** list.

ResetCustomLabel Method

Resets any custom attributes placed on a data point label in a chart to the series default.

Applies To

DataPointLabel Object

Syntax

*object.***ResetCustomLabel**

The object placeholder represents an object expression that evaluates to an object in the **Applies To** list.

Rotation Property

Returns or sets a value that describes the degree of rotation from which a three-dimensional chart is viewed.

Applies To

View3D Object

Syntax

*object.***Rotation** [= *degree*]

The **Rotation** property syntax has these parts:

Part	Description
object	An object expression that evaluates to an object in the **Applies To** list.
degree	Single. The degree of rotation.
	Rotation can range from 0 to 360 degrees. By default, degrees are used to measure rotation. However, these settings use the current settings for the **AngleUnits** property. The other options are: Grads and Radians.

Row Property (MSChart)

Returns or sets a specific row in the current column of a data grid associated with a chart.

Applies To

MSChart Control

Syntax

*object.***Row** [= *num*]

The **Row** property syntax has these parts:

Part	Description
object	An object expression that evaluates to an object in the **Applies To** list.
num	Integer. A row number in the current column. Rows are numbered from top to bottom beginning with 1.

RowCount Property (MSChart)

Returns or sets how many rows there are in each column of a data grid associated with a chart.

Applies To

MSChart Control, **DataGrid** Object

Syntax

object.**RowCount** [= *count*]

The **RowCount** property syntax has these parts:

Part	Description
object	An object expression that evaluates to an object in the **Applies To** list.
count	Integer. The number of rows in a column.

RowLabel Property (DataGrid)

Returns or sets a specific row label in the current data grid associated with a chart.

Applies To

DataGrid Object

Syntax

object.**RowLabel** (*row*, *labelIndex*) [= *text*]

The **RowLabel** property syntax has these parts:

Part	Description
object	An object expression that evaluates to an object in the **Applies To** list.
row	Integer. Specifies a row. Rows are numbered from top to bottom beginning at 1.
labelIndex	Integer. Specifies a specific level of row labels. Row labels are numbered from left to right beginning at 1.
Text	String. Text of the row label.

See Also

RowLabel Property (MSChart)

RowLabel Property (MSChart)

Returns or sets a data label that can be used to identify the current data point in a chart.

Applies To

MSChart Control

Syntax

*object.***RowLabel** [= *text*]

The **RowLabel** property syntax has these parts:

Part	Description
object	An object expression that evaluates to an object in the **Applies To** list.
text	String. The text for a row label. The label you specify sets the label for the data points identified by the **Row** property. This label appears along the category axis for most chart types and is used as the label for each individual pie in a pie chart. Label text may not be displayed if it is too long to fit on a chart.

See Also

RowLabel Property (DataGrid)

RowLabelCount Property

Returns or sets the number of levels of labels on the rows in a data grid associated with a chart.

Applies To

MSChart Control, **DataGrid** Object

Syntax

*object.***RowLabelCount** [= *count*]

The **RowLabelCount** property syntax has these parts:

Part	Description
object	An object expression that evaluates to an object in the **Applies To** list.
count	Integer. The number of label levels. Set this property to add or delete levels of labels from data grid rows. Row label levels are numbered from right to left, beginning at 1. Levels are added or subtracted from the left.

See Also

SetSize Method

RowLabelIndex Property

Returns or sets a value that specifies a level of row labels.

Applies To

MSChart Control

Syntax

object.**RowLabelIndex** [= *index*]

The **RowLabelIndex** property syntax has these parts:

Part	Description
object	An object expression that evaluates to an object in the **Applies To** list.
index	Integer. A row label level. To set a label on a row with more than one level of labels, or to return the current value for a label, you must first identify which level you want to affect. Row label levels are numbered from right to left, beginning at 1.

ScaleType Constants

VtChScaleType provides methods for plotting chart values and displaying the chart scale.

Constant	Description
VtChScaleTypeLinear	Chart values are plotted in a linear scale with values ranging from the minimum to the maximum chart range value.
VtChScaleTypeLogarithmic	Chart values are plotted in a logarithmic scale with values based on a specific log scale set with the *logBase* argument of this function.
VtChScaleTypePercent	Chart values are plotted in a linear scale with values based on the percentages of the chart range values.

See Also

Type Property (MSChart), **Visual Basic** Constants

SecondaryAxis Property

Returns or sets a value that determines whether the series is charted on the secondary axis.

Applies To

Series Object

Syntax

object.**SecondaryAxis** [= *boolean*]

The **SecondaryAxis** property syntax has these parts:

Part	Description
object	An object expression that evaluates to an object in the **Applies To** list.
boolean	A Boolean expression that controls whether the series is charted on the secondary axis, as described in **Settings**.

Settings

The settings for *boolean* are:

Setting	Description
True	The series is charted on the secondary axis.
False	The series is not charted on the secondary axis.

Select Method

Selects the specified chart element.

Applies To

DataPoint Object, **DataPointLabel** Object, **Footnote** Object, **Legend** Object, **Series** Object, **Title** Object

Syntax

object.**Select**

The object placeholder represents an object expression that evaluates to an object in the **Applies To** list.

SelectPart Method

Selects the specified chart part.

Applies To

MSChart Control

Syntax

object.**SelectPart** (*part, index1, index2, index3, index4*)

The **SelectPart** method syntax has these parts:

Part	Description
object	An object expression that evaluates to an object in the **Applies To** list.
part	Integer. Specifies the chart part. Valid constants are **VtChPartType**.

(continued)

Part	Description
index1	Integer. If *part* refers to a series or a data point, this argument specifies which series. Series are numbered in the order their corresponding columns appear in the data grid from left to right, beginning with 1. If *part* refers to an axis or axis label, this argument identifies the axis type with a **VtChAxisId** constant.
index2	Integer. If *part* refers to a data point, this argument specifies which data point in the series is identified by index1. Data points are numbered in the order their corresponding rows appear in the data grid from top to bottom, beginning with 1. If *part* refers to an axis, axis title, or axis label, this argument refers to the axis index which is currently not used. In this case, the only valid value for this argument is 1.
index3	Integer. If *part* refers to an axis label, this argument refers to the level of the label. Axis label levels are numbered from the axis out, beginning with 1. If *part* is not an axis label, the argument is unused.
index4	Integer. This argument is unused at this time.

See Also

AxisId Constants, **PartType** Constant

Series Collection

A collection of chart series.

Syntax

Series (*index*)

The **Series** collection syntax has these parts:

Part	Description
index	Integer. Identifies the series of the chart. Series are identified in the order of data grid columns, beginning with 1.

Properties

DataPoints Property, **GuidelinePen** Property, **LegendText Pen** Property, **Position** Property, **SecondaryAxis** Property, **SeriesMarker** Property, **SeriesType** Property, **ShowGuideLines** Property, **ShowLine** Property, **StatLine** Property, **TypeByChartType** Property

Methods

Select Method

See Also

Item Property (MSChart), **Series** Object

Example

The following example hides all the series in a chart.

```
Private Sub Command1_Click()
   Dim series As Object
   ' Hides All Series.
   For Each series In MSChart1.Plot.SeriesCollection
      Series.Position.Hidden = True
   Next
End Sub
```

Series Object

An item from a **SeriesCollection** collection that represents a group of data points on a chart.

Syntax

Series

Properties

DataPoints Property, **GuidelinePen** Property, **LegendText Pen** Property, **Position** Property, **SecondaryAxis** Property, **SeriesMarker** Property, **SeriesType** Property, **ShowGuideLines** Property, **ShowLine** Property, **StatLine** Property, **TypeByChartType** Method

Methods

Select Method

See Also

SeriesCollection Collection

Example

The following example sets smoothing for all series in a three-dimensional line chart.

```
Private Sub Command1_Click()
Dim Series As Object
   ' Change the chart type to 3D line and smoothing
   ' each line.
   Form1.MSChart1.ChartType = VtChChartType3dLine
   Form1.MSChart1.ColumnCount = 4
   For Each Series In _
   Form1.MSChart1.Plot.SeriesCollection
      Series.SmoothingType = _
      VtSmoothingTypeCubicBSpline
      Series.SmoothingFactor = 10
      Series.Pen.Style = 4
   Next
End Sub
```

SeriesActivated Event

Occurs when the user double clicks a chart series. You can replace the standard user interface by canceling the event and displaying your own dialog box.

Applies To

MSChart Control

Syntax

Private Sub *object*_**SeriesActivated** (*series* **As Integer**, *mouseFlag* **As Integer**,
↵ *cancel* **As Integer**)

The **SeriesActivated** event syntax has these parts:

Part	Description
object	An object expression that evaluates to an object in the **Applies To** list.
series	Integer. Identifies the series containing the data point. Series are numbered in the order that their columns appear in the data grid, beginning with 1.
mouseFlag	Integer. Indicates whether a key is held down when the mouse button is clicked, as described in **Settings**.
cancel	Integer. This argument is not used at this time.

Settings

The event handler determines if a key is held down when the mouse button is clicked and sets *mouseFlag* to:

Constants	Description
VtChMouseFlagShiftKeyDown	If the SHIFT key is held down.
VtChMouseFlagControlKeyDown	If the CONTROL key is held down.

SeriesCollection Collection

Provides information about the series that make up a chart.

Syntax

SeriesCollection(*index*)

The **SeriesCollection** collection syntax has these parts:

Part	Description
index	Identifies a specific series in the series collection.

Properties

Item Property (MSChart)

Methods

> **Count** Property

Example

> The following example hides all the series in a chart.

```
Private Sub Command1_Click()
   Dim series As Object
   ' Hides All Series.
   For Each series In MSChart1.Plot.SeriesCollection
      Series.Position.Hidden = True
   Next
End Sub
```

SeriesCollection Property

> Returns a reference to a **SeriesCollection** collection that provides information about the series that make up a chart.

Applies To

> **Plot** Object

Syntax

> *object*.**SeriesCollection**

> The object placeholder represents an object expression that evaluates to an object in the **Applies To** list.

SeriesColumn Property

> Returns or sets the column position for the current series data.

Applies To

> **MSChart** Control

Syntax

> *object*.**SeriesColumn** [= *pos*]

> The **SeriesColumn** property syntax has these parts:

Part	Description
object	An object expression that evaluates to an object in the **Applies To** list.
pos	Integer. The position of the column containing the current series data. You can use this property to reorder series. If two series are assigned the same position, they are stacked.

SeriesMarker Object

Describes a marker that identifies all data points within one series on a chart.

Syntax

SeriesMarker

Properties

Auto Property (SeriesMarker), **Show** Property

Example

The following example sets marker parameters for all series in a chart.

```
Private Sub Command1_Click()
    Dim series As Object
    ' Show markers and unshow the lines for all series.
    Form1.MSChart1.ChartType = VtChChartType2dLine
    For Each series In _
    Form1.MSChart1.Plot.SeriesCollection
        Series.SeriesMarker.Show = True
        Series.ShowLine = False
    Next
End Sub
```

SeriesMarker Property

Returns a reference to a **SeriesMarker** object that describes a marker that identifies all data points within one series on a chart.

Applies To

Series Object

Syntax

object.**SeriesMarker**

The object placeholder represents an object expression that evaluates to an object in the **Applies To** list.

SeriesPosition Object

The location where a chart series is drawn in relation to other series. If all series have the same order (position), then they are stacked.

Syntax

SeriesPosition

Properties

Excluded Property, **Hidden** Property (MSChart), **Order** Property, **StackOrder** Property

SeriesSelected Event

Occurs when the user clicks a chart series.

Applies To

MSChart Control

Syntax

Private Sub *object*_**SeriesSelected** (*series* **As Integer**, *mouseFlag* **As Integer**,
➥ *cancel* **As Integer**)

The **SeriesSelected** event syntax has these parts:

Part	Description
object	An object expression that evaluates to an object in the **Applies To** list.
series	Integer. Identifies the series containing the data point. Series are numbered in the order that their columns appear in the data grid, beginning with 1.
mouseFlag	Integer. Indicates whether a key is held down when the mouse button is clicked, as described in **Settings**.
cancel	Integer. This argument is not used at this time.

Settings

The event handler determines if a key is held down when the mouse button is clicked and sets *mouseFlag* to:

Constants	Description
VtChMouseFlagShiftKeyDown	If the SHIFT key is held down.
VtChMouseFlagControlKeyDown	If the CONTROL key is held down.

SeriesType Constants

The **VtChSeriesType** constants provide options for types of series.

Constant	Series Type
VtChSeriesType3dBar	3D Bar
VtChSeriesType2dBar	2D Bar
VtChSeriesType3dLine	3D Line
VtChSeriesType2dLine	2D Line
VtChSeriesType3dArea	3D Area
VtChSeriesType2dArea	2D Area
VtChSeriesType3dStep	3D Step
VtChSeriesType2dStep	2D Step
VtChSeriesType2dXY	XY
VtChSeriesType2dPie	2D Pie

See Also

TypeByChartType Method, **SeriesType** Property, **Visual Basic** Constants

SeriesType Property

Returns or sets the type used to display the current series.

Applies To

MSChart Control, **Series** Object

Syntax

*object.***SeriesType** [= *type*]

The **SeriesType** property syntax has these parts:

Part	Description
object	An object expression that evaluates to an object in the **Applies To** list.
type	Integer. A **VtChSeriesType** constant describing the method used to display the series. You must select the series to change using the **Column** property before using the **SeriesType** property.

See Also

SeriesType Constants

SeriesUpdated Event

Occurs when a chart series has changed.

Applies To

MSChart Control

Syntax

Private Sub *object*_**SeriesUpdated** (*series* **As Integer**, *updateFlags* **As Integer**)

The **SeriesUpdated** event syntax has these parts:

Part	Description
object	An object expression that evaluates to an object in the **Applies To** list.
series	Integer. Identifies the series containing the data point. Series are numbered in the order that their columns appear in the data grid, beginning with 1.
updateFlags	Integer. Provides information about the update of the series, as described in **Settings**.

Settings

The following table lists the constants for *updateFlags*.

Constant	Description
VtChNoDisplay	Absence of update flags; the chart display is not affected. (Defined as 0.)
VtChDisplayPlot	Update will cause the plot to repaint.
VtChLayoutPlot	Update will cause the plot to lay out.
VtChDisplayLegend	Update will cause the legend to repaint.
VtChLayoutLegend	Update will cause the legend to lay out.
VtChLayoutSeries	Update will cause the series to lay out.
VtChPositionSection	A chart section has been moved or resized.

Set Method (LightSource)

Sets the x, y, and z coordinates and the intensity for the **LightSource** object location.

Applies To

LightSource Object

Syntax

*object.***Set** (*x,y,z, intensity*)

The **Set** method syntax has these parts:

Part	Description
object	An object expression that evaluates to an object in the **Applies To** list.
x, y, z	Integers. Indicate the light source location.
intensity	Single. Indicate the light source intensity.

Set Method (MSChart)

Sets the x and y coordinate values for a chart.

Applies To

Coor Object, **LCoor** Object

Syntax

*object.***Set** (*x,y*)

The **Set** method syntax has these parts:

Part	Description
object	An object expression that evaluates to an object in the **Applies To** list.
x	Single. (Long for **LCoor** object.) Identifies the x value of the coordinate.
y	Single. (Long for **LCoor** object.) Identifies the y value of the coordinate.

See Also

    X Property, **Y** Property

Set Method (View3D)

Sets the rotation and degree of elevation for a three-dimensional chart.

Applies To

    View3D Object

Syntax

    object.**Set** (*rotation, elevation*)

The **Set** method syntax has these parts:

Part	Description
object	An object expression that evaluates to an object in the **Applies To** list.
rotation	Single. The degree of rotation.
	Rotation can range from 0 to 360 degrees. By default, degrees are used to measure rotation. However, these settings use the current settings for the **AngleUnits** property. The other options are: Grads and Radians.
degree	Single. The degree of elevation.
	Elevation can be any number from 0 to 90 degrees. If you set the elevation to 90 degrees, you look directly down onto the top of the chart. If you set the elevation to 0, you look directly at the side of the chart. The default elevation is 30 degrees. By default, degrees are used to measure elevation. However, these settings use the current settings for the **AngleUnits** property. The other options are: Grads and Radians.

Set Method (VtColor)

Sets the red, green and blue values of the **VtColor** object.

Applies To

    VtColor Object

Syntax

    object.**Set** (*red,green,blue*)

The **Set** method syntax has these parts:

Part	Description
object	An object expression that evaluates to an object in the **Applies To** list.
red, *green*, *blue*	Integer. The values for the red, green and blue components of color.

Remarks

RGB specifies the relative intensity of red, green, and blue to cause a specific color to be displayed. The valid range for a normal RGB color is 0 to 16,777,215. The value for any argument to RGB that exceeds 255 is assumed to be 255.

Set Method (Weighting)

Sets the basis and style of the **Weighting** object.

Syntax

object.**Set** (*basis, style*)

The **Set** method syntax has these parts:

Part	Description
object	An object expression that evaluates to an object in the **Applies To** list.
basis	A **VtChPieWeightBasis** constant that identifies the weighting type.
style	A **VtChPieWeightStyle** constant that identifies the weighting factor method.

See Also

PieWeightBasis Constants, **PieWeightStyle** Constants

SetData Method (MSChart)

Sets the value for a specific data point in the data grid associated with a chart.

Applies To

MSChart Control

Syntax

object.**SetData** *(row, column, dataPoint, nullFlag)*

The **SetData** method syntax has these parts:

Part	Description
object	An object expression that evaluates to an object in the **Applies To** list.
row	Integer. Identifies the row containing the data point value.
column	Integer. Identifies the column containing the data point value.

(continued)

Part	Description
dataPoint	Double. The data point value.
nullFlag	Integer. Indicates whether or not the data point value is a null.

SetSize Method

Resizes the number of data columns and rows, as well as the number of levels of column labels and row labels of a data grid associated with a chart at one time.

Applies To

DataGrid Object

Syntax

object.**SetSize** (*rowLabelCount, columnLabelCount, dataRowCount, columnLabelCount*)

The **SetSize** method syntax has these parts:

Part	Description
object	An object expression that evaluates to an object in the **Applies To** list.
rowLabelCount	Integer. Returns or sets the number of levels of row labels you want on the data grid.
columnLabelCount	Integer. Returns or sets the number of levels of column labels you want on the data grid.
dataRowCount	Integer. Returns or sets the number of data rows you want on the data grid.
dataColumnCount	Integer. Returns or sets the number of data columns you want on the data grid.

Remarks

This method can be used in place of **RowCount, ColumnCount**, **RowLabelCount** and **ColumnLabelCount**.

If you reduce the size of the data grid, data in deleted rows or columns is destroyed.

Shadow Object

Holds information about the appearance of a shadow on a chart element.

Syntax

Shadow

Properties

Brush Property, **Style** Property (MSChart), **Offset** Property

See Also

>   **Brush** Object, **Coor** Object

Example

>   The following example sets a shadow on a chart backdrop title.

```
Private Sub Command1_Click()
    ' Show shadow for title.
    With Form1.MSChart1.Title
        .Location.Visible = True
        .Text = "Chart Title"
    End With
    With Form1.MSChart1.Title.Backdrop.Frame
        .Width = 1
        .FrameColor.Set 255, 0, 0
        .Style = VtFrameStyleSingleLine
    End With
    With Form1.MSChart1.Title.Backdrop.Shadow
        .Style = VtShadowStyleDrop
        .Offset.x = 10
        .Offset.y = 10
    End With
End Sub
```

Shadow Property

>   Returns a reference to a **Shadow** object that describes the appearance of a shadow on chart elements.

Applies To

>   **Backdrop** Object

Syntax

>   *object*.**Shadow**

>   The object placeholder represents an object expression that evaluates to an object in the **Applies To** list.

ShadowStyle Constants

>   The **VtShadowStyle** constants provides shadow options.

Constant	Description
VtShadowStyleNull	No shadow.
VtShadowStyleDrop	Drop shadow.

See Also

>   **Style** Property (MSChart), **Visual Basic** Constants

Show Property

Returns or sets a value that determines whether series markers are displayed on a chart.

Applies To

SeriesMarker Object

Syntax

object.**Show** [= *boolean*]

The **Show** property syntax has these parts:

Part	Description
object	An object expression that evaluates to an object in the **Applies To** list.
boolean	A Boolean expression that controls whether series markers are displayed, as described in **Settings**.

Settings

The settings for *boolean* are:

Setting	Description
True	Series markers are displayed
False	Series markers are not displayed.

ShowGuideLines Property

Returns or sets a value that determines whether or not the connecting data point lines on a chart are displayed for a series.

Applies To

Series Object

Syntax

object.**ShowGuideLines** (axisId, *index*) [= *boolean*]

The **ShowGuideLine** property syntax has these parts:

Part	Description
object	An object expression that evaluates to an object in the **Applies To** list.
axisId	Integer. A **VtChAxisId** constant describing the series axis you want to set this property for.
index	Integer. An integer reserved for future use. For this version of **MSChart** control, 1 is the only valid value for this argument.
boolean	A Boolean expression that controls whether the series is charted on the secondary axis, as described in **Settings**.

Settings

The settings for *boolean* are:

Setting	Description
True	The series guidelines are displayed.
False	The series guidelines are not displayed.

See Also

AxisId Constants

ShowLegend Property

Returns or sets a value that indicates whether a legend is visible for a chart.

Applies To

MSChart Control

Syntax

object.**ShowLegend** [= *boolean*]

The **ShowLegend** property syntax has these parts:

Part	Description
object	An object expression that evaluates to an object in the **Applies To** list.
boolean	A Boolean expression that controls whether a legend is displayed on the chart, as described in **Settings**.

Settings

The settings for *boolean* are:

Setting	Description
True	The legend appears on the chart in the position indicated by the **Location** object.
False	The legend is not displayed on the chart. The default legend location is to the right side of the chart.

Remarks

The default legend location is to the right side of the chart.

ShowLine Property

Returns or sets a value that determines whether the lines connecting data points on a chart are visible.

Applies To

Series Object

Syntax

object.**ShowLine** [= *boolean*]

The **ShowLine** property syntax has these parts:

Part	Description
object	An object expression that evaluates to an object in the **Applies To** list.
boolean	A Boolean expression that controls whether lines are displayed, as described in **Settings**.

Settings

The settings for *boolean* are:

Setting	Description
True	The lines connecting data points appear on the chart.
False	The data point lines do not appear.

Size Property (MSChart)

Returns or sets the size of a chart element in points.

Applies To

Marker Object, **VtFont** Object

Syntax

object.**Size** [= *size*]

The **Size** property syntax has these parts:

Part	Description
object	An object expression that evaluates to an object in the **Applies To** list.
size	Single. Size of the chart element in points.

Sort Property (MSChart)

Returns or sets the type of sort order used in a pie chart.

Applies To

Plot Object

Syntax

object.**Sort** [= *type*]

The **Sort** property syntax has these parts:

Part	Description
object	An object expression that evaluates to an object in the **Applies To** list.
type	Integer. A **VtSortType** constant used to describe the plot sort order.

See Also

SortType Constants

SortType Constants

The **VtSortType** constants provide options for sorting pie charts.

Constant	Description
VtSortTypeNone	Pie slices are drawn in the order the data appears in the data grid.
VtSortTypeAscending	Pie slices are drawn, in order, from the smallest to the largest slice, starting at the defined starting angle and in the defined plot direction.
VtSortTypeDescending	Pie slices are drawn, in order, from the largest to the smallest slice, starting at the defined starting angle and in the defined plot direction.

See Also

Sort Property (MSChart), **Visual Basic** Constants

SpaceColor Property

Returns a reference to a **VtColor** object that specifies the color used fill the space between double frames around a chart element.

Applies To

Frame Object

Syntax

object.**SpaceColor**

The object placeholder represents an object expression that evaluates to an object in the **Applies To** list.

See Also

FrameColor Property

Example

The following example sets a blue, double-line frame on a chart backdrop.

```
Private Sub Command1_Click()
    With MSChart1.backdrop.Frame
        .Style = VtFrameStyleDoubleLine
        .Width = 2
        .FrameColor.Set 0, 0, 255        ' Blue frame.
        .SpaceColor.Set 255, 0, 0        ' Red spacing.
    End With
End Sub
```

Stacking Property

Sets a value that determines whether all the series in the chart are stacked.

Applies To

MSChart Control

Syntax

object.**Stacking** [= *boolean*]

The **Stacking** property syntax has these parts:

Part	Description
object	An object expression that evaluates to an object in the **Applies To** list.
boolean	A Boolean expression that controls whether all chart series are stacked, as described in **Settings**.

Settings

The settings for *boolean* are:

Setting	Description
True	All chart series are stacked.
False	Chart series are not stacked.

Remarks

The default legend location is to the right side of the chart.

StackOrder Property

Returns or sets in what position the current series is drawn if it is stacked with other series.

Applies To

SeriesPosition Object

Syntax

object.**StackOrder** [= *position*]

The **StackOrder** property syntax has these parts:

Part	Description
object	An object expression that evaluates to an object in the **Applies To** list.
position	Integer. The order of the series if stacked with other series. Lower stack orders are on the bottom of the stack.

Standing Property

Returns or sets a value that specifies whether axis labels are displayed horizontally in the x or z plane or vertically on the text baseline in the y plane.

Applies To

Label Object (Item)

Syntax

object.**Standing** [= *boolean*]

The **Standing** property syntax has these parts:

Part	Description
object	An object expression that evaluates to an object in the **Applies To** list.
boolean	A Boolean expression that specifies how to display the axis labels, as described in **Settings**.

Settings

The settings for *boolean* are:

Setting	Description
True	The axis labels are displayed vertically on the text baseline in the y plane.
False	The axis labels are displayed horizontally in the x or z plane.

StartingAngle Property

Returns or sets the position where you want to start drawing pie charts.

Applies To

Plot Object

Syntax

object.**StartingAngle** [= *angle*]

The **StartingAngle** property syntax has these parts:

Part	Description
object	An object expression that evaluates to an object in the **Applies To** list.

Part	Description
angle	Single. This angle can be measured in degrees, radians, or grads, depending on the current **AngleUnits** setting. A value of 0 degrees indicates the 3 o'clock position. Setting the starting angle to 90 degrees moves the starting position to 12 o'clock if the **Clockwise** property is set to counterclockwise, or to 6 o'clock if it's set to clockwise. Valid values range from -360 to 360 degrees.

StatLine Object

Describes how statistic lines are displayed on a chart.

Syntax

StatLine

Properties

Style Property (MSChart), **Width** Property (MSChart), **Flag** Property, **VtColor** Property

Example

The following example sets the color and pen parameters for a chart statistics line.

```
Private Sub Command1_Click()
    ' Show all statistic lines for series 2.
    Form1.MSChart1.chartType = VtChChartType2dLine
    With Form1.MSChart1.plot.SeriesCollection._
    Item(2).StatLine
        .VtColor.Set 128, 128, 255
        .Flag = VtChStatsMinimum Or VtChStatsMaximum _
        Or VtChStatsMean Or VtChStatsStddev Or _
        VtChStatsRegression
        .Style(vtChStatsMinimum) = VtPenStyleDotted
        .width = 2
    End With
End Sub
```

StatLine Property

Returns a reference to a **StatLine** object that describes how statistic lines are displayed on a chart.

Applies To

Series Object

Syntax

object.**StatLine**

The object placeholder represents an object expression that evaluates to an object in the **Applies To** list.

StatsType Constants

The **VtChStats** constants provide methods of displaying statistic lines on a chart.

Constant	Description
VtChStatsMinimum	Shows the minimum value in the series.
VtChStatsMaximum	Shows the maximum value in the series.
VtChStatsMean	Shows the mathematical mean of the values in the series.
VtChStatsStddev	Shows the standard deviation of the values in the series.
VtChStatsRegression	Shows a trend line indicated by the values in a series.

See Also

Flag Property, **Style** Property (StatLine), **Visual Basic** Constants

---

Style Property (MSChart)

Returns or sets the style used to draw certain chart elements

Applies To

Brush Object, **Fill** Object, **Frame** Object, **Marker** Object, **Pen** Object, **Shadow** Object, **Tick** Object, **VtFont** Object, **Weighting** Object

Syntax

object.**Style** [=*style*]

The **Style** property syntax has these parts:

Part	Description
object	An object expression that evaluates to an object in the **Applies To** list.
style	For the **Brush** object, a **VtBrushStyle** constant describing the brush pattern.
	For the **Fill** object, a **VtFillStyle** constant that describes the style of fill. A fill can have a brush, which is a solid color or patterned fill.
	For the **Frame** object, a **VtFrameStyle** constant that describes the type of frame**.**
	For the **Marker** object, a **VtMarkerStyle** constant that lists the marker type.
	For the **Pen** object, a **VtPenStyle** constant that describes the style of pen.
	For the **Shadow** object, a **VtShadowStyle** constant used to describe the shadow type.
	For the **Tick** object, a **VtChAxisTickStyle** constant used to describe the axis tick position.
	For the **VtFont** object, a **VtFontStyle** constant describing the style of font.
	For the **Weighting** object, a **VtChPieWeightStyle** constant that identifies the weighting factor method.

See Also

AxisTickStyle Constants, **BorderStyle** Constants (MSChart), **FillStyle** Constants, **FontStyle** Constants, **FrameStyle** Constants, **MarkerStyle** Constants, **PenStyle** Constants, **PieWeightStyle** Constants, **ShadowStyle** Constants, **Style** Property (StatLine), **StatsType** Constants

Style Property (StatLine)

Returns or sets the line type used to display the statistic line.

Applies To

StatLine Object

Syntax

object.**Style** (*type*)[= *style*]

The **Style** property syntax has these parts:

Part	Description
object	An object expression that evaluates to an object in the **Applies To** list.
type	Integer. A **VtChStats** constant used to describe the line type.
style	Integer. A **VtPenStyle** constant used to describe the stat line style.

See Also

Style Property (MSChart), **PenStyle** Constants

SubPlotLabelLocationType Constants

The **VtSubPlotLabelLocationType** constants provide methods for displaying the subplot label.

Constant	Description
VtChSubPlotLabelLocationTypeNone	No subplot label is displayed.
VtChSubPlotLabelLocationTypeAbove	The subplot label is displayed above the pie.
VtChSubPlotLabelLocationTypeBelow	The subplot label is displayed below the pie.
VtChSubPlotLabelLocationTypeCenter	The subplot label is centered on the pie.

See Also

SubPlotLabelPosition Property, **Visual Basic** Constants

SubPlotLabelPosition Property

Returns or sets the position used to display a label on each pie in a chart.

Applies To

Plot Object

Syntax

*object.***SubPlotLabelPosition** [= *pos*]

The **SubPlotLabelPosition** property syntax has these parts:

Part	Description
object	An object expression that evaluates to an object in the **Applies To** list.
pos	Integer. A **VtChSubPlotLabelLocationType** constant used to describe the position of the chart label.

See Also

SubPlotLabelPosition Property

Text Property (MSChart)

Returns or sets the text used to display a chart element such as an axis title, data point label, footnote, or chart title.

Applies To

AxisTitle Object, **DataPointLabel** Object, **Footnote** Object, **Title** Object

Syntax

*object.***Text** [= *text*]

The **Text** property syntax has these parts:

Part	Description
object	An object expression that evaluates to an object in the **Applies To** list.
text	String. A string that contains the text used for the chart element.

Remarks

The **Text** property is the default property for each of the objects to which it applies.

TextLayout Object

Represents text positioning and orientation.

Syntax

TextLayout

Properties

WordWrap Property(MSChart), **HorzAlignment** Property, **Orientation** Property (MSChart), **VertAlignment** Property

Example

The following example sets the title text position and orientation for a chart.

```
Private Sub Command1_Click()
   ' Sets the title text position and orientation.
   With Form1.MSChart1.Title
      .Location.Visible = True
      .Location.LocationType = VtChLocationTypeLeft
      .Text = "Title TextLayout"
   End With
   With Form1.MSChart1.Title.TextLayout
      .Orientation = VtOrientationUp
      .HorzAlignment = VtHorizontalAlignmentCenter
      .VertAlignment = VtVerticalAlignmentCenter
   End With
End Sub
```

TextLayout Property

Returns a reference to a **TextLayout** object that describes text positioning and orientation.

Applies To

AxisTitle Object, **DataPointLabel** Object**, Footnote** Object, **Label** Object (Item), **Legend** Object, **Title** Object

Syntax

object.**TextLayout**

The object placeholder represents an object expression that evaluates to an object in the **Applies To** list.

TextLength Property

Returns or sets the number of characters in the text of a chart axis title, data point label, footnote, or chart title.

Applies To

AxisTitle Object, **DataPointLabel** Object**, Footnote** Object, **Title** Object

Syntax

object.**TextLength** [= *size*]

The **TextLength** property syntax has these parts:

Part	Description
object	An object expression that evaluates to an object in the **Applies To** list.
size	Integer. The number of characters in the text.

TextLengthType Constants

The **VtTextLengthType** constants provide options for optimizing text layout for the screen or for the printer.

Constant	Description
VtTextLengthTypeVirtual	Choose this constant to use TrueType virtual font metrics to optimize text layout for printing. TrueType virtual font metrics may not be very accurate for text displayed on the screen. Text displayed on the screen may be a larger or smaller than the virtual metrics requested. Larger text may not fit where it is supposed to and part of a character, a whole character, or even in some cases words may be clipped.
VtTextLengthTypeDevice	Choose this constant to optimize text layout for the screen. Text in charts laid out for screen display always fits correctly within its chart area. The printed text is generally a bit smaller and so the text may appear in slightly different places.

See Also

TextLengthType Property, **Visual Basic** Constants

TextLengthType Property

Returns or sets a value that specifies how text is drawn to optimize the appearance either on the screen or printed page.

Applies To

MSChart Control

Syntax

*object.***TextLengthType** [= *type*]

The **TextLengthType** property syntax has these parts:

Part	Description
object	An object expression that evaluates to an object in the **Applies To** list.
type	Integer. A **VtTextLengthType** constant indicating the method used to draw text.

TextLengthType Constants

TextOutputType Constants

The **VtTextOutputType** constants provide methods of outputting text.

Constant	Description
VtTextOutputTypeHardware	Device context type Null.
VtTextOutputTypePolygon	Device context type Metafile.

Tick Object

A marker indicating a division along a chart axis.

Syntax

Tick

Properties

Style Property (MSChart), **Length** Property (MSChart)

Example

The following example sets the tick length and style for the y axis on a chart.

```
Private Sub Command1_Click()
    ' Set the tick for y axis.
    With Form1.MSChart1.Plot.Axis(VtChAxisIdY, 1).Tick
        .Length = 20
        .Style = VtChAxisTickStyleOutside
    End With
End Sub
```

Tick Property

Returns a reference to a **Tick** object that describes a marker indicating a division along a chart axis.

Applies To

Axis Object

Syntax

object.**Tick**

The object placeholder represents an object expression that evaluates to an object in the **Applies To** list.

Title Object

Text identifying the chart.

Syntax

Title

Properties

Text Property (MSChart), **TextLength** Property, **Backdrop** Property, **Font** Property (MSChart), **Location** Property, **TextLayout** Property, **VtFont** Property

Methods

Select Method

See Also

Backdrop Object

Title Property (MSChart)

Reference to a **Title** object that describes the text used to title a chart.

Applies To

MSChart Control

Syntax

*object***.Title**

The object placeholder represents an object expression that evaluates to an object in the **Applies To** list.

TitleActivated Event

Occurs when the user double clicks the chart title. You can replace the standard user interface by canceling the event and displaying your own dialog box.

Applies To

MSChart Control

Syntax

Private Sub *object*_**TitleActivated** (*mouseFlag* **As Integer**, *cancel* **As Integer**)

The **TitleActivated** event syntax has these parts:

Part	Description
object	An object expression that evaluates to an object in the **Applies To** list.
mouseFlag	Integer. Indicates whether a key is held down when the mouse button is clicked, as described in **Settings**.

(continued)

Part	Description
cancel	Integer. This argument is not used at this time.

Settings

The event handler determines if a key is held down when the mouse button is clicked and sets *mouseFlag* to:

Constants	Description
VtChMouseFlagShiftKeyDown	If the SHIFT key is held down.
VtChMouseFlagControlKeyDown	If the CONTROL key is held down.

TitleSelected Event

Occurs when the user clicks the chart title.

Applies To

MSChart Control

Syntax

Private Sub *object_***TitleSelected** (*mouseFlag* **As Integer**, *cancel* **As Integer**)

The **TitleSelected** event syntax has these parts:

Part	Description
object	An object expression that evaluates to an object in the **Applies To** list.
mouseFlag	Integer. Indicates whether a key is held down when the mouse button is clicked, as described in **Settings**.
cancel	Integer. This argument is not used at this time.

Settings

The event handler determines if a key is held down when the mouse button is clicked and sets *mouseFlag* to:

Constants	Description
VtChMouseFlagShiftKeyDown	If the SHIFT key is held down.
VtChMouseFlagControlKeyDown	If the CONTROL key is held down.

TitleText Property

Returns or sets the text displayed as the chart title.

Applies To

MSChart Control

Syntax

*object.***TitleText** [= *text*]

The **TitleText** property syntax has these parts:

Part	Description
object	An object expression that evaluates to an object in the **Applies To** list.
text	The text used to display a chart title.

Remarks

This property provides a simple means to set or return the chart title. This property is functionally identical to using MSChart.Title.Text.

TitleUpdated Event

Occurs when the chart title has changed.

Applies To

MSChart Control

Syntax

Private Sub *object_***TitleUpdated** (*updateFlags* **As Integer**)

The **TitleUpdated** event syntax has these parts:

Part	Description
object	An object expression that evaluates to an object in the **Applies To** list.
updateFlags	Provides information about the update of the title, as described in **Settings**.

Settings

The following table lists the constants for *updateFlags*.

Constant	Description
VtChNoDisplay	Absence of update flags; the chart display is not affected. (Defined as 0.)
VtChDisplayPlot	Update will cause the plot to repaint.
VtChLayoutPlot	Update will cause the plot to lay out.
VtChDisplayLegend	Update will cause the legend to repaint.
VtChLayoutLegend	Update will cause the legend to lay out.
VtChLayoutSeries	Update will cause the series to lay out.
VtChPositionSection	A chart section has been moved or resized.

ToDefaults Method

Returns the chart to its initial settings.

Applies To

MSChart Control

Syntax

*object.***ToDefaults**

The object placeholder represents an object expression that evaluates to an object in the **Applies To** list.

TwipsToChartPart Method

Identifies a chart part by using the x and y set of coordinates on to identify that part.

Applies To

MSChart Control

Syntax

*object.***TwipsToChartPart** (*xVal*, *yVal*, *part*, *index1*, *index2*, *index3*, *index4*)

The **TwipsToChartPart** method syntax has these parts:

Part	Description
object	An object expression that evaluates to an object in the **Applies To** list.
xVal,yVal	Long. The horizontal and vertical coordinates of the point.
part	Integer. A **VtChPartType** constant that identifies the chart part that is located at the *xVal* and *yVal* coordinates.
index1	Integer. If *part* refers to a series or a data point, this argument specifies which series. Series are numbered in the order their corresponding columns appear in the data grid from left to right, beginning with 1. If *part* refers to an axis or axis label, this argument identifies the axis type using the **VtChAxisId** constant.
index2	Integer. If *part* refers to a data point, this argument specifies which data point in the series identified by index1. Data points are numbered in the order their corresponding rows appear in the data grid from top to bottom, beginning with 1. If *part* refers to an axis, axis title, or axis label, this argument refers to the axis index which is currently not used. In this case, the only valid value for this argument is 1.
index3	Integer. If *part* refers to an axis label, this argument refers to the level of the label. Axis label levels are numbered from the axis out, beginning with 1. If *part* is not an axis label, the argument is unused.
index4	Integer. This argument is unused at this time.

See Also

AxisId Constants, **PartType** Constants

Type Property (MSChart)

Returns or sets the scale type of an axis.

Applies To

AxisScale Object

Syntax

object.**Type** [= *type*]

The **Type** property syntax has these parts:

Part	Description
object	An object expression that evaluates to an object in the **Applies To** list.
type	A **VtChScaleType** constant describing the axis scale type.

See Also

ScaleType Constants

TypeByChartType Method

Returns the series type used to draw a series if the chart type is set to *chType*. This method allows you to get the series type information based on a specified chart type without actually setting the chart type.

Applies To

Series Object

Syntax

object.**TypeByChartType** (*chtype*)

The **TypeByChartType** method syntax has these parts:

Part	Description
object	An object expression that evaluates to an object in the **Applies To** list.
seriestype	Integer. A **VtChSeriesType** constant that describes the returned type used to display a series.
chtype	Integer. A **VtChChartType** constant describing the chart type.

See Also

ChartType Constants, **SeriesType** Constants

UniformAxis Property

Returns or sets a value that specifies whether the unit scale for all value axes in a chart is uniform.

Applies To

Plot Object

Syntax

*object.***UniformAxis** [= *boolean*]

The **UniformAxis** property syntax has these parts:

Part	Description
object	An object expression that evaluates to an object in the **Applies To** list.
boolean	A Boolean expression that controls the unit scale, as described in **Settings**.

Settings

The settings for *boolean* are:

Setting	Description
True	The unit scale for all value axes is uniform.
False	The unit scale is not uniform. The unit scale is determined by the plot size and positioning set according to the **AutoLayout** or **LocationRect** property. If **AutoLayout** is **True**, the plot size and position are based on the size and position of other automatically laid out elements. If **False**, the coordinates specified by **LocationRect** are used to position the plot and determine the axes unit scale.

ValueFormat Property

Returns or sets the format used to display the label as a value.

Applies To

DataPointLabel Object

Syntax

*object.***ValueFormat** [= *format*]

The **ValueFormat** property syntax has these parts:

Part	Description
object	An object expression that evaluates to an object in the **Applies To** list.
format	String. Describes the format used to display a label as a value.

Remarks

Use the **DataPointLabel** object's **Component** property to change the label type.

ValueScale Object

Scale used to display a value axis.

Syntax

ValueScale

Properties

Auto Property (ValueScale), **MajorDivision** Property, **Maximum** Property, **Minimum** Property, **MinorDivision** Property

See Also

CategoryScale Object, **ValueScale** Property

Example

The following example sets the major and minor grid line color for a two-dimensional bar chart using the ValueScale object.

```
Private Sub Command1_Click()
   ' Set chart type to 2d bar.
   Form1.MSChart1.ChartType = VtChChartType2dBar
   ' Use manual scale to display y axis (value axis).
   With _
   Form1.MSChart1.Plot.Axis(VtChAxisIdY).ValueScale
      .Auto = False
      .MajorDivision = 2
      .MinorDivision = 5
   End With
   ' Show major grid line in red and minor grid line
   ' in blue.
   With Form1.MSChart1.Plot.Axis(VtChAxisIdY).AxisGrid
      .MajorPen.VtColor.Set 255, 0, 0
      .MajorPen.Width = 4
.MinorPen.VtColor.Set 0, 0, 255
      .MinorPen.Width = 2
   End With
End Sub
```

ValueScale Property

Returns a reference to a **ValueScale** object that describes the scale used to display a value axis.

Applies To

Axis Object

Syntax

object.**ValueScale**

The object placeholder represents an object expression that evaluates to an object in the **Applies To** list.

See Also

    CategoryScale Property

VertAlignment Property

    Returns or sets the method used to vertically align text.

Applies To

    TextLayout Object

Syntax

    *object.***VertAlignment** [= *type*]

    The **VertAlignment** property syntax has these parts:

Part	Description
object	An object expression that evaluates to an object in the **Applies To** list.
type	Integer. A **VtVerticalAlignment** constant used to describe the vertical alignment method of text.

See Also

    VerticalAlignment Constants

VerticalAlignment Constants

    The **VtVerticalAlignment** constants provide methods of vertically aligning text.

Constant	Description
VtVerticalAlignmentTop	All lines of text are aligned at the top margin.
VtVerticalAlignmentBottom	All lines of text are aligned at the bottom margin.
VtVerticalAlignmentCenter	All lines of text are centered vertically.

See Also

    VertAlignment Property, **Visual Basic** Constants

View3D Object

    Represents the physical orientation of a three-dimensional chart.

Syntax

    View3D

Properties

    Elevation Property, **Rotation** Property

Methods

Set Method (View3D)

Example

The following example sets the chart elevation and rotation for a three-dimensional bar chart using the view object.

```
Private Sub Command1_Click()
    ' Set the chart type to 3d bar.
    Form1.MSChart1.ChartType = VtChChartType3dBar
    With Form1.MSChart1.Plot.View3d
        .Elevation = 90    ' Look directly down onto the
                           ' top of the chart.
        .Rotation = 90
    End With
End Sub
```

View3D Property

Returns a reference to a **View3D** object that describes the physical orientation of a three-dimensional chart.

Applies To

Plot Object

Syntax

object.**View3D**

The object placeholder represents an object expression that evaluates to an object in the **Applies To** list.

Visible Property (MSChart)

Returns or sets a value that determines whether a chart element is displayed.

Applies To

MSChart Control, **AxisTitle** Object, **Location** Object, **Marker** Object

Syntax

object.**Visible** [= *boolean*]

The **Visible** property syntax has these parts:

Part	Description
object	An object expression that evaluates to an object in the **Applies To** list.
boolean	A Boolean expression that specifies whether the item is displayed, as described in **Settings**.

Settings

The settings for *boolean* are:

Setting	Description
True	The chart, axis title, label, or marker are displayed.
False	The elements are hidden.

VtColor Object

Describes a drawing color in a chart.

Syntax

VtColor

Properties

Automatic Property, **Blue** Property, **Green** Property, **Red** Property

Methods

Set Method (VtColor)

Example

The following example sets the fill color for a chart backdrop brush. The FillColor property returns a reference to the VtColor object.

```
Private Sub Command1_Click()
' Sets Backdrop to Fill - Brush Style.
  MSChart1.Backdrop.Fill.Style = VtFillStyleBrush
   ' Sets chart fill color to red.
  With MSChart1.Backdrop.Fill.Brush.FillColor
     .Red = 255  ' Use properties to set color.
     .Green = 0
     .Blue = 0
  End With
End Sub
```

VtColor Property

Returns a reference to a **VtColor** object that describes a drawing color in a chart.

Applies To

Pen Object, **StatLine** Object, **VtFont** Object

Syntax

object.**VtColor**

The object placeholder represents an object expression that evaluates to an object in the **Applies To** list.

VtFont Object

The font used to display chart text.

Syntax

VtFont

Properties

Style Property (MSChart), **Size** Property (MSChart), **VtColor** Property, **Effect** Property, **Name** Property (VtFont)

Example

The following example sets the font parameters for a chart title.

```
Private Sub Command1_Click()
    ' Make Chart Title visible.
    MSChart1.Title.Location.Visible = True
    ' Set font for Chart Title.
    With MSChart1.Title.VtFont
        .Name = "Times New Roman"
        .Size = 18
        .Style = VtfontStyleBoldItalic
        ' Use both StrikeThrough and Underline in the
        ' text.
        .Effect = VtFontEffectStrikeThrough Or _
    VtFontEffectUnderline
        ' Set text color to Blue.
        .VtColor.Set 0, 0, 255
    End With
End Sub
```

VtFont Property

Returns a reference to a **VtFont** object that describes the font used to display chart text.

Applies To

AxisTitle Object, **DataPointLabel** Object, **Footnote** Object, **Label** Object (Item), **Legend** Object, **Title** Object

Syntax

object.**VtFont**

The object placeholder represents an object expression that evaluates to an object in the **Applies To** list.

Wall Object

A planar area depicting the y axes on a three-dimensional chart.

Syntax

Wall

Properties

Brush Property, **Width** Property (MSChart), **Pen** Property

Methods

Set Method (Weighting)

See Also

Brush Object

Example

The following example displays a colored wall for a three-dimensional chart.

```
Private Sub Command1_Click()
    ' Displays a colored wall for a 3D chart.
    Form1.MSChart1.ChartType = VtChChartType3dBar
    With Form1.MSChart1.Plot.Wall
        .Brush.Style = VtBrushStylePattern
        .Brush.Index = VtBrushPatternChecks
        .Brush.FillColor.Set 255, 120, 120
        .Brush.PatternColor.Set 120, 120, 0
        .Width = 20
    End With
End Sub
```

Wall Property

Returns a reference to a **Wall** object that describes the planar area depicting the y axes on a three-dimensional chart.

Applies To

Plot Object

Syntax

object.**Wall**

The object placeholder represents an object expression that evaluates to an object in the **Applies To** list.

Weighting Object

Represents the size of a pie in relation to other pies in the same chart.

Syntax

Weighting

Properties

Style Property (MSChart), **Basis** Property

Methods

Set Method (Weighting)

Example

The following example shows the weighting of a pie chart.

```
Private Sub Command1_Click()
   ' Show the weighting of the pie.
   Form1.MSChart1.ChartType = VtChChartType2dPie
   With Form1.MSChart1.Plot.Weighting
      .Basis = VtChPieWeightBasisTotal
      .Style = VtChPieWeightStyleArea
   End With
End Sub
```

Weighting Property

Returns a reference to a **Weighting** object that describes the size of a pie in relation to other pies in the same chart.

Applies To

Plot Object

Syntax

object.**Weighting**

The object placeholder represents an object expression that evaluates to an object in the **Applies To** list.

Width Property (MSChart)

Returns or sets the width of a chart element, in points.

Applies To

MSChart Control, **Frame** Object, **Pen** Object, **StatLine** Object, **Wall** Object

Syntax

object.**Width** [= *width*]

The **Width** property syntax has these parts:

Part	Description
object	An object expression that evaluates to an object in the **Applies To** list.
width	Single. The width of the chart element.

WidthToHeightRatio Property

Returns or sets the percentage of the chart height to be used as the chart width.

Applies To

Plot Object

Syntax

object.**WidthToHeightRatio** [= *pctg*]

The **WidthToHeightRatio** property syntax has these parts:

Part	Description
object	An object expression that evaluates to an object in the **Applies To** list.
pctg	Single. The chart height percentage.

WordWrap Property(MSChart)

Returns or sets a value that determines whether text wraps.

Applies To

TextLayout Object

Syntax

object.**WordWrap** [= *boolean*]

The **WordWrap** property syntax has these parts:

Part	Description
object	An object expression that evaluates to an object in the **Applies To** list.
boolean	A Boolean expression that determines whether text wraps, as described in **Settings**.

Settings

The settings for *boolean* are:

Setting	Description
True	Text wraps.
False	Text does not wrap.

X Property

Returns or sets the x value in a floating coordinate pair for a chart.

Applies To

Coor Object, **LCoor** Object, **LightSource** Object

Syntax

object.**X** [= *x*]

The **X** property syntax has these parts:

Part	Description
object	An object expression that evaluates to an object in the **Applies To** list.
x	Single. (Long for **LCoor** object.) Identifies the x value of the coordinate.

See Also

Y Property, **Set** Method (MSChart)

XGap Property

Returns or sets the spacing of bars between divisions on the x axis. This space is measured as a percentage of the bar width.

Applies To

Plot Object

Syntax

object.**xGap** [= *spacing*]

The **xGap** property syntax has these parts:

Part	Description
object	An object expression that evaluates to an object in the **Applies To** list.
spacing	Single. The bar width percentage. A value of 0 results in the series of bars touching.

Y Property

Returns or sets the y value in a floating coordinate pair for a chart.

Applies To

Coor Object, **LCoor** Object, **LightSource** Object

Syntax

object.**Y** [= *y*]

The **Y** property syntax has these parts:

Part	Description
object	An object expression that evaluates to an object in the **Applies To** list.
y	Single. (Long for **LCoor** object.) Identifies the y value of the coordinate.

See Also

X Property, **Set** Method (MSChart)

Z Property

Returns or sets the z value in a coordinate location.

Applies To

LightSource Object

Syntax

*object.***Z** [= *z*]

The **Z** property syntax has these parts:

Part	Description
object	An object expression that evaluates to an object in the **Applies To** list.
z	Single. (Long for **LCoor** object.) Identifies the z value of the coordinate.

See Also

X Property, **Y** Property

ZGap Property

Returns or sets the spacing of three-dimensional bars between divisions on the z axis. This space is measured as a percentage of the bar depth.

Applies To

Plot Object

Syntax

*object.***zGap** [= *spacing*]

The **zGap** property syntax has these parts:

Part	Description
object	An object expression that evaluates to an object in the **Applies To** list.
spacing	Single. The bar depth percentage. A value of 0 results in the series of bars touching along the z axis.

MSComm Control

The **MSComm** control provides serial communications for your application by allowing the transmission and reception of data through a serial port.

Syntax

MSComm

Remarks

The **MSComm** control provides the following two ways for handling communications:

- Event-driven communications is a very powerful method for handling serial port interactions. In many situations you want to be notified the moment an event takes place, such as when a character arrives or a change occurs in the Carrier Detect (CD) or Request To Send (RTS) lines. In such cases, use the **MSComm** control's **OnComm** event to trap and handle these communications events. The **OnComm** event also detects and handles communications errors. For a list of all possible events and communications errors, see the **CommEvent** property.

- You can also poll for events and errors by checking the value of the **CommEvent** property after each critical function of your program. This may be preferable if your application is small and self-contained. For example, if you are writing a simple phone dialer, it may not make sense to generate an event after receiving every character, because the only characters you plan to receive are the OK response from the modem.

Each **MSComm** control you use corresponds to one serial port. If you need to access more than one serial port in your application, you must use more than one **MSComm** control. The port address and interrupt address can be changed from the Windows Control Panel.

Although the **MSComm** control has many important properties, there are a few that you should be familiar with first.

Properties	Description
CommPort	Sets and returns the communications port number.
Settings	Sets and returns the baud rate, parity, data bits, and stop bits as a string.
PortOpen	Sets and returns the state of a communications port. Also opens and closes a port.
Input	Returns and removes characters from the receive buffer.
Output	Writes a string of characters to the transmit buffer.

Properties

Break Property, **CDHolding** Property, **CommEvent** Property, **CommID** Property, **CommPort** Property, **CTSHolding** Property, **DSRHolding** Property, **DTREnable** Property, **EOFEnable** Property, **Handshaking** Property, **InBufferCount** Property, **InBufferSize** Property, **Index** Property (ActiveX Controls), **Index** Property (Control Array), **Input** Property, **InputLen** Property, **InputMode** Property, **Name** Property, **NullDiscard** Property, **MSComm** Control, **Object** Property, **OutBufferCount** Property, **OutBufferSize** Property, **Output** Property, **Parent** Property, **ParityReplace** Property, **PortOpen** Property, **RThreshold** Property, **RTSEnable** Property, **Settings** Property, **SThreshold** Property, **Tag** Property (ActiveX Controls)

Events

OnComm Event

See Also

OnComm Event, **MSComm** Control Constants, **Error Messages**

Example

The following simple example shows basic serial communications using a modem:

```
Private Sub Form_Load ()
    ' Buffer to hold input string
    Dim Instring As String
    ' Use COM1.
    MSComm1.CommPort = 1
    ' 9600 baud, no parity, 8 data, and 1 stop bit.
    MSComm1.Settings = "9600,N,8,1"
    ' Tell the control to read entire buffer when Input
    ' is used.
    MSComm1.InputLen = 0
    ' Open the port.
    MSComm1.PortOpen = True
    ' Send the attention command to the modem.
    MSComm1.Output = "AT" + Chr$(13)
    ' Wait for data to come back to the serial port.
    Do
        DoEvents
    Loop Until MSComm1.InBufferCount >= 2
    ' Read the "OK" response data in the serial port.
    Instring = MSComm1.Input
    ' Close the serial port.
    MSComm1.PortOpen = False
End Sub
```

Note The **MSComm** control can use polling or an event-driven method to retrieve data from the port. This simple example uses the polling method. For an example of the event-driven method, see **OnComm** event.

Break Property

Sets or clears the break signal state. This property is not available at design time.

Applies To

MSComm Control

Syntax

object.**Break** [= *value*]

The **Break** property syntax has these parts:

Part	Description
object	An object expression that evaluates to an object in the **Applies To** list.
value	A Boolean expression specifying whether the break signal state is set, as described in Settings.

Settings

The settings for *value* are:

Setting	Description
True	Sets the break signal state.
False	Clears the break signal state.

Remarks

When set to **True**, the **Break** property sends a break signal. The break signal suspends character transmission and places the transmission line in a break state until you set the **Break** property to **False**.

Typically, you set the break state for a short interval of time, and *only* if the device with which you are communicating requires that a break signal be set.

Data Type

Boolean

See Also

MSComm Control, **OnComm** Event

Example

The following example shows how to send a break signal for a tenth of a second:

```
' Set the Break condition.
MSComm1.Break = True
' Set duration to 1/10 second.
Duration! = Timer + .1
' Wait for the duration to pass.
Do Until Timer > Duration!
   Dummy = DoEvents()
Loop
' Clear the Break condition.
MSComm1.Break = False
```

CDHolding Property

Determines whether the carrier is present by querying the state of the Carrier Detect (CD) line. Carrier Detect is a signal sent from a modem to the attached computer to indicate that the modem is online. This property is not available at design time and is read-only at run time.

Applies To

MSComm Control

Syntax

object.**CDHolding**

The **CDHolding** property syntax has these parts:

Part	Description
object	An object expression that evaluates to an object in the **Applies To** list.

Settings

The settings for the **CDHolding** property are:

Setting	Description
True	Carrier Detect line is high
False	Carrier Detect line is low

Remarks

When the Carrier Detect line is high (**CDHolding = True**) and times out, the **MSComm** control sets the **CommEvent** property to **comEventCDTO** (Carrier Detect Timeout Error), and generates the **OnComm** event.

Note It is especially important to trap a loss of the carrier in a host application, such as a bulletin board, because the caller can hang up (drop the carrier) at any time.

The Carrier Detect is also known as the Receive Line Signal Detect (RLSD).

Data Type

Boolean

See Also

MSComm Control, **CTSHolding** Property, **DSRHolding** Property, **MSComm** Control Constants, **Error Messages**

CommEvent Property

Returns the most recent communication event or error. This property is not available at design time and is read-only at run time.

Applies To

MSComm Control

Syntax

object.**CommEvent**

The **CommEvent** property syntax has these parts:

Part	Description
object	An object expression that evaluates to an object in the **Applies To** list.

Remarks

Although the **OnComm** event is generated whenever a communication error or event occurs, the **CommEvent** property holds the numeric code for that error or event. To determine the actual error or event that caused the **OnComm** event, you must reference the **CommEvent** property.

The **CommEvent** property returns one of the following values for communication errors or events. These constants can also be found in the Object Library for this control.

Communication errors include the following settings:

Constant	Value	Description
comEventBreak	1001	A Break signal was received.
comEventCTSTO	1002	Clear To Send Timeout. The Clear To Send line was low for the system specified amount of time while trying to transmit a character.
comEventDSRTO	1003	Data Set Ready Timeout. The Data Set Ready line was low for the system specified amount of time while trying to transmit a character.
ComEventFrame	1004	Framing Error. The hardware detected a framing error.
ComEventOverrun	1006	Port Overrun. A character was not read from the hardware before the next character arrived and was lost.
ComEventCDTO	1007	Carrier Detect Timeout. The Carrier Detect line was low for the system specified amount of time while trying to transmit a character. Carrier Detect is also known as the Receive Line Signal Detect (RLSD).
ComEventRxOver	1008	Receive Buffer Overflow. There is no room in the receive buffer.
ComEventRxParity	1009	Parity Error. The hardware detected a parity error.
ComEventTxFull	1010	Transmit Buffer Full. The transmit buffer was full while trying to queue a character.
ComEventDCB	1011	Unexpected error retrieving Device Control Block (DCB) for the port.

Communications events include the following settings:

Constant	Value	Description
comEvSend	1	There are fewer than Sthreshold number of characters in the transmit buffer.
ComEvReceive	2	Received Rthreshold number of characters. This event is generated continuously until you use the Input property to remove the data from the receive buffer.
ComEvCTS	3	Change in Clear To Send line.
comEvDSR	4	Change in Data Set Ready line. This event is only fired when DSR changes from 1 to 0.
comEvCD	5	Change in Carrier Detect line.
comEvRing	6	Ring detected. Some UARTs (universal asynchronous receiver-transmitters) may not support this event.
comEvEOF	7	End Of File (ASCII character 26) character received.

Data Type

Integer

See Also

MSComm Control, **OnComm** Event, **MSComm** Control Constants, **Error Messages**

CommID Property

Returns a handle that identifies the communications device. This property is not available at design time and is read-only at run time.

Applies To

MSComm Control

Syntax

object.**CommID**

The **CommID** property syntax has these parts:

Part	Description
object	An object expression that evaluates to an object in the **Applies To** list.

Remarks

This is the same value that's returned by the Windows API **CreateFile** function. Use this value when calling any communications routines in the Windows API.

Data Type

Long

See Also

MSComm Control, **MSComm** Control Constants, **Error Messages**

CommPort Property

Sets and returns the communications port number.

Applies To

MSComm Control

Syntax

object.**CommPort**[= *value*]

The **CommPort** property syntax has these parts:

Part	Description
object	An object expression that evaluates to an object in the **Applies To** list.
value	A integer value specifying the port number.

Remarks

You can set *value* to any number between 1 and 16 at design time (the default is 1). However, the **MSComm** control generates error 68 (Device unavailable) if the port does not exist when you attempt to open it with the **PortOpen** property.

Warning You must set the **CommPort** property before opening the port.

Data Type

Integer

See Also

MSComm Control, **PortOpen** Property, **MSComm** Control Constants, **Error Messages**

CTSHolding Property

Determines whether you can send data by querying the state of the Clear To Send (CTS) line. Typically, the Clear To Send signal is sent from a modem to the attached computer to indicate that transmission can proceed. This property is not available at design time and is read-only at run time.

Applies To

MSComm Control

Syntax

object.**CTSHolding**

The **CTSHolding** property syntax has these parts:

Part	Description
object	An object expression that evaluates to an object in the **Applies To** list.

The following table lists the **CTSHolding** property settings for the **MSComm** control.

Setting	Description
True	Clear To Send line high.
False	Clear To Send line low.

Remarks

When the Clear To Send line is low (**CTSHolding = False**) and times out, the **MSComm** control sets the **CommEvent** property to **comEventCTSTO** (Clear To Send Timeout) and invokes the **OnComm** event.

The Clear To Send line is used in RTS/CTS (Request To Send/Clear To Send) hardware handshaking. The **CTSHolding** property gives you a way to manually poll the Clear To Send line if you need to determine its state.

For more information on handshaking protocols, see the Handshaking property.

Data Type

Boolean

See Also

MSComm Control, **CDHolding** Property, **DSRHolding** Property, **MSComm** Control Constants, **Error Messages**

DSRHolding Property

Determines the state of the Data Set Ready (DSR) line. Typically, the Data Set Ready signal is sent by a modem to its attached computer to indicate that it is ready to operate. This property is not available at design time and is read-only at run time.

Applies To

MSComm Control

Syntax

object.**DSRHolding**

The *object* placeholder represents an object expression that evaluates to an object in the **Applies To** list.

The **DSRHolding** property returns the following values:

Value	Description
True	Data Set Ready line high
False	Data Set Ready line low

Remarks

When the Data Set Ready line is high (**DSRHolding = True**) and has timed out, the **MSComm** control sets the **CommEvent** property to **comEventDSRTO** (Data Set Ready Timeout) and invokes the **OnComm** event.

This property is useful when writing a Data Set Ready/Data Terminal Ready handshaking routine for a Data Terminal Equipment (DTE) machine.

Data Type

Boolean

See Also

MSComm Control, **CDHolding** Property, **CTSHolding** Property, **MSComm** Control Constants, **Error Messages**

DTREnable Property

Determines whether to enable the Data Terminal Ready (DTR) line during communications. Typically, the Data Terminal Ready signal is sent by a computer to its modem to indicate that the computer is ready to accept incoming transmission.

Applies To

MSComm Control

Syntax

object.**DTREnable**[= *value*]

The **DTREnable** property syntax has these parts:

Part	Description
object	An object expression that evaluates to an object in the **Applies To** list.
Value	A Boolean expression specifying whether to enable the Data Terminal Ready (DTR) line, as described in Settings.

Settings

The settings for *value* are:

Setting	Description
True	Enable the Data Terminal Ready line.
False	(Default) Disable the Data Terminal Ready line.

Remarks

When **DTREnable** is set to **True**, the Data Terminal Ready line is set to high (on) when the port is opened, and low (off) when the port is closed. When **DTREnable** is set to **False**, the Data Terminal Ready always remains low.

Note In most cases, setting the Data Terminal Ready line to low hangs up the telephone.

Data Type

Boolean

See Also

MSComm Control, **MSComm** Control Constants, **Error Messages**, **EOFEnable**
Property

EOFEnable Property

The **EOFEnable** property determines if the **MSComm** control looks for End Of
File (EOF) characters during input. If an EOF character is found, the input will
stop and the **OnComm** event will fire with the **CommEvent** property set to
comEvEOF.

Applies To

MSComm Control

Syntax

object.**EOFEnable** [= *value*]

The **EOFEnable** property syntax has these parts:

Part	Description
object	An object expression that evaluates to an object in the **Applies To** list.
value	A Boolean expression that determines whether the **OnComm** event is fired when an EOF character is found, as described in Settings.

Settings

The settings for *value* are:

Setting	Description
True	The **OnComm** event is fired when an EOF character is found.
False	(Default) The **OnComm** event isn't fired when an EOF character is found.

Remarks

When **EOFEnable** property is set to **False**, the control will not scan the input stream
for EOF characters.

See Also

MSComm Control, **CommEvent** Property, **OnComm** Event, **MSComm** Control
Constants, **Error Messages**

Error Messages

The following table lists the trappable errors for the **MSComm** control.

Error Number	Message Explanation
8000	Operation not valid while the port is opened
8001	Timeout value must be greater than zero
8002	Invalid Port Number
8003	Property available only at run time
8004	Property is read only at runtime
8005	Port already open
8006	The device identifier is invalid or unsupported
8007	The device's baud rate is unsupported
8008	The specified byte size is invalid
8009	The default parameters are in error
8010	The hardware is not available (locked by another device)
8011	The function cannot allocate the queues
8012	The device is not open
8013	The device is already open
8014	Could not enable comm notification
8015	Could not set comm state
8016	Could not set comm event mask
8018	Operation valid only when the port is open
8019	Device busy
8020	Error reading comm device

See Also

MSComm Control

Handshaking Property

Sets and returns the hardware handshaking protocol.

Applies To

MSComm Control

Syntax

object.**Handshaking** [= *value*]

The **Handshaking** property syntax has these parts:

Part	Description
object	An object expression that evaluates to an object in the **Applies To** list.
value	An integer expression specifying the handshaking protocol, as described in Settings.

Settings

The settings for *value* are:

Setting	Value	Description
comNone	0	(Default) No handshaking.
comXOnXOff	1	XON/XOFF handshaking.
comRTS	2	RTS/CTS (Request To Send/Clear To Send) handshaking.
comRTSXOnXOff	3	Both Request To Send and XON/XOFF handshaking.

Remarks

Handshaking refers to the internal communications protocol by which data is transferred from the hardware port to the receive buffer. When a character of data arrives at the serial port, the communications device has to move it into the receive buffer so that your program can read it. If there is no receive buffer and your program is expected to read every character directly from the hardware, you will probably lose data because the characters can arrive very quickly.

A handshaking protocol insures data is not lost due to a buffer overrun, where data arrives at the port too quickly for the communications device to move the data into the receive buffer.

Data Type

Integer

See Also

MSComm Control, **MSComm** Control Constants, **Error Messages**

InBufferCount Property

Returns the number of characters waiting in the receive buffer. This property is not available at design time.

Applies To

MSComm Control

Syntax

object.**InBufferCount**[= *value*]

The **InBufferCount** property syntax has these parts:

Part	Description
object	An object expression that evaluates to an object in the **Applies To** list.
value	An integer expression specifying the number of characters waiting in the receive buffer.

Remarks

InBufferCount refers to the number of characters that have been received by the modem and are waiting in the receive buffer for you to take them out. You can clear the receive buffer by setting the **InBufferCount** property to 0.

Note Do not confuse this property with the **InBufferSize** property. The **InBufferSize** property reflects the total size of the receive buffer.

Data Type

Integer

See Also

MSComm Control, **InBufferSize** Property, **MSComm** Control Constants, **Error Messages**

InBufferSize Property

Sets and returns the size of the receive buffer in bytes.

Applies To

MSComm Control

Syntax

object.**InBufferSize**[= *value*]

The **InBufferSize** property syntax has these parts:

Part	Description
object	An object expression that evaluates to an object in the **Applies To** list.
value	An integer expression specifying the size of the receive buffer in bytes.

Remarks

InBufferSize refers to the total size of the receive buffer. The default size is 1024 bytes. Do not confuse this property with the **InBufferCount** property which reflects the number of characters currently waiting in the receive buffer.

Note Note that the larger you make the receive buffer, the less memory you have available to your application. However, if your buffer is too small, it runs the risk of overflowing unless handshaking is used. As a general rule, start with a buffer size of 1024 bytes. If an overflow error occurs, increase the buffer size to handle your application's transmission rate.

Data Type

Integer

Input Property

Returns and removes a stream of data from the receive buffer. This property is not available at design time and is read-only at run time.

Applies To

MSComm Control

Syntax

object.**Input**

The **Input** property syntax has these parts:

Part	Description
object	An object expression that evaluates to an object in the **Applies To** list.

Remarks

The **InputLen** property determines the number of characters that are read by the **Input** property. Setting **InputLen** to 0 causes the **Input** property to read the entire contents of the receive buffer.

The **InputMode** property determines the type of data that is retrieved with the **Input** property. If **InputMode** is set to **comInputModeText** then the **Input** property returns text data in a **Variant**. If **InputMode** is **comInputModeBinary** then the **Input** property returns binary data in an array of bytes in a **Variant**.

Data Type

Variant

See Also

MSComm Control, **InputLen** Property, **MSComm** Control Constants, **Error Messages**, **InputMode** Property

Example

This example shows how to retrieve data from the receive buffer:

```
Private Sub Command1_Click()
Dim InString as String
' Retrieve all available data.
MSComm1.InputLen = 0

' Check for data.
If MSComm1.InBufferCount Then
    ' Read data.
    InString = MSComm1.Input
End If
End Sub
```

InputLen Property

Sets and returns the number of characters the **Input** property reads from the receive buffer.

Applies To

MSComm Control

Syntax

object.**InputLen** [= *value*]

The **InputLen** property syntax has these parts:

Part	Description
object	An object expression that evaluates to an object in the **Applies To** list.
value	An integer expression specifying the number of characters the **Input** property reads from the receive buffer.

Remarks

The default value for the **InputLen** property is 0. Setting **InputLen** to 0 causes the **MSComm** control to read the entire contents of the receive buffer when **Input** is used.

If **InputLen** characters are not available in the receive buffer, the **Input** property returns a zero-length string (" "). The user can optionally check the **InBufferCount** property to determine if the required number of characters are present before using **Input**.

This property is useful when reading data from a machine whose output is formatted in fixed-length blocks of data.

Data Type

Integer

See Also

MSComm Control, **Input** Property, **MSComm** Control Constants, **Error Messages**, **InputMode** Property

Example

This example shows how to read 10 characters of data:

```
Private Command1_Click()
Dim CommData as String
' Specify a 10 character block of data.
MSComm1.InputLen = 10
' Read data.
CommData = MSComm1.Input
End Sub
```

InputMode Property

Sets or returns the type of data retrieved by the **Input** property.

Applies To

MSComm Control

Syntax

object.**InputMode** [= *value*]

The **InputMode** property syntax has these parts:

Part	Description
object	An object expression that evaluates to an object in the **Applies To** list.
value	A value or constant that specifies the input mode, as described in Settings.

Settings

The settings for *value* are:

Constant	Value	Description
comInputModeText	0	(Default) Data is retrieved through the **Input** property as text.
comInputModeBinary	1	Data is retrieved through the **Input** property as binary data.

Remarks

The **InputMode** property determines how data will be retrieved through the **Input** property. The data will either be retrieved as string or as binary data in a byte array.

Use **comInputModeText** for data that uses the ANSI character set. Use **comInputModeBinary** for all other data such as data that has embedded control characters, Nulls, etc.

See Also

MSComm Control, **Input** Property, **InputLen** Property, **MSComm** Control Constants, **Error Messages**

Example

This example reads 10 bytes of binary data from the communications port and assigns it to a byte array.

```
Private Sub Command1_Click()
Dim Buffer as Variant
Dim Arr() as Byte

' Set and open port
MSComm1.CommPort = 1
MSComm1.PortOpen = True

' Set InputMode to read binary data
MSComm1.InputMode = comInputModeBinary
```

```
' Wait until 10 bytes are in the input buffer
Do Until MSComm1.InBufferCount < 10
    DoEvents
Loop

' Store binary data in buffer
Buffer = MSComm1.Input

' Assign to byte array for processing
Arr = Buffer

End Sub
```

MSComm Control Constants

Handshake Constants

Constant	Value	Description
comNone	0	No handshaking.
comXonXoff	1	XOn/XOff handshaking.
comRTS	2	Request-to-send/clear-to-send handshaking.
comRTSXOnXOff	3	Both request-to-send and XOn/XOff handshaking.

OnComm Constants

Constant	Value	Description
comEvSend	1	Send event.
comEvReceive	2	Receive event.
comEvCTS	3	Change in clear-to-send line.
comEvDSR	4	Change in data-set ready line.
comEvCD	5	Change in carrier detect line.
comEvRing	6	Ring detect.
comEvEOF	7	End of file.

Error Constants

Constant	Value	Description
comEventBreak	1001	Break signal received
comEventCTSTO	1002	Clear-to-send timeout
comEventDSRTO	1003	Data-set ready timeout
comEventFrame	1004	Framing error
comEventOverrun	1006	Port overrun
comEventCDTO	1007	Carrier detect timeout
comEventRxOver	1008	Receive buffer overflow

(continued)

(continued)

Constant	Value	Description
comEventRxParity	1009	Parity error
comEventTxFull	1010	Transmit buffer full
comEventDCB	1011	Unexpected error retrieving Device Control Block (DCB) for the port

InputMode Constants

Constant	Value	Description
comInputModeText	0	(Default) Data is retrieved through the **Input** property as text.
comInputModeBinary	1	Data is retrieved through the **Input** property as binary data.

See Also

Error Messages, **MSComm** Control, **Visual Basic** Constants

NullDiscard Property

Determines whether null characters are transferred from the port to the receive buffer.

Applies To

MSComm Control

Syntax

object.**NullDiscard** [= *value*]

The **NullDiscard** property syntax has these parts:

Part	Description
object	An object expression that evaluates to an object in the **Applies To** list.
value	A Boolean expression specifying whether null characters are transferred from the port to the receive buffer, as described in Settings

Settings

The settings for *value* are:

Setting	Description
True	Null characters are *not* transferred from the port to the receive buffer.
False	(Default) Null characters are transferred from the port to the receive buffer.

Remarks

A null character is defined as ASCII character 0, `Chr$(0)`.

Data Type

Boolean

See Also

MSComm Control, **MSComm** Control Constants, **Error Messages**

OnComm Event

The **OnComm** event is generated whenever the value of the **CommEvent** property changes, indicating that either a communication event or an error occurred.

Applies To

MSComm Control

Syntax

Private Sub *object*_**OnComm** ()

The **OnComm** event syntax has these parts:

Part	Description
object	An object expression that evaluates to an object in the **Applies To** list.

Remarks

The **CommEvent** property contains the numeric code of the actual error or event that generated the **OnComm** event. Note that setting the **RThreshold** or **SThreshold** properties to 0 disables trapping for the **comEvReceive** and **comEvSend** events, respectively.

See Also

MSComm Control, **CommEvent** Property, **MSComm** Control Constants, **Error Messages**

Example

The following example shows how to handle communications errors and events. You can insert code after each related Case statement, to handle a particular error or event.

```
Private Sub MSComm_OnComm ()
   Select Case MSComm1.CommEvent
   ' Handle each event or error by placing
   ' code below each case statement

   ' Errors
      Case comEventBreak    ' A Break was received.
      Case comEventCDTO     ' CD (RLSD) Timeout.
      Case comEventCTSTO    ' CTS Timeout.
      Case comEventDSRTO    ' DSR Timeout.
      Case comEventFrame    ' Framing Error
      Case comEventOverrun  ' Data Lost.
      Case comEventRxOver   ' Receive buffer overflow.
      Case comEventRxParity ' Parity Error.
      Case comEventTxFull   ' Transmit buffer full.
      Case comEventDCB      ' Unexpected error retrieving DCB]
```

```
' Events
   Case comEvCD        ' Change in the CD line.
   Case comEvCTS       ' Change in the CTS line.
   Case comEvDSR       ' Change in the DSR line.
   Case comEvRing      ' Change in the Ring Indicator.
   Case comEvReceive   ' Received RThreshold # of
                       ' chars.
   Case comEvSend      ' There are SThreshold number of
                       ' characters in the transmit
                       ' buffer.
   Case comEvEof       ' An EOF charater was found in
                       ' the input stream
End Select
End Sub
```

OutBufferCount Property

Returns the number of characters waiting in the transmit buffer. You can also use it to clear the transmit buffer. This property is not available at design time.

Applies To

MSComm Control

Syntax

object.**OutBufferCount** [= *value*]

The **OutBufferCount** property syntax has these parts:

Part	Description
object	An object expression that evaluates to an object in the **Applies To** list.
value	An integer expression specifying the number of characters waiting in the transmit buffer.

Remarks

You can clear the transmit buffer by setting the **OutBufferCount** property to 0.

Note   Do not confuse the **OutBufferCount** property with the **OutBufferSize** property which reflects the total size of the transmit buffer.

Data Type

Integer

See Also

MSComm Control, **OutBufferSize** Property, **Output** Property, **MSComm** Control Constants, **Error Messages**

OutBufferSize Property

Sets and returns the size, in bytes, of the transmit buffer.

Applies To

MSComm Control

Syntax

object.**OutBufferSize** [= *object*]

The **OutBufferSize** property syntax has these parts:

Part	Description
object	An object expression that evaluates to an object in the **Applies To** list.
value	An integer expression specifying the size of the transmit buffer.

Remarks

OutBufferSize refers to the total size of the transmit buffer. The default size is 512 bytes. Do not confuse this property with the **OutBufferCount** which reflects the number of bytes currently waiting in the transmit buffer.

Note   The larger you make the transmit buffer, the less memory you have available to your application. However, if your buffer is too small, you run the risk of overflowing unless you use handshaking. As a general rule, start with a buffer size of 512 bytes. If an overflow error occurs, increase the buffer size to handle your application's transmission rate.

Data Type

Integer

See Also

MSComm Control, **OutBufferCount** Property, **Output** Property, **MSComm** Control Constants, **Error Messages**

Output Property

Writes a stream of data to the transmit buffer. This property is not available at design time and is write-only at run time.

Applies To

MSComm Control

Syntax

object.**Output** [= *value*]

The **Output** property syntax has these parts:

Part	Description
object	An object expression that evaluates to an object in the **Applies To** list.
value	A string of characters to write to the transmit buffer.

Remarks

The **Output** property can transmit text data or binary data. To send text data using the **Output** property, you must specify a **Variant** that contains a string. To send binary data, you must pass a **Variant** which contains a byte array to the **Output** property.

Normally, if you are sending an ANSI string to an application, you can send it as text data. If you have data that contains embedded control characters, Null characters, etc., then you will want to pass it as binary data.

Data Type

Variant

See Also

MSComm Control, **OutBufferCount** Property, **OutBufferSize** Property, **MSComm** Control Constants, **Error Messages**

Example

The following example shows how to send every character the user types to the serial port:

```
Private Sub Form_KeyPress (KeyAscii As Integer)
   Dim Buffer as Variant

   ' Set and open port
   MSComm1.CommPort = 1
   MSComm1.PortOpen = True

   Buffer = Chr$(KeyAscii)
   MSComm1.Output = Buffer
End Sub
```

ParityReplace Property

Sets and returns the character that replaces an invalid character in the data stream when a parity error occurs.

Applies To

MSComm Control

Syntax

object.**ParityReplace** [= *value*]

The **ParityReplace** property syntax has these parts:

Part	Description
object	An object expression that evaluates to an object in the **Applies To** list.
value	A string expression representing a character, as described in Remarks.

Remarks

The *parity bit* refers to a bit that is transmitted along with a specified number of data bits to provide a small amount of error checking. When you use a parity bit, the **MSComm** control adds up all the bits that are set (having a value of 1) in the data and tests the sum as being odd or even (according to the parity setting used when the port was opened).

By default, the control uses a question mark (?) character for replacing invalid characters. Setting **ParityReplace** to an empty string ("") disables replacement of the character where the parity error occurs. The **OnComm** event is still fired and the **CommEvent** property is set to **comEventRXParity**.

The **ParityReplace** character is used in a byte-oriented operation, and must be a single-byte character. You can specify any ANSI character code with a value from 0 to 255.

Data Type

String

See Also

MSComm Control, **CommEvent** Property, **OnComm** Event, **MSComm** Control Constants, **Error Messages**

PortOpen Property

Sets and returns the state of the communications port (open or closed). Not available at design time.

Applies To

MSComm Control

Syntax

object.**PortOpen** [= *value*]

The **PortOpen** property syntax has these parts:

Part	Description
object	An object expression that evaluates to an object in the **Applies To** list.
value	A Boolean expression specifying the state of the communications port.

Settings

The settings for *value* are:

Setting	Description
True	Port is opened
False	Port is closed

Remarks

Setting the **PortOpen** property to **True** opens the port. Setting it to **False** closes the port and clears the receive and transmit buffers. The **MSComm** control automatically closes the serial port when your application is terminated.

Make sure the **CommPort** property is set to a valid port number before opening the port. If the **CommPort** property is set to an invalid port number when you try to open the port, the **MSComm** control generates error 68 (Device unavailable).

In addition, your serial port device must support the current values in the **Settings** property. If the **Settings** property contains communications settings that your hardware does not support, your hardware may not work correctly.

If either the **DTREnable** or the **RTSEnable** properties is set to **True** before the port is opened, the properties are set to **False** when the port is closed. Otherwise, the DTR and RTS lines remain in their previous state.

Data Type

Boolean

See Also

MSComm Control, **CommPort** Property, **DTREnable** Property, **Settings** Property, **MSComm** Control Constants, **EOFEnable** Property

Example

The following example opens communications port number 1 at 9600 baud with no parity checking, 8 data bits, and 1 stop bit:

```
MSComm1.Settings = "9600,n,8,1"
MSComm1.CommPort = 1
MSComm1.PortOpen = True
```

RThreshold Property

Sets and returns the number of characters to receive before the **MSComm** control sets the **CommEvent** property to **comEvReceive** and generates the **OnComm** event.

Applies To

MSComm Control

Syntax

object.**Rthreshold** [= *value*]

The **Rthreshold** property syntax has these parts:

Part	Description
object	An object expression that evaluates to an object in the **Applies To** list.
value	An integer expression specifying the number of characters to receive before generating the **OnComm** event.

Remarks

Setting the **RThreshold** property to 0 (the default) disables generating the **OnComm** event when characters are received.

Setting **RThreshold** to 1, for example, causes the **MSComm** control to generate the **OnComm** event every time a single character is placed in the receive buffer.

Data Type

Integer

See Also

MSComm Control, **CommEvent** Property, **OnComm** Event, **MSComm** Control Constants, **Error Messages**

RTSEnable Property

Determines whether to enable the Request To Send (RTS) line. Typically, the Request To Send signal that requests permission to transmit data is sent from a computer to its attached modem.

Applies To

MSComm Control

Syntax

object.**RTSEnable**[= *value*]

The **RTSEnable** property syntax has these parts:

Part	Description
object	An object expression that evaluates to an object in the **Applies To** list.
value	A Boolean expression specifying whether the Request To Send (RTS) line is enabled, as described in Settings.

Settings

The settings for *value* are:

Setting	Description
True	Enables the Request To Send line.
False	(Default) Disables the Request To Send line.

Remarks

When **RTSEnable** is set to **True**, the Request To Send line is set to high (on) when the port is opened, and low (off) when the port is closed.

The Request To Send line is used in RTS/CTS hardware handshaking. The **RTSEnable** property allows you to manually poll the Request To Send line if you need to determine its state.

For more information on handshaking protocols, see the **Handshaking** property.

Data Type

Boolean

See Also

MSComm Control, **Handshaking** Property, **MSComm** Control Constants, **Error Messages**

Settings Property

Sets and returns the baud rate, parity, data bit, and stop bit parameters.

Applies To

MSComm Control

Syntax

object.**Settings** [= *value*]

The **Settings** property syntax has these parts:

Part	Description
object	An object expression that evaluates to an object in the **Applies To** list.
value	An string expression representing the communications port settings, as described below.

Remarks

If *value* is not valid when the port is opened, the **MSComm** control generates error 380 (Invalid property value).

Value is composed of four settings and has the following format:

`"BBBB,P,D,S"`

Where BBBB is the baud rate, P is the parity, D is the number of data bits, and S is the number of stop bits. The default value of *value* is:

`"9600,N,8,1"`

The following table lists the valid baud rates.

Setting

110

300

600

1200

2400

9600 (Default)

14400

19200

28800

38400 (reserved)

56000 (reserved)

128000 (reserved)

256000 (reserved)

The following table describes the valid parity values.

Setting	Description
E	Even
M	Mark
N	(Default)
None	
O	Odd
S	Space

The following table lists the valid data bit values.

Setting

4

5

6

7

8

(Default)

The following table lists the valid stop bit values.

Setting	
1	(Default)
1.5	
2	

Data Type

String

See Also

MSComm Control, **MSComm** Control Constants, **Error Messages**

Example

The following example sets the control's port to communicate at 9600 baud with no parity checking, 8 data bits, and 1 stop bit:

```
MSComm1.Settings = "9600,N,8,1"
```

SThreshold Property

Sets and returns the minimum number of characters allowable in the transmit buffer before the **MSComm** control sets the **CommEvent** property to **comEvSend** and generates the **OnComm** event.

Applies To

MSComm Control

Syntax

object.**SThreshold** [= *value*]

The **SThreshold** property syntax has these parts:

Part	Description
object	An object expression that evaluates to an object in the **Applies To** list.
value	An integer expression representing the minimum number of characters in the transmit buffer before the **OnComm** event is generated.

Remarks

Setting the **SThreshold** property to 0 (the default) disables generating the **OnComm** event for data transmission events. Setting the **SThreshold** property to 1 causes the **MSComm** control to generate the **OnComm** event when the transmit buffer is completely empty.

If the number of characters in the transmit buffer is less than *value*, the **CommEvent** property is set to **comEvSend**, and the **OnComm** event is generated. The **comEvSend** event is only fired once, when the number of characters crosses the **SThreshold**. For example, if **SThreshold** equals five, the **comEvSend** event occurs only when the number of characters drops from five to four in the output queue. If there are never more than **SThreshold** characters in the output queue, the event is never fired.

Data Type

Integer

See Also

MSComm Control, **CommEvent** Property, **OnComm** Event, **MSComm** Control Constants, **Error Messages**

MSFlexGrid Control

The **MSFlexGrid** control displays and operates on tabular data. It allows complete flexibility to sort, merge, and format tables containing strings and pictures. When bound to a **Data** control, **MsFlexGrid** displays read-only data.

Syntax

MSFlexGrid

Remarks

You can put text, a picture, or both in any cell of a **MSFlexGrid**. The **Row** and **Col** properties specify the current cell in a **MSFlexGrid**. You can specify the current cell in code, or the user can change it at run time using the mouse or the arrow keys. The **Text** property references the contents of the current cell.

If a cell's text is too long to be displayed in the cell, and the **WordWrap** property is set to **True**, the text wraps to the next line within the same cell. To display the wrapped text, you may need to increase the cell's column width (**ColWidth** property) or row height (**RowHeight** property).

Use the **Cols** and **Rows** properties to determine the number of columns and rows in a **MSFlexGrid** control.

Distribution Note   Before you can use a **MSFlexGrid** control in your application, you must add the MSFlxGrd.ocx file to your project. To automatically include the file in your project, put it in the Autoload file. When distributing your application, you should install the MSFlxGrd.ocx file in the user's Microsoft Windows System directory. For more information about adding an ActiveX control to a project, see the *Programmer's Guide*.

Properties

AllowBigSelection Property, **AllowResizing** Property, **Appearance** Property (ActiveX Controls), **BackColor**, **BackColorBkg**, **BackColorFixed**, **BackColorSel** Properties, **BackColor**, **ForeColor** Properties (ActiveX Controls), **BorderStyle** Property (ActiveX Controls), **CellAlignment** Property, **CellBackColor**, **CellForeColor** Properties, **CellFontBold** Property, **CellFontItalic** Property, **CellFontName** Property, **CellFontSize** Property, **CellFontStrikeThrough** Property, **CellFontUnderline** Property, **CellFontWidth** Property, **CellHeight**, **CellLeft**, **CellTop**, **CellWidth** Properties (MSFlexGrid), **CellPicture** Property, **CellPictureAlignment** Property, **CellTextStyle** Property, **Clip** Property (MSFlexGrid), **Col**, **Row** Properties (MSFlexGrid), **ColAlignment** Property (MSFlexGrid), **ColData**, **RowData** Properties, **CollsVisible** Property, **ColPos** Property, **ColPosition**, **RowPosition** Properties, **Cols**, **Rows** Properties (MSFlexGrid), **ColSel**, **RowSel** Properties, **ColWidth** Property (MSFlexGrid), **Container** Property, **DataBindings** Property, **DataSource** Property (ActiveX Controls), **DragIcon** Property, **DragMode** Property, **Enabled** Property, **FillStyle** Property (MSFlexGrid), **FixedAlignment** Property, **FixedCols**, **FixedRows** Properties (MSFlexGrid), **FocusRect** Property, **FontWidth** Property, **ForeColor**,

ForeColorFixed, ForeColorSel Properties, FormatString Property, GridColor, GridColorFixed Properties, GridLineWidth Property, Height, Width Properties (ActiveX Controls), HelpContextID Property, HighLight Property (MSFlexGrid), hWnd Property, Index Property (ActiveX Controls), Left, Top Properties (ActiveX Controls), LeftCol Property (MSFlexGrid), MergeCells Property, MergeCol, MergeRows Properties, MouseCol, MouseRow Properties, MouseIcon Property, MousePointer Property (ActiveX Controls), Name Property, Object Property, OLEDropMode Property (ActiveX Controls), Parent Property, Picture Property, PictureType Property, Redraw Property, RemoveItem Method (MSFlexGrid), RightToLeft Property (ActiveX Controls), RowHeight Property (MSFlexGrid), RowHeightMin Property, RowIsVisible Property, RowPos Property, ScrollBars Property (MSFlexGrid), ScrollTrack Property, SelectionMode Property, Sort Property (MSFlexGrid), TabIndex Property, TabStop Property, Tag Property (ActiveX Controls), Text Property, TextArray Property, TextMatrix Property, TextStyle, TextStyleFixed Properties, ToolTipText Property, TopRow Property (MSFlexGrid), Version Property (MSFlexGrid), Visible Property (ActiveX Controls), WhatsThisHelpID Property, WordWrap Property (MSFlexGrid)

Events

Click Event, Compare Event, DragDrop Event, DragOver Event, EnterCell Event, GotFocus Event, KeyDown, KeyUp Events, KeyPress Event, LeaveCell Event, LostFocus Event, MouseDown, MouseUp Events, MouseMove Event, OLECompleteDrag Event (ActiveX Controls), OLEDragDrop Event (ActiveX Controls), OLEDragOver Event (ActiveX Controls), OLEGiveFeedback Event (ActiveX Controls), OLESetData Event (ActiveX Controls), OLEStartDrag Event (ActiveX Controls), RowColChage Event (MSFlexGrid), Scroll Event (MSFlexGrid), SelChange Event (MSFlexGrid)

Methods

AddItem Method (MSFlexGrid), Clear Method (MSFlexGrid), Drag Method, Move Method, OLEDrag Method (ActiveX Controls), Refresh Method (ActiveX Controls), RemoveItem Method, SetFocus Method, ShowWhatsThis Method, ZOrder Method

See Also

MSFlexGrid Control Constants

AddItem Method (MSFlexGrid)

Adds a row to a **MSFlexGrid** control. Doesn't support named arguments.

Applies To

MSFlexGrid Control

Syntax

object.**AddItem** (*item* **As String**, *index*)

The **AddItem** method syntax has these parts:

Part	Description
object	An object expression that evaluates to an object in the **Applies To** list.
item	Required. A string expression displayed in the newly added row. To add multiple strings (for multiple columns in the row), use the tab character (**vbTab**) to separate each string.
Index	Optional. A Long representing the position within the control where the new row is placed. For the first row, *index*=0. If *index* is omitted, the new row becomes the last.

Example

This example uses the **AddItem** method to add 100 items to a **MSFlexGrid**. To try this example, paste the code into the Declarations section of a form with a **MSFlexGrid** control named MSFlexGrid1, and then press F5 and click the form.

```
Private Sub Form_Click ()
   Dim Entry, i, Msg                ' Declare variables.
   Msg = _
   "Choose OK to add 100 items to your MSFlexGrid."
   MsgBox Msg                       ' Display message.
   MSFlexGrid1.Cols = 2             ' Two strings per row.
   For i = 1 To 100                 ' Count from 1 to 100.
      Entry = "Entry " & Chr(9) & I ' Create entry.
      MSFlexGrid1.AddItem Entry     ' Add entry.
   Next i
   Msg = "Choose OK to remove every other entry."
   MsgBox Msg                       ' Display message.
   For i = 1 To 50                  ' Determine how to
      MSFlexGrid1.RemoveItem i      ' remove every other
   Next I                           ' item.
   Msg = "Choose OK to clear all items."
   MsgBox Msg                       ' Display message.
   MSFlexGrid1.Clear                ' Clear list box.
End Sub
```

AllowBigSelection Property

Returns or sets a value that determines whether clicking on a column or row header should cause the entire column or row to be selected.

Applies To

MSFlexGrid Control

Syntax

object.**AllowBigSelection** [= *boolean*]

The **AllowBigSelection** property syntax has these parts:

Part	Description
object	An object expression that evaluates to an object in the **Applies To** list.
boolean	Determines whether an entire column or row is selected when the header is clicked. The property is **True** by default.

Remarks

For example, the following code allows an entire column or row to be selected when the user clicks on the header:

```
Sub Form1_Load ()
   MSFlexGrid1.AllowBigSelection = True
End Sub
```

See Also

SelectionMode Property

AllowUserResizing Property

Returns or sets a value that determines whether the user should be allowed to resize rows and columns in the **MSFlexGrid** control with the mouse.

Applies To

MSFlexGrid Control

Syntax

object.**AllowUserResizing** [= *value*]

The **AllowUserResizing** property syntax has these parts:

Part	Description
object	An object expression that evaluates to an object in the **Applies To** list.
value	An integer or constant specifying whether a user can resize rows and columns, as described in **Settings**.

Settings

The settings for *value* are:

Constant	Value	Description
flexResizeNone	0	Default) None. The user can't resize with the mouse.
flexResizeColumns	1	Columns. The user can resize columns using the mouse.
flexResizeRows	2	Rows. The user can resize rows using the mouse.
flexResizeBoth	3	Both. The user can resize columns and rows using the mouse.

Remarks

To resize rows or columns, the mouse must be over the fixed area of the **MSFlexGrid** control, and close to a border between rows and columns. The mouse pointer will change into an appropriate sizing pointer and the user can drag the row or column to change the row height or column width. The following code allows this functionality:

```
Sub Form1_Load ()
   MSFlexGrid1.AllowUserResizing = True
End Sub
```

See Also

ColWidth Property (MSFlexGrid)

BackColor, BackColorBkg, BackColorFixed, BackColorSel Properties

Returns or sets the background color of various elements of the **MSFlexGrid**.

Applies To

MSFlexGrid Control

Syntax

object.**BackColor** [=*color*]
object.**BackColorBkg** [=*color*]
object.**BackColorFixed** [=*color*]
object.**BackColorSel** [=*color*]

The **BackColor**, **BackColorBkg**, **BackColorFixed**, **BackColorSel** properties syntax have these parts:

Part	Description
object	An object expression that evaluates to an object in the **Applies To** list.
color	A numeric expression that specifies the color.

Remarks

The picture below shows what part of the **MSFlexGrid** the properties refers to:

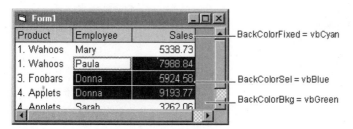

411

BackColor affects the color of all nonfixed cells. To set the background color of individual cells, use the **CellBackColor** property.

See Also

CellBackColor, CellForeColor Properties

Example

This example uses the **BackColorBkg**, **BackColorFixed**, and **BackColorSel** properties in **MSFlexGrid**. It resets the colors of the controls background, selected background, and fixed-cell background randomly twice each second for **MSFlexGrid** control. To try this example, paste the code into the Declarations section of a form with a **Timer** control and an **MSFlexGrid** control with the names Timer1 and MSFlexGrid1, and then load the form.

```
Private Sub Form_Load ()
   Timer1.Interval = 500
End Sub

Private Sub Timer1_Timer ()
   MSFlexGrid1.BackColorBkg = QBColor(Rnd * 15)
   MSFlexGrid1.BackColorFixed = QBColor(Rnd * 10)
   MSFlexGrid1.BackColorSel = QBColor(Rnd * 10)
End Sub
```

CellAlignment Property

Returns or sets a value that determines the alignment of data in a cell or range of selected cells. Not available at design time.

Applies To

MSFlexGrid Control

Syntax

object.**CellAlignment** [= *value*]

The **CellAlignment** property syntax has these parts:

Part	Description
object	An object expression that evaluates to an object in the **Applies To** list.
Value	An integer or constant specifying how text should be aligned within cells, as described in **Settings**.

Settings

The settings for *value* are:

Constant	Value	Description
flexAlignLeftTop	0	Left Top
flexAlignLeftCenter	1	Left Center (default for strings)
flexAlignLeftBottom	2	Left Bottom

(continued)

Constant	Value	Description
flexAlignCenterTop	3	Center Top
flexAlignCenterCenter	4	Center Center
flexAlignCenterBottom	5	Center Bottom
flexAlignRightTop	6	Right Top
flexAlignRightCenter	7	Right Center (default for numbers)
flexAlignRightBottom	8	Right Bottom
flexAlignGeneral	9	General: Left Center for strings, Right Center for numbers

Remarks

The following example sets the text alignment for each cell to Left Center using the constant setting.

```
Sub Form1_Load ()
    MSFlexGrid1.CellAlignment = flexAlignLeftCenter
End Sub
```

See Also

CellPicture Property, **ColAlignment** Property (MSFlexGrid)

CellBackColor, CellForeColor Properties

Returns or sets the background and foreground colors of individual cells or ranges of cells. Not available at design time.

Applies To

MSFlexGrid Control

Syntax

object.**CellBackColor** [= *color*]
object.**CellForeColor** [= *color*]

The **CellBackColor** and **CellForeColor** properties syntax has these parts:

Part	Description
object	An object expression that evaluates to an object in the **Applies To** list.
color	Integer (enumerated). A numeric expression specifying the color for the current cell selection. Setting either of these properties to zero paints the cell using standard background and foreground colors.

Remarks

Changing this property affects the current cell or the current selection, depending on the setting of the **FillStyle** property.

Setting either of these properties to zero causes **MSFlexGrid** to paint the cell using the standard background and foreground colors. If you want to set either of these properties to black, set them to one instead of zero.

To set the colors of various **MSFlexGrid** elements, use the **BackColorBkg**, **BackColorFixed**, **BackColorSel**, **ForeColorFixed**, and **ForeColorSel** properties. To set all nonfixed cells to the same background color, use the **BackColor** property.

See Also

BackColor, BackColorBkg, BackColorFixed, BackColorSel Properties, **FillStyle** Property (MSFlexGrid), **ForeColor, ForeColorFixed, ForeColorSel** Properties

Example

This example uses the **CellBackColor**, and **CellForeColor** properties in **MSFlexGrid**. It resets the colors of the focused cell's background color and text color randomly twice each second for **MSFlexGrid** control. To try this example, paste the following code into the Declarations section of a form with a **Timer** control and an **MSFlexGrid** control with the names Timer1 and MSFlexGrid1, and then load the form.

```
Private Sub Form_Load ()
   Timer1.Interval = 500
   MSFlexGrid1.Text = "Focus Here"
End Sub

Private Sub Timer1_Timer ()
   MSFlexGrid1.CellBackColor = QBColor(Rnd * 15)
   MSFlexGrid1.CellForeColor = QBColor(Rnd * 10)
End Sub
```

CellFontBold Property

Returns or sets the bold style for the current cell text. Not available at design time.

Applies To

MSFlexGrid Control

Syntax

object.**CellFontBold** [= *boolean*]

The **CellFontBold** property syntax has these parts:

Part	Description
object	An object expression that evaluates to an object in the **Applies To** list.
boolean	Determines whether the current cell text is bold. The property is **False** by default.

Remarks

Changing this property affects the current cell or the current selection, depending on the setting of the **FillStyle** property. The following code sets the text of the current cell to bold whenever the **MSFlexGrid** control is in focus:

```
Sub MSFlexGrid1_GotFocus()
   MSFlexGrid1.CellFontBold = 1
End Sub
```

See Also

CellFontItalic Property, **CellFontName** Property, **CellFontSize** Property, **CellFontUnderline** Property, **CellFontWidth** Property, **FillStyle** Property (MSFlexGrid)

CellFontItalic Property

Returns or sets the italic style for the current cell text. Not available at design time.

Applies To

MSFlexGrid Control

Syntax

object.**CellFontItalic** [= *boolean*]

The **CellFontItalic** property syntax has these parts:

Part	Description
object	An object expression that evaluates to an object in the **Applies To** list.
boolean	Determines whether the text style in the cell is italic. The property is **False** by default.

Remarks

Changing this property affects the current cell or the current selection, depending on the setting of the **FillStyle** property. The following code sets the text of the current cell to Italic whenever the **MSFlexGrid** control is in focus:

```
Sub MSFlexGrid1_GotFocus()
   MSFlexGrid1.CellFontItalic = True
End Sub
```

See Also

CellFontBold Property, **CellFontName** Property, **CellFontSize** Property, **CellFontUnderline** Property, **CellFontWidth** Property, **FillStyle** Property (MSFlexGrid)

CellFontName Property

Returns or sets the name of the font for the current cell text. Not available at design time.

Applies To
MSFlexGrid Control

Syntax

object.**CellFontName** [= *name*]

The **CellFontName** property syntax has these parts:

Part	Description
object	An object expression that evaluates to an object in the **Applies To** list.
name	A string expression naming of one of the available font faces.

Remarks

Changing this property affects the current cell or the current selection, depending on the setting of the **FillStyle** property. The following code sets the text of the current cell to a specific font type whenever the **MSFlexGrid** control is in focus:

```
Sub MSFlexGrid1_GotFocus()
   MSFlexGrid1.CellFontName = Screen.Fonts(3)
   MSFlexGrid1.Text = Screen.Fonts(3)        ' Displays font
                                             ' name.
End Sub
```

See Also

CellFontBold Property, **CellFontItalic** Property, **CellFontSize** Property, **CellFontUnderline** Property, **CellFontWidth** Property, **FillStyle** Property (MSFlexGrid)

CellFontSize Property

Returns or sets the size, in points, for the current cell text. Not available at design time.

Applies To
MSFlexGrid Control

Syntax

object.**CellFontSize** [= *value*]

The **CellFontSize** property syntax has these parts:

Part	Description
object	An object expression that evaluates to an object in the **Applies To** list.
value	Single. A numeric expression specifying the size of the current cell text.

Remarks

Changing this property affects the current cell or the current selection, depending on the setting of the **FillStyle** property. The following code sets the text of the current cell to 12 points whenever the **MSFlexGrid** control is in focus:

```
Sub MSFlexGrid1_GotFocus()
   MSFlexGrid1.CellFontSize = 12
End Sub
```

See Also

CellFontBold Property, **CellFontItalic** Property, **CellFontName** Property, **CellFontUnderline** Property, **CellFontWidth** Property, **FillStyle** Property (MSFlexGrid)

CellFontStrikeThrough Property

Returns or sets a value that determines if the FontStrikeThrough style is applied to the current cell text.

Applies To

MSFlexGrid Control

Syntax

object.**CellFontStrikeThrough** =[*boolean*]

Part	Description
object	An object expression that evaluates to an object in the **Applies To** list.
Boolean	A Boolean expression that specifies if the StrikeThrough style is applied to the cell text.

Settings

The settings for *boolean* are:

Setting	Description
True	The StrikeThrough style is applied to the cell.
False	(Default) The StrikeThrough style isn't applied to the cell.

Remarks

Changing this property affects the current cell or the current selection, depending on the setting of the **FillStyle** property. The following code sets the text of the current cell to Strike-Through whenever the **MSFlexGrid** control is in focus:

```
Sub MSFlexGrid1_GotFocus
   MSFlexGrid1.CellFontStrikeThrough = 1
End Sub
```

See Also

CellFontUnderline Property

CellFontUnderline Property

Returns or sets a value that specifies if the underline style is applied to the current cell text.

Applies To

MSFlexGrid Control

Syntax

object.**CellFontUnderline** =[*boolean*]

Part	Description
object	An object expression that evaluates to an object in the **Applies To** list.
boolean	A Boolean expression that specifies if the Underline style is applied to the cell text.

Settings

The settings for *boolean* are:

Setting	Description
True	The Underline style is applied to the cell.
False	(Default) The Underline style isn't applied to the cell.

Remarks

Changing this property affects the current cell or the current selection, depending on the setting of the **FillStyle** property. The following code sets the text of the current cell to Underline whenever the **MSFlexGrid** control is in focus:

```
Sub MSFlexGrid1_GotFocus
   MSFlexGrid1.CellFontUnderline = 1
End Sub
```

CellFontWidth Property

Returns or sets the width, in points, for the current cell text. Not available at design time.

Applies To

MSFlexGrid Control

Syntax

object.**CellFontWidth** [= *value*]

The **CellFontWidth** property syntax has these parts:

Part	Description
object	An object expression that evaluates to an object in the **Applies To** list.
value	Single. A numeric expression specifying the desired point width for the current cell's font.

Remarks

Changing this property affects the current cell or the current selection, depending on the setting of the **FillStyle** property. The following code sets the width of the text of the current cell when the **MSFlexGrid** control is in focus:

```
Sub MSFlexGrid1_GotFocus()
   MSFlexGrid1.CellFontWidth = 5
End Sub
```

See Also

CellFontBold Property, **CellFontItalic** Property, **CellFontName** Property, **CellFontSize** Property, **CellFontUnderline** Property, **FillStyle** Property (MSFlexGrid)

CellHeight, CellLeft, CellTop, CellWidth Properties (MSFlexGrid)

Returns the position and size of the current cell, in twips. Not available at design time.

Applies To

MSFlexGrid Control

Syntax

object.**CellHeight**
object.**CellLeft**
object.**CellTop**
object.**CellWidth**

The object placeholder represents an object expression that evaluates to an object in the **Applies To** list.

Remarks

These properties are useful if you want to emulate in-cell editing. By trapping the **MSFlexGrid** control's **KeyPress** event, you can place a text box or some other control over the current cell and let the user edit its contents.

The return values are always in twips, regardless of the form's **ScaleMode** setting.

See Also

FillStyle Property (MSFlexGrid)

CellPicture Property

Returns or sets an image to be displayed in the current cell or in a range of cells. Not available at design time.

Applies To

MSFlexGrid Control

Syntax

object.**CellPicture** [= *picture*]

The **CellPicture** property syntax has these parts:

Part	Description
object	An object expression that evaluates to an object in the **Applies To** list.
picture	Bitmap, icon, or metafile graphic. Can also be assigned to another control's **Picture** property.

Remarks

You can set this property at run time using the **LoadPicture** function on a bitmap, icon, or metafile, or by assigning to it another control's **Picture** property.

Changing this property affects the current cell or the current selection, depending on the setting of the **FillStyle** property.

Each cell may contain text and a picture. The relative position of the text and picture is determined by the **CellAlignment** and **CellPictureAlignment** properties.

See Also

CellAlignment Property, **CellPictureAlignment** Property, **FillStyle** Property (MSFlexGrid)

Example

This example loads icons from the Visual Basic icon library into two cells in an **MSFlexGrid** control. You can use any two icons. Paste the code into the Declarations section of a form that has the **MSFlexGrid** control. Press F5 to run the program, and then click the form.

```
Private Sub Form_Click ()
    ' Load the icons.
    MSFlexGrid1.Row = 1
    MSFlexGrid1.Col = 1
    Set MSFlexGrid1.CellPicture = _
    LoadPicture("Icons\Computer\Trash02a.ico")
    MSFlexGrid1.Row = 1
    MSFlexGrid1.Col = 2
    Set MSFlexGrid1.CellPicture = _
    LoadPicture("Icons\Computer\Trash02b.ico")
End Sub
```

CellPictureAlignment Property

Returns or sets the alignment of pictures in a cell or range of selected cells. Not available at design time.

Applies To

MSFlexGrid Control

Syntax

object.**CellPictureAlignment** [= *value*]

The **CellPictureAlignment** property syntax has these parts:

Part	Description
object	An object expression that evaluates to an object in the **Applies To** list.
value	An integer or constant specifying how pictures should be aligned within cells, as described in **Settings**.

Settings

The settings for *value* are:

Constant	Value	Description
flexAlignLeftTop	0	Left Top
flexAlignLeftCenter	1	Left Center
flexAlignLeftBottom	2	Left Bottom
flexAlignCenterTop	3	Center Top
flexAlignCenterCenter	4	Center Center
flexAlignCenterBottom	5	Center Bottom
flexAlignRightTop	6	Right Top
flexAlignRightCenter	7	Right Center
flexAlignRightBottom	8	Right Bottom

Remarks

Changing this property affects the current cell or the current selection, depending on the setting of the **FillStyle** property.

The following code sets the picture alignment of the current cell to Right Center using the constant value.

```
Sub Form1_Load
   MSFlexGrid1.CellPictureAlignment = _
   flexAlignRightCenter
End Sub
```

See Also

CellPicture Property, **FillStyle** Property (MSFlexGrid)

CellTextStyle Property

Returns or sets the three-dimensional style for text on a specific cell or range of cells. Not available at design time.

Applies To

MSFlexGrid Control

Syntax

object.**CellTextStyle** [= *value*]

The **CellTextStyle** property syntax has these parts:

Part	Description
object	An object expression that evaluates to an object in the **Applies To** list.
value	An integer or constant specifying one of the constants of the **CellTextStyle** property, as described in **Settings**.

Settings

The settings for *value* are:

Constant	Value	Description
flexTextFlat	0	Flat (normal text)
flexTextRaised	1	Raised
flexTextInset	2	Inset
flexTextRaisedLight	3	Raised Light
flexTextInsetLight	4	Inset Light

Remarks

Settings 1 and 2 work best for large and bold fonts. **Settings** 3 and 4 work best for small regular fonts. The cell's appearance is also affected by the backcolor settings; some backcolor settings do not show the raised or inset feature.

Changing this property affects the current cell or the current selection, depending on the setting of the **FillStyle** property.

The following code sets the text style of the current cell or current selection to Inset using the constant value.

```
Sub MSFlexGrid1_GotFocus
    MSFlexGrid1.CellTextStyle = flexTextInset
End Sub
```

See Also

FillStyle Property (MSFlexGrid), **Text** Property (MSFlexGrid), **TextStyle, TextStyleFixed** Properties

Clear Method (MSFlexGrid)

Clears the contents of the **MSFlexGrid**. This includes all text, pictures, and cell formatting. The **Clear** method does not affect the number of rows and columns on the **MSFlexGrid**.

Applies To

MSFlexGrid Control

Syntax

object.**Clear**

The object placeholder represents an object expression that evaluates to an object in the **Applies To** list.

Remarks

To remove cells instead of just clearing them, use the **RemoveItem** method on each row to be removed.

Example

This example puts "Flex" into the current cell whenever the user clicks on a cell. Whenever the user double-clicks, it clears the **MSFlexGrid** control. To run the program click F5.

```
Private Sub Form1_Load ()
   MSFlexGrid1.Rows = 8
   MSFlexGrid1.Cols = 5
End Sub

Private Sub MSFlexGrid1_Click ()
   ' Put text in current cell.
   MSFlexGrid1.Text = "Flex"
End Sub

Private Sub MSFlexGrid1.DblClick ()
   MSFlexGrid1.Clear
End Sub
```

Clip Property (MSFlexGrid)

Returns or sets the contents of the cells in **MSFlexGrid** control's selected region. Not available at design time.

Applies To

MSFlexGrid Control

Syntax

object.**Clip** [= *string*]

The **Clip** property syntax has these parts:

Part	Description
object	An object expression that evaluates to an object in the **Applies To** list.
string	A string expression with the contents of the selected area.

Remarks

The *string* may hold the contents of multiple rows and columns. In *string*, a tab character, **Chr** (9), or the constant **vbTab** indicates a new cell in a row, and a carriage return, **Chr** (13) or **vbCR** indicates the beginning of a new row. Use the **Chr** function or the vb constants to embed these characters in strings.

When placing data into a **MSFlexGrid** control, only the selected cells are affected. If there are more cells in the selected region than are described in *string*, the remaining cells are left alone. If there are more cells described in *string* than in the selected region, the unused portion of *string* is ignored.

See Also

ColPosition, **RowPosition** Properties

Example

This example puts "James," "Nancy," and "Lisa" into the selected cells whenever the user selects a group of cells. Whenever the user double-clicks, it clears the **MSFlexGrid** control. To run the program click F5.

```
Private Sub Form1_Load ()
   MSFlexGrid1.Rows = 8
   MSFlexGrid1.Cols = 5
End Sub

Private Sub MSFlexGrid1_MouseUp (Button As Integer, _
Shift as Integer, X As Single, Y As Single)
Dim myStr As String
   myStr = "James" + Chr(9) + "Nancy" + Chr(9) + "Lisa"
   MSFlexGrid1.Clip = myStr
End Sub
```

Col, Row Properties (MSFlexGrid)

Returns or sets the coordinates of the active cell in a **MSFlexGrid**. Not available at design time.

Applies To

MSFlexGrid Control

Syntax

object.**Col** [= *number*]
object.**Row** [= *number*]

The **Col**, **Row** syntax has these parts:

Part	Description
object	An object expression that evaluates to an object in the **Applies To** list.
number	Long. A numeric expression specifying the position of the active cell.

Remarks

Use these properties to specify a cell in a **MSFlexGrid** or to find out which row or column contains the current cell. Columns and rows are numbered from zero, beginning at the top for rows and at the left for columns.

Setting these properties automatically resets **RowSel** and **ColSel**, so the selection becomes the current cell. Therefore, to specify a block selection, you must set **Row** and **Col** first, then set **RowSel** and **ColSel**.

The value of the current cell, defined by the **Col** and **Row** settings, is the text contained in that cell. To modify a cell's value without changing the selected **Row** and **Col** properties, use the **TextMatrix** property.

See Also

Cols, Rows Properties (MSFlexGrid), **ColSel, RowSel** Properties, **SelChange** Event (MSFlexGrid), **Sort** Property (MSFlexGrid), **Text** Property (MSFlexGrid), **TextMatrix** Property

Example

This example puts "Here" into the current cell and then changes the active cell to the third cell in the third row and puts "There" into that cell. To run the program click F5, then click the grid.

```
Private Sub Form1_Load ()
   MSFlexGrid1.Rows = 8
   MSFlexGrid1.Cols = 5
End Sub

Private Sub MSFlexGrid1_Click ()
   ' Put text in current cell.
   MSFlexGrid1.Text = "Here"
   '  Put text in third row, third column.
   MSFlexGrid1.Col = 2
   MSFlexGrid1.Row = 2
   MSFlexGrid1.Text = "There"
End Sub
```

ColAlignment Property (MSFlexGrid)

Returns or sets the alignment of data in a column. Not available at design time (except indirectly through the **FormatString** property).

Applies To

MSFlexGrid Control

Syntax

object.**ColAlignment**(*number*) [= *value*]

The **ColAlignment** property syntax has these parts:

Part	Description
object	An object expression that evaluates to an object in the **Applies To** list.
number	Long. The number of the column in the **MSFlexGrid** control, or -1 to set all columns at once.
value	Integer or constant specifying the alignment of data in a column, as described in **Settings**.

Remarks

The settings for *value* are:

Constant	Value	Description
flexAlignLeft	0	Left Align
flexAlignRight	1	Right Align
flexAlignCenter	2	Center Data

Remarks

Any column can have an alignment that is different from other columns. This property affects all cells in the specified column, including those in fixed rows.

To set individual cell alignments, use the **CellAlignment** property. To set column alignments at design time, use the **FormatString** property.

The following code sets the column alignment of the third column to Right Align using the constant value.

```
Sub Form1_Load ()
   MSFlexGrid1.ColAlignment(3) = flexAlignRight
End Sub
```

See Also

CellAlignment Property, **FormatString** Property

ColData, RowData Properties

Returns or sets an arbitrary long value associated with each row and column. Not available at design time.

Applies To

MSFlexGrid Control

Syntax

object.**ColData**(*number*) [= *value*]
object.**RowData**(*number*) [= *value*]

The **ColData**, **RowData** syntax has these parts:

Part	Description
object	An object expression that evaluates to an object in the **Applies To** list.
number	Long. The number of the column or row in the **MSFlexGrid** control where to save or retrieve the data.
value	Long. A numeric expression specifying the contents of the **ColData** or **RowData** arrays.

Remarks

Use the **RowData** and **ColData** properties to associate a specific number with each row or column on a **MSFlexGrid** control. You can then use these numbers in code to identify the items.

For example, you can add rows containing totals to a **MSFlexGrid** and identify those rows by setting their **RowData** property to a nonzero value. To update the totals later, you can delete the old totals by scanning the **RowData** array and removing the appropriate rows.

Another typical use of the **RowData** property is to keep an index into an array of data structures associated with the items described on each row.

Example

The code below shows how to create a **MSFlexGrid** picture that includes only the current selection.

```
Sub CopySelectedPictureToClipboard (myFlex As _
MSFlexGrid)
   Dim i As Integer, tr As Long, lc As Long, _
   hl As Integer
   ' Get ready to operate.
   MyFlex.Redraw = False' To eliminate flicker.
   hl = MyFlex.HighLight' Save current settings.
   tr = MyFlex.TopRow
   lc = MyFlex.LeftCol
   MyFlex.HighLight = 0 ' No highlight on picture.
   ' Hide nonselected rows and columns.
   ' (Save original sizes in RowData/ColData
   ' properties.)
   For i = MyFlex.FixedRows To MyFlex.Rows - 1
      If i < MyFlex.Row Or i > MyFlex.RowSel Then
         MyFlex.RowData(i) = MyFlex.RowHeight(i)
         MyFlex.RowHeight(i) = 0
      End If
   Next
   For i = MyFlex.FixedCols To MyFlex.Cols - 1
      If i < MyFlex.Col Or i > MyFlex.ColSel Then
         MyFlex.ColData(i) = MyFlex.ColWidth(i)
         MyFlex.ColWidth(i) = 0
      End If
```

```
      Next
      ' Scroll to top left corner.
      MyFlex.TopRow = MyFlex.FixedRows

MyFlex.LeftCol = MyFlex.FixedCols
      ' Copy picture.
      clipboard.Clear
      On Error Resume Next
      MyFlex.PictureType = 0 ' Color.
      clipboard.SetData MyFlex.Picture
      If Error <> 0 Then
         MyFlex.PictureType = 1 ' Monochrome.
         clipboard.SetData MyFlex.Picture
      Endif
      ' Restore control.
      For i = MyFlex.FixedRows To MyFlex.Rows - 1
         If i < MyFlex.Row Or i > MyFlex.RowSel Then
            MyFlex.RowHeight(i) = MyFlex.RowData(i)

End If
      Next
      For i = MyFlex.FixedCols To MyFlex.Cols - 1
         If i < MyFlex.Col Or i > MyFlex.ColSel Then
            MyFlex.ColWidth(i) = MyFlex.ColData(i)
         End If
      Next
      MyFlex.TopRow = tr
      MyFlex.LeftCol = lc
      MyFlex.HighLight = hl
      MyFlex.Redraw = True
End Sub
```

ColIsVisible Property

Returns a Boolean value that indicates whether a specified column is currently visible.

Applies To

MSFlexGrid Control

Syntax

object.**ColIsVisible**(*index*)

The **ColIsVisible** property syntax has these parts:

Part	Description
object	An object expression that evaluates to an object in the **Applies To** list.
index	Long. The number of the column. The value must be in the range of 0 to **Cols** property −1.

Return Values

The return values for the **ColIsVisible** property are:

Setting	Description
True	The specified column is currently visible.
False	The specified column is not currently visible.

ColPos Property

Returns the distance in twips between the upper-left corner of the control and the upper-left corner of a specified column.

Applies To

MSFlexGrid Control

Syntax

object.**ColPos**(*index*)

The **ColPos** property syntax has these parts:

Part	Description
object	An object expression that evaluates to an object in the **Applies To** list.
index	Long. The number of the column. The value must be in the range of 0 to **Cols** property −1.

ColPosition, RowPosition Properties

Sets the position of a **MSFlexGrid** row or column, allowing you to move rows and columns to specific positions.

Applies To

MSFlexGrid Control

Syntax

object.**ColPosition**(*number*) [= *value*]
object.**RowPosition**(*number*) [= *value*]

The **ColPosition**, **RowPosition** properties syntax has these parts:

Part	Description
object	An object expression that evaluates to an object in the **Applies To** list.
number	Long. The number of the column or row to be moved.
value	Integer. A numeric expression specifying the new position of the column or row.

Remarks

The index and setting must correspond to valid row or column numbers (in the range 0 to **Rows** −1 or **Cols** −1) or an error will be generated.

For example, the following code moves a column to first position when the user clicks on it:

```
Sub MSFlexGrid1_Click ()
   MSFlexGrid1.ColPosition(MSFlexGrid1.MouseCol) = 0
End Sub
```

When a row or column is moved with these properties, all formatting information moves with it, including width, height, alignment, colors, fonts, and so on. To move text only, use the **Clip** property instead.

See Also

Clip Property (MSFlexGrid), **Cols, Rows** Properties (MSFlexGrid)

Cols, Rows Properties (MSFlexGrid)

Returns or sets the total number of columns or rows in a **MSFlexGrid**.

Applies To

MSFlexGrid Control

Syntax

object.**Cols** [= *value*]
object.**Rows** [= *value*]

The **Cols**, **Rows** syntax has these parts:

Part	Description
object	An object expression that evaluates to an object in the **Applies To** list.
value	Long. A numeric expression specifying the number of columns or rows.

Remarks

You can use these properties to expand and shrink **MSFlexGrid** dynamically at run time.

The minimum number of rows and columns is 0. The maximum number is limited by the memory available on your computer.

The value of **Cols** must be at least one greater than the value of **FixedCols**, unless they are both set to zero. The value of **Rows** must be at least one greater than the value of **FixedRows**, unless they are both set to zero.

See Also

Col, Row Properties (MSFlexGrid), **ColPosition, RowPosition** Properties, **FormatString** Property

Example

This example puts "Here" into the current cell and then changes the active cell to the third cell in the third row and puts "There" into that cell. To run the program click F5, then click the grid.

```
Private Sub Form_Load ()
    MSFlexGrid1.Rows = 8
    MSFlexGrid1.Cols = 5
End Sub

Private Sub MsFlexGrid1_Click ()
    ' Put text in current cell.
    MSFlexGrid1.Text = "Here"
    ' Put text in third row, third column.
    MSFlexGrid1.Col = 2
    MSFlexGrid1.Row = 2
    MSFlexGrid1.Text = "There"
End Sub
```

ColSel, RowSel Properties

Returns or sets the starting or ending row or column for a range of cells. Not available at design time.

Applies To

MSFlexGrid Control

Syntax

object.**ColSel** [= *value*]
object.**RowSel** [= *value*]

The **ColSel**, **RowSel** properties syntax has these parts:

Part	Description
object	An object expression that evaluates to an object in the **Applies To** list.
value	Long. A numeric expression specifying the starting or ending row or column for a range of cells.

Remarks

You can use these properties to select a specific region of **MSFlexGrid** from code, or to read into code the dimensions of an area that the user selects.

The **MSFlexGrid** cursor is the cell at **Row, Col**. The **MSFlexGrid** selection is the region between rows **Row** and **RowSel** and columns **Col** and **ColSel**. Note that **RowSel** may be above or below **Row**, and **ColSel** may be to the left or to the right of **Col**.

Whenever you set the **Row** and **Col** properties, **RowSel** and **ColSel** are automatically reset so the cursor becomes the current selection. If you want to select a block of cells from code, you must set the **Row** and **Col** properties first, then set **RowSel** and **ColSel**.

The following code writes in the current value of the **ColSel** property into the first cell of MSFlexGrid1. This value changes as the user clicks on various selections of cell groups.

```
Private Sub MSFlexGrid1_MouseUp _
(Button As Integer, Shift As Integer, x As Single, _
y As Single)
   MSFlexGrid1.Text = MSFlexGrid1.ColSel
End Sub
```

See Also

Col, Row Properties (MSFlexGrid), **SelChange** Event (MSFlexGrid), **Sort** Property (MSFlexGrid)

ColWidth Property (MSFlexGrid)

Returns or sets the width of the specified column in twips. Not available at design time.

Applies To

MSFlexGrid Control

Syntax

object.**ColWidth**(*number*) [= *value*]

The **ColWidth** property syntax has these parts:

Part	Description
object	An object expression that evaluates to an object in the **Applies To** list.
number	Long. The number of the column in the **MSFlexGrid** control, or −1 to set all columns at once.
value	A numeric expression specifying the width of the specified column in twips.

Remarks

You can use this property to set the width of any column at run time. For instructions on setting column widths at design time, see the **FormatString** property.

You can set **ColWidth** to zero to create invisible columns, or to −1 to reset the column width to its default value, which depends on the size of the current font.

The following code writes in the current value of the current size of the first column. This can be more apparent by setting the **AllowUserResizing** property to **True**, so that the value changes as the user resizes Column 1.

```
Sub Form1_Load()
   MSFlexGrid1.AllowUserResizing = True
End Sub
```

```
Sub MSFlexGrid1_MouseUp (Button As Integer, Shift As _
Integer, X As Single, Y As Single)
   MSFlexGrid1.Text = MSFlexGrid1.ColWidth(0)
End Sub
```

See Also

AllowUserResizing Property, **FormatString** Property

Compare Event

Occurs when the **Sort** property for the **MSFlexGrid** control is set to Custom Sort (9) so the user can customize the sort process.

Applies To

MSFlexGrid Control

Syntax

Private Sub *object*_**Compare**(*row1* **As Integer**, *row2* **As Integer**, *cmp* **As Integer**)

The **Compare** event syntax has these parts:

Part	Description
object	An object expression that evaluates to an object in the **Applies To** list.
row1	A Long representing the first row in a pair of rows being compared.
row2	A Long representing the second row in a pair of rows being compared.
cmp	Integer that represents the sort order of each pair, as described in **Settings**.

Settings

The event handler must compare rows *row1* and *row2* and set *cmp* to:

Setting	Description
−1	If *row1* should appear *before row2*.
0	If both rows are equal or either row can appear before the other.
1	If *row1* should appear *after row2*.

Remarks

When the **Sort** property is set to 9 (Custom Sort), the Compare event is triggered once for each pair of rows in the control that you want to compare. Because the Compare event uses row numbers instead of text values, you can use it to compare any property value for that row, including **RowData**. Custom sorts are always much slower that the built-in sorts. However, you can sort a row by any column or using any other cell property.

See Also

Sort Property (MSFlexGrid)

EnterCell Event

Occurs when the currently active cell changes to a different cell.

Applies To

MSFlexGrid Control

Syntax

Private Sub *object*_**EnterCell** ()

The object placeholder represents an object expression that evaluates to an object in the **Applies To** list.

Remarks

Dragging the mouse over a cell does not trigger the **EnterCell** event. Clicking the mouse on a fixed row will trigger this event on the first nonfixed column in that row.

FillStyle Property (MSFlexGrid)

Returns or sets a value that determines whether setting the **Text** property or one of the cell formatting properties of a **MSFlexGrid** applies the change to all selected cells.

Applies To

MSFlexGrid Control

Syntax

object.**FillStyle**[= *value*]

The **FillStyle** property syntax has these parts:

Part	Description
object	An object expression that evaluates to an object in the **Applies To** list.
value	Integer or constant that specifies the fill style, as described in **Settings**.

Settings

The settings for *value* are:

Constant	Value	Description
flexFillSingle	0	Single (default). Changing **Text** or any of the cell properties only affects the active cell.
flexFillRepeat	1	Repeat. Changing the **Text** or any of the cell properties affects all selected cells.

Remarks

The following code allows you to format individual cells differently.

```
Sub Form1_Load ()
   MSFlexGrid1.FillStyle = 0
End Sub
```

FillStyle must be set to 1(Repeat) whenever you want a cell change to apply to all cells.

See Also

CellAlignment Property, **CellBackColor, CellForeColor** Properties, **CellFontBold** Property, **CellFontItalic** Property, **CellFontName** Property, **CellFontSize** Property, **CellFontWidth** Property, **CellHeight, CellLeft, CellTop, CellWidth** Properties (MSFlexGrid), **CellPicture** Property, **CellPictureAlignment** Property, **CellTextStyle** Property, **Text** Property (MSFlexGrid)

FixedAlignment Property

Returns or sets the alignment of data in the fixed cells of a column in a grid.

Applies To

MSFlexGrid Control

Syntax

object.**FixedAlignment** (*index*)= [*value*]

The **FixedAlignment** property syntax has these parts:

Part	Description
object	An object expression that evaluates to an object in the **Applies To** list.
index	Long number that specifies the column.
value	Integer that determines the alignment of the data in the fixed cells, as described in **Settings**.

Settings

The settings for *value* are:

Constant	Value	Description
flexAlignLeftTop	0	Left Top
flexAlignLeftCenter	1	Left Center
flexAlignLeftBottom	2	Left Bottom
flexAlignCenterTop	3	Center Top
flexAlignCenterCenter	4	Center Center
flexAlignCenterBottom	5	Center Bottom
flexAlignRightTop	6	Right Top
flexAlignRightCenter	7	Right Center
flexAlignRightBottom	8	Right Bottom

Remarks

Fix the cells in a column using the **FixedCols** and **FixedRows** properties.

FixedCols, FixedRows Properties (MSFlexGrid)

Returns or sets the total number of fixed columns or fixed rows for a **MSFlexGrid** control. By default, **MSFlexGrid** has one fixed column and one fixed row.

Applies To

MSFlexGrid Control

Syntax

object.**FixedCols** [= *value*]
object.**FixedRows** [= *value*]

The **FixedCols**, **FixedRows** properties syntax have these parts:

Part	Description
object	An object expression that evaluates to an object in the **Applies To** list.
value	Long. A numeric expression specifying total number of fixed columns or fixed rows.

Remarks

Fixed columns and rows do not move when the other columns or rows in **MSFlexGrid** are scrolled. You can have zero or more fixed columns and zero or more fixed rows. You can select the colors, font, grid and text style use for the fixed columns and rows.

Selecting a fixed row or column at run time selects all cells in that row or column unless the **SelectionMode** property has a nonzero value.

If the value of the **AllowUserResizing** property is nonzero, having fixed rows or columns in your **MsFlexGrid** control allows you to resize them at run time using the mouse.

Fixed columns and rows are typically used in spreadsheet applications to display row numbers and column names or letters.

For example, the following code sets the first row to be fixed, and the first and second columns to be fixed:

```
Sub Form1_Load ()
   MSFlexGrid1.FixedCols = 2
   MSFlexGrid1.FixedRows = 1
End Sub
```

Specifics

FixedAlignment Property

FocusRect Property

Returns or sets a value that determines whether the **MSFlexGrid** control should draw a focus rectangle around the current cell.

Applies To

MSFlexGrid Control

Syntax

object.**FocusRect** [= *value*]

The **FocusRect** property syntax has these parts:

Part	Description
object	An object expression that evaluates to an object in the **Applies To** list.
value	Integer or constant that specifies the focus rectangle style, as described in **Settings**.

Settings

The settings for *value* are:

Constant	Value	Description
flexFocusNone	0	None. No focus rectangle around current cell.
flexFocusLight	1	Light (default). Light focus rectangle around current cell.
flexFocusHeavy	2	Heavy. Heavy focus rectangle around current cell.

Remarks

If a focus rectangle is drawn, then the current cell is painted in the background color, as in most spreadsheets and grids. Otherwise, the current cell is painted in the selection color, so you can see which cell is selected even without the focus rectangle.

For example, the following code sets the focus rectangle for the active cell to a Light Rectangle, using the constant value.

```
Sub Form1_Load ()
    MSFlexGrid1.FocusRect = flexFocusLight
End Sub
```

FontWidth Property

Returns or sets the width, in points, of the font to be used for text displayed in a **MSFlexGrid** control.

Applies To

MSFlexGrid Control

Syntax

object.**FontWidth** [= *value*]

The **FontWidth** property syntax has these parts:

Part	Description
object	An object expression that evaluates to an object in the **Applies To** list.
value	Single. A numeric expression specifying the desired point width for the current font.

Remarks

The font width is normally chosen by Windows to match the selected font height and provide a standard aspect ratio. **MSFlexGrid** allows you to specify fonts that are narrower or wider than the default so you can display more information in a cell or highlight certain cells.

When you specify a font width, Windows will try to select or generate a font to match your request. For best results, use TrueType fonts, which are more flexible. The Courier New font, for instance, looks very good when you make it a little narrower than its default.

To restore the default font width, set this property to zero.

To set the font of individual cells or cell ranges, use the **CellFontBold**, **CellFontItalic**, **CellFontName**, **CellFontSize**, and **CellFontWidth** properties.

ForeColor, ForeColorFixed, ForeColorSel Properties

Returns or sets the color used to draw text on each part of the **MSFlexGrid** control.

Applies To

MSFlexGrid Control

Syntax

object.**ForeColor** [= *color*]
object.**ForeColorFixed** [= *color*]
object.**ForeColorSel** [= *color*]

The **ForeColor**, **ForeColorFixed**, **ForeColorSel** properties syntax have these parts:

Part	Description
object	An object expression that evaluates to an object in the **Applies To** list.
color	A value or constant that determines the color used to paint text in the scrollable or fixed areas of **MSFlexGrid**.

Remarks

The picture below shows what part of **MSFlexGrid** the properties refer to:

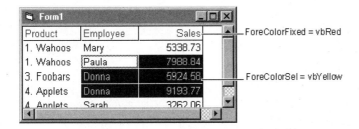

Use the **ForeColor** property to set the text color of all nonfixed cells. To set the text color of individual cells, use the **CellForeColor** property.

Example

This example sets the **ForeColorFixed** and the **ForeColorSel** Properties of **MSFlexGrid** to random colors every second:

```
Private Sub Form_Load ()
    Timer1.Interval = 500
    MSFlexGrid1.FillStyle = 2
    MSFlexGrid1.Text = "Color Me"
    MSFlexGrid1.FixedCols = 1
    MSFlexGrid1.FixedRows = 1
End Sub

Private Sub Timer1_Timer ()
    MSFlexGrid1.ForeColorFixed = QBColor(Rnd * 15)
    MSFlexGrid1.ForeColorSel = QBColor(Rnd * 10)
End Sub
```

FormatString Property

Sets a format string that sets up a **MSFlexGrid** control's column widths, alignments, and fixed row and column text.

Applies To

MSFlexGrid Control

Syntax

object.**FormatString**[= *string*]

The **FormatString** property syntax has these parts:

Part	Description
object	An object expression that evaluates to an object in the **Applies To** list.
string	A string expression for formatting text in rows and columns, as described in Remarks.

Remarks

MSFlexGrid parses the **FormatString** at design time and interprets it to get the following information: number of rows and columns, text for row and column headings, column width, and column alignment.

The **FormatString** property is made up of segments separated by pipe characters (|). The text between pipes defines a column, and it may contain the special alignment characters <, ^, or >, to align the entire column to the left, center, or right. The text is assigned to row zero, and its width defines the width of each column.

The **FormatString** may also contain a semi-colon (";"), which causes the remainder of the string to be interpreted as row heading and width information. The text is assigned to column zero, and the longest string defines the width of column zero.

MSFlexGrid will create additional rows and columns to accommodate all fields defined by the **FormatString**, but it will not delete rows or columns if only a few fields are specified. If you want, you can do this by setting the **Rows** and **Cols** properties.

See Also

ColAlignment Property (MSFlexGrid), **Cols, Rows** Properties (MSFlexGrid), **ColWidth** Property (MSFlexGrid)

Example

The examples below illustrate how the **FormatString** property works.

```
' Set column headers.
s$ = "<Region  |<Product  |<Employee  |>Sales    "
MSFlexGrid1.FormatString = s$
```

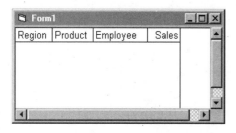

```
' Set row headers (note semicolon at start)
s$ = ";Name|Address|Telephone|Social Security#"
MSFlexGrid1.FormatString = s$
```

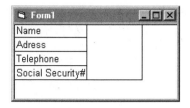

```
' Set column and row headers.
s$ = "|Name|Address|Telephone|Social Security#"
s$ = s$ + ";|Robert|Jimmy|Bonzo|John Paul"
MSFlexGrid.FormatString = s$
```

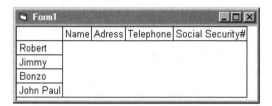

GridColor, GridColorFixed Properties

Returns or sets the color used to draw the lines between the **MSFlexGrid** control's cells.

Applies To

MSFlexGrid Control

Syntax

object.**GridColor** [= *color*]
object.**GridColorFixed** [= *color*]

The **GridColor**, **GridColorFixed** syntax has these parts:

Part	Description
object	An object expression that evaluates to an object in the **Applies To** list.
color	A value or constant that determines the color used to paint the gridlines in the scrollable or fixed areas of **MSFlexGrid**.

Remarks

The **GridColor** property is used only when the **GridLines** property is set to 1 (Lines), and **GridColorFixed** is used only when **GridLinesFixed** is set to 1 (Lines.) Raised and inset grid lines are always drawn in black and white.

See Also

GridLines, GridLinesFixed Properties (MSFlexGrid)

GridLines, GridLinesFixed Properties (MSFlexGrid)

Returns or sets a value that determines what type of lines should be drawn between cells.

Applies To

MSFlexGrid Control

Syntax

object.**GridLines** [= *value*]
object.**GridLinesFixed** [= *value*]

The **GridLines**, **GridLinesFixed** properties syntax have these parts:

Part	Description
object	An object expression that evaluates to an object in the **Applies To** list.
value	An integer or constant specifying the type of lines drawn, as described in **Settings**.

Settings

The settings for *value* are:

Constant	Value	Description
flexGridNone	0	No Lines. No lines in-between cells.
flexGridFlat	1	Lines(default for **GridLines**). Sets line style between cells to normal lines.
flexGridInset	2	Inset Lines (default for **GridLinesFixed**). Sets line style between cells to inset lines.
flexGridRaised	3	Raised Lines. Sets line style between cells to raised lines.

Remarks

When the **GridLines** property is set to 1 (Lines), the color of the lines is determined by the **GridColor** property. Raised and inset grid lines are always drawn in black and white.

See Also

MSFlexGrid Control, **GridColor, GridColorFixed** Properties, **GridLineWidth** Property

HighLight Property (MSFlexGrid)

Returns or sets a value that determines whether selected cells appear highlighted.

Applies To

MSFlexGrid Control

Syntax

object.**HighLight** [= *value*]

The **HighLight** property syntax has these parts:

Part	Description
object	An object expression that evaluates to an object in the **Applies To** list.
value	Integer or constant specifying when **MSFlexGrid** should highlight selected cells, as described in **Settings**.

Settings

The settings for *value* are:

Constant	Value	Description
flexHighlightNever	0	Never highlight selected cells.
flexHighlightAlways	1	Always highlight selected cells.
flexHighlightWithFocus	2	Highlight selected cells when control has focus.

Remarks

When this property is set to zero and the user selects a range of cells, there is no visual cue that shows which cells are currently selected. When the property is set to 2 (With Focus), the highlight appears only when the control has focus.

LeaveCell Event

Occurs immediately before the currently active cell changes to a different cell.

Applies To

MSFlexGrid Control

Syntax

Private Sub *object*_**LeaveCell** ()

The *object* placeholder represents an object expression that evaluates to an object in the **Applies To** list.

Remarks

This event is useful for validating a cell's contents. The **LeaveCell** event is not triggered when the focus moves to a different control.

LeftCol Property (MSFlexGrid)

Returns or sets the left-most visible column (other than a fixed column) in the **MSFlexGrid** control. Not available at design time.

Applies To

MSFlexGrid Control

Syntax

object.**LeftCol** [= *value*]

The **LeftCol** property syntax has these parts:

Part	Description
object	An object expression that evaluates to an object in the **Applies To** list.
value	Integer. A numeric expression specifying the left-most column.

Remarks

You can use this property in code to scroll **MSFlexGrid** programmatically. Use the **TopRow** property to determine the topmost visible row in the **MSFlexGrid**.

See Also

Scroll Event (MSFlexGrid), **TopRow** Property (MSFlexGrid)

MergeCells Property

Returns or sets a value that determines whether cells with the same contents should be grouped in a single cell spanning multiple rows or columns.

Applies To

MSFlexGrid Control

Syntax

object.**MergeCells** [= *value*]

The **MergeCells** property syntax has these parts:

Part	Description
object	An object expression that evaluates to an object in the **Applies To** list.
value	Integer or constant specifying the grouping of cells, as specified in **Settings**.

Settings

The settings for *value* are:

Constant	Value	Description
flexMergeNever	0	(Default) Never group cells with the same contents.
flexMergeFree	1	Free
flexMergeRestrictRows	2	Restrict Rows
flexMergeRestrictColumns	3	Restrict Columns
flexMergeRestrictBoth	4	Restrict Both

Remarks

This ability to merge cells allows you to present data in a clear, appealing way. Cell merging is can be used in concert with **MSFlexGrid** control's sorting and column ordering capabilities.

▶ **To use** MSFlexGrid **control's cell merging capabilities, you must do two things:**

1 Set **MergeCells** to a value other than zero. (The difference between the settings is explained below.)

2 Set the **MergeRow()** and **MergeCol()** array properties to **True** for the rows and columns you wish to merge.

MSFlexGrid will merge cells with the same contents, and will update the merging automatically whenever you change the contents of any cells.

With Free merging, cells with the same contents are always merged. With Restricted merging, only adjacent cells with the same content—to the left or to the top—are merged.

Note   When **MergeCells** is set to a value other than 0 (Never), selection highlighting is automatically turned off. This is done mainly to speed up repainting, but also because selection of ranges containing merged cells may lead to unexpected results.

See Also

MergeCol, MergeRow Properties

Example

The examples below show the same **MSFlexGrid** with each different setting for the **MergeCells** property.

No Merging

MergeCells = 0
MergeRow(0) = True
MergeRow(1) = True
MergeRow(2) = True
MergeRow(3) = False

This is the regular view.

Region	Product	Employee	Sales
1. Northwest	1. Wahoos	Mary	5338.73
1. Northwest	1. Wahoos	Paula	7988.84
1. Northwest	3. Foobars	Donna	5924.58
1. Northwest	4. Applets	Donna	9193.77
1. Northwest	4. Applets	Sarah	3262.06
2. Southwest	2. Trinkets	Donna	3640.19
2. Southwest	4. Applets	Donna	2613.68
2. Southwest	4. Applets	Mary	157.04
2. Southwest	4. Applets	Mary	2895.62

Free Merging

MergeCells = 1
MergeRow(0) = True
MergeRow(1) = True
MergeRow(2) = True
MergeRow(3) = False

Notice how the third employee cell (Donna) merges across products to its left and across sales to its right.

Region	Product	Employee	Sales
1. Northwest	1. Wahoos	Mary	5338.73
		Paula	7988.84
	3. Foobars	Donna	5924.58
	4. Applets		9193.77
		Sarah	3262.06
2. Southwest	2. Trinkets	Donna	3640.19
			2613.68
	4. Applets	Mary	157.04
			2895.62

Restricted Merging

MergeCells = 2
MergeRow(0) = True
MergeRow(1) = True
MergeRow(2) = True
MergeRow(3) = False

Notice how the third employee cell (Donna) no longer merges across sales.

Region	Product	Employee	Sales
1. Northwest	1. Wahoos	Mary	5338.73
		Paula	7988.84
	3. Foobars	Donna	5924.58
	4. Applets	Donna	9193.77
		Sarah	3262.06
2. Southwest	2. Trinkets	Donna	3640.19
		Donna	2613.68
	4. Applets	Mary	157.04
			2895.62

MergeCol, MergeRow Properties

Returns or sets a value that determines which rows and columns should have their contents merged when the **MergeCells** property is set to a value other than 0 (Never).

Applies To

MSFlexGrid Control

Syntax

object.**MergeCol**(*number*) [= *boolean*]
object.**MergeRow**(*number*) [= *boolean*]

The **MergeCol**, **MergeRows** properties syntax has these parts:

Part	Description
object	An object expression that evaluates to an object in the **Applies To** list.
number	Long. The number of the column or row in the **MSFlexGrid** control.
boolean	These properties are set to **False** by default.

Remarks

If the **MergeCells** property is set to a nonzero value, adjacent cells with identical values are merged if they are in a row with the **MergeRow** property set to **True** or in a column with the **MergeCol** property set to **True**.

For details on how **MSFlexGrid** control's merging technology works, see the **MergeCells** property.

MergeCells Property

MouseCol, MouseRow Properties

Returns the current mouse position, in row and column coordinates.

Applies To

MSFlexGrid Control

Syntax

object.**MouseCol**
object.**MouseRow**

The *object* placeholder represents an object expression that evaluates to an object in the **Applies To** list.

Remarks

You can use these properties in code to determine where the mouse is and act accordingly. These properties are especially useful to display context-sensitive help on the contents of individual cells or to test whether the user has clicked on a fixed row or column.

MSFlexGrid Control Constants

AllowUserResizing Property

Constant	Value	Description
flexResizeNone	0	Default. No resizing is allowed.
flexResizeColumns	1	Individual columns can be resized by user.
flexResizeRows	2	Individual rows can be resized by user.
flexResizeBoth	3	Individual columns and rows can be resized by user.

Appearance Property

Constant	Value	Description
flexFlat	0	Sets the overall look of **MSFlexGrid** to normal.
flex3D	1	Sets the overall look of **MSFlexGrid** to three-dimensional.

BorderStyle Property

Constant	Value	Description
flexBorderNone	0	No border.
flexBorderSingle	1	Single border.

CellAlignment Property

Constant	Value	Description
flexAlignLeftTop	0	Left top.
flexAlignLeftCenter	1	Left center. (Default for strings)
flexAlignLeftBottom	2	Left bottom.
flexAlignCenterTop	3	Center top.
flexAlignCenterCenter	4	Center center.
flexAlignCenterBottom	5	Center bottom.
flexAlignRightTop	6	Right top.
flexAlignRightCenter	7	Right center. (Default for numbers)
flexAlignRightBottom	8	Right bottom.
flexAlignGeneral	9	General.

CellPictureAlignment Property

Constant	Value	Description
flexAlignLeftTop	0	Left top.
flexAlignLeftCenter	1	Left center.
flexAlignLeftBottom	2	Left bottom.
flexAlignCenterTop	3	Center top.
flexAlignCenterCenter	4	Center center.
flexAlignCenterBottom	5	Center bottom.
flexAlignRightTop	6	Right top.
flexAlignRightCenter	7	Right center.
flexAlignRightBottom	8	Right bottom.

CellTextStyle, TextStyle, TextStyleFixed Properties

Constant	Value	Description
flexTextFlat	0	Regular text.
flexTextRaised	1	Text appears raised.
flexTextInset	2	Text appears inset.
flexTextRaisedLight	3	Text appears slightly raised.
flexTextInsetLight	4	Text appears slightly inset.

ColAlignment Properties

Constant	Value	Description
flexAlignCenter	2	Center data in column.
flexAlignLeft	0	Left-align data in column.
flexAlignRight	1	Right-align data in column.

FillStyle Property

Constant	Value	Description
flexFillSingle	0	Changing **Text** property setting affects only active cell.
flexFillRepeat	1	Changing **Text** property setting affects all selected cells.

FocusRect Property

Constant	Value	Description
flexFocusNone	0	No focus rectangle around current cell.
flexFocusLight	1	Default. Light focus rectangle around current cell.
flexFocusHeavy	2	Heavy focus rectangle around current cell.

GridLines, GridLinesFixed Properties

Constant	Value	Description
flexGridNone	0	Default for **GridLines**. No lines between cells.
flexGridFlat	1	Sets line style between cells to normal lines.
flexGridInset	2	Sets line style between cells to inset lines.
flexGridRaised	3	Default for **GridLinesFixed**. Sets line style between cells to raised lines.

HighLight Property

Constant	Value	Description
flexHighlightNever	0	Selected cells are never highlighted.
flexHighlightAlways	1	Default. Selected cells are always highlighted.
flexHighlightWithFocus	2	Selected cells are highlighted only when they are in focus.

MergeCells Property

Constant	Value	Description
flexMergeNever	0	Default. No merging.
flexMergeFree	1	All rows and columns set to **MergeRow** (or **MergeCol**) = **True** are free to merge in any direction.
flexMergeRestrictRows	2	Same as free merging except rows can only merge into cells on the left.
flexMergeRestrict-Columns	3	Same as free merging except columns can only merge into cells above.
flexMergeRestrictAll	4	All rows and columns set to **MergeRow** (or **MergeCol**) = **True** can merge either to the left or to the top.

MousePointer Property

Constant	Value	Description
flexDefault	0	Outline of **MSFlexGrid** control.
flexArrow	1	Arrow pointer.
flexCross	2	Cross-hairs.
flexIBeam	3	"I" shaped beam to allow for text entry.
flexIcon	4	A square within a square.
flexSize	5	Resizing pointer with arrows facing up, down, left and right.
flexSizeNESW	6	Resizing pointer with arrows pointing to the upper right and lower left.
flexSizeNS	7	Resizing pointer with arrows pointing up and down.
flexSizeNWSE	8	Resizing pointer with arrows pointing to the upper left and lower right.
flexSizeEW	9	Resizing pointer with arrows pointing left and right.
flexUpArrow	10	Arrow pointing up.
flexHourGlass	11	Hour glass symbol.
flexNoDrop	12	No drop pointer.
flexCustom	13	Custom style pointer.

PictureType Property

Constant	Value	Description
flexPictureColor	0	Allows full color.
flexPictureMonochrome	1	Monochrome only.

SelectionMode Property

Constant	Value	Description
flexSelectionFree	0	Default. Individual cells in **MSFlexGrid** can be selected.
flexSelectionByRow	1	Entire rows at a time are selected in **MSFlexGrid**.
flexSelectionByColumn	2	Entire columns at a time are selected in **MSFlexGrid**.

ScrollBars Property

Constant	Value	Description
flexScrollBarNone	0	**MSFlexGrid** has no scroll bars.
flexScrollBarHorizontal	1	**MSFlexGrid** has a horizontal scroll bar.
flexScrollBarVertical	2	**MSFlexGrid** has a vertical scroll bar.
flexScrollBarBoth	3	Default. **MSFlexGrid** has horizontal and vertical scroll bars.

Sort Property

Constant	Value	Description
flexSortNone	0	No sorting.
flexSortGenAscend	1	Ascending sort which guesses whether text is string or number.
flexSortGenDescend	2	Descending sort which guesses whether text is string or number.
flexSortNumAscend	3	Ascending sort which converts strings to numbers.
flexSortNumDescend	4	Descending sort which converts strings to numbers.
flexSortStrAscend	5	Ascending sort using case-insensitive string comparison.
flexSortStrDescend	6	Descending sort using case-insensitive string comparison.
flexSortStrAscendCase	7	Ascending sort using case-sensitive string comparison.
flexSortStrDescendCase	8	Descending sort using case-sensitive string comparison.
flexSortCustom	9	Uses Compare event to compare rows.

See Also

MSFlexGrid Control, **Visual Basic** Constants

Picture Property (MSFlexGrid)

Returns a picture of the **MSFlexGrid** control, suitable for printing, saving to disk, copying to the clipboard, or assigning to a different control.

Applies To

MSFlexGrid Control

Syntax

object.**Picture**

The *object* placeholder represents an object expression that evaluates to an object in the **Applies To** list.

Remarks

The **Picture** property creates a bitmap showing the **MSFlexGrid** control. The bitmap created looks exactly like the one on the screen, except it is extended to the right and to the bottom to accommodate all rows and columns. This means that if you have an **MSFlexGrid** control with 1000 rows, the bitmap will normally include all of them, and the picture will be huge.

If you want to create a picture of a part of the **MSFlexGrid** control, write a routine to hide all the elements you don't want to show, get the picture, and then restore the control.

If the **MSFlexGrid** is very large, the bitmap created will also be large. To reduce the size of the bitmap and increase speed, you may consider setting the **PictureType** property to 1 (Monochrome bitmap). The picture will not look as nice, but it will be much smaller in memory. The code in the example shows how you can trap out-of-memory errors and automatically switch to monochrome mode by using the **PictureType** property.

The following example shows how to set the **MSFlexGrid** control's **Picture** property to a **PictureBox** control:

```
Private Sub Form_Click ()
    Set Picture1.Picture = MSFlexGrid1.Picture
End Sub
```

See Also

PictureType Property

Example

The code below shows how to create a **MSFlexGrid** picture that includes only the current selection.

```
Sub CopySelectedPictureToClipboard (myFlex As _
MSFlexGrid)
    Dim i As Integer, tr As Long, lc As Long, _
    hl As Integer
    ' Get ready to operate.
    MyFlex.Redraw = False        ' To eliminate flicker.
    hl = MyFlex.HighLight        ' Save current settings.
    tr = MyFlex.TopRow
    lc = MyFlex.LeftCol
    MyFlex.HighLight = 0          ' No highlight on picture.
    ' Hide nonselected rows and columns.
    ' (Save original sizes in RowData/ColData
    ' properties.)
    For i = MyFlex.FixedRows To MyFlex.Rows - 1
        If i < MyFlex.Row Or i > MyFlex.RowSel Then
            MyFlex.RowData(i) = MyFlex.RowHeight(i)
            MyFlex.RowHeight(i) = 0
        End If
    Next
    For i = MyFlex.FixedCols To MyFlex.Cols - 1
        If i < MyFlex.Col Or i > MyFlex.ColSel Then
            MyFlex.ColData(i) = MyFlex.ColWidth(i)
            MyFlex.ColWidth(i) = 0
        End If
    Next
    ' Scroll to top left corner.
    MyFlex.TopRow = MyFlex.FixedRows
    MyFlex.LeftCol = MyFlex.FixedCols
```

```
' Copy picture.
clipboard.Clear
On Error Resume Next
MyFlex.PictureType = 0            ' Color.
clipboard.SetData MyFlex.Picture
If Error <> 0 Then
   MyFlex.PictureType = 1         ' Monochrome.
   clipboard.SetData MyFlex.Picture
Endif
' Restore control.
For i = MyFlex.FixedRows To MyFlex.Rows - 1
   If i < MyFlex.Row Or i > MyFlex.RowSel Then
      MyFlex.RowHeight(i) = MyFlex.RowData(i)
   End If
Next
For i = MyFlex.FixedCols To MyFlex.Cols - 1
   If i < MyFlex.Col Or i > MyFlex.ColSel Then
      MyFlex.ColWidth(i) = MyFlex.ColData(i)
   End If
Next
MyFlex.TopRow = tr
MyFlex.LeftCol = lc
MyFlex.HighLight = hl
MyFlex.Redraw = True
End Sub
```

PictureType Property

Returns or sets the type of picture that should be generated by the **Picture** property.

Applies To

MSFlexGrid Control

Syntax

object.**PictureType** [= *type*]

The **PictureType** property syntax has these parts:

Part	Description
object	An object expression that evaluates to an object in the **Applies To** list.
type	Integer or constant specifying the type of picture that should be generated, as described in **Settings**.

Settings

Settings for *type* are:

Constant	Value	Description
flexPictureColor	0	Display compatible bitmap.
flexPictureMonochrome	1	Monochrome bitmap.

Remarks

Set this property to 0 (Display compatible) to obtain a high-quality image.
Set it to 1 (Monochrome bitmap) to obtain a lower-quality image that consumes less memory.

See Also

Picture Property (MSFlexGrid)

Redraw Property

Returns or sets a value that determines whether the **MSFlexGrid** control should or not be automatically redrawn after each change.

Applies To

MSFlexGrid Control

Syntax

object.**Redraw** [= *boolean*]

The **Redraw** property syntax has these parts:

Part	Description
object	An object expression that evaluates to an object in the **Applies To** list.
boolean	The property is **True** by default.

Remarks

You can use this property in code to reduce flicker while making extensive updates to the contents of the **MSFlexGrid** control.

For example, the code below turns repainting off, makes several changes to the contents of **MSFlexGrid**, and then turns repainting back on to show the results:

```
Dim i As Integer
' Freeze MSFlexGrid to avoid flicker.
MSFlexGrid.Redraw = False
' Update MSFlexGrid contents.
For i = MSFlexGrid1.FixedRows To MSFlexGrid1.Rows - 1
    MSFlexGrid1.TextMatrix(i, 1) = GetName(i, 1)
    MSFlexGrid1.TextMatrix(i, 2) = GetName(i, 2)
Next
' Show results.
MSFlexGrid1.Redraw = True
```

RemoveItem Method (MSFlexGrid)

Removes a row from a **MSFlexGrid** control at run time. Doesn't support named arguments.

Applies To

MSFlexGrid Control

Syntax

object.**RemoveItem** *index*

The **RemoveItem** method syntax has these parts:

Part	Description
object	An object expression that evaluates to an object in the **Applies To** list.
index	Integer representing the row to remove.

Remarks

To remove the first row, use index = 0.

The **RemoveItem** method deletes the entire row specified. To clear data without removing the rows themselves, use the **Clear** method.

Example

This example uses the **AddItem** method to add 100 items to a **MSFlexGrid**. To try this example, paste the code into the Declarations section of a form with a **MSFlexGrid** control named **MSFlexGrid1**, and then press F5 and click the form.

```
Private Sub Form_Click ()
    Dim Entry, i, Msg              ' Declare variables.
    Msg = _
    "Choose OK to add 100 items to your MSFlexGrid."
    MsgBox Msg                     ' Display message.

MSFlexGrid1.Cols = 2               ' Two strings per row.

For i = 1 To 100   ' Count from 1 to 100.
     Entry = "Entry " & Chr(9) & I  ' Create entry.

MSFlexGrid1.AddItem Entry          ' Add entry.

Next i
    Msg = "Choose OK to remove every other entry."
    MsgBox Msg                     ' Display message.
    For i = 1 To 50                ' Determine how to
       MSFlexGrid1.RemoveItem i    ' remove every other
    Next I                         ' item.
    Msg = "Choose OK to clear all items."
    MsgBox Msg                     ' Display message.
    MSFlexGrid1.Clear              ' Clear list box.
End Sub
```

RowColChange Event (MSFlexGrid)

Occurs when the currently active cell changes to a different cell.

Applies To

MSFlexGrid Control

Syntax

Private Sub *object*_**RowColChange** ()

The *object* placeholder represents an object expression that evaluates to an object in the **Applies To** list.

Remarks

The order of events triggered when the active cell changes is: **LeaveCell**, **EnterCell**, **RowColChange**.

The **RowColChange** event occurs when a user clicks a new cell, but not while a user drags the selection across the **MSFlexGrid** control.

RowHeight Property (MSFlexGrid)

Returns or sets the height of the specified row, in twips. Not available at design time.

Applies To

MSFlexGrid Control

Syntax

object.**RowHeight**(*number*)[= *value*]

The **RowHeight** property syntax has these parts:

Part	Description
object	An object expression that evaluates to an object in the **Applies To** list.
number	Integer. The number of the row in the **MSFlexGrid** control, or -1 to set all rows at once.
value	Single. A numeric expression specifying the height of the row in twips.

Remarks

You can set **RowHeight** to zero to create invisible rows, or to −1 to reset the row height to its default value, which depends on the size of the current font.

RowHeight is independent of the form's scale mode.

See Also

RowHeightMin Property

RowHeightMin Property

Returns or sets the minimum row height for the entire control, in twips.

Applies To

MSFlexGrid Control

Syntax

object.**RowHeightMin** [= *value*]

The **RowHeightMin** property syntax has these parts:

Part	Description
object	An object expression that evaluates to an object in the **Applies To** list.
value	Single. A numeric expression specifying the minimum row height for **MSFlexGrid**.

Remarks

Use this property if you wish to use small fonts but want the rows to be tall. Setting this property is sometimes easier than setting individual row heights with the **RowHeight** property.

RowHeight is independent of the form's scale mode.

See Also

RowHeight Property (MSFlexGrid)

RowIsVisible Property

Returns a Boolean value that indicates whether a specified row is currently visible.

Applies To

MSFlexGrid Control

Syntax

object.**RowIsVisible**(*index*)

The **RowIsVisible** property syntax has these parts:

Part	Description
object	An object expression that evaluates to an object in the **Applies To** list.
index	Long. The number of the column. The value must be in the range of 0 to **Cols** property −1.

Return Values

The return values for the **RowIsVisible** property are:

Setting	Description
True	The specified row is currently visible.
False	The specified row is not currently visible.

RowPos Property

Returns the distance in twips between the upper-left corner of the control and the upper-left corner of a specified row.

Applies To

MSFlexGrid Control

Syntax

object.**RowPos** (*index*)

The **RowPos** property syntax has these parts:

Part	Description
object	An object expression that evaluates to an object in the **Applies To** list.
index	Long. The number of the column. The value must be in the range of 0 to **Cols** property −1.

Scroll Event (MSFlexGrid)

Occurs when the **MSFlexGrid** scrolls its contents, either through the scroll bars, keyboard, or code changing the **TopRow** or **LeftCol** properties.

Applies To

MSFlexGrid Control

Syntax

Private Sub *object*_**Scroll** ()

The *object* placeholder represents an object expression that evaluates to an object in the **Applies To** list.

If the **ScrollTrack** property is set to **True**, the scroll event is triggered while the user is dragging/scrolling the mouse; otherwise, it is not triggered until the drag is complete.

See Also

ScrollBars Property (MSFlexGrid), **ScrollTrack** Property

ScrollBars Property (MSFlexGrid)

Returns or sets a value that determines whether a **MSFlexGrid** has horizontal and/or vertical scroll bars.

Applies To

MSFlexGrid Control

Syntax

object.**ScrollBars** [= *value*]

The **ScrollBars** property syntax has these parts:

Part	Description
object	An object expression that evaluates to an object in the **Applies To** list.
value	Integer or constant specifying the type of scrollbars, as described in **Settings**.

Settings

The settings for *value* are:

Constant	Value	Description
flexScrollNone	0	None
flexScrollHorizontal	1	Horizontal
flexScrollVertical	2	Vertical
flexScrollBoth	3	Both

Remarks

Scroll bars appear on a **MSFlexGrid** only if its contents extend beyond the **MSFlexGrid** control's borders. For example, a vertical scroll bar appears when **MSFlexGrid** can't display all of its rows. If **ScrollBars** is set to **False**, **MSFlexGrid** will not have scroll bars, regardless of its contents.

Note that if **MSFlexGrid** has no scroll bars in either direction, it will not allow *any* scrolling in that direction, even if the user uses the keyboard to select a cell that is off the visible area of the control.

See Also

Scroll Event (MSFlexGrid), **ScrollTrack** Property

ScrollTrack Property

Returns or sets a value that determines whether **MSFlexGrid** should scroll its contents while the user moves the scroll box along the scroll bars.

Applies To

MSFlexGrid Control

Syntax

object.**ScrollTrack** [= *boolean*]

The **ScrollTrack** property syntax has these parts:

Part	Description
object	An object expression that evaluates to an object in the **Applies To** list.
boolean	This property is **False** by default.

Remarks

This property should normally be set to **False** to avoid excessive scrolling and flickering. Set it to **True** only if you want to emulate other controls that have this behavior, or when you want to view rows and columns as they are being scrolled.

See Also

Scroll Event (MSFlexGrid), **ScrollBars** Property (MSFlexGrid)

SelChange Event (MSFlexGrid)

Occurs when the selected range changes to a different cell or range of cells.

Applies To

MSFlexGrid Control

Syntax

Private Sub *object*_**SelChange** ()

The *object* placeholder represents an object expression that evaluates to an object in the **Applies To** list.

Remarks

The **SelChange** event occurs whenever the user clicks a cell other than the selected cell and as a user drags to select a new range of cells. A user can also select a range of cells by pressing the SHIFT key and using the arrow keys.

This event can be triggered in code by changing the selected region using the **Row**, **Col**, **RowSel**, or **ColSel** properties. The **RowColChange** event also occurs when a user clicks a new cell but does not occur while a user drags the selection across **MSFlexGrid**.

See Also

Col, Row Properties (MSFlexGrid), **ColSel, RowSel** Properties

SelectionMode Property

Returns or sets a value that determines whether a **MSFlexGrid** should allow regular cell selection, selection by rows, or selection by columns.

Applies To

MSFlexGrid Control

Syntax

object.**SelectionMode** [= *number*]

The **SelectionMode** property syntax has these parts:

Part	Description
object	An object expression that evaluates to an object in the **Applies To** list.
number	Integer or constant specifying the selection mode, as described in **Settings**.

Settings

The settings for *number* are:

Constant	Value	Description
flexSelectionFree	0	Free. Allows selections to be made normally, spreadsheet-style.
flexSelectionByRow	1	By Row. Forces selections to span entire rows, as in a multi-column list-box or record-based display.
flexSelectionByColumn	2	By Column. Forces selections to span entire columns, as if selecting ranges for a chart or fields for sorting.

See Also

AllowBigSelection Property

Sort Property (MSFlexGrid)

Sets a value that sorts selected rows according to selected criteria. Not available at design time.

Syntax

object.**Sort** [=*value*]

The **Sort** property syntax has these parts:

Part	Description
object	An object expression that evaluates to an object in the **Applies To** list.
value	Integer or constant specifying the type of sorting, as described in **Settings**.

Settings

The settings for *value* are:

Constant	Value	Description
flexSortNone	0	None
flexSortGenericAscending	1	Generic Ascending. Guesses whether text is string or number
flexSortGenericDescending	2	Generic Descending
flexSortNumericAscending	3	Numeric Ascending. Converts strings to numbers
flexSortNumericDescending	4	Numeric Descending
flexSortStringNoCaseAsending	5	String Ascending. Case-insensitive
flexSortNoCaseDescending	6	String Descending. Case-insensitive
flexSortStringAscending	7	String Ascending. Case-sensitive
flexSortStringDescending	8	String Descending. Case-sensitive
	9	Custom. Uses Compare event to compare rows

Remarks

The **Sort** property always sorts entire rows. The range to be sorted is specified by setting the **Row** and **RowSel** properties. If **Row** and **RowSel** are the same, **MSFlexGrid** assumes that you want to sort all nonfixed rows.

The keys used for sorting are determined by the **Col** and **ColSel** properties, always from the left to the right. For example, if **Col** = 3 and **ColSel** = 1, the sort would be done according to the contents of columns 1, then 2, then 3.

The method used to compare the rows is determined by the setting, as explained above. The 9 (Custom) setting is the most flexible, since it fires the **Compare** event that allows you to compare rows in any way you want, using any columns in any order (see the Compare event for details). However, this method is also much slower that the others, typically by a factor of ten, so it should be used only when really necessary.

An alternative to using the 9 (Custom) setting is to create an invisible column, fill it with the keys, then sort based on it with one of the other settings. This is a very good approach for sorting based on dates, for example.

See Also

Col, Row Properties (MSFlexGrid), **ColSel, RowSel** Properties, **Compare** Event

Example

The example below sorts a grid according to the value of a **ComboBox** control. To try the example, place an **MSFlexGrid** control and a **ComboBox** control on a form. Paste the code below into the Declarations section, and press F5.

```
Private Sub Combo1_Click()
    ' Select Column according to Sort method.
    Select Case Combo1.ListIndex
        Case 0 To 2
            MSFlexGrid1.Col = 1
```

```
      Case 3 To 4
         MSFlexGrid1.Col = 2
      Case 4 To 8
         MSFlexGrid1.Col = 1
   End Select
   ' Sort according to Combo1.ListIndex.
   MSFlexGrid1.Sort = Combo1.ListIndex
End Sub

Private Sub Form_Load()
   Dim i As Integer
   ' Fill MSFlexGrid with random data.
   MSFlexGrid1.Cols = 3                      ' Create three columns.

   For i = 1 To 11                           ' Add ten items.
      MSFlexGrid1.AddItem ""
      MSFlexGrid1.Col = 2
      MSFlexGrid1.TextMatrix(i, 1) = SomeName(i)
      MSFlexGrid1.TextMatrix(i, 2) = Rnd()
   Next i

   ' Fill combo box with Sort choices
   With Combo1
      .AddItem "flexSortNone"                     '0
      .AddItem "flexSortGenericAscending"         '1
      .AddItem "flexSortGenericDescending"        '2
      .AddItem "flexSortNumericAscending"         '3
      .AddItem "flexSortNumericDescending"        '4
      .AddItem "flexSortStringNoCaseAsending"     '5
      .AddItem "flexSortNoCaseDescending"         '6
      .AddItem "flexSortStringAscending"          '7
      .AddItem "flexSortStringDescending"         '8
      .ListIndex = 0
   End With
End Sub

Private Function SomeName(i As Integer) As String
   Select Case i
   Case 1
      SomeName = "Ann"
   Case 2
      SomeName = "Glenn"
   Case 3
      SomeName = "Sid"
   Case 4
      SomeName = "Anton"
   Case 5
      SomeName = "Hoagie"
   Case 6
      SomeName = "Traut 'Trane"
   Case 7
      SomeName = "MereD Wah"
   Case 8
      SomeName = "Kemp"
```

```
    Case 9
       SomeName = "Sandy"
    Case 10
       SomeName = "Lien"
    Case 11
       SomeName = "Randy"
    End Select
End Function
```

Text Property (MSFlexGrid)

Returns or sets the text contents of a cell or range of cells.

Applies To

MSFlexGrid Control

Syntax

object.**Text** [= *string*]

The **Text** property syntax has these parts:

Part	Description
object	An object expression that evaluates to an object in the **Applies To** list.
string	A string expression containing the text contents of a cell or range of cells.

Remarks

When retrieving, the **Text** property always retrieves the contents of the current cell, defined by the **Row** and **Col** properties.

When setting, the **Text** property sets the contents of the current cell or of the current selection, depending on the setting of the **FillStyle** property.

See Also

CellTextStyle Property, **Col, Row** Properties (MSFlexGrid), **FillStyle** Property (MSFlexGrid), **TextArray** Property, **TextMatrix** Property, **TextStyle, TextStyleFixed** Properties

Example

This example puts "Here" into the current cell and then changes the active cell to the third cell in the third row and puts "There" into that cell. To run the program click F5, then click the grid.

```
Private Sub Form1_Load ()
   MSFlexGrid1.Rows = 8
   MSFlexGrid1.Cols = 5
End Sub

Private Sub MSFlexGrid1_Click ()
   ' Put text in current cell.
   MSFlexGrid1.Text = "Here"
```

```
'  Put text in third row, third column.
   MSFlexGrid1.Col = 2
   MSFlexGrid1.Row = 2
   MSFlexGrid1.Text = "There"
End Sub
```

TextArray Property

Returns or sets the text contents of an arbitrary cell.

Applies To

MSFlexGrid Control

Syntax

object.**TextArray**(*cellindex*) [= *string*]

The **TextArray** property syntax has these parts:

Part	Description
object	An object expression that evaluates to an object in the **Applies To** list.
cellindex	Integer. A numeric expression specifying which cell to read or write. See Remarks.
string	A string expression containing the contents of an arbitrary cell.

Remarks

This property allows you to set or retrieve the contents of a cell without changing the **Row** and **Col** properties.

The *cellindex* argument determines which cell to use. It is calculated by multiplying the desired row by the **Cols** property and adding the desired column. The clearest and most convenient way to calculate *cellindex* is to define a function to do it, as shown below:

```
' Calculate index for use with TextArray property.
Function faIndex(row As Integer, col As Integer) As Long
    faIndex = row * MSFlexGrid1.Cols + col
End Function

Sub Form_Load()
Dim i as Integer
' Fill MSFlexGrid with data using TextArray property.
For i = MSFlexGrid1.FixedRows to MSFlexGrid1.Rows - 1
    ' ** column 1
    MSFlexGrid1.TextArray(faIndex(i, 1)) = RandomName()
    ' Column 2.
    MSFlexGrid1.TextArray(faIndex(i, 2)) = RandomNumber()
Next
```

See Also

Text Property (MSFlexGrid), **TextMatrix** Property

TextMatrix Property

Returns or sets the text contents of an arbitrary cell.

Applies To

MSFlexGrid Control

Syntax

object.**TextMatrix**(*rowindex, colindex*) [= *string*]

The **TextMatrix** property syntax has these parts:

Part	Description
object	An object expression that evaluates to an object in the **Applies To** list.
rowindex, colindex	Integer. Numeric expressions specifying which cell to read or write.
string	A string expression containing the contents of an arbitrary cell.

Remarks

This property allows you to set or retrieve the contents of a cell without changing the **Row** and **Col** properties.

See Also

Col, Row Properties (MSFlexGrid), **Text** Property (MSFlexGrid), **TextArray** Property

Example

The example below sorts a grid according to the value of a **ComboBox** control. To try the example, place an **MSFlexGrid** control and a **ComboBox** control on a form. Paste the code below into the Declarations section, and press F5.

```
Private Sub Combo1_Click()
   ' Select Column according to Sort method.
   Select Case Combo1.ListIndex
      Case 0 To 2
         MSFlexGrid1.Col = 1
      Case 3 To 4
         MSFlexGrid1.Col = 2
      Case 4 To 8
         MSFlexGrid1.Col = 1
   End Select
   ' Sort according to Combo1.ListIndex.
   MSFlexGrid1.Sort = Combo1.ListIndex
End Sub

Private Sub Form_Load()
   Dim i As Integer
   ' Fill MSFlexGrid with random data.
   MSFlexGrid1.Cols = 3 ' Create three columns.
```

```
For i = 1 To 11 ' Add ten items.
    MSFlexGrid1.AddItem ""
    MSFlexGrid1.Col = 2
    MSFlexGrid1.TextMatrix(i, 1) = SomeName(i)
    MSFlexGrid1.TextMatrix(i, 2) = Rnd()
Next i

' Fill combo box with Sort choices
With Combo1
    .AddItem "flexSortNone" ' 0
    .AddItem "flexSortGenericAscending" '1
    .AddItem "flexSortGenericDescending" '2
    .AddItem "flexSortNumericAscending" '3
    .AddItem "flexSortNumericDescending" '4
    .AddItem "flexSortStringNoCaseAsending" '5

.AddItem "flexSortNoCaseDescending" '6
    .AddItem "flexSortStringAscending" '7
    .AddItem "flexSortStringDescending" '8
    .ListIndex = 0
End With
End Sub

Private Function SomeName(i As Integer) As String
    Select Case i
    Case 1
        SomeName = "Ann"
    Case 2
        SomeName = "Glenn"
    Case 3
        SomeName = "Sid"
    Case 4
        SomeName = "Anton"
    Case 5
        SomeName = "Hoagie"
    Case 6
        SomeName = "Traut 'Trane"
    Case 7
        SomeName = "MereD Wah"

Case 8
    SomeName = "Kemp"
    Case 9
        SomeName = "Sandy"
    Case 10
        SomeName = "Lien"
    Case 11
        SomeName = "Randy"
    End Select
End Function
```

TextStyle, TextStyleFixed Properties

Returns or sets the three-dimensional style for text on a specific cell or range of cells. **TextStyle** determines the style of regular **MSFlexGrid** cells, and **TextStyleFixed** determines the style of fixed rows and columns.

Applies To

MSFlexGrid Control

Syntax

object.**TextStyle**[= *style*]
object.**TextStyleFixed**[= *style*]

The **TextStyle, TextStyleFixed** properties syntax have these parts:

Part	Description
object	An object expression that evaluates to an object in the **Applies To** list.
style	Integer or constant that specifies the text style, as described in **Settings**.

Settings

Settings for *style* are:

Constant	Value	Description
flexTextFlat	0	Flat (normal text)
flexTextRaised	1	Raised
flexTextInset	2	Inset
flexTextRaisedLight	3	Raised Light
flexTextInsetLight	4	Inset Light

Remarks

Settings 1 and 2 work best for large and bold fonts. **Settings** 3 and 4 work best for small regular fonts.

See Also

CellTextStyle Property, **Text** Property (MSFlexGrid)

TopRow Property (MSFlexGrid)

Returns or sets the uppermost visible row (other than a fixed row) in the **MSFlexGrid**. Not available at design time.

Applies To

MSFlexGrid Control

Syntax

object.**TopRow** [= *number*]

The **TopRow** property syntax has these parts:

Part	Description
object	An object expression that evaluates to an object in the **Applies To** list.
number	Long. A numeric expression specifying the uppermost row in **MSFlexGrid**.

Remarks

You can use this property in code to programmatically read or set the visible top row of the **MSFlexGrid**. Use the **LeftCol** property to determine the leftmost visible column in the **MSFlexGrid**.

When setting this property, the largest possible row number is the total number of rows minus the number of rows that can be visible in the **MSFlexGrid**. Attempting to set **TopRow** to a greater row number will cause the **MSFlexGrid** to set it to the largest possible value.

See Also

LeftCol Property (MSFlexGrid), **Scroll** Event (MSFlexGrid)

Version Property (MSFlexGrid)

Returns the version (as an integer) of the **MSFlexGrid** control currently loaded in memory.

Applies To

MSFlexGrid Control

Syntax

object.**Version**

The object placeholder represents an object expression that evaluates to an object in the **Applies To** list.

Remarks

The version number is a three-digit integer where the first digit represents the major version number and the last two represent the minor version number. For example, version 3.5 would return 350.

WordWrap Property (MSFlexGrid)

Returns or sets a value that determines whether text within a cell should be broken between words if a word would extend past the edge of the cell. Return characters – **Chr**(13) – also force line breaks.

Applies To

MSFlexGrid Control

Syntax

object.**WordWrap** [= *boolean*]

The **WordWrap** property syntax has these parts:

Part	Description
object	An object expression that evaluates to an object in the **Applies To** list.
boolean	Determines if the text within a cell wraps. This property is **False** by default.

Remarks

MSFlexGrid can display text slightly faster if you set **WordWrap** to **False**.

Multimedia MCI Control

The **Multimedia MCI** control manages the recording and playback of multimedia files on Media Control Interface (MCI) devices. Conceptually, this control is a set of push buttons that issues MCI commands to devices such as audio boards, MIDI sequencers, CD-ROM drives, audio CD players, videodisc players, and videotape recorders and players. The MCI control also supports the playback of Video for Windows (*.avi) files.

When you add the **Multimedia MCI** control to a form at design time, the control appears on the form as follows:

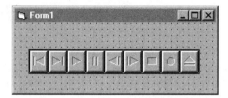

The buttons are defined as Prev, Next, Play, Pause, Back, Step, Stop, Record, and Eject, respectively.

Remarks

Your application should already have the MCI device open and the appropriate buttons in the **Multimedia MCI** control enabled before the user is allowed to choose a button from the **Multimedia MCI** control. In Visual Basic, place the MCI Open command in the **Form_Load** event.

When you intend to record audio with the **Multimedia MCI** control, open a new file. This action ensures that the data file containing the recorded sound will be in a form at compatible with your system's recording capabilities. Also, issue the MCI Save command before closing the MCI device to store the recorded data in the file.

The **Multimedia MCI** control is programmable in several ways:

- The control can be visible or invisible at run time.
- You can augment or completely redefine the functionality of the buttons in the control.
- You can control multiple devices in a form.

If you want to use the buttons in the **Multimedia MCI** control, set the **Visible** and **Enabled** properties to **True**. If you do not want to use the buttons in the control, but want to use the **Multimedia MCI** control for its multimedia functionality, set the **Visible** and **Enabled** properties to **False**. An application can control MCI devices with or without user interaction.

The events (button definitions) of the **Multimedia MCI** control are programmable. You can augment or completely redefine the functionality of these buttons by developing code for the button events.

The MCI extensions support multiple instances of the **Multimedia MCI** control in a single form to provide concurrent control of several MCI devices. You use one control per device.

Distribution Note When you create and distribute applications that use the **Multimedia MCI** control, you should install and register the appropriate files in the customer's Microsoft Windows System or System32 directory. The Setup Wizard included with Visual Basic provides tools to help you write setup programs that install your applications correctly.

Properties

AutoEnable Property (Multimedia MCI Control), **BorderStyle** Property, **ButtonEnabled** Property (Multimedia MCI Control), **ButtonVisible** Property (Multimedia MCI Control), **CanEject** Property (Multimedia MCI Control), **CanPlay** Property (Multimedia MCI Control), **CanRecord** Property (Multimedia MCI Control), **CanStep** Property (Multimedia MCI Control), **Command** Property (Multimedia MCI Control), **Container** Property, **DataBindings** Property, **DeviceID** Property (Multimedia MCI Control), **DeviceType** Property (Multimedia MCI Control), **DragIcon** Property, **DragMode** Property, **Enabled** Property (Multimedia MCI Control), **Error** Property (Multimedia MCI Control), **ErrorMessage** Property (Multimedia MCI Control), **FileName** Property (Multimedia MCI Control), **Frames** Property (Multimedia MCI Control), **From** Property (Multimedia MCI Control), **HelpContextID** Property, **hWnd** Property, **hWndDisplay** Property (Multimedia MCI Control), **Index** Property, **Length** Property (Multimedia MCI Control), **Mode** Property (Multimedia MCI Control), **MouseIcon** Property, **MousePointer** Property, **Name** Property, **Notify** Property (Multimedia MCI Control), **NotifyMessage** Property (Multimedia MCI Control), **NotifyValue** Property (Multimedia MCI Control), **Object** Property, **OLEDropMode** Property, **Orientation** Property (Multimedia MCI Control), **Parent** Property, **Position** Property (Multimedia MCI Control), **RecordMode** Property (Multimedia MCI Control), **Shareable** Property (Multimedia MCI Control), **Silent** Property (Multimedia MCI Control), **Start** Property (Multimedia MCI Control), **TabIndex** Property, **TabStop** Property, **Tag** Property, **TimeFormat** Property (Multimedia MCI Control), **To** Property (Multimedia MCI Control), **ToolTipText** Property, **Track** Property (Multimedia MCI Control), **TrackLength** Property (Multimedia MCI Control), **TrackPosition** Property (Multimedia MCI Control), **Tracks** Property (Multimedia MCI Control), **UpdateInterval** Property (Multimedia MCI Control), **UsesWindows** Property (Multimedia MCI Control), **Visible** Property (Multimedia MCI Control), **Wait** Property (Multimedia MCI Control), **WhatsThisHelpID** Property

Events

ButtonClick Event, **ButtonCompleted** Event, **ButtonGotFocus** Event, **ButtonLostFocus** Event, **Done** Event, **DragDrop** Event, **DragOver** Event, **GotFocus** Event, **LostFocus** Event, **OLECompleteDrag** Event, **OLEDragDrop**

Event, **OLEDragOver** Event, **OLEGiveFeedback** Event, **OLESetData** Event, **OLEStartDrag** Event, **StatusUpdate** Event

Methods

Drag Method, **Move** Method, **OLEDrag** Method, **Refresh** Method, **SetFocus** Method, **ShowWhatsThis** Method, **Zorder** Method

See Also

AutoEnable Property (Multimedia MCI Control), **ButtonEnabled** Property (Multimedia MCI Control), **Start** Property (Multimedia MCI Control), **TimeFormat** Property (Multimedia MCI Control)

AutoEnable Property (Multimedia MCI Control)

Determines if the **Multimedia MCI** control can automatically enable or disable individual buttons in the control. If the **AutoEnable** property is set to **True**, the **Multimedia MCI** control enables those buttons that are appropriate for the current mode of the specified MCI device type. This property also disables those buttons that the current mode of the MCI device does not support.

Applies To

Multimedia MCI Control

Syntax

[*form.*]*MMControl*.**AutoEnable**[= {**True** | **False**}]

Remarks

The effect of the **AutoEnable** property is superseded by the **Enabled** property. The **AutoEnable** property can automatically enable or disable individual buttons in the control when the **Multimedia MCI** control is enabled (**Enabled** property set to **True**). When the **Enabled** property is **False**, keyboard and mouse run-time access to the **Multimedia MCI** control are turned off, regardless of the **AutoEnable** property setting.

The following table lists the **AutoEnable** property settings for the **Multimedia MCI** control.

Setting	Description
False	Does not enable or disable buttons. The program controls the states of the buttons by setting the **Enabled** and **ButtonEnabled** properties.
True	(Default) Enables buttons whose functions are available and disables buttons whose functions are not.

The following tables show how the MCI mode settings are reflected in the control's property settings:

Play mode

Record mode

Pause mode

Stop mode

Open mode

Seek or Not Ready modes

The effect of the **AutoEnable** property supersedes the effects of *Button***Enabled** properties. When the **Enabled** and **AutoEnable** properties are both **True**, the *Button***Enable** properties are not used.

Data Type

Integer (Boolean)

Play mode

Button	Status
Back*	Enabled
Eject*	Enabled
Next	Enabled
Pause	Enabled
Play*	Disabled
Prev	Enabled
Record*	Disabled
Step*	Enabled
Stop	Enabled

*Button is enabled if the operation is supported by the open MCI device.

Record mode

Button	Status
Back*	Enabled
Eject*	Enabled
Next	Enabled
Pause	Enabled
Play*	Disabled
Prev	Enabled
Record*	Disabled
Step*	Enabled
Stop	Enabled

*Button is enabled if the operation is supported by the open MCI device.

Pause mode

Button	Status
Back*	Enabled
Eject*	Enabled
Next	Enabled
Pause	Enabled
Play*	Enabled
Prev	Enabled
Record*	Enabled
Step*	Enabled
Stop	Enabled

*Button is enabled if the operation is supported by the open MCI device.

Stop mode

Button	Status
Back*	Enabled
Eject*	Enabled
Next	Enabled
Pause	Disabled
Play*	Enabled
Prev	Enabled
Record*	Enabled
Step*	Enabled
Stop	Disabled

* Button is enabled if the operation is supported by the open MCI device.

Open mode

Button	Status
Back*	Disabled
Eject*	Enabled
Next	Disabled
Pause	Disabled
Play*	Disabled
Prev	Disabled
Record*	Disabled
Step*	Disabled
Stop	Disabled

* Button is enabled if the operation is supported by the open MCI device.

Seek or Not Ready modes

Button	Status
Back*	Disabled
Eject*	Disabled
Next	Disabled
Pause	Disabled
Play*	Disabled
Prev	Disabled
Record*	Disabled
Step*	Disabled
Stop	Disabled

*Button is enabled if the operation is supported by the open MCI device.

See Also

Multimedia MCI, **ButtonEnabled** Property (**Multimedia MCI** Control), **Enabled** Property (**Multimedia MCI** Control)

BorderStyle Property (ActiveX Controls)

Returns or sets the border style for an object.

Syntax

*object***.BorderStyle** [= *value*]

The **BorderStyle** property syntax has these parts:

Part	Description
object	An object expression that evaluates to an object.
value	A value or constant that determines the border style, as described in Settings.

Settings

The settings for *value* are:

Constant	Value	Description
ccNone	0	(Default) No border or border-related elements.
ccFixedSingle	1	Fixed single.

Note The cc prefix refers to the Windows 95 controls. For the other controls, prefixes for the settings change with the specific control or group of controls. However, the description remains the same unless indicated.

Remarks

Setting **BorderStyle** for a **ProgressBar** control decreases the size of the chunks the control displays.

ButtonClick Event (Multimedia MCI Control)

Occurs when the user presses and releases the mouse button over one of the buttons in the **Multimedia MCI** control.

Applies To

Multimedia MCI Control

Syntax

Private Sub *MMControl_**Button**Click* (*Cancel* **As Integer**)

Remarks

Button may be any of the following: Back, Eject, Next, Pause, Play, Prev, Record, Step, or Stop.

Each of the ***Button*Click** events, by default, perform an **MCI** command when the user chooses a button. The following table lists the **MCI** commands performed for each button in the control.

Button	Command
Back	MCI_STEP
Step	MCI_STEP
Play	MCI_PLAY
Pause	MCI_PAUSE
Prev	MCI_SEEK
Next	MCI_SEEK
Stop	MCI_STOP
Record	MCI_RECORD
Eject	MCI_SET with the MCI_SET_DOOR_OPEN parameter

Setting the *Cancel* parameter for the ***Button*Click** event to **True** prevents the default **MCI** command from being performed. The *Cancel* parameter can take either of the following settings.

Setting	Description
True	Prevents the default MCI command from being performed.
False	Performs the MCI command associated with the button after performing the body of the appropriate ***Button*Click** event.

The body of an event procedure is performed before performing the default **MCI** command associated with the event. Adding code to the body of the ***Button*Click** events augments the functionality of the buttons. If you set the *Cancel* parameter to **True** within the body of an event procedure or pass the value **True** as the argument to a ***Button*Click** event procedure, the default **MCI** command associated with the event will not be performed.

Note Issuing a **Pause** command to restart a paused device can end pending notifications from the original **Play** command if the device does not support the **MCI Resume** command. The **Multimedia MCI** control uses the **MCI Play** command to restart devices that do not support the **MCI Resume** command. Notifications from the **Play** command that restarts a paused device cancel callback conditions and supersede pending notifications from the original **Play** command.

See Also

Multimedia MCI, **Command** Property (Multimedia MCI Control)

ButtonCompleted Event (Multimedia MCI Control)

Occurs when the **MCI** command activated by a **Multimedia MCI** control button finishes.

Applies To

Multimedia MCI Control

Syntax

Private Sub *MMControl_**Button*Completed** (*Errorcode* **As Long**)

Remarks

Button may be any of the following: Back, Eject, Next, Pause, Play, Prev, Record, Step, or Stop.

The *Errorcode* argument can take the following settings.

Setting	Description
0	Command completed successfully.
Any other value	Command did not complete successfully.

If the *Cancel* argument is set to **True** during a ***Button*Click** event, the ***Button*Completed** event is not triggered.

See Also

Command Property (Multimedia MCI Control)

ButtonEnabled Property (Multimedia MCI Control)

Determines if a button in the control is enabled or disabled (a disabled button appears dimmed).

Applies To

Multimedia MCI Control

Syntax

[*form.*]*MMControl.**Button**Enabled[= {**True** | **False**}]

Remarks

The effects of the *Button***Enabled** properties are superseded by the **Enabled** and **AutoEnable** properties. Individual *Button***Enabled** properties enable or disable the associated buttons in the **Multimedia MCI** control when the **Multimedia MCI** control is enabled (**Enabled** property set to **True**) and the **AutoEnable** property is turned off (set to **False**).

For this property, *Button* may be any of the following: Back, Eject, Next, Pause, Play, Prev, Record, Step, or Stop. For example, to disable the Play button, use:

```
[form.]MMControl.PlayEnabled = False
```

To check whether the Record button is enabled, use:

```
If [form.]MMControl.RecordEnabled Then ..
```

The following table lists the *Button***Enabled** property settings for the **Multimedia MCI** control.

Setting	Description
False	(Default) Disables (dims) the button specified by *Button*. This button's function is not available in the control.
True	Enables the button specified by *Button*. This button's function is available in the control.

Data Type

Integer (Boolean)

See Also

Multimedia MCI, **AutoEnable** Property (Multimedia MCI Control), **Enabled** Property (Multimedia MCI Control)

ButtonGotFocus Event (Multimedia MCI Control)

Occurs when a button in the **Multimedia MCI** control receives the input focus.

Applies To

Multimedia MCI Control

Syntax

Private Sub *MMControl_Button***GotFocus** ()

Remarks

Button may be any of the following: Back, Eject, Next, Pause, Play, Prev, Record, Step, or Stop.

See Also

Multimedia MCI, **ButtonLostFocus** Event (Multimedia MCI Control)

ButtonLostFocus Event (Multimedia MCI Control)

Occurs when a button in the **Multimedia MCI** control loses the input focus.

Applies To

Multimedia MCI Control

Syntax

Private Sub *MMControl_Button***LostFocus** ()

Remarks

Button may be any of the following: Back, Eject, Next, Pause, Play, Prev, Record, Step, or Stop.

See Also

Multimedia MCI, **ButtonGotFocus** Event (Multimedia MCI Control)

ButtonVisible Property (Multimedia MCI Control)

Determines if the specified button is displayed in the control.

Applies To

Multimedia MCI Control

Syntax

[*form.*]*MMControl.****Button****Visible*[= {**True** | **False**}]

Remarks

The effects of the *Button***Visible** properties are superseded by the **Visible** property. Individual *Button***Visible** properties display and hide the associated buttons in the **Multimedia MCI** control when the **Multimedia MCI** control is visible (**Visible** property set to **True**). If the **Multimedia MCI** control is invisible, these properties are not used.

For this property, *Button* may be any of the following: Back, Eject, Next, Pause, Play, Prev, Record, Step, or Stop.

The following table lists the *Button***Visible** property settings for the **Multimedia MCI** control.

Setting	Description
False	Does not display the button specified by *Button*. This button's function is not available in the control.
True	(Default) Displays the button specified by *Button*.

Data Type

Integer (Boolean)

See Also

Multimedia MCI, **Multimedia MCI Control** Constants

CanEject Property (Multimedia MCI Control)

Determines if the open MCI device can eject its media. This property is not available at design time and is read-only at run time.

Applies To

Multimedia MCI Control

Syntax

[*form.*]*MMControl.***CanEject**

Remarks

The following table lists the **CanEject** property settings for the **Multimedia MCI** control.

Setting	Description
False	(Default) The device cannot eject its media.
True	The device can eject its media.

The value of **CanEject** is retrieved using MCI_GETDEVCAPS during the processing of an **Open** command.

Data Type

Integer (Boolean)

See Also

Multimedia MCI, **CanPlay** Property (Multimedia MCI Control), **CanRecord** Property (Multimedia MCI Control), **CanStep** Property (Multimedia MCI Control), **Command** Property (Multimedia MCI Control)

CanPlay Property (Multimedia MCI Control)

Determines if the open MCI device can play. This property is not available at design time and is read-only at run time.

Applies To

Multimedia MCI Control

Syntax

[*form.*]*MMControl*.**CanPlay**

Remarks

The following table lists the **CanPlay** property settings for the **Multimedia MCI** control.

Setting	Description
False	(Default) The device cannot play.
True	The device can play.

The value of **CanPlay** is retrieved using MCI_GETDEVCAPS during the processing of an **Open** command.

Data Type

Integer (Boolean)

See Also

Multimedia MCI, **CanEject** Property (Multimedia MCI Control), **CanRecord** Property (Multimedia MCI Control), **CanStep** Property (Multimedia MCI Control), **Command** Property (Multimedia MCI Control)

CanRecord Property (Multimedia MCI Control)

Determines if the open MCI device can record. This property is not available at design time and is read-only at run time.

Applies To

Multimedia MCI Control

Syntax

[*form.*]*MMControl*.**CanRecord**

Remarks

The following table lists the **CanRecord** property settings for the **Multimedia MCI** control.

Setting	Description
False	(Default) The device cannot record.
True	The device can record.

The value of **CanRecord** is retrieved using MCI_GETDEVCAPS during the processing of an **Open** command.

Data Type

Integer (Boolean)

See Also

Multimedia MCI, **CanEject** Property (Multimedia MCI Control), **CanPlay** Property (Multimedia MCI Control), **CanStep** Property (Multimedia MCI Control), **Command** Property (Multimedia MCI Control)

CanStep Property (Multimedia MCI Control)

Determines if the open MCI device can step a frame at a time. This property is not available at design time and is read-only at run time.

Applies To

Multimedia MCI Control

Syntax

[*form.*]*MMControl*.**CanStep**

Remarks

The following table lists the **CanStep** property settings for the **Multimedia MCI** control.

Setting	Description
False	(Default) The device cannot step a frame at a time.
True	The device can step a frame at a time.

Currently only MMMovie, Overlay, and VCR MCI devices can step a frame at a time. Because there is no way to check whether a device can step, programs set the value of this property by checking if the device type is MMMovie, Overlay, or VCR during the processing of an **Open** command.

Data Type

Integer (Boolean)

See Also

Multimedia MCI, **CanEject** Property (Multimedia MCI Control), **CanPlay** Property (Multimedia MCI Control), **CanRecord** Property (Multimedia MCI Control), **Command** Property (Multimedia MCI Control)

Command Property (Multimedia MCI Control)

Specifies an **MCI** command to execute. This property is not available at design time.

Applies To

Multimedia MCI Control

Syntax

[*form.*]*MMControl*.**Command**[= *cmdstring$*]

Remarks

The *cmdstring$* argument gives the name of the **MCI** command to execute: Open, Close, Play, Pause, Stop, Back, Step, Prev, Next, Seek, Record, Eject, Sound, or Save. The command is executed immediately, and the error code is stored in the **Error** property.

The following table describes each command and lists the properties it uses. If a property is not set, either a default value is used (shown in parentheses following the property name), or the property is not used at all (if no default value is shown).

Command	Description/Properties used
Open	Opens a device using the MCI_OPEN command.
	Notify (**False**)
	Wait (**True**)
	Shareable
	DeviceType
	FileName
Close	Closes a device using the MCI_CLOSE command.
	Notify (**False**)
	Wait (**True**)
Play	Plays a device using the MCI_PLAY command.
	Notify (**True**)
	Wait (**False**)
	From
	To
Pause	Pauses playing or recording using the MCI_PLAY command. If executed while the device is paused, tries to resume playing or recording using the MCI_RESUME command.
	Notify (**False**)
	Wait (**True**)
Stop	Stops playing or recording using the MCI_STOP command.
	Notify (**False**)
	Wait (**True**)
Back	Steps backward using the MCI_STEP command.
	Notify (**False**)
	Wait (**True**)
	Frames
Step	Steps forward using the MCI_STEP command.
	Notify (**False**)
	Wait (**True**)
	Frames
Prev	Goes to the beginning of the current track using the Seek command. If executed within three seconds of the previous Prev command, goes to the beginning of the previous track or to the beginning of the first track if at the first track.
	Notify (**False**)
	Wait (**True**)

(continued)

(continued)

Command	Description/Properties used
Next	Goes to the beginning of the next track (if at last track, goes to beginning of last track) using the Seek command.
	Notify (**False**)
	Wait (**True**)
Seek	If not playing, seeks a position using the MCI_SEEK command. If playing, continues playing from the given position using the MCI_PLAY command.
	Notify (**False**)
	Wait (**True**)
	To
Record	Records using the MCI_RECORD command.
	Notify (**True**)
	Wait (**False**)
	From
	To
	RecordMode (0–Insert)
Eject	Ejects media using the MCI_SET command.
	Notify (**False**)
	Wait (**True**)
Sound	Plays a sound using the MCI_SOUND command.
	Notify (**False**)
	Wait (**False**)
	FileName
Save	Saves an open file using the MCI_SAVE command.
	Notify (**False**)
	Wait (**True**)
	FileName

Data Type

String

See Also

Multimedia MCI Control, **CanEject** Property (Multimedia MCI Control), **CanPlay** Property (Multimedia MCI Control), **CanRecord** Property (Multimedia MCI Control), **CanStep** Property (Multimedia MCI Control), **Error** Property (Multimedia MCI Control), **ErrorMessage** Property (Multimedia MCI Control), **FileName** Property (Multimedia MCI Control), **Frames** Property (Multimedia MCI Control), **Length** Property (Multimedia MCI Control), **Notify** Property (Multimedia MCI Control), **RecordMode** Property (Multimedia MCI Control), **Shareable** Property (Multimedia MCI Control), **Silent** Property (Multimedia MCI Control), **Start** Property (Multimedia MCI Control), **To** Property (Multimedia MCI Control), **Track**

Property (Multimedia MCI Control), **TrackLength** Property (Multimedia MCI Control), **TrackPosition** Property (Multimedia MCI Control), **Tracks** Property (Multimedia MCI Control), **UpdateInterval** Property (Multimedia MCI Control), **UsesWindows** Property (Multimedia MCI Control), **Wait** Property (Multimedia MCI Control), **ButtonClick** Event (Multimedia MCI Control), **ButtonCompleted** Event (Multimedia MCI Control), **Done** Event (Multimedia MCI Control), **Error Messages** (Multimedia MCI Control)

Example

The following example illustrates the procedure used to open an MCI device with a compatible data file. By placing this code in the **Form_Load** procedure, your application can use the Multimedia MCI control "as is" to play, record, and rewind the file Gong.wav. To try this example, first create a form with a **Multimedia MCI** control.

```
Private Sub Form_Load ()
   ' Set properties needed by MCI to open.
   MMControl1.Notify = FALSE
   MMControl1.Wait = TRUE
   MMControl1.Shareable = FALSE
   MMControl1.DeviceType = "WaveAudio"
   MMControl1.FileName = "C:\WINDOWS\MMDATA\GONG.WAV"

   ' Open the MCI WaveAudio device.
   MMControl1.Command = "Open"
End Sub
```

To properly manage multimedia resources, you should close those MCI devices that are open before exiting your application. You can place the following statement in the **Form_Unload** procedure to close an open MCI device before exiting from the form containing the **Multimedia MCI** control.

```
Private Sub Form_Unload (Cancel As Integer)
   MMControl1.Command = "Close"
End Sub
```

DeviceID Property (Multimedia MCI Control)

Specifies the device ID for the currently open MCI device. This property is not available at design time and is read-only at run time.

Applies To

Multimedia MCI Control

Syntax

[*form.*]*MMControl*.**DeviceID**[= *id%*]

Remarks

The argument *id%* is the device ID of the currently open MCI device. This ID is obtained from MCI_OPEN as a result of an Open command. If no device is open, this argument is 0.

Data Type

Integer

See Also

Multimedia MCI, **Command** Property (Multimedia MCI Control), **DeviceType** Property (Multimedia MCI Control), **Error Messages** (Multimedia MCI Control)

DeviceType Property (Multimedia MCI Control)

Specifies the type of MCI device to open.

Applies To

Multimedia MCI Control

Syntax

[*form.*]*MMControl.***DeviceType**[= *device$*]

Remarks

The argument *device$* is the type of MCI device to open: AVIVideo, CDAudio, DAT, DigitalVideo, MMMovie, Other, Overlay, Scanner, Sequencer, VCR, Videodisc, or WaveAudio.

The value of this property must be set when opening simple devices (such as an audio CD that does not use files). It must also be set when opening compound MCI devices when the file-name extension does not specify the device to use.

Data Type

String

See Also

Multimedia MCI, **Command** Property (Multimedia MCI Control), **DeviceID** Property (Multimedia MCI Control)

Example

The following example illustrates the procedure used to open an MCI device with a compatible data file. By placing this code in the **Form_Load** procedure, your application can use the Multimedia MCI control "as is" to play, record, and rewind the file Gong.wav. To try this example, first create a form with a **Multimedia MCI** control.

```
Private Sub Form_Load ()
    ' Set properties needed by MCI to open.
```

```
    MMControl1.Notify = FALSE
    MMControl1.Wait = TRUE
    MMControl1.Shareable = FALSE
    MMControl1.DeviceType = "WaveAudio"
    MMControl1.FileName = "C:\WINDOWS\MMDATA\GONG.WAV"

    ' Open the MCI WaveAudio device.
    MMControl1.Command = "Open"
End Sub
```

To properly manage multimedia resources, you should close those MCI devices that are open before exiting your application. You can place the following statement in the **Form_Unload** procedure to close an open MCI device before exiting from the form containing the **Multimedia MCI** control.

```
Private Sub Form_Unload (Cancel As Integer)
    MMControl1.Command = "Close"
End Sub
```

Done Event (Multimedia MCI Control)

Occurs when an **MCI** command for which the **Notify** property is **True** finishes.

Applies To

Multimedia MCI Control

Syntax

Private Sub *MMControl_***Done** (*NotifyCode* **As Integer**)

Remarks

The *NotifyCode* argument indicates whether the **MCI** command succeeded. It can take any of the following settings.

Value	Setting/Result
1	**mciSuccessful**
	Command completed successfully.
2	**mciSuperseded**
	Command was superseded by another command.
4	**mciAborted**
	Command was aborted by the user.
8	**mciFailure**
	Command failed.

See Also

Multimedia MCI, **Notify** Property (Multimedia MCI Control), **NotifyMessage** Property (Multimedia MCI Control), **NotifyValue** Property (Multimedia MCI Control)

Enabled Property (Multimedia MCI Control)

Determines if the control can respond to user-generated events, such as the KeyPress and mouse events.

Applies To

Multimedia MCI Control

Syntax

[*form.*]*MMControl*.**Enabled**[= {**True** | **False**}]

Remarks

This property permits the **Multimedia MCI** control to be enabled or disabled at run time. The effect of the **Enabled** property supersedes the effects of the **AutoEnable** and *Button***Enabled** properties. For example, if the **Enabled** property is **False**, the **Multimedia MCI** control does not permit access to its buttons, regardless of the settings of the **AutoEnable** and *Button***Enabled** properties.

The following table lists the **Enabled** property settings for the **Multimedia MCI** control.

Setting	Description
False	All buttons on the control are disabled (dimmed).
True	(Default) The control is enabled. Use the **AutoEnable** property to let the **Multimedia MCI** control automatically enable or disable the buttons in the control. Or, use the **ButtonEnabled** properties to enable or disable individual buttons in the control.

Data Type

Integer (Boolean)

See Also

Multimedia MCI, **AutoEnable** Property (Multimedia MCI Control), **ButtonEnabled** Property (Multimedia MCI Control)

Error Messages (Multimedia MCI Control)

The following table lists the trappable errors for the **Multimedia MCI** control.

Constant	Value	Description
mciInvalidProcedureCall	5	Invalid procedure call.
MciInvalidProertyValue	380	invalid property value.
MciSetNotSupported	383	Property is read-only.
MciGetNotSupported	394	Property is write-only.
MciInvalidObjectUse	425	Invalid object use.
MciWrongClipboardFormat	461	Specified format doesn't match format of data.

(continued)

Constant	Value	Description
MciObjectLocked	672	**DataObject** formats list may not be cleared or expanded outside of the **OLEStartDrag** event.
MciExpectedArgument	673	Expected at least one argument.
MciRecursiveOleDrag	674	Illegal recursive invocation of OLE drag and drop
mciFormatNotByteArray	675	Non-intrinsic OLE drag and drop formats used with **SetData** require Byte array data. **GetData** may return more bytes than were given to **SetData**.
MciDataNotSetForFormat	676	Requested data was not supplied to the **DataObject** during the **OLESetData** event.
MciCantCreateButton	30001	Can't create button
mciCantCreateTimer	30002	Can't create a timer resource
mciUnsupportedFunction	30004	Unsupported function

Below is a list of the MCI error strings and numbers that are related to the **Multimedia MCI** control.

MCI Error Strings	MCI Error Numbers
MCIERR_BASE	256
MCIERR_INVALID_DEVICE_ID	257
MCIERR_UNRECOGNIZED_KEYWORD	259
MCIERR_UNRECOGNIZED_COMMAND	261
MCIERR_HARDWARE	262
MCIERR_INVALID_DEVICE_NAME	263
MCIERR_OUT_OF_MEMORY	264
MCIERR_DEVICE_OPEN	265
MCIERR_CANNOT_LOAD_DRIVER	266
MCIERR_MISSING_COMMAND_STRING	267
MCIERR_PARAM_OVERFLOW	268
MCIERR_MISSING_STRING_ARGUMENT	269
MCIERR_BAD_INTEGER	270
MCIERR_PARSER_INTERNAL	271
MCIERR_DRIVER_INTERNAL	272
MCIERR_MISSING_PARAMETER	273
MCIERR_UNSUPPORTED_FUNCTION	274
MCIERR_FILE_NOT_FOUND	275
MCIERR_DEVICE_NOT_READY	276
MCIERR_INTERNAL	277

(continued)

(continued)

MCI Error Strings	MCI Error Numbers
MCIERR_DRIVER	278
MCIERR_CANNOT_USE_ALL	279
MCIERR_MULTIPLE	280
MCIERR_EXTENSION_NOT_FOUND	281
MCIERR_OUTOFRANGE	282
MCIERR_FLAGS_NOT_COMPATIBLE	283
MCIERR_FILE_NOT_SAVED	286
MCIERR_DEVICE_TYPE_REQUIRED	287
MCIERR_DEVICE_LOCKED	288
MCIERR_DUPLICATE_ALIAS	289
MCIERR_BAD_CONSTANT	290
MCIERR_MUST_USE_SHAREABLE	291
MCIERR_MISSING_DEVICE_NAME	292
MCIERR_BAD_TIME_FORMAT	293
MCIERR_NO_CLOSING_QUOTE	294
MCIERR_DUPLICATE_FLAGS	295
MCIERR_INVALID_FILE	296
MCIERR_NULL_PARAMETER_BLOCK	297
MCIERR_UNNAMED_RESOURCE	298
MCIERR_NEW_REQUIRES_ALIAS	299
MCIERR_NOTIFY_ON_AUTO_OPEN	300
MCIERR_NO_ELEMENT_ALLOWED	301
MCIERR_NONAPPLICABLE_FUNCTION	302
MCIERR_ILLEGAL_FOR_AUTO_OPEN	303
MCIERR_FILENAME_REQUIRED	304
MCIERR_EXTRA_CHARACTERS	305
MCIERR_DEVICE_NOT_INSTALLED	306
MCIERR_GET_CD	307
MCIERR_SET_CD	308
MCIERR_SET_DRIVE	309
MCIERR_DEVICE_LENGTH	310
MCIERR_DEVICE_ORD_LENGTH	311
MCIERR_NO_INTEGER	312
MCIERR_WAVE_OUTPUTSINUSE	320
MCIERR_WAVE_SETOUTPUTINUSE	321
MCIERR_WAVE_INPUTSINUSE	322

(continued)

MCI Error Strings	MCI Error Numbers
MCIERR_WAVE_SETINPUTINUSE	323
MCIERR_WAVE_OUTPUTUNSPECIFIED	324
MCIERR_WAVE_INPUTUNSPECIFIED	325
MCIERR_WAVE_OUTPUTSUNSUITABLE	326
MCIERR_WAVE_SETOUTPUTUNSUITABLE	327
MCIERR_WAVE_INPUTSUNSUITABLE	328
MCIERR_WAVE_SETINPUTUNSUITABLE	329
MCIERR_SEQ_DIV_INCOMPATIBLE	336
MCIERR_SEQ_PORT_INUSE	337
MCIERR_SEQ_PORT_NONEXISTENT	338
MCIERR_SEQ_PORT_MAPNODEVICE	339
MCIERR_SEQ_PORT_MISCERROR	340
MCIERR_SEQ_TIMER	341
MCIERR_SEQ_PORTUNSPECIFIED	342
MCIERR_SEQ_NOMIDIPRESENT	343
MCIERR_NO_WINDOW	346
MCIERR_CREATEWINDOW	347
MCIERR_FILE_READ	348
MCIERR_FILE_WRITE	349
MCIERR_CUSTOM_DRIVER_BASE	512

See Also

Error Property (Multimedia MCI Control), **ErrorMessage** Property (Multimedia MCI Control)

Error Property (Multimedia MCI Control)

Specifies the error code returned from the last MCI command. This property is not available at design time and is read-only at run time.

Applies To

Multimedia MCI Control

Syntax

[*form.*]*MMControl*.**Error**

Remarks

If the last MCI command did not cause an error, this value is 0.

Data Type

> **Integer**

See Also

> **Multimedia MCI**, **Command** Property (Multimedia MCI Control), **ErrorMessage** Property (Multimedia MCI Control), **Error Messages** (Multimedia MCI Control)

ErrorMessage Property (Multimedia MCI Control)

Describes the error code stored in the **Error** property. This property is not available at design time and is read-only at run time.

Applies To

> **Multimedia MCI** Control

Syntax

> [*form.*]*MMControl*.**ErrorMessage**

Data Type

> **String**

See Also

> **Multimedia MCI**, **Command** Property (Multimedia MCI Control), **Error** Property (Multimedia MCI Control), **Error Messages** (Multimedia MCI Control)

FileName Property (Multimedia MCI Control)

Specifies the file to be opened by an **Open** command or saved by a **Save** command. To change the **FileName** property at run time, you must close and reopen the **Multimedia MCI** control.

Applies To

> **Multimedia MCI** Control

Syntax

> [*form.*]*MMControl*.**FileName**[= *stringexpression$*]

Remarks

> The argument *stringexpression$* specifies the file to be opened or saved.

Data Type

> **String**

See Also

Multimedia MCI, **Command** Property (Multimedia MCI Control)

Example

To change the **FileName** property of a **Multimedia MCI** control at run time, you must close and then reopen the **Multimedia MCI** control.

The following example finds a selected item, closes the **Multimedia MCI** Control, resets the **DeviceType** property, resets the **FileName** property with the selected item, then reopens the **Multimedia MCI** control. To try the example, place a **Multimedia MCI** control and a **FileListBox** on a form, and paste the code into the Declarations section of the form.

```
Private Sub File1_Click()
    Dim i As Integer
    For i = 0 To File1.ListCount - 1
        If File1.Selected(i) = True Then
            MMControl1.Command = "close"
            MMControl1.DeviceType = "WaveAudio"
            MMControl1.FileName = "c:\windows\" & File1.List(i)
            MMControl1.Command = "open"
        End If
    Next i
End Sub
```

Frames Property (Multimedia MCI Control)

Specifies the number of frames the **Step** command steps forward or the **Back** command steps backward. This property is not available at design time.

Applies To

Multimedia MCI Control

Syntax

[*form.*]*MMControl.***Frames**[= *frames&*]

Remarks

The argument *frames&* specifies the number of frames to step forward or backward.

Data Type

Long

See Also

Multimedia MCI, **Command** Property (Multimedia MCI Control)

From Property (Multimedia MCI Control)

Specifies the starting point, as defined by the **Multimedia MCI** control **TimeFormat** property, for the **Play** or **Record** command. This property is not available at design time.

Applies To

Multimedia MCI Control

Syntax

[*form.*]*MMControl*.**From**[= *location&*]

Remarks

The argument *location&* specifies the starting point for the play or record operation. The current time format is given by the **TimeFormat** property.

The value you assign to this property is used only with the next **MCI** command. Subsequent **MCI** commands ignore the **From** property until you assign it another (different or identical) value.

Data Type

Long

See Also

Multimedia MCI, **Command** Property (Multimedia MCI Control), **TimeFormat** Property (Multimedia MCI Control), **To** Property (Multimedia MCI Control)

---

hWndDisplay Property (Multimedia MCI Control)

Specifies the output window for MCI MMMovie or Overlay devices that use a window to display output. This property is not available at design time.

Applies To

Multimedia MCI Control

Syntax

[*form.*]*MMControl*.**hWndDisplay**

Remarks

This property is a handle to the window that the MCI device uses for output. If the handle is 0, a default window (also known as the "stage window") is used.

To determine whether a device uses this property, look at the **UsesWindows** property settings.

In Visual Basic, to get a handle to a control, first use the **SetFocus** method to set the focus to the desired control. Then call the Windows **GetFocus** function.

To get a handle to a Visual Basic form, use the **hWnd** property for that form.

Data Type

Integer

See Also

Multimedia MCI, **UsesWindows** Property (Multimedia MCI Control), **SetFocus** Method, **hWnd** Property, **GotFocus** Event

Length Property (Multimedia MCI Control)

Specifies the length, as defined by the **Multimedia MCI** control **TimeFormat** property, of the media in an open MCI device. This property is not available at design time and is read-only at run time.

Applies To

Multimedia MCI Control

Syntax

[*form.*]*MMControl*.**Length**

Data Type

Long

See Also

Multimedia MCI, **Command** Property (Multimedia MCI Control), **From** Property (Multimedia MCI Control), **TimeFormat** Property (Multimedia MCI Control)

Mode Property (Multimedia MCI Control)

Returns the current mode of an open MCI device. This property is not available at design time and is read-only at run time.

Applies To

Multimedia MCI Control

Syntax

[*form.*]*MMControl*.**Mode**

Remarks

The following table lists the **Mode** property return values for the **Multimedia MCI** control.

Value	Setting/Device mode	Description
524	**mciModeNotOpen**	Device is not open.
525	**mciModeStop**	Device is stopped.
526	**mciModePlay**	Device is playing.
527	**mciModeRecord**	Device is recording.
528	**mciModeSeek**	Device is seeking.
529	**mciModePause**	Device is paused.
530	**mciModeReady**	Device is ready.

Data Type

Long

See Also

Multimedia MCI

Multimedia MCI Control Constants

Mode Constants

Constant	Value	Description
mciModeNotOpen	524	Device not open.
mciModeStop	525	Device stop.
mciModePlay	526	Device play.
mciModeRecord	527	Device record.
mciModeSeek	528	Device seek.
mciModePause	529	Device pause.
mciModeReady	530	Device ready.

Notify Constants

Constant	Value	Description
mciNotifySuccessful	1	Command completed successfully.
mciNotifySuperseded	2	Command superseded by another command.
mciAborted	4	Command aborted by user.
mciFailure	8	Command failed.

Orientation Constants

Constant	Value	Description
mciOrientHorz	0	Buttons arranged horizontally.
mciOrientVert	1	Buttons arranged vertically.

RecordMode Constants

Constant	Value	Description
mciRecordInsert	0	Insert recording mode.
mciRecordOverwrite	1	Overwrite recording mode.

Format Constants

Constant	Value	Description
mciFormatMilliseconds	0	Milliseconds format.
mciFormatHms	1	Hours, seconds, and minutes format.
mciFormatMsf	2	Minutes, seconds, and frames format.
mciFormatFrames	3	Frames format.
mciFormatSmpte24	4	24-frame SMPTE format.
mciFormatSmpte25	5	25-frame SMPTE format.
mciFormatSmpte30	6	30-frame SMPTE format.
mciFormatSmpte30Drop	7	30-drop-frame SMPTE format.
mciFormatBytes	8	Bytes format.
mciFormatSamples	9	Samples format.
mciFormatTmsf	10	Tracks minutes, seconds, and frames format.

See Also

Multimedia MCI Control, **Mode** Property (Multimedia MCI Control), **Notify** Property (Multimedia MCI Control), **Orientation** Property (Multimedia MCI Control), **RecordMode** Property (Multimedia MCI Control), **TimeFormat** Property (Multimedia MCI Control)

Notify Property (Multimedia MCI Control)

Determines if the next **MCI** command uses MCI notification services. If set to **True**, the **Notify** property generates a callback event (Done), which occurs when the next **MCI** command is complete. This property is not available at design time.

Applies To

Multimedia MCI Control

Syntax

[*form.*]*MMControl*.**Notify**[= {**True** | **False**}]

Remarks

The following table lists the **Notify** property settings for the **Multimedia MCI** control.

Setting	Description
False	(Default) The next command does not generate the **Done** event.
True	The next command generates the **Done** event.

The value assigned to this property is used only with the next **MCI** command. Subsequent **MCI** commands ignore the **Notify** property until it is assigned another (different or identical) value.

Note A notification message is aborted when you send a new command that prevents the callback conditions set by a previous command, from being satisfied. For example, to restart a paused device that does not support the **MCI Resume** command, the **Multimedia MCI** control sends the **Play** command to the paused device. However, the **Play** command that restarts the device sets callback conditions, superseding callback conditions and pending notifications from earlier commands.

Data Type

Integer (Boolean)

See Also

Multimedia MCI, **Command** Property (Multimedia MCI Control), **NotifyMessage** Property (Multimedia MCI Control), **NotifyValue** Property (Multimedia MCI Control), **Done** Event (Multimedia MCI Control)

Example

The following example illustrates the procedure used to open an MCI device with a compatible data file. By placing this code in the **Form_Load** procedure, your application can use the Multimedia MCI control "as is" to play, record, and rewind the file Gong.wav. To try this example, first create a form with a **Multimedia MCI** control.

```
Private Sub Form_Load ()
    ' Set properties needed by MCI to open.
    MMControl1.Notify = FALSE
    MMControl1.Wait = TRUE
    MMControl1.Shareable = FALSE
    MMControl1.DeviceType = "WaveAudio"
    MMControl1.FileName = "C:\WINDOWS\MMDATA\GONG.WAV"

    ' Open the MCI WaveAudio device.
    MMControl1.Command = "Open"
End Sub
```

To properly manage multimedia resources, you should close those MCI devices that are open before exiting your application. You can place the following statement in the **Form_Unload** procedure to close an open MCI device before exiting from the form containing the **Multimedia MCI** control.

```
Private Sub Form_Unload (Cancel As Integer)
    MMControl1.Command = "Close"
End Sub
```

NotifyMessage Property (Multimedia MCI Control)

Describes the notify code returned in the **Done** event, triggered by the **Notify** Property. The **NotifyMessage** property is not available at design time and is read-only at run time.

Applies To

Multimedia MCI Control

Syntax

[*form.*]*MMControl***.NotifyMessage**

Data Type

String

See Also

Multimedia MCI, **Notify** Property (Multimedia MCI Control), **NotifyValue** Property (Multimedia MCI Control), **Done** Event (Multimedia MCI Control)

NotifyValue Property (Multimedia MCI Control)

Specifies the result of the last **MCI** command that requested a notification. This property is not available at design time and is read-only at run time.

Applies To

Multimedia MCI Control

Syntax

[*form.*]*MMControl***.NotifyValue**

Remarks

The following table lists the **NotifyValue** return values for the **Multimedia MCI** control.

Value	Setting/Device mode
1	**mciNotifySuccessful**
	Command completed successfully.
2	**mciNotifySuperseded**
	Command was superseded by another command.

(continued)

(continued)

Value	Setting/Device mode
4	**mciNotifyAborted**
	Command was aborted by the user.
8	**mciNotifyFailure**
	Command failed.

The program can check the **Notify** code returned in the **Done** event to determine this value for the most recent **MCI** command.

Data Type

Integer (Enumerated)

See Also

Multimedia MCI, **Notify** Property (Multimedia MCI Control), **NotifyMessage** Property (Multimedia MCI Control), **Done** Event (Multimedia MCI Control), **Multimedia MCI Control** Constants

Orientation Property (Multimedia MCI Control)

Determines whether buttons on the control are arranged vertically or horizontally.

Applies To

Multimedia MCI Control

Syntax

[*form.*]*MMControl.***Orientation**[= *orientation%*]

Remarks

The following table lists the **Orientation** property settings for the **Multimedia MCI** control.

Constant	Value	Description
mciOrientHorz	0	Buttons are arranged horizontally.
mciOrientVert	1	Buttons are arranged vertically.

Data Type

Integer (Enumerated)

See Also

Multimedia MCI, **Visible** Property (Multimedia MCI Control), **Multimedia MCI Control** Constants

Position Property (Multimedia MCI Control)

Specifies, as defined by the **Multimedia MCI** control **TimeFormat** property, the current position of an open MCI device. This property is not available at design time and is read-only at run time.

Applies To

Multimedia MCI Control

Syntax

[*form.*]*MMControl*.**Position**

Data Type

Long

See Also

Multimedia MCI, **TimeFormat** Property (Multimedia MCI Control)

RecordMode Property (Multimedia MCI Control)

Specifies the current recording mode for those MCI devices that support recording.

Applies To

Multimedia MCI Control

Syntax

[*form.*]*MMControl*.**RecordMode**[= *mode%*]

Remarks

The following table lists the **RecordMode** property settings for the **Multimedia MCI** control.

Constant	Value	Recording mode
mciRecordInsert	0	Insert
mciRecordOverwrite	1	Overwrite

To determine whether a device supports recording, check the **CanRecord** property.

A device that supports recording may support either or both of the recording modes. There is no way to check ahead of time which mode a device supports. If recording with a particular mode fails, try the other mode.

WaveAudio devices support Insert mode only.

503

Data Type

Integer (Enumerated)

See Also

Multimedia MCI, **CanRecord** Property (Multimedia MCI Control), **Command** Property (Multimedia MCI Control)

Shareable Property (Multimedia MCI Control)

Determines if more than one program can share the same MCI device.

Applies To

Multimedia MCI Control

Syntax

[*form.*]*MMControl*.**Shareable**[= {**True** | **False**}]

Remarks

The following table lists the **Shareable** property settings for the **Multimedia MCI** control.

Setting	Description
False	No other controls or applications can access this device.
True	More than one control or application can open this device.

Data Type

Integer (Boolean)

See Also

Multimedia MCI Control, **Command** Property (Multimedia MCI Control)

Example

The following example illustrates the procedure used to open an MCI device with a compatible data file. By placing this code in the **Form_Load** procedure, your application can use the Multimedia MCI control "as is" to play, record, and rewind the file Gong.wav. To try this example, first create a form with a **Multimedia MCI** control.

```
Private Sub Form_Load ()
    ' Set properties needed by MCI to open.
    MMControl1.Notify = FALSE
    MMControl1.Wait = TRUE
    MMControl1.Shareable = FALSE
    MMControl1.DeviceType = "WaveAudio"
    MMControl1.FileName = "C:\WINDOWS\MMDATA\GONG.WAV"
```

```
    ' Open the MCI WaveAudio device.
    MMControl1.Command = "Open"
End Sub
```

To properly manage multimedia resources, you should close those MCI devices that are open before exiting your application. You can place the following statement in the **Form_Unload** procedure to close an open MCI device before exiting from the form containing the **Multimedia MCI** control.

```
Private Sub Form_Unload (Cancel As Integer)
    MMControl1.Command = "Close"
End Sub
```

Silent Property (Multimedia MCI Control)

Determines if sound plays.

Applies To

Multimedia MCI Control

Syntax

[*form.*]*MMControl*.**Silent**[= {**True** | **False**}]

Remarks

The following table lists the **Silent** property settings for the **Multimedia MCI** control.

Setting	Description
False	Any sound present is played.
True	Sound is turned off.

Data Type

Integer (Boolean)

See Also

Multimedia MCI Control, **Command** Property (Multimedia MCI Control)

Start Property (Multimedia MCI Control)

Specifies, as defined in the **Multimedia MCI** control **TimeFormat** property, the starting position of the current media. This property is not available at design time and is read-only at run time.

Applies To

Multimedia MCI Control

Syntax

[*form.*]*MMControl*.**Start**

Data Type

> **Long**

See Also

> **Multimedia MCI** Control, **Command** Property (Multimedia MCI Control),
> **TimeFormat** Property (Multimedia MCI Control)

StatusUpdate Event (Multimedia MCI Control)

> Occurs automatically at intervals given by the **UpdateInterval** property.

Applies To

> **Multimedia MCI** Control

Syntax

> **Private Sub** *MMControl_***StatusUpdate** ()

Remarks

> This event allows an application to update the display to inform the user about the
> status of the current MCI device. The application can obtain status information from
> properties such as **Position**, **Length**, and **Mode**.

See Also

> **Multimedia MCI** Control, **Length** Property (Multimedia MCI Control), **Mode**
> Property (Multimedia MCI Control), **Position** Property (Multimedia MCI Control),
> **UpdateInterval** Property (Multimedia MCI Control)

TimeFormat Property (Multimedia MCI Control)

> Specifies the time format used to report all position information.

Applies To

> **Multimedia MCI** Control

Syntax

> *[form.]MMControl.***TimeFormat**[= *format&*]

Remarks

> The following table lists the **TimeFormat** property settings for the **Multimedia MCI**
> control.

Value	Setting/Time format
0	**mciFormatMilliseconds**
	Milliseconds are stored as a 4-byte integer variable.
1	**mciFormatHms**
	Hours, minutes, and seconds are packed into a 4-byte integer. From least significant byte to most significant byte, the individual data values are:
	Hours (least significant byte)
	Minutes
	Seconds
	Unused (most significant byte)
2	**mciFormatMsf**
	Minutes, seconds, and frames are packed into a 4-byte integer. From least significant byte to most significant byte, the individual data values are:
	Minutes (least significant byte)
	Seconds
	Frames
	Unused (most significant byte)
3	**mciFormatFrames**
	Frames are stored as a 4-byte integer variable.
4	**mciFormatSmpte24**
	24-frame SMPTE packs the following values in a 4-byte variable from least significant byte to most significant byte:
	Hours (least significant byte)
	Minutes
	Seconds
	Frames (most significant byte)
	SMPTE (Society of Motion Picture and Television Engineers) time is an absolute time format expressed in hours, minutes, seconds, and frames. The standard SMPTE division types are 24, 25, and 30 frames per second.
5	**mciFormatSmpte25**
	25-frame SMPTE packs data into the 4-byte variable in the same order as 24-frame SMPTE.
6	**mciFormatSmpte30**
	30-frame SMPTE packs data into the 4-byte variable in the same order as 24-frame SMPTE.
7	**mciFormatSmpte30Drop**
	30-drop-frame SMPTE packs data into the 4-byte variable in the same order as 24-frame SMPTE.
8	**mciFormatBytes**
	Bytes are stored as a 4-byte integer variable.

(continued)

507

(continued)

Value	Setting/Time format
9	**mciFormatSamples**
	Samples are stored as a 4-byte integer variable.
10	**mciFormatTmsf**
	Tracks, minutes, seconds, and frame are packed in the 4-byte variable from least significant byte to most significant byte:
	Tracks (least significant byte)
	Minutes
	Seconds
	Frames (most significant byte)
	Note MCI uses continuous track numbering.

Note   Not all formats are supported by every device. If you try to set an invalid format, the assignment is ignored.

The current timing information is always passed in a 4-byte integer. In some formats, the timing information returned is not really an integer, but single bytes of information packed in the long integer. Properties that access or send information in the current time format are: **From**, **Length**, **Position**, **Start**, **To**, **TrackLength**, **TrackPosition**.

Data Type

Long (Enumerated)

See Also

Multimedia MCI Control, **From** Property (Multimedia MCI Control), **Length** Property (Multimedia MCI Control), **Position** Property (Multimedia MCI Control), **Start** Property (Multimedia MCI Control), **To** Property (Multimedia MCI Control), **Track** Property (Multimedia MCI Control), **TrackLength** Property (Multimedia MCI Control), **TrackPosition** Property (Multimedia MCI Control)

To Property (Multimedia MCI Control)

Specifies the ending point, as defined in the **Multimedia MCI** control **TimeFormat** property, for the **Play** or **Record** command. This property is not available at design time.

Applies To

Multimedia MCI Control

Syntax

[*form.*]*MMControl*.**To**[= *location&*]

Remarks

The argument *location&* specifies the ending point for the play or record operation. The current time format is given by the **TimeFormat** property.

The value assigned to this property is used only with the next **MCI** command. Subsequent **MCI** commands ignore the **To** property until it is assigned another (different or identical) value.

Data Type

Long

See Also

Multimedia MCI, **Command** Property (Multimedia MCI Control), **From** Property (Multimedia MCI Control), **TimeFormat** Property (Multimedia MCI Control)

Track Property (Multimedia MCI Control)

Specifies the track about which the **TrackLength** and **TrackPosition** properties return information. This property is not available at design time.

Applies To

Multimedia MCI Control

Syntax

[*form.*]*MMControl*.**Track**[= *track&*]

Remarks

The argument *track&* specifies the track number.

This property is used only to get information about a particular track. It has no relationship to the current track.

Data Type

Long

See Also

Command Property (Multimedia MCI Control), **TrackLength** Property (Multimedia MCI Control), **TrackPosition** Property (Multimedia MCI Control)

TrackLength Property (Multimedia MCI Control)

Specifies the length, as defined in the **Multimedia MCI** control **TimeFormat** property, of the track given by the **Track** property. This property is not available at design time and is read-only at run time.

Applies To

Multimedia MCI Control

Syntax

> [*form.*]*MMControl*.**TrackLength**

Data Type

> **Long**

See Also

> **Multimedia MCI**, **Command** Property (Multimedia MCI Control), **Track** Property (Multimedia MCI Control), **TrackPosition** Property (Multimedia MCI Control)

TrackPosition Property (Multimedia MCI Control)

Specifies the starting position, as defined in the **Multimedia MCI** control **TimeFormat** property, of the track given by the **Track** property. This property is not available at design time and is read-only at run time.

Applies To

> **Multimedia MCI** Control

Syntax

> [*form.*]*MMControl*.**TrackPosition**

Data Type

> **Long**

See Also

> **Multimedia MCI**, **Command** Property (Multimedia MCI Control), **TimeFormat** Property (Multimedia MCI Control), **Track** Property (Multimedia MCI Control), **TrackLength** Property (Multimedia MCI Control)

Tracks Property (Multimedia MCI Control)

Specifies the number of tracks available on the current MCI device. This property is not available at design time and is read-only at run time.

Applies To

> **Multimedia MCI** Control

Syntax

> [*form.*]*MMControl*.**Tracks**

Data Type

Long

See Also

Multimedia MCI, **Command** Property (Multimedia MCI Control), **Track** Property (Multimedia MCI Control), **TrackLength** Property (Multimedia MCI Control), **TrackPosition** Property (Multimedia MCI Control)

UpdateInterval Property (Multimedia MCI Control)

Specifies the number of milliseconds between successive **StatusUpdate** events.

Applies To

Multimedia MCI Control

Syntax

[*form.*]*MMControl*.**UpdateInterval**[= *milliseconds%*]

Remarks

The argument *milliseconds%* specifies the number of milliseconds between events. If milliseconds is 0, no **StatusUpdate** events occur.

Data Type

Integer

See Also

Multimedia MCI, **Command** Property (Multimedia MCI Control), **StatusUpdate** Event (Multimedia MCI Control)

UsesWindows Property (Multimedia MCI Control)

Determines if the currently open MCI device uses a window for output. This property is not available at design time and is read-only at run time.

Applies To

Multimedia MCI Control

Syntax

[*form.*]*MMControl*.**UsesWindows**

Remarks

The following table lists the **UsesWindows** property return values for the **Multimedia MCI** control.

Value	Description
False	The current device does not use a window for output.
True	The current device uses a window.

Currently, only MMMovie and Overlay devices use windows for display. Because there is no way to determine whether a device uses windows, the value of **UsesWindows** is set during processing of an **Open** command by checking the device type. If the device type is MMMovie, Overlay, or VCR, the device uses windows.

For devices that use windows, you can use the **hWndDisplay** property to set the window that will display output.

Data Type

Integer (Boolean)

See Also

Multimedia MCI, **Command** Property (Multimedia MCI Control), **hWndDisplay** Property (Multimedia MCI Control)

Visible Property (Multimedia MCI Control)

Determines if the **Multimedia MCI** control is visible or invisible at run time.

Applies To

Multimedia MCI Control

Syntax

[*form.*]*MMControl*.**Visible**[= {**True** | **False**}]

Remarks

The effect of the **Visible** property supersedes the effects of the individual *Button***Visible** properties. When the **Multimedia MCI** control is visible, the individual *Button***Visible** properties govern the visibility of the associated buttons in the control. When the **Visible** property is **False**, the entire control is invisible, and the *Button***Visible** properties are not used.

The following table lists the **Visible** property settings for the **Multimedia MCI** control.

Setting	Description
False	The control is invisible.
True	(Default) Each button is visible or hidden individually, depending on its *Button*Visible property. This button's function is still available in the control.

Data Type

Integer (Boolean)

See Also

Multimedia MCI Control, ButtonVisible Property (Multimedia MCI Control)

Wait Property (Multimedia MCI Control)

Determines whether the Multimedia MCI control waits for the next MCI command to complete before returning control to the application. This property is not available at design time.

Applies To

Multimedia MCI Control

Syntax

[*form.*]*MMControl*.Wait[= {True | False}]

Remarks

The following table lists the Wait property settings for the Multimedia MCI control.

Setting	Description
False	Multimedia MCI does not wait until the MCI command completes before returning control to the application.
True	Multimedia MCI waits until the next MCI command completes before returning control to the application.

The value assigned to this property is used only with the next MCI command. Subsequent MCI commands ignore the Wait property until it is assigned another (different or identical) value.

Data Type

Integer (Boolean)

See Also

Multimedia MCI, Command Property (Multimedia MCI Control)

Example

The following example illustrates the procedure used to open an MCI device with a compatible data file. By placing this code in the **Form_Load** procedure, your application can use the Multimedia MCI control "as is" to play, record, and rewind the file Gong.wav. To try this example, first create a form with a **Multimedia MCI** control.

```
Private Sub Form_Load ()
   ' Set properties needed by MCI to open.
   MMControl1.Notify = FALSE
   MMControl1.Wait = TRUE
   MMControl1.Shareable = FALSE
   MMControl1.DeviceType = "WaveAudio"
   MMControl1.FileName = "C:\WINDOWS\MMDATA\GONG.WAV"

   ' Open the MCI WaveAudio device.
   MMControl1.Command = "Open"
End Sub
```

To properly manage multimedia resources, you should close those MCI devices that are open before exiting your application. You can place the following statement in the **Form_Unload** procedure to close an open MCI device before exiting from the form containing the **Multimedia MCI** control.

```
Private Sub Form_Unload (Cancel As Integer)
   MMControl1.Command = "Close"
End Sub
```

PictureClip Control

The **PictureClip** control allows you to select an area of a source bitmap and then display the image of that area in a form or picture box. **PictureClip** controls are invisible at run time.

File Name

PICCLP32.OCX

Class Name

PictureClip

Remarks

The **PictureClip** control provides an efficient mechanism for storing multiple picture resources. Instead of using multiple bitmaps or icons, create a source bitmap that contains all the icon images required by your application. When you need to display an individual icon, use the **PictureClip** control to select the region in the source bitmap that contains that icon.

For example, you could use this control to store all the images needed to display a toolbox for your application. It is more efficient to store all of the toolbox images in a single **PictureClip** control than it is to store each image in a separate picture box. To do this, first create a source bitmap that contains all of the toolbar icons. The picture at the top of this topic is an example of such a bitmap.

Note For international localized applications, resource files are sometimes a more useful way to store bitmaps. For more information, refer to Chapter 16, "International Issues," in the Visual Basic *Programmer's Guide.*

You can specify the clipping region in the source bitmap in one of two ways:

- Select any portion of the source bitmap as the clipping region. Specify the upper-left corner of the clipping region using the **ClipX** and **ClipY** properties. Specify the area of the clipping region using the **ClipHeight** and **ClipWidth** properties. This method is useful when you want to view a random portion of a bitmap.

- Divide the source bitmap into a specified number of rows and columns. The result is a uniform matrix of picture cells numbered 0, 1, 2, and so on. You can display individual cells using the **GraphicCell** property. This method is useful when the source bitmap contains a palette of icons that you want to display individually, such as in a toolbar bitmap.

Load the source bitmap into the **PictureClip** control using the **Picture** property. You can load only bitmap (.bmp) files into the **PictureClip** control.

Distribution Note When you create and distribute applications that use the **PictureClip** control, you should install PicClp32.ocx in the customer's Microsoft Windows System or System32 subdirectory. The Setup Kit included with Visual Basic provides tools to help you write setup programs that install your applications correctly.

Properties

CellHeight, CellWidth Properties, **Clip** Property, **ClipHeight** Property, **ClipWidth** Property, **ClipX** Property, **ClipY** Property, **Cols, Rows** Properties, **GraphicCell** Property, **Height, Width** Properties, **hWnd** Property, **Index** Property, **Name** Property, **Object** Property, **Parent** Property, **Picture** Property, **StretchX, StretchY** Properties, **Tag** Property

See Also

ClipHeight Property (PictureClip Control), **ClipWidth** Property (PictureClip Control), **ClipX** Property (PictureClip Control), **ClipY** Property (PictureClip Control), **GraphicCell** Property (PictureClip Control), **Error Messages** (PictureClip Control), **Picture** Property (ActiveX Controls), **PictureBox** Control

Example

The following example displays a **Clip** image in a picture box when the user specifies X and Y coordinates and then clicks a form. **First** create a form with a **PictureBox**, a **PictureClip** control, and two **TextBox** controls. At design time, use the **Properties** sheet to load a valid bitmap into the **PictureClip** control.

```
Private Sub Form_Click ()
    Dim SaveMode As Integer
    ' Save the current ScaleMode for the picture box.
    SaveMode = Picture1.ScaleMode
    ' Get X and Y coordinates of the clipping region.
    PicClip1.ClipX = Val(Text1.Text)
    PicClip1.ClipY = Val(Text2.Text)
    ' Set the area of the clipping region (in pixels).
    PicClip1.ClipHeight = 100
    PicClip1.ClipWidth = 100
    ' Set the picture box ScaleMode to pixels.
    Picture1.ScaleMode = 3
    ' Set the destination area to fill the picture box.

PicClip1.StretchX = Picture1.ScaleWidth
    PicClip1.StretchY = Picture1.ScaleHeight
    ' Assign the clipped bitmap to the picture box.
    Picture1.Picture = PicClip1.Clip
    ' Reset the ScaleMode of the picture box.
    Picture1.ScaleMode = SaveMode
End Sub
```

CellHeight, CellWidth Properties (PictureClip Control)

Returns the height and width, in pixels, of a **PictureClip** control's **GraphicCell** property.

Applies To

PictureClip Control

Syntax

object.**CellHeight**
object.**CellWidth**

The *object* placeholder represents an object expression that evaluates to a **PictureClip** control.

Remarks

The **CellHeight** and **CellWidth** properties are dependent upon the **Cols** and **Rows** properties of a **PictureClip** control. For example, dividing a picture into four columns and four rows would result in a **GraphicCell** that is twice the size of the same picture divided into eight columns and eight rows.

See Also

PictureClip Control, **Cols, Rows** Properties (PictureClip Control), **GraphicCell** Property (PictureClip Control), **Height, Width** Properties (PictureClip Control), **Error Messages** (PictureClip Control)

Clip Property (PictureClip Control)

Returns a bitmap of the area in the **PictureClip** control specified by the **ClipX**, **ClipY**, **ClipWidth**, and **ClipHeight** properties. This property is read-only at run time.

Applies To

PictureClip Control

Syntax

[*form.*]*PictureClip*.**Clip**

Remarks

Use this property to specify a random clipping region from the selected bitmap.

When assigning a **Clip** image to a picture control in Visual Basic, make sure that the **ScaleMode** property for the picture control is set to 3 (pixels). You must use pixels because the **ClipHeight** and **ClipWidth** properties that define the clipping region are measured in pixels.

Data Type

Integer

See Also

PictureClip Control, **ClipHeight** Property (PictureClip Control), **ClipWidth** Property (PictureClip Control), **ClipX** Property (PictureClip Control), **ClipY** Property (PictureClip Control), **GraphicCell** Property (PictureClip Control), **ScaleMode** Property

Example

The following example displays a **Clip** image in a picture box when the user specifies X and Y coordinates and then clicks a form. **First** create a form with a **PictureBox**, a **PictureClip** control, and two **TextBox** controls. At design time, use the Properties sheet to load a valid bitmap into the **PictureClip** control.

```
Private Sub Form_Click ()
   Dim SaveMode As Integer
   ' Save the current ScaleMode for the picture box.
   SaveMode = Picture1.ScaleMode
   ' Get X and Y coordinates of the clipping region.
   PicClip1.ClipX = Val(Text1.Text)
   PicClip1.ClipY = Val(Text2.Text)
   ' Set the area of the clipping region (in pixels).
   PicClip1.ClipHeight = 100
   PicClip1.ClipWidth = 100
   ' Set the picture box ScaleMode to pixels.
   Picture1.ScaleMode = 3
   ' Set the destination area to fill the picture box.
   PicClip1.StretchX = Picture1.ScaleWidth
   PicClip1.StretchY = Picture1.ScaleHeight
   ' Assign the clipped bitmap to the picture box.
   Picture1.Picture = PicClip1.Clip
   ' Reset the ScaleMode of the picture box.
   Picture1.ScaleMode = SaveMode
End Sub
```

ClipHeight Property (PictureClip Control)

Specifies the height of the bitmap section to be copied by the **Clip** property. This property is not available at design time.

Applies To

PictureClip Control

Syntax

[*form.*]*PictureClip*.**ClipHeight**[= *Height%*]

Remarks

This property is measured in pixels.

Data Type

Integer

See Also

ClipWidth Property (PictureClip Control), **ClipX** Property (PictureClip Control), **ClipY** Property (PictureClip Control)

Example

The following example displays a **Clip** image in a picture box when the user specifies X and Y coordinates and then clicks a form. **First** create a form with a **PictureBox**, a **PictureClip** control, and two **TextBox** controls. At design time, use the **Properties** sheet to load a valid bitmap into the **PictureClip** control.

```
Private Sub Form_Click ()
    Dim SaveMode As Integer
    ' Save the current ScaleMode for the picture box.
    SaveMode = Picture1.ScaleMode
    ' Get X and Y coordinates of the clipping region.
    PicClip1.ClipX = Val(Text1.Text)
    PicClip1.ClipY = Val(Text2.Text)
    ' Set the area of the clipping region (in pixels).
    PicClip1.ClipHeight = 100
    PicClip1.ClipWidth = 100
    ' Set the picture box ScaleMode to pixels.
    Picture1.ScaleMode = 3
    ' Set the destination area to fill the picture box.

PicClip1.StretchX = Picture1.ScaleWidth
    PicClip1.StretchY = Picture1.ScaleHeight
    ' Assign the clipped bitmap to the picture box.
    Picture1.Picture = PicClip1.Clip
    ' Reset the ScaleMode of the picture box.
    Picture1.ScaleMode = SaveMode
End Sub
```

ClipWidth Property (PictureClip Control)

Specifies the width of the bitmap section to be copied by the **Clip** property. This property is not available at design time.

Applies To

PictureClip Control

Syntax

[*form.*]*PictureClip*.**ClipWidth**[= *Width%*]

Remarks

This property is measured in pixels.

Data Type

Integer

See Also

ClipHeight Property (PictureClip Control), **ClipX** Property (PictureClip Control), **ClipY** Property (PictureClip Control)

Example

The following example displays a **Clip** image in a picture box when the user specifies X and Y coordinates and then clicks a form. **First** create a form with a **PictureBox**, a **PictureClip** control, and two **TextBox** controls. At design time, use the **Properties** sheet to load a valid bitmap into the **PictureClip** control.

```
Private Sub Form_Click ()
    Dim SaveMode As Integer
    ' Save the current ScaleMode for the picture box.
    SaveMode = Picture1.ScaleMode
    ' Get X and Y coordinates of the clipping region.
    PicClip1.ClipX = Val(Text1.Text)
    PicClip1.ClipY = Val(Text2.Text)
    ' Set the area of the clipping region (in pixels).
    PicClip1.ClipHeight = 100
    PicClip1.ClipWidth = 100
    ' Set the picture box ScaleMode to pixels.
    Picture1.ScaleMode = 3
    ' Set the destination area to fill the picture box.

PicClip1.StretchX = Picture1.ScaleWidth
    PicClip1.StretchY = Picture1.ScaleHeight
    ' Assign the clipped bitmap to the picture box.
    Picture1.Picture = PicClip1.Clip
    ' Reset the ScaleMode of the picture box.
    Picture1.ScaleMode = SaveMode
End Sub
```

ClipX Property (PictureClip Control)

Specifies the x-coordinate of the upper-left corner of the bitmap section to be copied by the **Clip** property. This property is not available at design time.

Applies To

PictureClip Control

Syntax

[*form.*]*PictureClip*.**ClipX**[= *X%*]

Remarks

This property is measured in pixels.

Data Type

Integer

See Also

Clip Property (PictureClip Control), **ClipHeight** Property (PictureClip Control), **ClipWidth** Property (PictureClip Control), **ClipY** Property (PictureClip Control)

Example

The following example displays a **Clip** image in a picture box when the user specifies X and Y coordinates and then clicks a form. **First** create a form with a **PictureBox**, a **PictureClip** control, and two **TextBox** controls. At design time, use the **Properties** sheet to load a valid bitmap into the **PictureClip** control.

```
Private Sub Form_Click ()
    Dim SaveMode As Integer
    ' Save the current ScaleMode for the picture box.
    SaveMode = Picture1.ScaleMode
    ' Get X and Y coordinates of the clipping region.
    PicClip1.ClipX = Val(Text1.Text)
    PicClip1.ClipY = Val(Text2.Text)
    ' Set the area of the clipping region (in pixels).
    PicClip1.ClipHeight = 100
    PicClip1.ClipWidth = 100
    ' Set the picture box ScaleMode to pixels.
    Picture1.ScaleMode = 3
    ' Set the destination area to fill the picture box.

PicClip1.StretchX = Picture1.ScaleWidth
    PicClip1.StretchY = Picture1.ScaleHeight
    ' Assign the clipped bitmap to the picture box.
    Picture1.Picture = PicClip1.Clip
    ' Reset the ScaleMode of the picture box.
    Picture1.ScaleMode = SaveMode
End Sub
```

ClipY Property (PictureClip Control)

Specifies the y-coordinate of the upper-left corner of the bitmap section to be copied by the **Clip** property. This property is not available at design time.

Applies To

PictureClip Control

Syntax

[*form.*]*PictureClip*.**ClipY**[= *Y%*]

Remarks

This property is measured in pixels.

Data Type

Integer

See Also

Clip Property (PictureClip Control), **ClipHeight** Property (PictureClip Control), **ClipWidth** Property (PictureClip Control), **ClipX** Property (PictureClip Control)

Example

The following example displays a **Clip** image in a picture box when the user specifies X and Y coordinates and then clicks a form. **First** create a form with a **PictureBox**, a **PictureClip** control, and two **TextBox** controls. At design time, use the **Properties** sheet to load a valid bitmap into the **PictureClip** control.

```
Private Sub Form_Click ()
    Dim SaveMode As Integer
    ' Save the current ScaleMode for the picture box.
    SaveMode = Picture1.ScaleMode
    ' Get X and Y coordinates of the clipping region.
    PicClip1.ClipX = Val(Text1.Text)
    PicClip1.ClipY = Val(Text2.Text)
    ' Set the area of the clipping region (in pixels).
    PicClip1.ClipHeight = 100
    PicClip1.ClipWidth = 100
    ' Set the picture box ScaleMode to pixels.
    Picture1.ScaleMode = 3
    ' Set the destination area to fill the picture box.

PicClip1.StretchX = Picture1.ScaleWidth
    PicClip1.StretchY = Picture1.ScaleHeight
    ' Assign the clipped bitmap to the picture box.
    Picture1.Picture = PicClip1.Clip
    ' Reset the ScaleMode of the picture box.
    Picture1.ScaleMode = SaveMode
End Sub
```

Cols, Rows Properties (PictureClip Control)

Set or return the total number of columns or rows in the picture.

Applies To

PictureClip Control

Syntax

[*form.*]*PictureClip*.**Cols**[= *cols%*]
[*form.*]*PictureClip*.**Rows**[= *rows%*]

Remarks

Use these properties to divide the source bitmap into a uniform matrix of picture cells. Use the **GraphicCell** property to specify individual cells.

A **PictureClip** control must have at least one column and one row.

The height of each graphic cell is determined by dividing the height of the source bitmap by the number of specified rows. Leftover pixels at the bottom of the source bitmap (caused by integer rounding) are clipped.

The width of each graphic cell is determined by dividing the width of the source bitmap by the number of specified columns. Leftover pixels at the right of the source bitmap (caused by integer rounding) are clipped.

Data Type

Integer

See Also

GraphicCell Property (PictureClip Control), **Height, Width** Properties (PictureClip Control), **Error Messages** (PictureClip Control)

Error Messages (PictureClip Control)

The following table lists the trappable errors for the **PictureClip** control.

Error Number	Constant	Description - Message Explanation
7	picOutOfMemory	Out of memory.
383	picSetNotPermitted picSetNotSupported	Property can't be set on this control. Property is read-only.
394	picGetNotSupported	Property is write-only.
32000	picInvalidPictureFormat	Picture format not supported.
		You can load only bitmap (.bmp) files into the **PictureClip** control.
32001	picDisplayContext	Unable to obtain display context.
32002	picMemDevContext	Unable to obtain memory device context.
32003	picBitmap	Unable to obtain bitmap.
32004	picSelBitmapObj	Unable to select bitmap object.
32005	picIntPicStruct	Unable to allocate internal picture structure.
32006	picBadIndex	Bad **GraphicCell** Index.
		The *index* argument for the **GraphicCell** property is out of range. This argument must be in the range 0 to (**PicClip.Rows** * **PicClip.Cols**)1.
32007	picNoPicSize	No **GraphicCell** picture size specified.
32008	picBitmapsOnly	Only bitmap GraphicCell pictures allowed.
32010	picBadClip	Bad **GraphicCell PictureClip** property request.

(continued)

(continued)

Error Number	Constant	Description - Message Explanation
32012	picGetObjFailed	GetObject() Windows function failure.
		A call to the Windows function **GetObject ()** failed.
32014	pic	GlobalAlloc() Windows function failure.
		A call to the Windows function **GlobalAlloc ()** failed.
32015	picClipBounds	Clip region boundary error.
		The **ClipHeight** and **ClipWidth** properties specify coordinates which are outside the boundary of the bitmap loaded in the **PictureClip** control.
32016	picCellTooSmall	Cell size too small (must be at least 1 by 1 pixel).
32017	picRowNotPositive	**Rows** property must be greater than zero.
32018	picColNotPositive	**Cols** property must be greater than zero.
32019	picStretchXNegative	**StretchX** property cannot be negative.
32020	picStretchYNegative	**StretchY** property cannot be negative.
32021	picNoPicture	No picture assigned.

See Also

PictureClip Control, **ClipHeight** Property (PictureClip Control), **ClipWidth** Property (PictureClip Control), **ClipX** Property (PictureClip Control), **ClipY** Property (PictureClip Control), **Cols, Rows** Properties (PictureClip Control), **GraphicCell** Property (PictureClip Control), **Picture** Property (PictureClip Control), **StretchX, StretchY** Properties (PictureClip Control), **Miscellaneous** Constants, **Visual Basic** Constants

GraphicCell Property (PictureClip Control)

A one-dimensional array of pictures representing all of the picture cells. This property is not available at design time and is read-only at run time.

Applies To

PictureClip Control

Syntax

[*form.*]*PictureClip*.**GraphicCell** (*Index%*)

Remarks

- Use the **Rows** and **Cols** properties to divide a picture into a uniform matrix of graphic cells.

- The cells specified by **GraphicCell** are indexed, beginning with 0, and increase from left to right and top to bottom.

- When reading this property, an error is generated when there is no picture or when the **Rows** or **Cols** property is set to 0.

Data Type

Integer

See Also

Cols, Rows Properties (PictureClip Control), **Height, Width** Properties (PictureClip Control), **Error Messages** (PictureClip Control)

Height, Width Properties (PictureClip Control)

Return the height and width (in pixels) of a bitmap contained in the control. These properties are not available at design time and are read-only at run time.

Applies To

PictureClip Control

Syntax

[*form.*]*PictureClip.***Height**
[*form.*]*PictureClip.***Width**

Remarks

These properties are only valid when the control contains a bitmap.

You can load a bitmap into a **PictureClip** control at design time using the Properties sheet. In Visual Basic, you can also load a bitmap into a **PictureClip** control at run time by using the **LoadPicture** function.

Data Type

Integer

See Also

Cols, Rows Properties (PictureClip Control), **GraphicCell** Property (PictureClip Control), **Error Messages** (PictureClip Control), **LoadPicture** Function

Picture Property (PictureClip Control)

This property is the same as the standard Visual Basic **Picture** property except that it supports only bitmap (.bmp) files.

Applies To

PictureClip Control

See Also

Error Messages (PictureClip Control), **Picture** Property, **Picture** Property (ActiveX Controls)

Example

The following example displays a **Clip** image in a picture box when the user specifies X and Y coordinates and then clicks a form. **First** create a form with a **PictureBox**, a **PictureClip** control, and two **TextBox** controls. At design time, use the Properties sheet to load a valid bitmap into the **PictureClip** control.

```
Private Sub Form_Click ()
   Dim SaveMode As Integer
   ' Save the current ScaleMode for the picture box.
   SaveMode = Picture1.ScaleMode
   ' Get X and Y coordinates of the clipping region.
   PicClip1.ClipX = Val(Text1.Text)
   PicClip1.ClipY = Val(Text2.Text)
   ' Set the area of the clipping region (in pixels).
   PicClip1.ClipHeight = 100
   PicClip1.ClipWidth = 100
   ' Set the picture box ScaleMode to pixels.
   Picture1.ScaleMode = 3
   ' Set the destination area to fill the picture box.

PicClip1.StretchX = Picture1.ScaleWidth
   PicClip1.StretchY = Picture1.ScaleHeight
   ' Assign the clipped bitmap to the picture box.
   Picture1.Picture = PicClip1.Clip
   ' Reset the ScaleMode of the picture box.
   Picture1.ScaleMode = SaveMode
End Sub
```

StretchX, StretchY Properties (PictureClip Control)

Specify the target size for the bitmap created with the **Clip** property. These properties are not available at design time.

Applies To

PictureClip Control

Syntax

[*form.*]*PictureClip*.**StretchX**[= *X%*]
[*form.*]*PictureClip*.**StretchY**[= *Y%*]

Remarks

Use these properties to define the area to which the Clip bitmap is copied. When the bitmap is copied, it is either stretched or condensed to fit the area defined by **StretchX** and **StretchY**.

StretchX and **StretchY** are measured in pixels.

Note In Visual Basic, the default **ScaleMode** for forms and picture boxes is twips. Set **ScaleMode** = 3 (pixels) for all controls that display pictures from a **PictureClip** control.

Data Type

Integer

See Also

Clip Property (PictureClip Control), **Error Messages** (PictureClip Control), **PictureBox** Control, **ScaleHeight**, **ScaleWidth** Properties, **ScaleMode** Property

Example

The following example displays a **Clip** image in a picture box when the user specifies X and Y coordinates and then clicks a form. **First** create a form with a **PictureBox**, a **PictureClip** control, and two **TextBox** controls. At design time, use the **Properties** sheet to load a valid bitmap into the **PictureClip** control.

```
Private Sub Form_Click ()
   Dim SaveMode As Integer
   ' Save the current ScaleMode for the picture box.
   SaveMode = Picture1.ScaleMode
   ' Get X and Y coordinates of the clipping region.
   PicClip1.ClipX = Val(Text1.Text)
   PicClip1.ClipY = Val(Text2.Text)
   ' Set the area of the clipping region (in pixels).
   PicClip1.ClipHeight = 100
   PicClip1.ClipWidth = 100
   ' Set the picture box ScaleMode to pixels.
   Picture1.ScaleMode = 3
   ' Set the destination area to fill the picture box.

PicClip1.StretchX = Picture1.ScaleWidth
   PicClip1.StretchY = Picture1.ScaleHeight
   ' Assign the clipped bitmap to the picture box.
   Picture1.Picture = PicClip1.Clip
   ' Reset the ScaleMode of the picture box.
   Picture1.ScaleMode = SaveMode
End Sub
```

ProgressBar Control

The **ProgressBar** control shows the progress of a lengthy operation by filling a rectangle with chunks from left to right.

Syntax

ProgressBar

Remarks

- The **ProgressBar** control monitors an operation's progress toward completion.

A **ProgressBar** control has a range and a current position. The range represents the entire duration of the operation. The current position represents the progress the application has made toward completing the operation. The **Max** and **Min** properties set the limits of the range. The **Value** property specifies the current position within that range. Because chunks are used to fill in the control, the amount filled in only approximates the **Value** property's current setting. Based on the control's size, the **Value** property determines when to display the next chunk.

The **ProgressBar** control's **Height** and **Width** properties determine the number and size of the chunks that fill the control. The more chunks, the more accurately the control portrays an operation's progress. To increase the number of chunks displayed, decrease the control's **Height** or increase its **Width**. The **BorderStyle** property setting also affects the number and size of the chunks. To accommodate a border, the chunk size becomes smaller.

You can use the **Align** property with the **ProgressBar** control to automatically position it at the top or bottom of the form.

Tip To shrink the chunk size until the progress increments most closely match actual progress values, make the **ProgressBar** control at least 12 times wider than its height.

The following example shows how to use the **ProgressBar** control, named ProgressBar1, to show the progress of a lengthy operation of a large array. Put a **CommandButton** control and a **ProgressBar** control on a form. The **Align** property in the sample code positions the **ProgressBar** control along the bottom of the form. The **ProgressBar** control displays no text.

```
Private Sub Command1_Click()
    Dim Counter As Integer
    Dim Workarea(250) As String
    ProgressBar1.Min = LBound(Workarea)
    ProgressBar1.Max = UBound(Workarea)
    ProgressBar1.Visible = True

'Set the Progress's Value to Min.
    ProgressBar1.Value = ProgressBar1.Min
```

```
'Loop through the array.
   For Counter = LBound(Workarea) To UBound(Workarea)
      'Set initial values for each item in the array.
      Workarea(Counter) = "Initial value" & Counter
      ProgressBar1.Value = Counter
   Next Counter
   ProgressBar1.Visible = False
   ProgressBar1.Value = ProgressBar1.Min
End Sub

Private Sub Form_Load()
   ProgressBar1.Align = vbAlignBottom
   ProgressBar1.Visible = False
   Command1.Caption = "Initialize array"
End Sub
```

Distribution Note The **ProgressBar** control is part of a group of **ActiveX** controls that are found in the COMCTL32.OCX file. To use the **ProgressBar** control in your application, you must add the COMCTL32.OCX file to the project. When distributing your application, install the COMCTL32.OCX file in the user's Microsoft Windows System or System32 directory. For more information on how to add an **ActiveX** control to a project, see the *Programmer's Guide*.

Properties

Align Property, **Appearance** Property, **BorderStyle** Property, **Container** Property, **DragIcon** Property, **DragMode** Property, **Enabled** Property, **Height, Width** Properties, **hWnd** Property, **Index** Property, **Left, Top** Properties, **Max, Min** Properties, **MouseIcon** Property, **MousePointer** Property, **Name** Property, **Negotiate** Property, **Object** Property, **OLEDropMode** Property, **Parent** Property, **TabIndex** Property, **Tag** Property, **ToolTipText** Property, **Value** Property, **WhatsThisHelpID** Property

Events

Click Event, **DragDrop** Event, **DragOver** Event, **MouseDown, MouseUp** Events, **MouseMove** Event, **OLECompleteDrag** Event, **OLEDragDrop** Event, **OLEDragOver** Event, **OLEGiveFeedback** Event, **OLESetData** Event, **OLEStartDrag** Event

Methods

Drag Method, **Move** Method, **OLEDrag** Method, **ShowWhatsThis** Method, **ZOrder** Method

See Also

Value Property (ActiveX Controls), **StatusBar** Control, **Align** Property, **Height**, **Width** Properties, **HScrollBar**, **VScrollBar** Controls

---

BorderStyle Property (ActiveX Controls)

Returns or sets the border style for an object.

Applies To

DBGrid Control, **ListView** Control, **Masked Edit** Control, **MSChart** Control,

MSFlexGrid Control, **Multimedia MCI** Control, **ProgressBar** Control, **RichTextBox** Control, **Slider** Control, **Toolbar** Control, **TreeView** Control

Syntax

object.**BorderStyle** [= *value*]

The **BorderStyle** property syntax has these parts:

Part	Description
object	An object expression that evaluates to an object in the **Applies To** list.
value	A value or constant that determines the border style, as described in **Settings**.

Settings

The settings for *value* are:

Constant	Value	Description
ccNone	0	(Default) No border or border-related elements.
ccFixedSingle	1	Fixed single.

Note The cc prefix refers to the Windows 95 controls. For the other controls, prefixes for the settings change with the specific control or group of controls. However, the description remains the same unless indicated.

Remarks

Setting **BorderStyle** for a **ProgressBar** control decreases the size of the chunks the control displays.

Value Property (ActiveX Controls)

Returns or sets the value of an object.

Applies To

ProgressBar Control, **Slider** Control, **Button** Object, **UpDown** Control

Syntax

object.**Value** [= *integer*]

The **Value** property syntax has these parts:

Part	Description
object	An object expression that evaluates to an object in the **Applies To** list.
integer	For a **Slider** control, a long integer that specifies the current position of the slider. For the **ProgressBar** control, an integer that specifies the value of the **ProgressBar** control. For other controls, see **Settings** below.

Settings

For the **Button** object, the settings for *integer* are:

Constant	Value	Description
tbrUnPressed	0	(Default). The button is not currently pressed or checked.
tbrPressed	1	The button is currently pressed or checked.

Remarks

- **Slider** control—returns or sets the current position of the slider. **Value** is always between the values for the **Max** and **Min** properties, inclusive, for a **Slider** control.

- **ProgressBar** control—returns or sets a value indicating an operation's approximate progress toward completion. Incrementing the **Value** property doesn't change the appearance of the **ProgressBar** control by the exact value of the **Value** property. **Value** is always in the range between the values for the **Max** and **Min** properties, inclusive. Not available at design time.

See Also

Toolbar Control Constants, **Click** Event

Example

This example uses the **Value** property to determine which icon from an associated **ImageList** control is displayed on the **Toolbar** control. To try the example, place a **Toolbar** control on a form and paste the code into the form's Declarations section. Then run the example.

```
Private Sub Toolbar1_ButtonClick(ByVal Button As Button)
   ' Use the Key value to determine which button has been clicked.
   Select Case Button.Key

   Case "Done"  ' A check button.
      If Button.Value = vbUnchecked Then
         ' The button is unchecked.
         Button.Value = vbChecked  ' Check the button.
         ' Assuming there is a ListImage object with
         ' key "down."
         Button.Image = "down"
      Else  ' Uncheck the button
         Button.Value = vbUnchecked
         ' Assuming there is a ListImage object with
         ' key " up."
         Button.Image = "up"
      End If

   ' More Cases are possible.
   End Select
End Sub
```

RichTextBox Control

The **RichTextBox** control allows the user to enter and edit text while also providing more advanced formatting features than the conventional **TextBox** control.

Syntax

RichTextBox

Remarks

The **RichTextBox** control provides a number of properties you can use to apply formatting to any portion of text within the control. To change the formatting of text, it must first be selected. Only selected text can be assigned character and paragraph formatting. Using these properties, you can make text bold or italic, change the color, and create superscripts and subscripts. You can also adjust paragraph formatting by setting both left and right indents, as well as hanging indents.

The **RichTextBox** control opens and saves files in both the RTF format and regular ASCII text format. You can use methods of the control (**LoadFile** and **SaveFile**) to directly read and write files, or use properties of the control such as **SelRTF** and **TextRTF** in conjunction with Visual Basic's file input/output statements.

The **RichTextBox** control supports object embedding by using the **OLEObjects** collection. Each object inserted into the control is represented by an **OLEObject** object. This allows you to create documents with the control that contain other documents or objects. For example, you can create a document that has an embedded Microsoft Excel spreadsheet or a Microsoft Word document or any other OLE object registered on your system. To insert objects into the **RichTextBox** control, you simply drag a file (from the Windows 95 Explorer for example), or a highlighted portion of a file used in another application (such as Microsoft Word), and drop the contents directly onto the control.

The **RichTextBox** control supports both clipboard and OLE drag/drop of OLE objects. When an object is pasted in from the clipboard, it is inserted at the current insertion point. When an object is dragged and dropped into the control, the insertion point will track the mouse cursor until the mouse button is released, causing the object to be inserted. This behavior is the same as Microsoft Word.

To print all or part of the text in a **RichTextBox** control use the **SelPrint** method.

Because the **RichTextBox** is a data-bound control, you can bind it with a **Data** control to a Binary or Memo field in a Microsoft Access database or a similar large capacity field in other databases (such as a TEXT data type field in SQL Server).

The **RichTextBox** control supports almost all of the properties, events and methods used with the standard **TextBox** control, such as **MaxLength**, **MultiLine**, **ScrollBars**, **SelLength**, **SelStart**, and **SelText**. Applications that already use **TextBox** controls can easily be adapted to make use of **RichTextBox** controls. However, the **RichTextBox** control doesn't have the same 64K character capacity limit of the conventional **TextBox** control.

Distribution Note To use the **RichTextBox** control in your application, you must add the RICHTX32.OCX file to the project. When distributing your application, install the RICHTX32.OCX file in the user's Microsoft Windows SYSTEM directory. For more information on how to add a custom control to a project, see the *Programmer's Guide*.

Properties

Appearance Property, **AutoVerbMenu** Property, **BackColor, ForeColor** Properties, **BorderStyle** Property, **BulletIndent** Property, **Container** Property, **DataBindings** Property, **DataChanged** Property, **DataField** Property, **DisableNoScroll** Property, **DragIcon** Property, **DragMode** Property, **Enabled** Property, **Font** Property, **HelpContextID** Property, **HideSelection** Property, **hWnd** Property, **Index** Property, **Left, Top** Properties, **Locked** Property, **MaxLength** Property, **MouseIcon** Property, **MousePointer** Property, **MultiLine** Property, **Name** Property, **Object** Property, **OLEDragMode** Property, **OLEDropMode** Property, **OLEObjects** Collection, **Parent** Property, **RightMargin** Property, **ScrollBars** Property, **SelAlignment** Property, **SelBold, SelItalic, SelStrikethru, SelUnderline** Properties, **SelBullet** Property, **SelCharOffset** Property, **SelColor** Property, **SelFontName** Property, **SelFontSize** Property, **SelHangingIndent, SelIndent, SelRightIndent** Properties, **SelLength, SelStart, SelText** Properties, **SelProtected** Property, **SelRTF** Property, **SelTabCount, SelTabs** Properties, **TabIndex** Property, **TabStop** Property, **Tag** Property, **Text** Property, **ToolTipText** Property, **Visible** Property, **WhatsThisHelpID** Property

Events

Change Event, **Click** Event, **DblClick** Event, **DragDrop** Event, **DragOver** Event, **GotFocus** Event, **KeyDown, KeyUp** Events, **KeyPress** Event, **LostFocus** Event, **MouseDown, MouseUp** Events, **SelChange** Event

Methods

Drag Method, **Find** Method, **GetLineFromChar** Method, **LoadFile** Method, **Move** Method, **OLEDrag** Method, **Refresh** Method, **SaveFile** Method, **SelPrint** Method, **SetFocus** Method, **ShowWhatsThis** Method, **Span** Method, **Upto** Method, **ZOrder** Method

See Also

Error Messages (RichTextBox Control), **LoadFile** Method, **SaveFile** Method, **SelPrint** Method, **SelRTF** Property, **TextRTF** Property, **RichTextBox** Control Constants, **Supported RTF Codes**, **OLEObject** Object, **OLEObjects** Collection, **MaxLength** Property (RichTextBox Control), **MultiLine** Property (RichTextBox Control), **ScrollBars** Property (RichTextBox Control), **SelLength, SelStart, SelText** Properties, **SupportedRTF Codes** (RichTextBox Control), **TextBox** Control

---

Add Method (OLEObjects Collection)

Adds an **OLEObject** object to an **OLEObjects** collection.

Applies To

RichTextBox Control, **OLEObjects** Collection

Syntax

object.**Add** *index, key, sourcedoc, class*

The **Add** Method syntax has these parts:

Part	Description
object	Required. An object expression that evaluates to an object in the **Applies To** list.
index	Optional. An integer that identifies a member of the object collection. If supplied, the new member will be inserted after the member specified by the index.
key	Optional. A unique string expression that can be used to access a member of the collection. The *key* and *index* arguments can be used interchangeably with the **Item** method of the collection to retrieve the **OLEObject** object.
sourcedoc	Required. The filename of a document used as a template for the embedded object. The **RichTextBox** control doesn't support linking, so the contents of the file will be copied into the **OLEObject** object. Must be a zero-length string ("") if you don't specify a source document.
class	Optional. The OLE class name for the object to be embedded. This argument is the **ProgID** used by OLE in the system registry. This argument is ignored if you specify a filename for *sourcedoc*.

Remarks

The following code adds a Microsoft Excel worksheet to the **RichTextBox** and sets its Key property to "SalesData":

```
RichTextBox1.OLEObjects.Add , "SalesData", , "Excel.Sheet.5"
```

When an object is added to the collection, it immediately becomes in-place active so the user can add data to it.

Specifics

Item Method, **OLEObject** Object, **OLEObjects** Collection

See Also

RichTextBox Control, **OLEObject** Object

Example

The following example presents a dialog box where you can find an **OLEObject** object (a bitmap) to add to a **RichTextBox** control. To try the example, place a **CommonDialog** and a **RichTextBox** control on a form, and paste the code into the Declarations section. Run the example and double-click on the control.

```
Private Sub RichTextBox1_DblClick()
   With CommonDialog1
      .Filter = ("bitmap (*.bmp)|*.bmp")
      .ShowOpen
   End With
   RichTextBox1.OLEObjects. _
   Add , , CommonDialog1.filename
End Sub
```

AutoVerbMenu Property (RichTextBox Control)

Returns or sets a value that determines if a pop-up menu containing the selected object's verbs is displayed when the user clicks the OLE object with the right mouse button.

Applies To

RichTextBox Control

Syntax

object.**AutoVerbMenu** [= *value*]

The **AutoVerbMenu** property has the following parts:

Part	Description
object	An object expression that evaluates to a **RichTextBox** control.
value	A Boolean expression that specifies whether a menu is displayed, as described in **Settings**.

Settings

The settings for *value* are:

Setting	Description
True	A pop-up menu is displayed when the user clicks the right mouse button on the object.
False	No pop-up menu is displayed.

Remarks

When this property is set to **True**, **Click** events and **MouseDown** events don't occur for the **RichTextBox** control when the OLE object is clicked with the right mouse button. Any other region of the control will generate the correct events.

See Also

OLEObject Object, **Click** Event, **MouseDown**, **MouseUp** Events

---

BulletIndent Property

Returns or sets the amount of indent used in a **RichTextBox** control when **SelBullet** is set to **True**.

Applies To

RichTextBox Control

Syntax

object.**BulletIndent** [= *integer*]

The **BulletIndent** property syntax has these parts:

Part	Description
object	An object expression that evaluates to an object in the **Applies To** list.
integer	An integer that determines the amount of indent. These properties use the scale mode units of the **Form** object containing the **RichTextBox** control.

Remarks

The **BulletIndent** property returns **Null** if the selection spans multiple paragraphs with different margin settings.

See Also

SelBullet Property, **Form** Object, **Forms** Collection

Class Property (OLEObject Object)

Returns the class name of the embedded object.

Applies To

RichTextBox Control, **OLEObject** Object

Syntax

object.**Class**

The *object* argument is an object expression that evaluates to an object in the **Applies To** list.

Remarks

A class name defines the type of an object. Applications that support OLE or Automation fully qualify the class names of their objects using either of the following syntaxes:

```
application.objecttype.version
objecttype.version
```

The syntax for OLE class names has the following parts:

Part	Description
application	The name of the application that supplies the object.
objecttype	The object's name as defined in the object library.
version	The version number of the object or application that supplies the object.

For example, Microsoft Excel version 5.0 supports a number of objects, including worksheets and charts. Their class names are Excel.Sheet.5 and Excel.Chart.5. Microsoft WordArt version 2.0 supports a single object with the class name MSWordArt.2.

Note Some OLE programming documentation refers to the class name syntax as a programmatic ID (ProgID).

Creating an object by using the **Add** method of the **OLEObjects** collection, automatically sets the **Class** property of the **OLEObject** object.

See Also

OLEObjects Collection, **Add** Method (OLEObjects Collection)

DisableNoScroll Property

Returns or sets a value that determines whether scroll bars in the **RichTextBox** control are disabled.

Applies To

RichTextBox Control

Syntax

object.**DisableNoScroll** [= *boolean*]

The **DisableNoScroll** property syntax has these parts:

Part	Description
object	An object expression that evaluates to an object in the **Applies To** list.
boolean	A Boolean expression specifying whether or not the scroll bars are enabled, as described in **Settings**.

Settings

The settings for *boolean* are:

Setting	Description
False	(Default) Scroll bars appear normally when displayed.
True	Scroll bars appear dimmed when displayed.

Remarks

The **DisableNoScroll** property is ignored when the **ScrollBars** property is set to 0 (None). However, when **ScrollBars** is set to 1 (Horizontal), 2 (Vertical), or 3 (Both), individual scroll bars are disabled when there are too few lines of text to scroll vertically or too few characters of text to scroll horizontally in the **RichTextBox** control.

See Also

ScrollBars Property (RichTextBox Control)

DisplayType Property (OLEObject Object)

Returns or sets a value indicating whether an object displays its contents or an icon.

Applies To

RichTextBox Control, **OLEObject** Object

Syntax

object.**DisplayType** [= *value*]

The **DisplayType** property syntax has these parts:

Part	Description
object	An object expression that evaluates to an object in the **Applies To** list.
value	An integer or constant specifying whether an object displays its contents or an icon, as described in **Settings**.

Settings

The settings for *value* are:

Constant	Value	Description
rtfDisplayContent	0	Content. When the **RichTextBox** control contains an object, the object's data is displayed in the control.
rtfDisplayIcon	1	Icon. When the **RichTextBox** control contains an object, the object's icon is displayed in the control.

Remarks

After adding the object to the **OLEObjects** Collection, use the **DisplayType** property to change how that object is displayed.

See Also

RichTextBox Control Constants, **OLEObjects** Collection

DoVerb Method (OLEObject Object)

Opens an object for an operation, such as editing.

Applies To

RichTextBox Control, **OLEObject** Object

Syntax

object.**DoVerb** (*verb*)

The **DoVerb** method syntax has these parts:

Part	Description
object	An object expression that evaluates to an object in the **Applies To** list.
verb	Optional. The verb to execute of the **OLEObject** object within **RichTextBox** control. If not specified, the default verb is executed. The value of this argument can be one of the standard verbs supported by all objects or an index of the **ObjectVerbs** property array.

Remarks

The **DoVerb** method executes a verb of the specified **OLEObject** object. The verb argument is an index of one of the verbs listed in the **ObjectVerbs** property array or one of the standard verbs listed below.

Each object can support its own set of verbs. The following values represent standard verbs every object should support:

Constant	Value	Description
vbOLEPrimary	0	The default action for the object.
vbOLEShow	-1	Activates the object for editing. If the application that created the object supports in-place activation, the object is activated within the **RichTextBox** control.
vbOLEOpen	-2	Opens the object in a separate application window. If the application that created the object supports in-place activation, the object is activated in its own window.
vbOLEHide	-3	For embedded objects, hides the application that created the object.
vbOLEUIActivate	-4	If the object supports in-place activation, activates the object for in-place activation and shows any user interface tools. If the object doesn't support in-place activation, the object doesn't activate, and an error occurs.
vbOLEInPlaceActivate	-5	If the user moves the focus to the embedded object, creates a window for the object and prepares the object to be edited. An error occurs if the object doesn't support activation on a single mouse click.
vbOLEDiscardUndoState	-6	Used when the object is activated for editing to discard all record of changes that the object's application can undo.

Note   These verbs may not be listed in the **ObjectVerbs** property array.

See Also

RichTextBox Control Constants, **OLEObjects** Collection, **ObjectVerbs** Property (OLEObject Object)

FileName Property (RichTextBox Control)

Returns or sets the filename of the file loaded into the **RichTextBox** control at design time.

Applies To

RichTextBox Control

Syntax

object.**FileName**

The *object* placeholder represents an object expression that evaluates to an object in the **Applies To** list.

Settings

You can only specify the names of text files or valid .RTF files for this property.

Find Method

Searches the text in a **RichTextBox** control for a given string.

Applies To

RichTextBox Control

Syntax

object.**Find**(*string, start, end, options*)

The **Find** method syntax has these parts:

Part	Description
object	Required. An object expression that evaluates to an object in the **Applies To** list.
string	Required. A string expression you want to find in the control.
start	Optional. An integer character index that determines where to begin the search. Each character in the control has an integer index that uniquely identifies it. The first character of text in the control has an index of 0.
end	Optional. An integer character index that determines where to end the search.
options	Optional. One or more constants used to specify optional features, as described in **Settings**.

Settings

The setting for *options* can include:

Constant	Value	Description
rtfWholeWord	2	Determines if a match is based on a whole word or a fragment of a word.
rtfMatchCase	4	Determines if a match is based on the case of the specified string as well as the text of the string.
rtfNoHighlight	8	Determines if a match appears highlighted in the **RichTextBox** control.

You can combine multiple options by using the **Or** operator.

Remarks

If the text searched for is found, the **Find** method highlights the specified text and returns the index of the first character highlighted. If the specified text is not found, the **Find** method returns −1.

If you use the **Find** method without the **rtfNoHighlight** option while the **HideSelection** property is **True** and the **RichTextBox** control does not have the focus, the control still highlights the found text. Subsequent uses of the **Find** method will search only for the highlighted text until the insertion point moves.

The search behavior of the **Find** method varies based on the combination of values specified for the *start* and *end* arguments. This table describes the possible behaviors:

Start	End	Search Behavior
Specified	Specified	Searches from the specified start location to the specified end location.
Specified	Omitted	Searches from the specified start location to the end of the text in the control.
Omitted	Specified	Searches from the current insertion point to the specified end location.
Omitted	Omitted	Searches the current selection if text is selected or the entire contents of the control if no text is selected.

See Also

RichTextBox Control Constants

Example

This example finds a string in a **RichTextBox** control based on a word entered in a **TextBox** control. After it finds the specified string, it displays a message box that shows the number of the line containing the specified word. To try this example, put a **RichTextBox** control, a **CommandButton** control and a **TextBox** control on a form. Load a file into the **RichTextBox,** and paste this code into the General Declarations section of the form. Then run the example, enter a word in the **TextBox**, and click the **CommandButton**.

```
Private Sub Command1_Click()
    Dim FoundPos As Integer
    Dim FoundLine As Integer
    ' Find the text specified in the TextBox control.
    FoundPos = RichTextBox1.Find(Text1.Text, , , rtfWholeWord)

    ' Show message based on whether the text was found or not.

    If FoundPos <> -1 Then
        ' Returns number of line containing found text.
        FoundLine = RichTextBox1.GetLineFromChar(FoundPos)
        MsgBox "Word found on line " & CStr(FoundLine)
    Else
        MsgBox "Word not found."
    End If
End Sub
```

GetLineFromChar Method

Returns the number of the line containing a specified character position in a **RichTextBox** control.

Applies To

RichTextBox Control

Syntax

object.**GetLineFromChar**(*charpos*)

The **GetLineFromChar** method syntax has these parts:

Part	Description
object	Required. An object expression that evaluates to an object in the **Applies To** list.
charpos	Required. A long integer that specifies the index of the character whose line you want to identify. The index of the first character in the **RichTextBox** control is 0.

Remarks

You use the **GetLineFromChar** method to find out which line in the text of a **RichTextBox** control contains a certain character position in the text. You might need to do this because the number of characters in each line of text can vary, making it very difficult to find out which line in the text contains a particular character, identified by its position in the text.

See Also

SelCharOffset Property

Example

This example finds a string in a **RichTextBox** control based on a word entered in a **TextBox** control. After it finds the specified string, it displays a message box that shows the number of the line containing the specified word. To try this example, put a **RichTextBox** control, a **CommandButton** control and a **TextBox** control on a form. Load a file into the **RichTextBox,** and paste this code into the General Declarations section of the form. Then run the example, enter a word in the **TextBox**, and click the **CommandButton**.

```
Private Sub Command1_Click()
    Dim FoundPos As Integer
    Dim FoundLine As Integer
    ' Find the text specified in the TextBox control.
    FoundPos = RichTextBox1.Find(Text1.Text, , , rtfWholeWord)

    ' Show message based on whether the text was found or not.

    If FoundPos <> -1 Then
        ' Returns number of line containing found text.
        FoundLine = RichTextBox1.GetLineFromChar(FoundPos)
        MsgBox "Word found on line " & CStr(FoundLine)
    Else
        MsgBox "Word not found."
    End If
End Sub
```

LoadFile Method

Loads an .RTF file or text file into a **RichTextBox** control.

Applies To

RichTextBox Control

Syntax

object.**LoadFile** *pathname, filetype*

The **LoadFile** method syntax has these parts:

Part	Description
object	Required. An object expression that evaluates to an object in the **Applies To** list.
pathname	Required. A string expression defining the path and filename of the file to load into the control.
filetype	Optional. An integer or constant that specifies the type of file loaded, as described in **Settings**.

Settings

The settings for *filetype* are:

Constant	Value	Description
rtfRTF	0	(Default) RTF. The file loaded must be a valid .RTF file.
rtfText	1	Text. The **RichTextBox** control loads any text file.

Remarks

When loading a file with the **LoadFile** method, the contents of the loaded file replaces the entire contents of the **RichTextBox** control. This will cause the values of the **Text** and **RTFText** properties to change.

You can also use the **Input** function in Visual Basic and the **TextRTF** and **SelRTF** properties of the **RichTextBox** control to read .RTF files. For example, you can load the contents of an .RTF file to the **RichTextBox** control as follows:

```
Open "mytext.rtf" For Input As 1

RichTextBox1.TextRTF = Input$(LOF(1), 1)
```

See Also

FileName Property (RichTextBox Control), **SaveFile** Method, **SelRTF** Property, **TextRTF** Property, **RichTextBox** Control Constants, **Supported RTF Codes** (RichTextBox Control)

Example

This example displays a dialog box to choose an .RTF file, then loads that file into a **RichTextBox** control. To try this example, put a **RichTextBox** control, a **CommandButton** control, and a **CommonDialog** control on a form. Paste this code into the General Declarations section of the form. Then run the example.

```
Private Sub Command1_Click()
    CommonDialog1.Filter = "Rich Text Format files|*.rtf"
    CommonDialog1.ShowOpen
    RichTextBox1.LoadFile CommonDialog1.Filename, rtfRTF
End Sub
```

Locked Property (RichTextBox Control)

Returns or sets a value indicating whether the contents in a **RichTextBox** control can be edited.

Applies To

RichTextBox Control

Syntax

object.**Locked** [= *boolean*]

The **Locked** property syntax has these parts:

Part	Description
object	An object expression that evaluates to a **RichTextBox** control.
boolean .	A Boolean expression specifying whether the contents of the control can be edited, as described in **Settings**.

Settings

The settings for *boolean* are:

Setting	Description
True	You can scroll and highlight the text in the control, but you can't edit it. The program can still modify the text by changing the **Text** property.
False	(Default) You can edit the text in the control.

See Also

ReadOnly Property

MaxLength Property (RichTextBox Control)

Returns or sets a value indicating whether there is a maximum number of characters a **RichTextBox** control can hold and, if so, specifies the maximum number of characters.

Applies To

RichTextBox Control

Syntax

object.**MaxLength** [= *long*]

The **MaxLength** property syntax has these parts:

Part	Description
object	An object expression that evaluates to a **RichTextBox** control.
long	A long integer specifying the maximum number of characters a user can enter in the control. The default for the **MaxLength** property is 0, indicating no maximum other than that created by memory constraints on the user's system. Any number greater than 0 indicates the maximum number of characters.

Remarks

Use the **MaxLength** property to limit the number of characters a user can enter in a **RichTextBox**.

If text that exceeds the **MaxLength** property setting is assigned to a **RichTextBox** from code, no error occurs; however, only the maximum number of characters is assigned to the **Text** property, and extra characters are truncated. Changing this property doesn't affect the current contents of a **RichTextBox**, but will affect any subsequent changes to the contents.

MultiLine Property (RichTextBox Control)

Returns or sets a value indicating whether a **RichTextBox** control can accept and display multiple lines of text. Read-only at run time.

Applies To

RichTextBox Control

Syntax

object.**MultiLine**

The *object* placeholder represents an object expression that evaluates to a **RichTextBox** control.

Settings

The **MultiLine** property settings are:

Setting	Description
True	Allows multiple lines of text.
False	(Default) Ignores carriage returns and restricts data to a single line.

Remarks

A multiple-line **RichTextBox** control wraps text as the user types text extending beyond the text box.

You can also add scroll bars to a larger **RichTextBox** control using the **ScrollBars** property. If no **HScrollBar** control (horizontal scroll bar) is specified, the text in a multiple-line **RichTextBox** automatically wraps.

Note On a form with no default button, pressing ENTER in a multiple-line **RichTextBox** control moves the focus to the next line. If a default button exists, you must press CTRL+ENTER to move to the next line.

See Also

ScrollBars Property (RichTextBox Control), **Default** Property

ObjectVerbFlags Property (OLEObject Object)

Returns the menu state for each verb in the **ObjectVerbs** array.

Applies To

RichTextBox Control, **OLEObject** Object

Syntax

object.**ObjectVerbFlags**(*value*)

The **ObjectVerbFlags** property syntax has these parts:

Part	Description
object	An object expression that evaluates to an object in the **Applies To** list.
value	A numeric expression indicating the element in the array.

Return Values

The **ObjectVerbFlags** property returns the following values:

Constant	Value	Description
vbOLEFlagChecked	&H0008	The menu item is checked.
vbOLEFlagDisabled	&H0002	The menu item is disabled (but not dimmed).
vbOLEFlagEnabled	&H0000	The menu item is enabled.
vbOLEFlagGrayed	&H0001	The menu item is dimmed.
vbOLEFlagSeparator	&H0800	The menu item is a separator bar.

Note   These constants are listed in the Visual Basic (VB) object library in the Object Browser.

Remarks

The first verb in the **ObjectVerbs** array is the default verb. The remaining verbs in this array are suitable for displaying on a menu. The **ObjectVerbFlags** array contains information about the menu state (such as dimmed, checked, and so on) for each verb in the **ObjectVerbs** array.

When displaying a menu containing an object's verbs, check the value of this property to see how the item is displayed.

See Also

OLEObjects Collection, **ObjectVerbs** Property (OLEObject Object),
ObjectVerbsCount Property (OLEObject Object)

ObjectVerbs Property (OLEObject Object)

Returns the list of verbs an object supports.

Applies To

RichTextBox Control, **OLEObject** Object

Syntax

object.**ObjectVerbs**(value)

The **ObjectVerbs** property syntax has these parts:

Part	Description
object	An object expression that evaluates to an object in the **Applies To** list.
value	A numeric expression indicating the element in the array.

Remarks

ObjectVerbs is a zero-based string array. Use this property along with the **ObjectVerbsCount** property to get the verbs supported by an object. These verbs are used to determine an action to perform when an object is activated with the **DoVerb** method. The list of verbs in the array varies from object to object and depends on the current conditions.

Each object can support its own set of verbs. The following values represent standard verbs supported by every object:

Constant	Value	Description
vbOLEPrimary	0	The default action for the object.
vbOLEShow	-1	Activates the object for editing. If the application that created the object supports in-place activation, the object is activated within the **RichTextBox** control.
vbOLEOpen	-2	Opens the object in a separate application window. If the application that created the object supports in-place activation, the object is activated in its own window.
vbOLEHide	-3	For embedded objects, hides the application that created the object.
vbOLEUIActivate	-4	If the object supports in-place activation, activates the object for in-place activation and shows any user interface tools. If the object doesn't support in-place activation, the object doesn't activate, and an error occurs.

(continued)

(continued)

Constant	Value	Description
vbOLEInPlaceActivate	-5	If the user moves the focus to the embedded object, creates a window for the object and prepares the object to be edited. An error occurs if the object doesn't support activation on a single mouse click.
vbOLEDiscardUndoState	-6	Used when the object is activated for editing to discard all record of changes that the object's application can undo.

Note These verbs may not be listed in the **ObjectVerbs** property array.

The first verb in the **ObjectVerbs** array, ObjectVerbs(0), is the default verb. Unless otherwise specified, this verb activates the object.

The remaining verbs in the array can be displayed on a menu. If it's appropriate to display the default verb in a menu, the default verb has two entries in the **ObjectVerbs** array.

Applications that display objects typically include an **Object** command on the Edit menu. When the user chooses Edit Object, a menu displays the object's verbs. Use the **ObjectVerbs**, **ObjectVerbsCount**, and **ObjectVerbFlags** properties to create such a menu at run time.

To automatically display the verbs in the **ObjectVerbs** array in a pop-up menu when the user clicks an object with the right mouse button, set the **AutoVerbMenu** property to **True**.

See Also

RichTextBox Control Constants, **AutoVerbMenu** Property (RichTextBox Control), **OLEObjects** Collection, **ObjectVerbsCount** Property (OLEObject Object), **ObjectVerbFlags** Property (OLEObject Object), **DoVerb** Method (OLEObject Object)

ObjectVerbsCount Property (OLEObject Object)

Returns the number of verbs supported by an object.

Applies To

RichTextBox Control, **OLEObject** Object

Syntax

object.**ObjectVerbsCount**

The *object* is an object expression that evaluates to an object in the **Applies To** list.

Remarks

Use this property to determine the number of elements in the **ObjectVerbs** property array.

The list of verbs an object supports may vary, depending on the state of the object.

See Also

OLEObjects Collection, **ObjectVerbs** Property (OLEObject Object)

OLEObject Object

An **OLEObject** object represents an insertable object within a **RichTextBox** control.

Remarks

The **RichTextBox** control enables you to add insertable objects to an RTF file. Insertable objects are represented by the **OLEObject** object.

Each embedded **OLEObject** object counts as one character in the **RichTextbox** control. That is, when counting from the beginning of the control, the object will take up one character position. OLE objects can be highlighted, cut or copied by the user, but they do not support any of the **Selxxx** properties (i.e. **SelBold**, **SelItalic**, etc.).

Each object supports a context menu that contains the standard Cut, Copy, Paste, and Delete commands, as well as Open and Edit. Open will cause the object's application to be opened in its own window so that the object can be edited. Edit will cause the object to in-place activate if the object supports in-place activation.

You can manually add **OLEObject** objects to the **OLEObjects** collection at run time by using the **Add** method, or by dragging an object from the Windows Explorer into the **RichTextBox** control.

Properties

Class Property (OLEObject Object), **DisplayType** Property (OLEObject Object), **ObjectVerbs** Property (OLEObject Object), **ObjectVerbsCount** Property (OLEObject Object), **ObjectVerbFlags** Property (OLEObject Object), **ObjectVerbs** Property (OLEObject Object)

Methods

DoVerb Method (OLEObject Object)

See Also

OLEObjects Collection, **Add** Method (OLEObjects Collection)

OLEObjects Collection

An **OLEObjects** collection contains a collection of **OLEObject** objects.

Syntax

object.**OLEObjects**(*index*)
object.**OLEObjects.Item**(*index*)

The **OLEObjects** collection syntax has these parts:

Part	Description
object	An object expression that evaluates to an object in the **Applies To** list.
index	The value of either the Index property or the Key property which uniquely identifies the **OLEObject** object.

Remarks

Every embedded OLE object created in the **RichTextBox** control is represented in the **OLEObjects** collection. You can manually add objects to the **OLEObjects** collection at run time by using the **Add** method, or by dragging an object from the Windows Explorer into the **RichTextBox** control.

The **OLEObjects** collection is a standard collection and supports the **Add**, **Item**, and **Remove** methods, as well as the **Count** property.

Properties

Count Property (VB Collections), **Item** Property

Methods

Add Method (OLEObjects Collection)

See Also

OLEObject Object, **Add** Method (OLEObjects Collection), **Item** Method (Add-In), **Remove** Method (Visual Basic Extensibility), **Key** Object

RichTextBox Control Constants

Appearance Property

Constant	Value	Description
rtfFlat	0	Flat. Paints without visual effects.
rtfThreeD	1	(Default). 3D. Paints with three-dimensional effects.

Find Method

Constant	Value	Description
rtfWholeWord	2	Determines if a match is based on a whole word or a fragment of a word.
rtfMatchCase	4	Determines if a match is based on the case of the specified string as well as the text of the string.
rtfNoHighlight	8	Determines if a match appears highlighted in the **RichTextBox** control.

Loadfile, Savefile Methods

Constant	Value	Description
rtfRTF	0	(Default) RTF. The file loaded must be a valid .RTF file (**LoadFile** method) or the contents in the control are saved to an .RTF file (**SaveFile** method).
rtfText	1	Text. The **RichTextBox** control loads any text file (**LoadFile** method) or the contents in the control are saved to a text file (**SaveFile** method).

Mousepointer Property

Constant	Value	Description
rtfDefault	0	(Default) Shape determined by the object.
rtfArrow	1	Arrow.
rtfCross	2	Cross (cross-hair pointer).
rtfIbeam	3	I Beam.
rtfIcon	4	Icon (small square within a square).
rtfSize	5	Size (four-pointed arrow pointing north, south, east, and west).
rtfSizeNESW	6	Size NE SW (double arrow pointing northeast and southwest).
rtfSizeNS	7	Size N S (double arrow pointing north and south).
rtfSizeNWSE	8	Size NW, SE.
rtfSizeEW	9	Size E W (double arrow pointing east and west).
rtfUpArrow	10	Up Arrow.
rtfHourglass	11	Hourglass (wait).
rtfNoDrop	12	No Drop.
rtfArrowHourglass	13	Arrow and hourglass.
rtfArrowQuestion	14	Arrow and question mark.
rtfSizeAll	15	Size all.
rtfCustom	99	Custom icon specified by the **MouseIcon** property.

Selalignment Property

Constant	Value	Description
rtfLeft	0	(Default) Left. The paragraph is aligned along the left margin.
rtfRight	1	Right. The paragraph is aligned along the right margin.
rtfCenter	2	Center. The paragraph is centered between the left and right margins.

Scrollbars Property

Constant	Value	Description
rtfNone	0	(Default) None.
rtfHorizontal	1	Horizontal scroll bar only.
rtfVertical	2	Vertical scroll bar only.
rtfBoth	3	Both horizontal and vertical scroll bars.

See Also

RichTextBox Control, **Find** Method, **LoadFile** Method, **SaveFile** Method, **SelAlignment** Property, **ScrollBars** Property, **Visual Basic** Constants

---

RightMargin Property

Returns or sets the right margin for the text in a **RichTextBox** control..

Applies To

RichTextBox Control

Syntax

object.**RightMargin** [= *value*]

The **RightMargin** property syntax has these parts:

Part	Description
object	An object expression that evaluates to a **RichTextBox** control.
value	A numeric expression specifying the indent in twips from the right edge of the text to the right edge of the control, as described below.

Remarks

The **RightMargin** property is used to set the right most limit for text wrapping, centering, and indentation. Centering a paragraph is based on the left most part of the text portion (doesn't include borders) of the **RichTextBox** control and the **RightMargin** property. Also, when setting the **SelRightIndent** property, it will be based on the current setting of the **RightMargin** property.

The default for the **RightMargin** property is 0 and will cause the control to set text wrapping equal to the right most part of the **RichTextBox** control so all text is viewable.

Note When calculating a value for the **RightMargin** property, you must take in to account the width of the borders of the **RichTextBox** control if **BorderStyle** is set to **rtfFixedSingle**.

See Also

SelHangingIndent, SelIndent, SelRightIndent Properties, **RichTextBox** Control Constants, **BorderStyle** Property (ActiveX Controls)

SaveFile Method

Saves the contents of a **RichTextBox** control to a file.

Applies To

RichTextBox Control

Syntax

object.**SaveFile**(*pathname*, *filetype*)

The **SaveFile** method syntax has these parts:

Part	Description
object	Required. An object expression that evaluates to an object in the **Applies To** list.
pathname	Required. A string expression defining the path and filename of the file to receive the contents of the control.
filetype	Optional. An integer or constant that specifies the type of file loaded, as described in **Settings**.

Settings

The settings for *filetype* are:

Constant	Value	Description
rtfRTF	0	(Default) RTF. The **RichTextBox** control saves its contents as an .RTF file.
rtfText	1	Text. The **RichTextBox** control saves its contents as a text file.

Remarks

You can also use the **Write** function in Visual Basic and the **TextRTF** and **SelRTF** properties of the **RichTextBox** control to write .RTF files. For example, you can save the highlighted contents of a **RichTextBox** control to an .RTF file as follows:

```
Open "mytext.rtf" For Output As 1

Print #1, RichTextBox1.SelRTF
```

See Also

LoadFile Method, **SelRTF** Property, **TextRTF** Property, **RichTextBox** Control Constants, **Supported RTF Codes** (RichTextBox Control)

Example

This example displays a dialog box to choose an .RTF file to which you will save the contents of a **RichTextBox** control. To try this example, put a **RichTextBox** control, a **CommandButton** control, and a **CommonDialog** control on a form. Paste this code into the **Click** event of the **CommandButton** control. Then run the example.

```
Private Sub Command1_Click()
    CommonDialog1.ShowSave
    RichTextBox1.SaveFile CommonDialog1.Filename, rtfRTF
End Sub
```

ScrollBars Property (RichTextBox Control)

Returns or sets a value indicating whether a **RichTextBox** control has horizontal or vertical scroll bars. Read-only at run time.

Applies To

RichTextBox Control

Syntax

object.**ScrollBars**

The *object* placeholder represents an object expression that evaluates to a **RichTextBox** control.

Settings

The **ScrollBars** property settings are:

Constant	Value	Description
rtfNone	0	(Default) No scroll bars shown.
rtfHorizontal	1	Horizontal scroll bar only.
rtfVertical	2	Vertical scroll bar only.
rtfBoth	3	Both horizontal and vertical scroll bars shown.

Remarks

For a **RichTextBox** control with setting 1 (Horizontal), 2 (Vertical), or 3 (Both), you must set the **MultiLine** property to **True**.

At run time, the Microsoft Windows operating environment automatically implements a standard keyboard interface to allow navigation in **RichTextBox** controls with the arrow keys (UP ARROW, DOWN ARROW, LEFT ARROW, and RIGHT ARROW), the HOME and END keys, and so on.

Scroll bars are displayed only if the contents of the **RichTextBox** extend beyond the control's borders. If **ScrollBars** is set to **False**, the control won't have scroll bars, regardless of its contents.

See Also

RichTextBox Control Constants, **MultiLine** Property (RichTextBox Control)

SelAlignment Property

Returns or sets a value that controls the alignment of the paragraphs in a **RichTextBox** control. Not available at design time.

Applies To

RichTextBox Control

Syntax

object.**SelAlignment** [= *value*]

The **SelAlignment** property syntax has these parts:

Part	Description
object	An object expression that evaluates to an object in the **Applies To** list.
value	An integer or constant that determines paragraph alignment, as described in **Settings**.

Settings

The settings for *value* are:

Constant	Value	Description
	Null	Neither. The current selection spans more than one paragraph with different alignments.
rtfLeft	0	(Default) Left. The paragraph is aligned along the left margin.
rtfRight	1	Right. The paragraph is aligned along the right margin.
rtfCenter	2	Center. The paragraph is centered between the left and right margins.

Remarks

The **SelAlignment** property determines paragraph alignment for all paragraphs that have text in the current selection or for the paragraph containing the insertion point if no text is selected.

To distinguish between the values of **Null** and 0 when reading this property at run time, use the **IsNull** function with the **If...Then...Else** statement. For example:

```
If IsNull(RichTextBox1.SelAlignment) = True Then
    ' Code to run when selection is mixed.
ElseIf RichTextBox1.SelAlignment = 0 Then
    ' Code to run when selection is left aligned.
...
End If
```

See Also

SelHangingIndent, SelIndent, SelRightIndent Properties, **SelBullet** Property, **SelTabCount, SelTabs** Properties, **RichTextBox** Control Constants

Example

This example uses an array of **OptionButton** controls to change the paragraph alignment of selected text in a **RichTextBox** control, but only if text is selected. The indices of the controls in the array correspond to settings for the **SelAlignment** property. To try this example, put a **RichTextBox** control and three **OptionButton** controls on a form. Give all three of the **OptionButton** controls the same name and set their **Index** property to 0, 1, and 2. Paste this code into the **Click** event of the **OptionButton** control. Then run the example.

```
Private Sub Option1_Click(Index As Integer)
   If RichTextBox1.SelLength > 0 Then
      RichTextBox1.SelAlignment = Index
   End If
End Sub
```

SelBold, SelItalic, SelStrikethru, SelUnderline Properties

Return or set font styles of the currently selected text in a **RichTextBox** control. The font styles include the following formats: **Bold**, *Italic*, ~~Strikethru~~, and <u>Underline</u>. Not available at design time.

Applies To

RichTextBox Control

Syntax

object.**SelBold** [= *value*]
object.**SelItalic** [= *value*]
object.**SelStrikethru** [= *value*]
object.**SelUnderline** [= *value*]

The **SelBold**, **SelItalic**, **SelStrikethru**, and **SelUnderline** properties syntax has these parts:

Part	Description
object	An object expression that evaluates to an object in the **Applies To** list.
value	A Boolean expression or constant that determines the font style, as described in **Settings**.

Settings

The settings for *value* are:

Setting	Description
Null	Neither. The selection or character following the insertion point contains characters that have a mix of the appropriate font styles.

(continued)

Setting	Description
True	All the characters in the selection or character following the insertion point have the appropriate font style.
False	(Default) None of the characters in the selection or character following the insertion point have the appropriate font style.

Remarks

These properties behave like the **Bold**, **Italic**, **Strikethru**, and **Underline** properties of a **Font** object. The **RichTextBox** control has a **Font** property and therefore the ability to apply font styles to all the text in the control through the properties of the control's **Font** object. Use these properties to apply font styles to selected text or to characters entered at the insertion point.

Typically, you access these properties by creating a toolbar in your application with buttons to toggle these properties individually.

To distinguish between the values of **Null** and **False** when reading these properties at run time, use the **IsNull** function with the **If...Then...Else** statement. For example:

```
If IsNull(RichTextBox1.SelBold) = True Then
    ' Code to run when selection is mixed.
ElseIf RichTextBox1.SelBold = False Then
    ' Code to run when selection is not bold.
...
End If
```

See Also

SelCharOffset Property, **SelColor** Property, **SelFontName** Property, **SelFontSize** Property

SelBullet Property

Returns or sets a value that determines if a paragraph in the **RichTextBox** control containing the current selection or insertion point has the bullet style. Not available at design time.

Applies To

RichTextBox Control

Syntax

object.**SelBullet** [= *value*]

The **SelBullet** property syntax has these parts:

Part	Description
object	An object expression that evaluates to an object in the **Applies To** list.
Value	An integer or constant that determines the bullet style of the paragraph(s), as described in **Settings**.

Settings

The settings for *value* are:

Setting	Description
Null	Neither. The selection spans more than one paragraph and contains a mixture of bullet and non-bullet styles.
True	The paragraphs in the selection have the bullet style.
False	(Default) The paragraphs in the selection don't have the bullet style.

Remarks

Use the **SelBullet** property to build a list of bulleted items in a **RichTextBox** control.

To distinguish between the values of **Null** and **False** when reading this property at run time, use the **IsNull** function with the **If...Then...Else** statement. For example:

```
If IsNull(RichTextBox1.SelBullet) = True Then
   ' Code to run when selection is mixed.
ElseIf RichTextBox1.SelBullet = False Then
   ' Code to run when selection doesn't have bullet style.
...
End If
```

See Also

SelHangingIndent, SelIndent, SelRightIndent Properties, **SelAlignment** Property, **SelTabCount, SelTabs** Properties

Example

This example changes the state of a **CheckBox** control on a form to show the bullet status of selected text in a **RichTextBox** control. To try this example, put a **RichTextBox** control and a **CheckBox** control on a form. Paste this code into the **SelChange** event of the **RichTextBox** control. Then run the example.

```
Private Sub RichTextBox1_SelChange()
   If IsNull(RichTextBox1.SelBullet) = True Then
      Check1.Value = vbGrayed
   ElseIf RichTextBox1.SelBullet = True Then
      Check1.Value = vbChecked
   ElseIf RichTextBox1.SelBullet = False Then
      Check1.Value = vbUnchecked
   End If
End Sub
```

SelChange Event

Occurs when the current selection of text in the **RichTextBox** control has changed or the insertion point has moved.

Applies To

RichTextBox Control

Syntax

Private Sub *object*_**SelChange**([*index* **As Integer**])

The SelChange event syntax has these parts:

Part	Description
object	An object expression that evaluates to an object in the **Applies To** list.
index	An integer that uniquely identifies a control if it's in a control array.

Remarks

You can use the **SelChange** event to check the various properties that give information about the current selection (such as **SelBold**) so you can update buttons in a toolbar, for example.

See Also

SelHangingIndent, SelIndent, SelRightIndent Properties, **SelBold, SelItalic, SelStrikethru, SelUnderline** Properties, **SelFontName** Property, **SelFontSize** Property, **SelTabCount, SelTabs** Properties

Example

This example checks the size of the current selection to see if the menu commands for cutting or copying text to the Clipboard should be enabled. To try this example, put a **RichTextBox** control and three **Menu** controls on a form to create a menu with commands to cut and copy. Paste this code into the **SelChange** event of the **RichTextBox** control. Then run the example.

```
Private Sub RichTextBox1_SelChange()
   If RichTextBox1.SelLength > 0 Then
      EditCutMenu.Enabled = True
      EditCopyMenu.Enabled = True
   Else
      EditCutMenu.Enabled = False
      EditCopyMenu.Enabled = False
   End If
End Sub
```

SelCharOffset Property

Returns or sets a value that determines whether text in the **RichTextBox** control appears on the baseline (normal), as a superscript above the baseline, or as a subscript below the baseline. Not available at design time.

Applies To

RichTextBox Control

Syntax

object.**SelCharOffset** [= *offset*]

The **SelCharOffset** property syntax has these parts:

Part	Description
object	An object expression that evaluates to an object in the **Applies To** list.
offset	An integer that determines how far the characters in the current selection or that following the insertion point are offset from the baseline of the text, as described in **Settings**.

Settings

The settings for *offset* are:

Setting	Description
Null	Neither. The selection has a mix of characters with different offsets.
0	(Default) Normal. The characters all appear on the normal text baseline.
Positive integer	Superscript. The characters appear above the baseline by the number of twips specified.
Negative integer	Subscript. The characters appear below the baseline by the number of twips specified.

Remarks

To distinguish between the values of **Null** and 0 when reading this property at run time, use the **IsNull** function with the **If...Then...Else** statement. For example:

```
If IsNull(RichTextBox1.SelCharOffset) = True Then
    ' Code to run when selection is mixed.
ElseIf RichTextBox1.SelCharOffset = 0 Then
    ' Code to run when selection is all on the baseline.
...
End If
```

See Also

SelBold, SelItalic, SelStrikethru, SelUnderline Properties, **SelColor** Property, **SelFontName** Property, **SelFontSize** Property

Example

This example uses a scroll bar to move selected text above or below the baseline. The minimum and maximum amount of offset is established by the font size of the text within the **RichTextBox** control. To try this example, put a **RichTextBox** control and a **VScrollBar** control on a form. Paste this code into the **Change** event of the **VScrollBar** control. Then run the example.

```
Private Sub VScroll1_Change ()
   VScroll1.Max = RichTextBox1.SelFontSize
   VScroll1.Min = -(VScroll1.Max)
   RichTextBox1.SelCharOffset = VScroll1.Value
End Sub
```

SelColor Property

Returns or sets a value that determines the color of text in the **RichTextBox** control. Not available at design time.

Applies To

RichTextBox Control

Syntax

object.**SelColor** [= *color*]

The **SelColor** property syntax has these parts:

Part	Description
object	An object expression that evaluates to an object in the **Applies To** list.
color	A value that specifies a color, as described in **Settings**.

Settings

The settings for *color* are:

Setting	Description
Null	The text contains a mixture of different color settings.
RGB colors	Colors specified in code with the **RGB** or **QBColor** functions.
System	Colors specified with the system color constants in the Visual Basic object library in the Object Browser. The color of the text then matches user selections for the specified constant in the Windows Control Panel.

Remarks

If there is no text selected in the **RichTextBox** control, setting this property determines the color of all new text entered at the current insertion point.

See Also

Object Browser, QBColor Function, **RGB** Function, **SelBold, SelItalic, SelStrikethru, SelUnderline** Properties, **SelCharOffset** Property, **SelFontName** Property, **SelFontSize** Property

Example

This example displays a color dialog box from a **CommonDialog** control to specify the color of selected text in a **RichTextBox** control. To try this example, put a **RichTextBox** control, a **CommandButton** control, and a **CommonDialog** control on a form. Paste this code into the **Click** event of the **CommandButton** control. Then run the example.

```
Private Sub Command1_Click()
   CommonDialog1.ShowColor
   RichTextBox1.SelColor = CommonDialog1.Color
End Sub
```

SelFontName Property

Returns or sets the font used to display the currently selected text or the character(s) immediately following the insertion point in the **RichTextBox** control. Not available at design time.

Applies To

RichTextBox Control

Syntax

object.**SelFontName** [= *string*]

The **SelFontName** property syntax has these parts:

Part	Description
object	An object expression that evaluates to an object in the **Applies To** list.
string	A string expression that identifies a font installed on the system.

Remarks

The **SelFontName** property returns **Null** if the selected text contains different fonts.

See Also

SelBold, SelItalic, SelStrikethru, SelUnderline Properties, **SelCharOffset** Property, **SelColor** Property, **SelFontSize** Property

Example

This example displays a font dialog box from a **CommonDialog** control to specify font attributes of selected text in a **RichTextBox** control. To try this example, put a **RichTextBox** control, a **CommandButton** control, and a **CommonDialog** control on a form. Paste this code into the **Click** event of the **CommandButton** control. Then run the example.

```
Private Sub Command1_Click ()
   CommonDialog1.Flags = cdlCFBoth
   CommonDialog1.ShowFont
   With RichTextBox1
      .SelFontName = CommonDialog1.FontName
      .SelFontSize = CommonDialog1.FontSize
      .SelBold = CommonDialog1.FontBold
      .SelItalic = CommonDialog1.FontItalic
      .SelStrikethru = CommonDialog1.FontStrikethru
      .SelUnderline = CommonDialog1.FontUnderline
   End With
End Sub
```

SelFontSize Property

Returns or sets a value that specifies the size of the font used to display text in a **RichTextBox** control. Not available at design time.

Applies To

RichTextBox Control

Syntax

object.**SelFontSize** [= *points*]

The **SelFontSize** property syntax has these parts:

Part	Description
object	An object expression that evaluates to an object in the **Applies To** list.
points	An integer that specifies the size in points of the currently selected text or the characters immediately following the insertion point.

Remarks

The maximum value for **SelFontSize** is 2160 points.

In general, you should change the **SelFontName** property before you set the size and style attributes. However, when you set TrueType fonts to smaller than 8 points, you should set the point size to 3 with the **SelFontSize** property, then set the **SelFontName** property, and then set the size again with the **SelFontSize** property.

Note Available fonts depend on your system configuration, display devices, and printing devices, and therefore may vary from system to system.

The **SelFontSize** property returns **Null** if the selected text contains different font sizes.

See Also

SelBold, SelItalic, SelStrikethru, SelUnderline Properties, **SelCharOffset** Property, **SelColor** Property, **SelFontName** Property

Example

This example displays a font dialog box from a **CommonDialog** control to specify font attributes of selected text in a **RichTextBox** control. To try this example, put a **RichTextBox** control, a **CommandButton** control, and a **CommonDialog** control on a form. Paste this code into the **Click** event of the **CommandButton** control. Then run the example.

```
Private Sub Command1_Click ()
   CommonDialog1.Flags = Both
   CommonDialog1.ShowFont
   With RichTextBox1
      .SelFontName = CommonDialog1.FontName
      .SelFontSize = CommonDialog1.FontSize
      .SelBold = CommonDialog1.FontBold
      .SelItalic = CommonDialog1.FontItalic
      .SelStrikethru = CommonDialog1.FontStrikethru
      .SelUnderline = CommonDialog1.FontUnderline
   End With
End Sub
```

SelHangingIndent, SelIndent, SelRightIndent Properties

Returns or sets the margin settings for the paragraph(s) in a **RichTextBox** control that either contain the current selection or are added at the current insertion point. Not available at design time.

Applies To

RichTextBox Control

Syntax

object.**SelHangingIndent** [= *integer*]
object.**SelIndent** [= *integer*]
object.**SelRightIndent** [= *integer*]

The **SelHangingIndent**, **SelIndent**, and **SelRightIndent** properties syntax has these parts:

Part	Description
object	An object expression that evaluates to an object in the **Applies To** list.
integer	An integer that determines the amount of indent. These properties use the scale mode units of the **Form** object containing the **RichTextBox** control.

Remarks

For the affected paragraph(s), the **SelIndent** property specifies the distance between the left edge of the **RichTextBox** control and the left edge of the text that is selected or added. Similarly, the **SelRightIndent** property specifies the distance between the right edge of the **RichTextBox** control and the right edge of the text that is selected or added.

The **SelHangingIndent** property specifies the distance between the left edge of the first line of text in the selected paragraph(s) (as specified by the **SelIndent** property) and the left edge of subsequent lines of text in the same paragraph(s).

These properties return zero (0) if the selection spans multiple paragraphs with different margin settings.

See Also

SelAlignment Property, **SelBullet** Property, **SelTabCount, SelTabs** Properties, **Form** Object, **Forms** Collection

Example

This example selects all the text in a **RichTextBox** control, then sets both the left and right indents to create margins. To try this example, put a **RichTextBox** control, a **CommandButton** control, and a **TextBox** control on a form. Load a file into the **RichTextBox**, and paste this code into the General Declarations section of the form. Then run the example.

```
Private Sub Command1_Click()
    Dim Margins As Integer
    Margins = CInt(Text1.Text)
    With RichTextBox1
        .SelStart = 1
        .SelLength = Len(RichTextBox1.Text)
        .SelIndent = Margins
        .SelRightIndent = Margins
    End With
End Sub
```

SelPrint Method

Sends formatted text in a **RichTextBox** control to a device for printing.

Applies To

RichTextBox Control

Syntax

object.**SelPrint**(*hdc*)

The **SelPrint** method syntax has these parts:

Part	Description
object	An object expression that evaluates to an object in the **Applies To** list.
hdc	The device context of the device you plan to use to print the contents of the control.

Remarks

If text is selected in the **RichTextBox** control, the **SelPrint** method sends only the selected text to the target device. If no text is selected, the entire contents of the **RichTextBox** are sent to the target device.

The **SelPrint** method does not print text from the **RichTextBox** control. Rather, it sends a copy of formatted text to a device which can print the text. For example, you can send the text to the **Printer** object using code as follows:

```
RichTextBox1.SelPrint(Printer.hDC)
```

Notice that the **hDC** property of the **Printer** object is used to specify the device context argument of the **SelPrint** method.

Note   If you use the **Printer** object as the destination of the text from the **RichTextBox** control, you must first initialize the device context of the **Printer** object by printing something like a zero-length string.

See Also

SelBold, SelItalic, SelStrikethru, SelUnderline Properties, **hDC** Property, **Printer** Object, **Printers** Collection

Example

This example prints the formatted text in a **RichTextBox** control. To try this example, put a **RichTextBox** control, a **CommonDialog** control, and a **CommandButton** control on a form. Paste this code into the **Click** event of the **CommandButton** control. Then run the example.

```
Private Sub Command1_Click()
    CommonDialog1.Flags = cdlPDReturnDC + cdlPDNoPageNums
    If RichTextBox1.SelLength = 0 Then
        CommonDialog1.Flags = CommonDialog1.Flags + cdlPDAllPages
    Else
        CommonDialog1.Flags = CommonDialog1.Flags + cdlPDSelection
    End If
    CommonDialog1.ShowPrinter
    Printer.Print ""
    RichTextBox1.SelPrint CommonDialog1.hDC
End Sub
```

SelProtected Property

Returns or sets a value which determines if the current selection is protected. Not available at design time.

Applies To

RichTextBox Control

Syntax

object.**SelProtected** [= *value*]

The **SelProtected** property syntax has the following parts:

Part	Description
object	An object expression that evaluates to a **RichTextBox** control.
value	A variant value that determines if the current selection is protected, as described in **Settings**.

Settings

Setting	Description
Null	The selection contains a mix of protected and non-protected characters.
True	All the characters in the selection are protected.
False	None of the characters in the selection are protected.

Remarks

Protected text looks the same a regular text, but cannot be modified by the end-user. That is, the text cannot be changed during run time. This allows you to create forms with the **RichTextbox** control, and have areas that cannot be modified by the end user.

See Also

SelBold, SelItalic, SelStrikethru, SelUnderline Properties

SelRTF Property

Returns or sets the text (in .RTF format) in the current selection of a **RichTextBox** control. Not available at design time.

Applies To

RichTextBox Control

Syntax

object.**SelRTF** [= *string*]

The **SelRTF** property syntax has these parts:

Part	Description
object	An object expression that evaluates to an object in the **Applies To** list.
string	A string expression in .RTF format.

Remarks

Setting the **SelRTF** property replaces any selected text in the **RichTextBox** control with the new string. This property returns a zero-length string ("") if no text is selected in the control.

You can use the **SelRTF** property along with the **Print** function to write .RTF files.

See Also

TextRTF Property, **Supported RTF Codes** (RichTextBox Control)

Example

This example saves the highlighted contents of a **RichTextBox** control to an .RTF file. To try this example, put a **RichTextBox** control and a **CommandButton** control on a form. Paste this code into the **Click** event of the **CommandButton** control. Then run the example.

```
Private Sub Command1_Click ()
   Open "mytext.rtf" For Output As 1
   Print #1, RichTextBox1.SelRTF
   Close 1
End Sub
```

SelTabCount, SelTabs Properties

Returns or sets the number of tabs and the absolute tab positions of text in a **RichTextBox** control. Not available at design time.

Applies To

RichTextBox Control

Syntax

object.**SelTabCount** [= *count*]
object.**SelTabs**(*index*) [= *location*]

The **SelTabCount** and **SelTabs** properties syntaxes have these parts:

Part	Description
object	An object expression that evaluates to an object in the **Applies To** list.
count	An integer that determines the number of tab positions in the selected paragraph(s) or in those paragraph(s) following the insertion point.
index	An integer that identifies a specific tab. The first tab location has an index of zero (0). The last tab location has an index equal to **SelTabCount** minus.
location	An integer that specifies the location of the designated tab. The units used to express tab positions are determined by the scale mode of the **Form** object or other object containing the **RichTextBox** control.

Remarks

By default, pressing TAB when typing in a **RichTextBox** control causes focus to move to the next control in the tab order, as specified by the **TabIndex** property. One way to insert a tab in the text is by pressing CTRL+TAB. However, users who are accustomed to working with word processors may find the CTRL+TAB key combination contrary to their experience. You can enable use of the TAB key to insert a tab in a **RichTextBox** control by temporarily switching the **TabStop** property of all the controls on the **Form** object to **False** while the **RichTextBox** control has focus. For example:

```
Private Sub RichTextBox1_GotFocus()
   ' Ignore errors for controls without the TabStop property.
   On Error Resume Next
   ' Switch off the change of focus when pressing TAB.
   For Each Control In Controls
      Control.TabStop = False
   Next Control
End Sub
```

Make sure to reset the **TabStop** property of the other controls when the **RichTextBox** control loses focus.

See Also

SelHangingIndent, SelIndent, SelRightIndent Properties, **SelAlignment** Property, **SelBullet** Property, **Form** Object, **Forms** Collection, **TabIndex** Property, **TabStop** Property

Example

This example sets the number of tabs in a **RichTextBox** control to a total of five and then sets the positions of the tabs to multiples of five. To try this example, put a **RichTextBox** control and a **CommandButton** control on a form. Paste this code into the **Click** event of the **CommandButton** control. Then run the example.

```
Private Sub Command1_Click()
    With RichTextBox1
        .SelTabCount = 5
        For X = 0 To .SelTabCount - 1
            .SelTabs(X) = 5 * X
        Next X
    End With
End Sub
```

Span Method

Selects text in a **RichTextBox** control based on a set of specified characters.

Applies To

RichTextBox Control

Syntax

object.**Span** *characterset*, *forward*, *negate*

The **Span** method syntax has these parts:

Part	Description
object	Required. An object expression that evaluates to an object in the **Applies To** list.
characterset	Required. A string expression that specifies the set of characters to look for when extending the selection, based on the value of *negate*.
forward	Optional. A Boolean expression that determines which direction the insertion point moves, as described in **Settings**.
negate	Optional. A Boolean expression that determines whether the characters in *characterset* define the set of target characters or are excluded from the set of target characters, as described in **Settings**.

Settings

The settings for *forward* are:

Setting	Description
True	(Default) Selects text from the current insertion point or the beginning of the current selection forward, toward the end of the text.
False	Selects text from the current insertion point or the beginning of the current selection backward, toward the start of the text.

The settings for *negate* are:

Setting	Description
True	The characters included in the selection are those which do not appear in the *characterset* argument. The selection stops at the first character found that appears in the *characterset* argument.
False	(Default) The characters included in the selection are those which appear in the *characterset* argument. The selection stops at the first character found that does not appear in the *characterset* argument.

Remarks

The **Span** method is primarily used to easily select a word or sentence in the **RichTextBox** control.

If the **Span** method cannot find the specified characters based on the values of the arguments, then the current insertion point or selection remains unchanged.

The **Span** method does not return any data.

See Also

Upto Method

Example

This example defines a pair of keyboard shortcuts that selects text in a **RichTextBox** control to the end of a sentence (CTRL+S) or the end of a word (CTRL+W). To try this example, put a **RichTextBox** control on a form. Paste this code into the **KeyUp** event of the **RichTextBox** control. Then run the example.

```
Private Sub RichTextBox1_KeyUp (KeyCode As Integer, Shift As Integer)
   If Shift = vbCtrlMask Then
      Select Case KeyCode
         ' If Ctrl+S:
         Case vbKeyS
            ' Select to the end of the sentence.
            RichTextBox1.Span ".?!:", True, True
            ' Extend selection to include punctuation.
            RichTextBox1.SelLength = RichTextBox1.SelLength + 1
         ' If Ctrl+W:
         Case vbKeyW
            ' Select to the end of the word.
            RichTextBox1.Span " ,;:.?!", True, True
      End Select
   End If
End Sub
```

Supported RTF Codes

The **RichTextBox** control recognizes the following RTF (Rich Text Format) codes. All other RTF codes are ignored by the control when loading text.

RTF Code	Description	RTF Code	Description
-	**OptionalHyphen**	objcropl	**CropLeft**
\n	**EndParagraph**	objcropr	**CropRight**
\r	**EndParagraph**	objcropt	**CropTop**
_	**NonBreakingHyphen**	objdata	**ObjectData**
|	**FormulaCharacter**	object	**Object**
~	**NonBreakingSpace**	objemb	**ObjectEmbedded**
ansi	**CharSetAnsi**	objh	**Height**

(continued)

RTF Code	Description	RTF Code	Description
b	**Bold**	objicemb	**ObjectMacICEmbedder**
bin	**BinaryData**	objlink	**ObjectLink**
blue	**ColorBlue**	objname	**ObjectName**
bullet	**ANSI Character 149**	objpub	**ObjectMacPublisher**
cb	**ColorBackground**	objscalex	**ScaleX**
cell	**Cell**	objscaley	**ScaleY**
cf	**ColorForeground**	objsetsize	**ObjectSetSize**
colortbl	**ColorTable**	objsub	**ObjectMacSubscriber**
cpg	**CodePage**	objw	**Width**
deff	**DefaultFont**	par	**EndParagraph**
deflang	**DefaultLanguage**	pard	**ParagraphDefault**
deftab	**DefaultTabWidth**	pc	**CharSetPc**
deleted	**Deleted**	pca	**CharSetPs2**
dibitmap	**PictureWindowsDIB**	piccropb	**CropBottom**
dn	**Down**	piccropl	**CropLeft**
dy	**TimeDay**	piccropr	**CropRight**
emdash	**ANSI Character 151**	piccropt	**CropTop**
endash	**ANSI Character 150**	pich	**Height**
f	**FontSelect**	pichgoal	**DesiredHeight**
fbidi	**FontFamilyBidi**	picscalex	**ScaleX**
fchars	**FollowingPunct**	picscaley	**ScaleY**
fcharset	**CharSet**	pict	**Picture**
fdecor	**FontFamilyDecorative**	picw	**Width**
fi	**IndentFirst**	picwgoal	**DesiredWidth**
field	**Field**	plain	**CharacterDefault**
fldinst	**FieldInstruction**	pmmetafile	**PictureOS2Metafile**
fldrslt	**FieldResult**	pn	**ParaNum**
fmodern	**FontFamilyModern**	pnindent	**ParaNumIndent**
fname	**RealFontName**	pnlvlblt	**ParaNumBullet**
fnil	**FontFamilyDefault**	pntext	**ParaNumText**
fontemb	**FontEmbedded**	pntxta	**ParaNumAfter**
fontfile	**FontFile**	pntxtb	**ParaNumBefore**
fonttbl	**FontTable**	protect	**Protect**
footer	**NullDestination** (Footer)	qc	**AlignCenter**
footerf	**NullDestination** (Footer, first)	ql	**AlignLeft**

(continued)

(continued)

RTF Code	Description	RTF Code	Description
footerl	**NullDestination** (Footer, left)	qr	**AlignRight**
footerr	**NullDestination** (Footer, right)	rdblquote	**ANSI Character 34**
footnote	**NullDestination** (footnote)	red	**ColorRed**
fprq	**Pitch**	result	**ObjectResult**
froman	**FontFamilyRoman**	revauth	**RevAuthor**
fs	**FontSize**	revised	**Revision**
fscript	**FontFamilyScript**	ri	**IndentRight**
fswiss	**FontFamilySwiss**	row	**Row**
ftech	**FontFamilyTechnical**	rquote	**ANSI Character 39**
ftncn	**NullDestination** (Footnote cont.)	rtf	**Rtf**
ftnsep	**NullDestination** (Footnote separ)	rtlch	**RightToLeftChars**
ftnsepc	**NullDestination** (Footnote cont. separ)	rtldoc	**RightToLeftDocument**
green	**ColorGreen**	rtlmark	**DisplayRightToLeft**
header	**NullDestination** (Header)	rtlpar	**RightToLeftParagraph**
headerf	**NullDestination** (Header, first)	sec	**TimeSecond**
headerl	**NullDestination** (Header, left)	sect	**EndSection**
headerr	**NullDestination** (Header, right)	sectd	**SectionDefault**
horzdoc	**HorizontalRender**	strike	**StrikeOut**
hr	**TimeHour**	stylesheet	**StyleSheet**
i	**Italic**	sub	**Subscript**
info	**DocumentArea** (Info fields)	super	**Superscript**
intbl	**InTable**	tb	**TabPosition**
lang	**Language**	tc	**NullDestination** (Table of contents)
lchars	**LeadingPunct**	tx	**TabPosition**
ldblquote	**ANSI Character 34**	ul	**Underline**
li	**IndentLeft**	uld	**UnderlineDotted**
line	**SoftBreak**	uldash	**UnderlineDash**
lquote	**ANSI Character 39**	uldashd	**UnderlineDashDotted**
ltrch	**LeftToRightChars**	uldashdd	**UnderlineDashDotDotted**
ltrdoc	**LeftToRightDocument**	uldb	**UnderlineDouble**
ltrmark	**DisplayLeftToRight**	ulhair	**UnderlineHairline**
ltrpar	**LeftToRightParagraph**	ulnone	**StopUnderline**
mac	**CharSetMacintosh**	ulth	**UnderlineThick**
macpict	**PictureQuickDraw**	ulw	**UnderlineWord**
margl	**MarginLeft**	ulwave	**UnderlineWave**

(continued)

RTF Code	Description	RTF Code	Description
marglsxn	**SectionMarginLeft**	up	**Up**
margr	**MarginRight**	v	**HiddenText**
margrsxn	**SectionMarginRight**	vertdoc	**VerticalRender**
min	**TimeMinute**	wbitmap	**PictureWindowsBitmap**
mo	**TimeMonth**	wbmbitspixel	**BitmapBitsPerPixel**
nocwrap	**NoWordBreak**	wbmplanes	**BitmapNumPlanes**
nooverflow	**NoOverflow**	wbmwidthbytes	**BitmapWidthBytes**
nosupersub	**NoSuperSub**	wmetafile	**PictureWindowsMetafile**
nowwrap	**NoWordWrap**	xe	**NullDestination** (index entry)
objautlink	**ObjectAutoLink**	yr	**TimeYear**
objclass	**ObjectClass**	zwj	**ZeroWidthJoiner**
objcropb	**CropBottom**	zwnj	**ZeroWidthNonJoiner**

See Also

RichTextBox Control, **FileName** Property (RichTextBox Control), **LoadFile** Method, **SaveFile** Method, **SelRTF** Property, **TextRTF** Property

TextRTF Property

Returns or sets the text of a **RichTextBox** control, including all .RTF code.

Applies To

RichTextBox Control

Syntax

object.**TextRTF** [= *string*]

The **TextRTF** property syntax has these parts:

Part	Description
object	An object expression that evaluates to an object in the **Applies To** list.
string	A string expression in .RTF format.

Remarks

Setting the **TextRTF** property replaces the entire contents of a **RichTextBox** control with the new string.

You can use the **TextRTF** property along with the **Print** function to write .RTF files. The resulting file can be read by any other word processor capable of reading RTF-encoded text.

See Also

SaveFile Method, **SelRTF** Property, **Supported RTF Codes** (Rich TextBox Control)

Example

This example saves the entire contents of a **RichTextBox** control to an .RTF file. To try this example, put a **RichTextBox** control and a **CommandButton** control on a form. Paste this code into the **Click** event of the **CommandButton** control. Then run the example.

```
Private Sub Command1_Click ()
    Open "mytext.rtf" For Output As 1
    Print #1, RichTextBox1.TextRTF
    Close 1
End Sub
```

Upto Method

Moves the insertion point up to, but not including, the first character that is a member of the specified character set in a **RichTextBox** control.

Applies To

RichTextBox Control

Syntax

object.**Upto**(*characterset, forward, negate*)

The **Upto** method syntax has these parts:

Part	Description
object	Required. An object expression that evaluates to an object in the **Applies To** list.
characterset	Required. A string expression that specifies the set of characters to look for when moving the insertion point, based on the value of *negate*.
forward	Optional. A Boolean expression that determines which direction the insertion point moves, as described in **Settings**.
negate	Optional. A Boolean expression that determines whether the characters in *characterset* define the set of target characters or are excluded from the set of target characters, as described in **Settings**.

Settings

The settings for *forward* are:

Setting	Description
True	(Default) Moves the insertion point forward, toward the end of the text.
False	Moves the insertion point backward, toward the start of the text.

The settings for *negate* are:

Setting	Description
True	The characters not specified in the *characterset* argument are used to move the insertion point.
False	(Default) The characters specified in the *characterset* argument are used to move the insertion point.

See Also

Span Method

Example

This example defines a pair of keyboard shortcuts that moves the insertion point in a **RichTextBox** control to the end of a sentence (ALT+S) or the end of a word (ALT+W). To try this example, put a **RichTextBox** control on a form. Paste this code into the **KeyUp** event of the **RichTextBox** control. Then run the example.

```
Private Sub RichTextBox1_KeyUp (KeyCode As Integer, Shift As Integer)
    If Shift = vbAltMask Then
        Select Case KeyCode
            ' If Alt+S:
            Case vbKeyS
                ' Move insertion point to the end of the sentence.
                RichTextBox1.Upto ".?!:", True, False
            ' If Alt+W:
            Case vbkeyW
                ' Move insertion point to the end of the word.
                RichTextBox1.Upto " .?!:", True, False
        End Select
    End If
End Sub
```

Slider Control

A **Slider** control is a window containing a slider and optional tick marks. You can move the slider by dragging it, clicking the mouse to either side of the slider, or using the keyboard.

Syntax

> **Slider**

Remarks

> **Slider** controls are useful when you want to select a discrete value or a set of consecutive values in a range. For example, you could use a **Slider** to set the size of a displayed image by moving the slider to a given tick mark rather than by typing a number. To select a range of values, set the **SelectRange** property to **True**, and program the control to select a range when the SHIFT key is down.
>
> The **Slider** control can be oriented either horizontally or vertically.
>
> **Distribution Note**   To use the **Slider** control in your application, you must add the COMCTL32.OCX file to the project. When distributing your application, install the COMCTL32.OCX file in the user's Microsoft Windows System or System32 directory. For more information on how to add an **ActiveX** control to a project, see the *Programmer's Guide*.

Properties

> **BorderStyle** Property, **Container** Property, **DataBindings** Property, **DragIcon** Property, **DragMode** Property, **Enabled** Property, **Height, Width** Properties, **HelpContextID** Property, **hWnd** Property, **Index** Property, **LargeChange, SmallChange** Properties, **Left, Top** Properties, **Max, Min** Properties, **MouseIcon** Property, **MousePointer** Property, **Name** Property, **Object** Property, **OLEDropMode** Property, **Orientation** Property, **Parent** Property, **SelectRange** Property, **SelLength, SelStart** Properties, **TabIndex** Property, **TabStop** Property, **Tag** Property, **TickFrequency** Property, **TickStyle** Property, **ToolTipText** Property, **Value** Property, **Visible** Property, **WhatsThisHelpID** Property

Events

> **Change** Event, **Click** Event, **DragDrop** Event, **DragOver** Event, **GotFocus** Event, **KeyDown, KeyUp** Events, **KeyPress** Event, **LostFocus** Event, **MouseDown, MouseUp** Events, **MouseMove** Event, **OLECompleteDrag** Event, **OLEDragDrop** Event, **OLEDragOver** Event, **OLEGiveFeedback** Event, **OLESetDate** Event, **OLEStartDrag** Event, **Scroll** Event

Methods

> **ClearSel** Method, **GetNumTicks** Method, **Drag** Method, **Move** Method, **OLEDrag** Method, **Refresh** Method, **SetFocus** Method, **ShowWhatsThis** Method, **ZOrder** Method

See Also

> **Slider** Constants

Change Event (ToolBar, Slider Controls)

Indicates that the contents of a control have changed. How and when this event occurs varies with the control.

Applies To

ComboBox Control, **DBCombo** Control, **DBGrid** Control, **DirListBox** Control, **DriveListBox** Control, **HScrollBar, VScrollBar** Controls, **Label** Control, **Picturebox** Control, **TextBox** Control

Syntax

Private Sub *object*_**Change**([*index* **As Integer**])

The **Change** event syntax has these parts:

Part	Description
object	An object expression that evaluates to a control in the **Applies To** list.
index	An integer that uniquely identifies a control if it's in a control array.

Remarks

- Slider—generated when the **Value** property changes, either through code, or when the user moves the control's slider.

- Toolbar—generated after the end user customizes a **Toolbar** control's toolbar using the Customize Toolbar dialog box.

The **Change** event procedure can synchronize or coordinate data display among controls. For example, you can use a **Slider** control's **Change** event procedure to update the control's **Value** property setting in a **TextBox** control. Or you could use a **Change** event procedure to display data and formulas in a work area and results in another area.

Note A **Change** event procedure can sometimes cause a cascading event. This occurs when the control's **Change** event alters the control's contents by setting a property in code that determines the control's value, such as the **Text** property setting for a **TextBox** control. To prevent a cascading event:

- If possible, avoid writing a **Change** event procedure for a control that alters that control's contents. If you do write such a procedure, be sure to set a flag that prevents further changes while the current change is in progress.

- Avoid creating two or more controls whose **Change** event procedures affect each other, for example, two **TextBox** controls that update each other during their **Change** events.

See Also

Text Property (MaskedEdit Control), **Value** Property (ActiveX Controls), **AllowCustomize** Property, **Customize** Method, **RestoreToolbar** Method, **SaveToolbar** Method, **Style** Property, **Picture** Property, **PathChange** Event, **PatternChange** Event, **Path** Property, **LostFocus** Event, **LinkTopic** Property, **KeyPress** Event, **KeyDown**, **KeyUp** Events, **Drive** Property, **Caption** Property

Example

This example displays the numeric setting of a horizontal scroll bar's **Value** property in a **TextBox** control. To try this example, create a form with a **TextBox** control and an **HScrollBar** control and then paste the code into the Declarations section of a form that contains a horizontal scroll bar (HScrollBar control) and a **TextBox** control. Press F5 and click the horizontal scroll bar.

```
Private Sub Form_Load ()
    HScroll1.Min = 0             ' Set Minimum.
    HScroll1.Max = 1000          ' Set Maximum.
    HScroll1.LargeChange = 100   ' Set LargeChange.
    HScroll1.SmallChange = 1     ' Set SmallChange.
End Sub

Private Sub HScroll1_Change ()
    Text1.Text = HScroll1.Value
End Sub
```

ClearSel Method

Clears the current selection of a **Slider** control.

Applies To

Slider Control

Syntax

object.**ClearSel**

The object placeholder represents an object expression that evaluates to a **Slider** control.

Remarks

This method sets the **SelStart** property to the value of the **Value** property and sets the **SelLength** property to 0.

See Also

Value Property (ActiveX Controls), **SelectRange** Property, **SelLength, SelStart** Properties (Slider Control)

GetNumTicks Method

Returns the number of ticks between the **Min** and **Max** properties of the **Slider** control.

Applies To

Slider Control

Syntax

object.**GetNumTicks**

The object placeholder represents an object expression that evaluates to a **Slider** control.

Remarks

To change the number of ticks, reset the **Min** or **Max** properties or the **TickFrequency** property.

See Also

Max, Min Properties (CommonDialog), **TickFrequency** Property

Example

This example displays the current number of ticks on a **Slider** control, then increments the **Max** property by 10. To try this example, place a **Slider** control onto a form and paste the code into the form's Declarations section. Run the example, and click the **Slider** control to get the number of ticks. Every click on the control increases the ticks.

```
Private Sub Slider1_Click()
   MsgBox Slider1.GetNumTicks
   Slider1.Max = Slider1.Max + 10
End Sub
```

LargeChange, SmallChange Properties (Slider Control)

- The **LargeChange** property sets the number of ticks the slider will move when you press the PAGEUP or PAGEDOWN keys, or when you click the mouse to the left or right of the slider.

- The **SmallChange** property sets the number of ticks the slider will move when you press the left or right arrow keys.

Applies To

Slider Control

Syntax

object.**LargeChange** = *number*
object.**SmallChange** = *number*

The **LargeChange** and **SmallChange** property syntaxes have these parts:

Part	Description
object	An object expression that evaluates to a **Slider** control.
number	A Long integer specifying how many ticks the slider moves.

Remarks

The default for the **LargeChange** property is 5. The default for the **SmallChange** property is 1.

See Also

Value Property (ActiveX Controls), **Slider** Control, **Change** Event, **Max**, **Min** Properties (Scroll Bar)

Example

This example matches a **TextBox** control's width to that of a **Slider** control. While the **Slider** control's **Value** property is above a certain value, the **TextBox** control's width matches the **Slider** control's value. The **SmallChange** and **LargeChange** properties depend on the value of the **Slider** control's **Max** property. To try the example, place a **Slider** control and a **TextBox** control on a form and paste the code into the form's Declarations section. Run the example and press the PAGEDOWN, PAGEUP, and LEFT and RIGHT ARROW keys.

```
Private Sub Form_Load()
    Text1.Width = 4500          ' Set a minimum width for the TextBox.
    Slider1.Left = Text1.Left   ' Align the Slider to the TextBox.
    ' Match the width of the Slider to the TextBox.
    Slider1.Max = Text1.Width
    ' Place the Slider a little below the Textbox.
    Slider1.Top = Text1.Top + Text1.Height + 50
    ' Set TickFrequency to a fraction of the Max value.
    Slider1.TickFrequency = Slider1.Max * 0.1
    ' Set LargeChange and SmallChange value to a fraction of Max.
    Slider1.LargeChange = Slider1.Max * 0.1
    Slider1.SmallChange = Slider1.Max * 0.01
End Sub

Private Sub Slider1_Change()
    ' If the slider is under 1/3 the size of the textbox, no change.
    ' Else, match the width of the textbox to the Slider's value.
    If Slider1.Value > Slider1.Max / 3 Then
        Text1.Width = Slider1.Value
    End If
End Sub
```

Orientation Property (Slider Control)

Sets a value that determines whether the **Slider** control is oriented horizontally or vertically.

Applies To

Slider Control

Syntax

object.**Orientation** = *number*

The **Orientation** property syntax has these parts:

Part	Description
object	An object expression that evaluates to a **Slider** control.
number	A constant or value specifying the orientation, as described in **Settings**.

Settings

The settings for *number* are:

Constant	Value	Description
sldHorizontal	0	(Default) Horizontal. The slider moves horizontally and tick marks can be placed on either the top or bottom, both, or neither.
sldVertical	1	Vertical. The slider moves vertically and tick marks can be placed on either the left or right sides, both, or neither.

See Also

Slider Constants

Example

This example toggles the orientation of a **Slider** control on a form. To try the example, place a **Slider** control onto a form and paste the code into the form's Declarations section, and then run the example. Click the form to toggle the **Slider** control's orientation.

```
Private Sub Form_Click()
    If Slider1.Orientation = 0 Then
        Slider1.Orientation = 1
    Else
        Slider1.Orientation = 0
    End If
End Sub
```

Scroll Event (Slider Control)

Occurs when you move the slider on a **Slider** control, either by clicking on the control or using keyboard commands.

Applies To
Slider Control

Syntax

Private Sub *object*_**Scroll( )**

The object placeholder represents an object expression that evaluates to a **Slider** control.

Remarks

The **Scroll** Event occurs before the **Click** event.

The **Scroll** Event continuously returns the value of the **Value** property as the slider is moved. You can use this event to perform calculations to manipulate controls that must be coordinated with ongoing changes in the **Slider** control. In contrast, use the **Change** event when you want an update to occur only once, after a **Slider** control's **Value** property has changed.

Note Avoid using a **MsgBox** statement or function in this event.

See Also

Change Event, **LargeChange**, **SmallChange** Properties (Slider Control), **MsgBox** Function, **Slider** Control, **Value** Property (ActiveX Controls)

SelectRange Property

Sets a value that determines if a **Slider** control can have a selected range.

Applies To
Slider Control

Syntax

object.**SelectRange** = *boolean*

The **SelectRange** property syntax has these parts:

Part	Description
object	An object expression that evaluates to a **Slider** control.
boolean	A Boolean expression that determines whether or not the **Slider** can have a selected range, as described in **Settings**.

Settings

The settings for *boolean* are:

Setting	Description
True	The **Slider** can have a selected range.
False	The **Slider** can't have a selected range.

Remarks

If **SelectRange** is set to **False**, then the **SelStart** property setting is the same as the **Value** property setting. Setting the **SelStart** property also changes the **Value** property, and vice-versa, which will be reflected in the position of the slider on the control. Setting **SelLength** when the **SelectRange** property is **False** has no effect.

See Also

ClearSel Method, **SelLength**, **SelStart** Properties (Slider Control), **Value** Property (ActiveX Controls)

Example

This example allows the user to select a range when the SHIFT key is held down. To try the example, place a **Slider** control on a form and paste the code into the form's Declarations section. Run the example and select a range by holding down the SHIFT key and dragging or clicking the mouse on the **Slider** control.

```
Private Sub Form_Load()
                                'Set slider control settings
    Slider1.Max = 20
End Sub


Private Sub Slider1_MouseDown(Button As Integer, Shift As Integer,
x As Single, y As Single)
    If Shift = 1 Then                   ' If Shift button is down then
        Slider1.SelectRange = True      ' turn SelectRange on.
        Slider1.SelStart = Slider1.Value ' Set the SelStart value
        Slider1.SelLength = 0    ' Set previous SelLength (if any) to 0.
    End If
End Sub


Private Sub Slider1_MouseUp(Button As Integer, Shift As Integer,
x As Single, y As Single)

    If Shift = 1 Then
    ' If user selects backwards from a point, an error will occur.
    On Error Resume Next
    ' Else set SelLength using SelStart and current value.
        Slider1.SelLength = Slider1.Value - Slider1.SelStart
    Else
        Slider1.SelectRange = False     ' If user lifts SHIFT key.
    End If
End Sub
```

SelLength, SelStart Properties (Slider Control)

- **SelLength** returns or sets the length of a selected range in a **Slider** control.
- **SelStart** returns or sets the start of a selected range in a **Slider** control.

Applies To

Slider Control

Syntax

object.**SelLength** [= *value*]
object.**SelStart** [= *value*]

The **SelLength** and **SelStart** property syntaxes have these parts:

Part	Description
object	An object expression that evaluates to a **Slider** control.
value	A value that falls within the **Min** and **Max** properties.

Remarks

The **SelLength** and **SelStart** properties are used together to select a range of contiguous values on a **Slider** control. The **Slider** control then has the additional advantage of being a visual analog of the range of possible values.

The **SelLength** property can't be less than 0, and the sum of **SelLength** and **SelStart** can't be greater than the **Max** property.

See Also

SelectRange Property, **ClearSel** Method, **Max**, **Min** Properties (Common Dialog)

Example

This example selects a range on a **Slider** control. To try this example, place a **Slider** control onto a form with three **TextBox** controls, named Text1, Text2, and Text3. The **Slider** control's **SelectRange** property must be set to **True**. Paste the code below into the form's Declarations section, and run the example. While holding down the SHIFT key, you can select a range on the slider, and the various values will be displayed in the text boxes.

```
Private Sub Form_Load()
   ' Make sure SelectRange is True so selection can occur.
   Slider1.SelectRange = True
End Sub

Private Sub Slider1_MouseDown(Button As Integer, Shift As Integer,
x As Single, y As Single)
   If Shift = 1 Then    ' If SHIFT is down, begin the range selection.
      Slider1.ClearSel  ' Clear any previous selection.
```

```
            Slider1.SelStart = Slider1.Value
            Text2.Text = Slider1.SelStart  ' Show the beginning
                                           ' of the range in the textbox.
        Else
            Slider1.ClearSel              ' Clear any previous selection.
        End If
End Sub

Private Sub Slider1_MouseUp(Button As Integer, Shift As Integer,
x As Single, y As Single)
    ' When SHIFT is down and SelectRange is True,
    ' this event is triggered.
    If Shift = 1 And Slider1.SelectRange = True Then
        ' Make sure the current value is larger than SelStart or
        ' an error will occur--SelLength can't be negative.
        If Slider1.Value >= Slider1.SelStart Then
            Slider1.SelLength = Slider1.Value - Slider1.SelStart
            Text1.Text = Slider1.Value  ' To see the end of the range.
            ' Text3 is the difference between the end and start values.
            Text3.Text = Slider1.SelLength
        End If
    End If
End Sub
```

Slider Constants

Orientation Constants

Constant	Value	Description
sldHorizontal	0	Horizontal orientation.
sldVertical	1	Vertical orientation.

Tickstyle Constants

Constant	Value	Description
sldBottomRight	0	Bottom/Right. Tick marks are positioned along the bottom of the **Slider** if the control is oriented horizontally, or along the right side if it is oriented vertically.
sldTopLeft	1	Top/Left. Tick marks are positioned along the top of the **Slider** if the control is oriented horizontally, or along the left side if it is oriented vertically.
sldBoth	2	Both. Tick marks are positioned on both sides or top and bottom of the **Slider**.
sldNoTicks	3	None. No tick marks appear on the **Slider**.

See Also

Orientation Property (Slider Control), **TickStyle** Property, **Visual Basic** Constants

TickFrequency Property

Returns or sets the frequency of tick marks on a **Slider** control in relation to its range. For example, if the range is 100, and the **TickFrequency** property is set to 2, there will be one tick for every 2 increments in the range.

Applies To

Slider Control

Syntax

object.**TickFrequency** [= *number*]

The **TickFrequency** property syntax has these parts:

Part	Description
object	An object expression that evaluates to a **Slider** control.
number	A numeric expression specifying the frequency of tick marks.

See Also

GetNumTicks Method

Example

This example matches a **TextBox** control's width to that of a **Slider** control. While the **Slider** control's **Value** property is above a certain value, the **TextBox** control's width matches the **Slider** control's value. The **TickFrequency** depends on the value of the **Slider** control's **Max** property. To try the example, place a **Slider** and a **TextBox** control on a form and paste the code into the form's Declarations section. Run the example and click the slider several times.

```
Private Sub Form_Load()
    Text1.Width = 4500          ' Set a minimum width for the TextBox.
    Slider1.Left = Text1.Left   ' Align the Slider to the TextBox.
    ' Match the width of the Slider to the TextBox.
    Slider1.Max = Text1.Width
    ' Place the Slider a little below the Textbox.
    Slider1.Top = Text1.Top + Text1.Height + 50
    ' Set TickFrequency to a fraction of the Max value.
    Slider1.TickFrequency = Slider1.Max * 0.1
    ' Set LargeChange and SmallChange value to a fraction of Max.
    Slider1.LargeChange = Slider1.Max * 0.1
    Slider1.SmallChange = Slider1.Max * 0.01
End Sub

Private Sub Slider1_Change()
    ' If the slider is under 1/3 the size of the textbox, no change.
    ' Else, match the width of the textbox to the Slider's value.
    If Slider1.Value > Slider1.Max / 3 Then
        Text1.Width = Slider1.Value
    End If
End Sub
```

TickStyle Property

Returns or sets the style (or positioning) of the tick marks displayed on the **Slider** control.

Applies To

Slider Control

Syntax

object.**TickStyle** [= *number*]

The **TickStyle** property syntax has these parts:

Part	Description
object	An object expression that evaluates to a **Slider** control.
number	A constant or integer that specifies the **TickStyle** property, as described in **Settings**.

Settings

The settings for *number* are:

Constant	Value	Description
sldBottomRight	0	(Default) Bottom/Right. Tick marks are positioned along the bottom of the **Slider** if the control is oriented horizontally, or along the right side if it is oriented vertically.
sldTopLeft	1	Top/Left. Tick marks are positioned along the top of the **Slider** if the control is oriented horizontally, or along the left side if it is oriented vertically.
sldBoth	2	Both. Tick marks are positioned on both sides or top and bottom of the **Slider**.
sldNoTicks	3	None. No tick marks appear on the **Slider**.

See Also

GetNumTicks Method, **Slider** Constants

Example

This example allows you to see the various tick styles available in a drop-down list. To try the example, place a **Slider** control and a **ComboBox** control on a form. Paste the code into the Declarations section of the form, and run the example. **Click** on the **ComboBox** to change the **TickStyle** property value.

```
Private Sub Form_Load()
   With combo1
      .AddItem "Bottom/Right"
      .AddItem "Top/Left"
      .AddItem "Both"
      .AddItem "None"
      .ListIndex = 0
   End With
End Sub

Private Sub combo1_Click()
   Slider1.TickStyle = combo1.ListIndex
End Sub
```

StatusBar Control

A **StatusBar** control provides a window, usually at the bottom of a parent form, through which an application can display various kinds of status data. The **StatusBar** can be divided up into a maximum of sixteen **Panel** objects that are contained in a **Panels** collection.

Syntax

StatusBar

Remarks

A **StatusBar** control consists of **Panel** objects, each of which can contain text and/or a picture. Properties to control the appearance of individual panels include **Width**, **Alignment** (of text and pictures), and **Bevel**. Additionally, you can use one of seven values of the **Style** property to automatically display common data such as date, time, and keyboard states.

At design time, you can create panels and customize their appearance by setting values in the Panel tab of the Properties Page of the **StatusBar** control. At run time, the **Panel** objects can be reconfigured to reflect different functions, depending on the state of the application. For detailed information about the properties, events, and methods of **Panel** objects, see the **Panel** Object and **Panels** Collection topics.

A **StatusBar** control typically displays information about an object being viewed on the form, the object's components, or contextual information that relates to that object's operation. The **StatusBar**, along with other controls such as the **Toolbar** control, gives you the tools to create an interface that is economical and yet rich in information.

Distribution Note   The **StatusBar** control is part of a group of custom controls that are found in the COMCTL32.OCX file. To use the **StatusBar** control in your application, you must add the COMCTL32.OCX file to the project. When distributing your application, install the COMCTL32.OCX file in the user's Microsoft Windows SYSTEM directory. For more information on how to add a custom control to a project, see the *Programmer's Guide.*

Properties

Align Property, **Container** Property, **DragIcon** Property, **DragMode** Property, **Enabled** Property, **Font** Property, **Height, Width** Properties, **hWnd** Property, **Index** Property, **MouseIcon** Property, **MousePointer** Property, **Name** Property, **Object** Property, **OLEDropMode** Property, **Panels** Property, **Parent** Property, **ShowTips** Property, **Simple** Property, **Style** Property, **TabIndex** Property, **Tag** Property, **ToolTipText** Property, **Visible** Property, **WhatsThisHelpID** Property

Events

Click Event, **DblClick** Event, **DragDrop** Event, **DragOver** Event, **MouseDown, MouseUp** Events, **MouseMove** Event, **OLECompleteDrag** Event, **OLEDragDrop** Event, **OLEDragOver** Event, **OLEGiveFeedback** Event, **OLESetData** Event, **OLEStartDrag** Event, **PanelClick** Event, **PanelDblClick** Event

Methods

Drag Method, **Move** Method, **OLEDrag** Method, **Refresh** Method, **ShowWhatsThis** Method, **ZOrder** Method

See Also

StatusBar Control Constants, **Panel** Object, **Panels** Collection, **Alignment** Property (Panel Object), **Bevel** Property (Panel Object), **Width** Property (Panel Object), **Toolbar** Control

---

Add Method (Panels Collection)

Adds a **Panel** object to a **Panels** collection and returns a reference to the newly created **Panel** object.

Applies To

StatusBar Control, **Panels** Collection

Syntax

object.**Add**(*index, key, text, style, picture*)

The **Add** method syntax has these parts:

Part	Description
object	An object expression that evaluates to a **Panels** collection.
index	Optional. An integer specifying the position where the **Panel** object is to be inserted. If no *index* is specified, the **Panel** is added to the end of the **Panels** collection.
key	Optional. A unique string that identifies the **Panel**. Use *key* to retrieve a specific **Panel**. This is equivalent to setting the **Key** property of the new **Panel** object after the object has been added.
text	Optional. A string that appears in the **Panel**. This is equivalent to setting the **Text** property of the new **Panel** object after the object has been added.
style	Optional. The style of the panel. The available styles are detailed in the **Style** Property (Panel Object). This is equivalent to setting the **Style** property of the new **Panel** object after the object has been added.
picture	Optional. Specifies the bitmap displayed in the active **Panel**. For more information, see the **LoadPicture** function. This is equivalent to setting the **Picture** property of the new **Panel** object after the object has been added.

Remarks

At run time, the **Add** method returns a reference to the newly inserted **Panel** object. With this reference, you can set properties for every new **Panel** in the following manner:

```
Dim pnlX As Panel
Dim i As Integer
For i = 1 To 6                    ' Add six Panel objects.
    ' Create a panel and get a reference to it simultaneously.
    Set pnlX = StatusBar1.Panels.Add(, "Panel" & i)  ' Set Key property.
    pnlX.Style = i               ' Set Style property.
    pnlX.AutoSize = sbrContents  ' Set AutoSize property.
Next i
```

The value of the **Text** property is displayed in a **Panel** object when the **Panel** object's **Style** property is set to **sbrText**.

The **Panels** collection is a 1-based collection. In order to get a reference to the first (default) **Panel** in a collection, you can use its **Index** or **Key** (if there is one) properties, or the **Item** method. The following code references the first **Panel** object using its index.

```
Dim pnlX As Panel
                                   ' Get a reference to first Panel.
Set pnlX = StatusBar1.Panels(1)  ' Use the index
pnlX.Text = "Changed text"       ' Alter the Panel object's text.
```

By default, one **Panel** already exists on the control. Therefore, after adding panels to a collection, the **Count** will be one more than the number of panels added. For example:

```
Dim i as Integer
For i = 1 to 4                   ' Add four panels.
    StatusBar1.Panels.Add        ' Add panels without any properties.
Next i
MsgBox StatusBar1.Panels.Count   ' Returns 5 panels.
```

See Also

StatusBar Control Constants, **Alignment** Property (Panel Object), **AutoSize** Property (Panel Object), **Count** Property (VB Collections), **Index** Property (ActiveX Controls), **Key** Property (ActiveX Controls), **LoadPicture** Function, **Picture** Property (ActiveX Controls), **Style** Property, **Text** Property (ActiveX Controls)

Example

This example uses the **Add** method to add three new **Panel** objects to a **StatusBar** control. To use the example, place a **StatusBar** control on a form and paste the code into the form's Declarations section. Run the example.

```
Private Sub Form_Load()
Dim pnlX As Panel
    ' Add blank panel as a spacer
    Set pnlX = StatusBar1.Panels.Add()
    pnlX.AutoSize = sbrSpring
    pnlX.MinWidth = 1
```

```
' Add a panel with a clock icon and time style.
Set pnlX = StatusBar1.Panels.Add _
(, , , sbrTime, LoadPicture("Graphics\icons\misc\clock03.ico"))
' Add second panel, with bitmap and Date style.
Set pnlX = StatusBar1.Panels.Add _
(, , , sbrDate, LoadPicture("Graphics\bitmaps\assorted\calendar.bmp"))
' Set Bevel property for last Panel object.
pnlX.Bevel = sbrInset        ' Inset bevel.
pnlX.Alignment = sbrRight  ' Set Alignment property for last object.
' Set Text and AutoSize properties for first (default )Panel object.
StatusBar1.Panels(1).Text = "Add Panel Example"
StatusBar1.Panels(1).AutoSize = sbrContents
End Sub
```

Alignment Property (Panel Object)

Returns or sets the alignment of text in the caption of a **Panel** object in a **StatusBar** control.

Applies To

StatusBar Control, **Panel** Object

Syntax

object.**Alignment** [= *number*]

The **Alignment** property syntax has these parts:

Part	Description
object	An object expression that evaluates to a **Panel** object.
number	A constant or value specifying the type of action, as described in Settings.

Settings

The settings for *number* are:

Constant	Value	Description
sbrLeft	0	(Default). Text appears left-justified and to right of bitmap.
sbrCenter	1	Text appears centered and to right of bitmap.
sbrRight	2	Text appears right-justified and to left of bitmap.

Remarks

As well as positioning the text, the **Alignment** property specifies the position of the bitmap, as described in **Settings**. There is no way to independently position the bitmap within the panel.

See Also

StatusBar Control Constants, **Add** Method (Panels Collection), **Clear** Method (ActiveX Controls), **Remove** Method (ActiveX Controls)

Example

This example adds two **Panel** objects to a **StatusBar** control and aligns the text in each panel using one of the three available styles. To try the example, place a **StatusBar** control on a form and paste the code into the Declarations section of the form. Run the example.

```
Private Sub Form_Load()
    ' Declare variables.
    Dim pnlX As Panel
    Dim I As Integer

    For I = 1 To 2     ' Add two panels.
       StatusBar1.Panels.Add
    Next I

    For I = 1 To 3     ' Add pictures to each Panel.
       Set pnlX = StatusBar1.Panels(I)
       Set pnlX.Picture = LoadPicture("Graphics\icons\comm\net12.ico")
       ' Set AutoSize and MinWidth so that panels
       ' are always in view.
       pnlX.AutoSize = sbrSpring
       pnlX.MinWidth = 1
    Next I

    ' Set styles and alignment.
    With StatusBar1.Panels
       .Item(1).Text = "Left"
       .Item(1).Alignment = sbrLeft     ' Left alignment.
       .Item(2).Text = "Center"
       .Item(2).Alignment = sbrCenter   ' Centered alignment.
       .Item(3).Text = "Right"
       .Item(3).Alignment = sbrRight    ' Right alignment.
    End With
End Sub
```

AutoSize Property (Panel Object)

Returns or sets a value that determines the width of a **Panel** object after the **StatusBar** control has been resized.

Applies To

StatusBar Control, **Panel** Object

Syntax

object.**AutoSize** [= *number*]

The **AutoSize** property syntax has these parts:

Part	Description
object	An object expression that evaluates to a **Panel** object.
number	A constant or value specifying the type of action, as described in Settings.

Settings

The settings for *number* are:

Constant	Value	Description
sbrNoAutoSize	0	(Default) None. No autosizing occurs. The width of the **Panel** is always and exactly that specified by the **Width** property.
sbrSpring	1	Spring. When the parent form resizes and there is extra space available, all panels with this setting divide the space and grow accordingly. However, the panels' width never falls below that specified by the **MinWidth** property.
sbrContents	2	Content. The **Panel** is resized to fit its contents, however, the width will never fall below the width specified by the **MinWidth** property.

Remarks

Panel objects with the Contents style have precedence over those with the Spring style. This means that a Spring-style **Panel** is shortened if a **Panel** with the Contents style requires that space.

See Also

StatusBar Control Constants, **MinWidth** Property, **Width** Property (Panel Object)

Example

This example adds two **Panel** objects to a **StatusBar** control and sets the **AutoSize** property to Content for all panels. As the cursor is moved over the objects on the form, the x and y coordinates are displayed as well as the **Tag** property value for each control. To try the example, place a **StatusBar**, a **PictureBox**, and a **CommandButton** on a form, then paste the code into the Declarations section. Run the example and move the cursor over the various controls.

```
Private Sub Form_Load()
    Dim pnlX As Panel
    ' Set long tags for each object.
    Form1.Tag = "Project 1 Form"
    Command1.Tag = "A command button"
    Picture1.Tag = "Picture Box Caption"
    StatusBar1.Tag = "Application StatusBar1"
    ' Set the AutoSize style of the first panel to Contents.
    StatusBar1.Panels(1).AutoSize = sbrContents
    ' Add 2 more panels, and set them to Contents.
    Set pnlX = StatusBar1.Panels.Add
    pnlX.AutoSize = sbrContents
    Set pnlX = StatusBar1.Panels.Add
    pnlX.AutoSize = sbrContents
End Sub

Private Sub Form_MouseMove(Button As Integer, Shift As Integer,
x As Single, y As Single)
    ' Display the control's tag in panel 1, and x and y
    ' coordinates in panels 2 and 3. Because AutoSize = Contents,
    ' the first panel stretches to accommodate the varying text.
```

```
      StatusBar1.Panels(1).Text = Form1.Tag
      StatusBar1.Panels(2).Text = "X = " & x
      StatusBar1.Panels(3).Text = "Y = " & y
   End Sub

   Private Sub Command1_MouseMove(Button As Integer, Shift As Integer,
   x As Single, y As Single)
      StatusBar1.Panels(1).Text = Command1.Tag
      StatusBar1.Panels(2).Text = "X = " & x
      StatusBar1.Panels(3).Text = "Y = " & y
   End Sub

   Private Sub Picture1_MouseMove(Button As Integer, Shift As Integer,
   x As Single, y As Single)
      StatusBar1.Panels(1).Text = Picture1.Tag
      StatusBar1.Panels(2).Text = "X = " & x
      StatusBar1.Panels(3).Text = "Y = " & y
   End Sub

   Private Sub StatusBar1_MouseMove(Button As Integer, Shift As Integer,
   x As Single, y As Single)
      StatusBar1.Panels(1).Text = StatusBar1.Tag
      StatusBar1.Panels(2).Text = "X = " & x
      StatusBar1.Panels(3).Text = "Y = " & y
   End Sub
```

Bevel Property (Panel Object)

Returns or sets the bevel style of a **StatusBar** control's **Panel** object.

Applies To

StatusBar Control, **Panel** Object

Syntax

*object.***Bevel** [= *value*]

The **Bevel** property syntax has these parts:

Part	Description
object	An object expression that evaluates to a **Panel** object.
value	A constant or value which determines the bevel style, as specified in Settings.

Settings

The settings for *value* are:

Constant	Value	Description
sbrNoBevel	0	None. The **Panel** displays no bevel, and text looks like it is displayed right on the status bar.
sbrInset	1	(Default). Inset. The **Panel** appears to be sunk into the status bar.
sbrRaised	2	Raised. The **Panel** appears to be raised above the status bar.

See Also

StatusBar Control Constants, **Add** Method (Panels Collection)

Example

This example adds two **Panel** objects to a **StatusBar** control, and gives each **Panel** a different bevel style. To use the example, place a **StatusBar** control on a form and paste the code into the Declarations section. Run the example.

```
Private Sub Form_Load()
   Dim pnlX As Panel
   Dim I as Integer

   For I = 1 to 2
      Set pnlX = StatusBar1.Panels.Add()     ' Add 2 panels.
   Next I

   With StatusBar1.Panels
      .Item(1).Style = sbrCaps               ' Caps Lock
      .Item(1).Bevel = sbrInset              ' Inset
      .Item(2).Style = sbrNum                ' NumLock
      .Item(2).Bevel = sbrNoBevel            ' No bevel
      .Item(3).Style = sbrDate               ' Date
      .Item(3).Bevel = sbrRaised             ' Raised bevel
   End With
End Sub
```

MinWidth Property

Returns or sets the minimum width of a **StatusBar** control's **Panel** object.

Applies To

StatusBar Control, **Panel** Object

Syntax

object.**MinWidth** [= *value*]

The **MinWidth** property syntax has these parts:

Part	Description
object	An object expression that evaluates to a **Panel** object.
value	An integer that determines the minimum width of a **Panel** object. The scale mode for this value is determined by the container of the control.

Remarks

The **MinWidth** property is used when the **AutoSize** property is set to Contents or Spring, to prevent the panel from autosizing to a width that is too small. When the **AutoSize** property is set to None, the **MinWidth** property is always set to the same value as the **Width** property.

The default value is the same as the default of the Width property. The value argument uses the same scale units as the scale mode of the parent form or container.

See Also

AutoSize Property (Panel Object), **Width** Property (Panel Object)

Example

This example uses the default panel of a **StatusBar** control to display the current date. The **MinWidth** property is set so that when you click on the panel, the date is cleared but the panel remains the same size. To use the example, place a **StatusBar** control on a form, and paste the code into the Declarations section. Run the example and click on the **Panel** object to clear the date.

```
Private Sub Form_Load()
    StatusBar1.Panels(1).AutoSize = sbrContents
    StatusBar1.Panels(1).Text = "Today's Date is: " & Str(Now)
    ' Set minimum width to the current size of panel
    StatusBar1.Panels(1).MinWidth = StatusBar1.Panels(1).Width
End Sub

Private Sub StatusBar1_PanelClick(ByVal Panel As ComctlLib.Panel)
    ' Clear today's date but keep size at minimum width.
    Panel.Text = "Today's Date is: "
End Sub
```

Panel Object

A **Panel** object represents an individual panel in the **Panels** collection of a **StatusBar** control.

Remarks

A **Panel** object can contain text and a bitmap which may be used to reflect the status of an application.

Use the **Panels** collection to retrieve, add, or remove an individual **Panel** object.

To change the look of a panel, change the properties of the **Panel** object. To modify the properties at design-time, you can change the properties of the **Panel** object in the Panels tab of the Properties Page. At run-time, you can change the **Panel** object properties in code.

Properties

Alignment Property, **AutoSize** Property, **Bevel** Property, **Enabled** Property, **Index** Property, **Key** Property, **Left, Top** Properties, **MinWidth** Property, **Picture** Property, **Style** Property, **Tag** Property, **ToolTipText** Property, **Visible** Property, **Width** Property

See Also

StatusBar Control, **Add** Method (Panels Collection), **Panels** Property, **Properties** Window, **Property Pages Dialog Box**

PanelClick Event

The **PanelClick** event is similar to the standard **Click** event but occurs when a user presses and then releases a mouse button over any of the **StatusBar** control's **Panel** objects.

Applies To

StatusBar Control

Syntax

Private Sub *object*_**PanelClick(ByVal** *panel* **As Panel)**

The **PanelClick** event syntax has these parts:

Part	Description
object	An object expression that evaluates to a **StatusBar** control.
panel	A reference to a **Panel** object.

Remarks

The standard **Click** event also occurs when a **Panel** object is clicked.

The **PanelClick** event is only generated when the click occurs over a **Panel** object. When the **StatusBar** control's **Style** property is set to Simple style, panels are hidden, and therefore the **PanelClick** event is not generated.

You can use the reference to the **Panel** object to set properties for that panel. For example, the following code resets the **Bevel** property of a clicked **Panel**:

```
Private Sub StatusBar1_PanelClick(ByVal Panel As Panel)
   Select Case Panel.Key
   Case "DisplayFileName"     ' Key="DisplayFileName"
     Panel.Bevel = sbrRaised  ' Reset Bevel property
   ' Add other case statements for other panels
   End Select
End Sub
```

See Also

Panel Object, **Bevel** Property (Panel Object), **PanelDblClick** Event, **Style** Property (Panel Object)

Example

This example adds two **Panel** objects to a **StatusBar** control; when each **Panel** is clicked, the value of the **Key** and **Width** properties of the clicked **Panel** are displayed in the third **Panel**. To try the example, place a **StatusBar** control on a form and paste the code into the Declarations section. Run the example.

```
Private Sub Form_Load()
   Dim I as Integer
   For I = 1 to 2
      StatusBar1.Panels.Add
   Next I
```

```
    With StatusBar1.Panels
        .Item(1).Style = sbrDate
        .Item(1).Key = "Date panel"
        .Item(1).AutoSize = sbrContents
        .Item(1).MinWidth = 2000
        .Item(2).Style = sbrTime
        .Item(2).Key = "Time panel"
        .Item(3).AutoSize = sbrContents ' Content
        .Item(3).Text = "Panel 3"
        .Item(3).Key = "Panel 3"
    End With
End Sub

Private Sub StatusBar1_PanelClick(ByVal Panel As Panel)
    ' Show clicked panel's key and width in Panel 3.
    StatusBar1.Panels("Panel 3").Text = Panel.Key & " Width = " & Panel.Width
End Sub
```

PanelDblClick Event

The **PanelDblClick** event is similar to the standard **DblClick** Event but occurs when a user presses and then releases a mouse button twice over a **StatusBar** control's **Panel** object.

Applies To

StatusBar Control

Syntax

Sub *object*_**PanelDblClick(ByVal** *panel* **As Panel)**

The **PanelDblClick** event syntax has these parts:

Part	Description
object	An object expression that evaluates to a **StatusBar** control.
panel	A reference to the double-clicked **Panel**.

Remarks

The standard **DblClick** event also occurs when a **Panel** is double-clicked.

The **PanelDblClick** event is only generated when the double-click occurs over a **Panel** object. When the **StatusBar** control's **Style** property is set to Simple style, panels are hidden, and therefore the **PanelDblClick** event is not generated.

See Also

Panel Object, **PanelClick** Event, **Style** Property (Panel Object)

Example

This example adds two **Panel** objects to a **StatusBar** control. When the user double-clicks on the control, the text of the clicked **Panel** object is displayed. To try the example, place a **StatusBar** control on a form and paste the code into the form's Declarations section. Run the example and double-click on the control.

```
Private Sub Form_Load()
Dim I as Integer
    For I = 1 to 2
        StatusBar1.Panels.Add
    Next I

    With StatusBar1.Panels
        .Item(1).Text = "A long piece of information."
        .Item(1).AutoSize = sbrContents ' Content
        .Item(2).Style = sbrDate        ' Date style
        .Item(2).AutoSize = sbrContents ' Content
        .Item(3).Style = sbrTime        ' Time style
    End With
End Sub

Private Sub StatusBar1_PanelDblClick(ByVal Panel As Panel)
    MsgBox "Panel.Style = " & Panel.Style
End Sub
```

Panels Collection

A **Panels** collection contains a collection of **Panel** objects.

Syntax

statusbar.**Panels**(*index*)

The **Panels** collection syntax has these parts.

Part	Description
statusbar	An object expression that evaluates to a **StatusBar** control.
Index	An integer or string that uniquely identifies the object in the collection. The integer is the value of the **Index** property of the desired **Panel** object; the string is the value of the **Key** property of the desired **Panel** object.

Remarks

The **Panels** collection is a 1-based array of **Panel** objects. By default, there is one **Panel** object on a **StatusBar** control. Therefore, if you want three panels to be created, you only need to add two objects to the **Panels** collection.

The **Panels** property returns a reference to a **Panels** collection.

To add a **Panel** object to a collection, use the **Add** method for **Panel** objects at run time, or the Panels tab on the Properties Page of the **StatusBar** control at design time.

Each item in the collection can be accessed by its **Index** property or its **Key** property. For example, to get a reference to the third **Panel** object in a collection, use the following syntax:

```
Dim pnlX As Panel
Set pnlX = StatusBar1.Panels(3)          ' Reference by index number.
                                         ' or
Set pnlX = StatusBar1.Panels("Third")    ' Reference by unique key.
                                         ' or
Set pnlX = StatusBar1.Panels.Item(3)     ' Use Item method.
```

Properties

Count Property, **Item** Property

Methods

Add Method (Panels Collection), **Clear** Method, **Remove** Method

See Also

Index Property (ActiveX Controls), **Key** Property (ActiveX Controls), **Panel** Object, **Panels** Property, **Property Pages Dialog Box**

Panels Property

Returns a reference to a collection of **Panel** objects.

Applies To

StatusBar Control

Syntax

object.**Panels**

The *object* placeholder is an object expression that evaluates to a **StatusBar** control.

See Also

Panels Collection, **Panel** Object, **AutoSize** Property (Panel Object), **Width** Property (Panel Object)

ShowTips Property (ActiveX Controls)

Returns a value that determines whether **ToolTips** are displayed for an object.

Applies To

StatusBar Control, **TabStrip** Control, **Toolbar** Control

Syntax

object.**ShowTips** [= *value*]

The **ShowTips** property syntax has these parts:

Part	Description
object	An object expression that evaluates to an object in the **Applies To** list.
value	A Boolean expression specifying whether **ToolTips** are displayed, as described in Settings.

Settings

The settings for *value* are:

Setting	Description
True	(Default) Each object in the control may display an associated string, which is the setting of the **ToolTipText** property, in a small rectangle below the object. This **ToolTip** appears when the user's cursor hovers over the object at run time for about one second.
False	An object will not display a **ToolTip** at run time.

Remarks

At design time you can set the **ShowTips** property on the General tab in the control's Property Pages dialog box.

See Also

ToolTipText Property

SimpleText Property

Returns or sets the text displayed when a **StatusBar** control's **Style** property is set to Simple.

Applies To

StatusBar Control

Syntax

object.**SimpleText** [= *string*]

The **SimpleText** property syntax has these parts:

Part	Description
object	An object expression that evaluates to a **StatusBar** control.
string	A string that is displayed when the **Style** property is set to Simple.

Remarks

The **StatusBar** control has a **Style** property which can be toggled between Simple and Normal styles. When in Simple style, the status bar displays only one panel. The text displayed in Simple style is also different from that displayed in Normal style. This text is set with the **SimpleText** property.

The **SimpleText** property can be used in situations where an application's mode of operation temporarily switches. For example, when a menu is pulled down, the **SimpleText** could describe the menu's purpose.

See Also

Style Property (StatusBar Control)

Example

This example adds two **Panel** objects to a **StatusBar** control that appear in Normal style, and then adds a string (using the **SimpleText** property) that appears when the **Style** property is set to Simple. The control toggles between the Simple style and the Normal style. To try the example, place a **StatusBar** control on a form and paste the code into the Declarations section of the form. Run the example and click on the **StatusBar** control.

```
Private Sub Form_Load()
   Dim I As Integer
   For I = 1 to 2
      StatusBar1.Panels.Add          ' Add 2 Panel objects.
   Next I

   With StatusBar1.Panels
      .Item(1).Style = sbrNum        ' Number lock
      .Item(2).Style = sbrCaps       ' Caps lock
      .Item(3).Style = sbrScrl       ' Scroll lock
   End With
End Sub

Private Sub StatusBar1_Click()
   ' Toggle between simple and normal style.
   With StatusBar1
      If .Style = 0 Then
         ' This text will be displayed when the StatusBar is in Simple style.
         .SimpleText = "Date and Time: " & Now
         .Style = sbrSimple          ' Simple style.
      Else
         .Style = sbrNormal          ' Normal style.
      End If
   End With
End Sub
```

StatusBar Control Constants

StatusBar Style Constants

Constant	Value	Description
sbrNormal	0	Normal. **StatusBar** is divided into panels.
sbrSimple	1	Simple. **StatusBar** has only one large panel and **SimpleText**.

Panel Alignment Constants

Constant	Value	Description
sbrLeft	0	Text to left.
sbrCenter	1	Text centered.
sbrRight	2	Text to right.

Panel Autosize Constants

Constant	Value	Description
sbrNoAutoSize	0	No Autosizing.
sbrSpring	1	Extra space divided among panels.
sbrContents	2	Fit to contents.

Panel Bevel Constants

Constant	Value	Description
sbrNoBevel	0	No bevel.
sbrInset	1	Bevel inset.
sbrRaised	2	Bevel raised.

Panel Style Constants

Constant	Value	Description
sbrText	0	Text and/or bitmap displayed.
sbrCaps	1	Caps Lock status displayed.
sbrNum	2	Number Lock status displayed.
sbrIns	3	Insert key status displayed.
sbrScrl	4	Scroll Lock status displayed.
sbrTime	5	Time displayed in System format.
sbrDate	6	Date displayed in System format.
sbrKana	7	Kana. displays the letters KANA in bold when scroll lock is enabled, and dimmed when disabled.

See Also

ActiveX Control Constants, **Alignment** Property (Panel Object), **AutoSize** Property (Panel Object), **Bevel** Property (Panel Object), **SimpleText** Property, **Style** Property (StatusBar Control), **Style** Property (Panel Object), **Visual Basic** Constants

Style Property (Panel Object)

Returns or sets the style of a **StatusBar** control's **Panel** object.

Applies To

StatusBar Control, **Panel** Object

Syntax

object.**Style** [= *number*]

The **Style** property syntax has these parts:

Part	Description
object	An object expression that evaluates to a **Panel** object.
number	An integer or constant specifying the style of the **Panel**, as described in Settings.

Settings

The settings for *number* are:

Constant	Value	Description
sbrText	0	(Default). Text and/or a bitmap. Set text with the **Text** property.
sbrCaps	1	Caps Lock key. Displays the letters CAPS in bold when Caps Lock is enabled, and dimmed when disabled.
sbrNum	2	Number Lock. Displays the letters NUM in bold when the number lock key is enabled, and dimmed when disabled.
sbrIns	3	Insert key. Displays the letters INS in bold when the insert key is enabled, and dimmed when disabled.
sbrScrl	4	Scroll Lock key. Displays the letters SCRL in bold when scroll lock is enabled, and dimmed when disabled.
sbrTime	5	Time. Displays the current time in the system format.
sbrDate	6	Date. Displays the current date in the system format.
sbrKana	7	Kana. displays the letters KANA in bold when scroll lock is enabled, and dimmed when disabled.

Remarks

If you set the **Style** property to any style except 0 (text and bitmap), any text set with the **Text** property will not display unless the **Style** property is set to 0.

The **Style** property can be set as **Panel** objects are added to a collection. See the **Add** method for more information.

Note   The **StatusBar** control also has a **Style** property. When the **StatusBar** control's **Style** is set to Simple, the control displays only one large panel and its string (set with the **SimpleText** property).

See Also

StatusBar Control Constants, **Panels** Collection, **Add** Method (Panels Collection), **SimpleText** Property, **Style** Property (StatusBar Control), **Text** Property (ActiveX Controls)

Example

This example displays data in the various styles on a **StatusBar** control. To try this example, place a **StatusBar** control on a form and paste the code into the form's Declarations section, and run the example.

```
Private Sub Form_Load()
    ' Dim variables.
    Dim I as Integer
    Dim pnlX as Panel

    For I = 1 to 5                    ' Add 5 panels.
       Set pnlX = StatusBar1.Panels.Add( )
    Next I

                                     ' Set the style of each panel.
    With StatusBar1.Panels
       .Item(1).Style = sbrDate      ' Date
       .Item(2).Style = sbrTime      ' Time
       .Item(3).Style = sbrCaps      ' Caps lock
       .Item(4).Style = sbrNum       ' Number lock
       .Item(5).Style = sbrIns       ' Insert key
       .Item(6).Style = sbrScrl      ' Scroll lock
    End With
    Form1.Width = 9140               ' Widen form to show all panels.
End Sub
```

Style Property (StatusBar Control)

Returns or sets the style of a **StatusBar** control.

Applies To

StatusBar Control

Syntax

object.**Style** [= *number*]

The **Style** property syntax has these parts:

Part	Description
object	An object expression that evaluates to a **StatusBar** control.
number	An integer or constant that determines the appearance of the **StatusBar** control, as specified in Settings.

Settings

The settings for *number* are:

Constant	Value	Description
sbrNormal	0	(Default). Normal. The **StatusBar** control shows all **Panel** objects.
sbrSimple	1	Simple. The control displays only one large panel.

Remarks

The **StatusBar** can toggle between two modes: Normal and Simple. When in Simple style, the **StatusBar** displays only one panel. The appearance also changes: the bevel style is raised with no borders. This allows the control to have two appearances, both of which are maintained separately from each other.

You can display different strings depending on the control's style. Use the **SimpleText** property to set the text of the string to be displayed when the **Style** property is set to Simple.

Note When the **Style** property is set to Simple, the **StatusBar** control displays a large panel (the width of the control) which cannot be controlled through the Panels collection.

See Also

StatusBar Control Constants, **Panel** Object, **SimpleText** Property, **Style** Property (Panel Object)

Example

This example adds two **Panel** objects to a **StatusBar** control that appear in Normal style, and then adds a string (using the **SimpleText** property) that will appear when the **Style** property is set to Simple. The control toggles between the Simple style and the Normal style to show the **SimpleText** property string. To try the example, place a **StatusBar** control on a form and paste the code into the Declarations section of the form. Run the example and click on the **StatusBar** control.

```
Private Sub Form_Load()
   Dim I As Integer
   For I = 1 to 2
      StatusBar1.Panels.Add
   Next I
   With StatusBar1.Panels
      .Item(1).Style = sbrDate        ' Date
      .Item(2).Style = sbrCaps        ' Caps lock
      .Item(3).Style = sbrScrl        ' Scroll lock
   End With

End Sub


Private Sub StatusBar1_Click()
   With StatusBar1
      If .Style = sbrNormal Then
         .SimpleText = Time           ' Show the time.
         .Style = sbrSimple           ' Simple style
      Else
         .Style = sbrNormal           ' Normal style
      End If
   End With
End Sub
```

Width Property (Panel Object)

Returns or sets the current width of a **StatusBar** control's **Panel** object.

Applies To

StatusBar Control, **Panel** Object

Syntax

*object.***Width**[= *number*]

The **Width** property syntax has these parts:

Part	Description
object	An object expression that evaluates to a **Panel** object.
number	An integer that determines the width of the **Panel**.

Remarks

The **Width** property always reflects the actual width of a **Panel** and can't be smaller than the **MinWidth** property.

See Also

MinWidth Property

Example

This example creates three **Panel** objects and sets their **Width** property to different values. When you click on the form, the **Width** property of the first **Panel** is reset. To try the example, place a **StatusBar** control on a form, and paste the code into the Declarations section. Run the example and click on each panel to see its width.

```
Private Sub Form_Load()
   Dim X As Panel
   Dim I as Integer
   For I = 1 to 2        ' Add 2 panels.
      Set X = StatusBar1.Panels.Add()
   Next I
   With StatusBar1.Panels
      .Item(1).Text = "Path = " & App.Path
      .Item(1).AutoSize = sbrContents        ' Contents
      .Item(1).Width = 2000                  ' A long panel
      .Item(2).Text = "Record Field"
      .Item(2).AutoSize = sbrSpring          ' Spring
      .Item(2).Width = 1000                  ' A medium panel
      .Item(3).Style = sbrTime               ' Time
      .Item(3).AutoSize = sbrSpring          ' Spring
      .Item(3).Width = 500                   ' A medium panel
   End With
End Sub

Private Sub Form_Click()
                                           ' Change Width.
   StatusBar1.Panels(1). Width = 800
End Sub
```

TabStrip Control

A **TabStrip** control is like the dividers in a notebook or the labels on a group of file folders. By using a **TabStrip** control, you can define multiple pages for the same area of a window or dialog box in your application.

Syntax

TabStrip

Remarks

The control consists of one or more **Tab** objects in a **Tabs** collection. At both design time and run time, you can affect the **Tab** object's appearance by setting properties. You can also add and remove tabs using the Properties Page of the **TabStrip** control at design time, or add and remove **Tab** objects at run time using methods.

The **Style** property determines whether the **TabStrip** control looks like push buttons (Buttons) or notebook tabs (Tabs). At design time when you put a **TabStrip** control on a form, it has one notebook tab. If the **Style** property is set to **tabTabs**, then there will be a border around the **TabStrip** control's internal area. When the **Style** property is set to **tabButtons**, no border is displayed around the internal area of the control, however, that area still exists.

To set the overall size of the **TabStrip** control, use its drag handles and/or set the **Top**, **Left**, **Height**, and **Width** properties. Based on the control's overall size at run time, Visual Basic automatically determines the size and position of the internal area and returns the Client-coordinate properties–**ClientLeft**, **ClientTop**, **ClientHeight**, and **ClientWidth**. The **MultiRow** property determines whether the control can have more than one row of tabs, the **TabWidthStyle** property determines the appearance of each row, and, if **TabWidthStyle** is set to **tabFixed**, you can use the **TabFixedHeight** and **TabFixedWidth** properties to set the same height and width for all tabs in the **TabStrip** control.

The **TabStrip** control is not a container. To contain the actual pages and their objects, you must use **Frame** controls or other containers that match the size of the internal area which is shared by all **Tab** objects in the control. If you use a control array for the container, you can associate each item in the array with a specific **Tab** object, as in the following example:

```
Option Explicit
Private mintCurFrame As Integer        ' Current Frame visible

Private Sub Tabstrip1_Click()
   If Tabstrip1.SelectedItem.Index = mintCurFrame _
      Then Exit Sub              ' No need to change frame.
   ' Otherwise, hide old frame, show new.
   Frame1(Tabstrip1.SelectedItem.Index).Visible = True
   Frame1(mintCurFrame).Visible = False
   ' Set mintCurFrame to new value.
   mintCurFrame = Tabstrip1.SelectedItem.Index
End Sub
```

Note   When grouping controls on a container, you must use the show/hide strategy shown above instead of using the **Zorder Method** to bring a frame to the front. Otherwise, controls that implement access keys (ALT + access key) will still respond to keyboard commands, even if the container is not the topmost control. Also note that you must segregate groups of **OptionButton** controls by placing each group on its own container, or else all **OptionButtons** on the form will behave as one large group of **OptionButtons**.

Tip   Use a **Frame** control with its **BorderStyle** set to None as the container instead of a **PictureBox** control. A **Frame** control uses less overhead than a **PictureBox** control.

The **Tabs** property of the **TabStrip** control is the collection of all the **Tab** objects. Each **Tab** object has properties associated with its current state and appearance. For example, you can associate an **ImageList** control with the **TabStrip** control, and then use images on individual tabs. You can also associate a ToolTip with each **Tab** object.

Distribution Note   The **TabStrip** control is part of a group of custom controls that are found in the COMCTL32.OCX file. To use the **TabStrip** control in your application, you must add the COMCTL32.OCX file to the project. When distributing your application, install the COMCTL32.OCX file in the user's Microsoft Windows SYSTEM directory. For more information on how to add a custom control to a project, see the *Programmer's Guide*.

Properties

ClientHeight, ClientWidth, ClientLeft, ClientTop Properties**, Container** Property, **DataBinding** Object, **DataBindings** Property, **DragIcon** Property, **DragMode** Property, **Enabled** Property, **Font** Property, **Height, Width** Properties**, HelpContextID** Property, **hWnd** Property, **ImageList** Property, **Index** Property, **Left, Top** Properties, **MouseIcon** Property, **MousePointer** Property, **MultiRow** Property, **Name** Property, **Object** Property, **OLEDropMode** Property, **Parent** Property, **SelectedItem** Property, **ShowTips** Property, **Style** Property, **Tab** Object, **TabFixedHeight, TabFixedWidth** Properties, **T abIndex** Property, **Tabs** Collection, **Tabs** Property, **TabStop** Property, **TabWidthStyle** Property, **Tag** Property, **ToolTipText** Property, **Visible** Property, **WhatsThisHelpID** Property

Events

BeforeClick Event, **Click** Event, **DragDrop** Event, **DragOver** Event, **GotFocus** Event, **KeyDown, KeyUp** Events**, KeyPress** Event, **LostFocus** Event, **MouseDown, MouseUp** Events**, MouseMove** Event, **OLECompleteDrag** Event, **OLEDragDrop** Event, **OLEDragOver** Event, **OLEGiveFeedback** Event, **OLESetData** Event, **OLEStartDrag** Event

Methods

Drag Method, **Move** Method, **OLEDrag** Method, **Refresh** Method, **SetFocus** Method, **ShowWhatsThis** Method, **ZOrder** Method

See Also

ImageList Control, **Tab** Object, **Tabs** Collection, **TabStrip** Control Constants, **ClientHeight, ClientWidth, ClientLeft, ClientTop** Properties, **MultiRow** Property, **Style** Property (TabStrip Control), **Selected** Property (ActiveX Controls), **SelectedItem** Property (ActiveX Controls), **BorderStyle** Property, **Frame** Control, **Height, Width** Properties, **PictureBox** Control, **ZOrder** Method, **Left, Top** Properties, **PictureBox** Control

Add Method (Tabs Collection)

Adds a **Tab** object to a **Tabs** collection in a **TabStrip** control.

Applies To

TabStrip Control, **Tabs** Collection

Syntax

object.**Add**(*index, key, caption, image*)

The **Add** method syntax has these parts:

Part	Description
object	An object expression that evaluates to a **Tabs** collection.
index	Optional. An integer specifying the position where you want to insert the **Tab**. If you don't specify an index, the **Tab** is added to the end of the **Tabs** collection.
key	Optional. A unique string that identifies the **Tab**. Use key to retrieve a specific Tab. This is equivalent to setting the **Key** property of the new **Tab** object after the object has been added to the **Tabs** collection.
caption	Optional. The string that appears on the **Tab**. This is equivalent to setting the **Caption** property of the new **Tab** object after the object has been added to the **Tabs** collection.
image	Optional. The index of an image in an associated **ImageList** control. This image is displayed on the tab. This is equivalent to setting the **Image** property of the new **Tab** object after the object has been added to the **Tabs** collection.

Remarks

To add tabs to the **TabStrip** control at design time, click the Insert Tab button on the Tab tab in the Properties Page of the **TabStrip** control, and then fill in the appropriate fields for the new tab.

To add tabs to the **TabStrip** control at run time, use the **Add** method, which returns a reference to the newly inserted **Tab** object. For example, the following code adds a tab with the *caption*, "Howdy!" whose *key* is "MyTab," as the second tab (its *index* is 2):

```
Set X = TabStrip1.Tabs.Add(2,"MyTab","Howdy!")
```

See Also

Caption Property (Tab Object), **ImageList** Control, **Tab** Object, **Properties** Window, **Property Pages** Dialog Box

Example

This example adds three **Tab** objects, each with captions and images from an **ImageList** control, to a **TabStrip** control. To try this example, put an **ImageList** and a **TabStrip** control on a form. The **ImageList** control supplies the images for the **Tab** objects, so add three images to the **ImageList** control. Paste the following code into the Load event of the Form object, and run the program.

```
Private Sub Form_Load()
   Dim X As Integer
   Set TabStrip1.ImageList = ImageList1
   TabStrip1.Tabs(1).Caption = "Time"
   TabStrip1.Tabs.Add 2, , "Date"
   TabStrip1.Tabs.Add 3, , "Mail"
   For X = 1 To TabStrip1.Tabs.Count
      TabStrip1.Tabs(X).Image = X
   Next X
End Sub
```

BeforeClick Event

Generated when a **Tab** object in a **TabStrip** control is clicked, or a **Tab** object's **Selected** setting has changed.

Applies To

TabStrip Control

Syntax

Private Sub *object*_**BeforeClick**(*cancel* **As Integer**)

The **BeforeClick** event syntax has these parts:

Part	Description
object	An object expression that evaluates to a **TabStrip** control.
cancel	Evaluates to an integer with values of 0 (False) and -1 (True). The initial value is 0.

Remarks

Use the **BeforeClick** event to validate the information on the old **Tab** object before actually generating a **Click** event that selects the new **Tab** object. Setting the *cancel* argument to **True** allows you to stop a change to the new selection.

Note Setting the *cancel* argument to **True** prevents the focus from switching to another tab but doesn't stop the **Click** event from occurring.

Note If you use the **MsgBox** or **InputBox** functions during the **BeforeClick** event procedure, the **TabStrip** control will not receive a **Click** event, regardless of the setting of the *cancel* argument.

See Also

InputBox Function, **MsgBox** Function, **SelectedItem** Property (ActiveX Controls), **Tab** Object

Example

This example uses the **BeforeClick** event to demonstrate how to prevent a user from switching to another tab. This is useful when you want to verify information on the current tab before displaying the newly selected tab.

To try this example, place a **TabStrip** control and a two-element **Frame** control array on the form (set the **BorderStyle** properties to None). In the first **Frame** control, add a **CheckBox** control and in the second, add a **TextBox**. Paste the following code into the Load event of the Form object, and run the program. Click the tab labeled Text after you select/deselect the **CheckBox** on the tab labeled Check.

```
Private Sub Form_Load()
Dim i As Integer
Dim Tabx As Object
' Sets the caption of the first tab to "Check."
TabStrip1.Tabs(1).Caption = "Check"
' Adds a second tab with "Text" as its caption.
Set Tabx = TabStrip1.Tabs.Add(2, , "Text")
' Labels the checkbox.
Check1.Caption = "Cancel tab switch"
   ' Aligns the Frames with the internal area
   ' of the Tabstrip Control.
   For i = 0 To 1
      Frame1(i).Left = TabStrip1.ClientLeft
      Frame1(i).Top = TabStrip1.ClientTop
      Frame1(i).Height = TabStrip1.ClientHeight
      Frame1(i).Width = TabStrip1.ClientWidth
   Next
   ' Puts the first tab's Frame container on top.
   Frame1(0).ZOrder 0
End Sub


' The BeforeClick event verifies the check box value
' to determine whether to proceed with the Click event.
Private Sub TabStrip1_BeforeClick(Cancel As Integer)
   If TabStrip1.Tabs(1).Selected Then
      If Check1.Value = 1 Then Cancel = True
   End If
End Sub

Private Sub TabStrip1_Click()
   Frame1(TabStrip1.SelectedItem.Index-1).ZOrder 0
End Sub
```

Caption Property (Tab Object)

Returns or sets the caption that appears on the tab or button of a **Tab** object in a **TabStrip** control.

Applies To

SSTab Control, **TabStrip** Control, **Tab** Object

Syntax

object.**Caption** [= *string*]

The **Caption** property syntax has these parts:

Part	Description
object	An object expression that evaluates to a **Tab** object.
string	A string expression that evaluates to the text displayed as the caption.

Remarks

You can set the **Caption** property for a **Tab** object in the **TabStrip** control at design time or at run time.

- Design time—On the Tab tab in the Properties Page of the **TabStrip** control, type the caption string in the Caption text box.

- Run time—Set the caption as follows:

```
TabStrip1.Tabs(1).Caption = "First Tab"
```

Or

```
TabStrip1.Tabs.Add 2, , "Second Tab"
```

See Also

Add Method (Tabs Collection)

Example

This example sets the **Caption** property for each of three **Tab** objects it adds to a **TabStrip** control. The caption strings are "Time," "Date," and "Mail." Each **Tab** object also displays an image from an **ImageList** control. To try this example, place an **ImageList** and a **TabStrip** control on a form. Place three sample bitmaps in the **ImageList** control. The **ImageList** control supplies the images for the **Tab** objects. Paste the following code into the Load event of the Form object, and run the program.

```
Private Sub Form_Load()
    Dim X As Integer
    ' Associate an ImageList with the TabStrip control.
    Set TabStrip1.ImageList = ImageList1
    ' Set the captions.
    TabStrip1.Tabs(1).Caption = "Time"
    TabStrip1.Tabs.Add 2, , "Date"
    TabStrip1.Tabs.Add 3, , "Mail"
    For X = 1 To TabStrip1.Tabs.Count
        ' Associate an image with a tab.
        TabStrip1.Tabs(X).Image = X
    Next X
End Sub
```

ClientHeight, ClientWidth, ClientLeft, ClientTop Properties

Return the coordinates of the internal area (display area) of the **TabStrip** control. Read-only at run time; not available at design time.

Applies To

TabStrip Control

Syntax

object.**ClientHeight**
object.**ClientWidth**
object.**ClientLeft**
object.**ClientTop**

The *object* placeholder represents an object expression that evaluates to a **TabStrip** control.

Remarks

At run time, the client-coordinate properties **ClientLeft**, **ClientTop**, **ClientHeight**, and **ClientWidth** automatically store the coordinates of the **TabStrip** control's internal area, which is shared by all **Tab** objects in the control. So that the controls associated with a specific **Tab** appear when that **Tab** object is selected, place the **Tab** object's controls inside a container, such as a **Frame** control, whose size and position match the client-coordinate properties. To associate a container (and its controls) with a **Tab** object, create a control array, such as a **Frame** control array.

All client-coordinate properties use the scale mode of the parent form. To place a **Frame** control so it fits perfectly in the internal area, use the following code:

```
Frame1.Left = TabStrip1.ClientLeft
Frame1.Top = TabStrip1.ClientTop
Frame1.Width = TabStrip1.ClientWidth
Frame1.Height = TabStrip1.ClientHeight
```

To create the effect of placing a new tab and its associated container on top when the tab is selected:

- Set the size and location of the container in the **TabStrip** control's internal area to the client-coordinate properties; and

- Use the **ZOrder** method to place the selected tab's container control at the front or back of the z-order.

See Also

Tab Object, **Frame** Control, **ZOrder** Method

Example

The following example demonstrates using the Client-coordinate properties—
ClientLeft, ClientTop, ClientWidth, and **ClientHeight**—along with a **Frame**
control array to display tab—specific objects in the internal area of the **TabStrip**
control when switching tabs. The example uses the **ZOrder** method to display the
appropriate **Frame** control and the objects it contains.

To try this example, place a **TabStrip** control and a three-element **Frame** control
array on the form. In one **Frame** control, place a **CheckBox** control, in another, place
a **CommandButton** control, and in the third, place a **TextBox** control. Paste the
following code into the **Load** event of the **Form** object, and run the program. **Click**
the various tabs to select them and their contents.

```
Private Sub Form_Load()
Dim Tabx As Object
Dim i As Integer
    ' Sets the caption of the first tab to "Check."
    TabStrip1.Tabs(1).Caption = "Check"
    ' Adds a second tab with "Command" as its caption.
    Set Tabx = TabStrip1.Tabs.Add(2, , "Command")
    ' Adds a third tab with "Text" as its caption.
    Set Tabx = TabStrip1.Tabs.Add(3, , "Text")

    ' Aligns the frame containers with the internal
    ' area of the TabStrip control.
    For i = 0 To 2
        With TabStrip1
            Frame1(i).Move .ClientLeft, .ClientTop, _
            .ClientWidth, .ClientHeight
        End With
    Next
    ' Puts the first tab's picture box container on top
    ' at startup.
    Frame1(0).ZOrder 0
End Sub

Private Sub TabStrip1_Click()
    Frame1(TabStrip1.SelectedItem.Index - 1).ZOrder 0
End Sub
```

MultiRow Property

Returns or sets a value indicating whether a **TabStrip** control can display more than
one row of tabs.

Applies To

TabStrip Control

Syntax

*object.***MultiRow** [= *boolean*]

The **MultiRow** property syntax has these parts:

Part	Description
object	An object expression that evaluates to a **TabStrip** control.
boolean	A Boolean expression that specifies whether the control has more than one row of tabs, as described in **Settings**.

Settings

The settings for *boolean* are:

Setting	Description
True	Allows more than one row of tabs.
False	Restricts tabs to a single row.

Remarks

The number of rows is automatically set by the width and number of the tabs. The number of rows can change if the control is resized, which ensures that the tab wraps to the next row. If **MultiRow** is set to **False**, and the last tab exceeds the width of the control, a horizontal spin control is added at the right end of the **TabStrip** control.

At design time, set the **MultiRow** property on the General tab in the Properties Page of the **TabStrip** control. At run time, use code like the following to set the **MultiRow** property:

```
'Allows more than one row of tabs in the TabStrip control.
TabStrip1.MultiRow = TRUE
```

See Also

TabStrip Control Constants, **ClientHeight, ClientWidth, ClientLeft, ClientTop** Properties, **TabFixedHeight, TabFixedWidth** Properties, **TabWidthStyle** Property

ShowTips Property (ActiveX Controls)

Returns a value that determines whether **ToolTips** are displayed for an object.

Applies To

StatusBar Control, **TabStrip** Control, **Toolbar** Control

Syntax

object.**ShowTips** [= *value*]

The **ShowTips** property syntax has these parts:

Part	Description
object	An object expression that evaluates to an object in the **Applies To** list.
value	A Boolean expression specifying whether **ToolTips** are displayed, as described in **Settings**.

Settings

The settings for *value* are:

Setting	Description
True	(Default) Each object in the control may display an associated string, which is the setting of the **ToolTipText** property, in a small rectangle below the object. This **ToolTip** appears when the user's cursor hovers over the object at run time for about one second.
False	An object will not display a **ToolTip** at run time.

Remarks

At design time you can set the **ShowTips** property on the General tab in the control's Property Pages dialog box.

See Also

ToolTipText Property

Style Property (TabStrip Control)

Returns or sets the appearance—tabs or buttons—of a **TabStrip** control.

Applies To

TabStrip Control

Syntax

object.**Style** [= *value*]

The **Style** property syntax has these parts:

Part	Description
object	An object expression that evaluates to a **TabStrip** control.
value	A constant or integer that determines the appearance of the tabbed dialog box, as described in **Settings**.

Settings

The settings for *value* are:

Constant	Value	Description
tabTabs	0	(Default) Tabs. The tabs appear as notebook tabs, and the internal area has a three-dimensional border around it.
tabButtons	1	Buttons. The tabs appear as regular push buttons, and the internal area has no border around it.

Remarks

At design time, select the **Style** property you want—tabs or buttons—from the Style list on the General tab of the Properties Page of the **TabStrip** control.

At run time, use code like the following to set the **Style** property:

```
' Style property set to the Tabs style.
TabStrip1.Style = tabTabs

' Style property set to the Buttons style:
TabStrip1.Style = tabButtons
```

See Also

TabStrip Control Constants, **ClientHeight, ClientWidth, ClientLeft, ClientTop** Properties, **MultiRow** Property, **TabFixedHeight, TabFixedWidth** Properties, **TabWidthStyle** Property, **Properties** Window, **Property Pages** Dialog Box

Tab Object

A **Tab** object represents an individual tab in the **Tabs** collection of a **TabStrip** control.

Remarks

For each **Tab** object, you can use various properties to specify its appearance, and you can specify its state with the **Selected** property.

At design time, use the Insert Tab and Remove Tab buttons on the Tabs tab in the Properties Page of the **TabStrip** control to insert and remove tabs, and use the text boxes to specify any of these properties for a **Tab** object: **Caption, Image, ToolTipText, Tag, Index**, and/or **Key**. You can also specify these properties at run time.

Use the **Caption** and **Image** properties, separately or together, to label or put an icon on a tab.

- To use the **Caption** property, in the Caption text box on the Tabs tab in the Properties Page of the **TabStrip** control, type the text you want to appear on the tab or button at run time.

- To use the **Image** property, put an **ImageList** control on the form and fill the **ListImages** collection with **ListImage** objects, each of which has an index number and an optional key, if you add one. On the General tab in the Properties Page of the **TabStrip** control, select that **ImageList** to associate it with the **TabStrip** control. In the Image text box on the Tabs tab, type the index number or key of the **ListImage** object that should appear on the **Tab** object.

Use the **ToolTipText** property to temporarily display a string of text in a small rectangular box at run time when the user's cursor hovers over the tab. To set the **ToolTipText** property at design time, select the **ShowTips** checkbox on the General tab, and then in the **ToolTipText** text box on the Tabs tab, type the **ToolTip** string.

To return a reference to a **Tab** object a user has selected, use the **SelectedItem** property; to determine whether a specific tab is selected, use the **Selected** property. These properties are useful in conjunction with the **BeforeClick** event to verify or record data associated with the currently-selected tab before displaying the next tab the user selects.

Each **Tab** object also has read-only properties you can use to reference a single **Tab** object in the **Tabs** collection: **Left**, **Top**, **Height** and **Width**.

Properties

Caption Property, **Height, Width** Properties (ActiveX Controls), **Image** Property (ActiveX Controls), **Index** Property (ActiveX Controls), **Key** Property (ActiveX Controls), **Left, Top** Properties (ActiveX Controls), **Selected** Property (ActiveX Controls), **Tag** Property (ActiveX Controls), **ToolTipText** Property

Methods

Add Method (Tabs Collection), **Clear** Method, **Remove** Method

See Also

ImageList Control, **ListImage** Object, **ListImages** Collection, **Tabs** Collection, **BeforeClick** Event, **Caption** Property (Tab Object), **Selected** Property (ActiveX Controls), **SelectedItem** Property (ActiveX Controls), **General** Tab (Options Dialog Box), **Index** Property (Control Array), **Properties** Window, **Property Pages** Dialog Box, **Tag** Property, **ToolTipText** Property

TabFixedHeight, TabFixedWidth Properties

Return or set the fixed height and width of all **Tab** objects in a **TabStrip** control, but only if the **TabWidthStyle** property is set to **tabFixed**.

Applies To

TabStrip Control, **Tab** Object

Syntax

object.**TabFixedHeight** [= *integer*]
object.**TabFixedWidth** [= *integer*]

The **TabFixedHeight** and **TabFixedWidth** properties syntax has these parts:

Part	Description
object	An object expression that evaluates to a **TabStrip** control.
integer	The number of pixels or twips of the height or width of a **TabStrip** control. The scale used for *integer* is dependent on the **ScaleMode** of the container.

Remarks

The **TabFixedHeight** property applies to all **Tab** objects in the **TabStrip** control. It defaults either to the height of the font as specified in the **Font** property, or the height of the **ListImage** object specified by the **Image** property, whichever is higher, plus a few extra pixels as a border. If the **TabWidthStyle** property is set to **tabFixed**, and the value of the **TabFixedWidth** property is set, the width of each **Tab** object remains the same whether you add or delete **Tab** objects in the control.

ListImage Object**, ListImages** Collection, **TabStrip** Control Constants, **ClientHeight, ClientWidth, ClientLeft, ClientTop** Properties, **TabWidthStyle** Property, **Font** Property, **Image** Property, **ScaleMode** Property

---

Tabs Collection

A **Tabs** collection contains a collection of **Tab** objects.

Syntax

tabstrip.**Tabs**(*index*)
tabstrip.**Tabs**.**Item**(*index*)

The **Tabs** collection syntax has these parts:

Part	Description
tabstrip	An object expression that evaluates to a **TabStrip** control.
index	An integer or string that uniquely identifies a member of an object collection. The integer is the value of the **Index** property of the desired **Tab** object; the string is the value of the **Key** property of the desired **Tab** object.

At design time, use the Insert Tab and Remove Tab buttons on the Tabs tab in the Properties Page of the **TabStrip** control to add and remove **Tab** objects from the **Tabs** collection.

The **Tabs** collection uses the **Count** property to return the number of tabs in the collection. To manipulate the **Tab** objects in the **Tabs** collection, use these methods at run time:

- **Add** — adds **Tab** objects to the **TabStrip** control.
- **Item** — retrieves the **Tab** identified by its **Key** or **Index** from the collection.
- **Clear** — removes all **Tab** objects from the collection.
- **Remove** — removes the **Tab** identified by its **Key** or **Index** from the collection.

Properties

Count Property, **Item** Property

Methods

Add Method (Tabs Collection), **Clear** Method, **Remove** Method

See Also

Tab Object, **Count** Property, **Index** Property

Tabs Property (TabStrip Control)

Returns a reference to the collection of **Tab** objects in a **TabStrip** control.

Applies To

TabStrip Control

Syntax

object.**Tabs**(*index*)

The **Tabs** property syntax has these parts:

Part	Description
object	An object expression that evaluates to a **TabStrip** control.
index	A value that identifies a **Tab** object in the **Tabs** collection. This may either be the **Index** property or the **Key** property of the desired **Tab** object.

Remarks

The **Tabs** collection can be accessed by using the standard collection methods, such as the **Item** method.

See Also

Add Method (Tabs Collection), **Clear** Method, **Item** Method, **Remove** Method, **Tab** Object

---

TabStrip Control Constants

Tab Style Constants

Constant	Value	Description
tabTabs	0	Tabs appear as notebook tabs, and the internal area has a three-dimensional border enclosing it.
tabButtons	1	Tabs appear as push buttons, and the internal area has no border around it.

Tab Width Style Constants

Constant	Value	Description
tabJustified	0	Each tab is wide enough to accommodate its contents, and the width of each tab is increased, if needed, so that each row of tabs spans the width of the control. If there is only a single row of tabs, this style has no effect.
tabNonJustified	1	Each tab is just wide enough to accommodate its contents. The rows are not justified, so multiple rows of tabs are jagged.
tabFixed	2	The height and width of all tabs are identical, and are set by the **TabFixedHeight** and **TabFixedWidth** properties.

See Also

TabStrip Control, **Tab** Object, **MultiRow** Property, **Style** Property (TabStrip Control), **TabFixedHeight, TabFixedWidth** Properties, **TabWidthStyle** Property, **Visual Basic** Constants

TabWidthStyle Property

Returns or sets a value that determines the justification or width of all **Tab** objects in a **TabStrip** control.

Applies To

TabStrip Control

Syntax

object.**TabWidthStyle** [=*value*]

The **TabWidthStyle** property syntax has these parts:

Part	Description
object	An object expression that evaluates to a **TabStrip** control.
value	An integer or constant that determines whether tabs are justified or set to a fixed width, as described in **Settings**.

Settings

The settings for *value* are:

Constant	Value	Description
tabJustified	0	(Default) Justified. If the **MultiRow** property is set to **True**, each tab is wide enough to accommodate its contents and, if needed, the width of each tab is increased so that each row of tabs spans the width of the control. If the **MultiRow** property is set to **False**, or if there is only a single row of tabs, this setting has no effect.
tabNonJustified	1	Nonjustified. Each tab is just wide enough to accommodate its contents. The rows are not justified, so multiple rows of tabs are jagged.
tabFixed	2	Fixed. All tabs have an identical width, which is determined by the **TabFixedWidth** property.

Remarks

At design time you can set the **TabWidthStyle** property on the General tab of the Properties Page of the **TabStrip** control. The setting of the **TabWidthStyle** property affects how wide each **Tab** object appears at run time.

At run time, you can set the **TabWidthStyle** property as follows:

```
' Justifies all the tabs in a row to fit the width of the control.
TabStrip1.MultiRow = True
TabStrip1.TabWidthStyle = tabJustified

' Creates ragged rows of tabs.
TabStrip1.MultiRow = True
TabStrip1.TabWidthStyle = tabNonJustified

' Sets the same width for all tabs.
TabStrip1.TabFixedWidth = 500
TabStrip1.TabWidthStyle = tabFixed
```

See Also

Tab Object, **TabStrip** Control Constants, **ClientHeight, ClientWidth, ClientLeft, ClientTop** Properties, **MultiRow** Property, **TabFixedHeight, TabFixedWidth** Properties

Toolbar Control

A **Toolbar** control contains a collection of **Button** objects used to create a toolbar that is associated with an application.

Syntax

Toolbar

Remarks

Typically, a toolbar contains buttons that correspond to items in an application's menu, providing a graphic interface for the user to access an application's most frequently used functions and commands. The **Toolbar** control allows you to create toolbars by adding **Button** objects to a **Buttons** collection. Each **Button** object can have optional text or an image, or both, supplied by an associated **ImageList** control. You can display an image on a button with the **Image** property, or display text with the **Caption** property, or both, for each **Button** object. At design time, you can add **Button** objects to the control using the Properties Page of the **Toolbar** control. At run time, you can add or remove buttons from the **Buttons** collection using the **Add** and **Remove** methods.

To program the **Toolbar**, add code to the **ButtonClick** event to respond to the selected button. You can also determine the behavior and appearance of each **Button** object using the **Style** property. For example, if four buttons are assigned the ButtonGroup style, only one button can be pressed at any time and at least one button is always pressed.

You can create space for other controls on the toolbar by assigning a **Button** object the PlaceHolder style, then positioning a control over the placeholder. For example, to place a drop-down combo box on a toolbar at design time, add a **Button** object with the PlaceHolder style and size it as wide as a **ComboBox** control. Then place a **ComboBox** control on the placeholder.

Double clicking a toolbar at run time invokes the Customize Toolbar dialog box, which allows the user to hide, display, or rearrange toolbar buttons. To enable or disable the dialog box, use the **AllowCustomize** property. You can also invoke the Customize Toolbar dialog box using the **Customize** method. If you wish to save and restore the state of a toolbar, or allow the user to do so, two methods are provided: the **SaveToolbar** and **RestoreToolbar** methods. The **Change** event, generated when a toolbar is altered, is typically used to invoke the **SaveToolbar** method.

Note The Customize dialog box also includes a Help button. Use the **HelpFile** and **HelpContextID** properties to determine which (if any) help file is displayed when the end user clicks the Help button.

Usability is further enhanced by programming **ToolTipText** descriptions of each **Button** object. To display ToolTips, the **ShowTips Property** must be set to **True**. When the user invokes the Customize Toolbar dialog box, clicking a button causes a description of the button to be displayed in the dialog box; this description can be programmed by setting the **Description** property.

Distribution Note The **Toolbar** control is part of a group of **ActiveX** controls that are found in the COMCTL32.OCX file. To use the **Toolbar** control in your application, you must add the COMCTL32.OCX file to the project. When distributing your application, install the COMCTL32.OCX file in the user's Microsoft Windows System or System32 (on Windows NT platforms) folder. For more information on how to add an **ActiveX** control to a project, see "Loading ActiveX Controls," in the *Component Tools Guide*.

Properties

Align Property, **AllowCustomize** Property, **Appearance** Property, **BorderStyle** Property, **ButtonHeight, ButtonWidth** Properties, **Buttons** Property, **Container** Property, **Controls** Property, **DataBinding** Object, **DataBindings** Property, **DragIcon** Property, **DragMode** Property, **Enabled** Property, **Height, Width** Properties, **HelpContextID** Property, **HelpFile** Property, **hWnd** Property, **ImageList** Property, **Index** Property, **Left, Top** Properties, **MouseIcon** Property, **MousePointer** Property, **Name** Property, **Object** Property, **OLEDropMode** Property, **Parent** Property, **ShowTips** Property, **TabIndex** Property, **Tag** Property, **ToolTipText** Property, **Visible** Property, **WhatsThisHelpID** Property, **Wrappable** Property

Events

Button Event, **Change** Event, **Click** Event, **DblClick** Event, **DragDrop** Event, **DragOver** Event, **MouseDown, MouseUp** Events, **MouseMove** Event, **OLECompleteDrag** Event, **OLEDragDrop** Event, **OLEDragOver** Event, **OLEGiveFeedback** Event, **OLESetData** Event, **OLEStartDrag** Event

Methods

Customize Method, **Drag** Method, **Move** Method, **OLEDrag** Method, **Refresh** Method, **Restore** Method, **SaveToolbar** Method, **ShowWhatsThis** Method, **ZOrder** Method

See Also

ImageList Control, **ShowTips** Property (ActiveX Controls), **Button** Object, **Buttons** Collection, **Add** Method (Buttons Collection), **AllowCustomize** Property, **Customize** Method, **Description** Property (Button Object), **RestoreToolbar** Method, **SaveToolbar** Method, **Style** Property (Button Object), **Toolbar** Control Constants, **Caption** Property, **ComboBox** Control, **Customize Dialog Box, ToolTipText** Property

Example

This example adds **Button** objects to a **Toolbar** control using the **Add** method and assigns images supplied by the **ImageList** control. The behavior of each button is determined by the **Style** property. The code creates buttons that can be used to open and save files and includes a **ComboBox** control that is used to change the backcolor of the form. To try the example, place a **Toolbar**, **ImageList**, and a **ComboBox** on a form and paste the code into the form's Declarations section. Make sure that you insert the **ComboBox** directly on the **Toolbar** control. Run the example, click the various buttons and select from the combo box.

```
Private Sub Form_Load()
   ' Create object variable for the ImageList.
   Dim imgX As ListImage

   ' Load pictures into the ImageList control.
   Set imgX = ImageList1.ListImages. _
   Add(, "open", LoadPicture("Graphics\bitmaps\tlbr_w95\open.bmp"))
   Set imgX = ImageList1.ListImages. _
   Add(, "save", LoadPicture("Graphics\bitmaps\tlbr_w95\save.bmp"))
   Toolbar1.ImageList = ImageList1

   ' Create object variable for the Toolbar.
   Dim btnX As Button
   ' Add button objects to Buttons collection using
   ' the
   ' Add method. After creating each button, set both
   ' Description and ToolTipText properties.
   Toolbar1.Buttons.Add , , , tbrSeparator
   Set btnX = Toolbar1.Buttons.Add(, "open", , tbrDefault, "open")
   btnX.ToolTipText = "Open File"
   btnX.Description = btnX.ToolTipText
   Set btnX = Toolbar1.Buttons.Add(, "save", , tbrDefault, "save")
   btnX.ToolTipText = "Save File"
   btnX.Description = btnX.ToolTipText
   Set btnX = Toolbar1.Buttons.Add(, , , tbrSeparator)

   ' The next button has the Placeholder style. A
   ' ComboBox control will be placed on top of this
   ' button.
   Set btnX = Toolbar1.Buttons.Add(, "combo1", , tbrPlaceholder)
   btnX.Width = 1500 ' Placeholder width to accommodate a combobox.

   Show ' Show form to continue configuring ComboBox.

   ' Configure ComboBox control to be at same location
   ' as the
   ' Button object with the PlaceHolder style (key =
   ' "combo1").
   With Combo1
      .Width = Toolbar1.Buttons("combo1").Width
      .Top = Toolbar1.Buttons("combo1").Top
      .Left = Toolbar1.Buttons("combo1").Left
      .AddItem "Black" ' Add colors for text.
```

```
            .AddItem "Blue"
            .AddItem "Red"
            .ListIndex = 0
        End With

End Sub

Private Sub Form_Resize()
    ' Configure ComboBox control.
    With Combo1
        .Width = Toolbar1.Buttons("combo1").Width
        .Top = Toolbar1.Buttons("combo1").Top
        .Left = Toolbar1.Buttons("combo1").Left
    End With

End Sub
Private Sub toolbar1_ButtonClick(ByVal Button As Button)
    ' Use the Key property with the SelectCase statement to specify
    ' an action.
    Select Case Button.Key
    Case Is = "open"            ' Open file.
       MsgBox "Add code to open file here!"
    Case Is = "save"            ' Save file.
       MsgBox "Add code to save file here!"
    End Select
End Sub

Private Sub Combo1_Click()
    ' Change backcolor of form using the ComboBox.
    Select Case Combo1.ListIndex
    Case 0
       Form1.BackColor = vbBlack
    Case 1
       Form1.BackColor = vbBlue
    Case 2
       Form1.BackColor = vbRed
    End Select
End Sub
```

Add Method (Buttons Collection)

Adds a **Button** object to a **Buttons** collection and returns a reference to the newly created object.

Applies To

Toolbar Control, **Buttons** Collection

Syntax

object.**Add**(*index, key, caption, style, image*)

The **Add** method syntax has these parts:

Part	Description
object	Required. An object expression that evaluates to a **Buttons** collection.
index	Optional. An integer specifying the position where you want to insert the **Button** object. If no *index* is specified, the **Button** is added to the end of the **Buttons** collection.
key	Optional. A unique string that identifies the **Button** object. Use this value to retrieve a specific **Button** object.
caption	Optional. A string that will appear beneath the **Button** object.
style	Optional. The style of the **Button** object. The available styles are detailed in the **Style** Property (Button Object).
image	Optional. An integer or unique key that specifies a **ListImage** object in an associated **ImageList** control.

Remarks

You can add **Button** objects at design time using the Buttons tab of the Properties Page of the **Toolbar** control. At run time, use the **Add** method to add **Button** objects as in the following code:

```
Dim btnButton as Button
Set btnButton = Toolbar1.Buttons.Add(, "open", , tbrDefault, "open")
```

You associate an **ImageList** control with the **Toolbar** through the **Toolbar** control's **ImageList** property.

See Also

ImageList Control, **ListImage** Object, **ListImages** Collection, **Toolbar** Control, **Button** Object, **Style** Property (Button Object)

AllowCustomize Property

Returns or sets a value determining if a **Toolbar** control can be customized by the end user with the Customize Toolbar dialog box.

Applies To

Toolbar Control

Syntax

object.**AllowCustomize** [= *boolean*]

The **AllowCustomize** property syntax has these parts:

Part	Description
object	An object expression that evaluates to a **Toolbar** control.
boolean	A constant or value that determines if the user can customize a **Toolbar** control, as described in **Settings**.

Settings

The settings for *boolean* are:

Setting	Description
True	Allows the end user to invoke the Customize Toolbar dialog box by double clicking a **Toolbar** control.
False	Customization of the **Toolbar** control with the Customize Toolbar dialog box is not allowed.

Remarks

If the **AllowCustomize** property is set to **True**, double-clicking a **Toolbar** control at run time invokes the Customize Toolbar dialog box.

The Customize Toolbar can also be invoked with the **Customize** method.

See Also

Customize Method, **RestoreToolbar** Method, **SaveToolbar** Method

Button Object

A **Button** object represents an individual button in the **Buttons** collection of a **Toolbar** control.

Remarks

For each **Button** object, you can add text or a bitmap image, or both, from an **ImageList** control, and set properties to change its state and style.

At design time, use the Insert Button and Remove Button buttons on the Buttons tab in the Properties Page of the **Toolbar** control to insert and remove **Button** objects from the **Buttons** collection. At run time, you can also add **Button** objects by using the **Add** method of the **Buttons** collection.

At design time and run time, you can set the **Caption**, **Image**, **Value**, **MixedState**, and **ToolTipText** properties to change the appearance of each **Button** object.

Whenever a button is clicked on the **Toolbar** control, the **ButtonClick** event is called with the selected **Button** object passed in as a parameter. To cause some action to occur when a button is clicked, use the **Index** or **Key** properties in a **Select Case** statement as in the following code:

```
Select Case Button.Key
    Case Is = "open"        ' Open file.
    ' Add code to Open a file here
    Case Is = "save"        ' Save file.
    ' Add code to Save a file here
    Case Else
    ' If any other button is pressed
End Select
```

Properties

Caption Property, **Description** Property, **Enabled** Property, **Height, Width**
Properties, **Image** Property, **Index** Property, **Key** Property, **Left, Top** Properties,
MixedState Property, **Style** Property, **Tag** Property, **ToolTipText** Property, **Value**
Property, **Visible** Property

See Also

Add Method (Buttons Collection), **Buttons** Collection, **Caption** Property, **ImageList**
Control, **MixedState** Property, **SelectCase** Statement, **Toolbar** Control, **ToolTipText**
Property, **Value** Property

ButtonClick Event

Occurs when the user clicks on a **Button** object in a **Toolbar** control.

Applies To

Toolbar Control

Syntax

Private Sub *object*_**ButtonClick**(**ByVal** *button* **As Button**)

The **ButtonClick** event syntax has these parts:

Part	Description
object	An object expression that evaluates to a **Toolbar** control.
button	A reference to the clicked **Button** object.

Remarks

To program an individual **Button** object's response to the **ButtonClick** event, use the
value of the *button* argument. For example, the following code uses the **Key** property
of the **Button** object to determine the appropriate action.

```
Private Sub Toolbar1_ButtonClick(ByVal Button As Button)
   Select Case Button.Key
   Case "Open"
      CommonDialog1.ShowOpen
   Case "Save"
      CommonDialog1.ShowSave
   End Select
End Sub
```

Note Because the user can rearrange **Button** objects using the Customize Toolbar dialog box,
the value of the **Index** property may not always indicate the position of the button. Therefore, it's
preferable to use the value of the **Key** property to retrieve a **Button** object.

See Also

Value Property (ActiveX Controls), **Button** Object, **Index** Property (Control Array)

ButtonHeight, ButtonWidth Properties

Return or set the height and width of a **Toolbar** control's buttons.

Applies To

Toolbar Control

Syntax

object.**ButtonHeight** [= *number*]
object.**ButtonWidth** [= *number*]

The **ButtonHeight, ButtonWidth** properties syntax has these parts:

Part	Description
object	An object expression that evaluates to a **Toolbar** control.
number	A numeric expression specifying the dimensions of all buttons on the control that have the Button, Check, or ButtonGroup style.

Remarks

ButtonHeight and **ButtonWidth** use the scale unit of the Toolbar control's container. The scale unit is determined by the **ScaleMode** property of the container.

By default, the **ButtonWidth** and **ButtonHeight** properties are automatically updated to accommodate the string in the **Caption** property or image in the **Image** property of the **Button** object.

See Also

Button Object, **Caption** Property, **Image** Property, **ScaleMode** Property

Buttons Collection

A **Buttons** collection is a collection of **Button** objects for a **Toolbar** control.

Syntax

toolbar.**Buttons**(*index*)
toolbar.**Buttons.Item**(*index*)

The **Buttons** collection syntax has these parts:

Part	Description
toolbar	An object expression that evaluates to a **Toolbar** control.
index	An integer or string that uniquely identifies the object in the collection. The integer is the value of the **Index** property; the string is the value of the **Key** property.

Remarks

The **Buttons** collection is a 1-based collection, which means the collection's **Index** property begins with the number 1 (versus 0 in a 0-based collection).

Each item in the collection can be accessed by its index or unique key. For example, to get a reference to the third **Button** object in a collection, use the following syntax:

```
Dim btnX As Button
    ' Reference by index number.
Set btnX = Toolbar1.Buttons(3)
    ' Or reference by unique key.
Set btnX = Toolbar1.Buttons("third") ' Assuming Key is "third."
    ' Or use Item method.
Set btnX = Toolbar1.Buttons.Item(3)
```

Properties

Count Property, **Item** Property

Methods

Add Method (Buttons Collection), **Clear** Method, **Remove** Method

See Also

Toolbar Control, **Button** Object, **Add** Method (Buttons Collection), **Index** Property (Control Array)

Buttons Property

Returns a reference to a **Toolbar** control's collection of **Button** objects.

Applies To

Toolbar Control

Syntax

object.**Buttons**

The *object* placeholder is an object expression that evaluates to a **Toolbar** control.

Remarks

You can manipulate **Button** objects using standard collection methods (for example, the **Add** and **Remove** methods). Each element in the collection can be accessed by its index, the value of the **Index** property, or by a unique key, the value of the **Key** property.

See Also

Buttons Collection, **Add** Method (Buttons Collection), **Index** Property (Control Array)

Change Event (ToolBar, Slider Controls)

Indicates that the contents of a control have changed. How and when this event occurs varies with the control.

Applies To

ComboBox Control, **DBCombo** Control, **DBGrid** Control, **DirListBox** Control, **DriveListBox** Control, **HScrollBar, VScrollBar** Controls, **Label** Control, **PictureBox** Control, **TextBox** Control

Syntax

Private Sub *object*_**Change**([*index* **As Integer**])

The **Change** event syntax has these parts:

Part	Description
object	An object expression that evaluates to a control in the **Applies To** list.
index	An integer that uniquely identifies a control if it's in a control array.

Remarks

- Slider—generated when the **Value** property changes, either through code, or when the user moves the control's slider.

- Toolbar—generated after the end user customizes a **Toolbar** control's toolbar using the Customize Toolbar dialog box.

The **Change** event procedure can synchronize or coordinate data display among controls. For example, you can use a **Slider** control's **Change** event procedure to update the control's **Value** property setting in a **TextBox** control. Or you could use a **Change** event procedure to display data and formulas in a work area and results in another area.

Note   A **Change** event procedure can sometimes cause a cascading event. This occurs when the control's **Change** event alters the control's contents by setting a property in code that determines the control's value, such as the **Text** property setting for a **TextBox** control. To prevent a cascading event:

- If possible, avoid writing a **Change** event procedure for a control that alters that control's contents. If you do write such a procedure, be sure to set a flag that prevents further changes while the current change is in progress.

- Avoid creating two or more controls whose **Change** event procedures affect each other, for example, two **TextBox** controls that update each other during their **Change** events.

See Also

Text Property (MaskedEdit Control), **Value** Property (ActiveX Controls),
AllowCustomize Property, **Customize** Method, **RestoreToolbar** Method,
SaveToolbar Method, **Style** Property, **Picture** Property, **PathChange** Event,
PatternChange Event, **Path** Property, **LostFocus** Event, **LinkTopic** Property,
KeyPress Event, **KeyDown**, **KeyUp** Events, **Drive** Property, **Caption** Property

Controls Property (Toolbar Control)

Returns a reference to a collection of controls contained on an object.

Applies To

Toolbar Control

Syntax

object.**Controls**(*index*)
object.**Controls.Item**(*index*)

The **Controls** property syntax has these parts:

Part	Description
object	An object expression that evaluates to an object in the **Applies To** list.
index	A value that identifies a member of a **Controls** collection.

Remarks

The **Controls** property is similar to the **Controls** collection on the **Form** object, and is accessed in a similar manner. For example, use the following code to get the **Top** property of the second control on a **Toolbar** control:

```
MsgBox Toolbar1.Controls(2).Top
```

With the **Controls** property, you can iterate through all the controls on a **Tab** object or a **Toolbar** control and change the properties of each control as in the following code:

```
For Each ContainedControl in Toolbar1.Controls
    ContainedControl.Width = Toolbar1.Width / Toolbar1.Buttons.Count
Next
```

Note The **Controls** collection refers to controls contained by the **Toolbar** control, such as a **ComboBox** control, and not the **Button** objects, which are part of the control itself.

See Also

Tab Object, **Button** Object, **ComboBox** Control, **Controls** Collection, **Form** Object, **Forms** Collection, **Index** Property (Control Array), **Left**, **Top** Properties

Customize Method

Invokes the Customize Toolbar dialog box which allows the end user to rearrange or hide **Button** objects on a **Toolbar** control.

Applies To

Toolbar Control

Syntax

object.**Customize**

The *object* placeholder is an object expression that evaluates to a **Toolbar** control.

Remarks

The **Toolbar** control contains a built-in dialog box that allows the user to hide, display, or rearrange buttons on a toolbar. Double-clicking the toolbar calls the **Customize** method, which invokes the dialog box.

Use the **Customize** method when you wish to restrict the alteration of the toolbar. For example, the code below allows the user to customize the toolbar only if a password is given:

```
Private Sub Command1_Click()
    If InputBox("Password:") = "Chorus&Line9" Then
        Toolbar1.Customize    ' Invoke Customize method.
    End If
End Sub
```

To preserve the state of a **Toolbar** control, the **SaveToolbar** method writes to the Windows registry. You can restore a **Toolbar** control to a previous state using the **RestoreToolbar** method to read the information previously saved in the registry.

See Also

Button Object, **AllowCustomize** Property, **Description** Property (Button Object), **RestoreToolbar** Method, **SaveToolbar** Method

Description Property (Button Object)

Returns or sets the text for a **Button** object's description, which is displayed in the Customize Toolbar dialog box.

Applies To

Toolbar Control, **Button** Object

Syntax

object.**Description** [= *string*]

The **Description** property syntax has these parts:

Part	Description
object	An object expression that evaluates to a **Button** object.
string	The string displayed in the Customize Toolbar dialog box when the button is selected.

Remarks

At run time, the Customize Toolbar dialog box can be invoked either by a user double-clicking the **Toolbar** control or programmatically using the **Customize** method. In either case, when the user selects a button in the dialog box, a description of the button is displayed in the lower-left corner of the dialog box. The text for that description is set with the **Description** property.

You can set the **Description** text when you add a **Button** object, as follows:

```
Dim btnX As Button
' Add a button with the Key "save."
Set btnX = Toolbar1.Buttons.Add(,"save")
btnX.Description = "Save a file."
```

See Also

AllowCustomize Property, **Customize** Method

HelpContextID Property (Toolbar Control)

Returns or sets an associated context number for an object. Used to provide context-sensitive Help for your application.

Note The **HelpContextID** property for the **Toolbar** control enables a link to Help from the Customize Toolbar dialog box rather than from the control itself. This behavior is different from that of other Visual Basic controls that contain the **HelpContextID** property.

Applies To

Toolbar Control

Syntax

object.**HelpContextID** [= *number*]

The **HelpContextID** property syntax has these parts:

Part	Description
object	An object expression that evaluates to an object in the **Applies To** list. If *object* is omitted, the form associated with the active form module is assumed to be *object*.
number	A numeric expression that specifies the context number of the Help topic associated with *object*.

Settings

The settings for *number* are:

Setting	Description
0	(Default) No context number specified.
> 0	An integer specifying a valid context number.

Remarks

For context-sensitive Help on an object in your application, you must assign the same context number to both *object* and to the associated Help topic when you compile your Help file.

If you've created a Microsoft Windows operating environment Help file for your application and set the application's **HelpFile** property, when a user presses the F1 key, Visual Basic automatically calls Help and searches for the topic identified by the current context number.

The current context number is the value of **HelpContextID** for the object that has the focus. If **HelpContextID** is set to 0, then Visual Basic looks in the **HelpContextID** of the object's container, and then that object's container, and so on. If a nonzero current context number can't be found, the F1 key is ignored.

For a **Menu** control, **HelpContextID** is normally read/write at run time. But **HelpContextID** is read-only for menu items that are exposed or supplied by Visual Basic to add-ins, such as the Add-In Manager command on the Add-Ins menu.

Note Building a Help file requires the Microsoft Windows Help Compiler, which is included with the Visual Basic Professional Edition.

See Also

Customize Dialog Box, HelpFile Property (Toolbar Control), **Menu** Control

---

HelpFile Property (Toolbar Control)

Specifies the path and filename of a Microsoft Windows Help file used by your application to display Help or online documentation.

Note The **HelpFile** property for the **Toolbar** control enables a link to Help from the Customize Toolbar dialog box rather than from the control itself. This behavior is different from that of other Visual Basic controls that contain the **HelpFile** property.

AppliesTo

Toolbar Control

Syntax

object.**HelpFile**[= *filename*]

The **HelpFile** property syntax has these parts:

Part	Description
object	An object expression that evaluates to an object in the **Applies To** list.
filename	A string expression specifying the path and filename of the Windows Help file for your application.

Remarks

If you've created a Windows Help file for your application and set the application's **HelpFile** property, Visual Basic automatically calls Help when a user presses the F1 key. If there is a context number in the **HelpContextID** property for either the active control or the active form, Help displays a topic corresponding to the current Help context; otherwise it displays the main contents screen.

You can also use the **HelpFile** property to determine which Help file is displayed when a user requests Help from the Object Browser for an **ActiveX** component.

Note Building a Help file requires the Microsoft Windows Help Compiler, which is available with Visual Basic, Professional Edition.

MixedState Property

Returns or sets a value that determines if a **Button** object in a **Toolbar** control appears in an indeterminate state.

Applies To

Toolbar Control, **Button** Object

Syntax

object.**MixedState** [= *boolean*]

The **MixedState** property syntax has these parts:

Part	Description
object	An object expression that evaluates to a **Button** object.
boolean	A Boolean expression that determines if a **Button** shows the indeterminate state, as specified in **Settings**.

Settings

The settings for *boolean* are:

Setting	Description
True	The **Button** object is in the indeterminate state and becomes dimmed.
False	The **Button** object is not in the indeterminate state and looks normal.

Remarks

The **MixedState** property is typically used when a selection contains a variety of attributes. For example, if you select text that contains both plain (normal) characters and bold characters, the **MixedState** property is used. The image displayed by the **Button** object could then be changed to indicate its state, which would differ from the Checked and Unchecked value returned by the **Value** property.

See Also

Value Property (ActiveX Controls)

RestoreToolbar Method

Restores a toolbar, created with a **Toolbar** control, to its original state after being customized.

Applies To

Toolbar Control

Syntax

object.**RestoreToolbar**(*key* **As String**, *subkey* **As String**, *value* **As String**)

The **RestoreToolbar** method syntax has these parts:

Part	Description
object	Required. An object expression that evaluates to a **Toolbar** control.
key	Required. A string expression that specifies the key in the Windows registry where the method retrieves the **Toolbar** information.
subkey	Required. A string expression that specifies a subkey under the *key* parameter in the registry.
value	Required. A string expression that identifies the value under the *subkey* where the **Toolbar** information is stored in the registry.

Remarks

Warning When the **RestoreToolbar** method is used, any toolbar buttons that do not contain **ImageList ListImage** object will disappear. A user can make them visible again by using the Reset button on the Customize Toolbar dialog box. You can use the **Customize** method to programmatically invoke this dialog box for the user.

To customize the **Toolbar** control at run time, use the **Customize** method in code or if the **AllowCustomize** property is **True**, the user can customize it by double clicking the control.

The state of the toolbar can be saved in the registry using the **SaveToolbar** method. The **RestoreToolbar** method restores the state of a toolbar by reading the registry.

The following code restores the **Toolbar** control's settings for the current user, assuming they have previously been saved with the **SaveToolbar** method.

```
Toolbar1.RestoreToolbar "AppName", "User1", "Toolbar1"
```

See Also

AllowCustomize Property, **Customize** Method, **SaveToolbar** Method

---

SaveToolbar Method

At run time, saves the state of a toolbar, created with the **Toolbar** control, in the registry.

Applies To

Toolbar Control

Syntax

object.**SaveToolbar**(*key* **As String,** *subkey* **As String,** *value* **As String**)

The **SaveToolbar** method syntax has these parts:

Part	Description
object	Required. An object expression that evaluates to a **Toolbar** control.
key	Required. A string expression specifying the key in the registry where the method stores the **Toolbar** information.
subkey	Required. A string expression that specifies a location in the registry under the *key* parameter.
value	Required. The **Toolbar** information to be stored in the *subkey*.

Remarks

To customize the **Toolbar** control at run time, use the **Customize** method in code or if the **AllowCustomize** property is **True**, the user can customize it by double clicking the control.

If the *key, subkey, or value* you specify doesn't exist in the registry, it is created.

To save more than one version of the toolbar, you can change the *subkey* or *value* parameter. This causes the toolbar to write to a different part of the registry. The following code saves two different states of a toolbar after it has been customized.

```
' Save settings for User1
Toolbar1.SaveToolbar "AppName", "User1", "Toolbar1"

' Save settings for User2
Toolbar1.SaveToolbar "AppName", "User2", "Toolbar1"
```

Since the **Change** event for the **Toolbar** control occurs after the toolbar has been customized, in most cases the above code can be placed in the **Change** event for the toolbar.

See Also

AllowCustomize Property, **Customize** Method, **RestoreToolbar** Method

---

ShowTips Property (ActiveX Controls)

Returns a value that determines whether **ToolTips** are displayed for an object.

Applies To

StatusBar Control, **TabStrip** Control, **Toolbar** Control

Syntax

object.**ShowTips** [= *value*]

The **ShowTips** property syntax has these parts:

Part	Description
object	An object expression that evaluates to an object in the **Applies To** list.
value	A Boolean expression specifying whether **ToolTips** are displayed, as described in **Settings**.

Settings

The settings for *value* are:

Setting	Description
True	(Default) Each object in the control may display an associated string, which is the setting of the **ToolTipText** property, in a small rectangle below the object. This **ToolTip** appears when the user's cursor hovers over the object at run time for about one second.
False	An object will not display a **ToolTip** at run time.

Remarks

At design time you can set the **ShowTips** property on the General tab in the control's Property Pages dialog box.

See Also

ToolTipText Property

Style Property (Button Object)

Returns or sets a constant or value that determines the appearance and behavior of a **Button** object in a **Toolbar** control.

Applies To

Toolbar Control, **Button** Object

Syntax

object.**Style** [*=value*]

The **Style** property syntax has these parts:

Part	Description
object	An object expression that evaluates to a **Button** object.
value	A constant or integer that determines the appearance and behavior of a **Button** object, as specified in **Settings**.

Settings

The settings for *value* are:

Constant	Value	Description
tbrDefault	0	(Default) Button. The button is a regular push button.
tbrCheck	1	Check. The button is a check button, which can be checked or unchecked.
tbrButtonGroup	2	ButtonGroup. The button remains pressed until another button in the group is pressed. Exactly one button in the group can be pressed at any one moment.
tbrSeparator	3	Separator. The button functions as a separator with a fixed width of 8 pixels.
tbrPlaceholder	4	Placeholder. The button is like a separator in appearance and functionality, but has a settable width.

Remarks

Buttons that have the ButtonGroup style must be grouped. To distinguish a group, place all **Button** objects with the same style (ButtonGroup) between two **Button** objects with the Separator style.

You can also place another control on a toolbar by assigning a **Button** object the PlaceHolder style, then drawing a control on to the toolbar. For example, to place a drop-down combo box on a toolbar at design time, add a **Button** object with the PlaceHolder style and size it to the size of a **ComboBox** control. Then place a **ComboBox** on the placeholder.

When a **Button** object is assigned the PlaceHolder style, you can set the value of the **Width** property to accommodate another control placed on the **Button**. If a **Button** object has the Button, Check, or ButtonGroup style, the height and width are determined by the **ButtonHeight** and **ButtonWidth** properties.

If you place a control on a button with the PlaceHolder style, you must use code to align and size the control if the form is resized, as shown below:

```
Private Sub Form_Resize()
    ' Track a ComboBox by setting its Top, Left, and
    ' Width properties
    ' to the Top, Left, and Width properties of a
    ' Button object
With Toolbar1.Buttons("Combo1")
    Combo1.Move .Left,.Top,.Width
End With
End Sub
```

See Also

ButtonHeight, ButtonWidth Properties, **Toolbar** Control Constants, **ComboBox** Control, **Height**, **Width** Properties

---

Toolbar Control Constants

Style Constants

Constant	Value	Description
tbrDefault	0	The button is a regular push button.
tbrCheck	1	The button is a check button.
tbrButtonGroup	2	The button remains pressed until another button in the group is pressed. Exactly one button in the group is pressed at any time.
tbrSeparator	3	The button functions as a separator with a fixed width of 8 pixels.
tbrPlaceholder	4	The button is like a separator in appearance and functionality but has a settable width.

Value Constants

Constant	Value	Description
tbrUnpressed	0	The button is not currently pressed or checked.
tbrPressed	1	The button is currently pressed or checked.

See Also

Value Property (ActiveX Controls), **Toolbar** Control, **Style** Property (Button Object), **Visual Basic** Constants

Wrappable Property

Returns or sets a value that determines if **Toolbar** control buttons will automatically wrap when the window is resized.

Applies To

Toolbar Control

Syntax

object.**Wrappable** [= *boolean*]

The **Wrappable** property syntax has these parts:

Part	Description
object	An object expression that evaluates to a **Toolbar** control.
boolean	A Boolean expression that determines if the **Button** objects on a **Toolbar** control will wrap, as described in **Settings**.

Settings

The settings for *boolean* are:

Value	Description
True	The buttons on the **Toolbar** control wrap if the form is resized.
False	The buttons on the **Toolbar** control won't wrap if the form is resized.

See Also

Button Object

TreeView Control

A **TreeView** control displays a hierarchical list of **Node** objects, each of which consists of a label and an optional bitmap. A **TreeView** is typically used to display the headings in a document, the entries in an index, the files and directories on a disk, or any other kind of information that might usefully be displayed as a hierarchy.

Syntax

Treeview

Remarks

After creating a **TreeView** control, you can add, remove, arrange, and otherwise manipulate **Node** objects by setting properties and invoking methods. You can programmatically expand and collapse **Node** objects to display or hide all child nodes. Three events, the **Collapse**, **Expand**, and **NodeClick** event, also provide programming functionality.

You can navigate through a tree in code by retrieving a reference to **Node** objects using **Root**, **Parent**, **Child**, **FirstSibling**, **Next**, **Previous**, and **LastSibling** properties. Users can navigate through a tree using the keyboard as well. UP ARROW and DOWN ARROW keys cycle downward through all expanded **Node** objects. **Node** objects are selected from left to right, and top to bottom. At the bottom of a tree, the selection jumps back to the top of the tree, scrolling the window if necessary. RIGHT ARROW and LEFT ARROW keys also tab through expanded **Node** objects, but if the RIGHT ARROW key is pressed while an unexpanded **Node** is selected, the **Node** expands; a second press will move the selection to the next **Node**. Conversely, pressing the LEFT ARROW key while an expanded **Node** has the focus collapses the **Node**. If a user presses an ANSI key, the focus will jump to the nearest **Node** that begins with that letter. Subsequent pressings of the key will cause the selection to cycle downward through all expanded nodes that begin with that letter.

Several styles are available which alter the appearance of the control. **Node** objects can appear in one of eight combinations of text, bitmaps, lines, and plus/minus signs.

The **TreeView** control uses the **ImageList** control, specified by the **ImageList** property, to store the bitmaps and icons that are displayed in **Node** objects. A **TreeView** control can use only one **ImageList** at a time. This means that every item in the **TreeView** control will have an equal-sized image next to it when the **TreeView** control's **Style** property is set to a style which displays images.

Distribution Note The **TreeView** control is part of a group of **ActiveX** controls that are found in the COMCTL32.OCX file. To use the **TreeView** control in your application, you must add the COMCTL32.OCX file to the project. When distributing your application, install the COMCTL32.OCX file in the user's Microsoft Windows System or System32 directory.

Properties

Appearance Property, BorderStyle Property, Container Property, DragIcon Property, DragMode Property, DropHighlight Property, Enabled Property, Font Property, Height, Width Properties, HelpContextID Property, HideSelection Property, hWnd Property, ImageList Property, Indentation Property, Index Property, LabelEdit Property, Left, Top Properties, LineStyle Property, MouseIcon Property, MousePointer Property, Name Property, Nodes Property, Object Property, OLEDragMode Property, OLEDropMode Property, Parent Property, PathSeparator Property, SelectedItem Property, Sorted Property, Style Property, TabIndex Property, TabStop Property, Tag Property, ToolTipText Property, Visible Property, WhatsThisHelpID Property

Events

AfterLabelEdit Event, BeforeLabelEdit Event, Click Event, Collapse Event, DblClick Event, DragDrop Event, DragOver Event, Expand Event, GotFocus Event, KeyDown, KeyUp Events, KeyPress Event, LostFocus Event, MouseDown, MouseUp Events, MouseMove Event, NodeClick Event, OLECompleteDrag Event, OLEDragDrop Event, OLEDragOver Event, OLEGiveFeedback Event, OLESetData Event, OLEStartDrag Event

Methods

Drag Method, GetVisibleCount Method, HitTest Method, Move Method, OLEDrag Method, Refresh Method, SetFocus Method, ShowWhatsThis Method, StartLabelEdit Method, ZOrder Method

See Also

ImageList Control, TreeView Control Constants, Node Object, Nodes Collection, Child Property (TreeView Control), Collapse Event (TreeView Control), Expand Event (TreeView Control), FirstSibling Property, LastSibling Property, Next Property, NodeClick Event, Parent Property (Node Object), Previous Property (Node Object), Root Property (Node Object), Style Property (TreeView Control), ImageList Property (ActiveX Controls)

Add Method (Nodes Collection)

Adds a **Node** object to a **Treeview** control's **Nodes** collection.

Applies To

TreeView Control

Syntax

object.**Add**(*relative, relationship, key, text, image, selectedimage*)

The **Add** method syntax has these parts:

Part	Description
object	Required. An object expression that evaluates to an object in the **Applies To** list.
relative	Optional. The index number or key of a pre-existing **Node** object. The relationship between the new node and this pre-existing node is found in the next argument, *relationship*.
relationship	Optional. Specifies the relative placement of the **Node** object, as described in **Settings**.
key	Optional. A unique string that can be used to retrieve the **Node** with the **Item** method.
text	Required. The string that appears in the **Node**.
image	Optional. The index of an image in an associated **ImageList** control.
selectedimage	Optional. The index of an image in an associated **ImageList** control that is shown when the **Node** is selected.

Settings

The settings for *relationship* are:

Constant	Value	Description
tvwFirst	0	First. The **Node** is placed before all other nodes at the same level of the node named in *relative*.
tvwLast	1	Last. The **Node** is placed after all other nodes at the same level of the node named in *relative*. Any **Node** added subsequently may be placed after one added as Last.
tvwNext	2	(Default) Next. The **Node** is placed after the node named in *relative*.
tvwPrevious	3	Previous. The **Node** is placed before the node named in *relative*.
tvwChild	4	Child. The **Node** becomes a child node of the node named in *relative*.

Note If no **Node** object is named in *relative*, the new node is placed in the last position of the top node hierarchy.

Remarks

The **Nodes** collection is a 1-based collection.

As a **Node** object is added it is assigned an index number, which is stored in the **Node** object's **Index** property. This value of the newest member is the value of the **Node** collection's **Count** property.

Because the **Add** method returns a reference to the newly created **Node** object, it is most convenient to set properties of the new **Node** using this reference. The following example adds several **Node** objects with identical properties:

```
Dim nodX As Node    ' Declare the object variable.
Dim I as Integer    ' Declare a counter variable.
For I = 1 to 4
   Set nodX = TreeView1.Nodes.Add(,,,"Node " & Cstr(i))
   ' Use the reference to set other properties, such as Enabled.
   nodX.Enabled = True
   ' Set image property to image 3 in an associated ImageList.
   nodX.ExpandedImage = 3
Next I
```

See Also

Count Property (VB Collections), **ImageList** Control, **Item** Method, **Index** Property (ActiveX Controls), **Key** Property (ActiveX Controls), **Remove** Method (ActiveX Controls)

Example

The following example adds two **Node** objects to a **TreeView** control. To try the example, place a **TreeView** control on a form, and paste the code into the form's Declarations section. Run the example, and click the **Node** object to expand it.

```
Private Sub Form_Load()
   ' Set Treeview control properties.
   TreeView1.LineStyle = tvwRootLines        ' Linestyle 1

   ' Add Node objects.
   Dim nodX As Node                          ' Declare Node variable.
   ' First node with 'Root' as text.
   Set nodX = TreeView1.Nodes.Add(, , "r", "Root")

   ' This next node is a child of Node 1 ("Root").
   Set nodX = TreeView1.Nodes.Add("r", tvwChild, "child1", "Child")

End Sub
```

AfterLabelEdit Event (ListView, TreeView Controls)

Occurs after a user edits the label of the currently selected **Node** or **ListItem** object.

Applies To

ListView Control, **TreeView** Control

Syntax

Private Sub *object*_**AfterLabelEdit**(*cancel* **As Integer**, *newstring* **As String**)

The **AfterLabelEdit** event syntax has these parts:

Part	Description
object	An object expression that evaluates to an object in the **Applies To** list.

(continued)

Part	Description
cancel	An integer that determines if the label editing operation is canceled. Any nonzero integer cancels the operation. Boolean values are also accepted.
newstring	The string the user entered, or **Null** if the user canceled the operation.

Remarks

Both the **AfterLabelEdit** and the **BeforeLabelEdit** events are generated only if the **LabelEdit** property is set to 0 (`Automatic`), or if the **StartLabelEdit** method is invoked.

The **AfterLabelEdit** event is generated after the user finishes the editing operation, which occurs when the user clicks on another **Node** or **ListItem** or presses the ENTER key.

To cancel a label editing operation, set *cancel* to any nonzero number or to **True**. If a label editing operation is canceled, the previously existing label is restored.

The *newstring* argument can be used to test for a condition before canceling an operation. For example, the following code cancels the operation if *newstring* is a number:

```
Private Sub TreeView1_AfterLabelEdit(Cancel As Integer,
NewString As String)
    If IsNumeric(NewString) Then
        MsgBox "No numbers allowed"
        Cancel = True
    End If
End Sub
```

See Also

ListItem Object, **ListItems** Collection, **Node** Object, **Nodes** Collection, **BeforeLabelEdit** Event (ListView, TreeView Controls), **LabelEdit** Property, **NodeClick** Event, **StartLabelEdit** Method

Examples

This example adds three **Node** objects to a **TreeView** control. When you attempt to edit a **Node** object's label, the object's index is checked. If it is 1, the operation is canceled. To try the example, place a **TreeView** control on a form and paste the code into the form's Declarations section. Run the example, click twice on the top **Node** object's label to edit it, type in some text, and press ENTER.

```
Private Sub Form_Load()
    TreeView1.Style = tvwTreelinesText   ' Lines and text.
    Dim nodX As Node
    Set nodX = TreeView1.Nodes.Add(,,,"Parent")
    Set nodX = TreeView1.Nodes.Add(1,tvwChild,,"Child1")
    Set nodX = TreeView1.Nodes.Add(1,tvwChild,,"Child2")
    nodX.EnsureVisible   ' Make sure all nodes are visible.
End Sub
```

```
Private Sub TreeView1_AfterLabelEdit _
(Cancel As Integer, NewString As String)
   ' If current node's index is 1, edit is canceled.
   If TreeView1.SelectedItem.Index = 1 Then
      Cancel = True
      MsgBox "Can't replace " & TreeView1.SelectedItem.Text & _
      " with " & NewString
   End If
End Sub
```

This example adds three **ListItem** objects to a **ListView** control. When you attempt to edit a **ListItem** object's label, the object's index is checked. If it is 1, the operation is canceled. To try the example, place a **ListView** control on a form and paste the code into the form's Declarations section. Run the example, click twice on any **ListItem** object's label to edit it, type in some text, and press ENTER.

```
Private Sub Form_Load()
   Dim itmX As ListItem
   Set itmX = ListView1.ListItems.Add(,,"Item1")
   Set itmX = ListView1.ListItems.Add(,,"Item 2")
   Set itmX = ListView1.ListItems.Add(,,"Item 3")
End Sub

Private Sub ListView1_AfterLabelEdit _
(Cancel As Integer, NewString As String)
   ' If current ListItem's index is 1, edit is canceled.
   If ListView1.SelectedItem.Index = 1 Then
      Cancel = True
      MsgBox "Can't replace " & ListView1.SelectedItem.Text & _
      " with " & NewString
   End If
End Sub
```

BeforeLabelEdit Event (ListView, TreeView Controls)

Occurs when a user attempts to edit the label of the currently selected **ListItem** or **Node** object.

Applies To

ListView Control, **TreeView** Control

Syntax

Private Sub *object*_**BeforeLabelEdit**(*cancel* **As Integer**)

The **BeforeLabelEdit** event syntax has these parts:

Part	Description
object	An object expression that evaluates to an object in the **Applies To** list.
cancel	An integer that determines if the operation is canceled. Any nonzero integer cancels the operation. The default is 0.

Remarks

Both the **AfterLabelEdit** and the **BeforeLabelEdit** events are generated only if the **LabelEdit** property is set to 0 (`Automatic`), or if the **StartLabelEdit** method is invoked.

The **BeforeLabelEdit** event occurs after the standard **Click** event.

To begin editing a label, the user must first click the object to select it, and click it a second time to begin the operation. The **BeforeLabelEdit** event occurs after the second click.

To determine which object's label is being edited, use the **SelectedItem** property. The following example checks the index of a selected **Node** before allowing an edit. If the index is 1, the operation is cancelled.

```
Private Sub TreeView1_BeforeLabelEdit(Cancel As Integer)
    If TreeView1.SelectedItem.Index = 1 Then
        Cancel = True                 ' Cancel the operation
    End If
End Sub
```

See Also

ListItem Object, **ListItems** Collection, **Node** Object, **Nodes** Collection, **AfterLabelEdit** Event (ListView, TreeView Controls), **LabelEdit** Property, **SelectedItem** Property (ActiveX Controls), **StartLabelEdit** Method, **Click** Event

Examples

This example adds several **Node** objects to a **TreeView** control. If you try to edit a label, the **Node** object's index is checked. If it is 1, the edit is prevented. To try the example, place a **TreeView** control on a form and paste the code into the form's Declarations section. Run the example, and try to edit the labels.

```
Private Sub Form_Load()
    Dim nodX As Node
    Set nodX = TreeView1.Nodes.Add(,,"P1","Parent 1")
    Set nodX = TreeView1.Nodes.Add("P1",tvwChild,,"Child 1")
    Set nodX = TreeView1.Nodes.Add("P1",tvwChild,,"Child 2")
    nodX.EnsureVisible' Make sure all nodes are visible.
End Sub

Private Sub TreeView1_BeforeLabelEdit(Cancel As Integer)
    ' Check selected node's index. If it is 1,
    ' then cancel the editing operation.
    If TreeView1.SelectedItem.Index = 1 Then
        MsgBox "Can't edit " + TreeView1.SelectedItem.Text
        Cancel = True
    End If
End Sub
```

This example adds several **ListItem** objects to a **ListView** control. If you try to edit a label, the **ListItem** object's index is checked. If it is 1, the edit is prevented. To try the example, place a **ListView** control on a form and paste the code into the form's Declarations section. Run the example, and try to edit the labels.

```
Private Sub Form_Load()
    Dim nodX As ListViewItem
    Set nodX = ListView1.ListItems.Add(, , "Item 1")
    Set nodX = ListView1.ListItems.Add(, , "Item 2")
    Set nodX = ListView1.ListItems.Add(, , "Item 3")
End Sub

Private Sub ListView1_BeforeLabelEdit(Cancel As Integer)
    ' Check selected item's index. If it is 1,
    ' then cancel the editing operation.
    If ListView1.SelectedItem.Index = 1 Then
        MsgBox "Can't edit " + ListView1.SelectedItem.Text
            Cancel = True
    End If
End Sub
```

Child Property (TreeView Control)

Returns a reference to the first child of a **Node** object in a **TreeView** control.

Applies To

TreeView Control, **Node** Object, **Nodes** Collection

Syntax

object.**Child**

The *object* placeholder represents an object expression that evaluates to an object in the **Applies To** list.

Remarks

The **Child**, **FirstSibling**, **LastSibling**, **Previous**, **Parent**, **Next**, and **Root** properties all return a reference to another **Node** object. Therefore, you can simultaneously reference and perform operations on a **Node**, as follows:

```
With TreeView1.Nodes(TreeView1.SelectedItem.Index).Child
    .Text = "New text"
    .Key = "New key"
    .SelectedImage = 3
End With
```

You can also set an object variable to the referenced **Node**, as follows:

```
Dim NodChild As Node
' Get a reference to the child of the selected node.
Set NodChild = TreeView1.Nodes(TreeView1.SelectedItem.Index).Child
' Use this reference to perform operations on the child Node.
With nodChild
```

```
   .Text = "New text"      ' Change the text.
   .Key = "New key"        ' Change key.
   .SelectedImage = 3      ' Change SelectedImage.
End With
```

See Also

Children Property, **FirstSibling** Property, **LastSibling** Property, **Next** Property, **Parent** Property (Node Object), **Previous** Property (Node Object), **Root** Property (Node Object)

Example

This example creates several **Node** objects. When you click on a **Node** object, the code first uses the **Children** property to determine if the **Node** has children nodes. If so, the caption of the form displays the text of the **Child** node.

```
Option Explicit

Private Sub Form_Load()
' This code creates a tree with 3 Node objects.
   TreeView1.Style = tvwTreelinesPlusMinusText  ' Style 6.
   TreeView1.LineStyle = tvwRootLines            'Linestyle 1.

   ' Add several Node objects.
   Dim nodX As Node                             ' Create variable.

   Set nodX = TreeView1.Nodes.Add(, , "r", "Root")
   Set nodX = TreeView1.Nodes.Add("r", tvwChild, "c1", "Child 1")

   nodX.EnsureVisible                           ' Show all nodes.
   Set nodX = TreeView1.Nodes.Add("c1", tvwChild, "c2", "Child 2")
   Set nodX = TreeView1.Nodes.Add("c1", tvwChild, "c3", "Child 3")
   nodX.EnsureVisible                           ' Show all nodes.
End Sub

Private Sub TreeView1_NodeClick(ByVal Node As Node)
   ' If the Node does have children, then display the text of
   ' the child Node.
   If Node.Children Then
      Caption = Node.Child.Text
   End If
End Sub
```

Children Property

Returns the number of child **Node** objects contained in a **Node** object.

Applies To

TreeView Control, **Node** Object, **Nodes** Collection

Syntax

object.**Children**

The *object* placeholder represents an object expression that evaluates to an object in the **Applies To** list.

Remarks

The **Children** property can be used to check if a **Node** object has any children before performing an operation that affects the children. For example, the following code checks for the presence of child nodes before retrieving the **Text** property of the first **Node**, using the **Child** property.

```
Private Sub TreeView1_NodeClick(ByVal Node As Node)
    If Node.Children > 0 Then
        MsgBox Node.Child.Text
    End If
End Sub
```

See Also

Child Property (TreeView Control), **Text** Property

Example

This example puts several **Node** objects in a **TreeView** control. The code checks to see if a **Node** has children nodes. If so, then it displays the text of the children nodes. To try the example, place a **TreeView** control on a form and paste the code into the form's Declarations section. Run the example, click a **Node** object to select it, then click the form to see the text of the **Node** object's children.

```
Option Explicit
Private Sub Form_Click()
    Dim strC As String
    Dim N As Integer
    If TreeView1.SelectedItem.Children > 0 Then ' There are children.

        ' Get first child's text, and set N to its index value.
        strC = TreeView1.SelectedItem.Child.Text & vbLF
        N = TreeView1.SelectedItem.Child.Index

        ' While N is not the index of the child node's
        ' last sibling, get next sibling's text.
        While N <> TreeView1.SelectedItem.Child.LastSibling.Index
            strC = strC & TreeView1.Nodes(N).Next.Text & vbLF
            ' Reset N to next sibling's index.
            N = TreeView1.Nodes(N).Next.Index
        Wend
        ' Show results.
        MsgBox "Children of " & TreeView1.SelectedItem.Text & _
        " are: " & vbLF & strC
    Else                            ' There are no children.
        MsgBox TreeView1.SelectedItem.Text & " has no children"
    End If
End Sub

Private Sub Form_Load()
    TreeView1.BorderStyle = 1  ' Ensure border is visible
    Dim nodX As Node
```

```
Set nodX = TreeView1.Nodes.Add(,,"d","Dates")
Set nodX = TreeView1.Nodes.Add("d",tvwChild,"d89","1989")
Set nodX = TreeView1.Nodes.Add("d",tvwChild,"d90","1990")

' Create children of 1989 node.
Set nodX = TreeView1.Nodes.Add("d89",tvwChild, ,"John")
Set nodX = TreeView1.Nodes.Add("d89",tvwChild, ,"Brent")
Set nodX = TreeView1.Nodes.Add("d89",tvwChild, ,"Eric")
Set nodX = TreeView1.Nodes.Add("d89",tvwChild, ,"Ian")
nodX.EnsureVisible ' Show all nodes.

' Create children of 1990 node.
Set nodX = TreeView1.Nodes.Add("d90",tvwChild, ,"Randy")
Set nodX = TreeView1.Nodes.Add("d90",tvwChild, ,"Ron")
nodX.EnsureVisible ' Show all nodes.
End Sub
```

Collapse Event (TreeView Control)

Generated when any **Node** object in a **TreeView** control is collapsed.

Applies To

TreeView Control, **Node** Object, **Nodes** Collection

Syntax

Private Sub *object*_**Collapse(ByVal** *node* **As Node)**

The **Collapse** event syntax has these parts:

Part	Description
object	An object expression that evaluates to an object in the **Applies To** list.
node	A reference to the clicked **Node** object.

Remarks

The Collapse event occurs before the standard **Click** event.

There are three methods of collapsing a **Node**: by setting the **Node** object's **Expanded** property to **False**, by double-clicking a **Node** object, and by clicking a plus/minus image when the **TreeView** control's **Style** property is set to a style that includes plus/minus images. All of these methods generate the **Collapse** event.

The event passes a reference to the collapsed **Node** object. The reference can validate an action, as in the following example:

```
Private Sub TreeView1_Collapse(ByVal Node As Node)
    If Node.Index = 1 Then
        Node.Expanded = True ' Expand the node again.
    End If
End Sub
```

See Also

Expand Event (TreeView Control), **Expanded** Property, **NodeClick** Event, **SelectedItem** Property (ActiveX Controls), **Style** Property (TreeView Control)

Example

This example adds one **Node** object, with several child nodes, to a **TreeView** control. When the user collapses a **Node,** the code checks to see how many children the **Node** has. If it has more than one child, the **Node** is re-expanded. To try the example, place a **TreeView** control on a form and paste the code into the form's Declarations section. Run the example, and double-click a **Node** to collapse it and generate the event.

```
Private Sub Form_Load()
    TreeView1.Style = tvwTreelinesPlusMinusText ' Style 6.
    Dim nodX As Node
    Set nodX = TreeView1.Nodes.Add(,,"DV","Da Vinci")
    Set nodX = TreeView1.Nodes.Add("DV",tvwChild,"T","Titian")
    Set nodX = TreeView1.Nodes.Add("T",tvwChild,"R","Rembrandt")
    Set nodX = TreeView1.Nodes.Add("R",tvwChild,,"Goya")
    Set nodX = TreeView1.Nodes.Add("R",tvwChild,,"David")
    nodX.EnsureVisible' Show all nodes.
End Sub

Private Sub TreeView1_Collapse(ByVal Node As Node)
    ' If the Node has more than one child node,
    ' keep the node expanded.
    Select Case Node.Children
       Case Is > 1
           Node.Expanded = True
    End Select
End Sub
```

CreateDragImage Method

Creates a drag image using a dithered version of an object's associated image. This image is typically used in drag-and-drop operations.

Applies To

ListView Control, **ListItem** Object, **ListItems** Collection, **TreeView** Control, **Node** Object, **Nodes** Collection

Syntax

object.**CreateDragImage**

The *object* placeholder represents an object expression that evaluates to an object in the **Applies To** list.

Remarks

The **CreateDragImage** method is typically used to assign an image to a **DragIcon** property at the start of a drag-and-drop operation.

See Also

DropHighlight Property (ListView, TreeView Controls), **HitTest** Method (ListView, TreeView Controls), **DragIcon** Property

Example

This example adds several **Node** objects to a **TreeView** control. After you select a **Node** object, you can drag it to any other **Node**. To try the example, place **TreeView** and **ImageList** controls on a form and paste the code into the form's Declaration section. Run the example and drag **Node** objects around to see the result.

```
' Declare global variables.
Dim indrag As Boolean    ' Flag that signals a Drag Drop operation.
Dim nodX As Object       ' Item that is being dragged.

Private Sub Form_Load()
    ' Load a bitmap into an Imagelist control.
    Dim imgX As ListImage
    Dim BitmapPath As String
    BitmapPath = "icons\mail\mail01a.ico"
    Set imgX = imagelist1.ListImages.Add(, , LoadPicture(BitmapPath))

    ' Initialize TreeView control and create several nodes.
    TreeView1.ImageList = imagelist1
    Dim nodX As Node     ' Create a tree.
    Set nodX = TreeView1.Nodes.Add(, , , "Parent1", 1)
    Set nodX = TreeView1.Nodes.Add(, , , "Parent2", 1)
    Set nodX = TreeView1.Nodes.Add(1, tvwChild, , "Child 1", 1)
    Set nodX = TreeView1.Nodes.Add(1, tvwChild, , "Child 2", 1)
    Set nodX = TreeView1.Nodes.Add(2, tvwChild, , "Child 3", 1)
    Set nodX = TreeView1.Nodes.Add(2, tvwChild, , "Child 4", 1)
    Set nodX = TreeView1.Nodes.Add(3, tvwChild, , "Child 5", 1)
    nodX.EnsureVisible    ' Expand tree to show all nodes.
End Sub

Private Sub TreeView1_MouseDown_
(Button As Integer, Shift As Integer, x As Single, y As Single)
    Set nodX = TreeView1.SelectedItem  ' Set the item being dragged.
End Sub

Private Sub TreeView1_MouseMove _
(Button As Integer, Shift As Integer, x As Single, y As Single)
    If Button = vbLeftButton Then      ' Signal a Drag operation.
        indrag = True                  ' Set the flag to true.
        ' Set the drag icon with the CreateDragImage method.
        TreeView1.DragIcon = TreeView1.SelectedItem.CreateDragImage
        TreeView1.Drag vbBeginDrag     ' Drag operation.
    End If
End Sub

Private Sub TreeView1_DragDrop_
(Source As Control, x As Single, y As Single)
    If TreeView1.DropHighlight Is Nothing Then
        Set TreeView1.DropHighlight = Nothing
```

```
                indrag = False
                Exit Sub
            Else
                If nodX = TreeView1.DropHighlight Then Exit Sub
                Cls
                Print nodX.Text & " dropped on " & TreeView1.DropHighlight.Text
                Set TreeView1.DropHighlight = Nothing
                indrag = False
            End If
        End Sub

        Private Sub TreeView1_DragOver(Source As Control, x As Single,
        y As Single, State As Integer)
            If indrag = True Then
                ' Set DropHighlight to the mouse's coordinates.
                Set TreeView1.DropHighlight = TreeView1.HitTest(x, y)
            End If
        End Sub
```

DropHighlight Property (ListView, TreeView Controls)

Returns or sets a reference to a **Node** or **ListItem** object that is highlighted with the system highlight color when the cursor moves over it.

Applies To

ListView Control, **TreeView** Control

Syntax

object.**DropHighlight** [= *value*]

The **DropHighlight** property syntax has these parts:

Part	Description
object	An object expression that evaluates to an object in the **Applies To** list.
value	A **Node** or **ListItem** object.

Remarks

The **DropHighlight** property is typically used in combination with the **HitTest** method in drag-and-drop operations. As the cursor is dragged over a **ListItem** or **Node** object, the **HitTest** method returns a reference to any object it is dragged over. In turn, the **DropHighlight** property is set to the hit object, and simultaneously returns a reference to that object. The **DropHighlight** property then highlights the hit object with the system highlight color. The following code sets the **DropHighlight** property to the object hit with the **HitTest** method.

```
Private Sub TreeView1_DragOver _
(Source As Control, X As Single, Y As Single, State As Integer)
   Set TreeView1.DropHighlight = TreeView1.HitTest(X,Y)
End Sub
```

Subsequently, you can use the **DropHighlight** property in the **DragDrop** event to return a reference to the last object the source control was dropped over, as shown in the following code:

```
Private Sub TreeView1_DragDrop _
(Source As Control, x As Single, y As Single)
   ' DropHighlight returns a reference to object drop occurred over.
   Me.Caption = TreeView1.DropHighlight.Text
   ' To release the DropHighlight reference, set it to Nothing.
   Set TreeView1.DropHighlight = Nothing
End Sub
```

Note that in the preceding example, the **DropHighlight** property is set to Nothing after the procedure is completed. This must be done to release the highlight effect.

See Also

ListItem Object, **ListItems** Collection, **Node** Object, **Nodes** Collection, **HitTest** Method (ListView, TreeView Controls), **DragDrop** Event

Example

This example adds several **Node** objects to a **TreeView** control. After you select a **Node** object, you can drag it to any other **Node**. To try the example, place **TreeView** and **ImageList** controls on a form and paste the code into the form's Declaration section. Run the example and drag **Node** objects around to see the result.

```
' Declare global variables.
Dim indrag As Boolean       ' Flag that signals a Drag Drop operation.
Dim nodX As Object          ' Item that is being dragged.

Private Sub Form_Load()
   ' Load a bitmap into an Imagelist control.
   Dim imgX As ListImage
   Dim BitmapPath As String
   BitmapPath = "icons\mail\mail01a.ico"
   Set imgX = imagelist1.ListImages.Add(, , LoadPicture(BitmapPath))

   ' Initialize TreeView control and create several nodes.
   TreeView1.ImageList = imagelist1
   Dim nodX As Node       ' Create a tree.
   Set nodX = TreeView1.Nodes.Add(, , , "Parent1", 1)
   Set nodX = TreeView1.Nodes.Add(, , , "Parent2", 1)
   Set nodX = TreeView1.Nodes.Add(1, tvwChild, , "Child 1", 1)
   Set nodX = TreeView1.Nodes.Add(1, tvwChild, , "Child 2", 1)
   Set nodX = TreeView1.Nodes.Add(2, tvwChild, , "Child 3", 1)
   Set nodX = TreeView1.Nodes.Add(2, tvwChild, , "Child 4", 1)
   Set nodX = TreeView1.Nodes.Add(3, tvwChild, , "Child 5", 1)
   nodX.EnsureVisible       ' Expand tree to show all nodes.
End Sub
```

```
        Private Sub TreeView1_MouseDown_
        (Button As Integer, Shift As Integer, x As Single, y As Single)
            Set nodX = TreeView1.SelectedItem ' Set the item being dragged.
        End Sub

        Private Sub TreeView1_MouseMove _
        (Button As Integer, Shift As Integer, x As Single, y As Single)
            If Button = vbLeftButton Then      ' Signal a Drag operation.
                indrag = True                  ' Set the flag to true.
                ' Set the drag icon with the CreateDragImage method.
                TreeView1.DragIcon = TreeView1.SelectedItem.CreateDragImage
                TreeView1.Drag vbBeginDrag      ' Drag operation.
            End If
        End Sub

        Private Sub TreeView1_DragDrop_
        (Source As Control, x As Single, y As Single)
            If TreeView1.DropHighlight Is Nothing Then
                Set TreeView1.DropHighlight = Nothing
                indrag = False
                Exit Sub
            Else
                If nodX = TreeView1.DropHighlight Then Exit Sub
                Cls
                Print nodX.Text & " dropped on " & TreeView1.DropHighlight.Text
                Set TreeView1.DropHighlight = Nothing
                indrag = False
            End If
        End Sub

        Private Sub TreeView1_DragOver(Source As Control, x As Single,
        y As Single, State As Integer)
            If indrag = True Then
                ' Set DropHighlight to the mouse's coordinates.
                Set TreeView1.DropHighlight = TreeView1.HitTest(x, y)
            End If
        End Sub
```

EnsureVisible Method

Ensures that a specified **ListItem** or **Node** object is visible. If necessary, this method expands **Node** objects and scrolls the **TreeView** control. The method only scrolls the **ListView** control.

Applies To

ListView Control, **ListItem** Object, **ListItems** Collection, **TreeView** Control, **Node** Object, **Nodes** Collection

Syntax

object.**EnsureVisible**

The *object* placeholder represents an object expression that evaluates to an object in the **Applies To** list.

Return Values

Value	Description
True	The method returns **True** if the **ListView** or **TreeView** control must scroll and/or expand to expose the object.
False	The method returns **False** if no scrolling and/or expansion is required.

Remarks

Use the **EnsureVisible** method when you want a particular **Node** or **ListItem** object, which might be hidden deep in a **TreeView** or **ListView** control, to be visible.

See Also

ListItem Object, **ListItems** Collection, **Node** Object, **Nodes** Collection, **Expand** Event (TreeView Control), **Expanded** Property

Example

This example adds many nodes to a **TreeView** control, and uses the **EnsureVisible** method to scroll and expand the tree. To try the example, place a **TreeView** control on a form and paste the code into the form's Declarations section. Run the example, and click the form to see the **TreeView** expand.

```
Private Sub Form_Load()
    Dim nodX As Node
    Dim i as Integer
    TreeView1.BorderStyle = FixedSingle            ' Show borders.

    Set nodX = TreeView1.Nodes.Add(,,,"Root")      ' Add first node.
    For i = 1 to 15' Add 15 nodes
        Set nodX = TreeView1.Nodes.Add(i,,,"Node " & CStr(i))
    Next i

    Set nodX = TreeView1.Nodes.Add(,,,"Bottom")        ' Add one with text.
    Set nodX = TreeView1.Nodes.Add(i,,,"Expanded")     ' Add child to node.
    Set nodX = TreeView1.Nodes.Add(i+1,,,"Show me")    ' Add a final child.
End Sub

Private Sub Form_Click()
    ' Tree will scroll and expand when you click the form.
    TreeView1.Nodes(TreeView1.Nodes.Count).EnsureVisible
End Sub
```

Expand Event (TreeView Control)

Occurs when a **Node** object in a **TreeView** control is expanded, that is, when its child nodes become visible.

Applies To

TreeView Control, **Node** Object, **Nodes** Collection

Syntax

Private Sub *object*_**Expand(ByVal** *node* **As Node)**

The **Expand** event syntax has these parts:

Part	Description
object	An object expression that evaluates to an object in the **Applies To** list.
node	A reference to the expanded **Node** object.

Remarks

The **Expand** event occurs after the **Click** and **DblClick** events.

The **Expand** event is generated in three ways: when the user double-clicks a **Node** object that has child nodes; when the **Expanded** property for a **Node** object is set to **True**; and when the plus/minus image is clicked. Use the **Expand** event to validate an object, as in the following example:

```
Private Sub TreeView1_Expand(ByVal Node As Node)
    If Node.Index <> 1 Then
        Node.Expanded = False         ' Prevent expand.
    End If
End Sub
```

See Also

Expanded Property, **Click** Event, **DblClick** Event

Example

This example adds several **Node** objects to a **TreeView** control. When a **Node** is expanded, the Expand event is generated, and information about the **Node** is displayed. To try the example, place a **TreeView** control on a form and paste the code into the form's Declarations section. Run the example, and expand the nodes.

```
Private Sub Form_Load()
    Dim nodX As Node
    Set nodX = TreeView1.Nodes.Add(, , "RP", "Root Parent")
    Set nodX = TreeView1.Nodes.Add("RP", tvwChild, "C1", "Child1")
    Set nodX = TreeView1.Nodes.Add("C1", tvwChild, "C2", "Child2")
    Set nodX = TreeView1.Nodes.Add("C2", tvwChild, "C3", " Child3")
    Set nodX = TreeView1.Nodes.Add("C2", tvwChild, "C4", " Child4")
    TreeView1.Style = tvwTreelinesPlusMinusText     ' Style 6.
    TreeView1.LineStyle = tvwRootLines              ' Style 1
End Sub

Private Sub TreeView1_Expand(ByVal Node As Node)
    Select Case Node.Key Like "C*"
    Case Is = True
        MsgBox Node.Text & " is a child node."
    End Select
End Sub
```

Expanded Property

Returns or sets a value that determines whether a **Node** object in a **TreeView** control is currently expanded or collapsed.

Applies To

TreeView Control, **Node** Object, **Nodes** Collection

Syntax

object.**Expanded**[= *boolean*]

The **Expanded** property syntax has these parts:

Part	Description
object	An object expression that evaluates to an object in the **Applies To** list.
boolean	A Boolean expression that specifies whether the node is expanded or collapsed.

The settings for *boolean* are:

Setting	Description
True	The **Node** is currently expanded.
False	The **Node** is currently collapsed.

Remarks

You can use the **Expanded** property to programmatically expand a **Node** object. The following code has the same effect as double-clicking the first **Node**:

```
TreeView1.Nodes(1).Expanded = True
```

When a **Node** object is expanded, the **Expand** event is generated.

If a **Node** object has no child nodes, the property value is ignored.

See Also

EnsureVisible Method, **Expand** Event (TreeView Control)

Example

This example adds several **Node** objects to a **TreeView** control. When you click the form, the **Expanded** property for each **Node** is set to **True**. To try the example, place a **TreeView** control on a form and paste the code into the form's Declarations section. Run the example, and click the form to expand all the **Node** objects.

```
Private Sub Form_Load()
    Dim nodX As Node
    Dim i as Integer
    TreeView1.BorderStyle = vbFixedSingle      ' Show border.

    ' Create a root node.
    Set nodX = TreeView1.Nodes.Add(,,"root","Root")
```

```
        For i = 1 to 5                              ' Add 5 child nodes.
           Set nodX = TreeView1.Nodes.Add(i,tvwChild,,"Node " & CStr(i))
        Next i
     End Sub

     Private Sub Form_Click()
        Dim I as Integer
        For I = 1 to TreeView1.Nodes.Count
           ' Expand all nodes.
           TreeView1.Nodes(i).Expanded = True
        Next I
     End Sub
```

ExpandedImage Property

Returns or sets the index or key value of a **ListImage** object in an associated **ImageList** control; the **ListImage** is displayed when a **Node** object is expanded.

Applies To

TreeView Control, **Node** Object, **Nodes** Collection

Syntax

object.**ExpandedImage**[= *number*]

The **ExpandedImage** property syntax has these parts:

Part	Description
object	An object expression that evaluates to an object in the **Applies To** list.
number	A numeric expression or string expression that specifies, respectively, the index value or the key value of the image to be displayed.

Remarks

This property allows you to change the image associated with a **Node** object when the user double-clicks the node or when the **Node** object's **Expanded** property is set to **True**.

See Also

ImageList Control, **ListImage** Object, **ListImages** Collection, **Expand** Event (TreeView Control), **Expanded** Property, **SelectedImage** Property, **Image** Property (ActiveX Controls), **ImageList** Property (ActiveX Controls)

FirstSibling Property

Returns a reference to the first sibling of a **Node** object in a **TreeView** control.

Applies To

TreeView Control, **Node** Object, **Nodes** Collection

Syntax

object.**FirstSibling**

The *object* placeholder represents an object expression that evaluates to an object in the **Applies To** list.

Remarks

The first sibling is the **Node** that appears in the first position in one level of a hierarchy of nodes. Which **Node** actually appears in the first position depends on whether or not the **Node** objects at that level are sorted, which is determined by the **Sorted** property.

The **Child**, **FirstSibling**, **LastSibling**, **Previous**, **Parent**, **Next**, and **Root** properties all return a reference to another **Node** object. Therefore you can simultaneously reference and perform operations on a **Node**, as follows:

```
With TreeView1.Nodes(x).FirstSibling
    .Text = "New text"
    .Key = "New key"
    .SelectedImage = 3
End With
```

You can also set an object variable to the referenced **Node**, as follows:

```
Dim NodFirstSib As Node
' Get a reference to the first sibling of Node x.
Set NodFirstSib = TreeView1.Nodes(x).FirstSibling
' Use this reference to perform operations on the first sibling Node.
With nodFirstSib
    .Text = "New text"        '  Change the text.
    .Key = "New key"          ' Change key.
    .SelectedImage = 3        ' Change SelectedImage.
End With
```

See Also

Child Property (TreeView Control), **LastSibling** Property, **Next** Property, **Parent** Property (Node Object), **Previous** Property (Node Object), **Root** Property (Node Object), **Sorted** Property (TreeView Control)

Example

This example adds several nodes to a **TreeView** control. The **FirstSibling** property, in conjunction with the **Next** property and the **LastSibling** property, is used to navigate through a clicked **Node** object's hierarchy . To try the example, place a **TreeView** control on a form and paste the code into the form's Declarations section. Run the example and click the various nodes to see what is returned.

```
Private Sub Form_Load()
    Dim nodX As Node
    Set nodX = TreeView1.Nodes.Add(,,"dad","Mike") ' A first sibling.
    Set nodX = TreeView1.Nodes.Add(,,"mom","Carol")
    Set nodX = TreeView1.Nodes.Add(,,,"Alice")
```

```
      ' Marsha is the FirstSibling.
      Set nodX = TreeView1.Nodes.Add("mom",tvwChild,,"Marsha")
      Set nodX = TreeView1.Nodes.Add("mom",tvwChild,,"Jan")
      Set nodX = TreeView1.Nodes.Add("mom",tvwChild,,"Cindy")
      nodX.EnsureVisible ' Show all nodes.

      ' Greg is the FirstSibling.
      Set nodX = TreeView1.Nodes.Add("dad",tvwChild,,"Greg")
      Set nodX = TreeView1.Nodes.Add("dad",tvwChild,,"Peter")
      Set nodX = TreeView1.Nodes.Add("dad",tvwChild,,"Bobby")
      nodX.EnsureVisible          ' Show all nodes.
   End Sub

   Private Sub TreeView1_NodeClick(ByVal Node As Node)
      Dim strText As String
      Dim n As Integer
      ' Set n to FirstSibling's index.
      n = Node.FirstSibling.Index
      ' Place FirstSibling's text & linefeed in string variable.
      strText = Node.FirstSibling.Text & vbLF
      While n <> Node.LastSibling.Index
      ' While n is not the index of the last sibling, go to the
      ' next sibling and place its text into the string variable.
         strText = strText & TreeView1.Nodes(n).Next.Text & vbLF
      ' Set n to the next node's index.
         n = TreeView1.Nodes(n).Next.Index
      Wend
      MsgBox strText              ' Display results.
   End Sub
```

FullPath Property

Returns the fully qualified path of the referenced **Node** object in a **TreeView** control. When you assign this property to a string variable, the string is set to the **FullPath** of the node with the specified index.

Applies To

Node Object, **Nodes** Collection

Syntax

object.**FullPath**

The *object* placeholder represents an object expression that evaluates to an object in the **Applies To** list.

Remarks

The fully qualified path is the concatenation of the text in the referenced **Node** object's **Text** property with the **Text** property values of all its ancestors. The value of the **PathSeparator** property determines the delimiter.

See Also

TreeView Control, **Node** Object, **Nodes** Collection, **PathSeparator** Property (TreeView Control), **Text** Property

Example

This example adds several **Node** objects to a **TreeView** control and displays the fully qualified path of each when selected. To try the example, place a **TreeView** control on a form and paste the code into the form's Declarations section. Run the example, then select a node and click the form to display the **Node** object's full path.

```
Private Sub Form_Load()
   Dim nodX As Node
   Set nodX = TreeView1.Nodes.Add(,,,"Root")
   Set nodX = TreeView1.Nodes.Add(1,tvwChild,,"Dir1")
   Set nodX = TreeView1.Nodes.Add(2,tvwChild,,"Dir2")
   Set nodX = TreeView1.Nodes.Add(3,tvwChild,,"Dir3")
   Set nodX = TreeView1.Nodes.Add(4,tvwChild,,"Dir4")
   nodX.EnsureVisible' Show all nodes.
   TreeView1.Style = tvwTreelinesText ' Style 4.
End Sub

Private Sub TreeView1_NodeClick(ByVal Node As Node)
   MsgBox Node.FullPath
End Sub
```

GetVisibleCount Method

Returns the number of **Node** objects that fit in the internal area of a **TreeView** control.

Applies To

TreeView Control, **Node** Object, **Nodes** Collection

Syntax

object.**GetVisibleCount**

The *object* placeholder represents an object expression that evaluates to an object in the **Applies To** list.

Remarks

The number of **Node** objects is determined by how many lines can fit in a window. The total number of lines possible is determined by the height of the control and the **Size** property of the **Font** object. The count includes the partially visible item at the bottom of the list.

You can use the **GetVisibleCount** property to make sure that a minimum number of lines are visible so the user can accurately assess a hierarchy. If the minimum number of lines is not visible, you can reset the size of the **TreeView** using the **Height** property.

If a particular **Node** object must be visible, use the **EnsureVisible** method to scroll and expand the **TreeView** control.

See Also

EnsureVisible Method, **Font** Object, **Height**, **Width** Properties, **Size** Property (Font)

Example

This example adds several **Node** objects to a **TreeView** control. When you click the form, the code uses the **GetVisibleCount** method to check how many lines are visible, and then enlarges the control to show all the objects. To try the example, place a **TreeView** control on a form and paste the code into the form's Declarations section. Run the example, and click the form to enlarge the control.

```
Private Sub Form_Load()
   Dim nodX As Node
   Dim i as Integer
   TreeView1.BorderStyle = 1  ' Show border.
   For i = 1 to 20
      Set nodX = TreeView1.Nodes.Add(,,,"Node " & CStr(i))
   Next I
   TreeView1.Height = 1500  ' TreeView is short, for comparison's sake.
End Sub

Private Sub Form_Click()
   While Treeview1.GetVisibleCount < 20
      ' Make the treeview larger.
      TreeView1.Height = TreeView1.Height + TreeView1.Font.Size
   Wend
End Sub
```

HitTest Method (ListView, TreeView Controls)

Returns a reference to the **ListItem** object or **Node** object located at the coordinates of x and y. Most often used with drag-and-drop operations to determine if a drop target item is available at the present location.

Applies To

ListView Control, **ListItem** Object, **ListItems** Collection, **TreeView** Control, **Node** Object, **Nodes** Collection

Syntax

object.**HitTest** (*x* **As Single,** *y* **As Single**)

The **HitTest** method syntax has these parts:

Part	Description
object	An object expression that evaluates to an object in the **Applies To** list.
x,y	Coordinates of a target object, which is either a **Node** object or a **ListItem** object.

Remarks

If no object exists at the specified coordinates, the **HitTest** method returns **Nothing**.

The **HitTest** method is most frequently used with the **DropHighlight** property to highlight an object as the mouse is dragged over it. The **DropHighlight** property requires a reference to a specific object that is to be highlighted. In order to determine that object, the **HitTest** method is used in combination with an event that returns x and y coordinates, such as the **DragOver** event, as follows:

```
Private Sub TreeView1_DragOver _
(Source As Control, X As Single, Y As Single, State As Integer)
    Set TreeView1.DropHighlight = TreeView1.HitTest(X,Y)
End Sub
```

Subsequently, you can use the **DropHighlight** property in the **DragDrop** event to return a reference to the last object the source control was dropped over, as shown in the following code:

```
Private Sub TreeView1_DragDrop _
(Source As Control, x As Single, y As Single)
    ' DropHighlight returns a reference to object drop occurred over.
    Me.Caption = TreeView1.DropHighlight.Text
    ' To release the DropHighlight reference, set it to Nothing.
    Set TreeView1.DropHighlight = Nothing
End Sub
```

Note in the preceding example that the **DropHighlight** property is set to **Nothing** after the procedure is completed. This must be done to release the highlight effect.

See Also

DropHighlight Property (ListView, TreeView Controls), **DragDrop** Event, **DragOver** Event

Example

This example adds several **Node** objects to a **TreeView** control. After you select a **Node** object, you can drag it to any other **Node**. To try the example, place **TreeView** and **ImageList** controls on a form and paste the code into the form's Declaration section. Run the example and drag **Node** objects around to see the result.

```
' Declare global variables.
Dim indrag As Boolean      ' Flag that signals a Drag Drop operation.
Dim nodX As Object         ' Item that is being dragged.

Private Sub Form_Load()
    ' Load a bitmap into an Imagelist control.
    Dim imgX As ListImage
    Dim BitmapPath As String
```

```
        BitmapPath = "icons\mail\mail01a.ico"
        Set imgX = imagelist1.ListImages.Add(, , LoadPicture(BitmapPath))

        ' Initialize TreeView control and create several nodes.
        TreeView1.ImageList = imagelist1
        Dim nodX As Node                    ' Create a tree.
        Set nodX = TreeView1.Nodes.Add(, , "Parent1", 1)
        Set nodX = TreeView1.Nodes.Add(, , "Parent2", 1)
        Set nodX = TreeView1.Nodes.Add(1, tvwChild, , "Child 1", 1)
        Set nodX = TreeView1.Nodes.Add(1, tvwChild, , "Child 2", 1)
        Set nodX = TreeView1.Nodes.Add(2, tvwChild, , "Child 3", 1)
        Set nodX = TreeView1.Nodes.Add(2, tvwChild, , "Child 4", 1)
        Set nodX = TreeView1.Nodes.Add(3, tvwChild, , "Child 5", 1)
        nodX.EnsureVisible                  ' Expand tree to show all nodes.
End Sub

Private Sub TreeView1_MouseDown_
(Button As Integer, Shift As Integer, x As Single, y As Single)
        Set nodX = TreeView1.SelectedItem ' Set the item being dragged.
End Sub

Private Sub TreeView1_MouseMove _
(Button As Integer, Shift As Integer, x As Single, y As Single)
        If Button = vbLeftButton Then      ' Signal a Drag operation.
            indrag = True                  ' Set the flag to true.
            ' Set the drag icon with the CreateDragImage method.
            TreeView1.DragIcon = TreeView1.SelectedItem.CreateDragImage
            TreeView1.Drag vbBeginDrag     ' Drag operation.
        End If
End Sub

Private Sub TreeView1_DragDrop_
(Source As Control, x As Single, y As Single)
        If TreeView1.DropHighlight Is Nothing Then
            Set TreeView1.DropHighlight = Nothing
            indrag = False
            Exit Sub
        Else
            If nodX = TreeView1.DropHighlight Then Exit Sub
            Cls
            Print nodX.Text & " dropped on " & TreeView1.DropHighlight.Text
            Set TreeView1.DropHighlight = Nothing
            indrag = False
        End If
End Sub

Private Sub TreeView1_DragOver(Source As Control, x As Single,
y As Single, State As Integer)
        If indrag = True Then
            ' Set DropHighlight to the mouse's coordinates.
            Set TreeView1.DropHighlight = TreeView1.HitTest(x, y)
        End If
End Sub
```

Indentation Property

Returns or sets the width of the indentation for a **TreeView** control. Each new child **Node** object is indented by this amount.

Applies To

TreeView Control

Syntax

object.**Indentation**[= *number*]

The **Indentation** property syntax has these parts:

Part	Description
object	An object expression that evaluates to an object in the **Applies To** list.
number	An integer specifying the width that each child **Node** is indented.

Remarks

If you change the **Indentation** property at run time, the **TreeView** is redrawn to reflect the new width. The property value cannot be negative.

See Also

Node Object, **Nodes** Collection

Example

This example adds several **Node** objects to a **TreeView** control, while the **Indentation** property is shown in the form's caption. An **OptionButton** control array provides alternate values for the **Indentation** width. To try the example, place a **TreeView** control and a control array of three **OptionButton** controls on a form, and paste the code into the form's Declarations section. Run the example, and click an **OptionButton** to change the **Indentation** property.

```
Private Sub Form_Load()
   ' Label OptionButton controls with Indentation choices.
   Option1(0).Caption = "250"
   Option1(1).Caption = "500"
   Option1(2).Caption = "1000"

   ' Select the first option, and set the indentation to 250 initially
   Option1(0).Value = True
   Treeview1.Indentation = 250

   Dim nodX As Node
   Dim i As Integer

   Set nodX = TreeView1.Nodes.Add(,,,CStr(1)) ' Add first node.

   For i = 1 To 6          ' Add 6 nodes.
      Set nodX = TreeView1.Nodes.Add(i,tvwChild,,CStr(i + 1))
   Next i
```

```
      nodX.EnsureVisible      ' Makes sure all nodes are visible.
      Form1.Caption = "Indentation = " & TreeView1.Indentation
   End Sub

   Private Sub Option1_Click(Index as Integer)
      ' Change Indentation with OptionButton value.
      TreeView1.Indentation = Val(Option1(Index).Caption)
      Form1.Caption = "Indentation = " & TreeView1.Indentation
   End Sub
```

LabelEdit Property

Returns or sets a value that determines if a user can edit labels of **ListItem** or **Node** objects in a **ListView** or **TreeView** control.

Applies To

ListView Control, **TreeView** Control

Syntax

object.**LabelEdit** [= *integer*]

The **LabelEdit** property syntax has these parts:

Part	Description
object	An object expression that evaluates to an object in the **Applies To** list.
integer	An integer that determines whether the label of a **Node** or **ListItem** object can be edited, as specified in **Settings**.

Settings

The settings for *integer* are:

Constant	Value	Description
ListView: **lvwAutomatic** TreeView: **tvwAutomatic**	0	(Default) Automatic. The **BeforeLabelEdit** event is generated when the user clicks the label of a selected node.
ListView: **lvwManual** TreeView: **tvwManual**	1	Manual. The **BeforeLabelEdit** event is generated only when the **StartLabelEdit** method is invoked.

Remarks

Label editing of an object is initiated when a selected object is clicked (if the **LabelEdit** property is set to Automatic). That is, the first click on an object will select it; a second (single) click on the object will initiate the label editing operation.

The **LabelEdit** property, in combination with the **StartLabelEdit** method, allows you to programmatically determine when and which labels can be edited. When the **LabelEdit** property is set to 1, no label can be edited unless the **StartLabelEdit** method is invoked. For example, the following code allows the user to edit a **Node** object's label by clicking a Command button:

```
Private Sub Command1_Click()
    ' Determine if the right Node is selected.
    If TreeView1.SelectedItem.Index = 1 Then
        TreeView1.StartLabelEdit          ' Let user begin editing.
    End If
End Sub
```

ListItem Object, **ListItems** Collection, **ListView** Control Constants, **TreeView** Control Constants, **Node** Object, **Nodes** Collection, **AfterLabelEdit** Event (ListView, TreeView Controls), **BeforeLabelEdit** Event (ListView, TreeView Controls), **StartLabelEdit** Method

Example

This example initiates label editing when you click the Command button. It allows a **Node** object to be edited unless it is a root **Node**. The **LabelEdit** property must be set to **Manual**. To try the example, place a **TreeView** control and a **CommandButton** on a form. Paste the code into the form's Declarations section. Run the example, select a node to edit, and press the **CommandButton**.

```
Private Sub Form_Load()
    Dim nodX As Node
    Dim i As Integer
    TreeView1.LabelEdit = tvwManual        ' Set property to manual.
    Set nodX = TreeView1.Nodes.Add(,,," Node 1")  ' Add first node.

    For i = 1 to 5                          ' Add 5 nodes.
        Set nodX = TreeView1.Nodes.Add(i,tvwChild,,"Node " & CStr(i + 1))
    Next I

    nodX.EnsureVisible                      ' Show all nodes.
End Sub

Private Sub Command1_Click()
    ' Invoke the StartLabelEdit method on the selected node,
    ' which triggers the BeforeLabelEdit event.
    TreeView1.StartLabelEdit
End Sub

Private Sub TreeView_BeforeLabelEdit (Cancel as Integer)
    ' If the selected item is the root, then cancel the edit.
    If TreeView1.SelectedItem Is TreeView1.SelectedItem.Root Then
        Cancel = True
    End If
End Sub
```

```
Private Sub TreeView_AfterLabelEdit _
(Cancel As Integer, NewString As String)
   ' Assume user has entered some text and pressed the ENTER key.
   ' Any nonempty string will be valid.
   If Len(NewString) = 0 Then
      Cancel = True
   End If
End Sub
```

LastSibling Property

Returns a reference to the last sibling of a **Node** object in a **TreeView** control.

Applies To

TreeView Control, **Node** Object, **Nodes** Collection

Syntax

object.**LastSibling**

The *object* placeholder represents an object expression that evaluates to an object in the **Applies To** list.

Remarks

The last sibling is the **Node** that appears in the last position in one level of a hierarchy of nodes. Which **Node** actually appears in the last position depends on whether or not the **Node** objects at that level are sorted, which is determined by the **Sorted** property. To sort the **Node** objects at one level, set the **Sorted** property of the **Parent** node to **True**. The following code demonstrates this:

```
Private Sub TreeView1_NodeClick(ByVal Node As Node)
   Node.Parent.Sorted = True
End Sub
```

The **Child**, **FirstSibling**, **LastSibling**, **Previous**, **Parent**, **Next**, and **Root** properties all return a reference to another **Node** object. Therefore, you can simultaneously reference and perform operations on a **Node**, as follows:

```
With TreeView1.Nodes(x).LastSibling
   .Text = "New text"
   .Key = "New key"
   .SelectedImage = 3
End With
```

You can also set an object variable to the referenced **Node**, as follows:

```
Dim NodLastSib As Node
' Get a reference to the last sibling of Node x.
Set NodLastSib = TreeView1.Nodes(x).LastSibling
' Use this reference to perform operations on the sibling Node.
With nodLastSib
   .Text = "New text"    '  Change the text.
   .Key = "New key"      ' Change key.
   .SelectedImage = 3    ' Change SelectedImage.
End With
```

See Also

Node Object**, Nodes** Collection, **Child** Property (TreeView Control), **FirstSibling** Property, **Next** Property, **Parent** Property (Node Object), **Previous** Property (Node Object), **Root** Property (Node Object), **Sorted** Property (TreeView Control)

Example

This example adds several **Node** objects to a **TreeView** control. The **LastSibling** property, in conjunction with the **Next** property and the **FirstSibling** property, is used to navigate through a clicked **Node** object's hierarchy level. To try the example, place a **TreeView** control on a form and paste the code into the form's Declarations section. Run the example, and click the various nodes to see what is returned.

```
Private Sub Form_Load()
   Dim nodX As Node
   Set nodX = TreeView1.Nodes.Add(,,"dad","Mike")
   Szet nodX = TreeView1.Nodes.Add(,,"mom","Carol")
   ' Alice is the LastSibling.
   Set nodX = TreeView1.Nodes.Add(,,,"Alice")

   Set nodX = TreeView1.Nodes.Add("mom",tvwChild,,"Marsha")
   Set nodX = TreeView1.Nodes.Add("mom",tvwChild,,"Jan")
   ' Cindy is the LastSibling.
   Set nodX = TreeView1.Nodes.Add("mom",tvwChild,,"Cindy")
   nodX.EnsureVisible                 ' Show all nodes.

   Set nodX = TreeView1.Nodes.Add("dad",tvwChild,,"Greg")
   Set nodX = TreeView1.Nodes.Add("dad",tvwChild,,"Peter")
   ' Bobby is the LastSibling.
   Set nodX = TreeView1.Nodes.Add("dad",tvwChild,,"Bobby")
   nodX.EnsureVisible                 ' Show all nodes.
End Sub

Private Sub TreeView1_NodeClick(ByVal Node As Node)
   Dim strText As String
   Dim n As Integer
   ' Set n to FirstSibling's index.
   n = Node.FirstSibling.Index
   ' Place FirstSibling's text & linefeed in string variable.
   strText = Node.FirstSibling.Text & vbLF
   While n <> Node.LastSibling.Index
   ' While n is not the index of the last sibling, go to the
   ' next sibling and place its text into the string variable
      strText = strText & TreeView1.Nodes(n).Next.Text & vbLF
   ' Set n to the next node's index.
      n = TreeView1.Nodes(n).Next.Index
   Wend
   MsgBox strText                     ' Display results.
End Sub
```

LineStyle Property

Returns or sets the style of lines displayed between **Node** objects.

Applies To

TreeView Control

Syntax

object.**LineStyle** [= *number*]

The **LineStyle** property syntax has these parts:

Part	Description
object	An object expression that evaluates to an object in the **Applies To** list.
number	A value or constant that specifies the line style as shown in **Settings**.

Settings

The settings for *number* are:

Constant	Value	Description
tvwTreeLines	0	(Default) Tree lines. Displays lines between **Node** siblings and their parent **Node**.
tvwRootLines	1	Root Lines. In addition to displaying lines between **Node** siblings and their parent **Node**, also displays lines between the root nodes.

Remarks

You must set the **Style** property to a style that includes tree lines.

See Also

TreeView Control, **TreeView** Control Constants, **Style** Property (TreeView Control))

Example

This example adds several **Node** objects with images to a **TreeView** control. You can change the **LineStyle** and **Style** properties by selecting the alternate styles in two **OptionButton** control arrays. To try the example, place a **TreeView** control, an **ImageList** control, and two **OptionButton** control arrays (one with two buttons and one with eight) on a form, and paste the code into the form's Declarations section. Run the example, and click any **OptionButton** to change the **LineStyle** and **Style** properties.

```
Private Sub Form_Load()
    ' Add an image to the ImageList control.
    Dim imgX As ListImage
    Set imgX = ImageList1.ListImages. _
    Add(,,LoadPicture("bitmaps\outline\leaf.bmp"))

    TreeView1.ImageList = ImageList1          ' Initialize ImageList.

    ' Label OptionButton controls with line styles choices.
    Option1(0).Caption = "TreeLines"
    Option1(1).Caption = "RootLines"
```

```
    ' Select the first option, and set the LineStyle to TreeLines initially
    Option1(0).Value = True
    Treeview1.LineStyle = tvwTreeLines

    ' Label OptionButton controls with Style choices.
    Option2(0).Caption = "Text only"
    Option2(1).Caption = "Image & text"
    Option2(2).Caption = "Plus/minus & text"
    Option2(3).Caption = "Plus/minus, image & text"
    Option2(4).Caption = "Lines & text"
    Option2(5).Caption = "Lines, image & Text"
    Option2(6).Caption = "Lines, plus/minus & Text"
    Option2(7).Caption = "Lines, plus/minus, image & text"

    ' Select the last option, and set the initial Style
    Option2(7).Value = True
    Treeview1.Style = tvwTreelinesPlusMinusPictureText

    Dim nodX As Node
    Dim i as Integer
    ' Create root node.
    Set nodX = TreeView1.Nodes.Add(,,,"Node " & "1",1)

    For i = 1 to 5              ' Add 5 nodes.
       Set nodX = TreeView1.Nodes. _
       Add(i,tvwChild,,"Node " & CStr(i + 1),1)
    Next I
    nodX.EnsureVisible          ' Show all nodes.
End Sub

Private Sub Option1_Click(Index as Integer)
    ' Change line style from OptionButton.
    TreeView1.LineStyle = Index
End Sub

Private Sub Option2_Click(Index as Integer)
' Change Style with OptionButton.
    TreeView1.Style = Index
    Form1.Caption = "TreeView Style = " & Option2(Index).Caption
End Sub
```

Next Property

Returns a reference to the next sibling **Node** of a **TreeView** control's **Node** object.

Applies To

Node Object, **Nodes** Collection

Syntax

object.**Next**

The *object* placeholder represents an object expression that evaluates to an object in the **Applies To** list.

Remarks

The **Child**, **FirstSibling**, **LastSibling**, **Previous**, **Parent**, **Next**, and **Root** properties all return a reference to another **Node** object. Therefore you can simultaneously reference and perform operations on a **Node**, as follows:

```
With TreeView1.Nodes(x).Child
    .Text = "New text"
    .Key = "New key"
    .SelectedImage = 3
End With
```

You can also set an object variable to the referenced **Node**, as follows:

```
Dim NodChild As Node
' Get a reference to the child of Node x.
Set NodChild = TreeView1.Nodes(x).Child
' Use this reference to perform operations on the child Node.
With nodChild
    .Text = "New text"'  Change the text.
    .Key = "New key"   ' Change key.
    .SelectedImage = 3' Change SelectedImage.
End With
```

See Also

TreeView Control, **Child** Property (TreeView Control), **FirstSibling** Property, **LastSibling** Property, **Parent** Property (Node Object), **Previous** Property (Node Object), **Root** Property (Node Object)

Example

This example adds several **Node** objects to a **TreeView** control. The **LastSibling** property, in conjunction with the **Next** property and the **FirstSibling** property, is used to navigate through a clicked **Node** object's hierarchy level. To try the example, place a **TreeView** control on a form and paste the code into the form's Declarations section. Run the example, and click the various nodes to see what is returned.

```
Private Sub Form_Load()
    Dim nodX As Node
    Set nodX = TreeView1.Nodes.Add(,,"dad","Mike")
    Set nodX = TreeView1.Nodes.Add(,,"mom","Carol")
    ' Alice is the LastSibling.
    Set nodX = TreeView1.Nodes.Add(,,,"Alice")

    Set nodX = TreeView1.Nodes.Add("mom",tvwChild,,"Marsha")
    Set nodX = TreeView1.Nodes.Add("mom",tvwChild,,"Jan")
    ' Cindy is the LastSibling.
    Set nodX = TreeView1.Nodes.Add("mom",tvwChild,,"Cindy")
    nodX.EnsureVisible                ' Show all nodes.
```

```
      Set nodX = TreeView1.Nodes.Add("dad",tvwChild,,"Greg")
      Set nodX = TreeView1.Nodes.Add("dad",tvwChild,,"Peter")
      ' Bobby is the LastSibling.
      Set nodX = TreeView1.Nodes.Add("dad",tvwChild,,"Bobby")
      nodX.EnsureVisible               ' Show all nodes.
   End Sub

   Private Sub TreeView1_NodeClick(ByVal Node As Node)
      Dim strText As String
      Dim n As Integer
      ' Set n to FirstSibling's index.
      n = Node.FirstSibling.Index
      ' Place FirstSibling's text & linefeed in string variable.
      strText = Node.FirstSibling.Text & vbLF
      ' While n is not the index of the last sibling, go to the
      ' next sibling and place its text into the string variable.
      While n <> Node.LastSibling.Index
         strText = strText & TreeView1.Nodes(n).Next.Text & vbLF
      ' Set n to the next node's index.
         n = TreeView1.Nodes(n).Next.Index
      Wend
      MsgBox strText                    ' Display results.
   End Sub
```

Node Object, Nodes Collection

- A **Node** object is an item in a **TreeView** control that can contain images and text.
- A **Nodes** collection contains one or more **Node** objects.

Syntax

treeview.**Nodes**
treeview.**Nodes.Item**(*index*)

The syntax lines above refer to the collection and to individual elements in the collection, respectively, according to standard collection syntax.

The **Node** object and **Nodes** collection syntax have these parts:

Part	Description
treeview	An object expression that evaluates to a **TreeView** control.
index	Either an integer or string that uniquely identifies a member of a **Nodes** collection. The integer is the value of the **Index** property; the string is the value of the **Key** property.

Remarks

Nodes can contain both text and pictures. However, to use pictures, you must associate an **ImageList** control using the **ImageList** property.

Pictures can change depending on the state of the node; for example, a selected node can have a different picture from an unselected node if you set the **SelectedImage** property to an image from the associated **ImageList**.

Properties

Child Property, **Children** Property, **Count** Property, **Expanded** Property, **ExpandedImage** Property, **FirstSibling** Property, **FullPath** Property, **Image** Property, **Index** Property, **Item** Property, **Key** Property, **LastSibling** Property, **Next** Property, **Parent** Property, **Previous** Property, **Root** Property, **Selected** Property, **SelectedImage** Property, **Sorted** Property, **Tag** Property, **Text** Property, **Visible** Property

Methods

Add Method (Nodes Collection)**, CreateDragImage** Method**, EnsureVisible** Method, **Clear** Method, **Remove** Method

See Also

ImageList Control, **ImageList** Property (ActiveX Controls), **TreeView** Control, **Nodes** Property, **SelectedImage** Property, **Index** Property (Control Array)

NodeClick Event

Occurs when a **Node** object is clicked.

Applies To

TreeView Control, **Node** Object, **Nodes** Collection

Syntax

Private Sub *object*_**NodeClick(ByVal** *node* **As Node)**

The **NodeClick** event syntax has these parts:

Part	Description
object	An object expression that evaluates to an object in the **Applies To** list.
node	A reference to the clicked **Node** object.

Remarks

The standard **Click** event is generated when the user clicks any part of the **TreeView** control outside a node object. The **NodeClick** event is generated when the user clicks a particular **Node** object; the **NodeClick** event also returns a reference to a particular **Node** object which can be used to validate the **Node** before further action is taken.

The **NodeClick** event occurs before the standard **Click** event.

See Also

SelectedItem Property (ActiveX Controls), **Click** Event

Example

This example adds several **Node** objects to a **TreeView** control. When a **Node** is clicked, the **NodeClick** event is triggered and is used to get the **Node** object's index and text. To try the example, place a **TreeView** control on a form and paste the code into the form's Declarations section. Run the example, and click any **Node**.

```
Private Sub Form_Load()
   Dim nodX As Node
   Set nodX = TreeView1.Nodes.Add(,,"R","Root")
   nodX.Expanded = True
   Set nodX = TreeView1.Nodes.Add(,,"P","Parent")
   nodX.Expanded = True
   Set nodX = TreeView1.Nodes.Add("R",tvwChild,,"Child 1")
   Set nodX = TreeView1.Nodes.Add("R",tvwChild,,"Child 2")
   Set nodX = TreeView1.Nodes.Add("R",tvwChild,,"Child 3")
   Set nodX = TreeView1.Nodes.Add("P",tvwChild,,"Child 4")
   Set nodX = TreeView1.Nodes.Add("P",tvwChild,,"Child 5")
   Set nodX = TreeView1.Nodes.Add("P",tvwChild,,"Child 6")
End Sub

Private Sub TreeView1_NodeClick(ByVal Node As Node)
   Form1.Caption = "Index = " & Node.Index & " Text:" & Node.Text
End Sub
```

Nodes Property

Returns a reference to a collection of **TreeView** control **Node** objects.

Applies To

TreeView Control, **Node** Object, **Nodes** Collection

Syntax

object.**Nodes**

The *object* placeholder represents an object expression that evaluates to an object in the **Applies To** list.

Remarks

You can manipulate **Node** objects using standard collection methods (for example, the **Add** and **Remove** methods). You can access each element in the collection by its index, or by a unique key that you store in the **Key** property.

See Also

Add Method (Nodes Collection), **Remove** Method (ActiveX Controls)

Example

This example adds several **Node** objects to a **TreeView** control. When the form is clicked, a reference to each **Node** is used to display each **Node** object's text. To try the example, place a **TreeView** control on a form and paste the code into the form's Declarations section. Run the example, and click the form.

```
Private Sub Form_Load()
   Dim nodX As Node
   Set nodX = TreeView1.Nodes.Add(,,"R","Root")
   Set nodX = TreeView1.Nodes.Add("R", tvwChild,"C1","Child 1")
   Set nodX = TreeView1.Nodes.Add("R", tvwChild,"C2","Child 2")
   Set nodX = TreeView1.Nodes.Add("R", tvwChild,"C3","Child 3")
   Set nodX = TreeView1.Nodes.Add("R", tvwChild,"C4","Child 4")
   nodX.EnsureVisible
   TreeView1.Style = tvwTreelinesText          ' Style 4.
   TreeView1.BorderStyle = vbFixedSingle
End Sub

Private Sub Form_Click()
   Dim i As Integer
   Dim strNodes As String
   For i = 1 To TreeView1.Nodes.Count
   strNodes = strNodes & TreeView1.Nodes(i).Index & " " & _
   "Key: " & TreeView1.Nodes(i).Key & " " & _
   "Text: " & TreeView1.Nodes(i).Text & vbLF
   Next i
   MsgBox strNodes
End Sub
```

Parent Property (Node Object)

Returns or sets the parent object of a **Node** object. Available only at run time.

Applies To

TreeView Control, **Node** Object, **Nodes** Collection

Syntax

object.**Parent**[= *node*]

The **Parent** property syntax has these parts:

Part	Description
object	An object expression that evaluates to an object in the **Applies To** list.
node	A **Node** object that becomes the parent of the object.

Remarks

At run time, an error occurs if you set this property to an object that creates a loop. For example, you cannot set any **Node** to become a child **Node** of its own descendants.

The **Child**, **FirstSibling**, **LastSibling**, **Previous**, **Parent**, **Next**, and **Root** properties all return a reference to another **Node** object. Therefore, you can simultaneously reference and perform operations on a **Node**, as follows:

```
With TreeView1.Nodes(x).Parent
    .Text = "New text"
    .Key = "New key"
    .SelectedImage = 3
End With
```

You can also set an object variable to the referenced **Node**, as follows:

```
Dim NodParent As Node
' Get a reference to the parent of Node x.
Set NodParent = TreeView1.Nodes(x).Parent
' Use this reference to perform operations on the Parent Node.
With nodParent
    .Text = "New text"     '  Change the text.
    .Key = "New key"       '  Change key.
    .SelectedImage = 3     '  Change SelectedImage.
End With
```

See Also

Node Object, **Nodes** Collection, **Child** Property (TreeView Control), **FirstSibling** Property, **LastSibling** Property, **Next** Property, **Previous** Property (Node Object), **Root** Property (Node Object), **Form** Object, **Forms** Collection, **MDIChild** Property, **MDIForm** Object

Example

This example adds several **Node** objects to a **TreeView** control. After you select a **Node** object, you can then click and drag it to any other **Node** to make it a child of the target **Node**. To try the example, place **TreeView** and **ImageList** controls on a form and paste the code into the form's Declaration section. Run the example and drag **Node** objects onto other **Node** objects to see the result.

```
' Declare global variables.
Dim indrag As Boolean      ' Flag that signals a Drag Drop operation.
Dim nodX As Object         ' Item that is being dragged.

Private Sub Form_Load()
    ' Load a bitmap into an Imagelist control.
    Dim imgX As ListImage
    Dim BitmapPath As String
    BitmapPath = "icons\mail\mail01a.ico"
    Set imgX = ImageList1.ListImages.Add(, , LoadPicture(BitmapPath))

    ' Initialize TreeView control and create several nodes.
    TreeView1.ImageList = ImageList1
    Dim nodX As Node           ' Create a tree.
    Set nodX = TreeView1.Nodes.Add(, , , "Parent1", 1)
    Set nodX = TreeView1.Nodes.Add(, , , "Parent2", 1)
    Set nodX = TreeView1.Nodes.Add(1, tvwChild, , "Child 1", 1)
    Set nodX = TreeView1.Nodes.Add(1, tvwChild, , "Child 2", 1)
    Set nodX = TreeView1.Nodes.Add(2, tvwChild, , "Child 3", 1)
    Set nodX = TreeView1.Nodes.Add(2, tvwChild, , "Child 4", 1)
    Set nodX = TreeView1.Nodes.Add(3, tvwChild, , "Child 5", 1)
    nodX.EnsureVisible      ' Expand tree to show all nodes.
End Sub
```

```
Private Sub TreeView1_MouseDown(Button As Integer, Shift As Integer,
x As Single, y As Single)
    Set nodX = TreeView1.SelectedItem   ' Set the item being dragged.
    Set TreeView1.DropHighlight = Nothing
End Sub

Private Sub TreeView1_MouseMove _
(Button As Integer, Shift As Integer, x As Single, y As Single)
    If Button = vbLeftButton Then       ' Signal a Drag operation.
        indrag = True                   ' Set the flag to true.
        ' Set the drag icon with the CreateDragImage method.
        TreeView1.DragIcon = TreeView1.SelectedItem.CreateDragImage
        TreeView1.Drag vbBeginDrag      ' Drag operation.
    End If
End Sub

Private Sub TreeView1_DragDrop(Source As Control, x As Single, y As Single)
    ' If user didn't move mouse or released it over an invalid area.
    If TreeView1.DropHighlight Is Nothing Then
        indrag = False
        Exit Sub
    Else
        ' Set dragged node's parent property to the target node.
        On Error GoTo checkerror         ' To prevent circular errors.
        Set nodX.Parent = TreeView1.DropHighlight
        Cls
        Print TreeView1.DropHighlight.Text & _
        " is parent of " & nodX.Text
        ' Release the DropHighlight reference.
        Set TreeView1.DropHighlight = Nothing
        indrag = False
        Exit Sub                         ' Exit if no errors occured.
    End If

checkerror:
    ' Define constants to represent Visual Basic errors code.
    Const CircularError = 35614
    If Err.Number = CircularError Then
        Dim msg As String
        msg = "A node can't be made a child of its own children."
        ' Display the message box with an exclamation mark icon
        ' and with OK and Cancel buttons.
        If MsgBox(msg, vbExclamation & vbOKCancel) = vbOK Then
            ' Release the DropHighlight reference.
            indrag = False
            Set TreeView1.DropHighlight = Nothing
            Exit Sub
        End If
    End If
End Sub

Private Sub TreeView1_DragOver(Source As Control, x As Single,
y As Single, State As Integer)
    Set TreeView1.DropHighlight = TreeView1.HitTest(x, y)
End Sub
```

PathSeparator Property (TreeView Control)

Returns or sets the delimiter character used for the path returned by the **FullPath** property.

Applies To

TreeView Control

Syntax

object.**PathSeparator** [= *string*]

The **PathSeparator** syntax has these parts:

Part	Description
object	An object expression that evaluates to an object in the **Applies To** list.
string	A string that determines the **PathSeparator**, usually a single character.

Remarks

The default character is "\."

See Also

FullPath Property

Example

This example adds several **Node** objects to a **TreeView** control, and uses an **OptionButton** control array to change the **PathSeparator** property. To try the example, place a **TreeView** control and an **OptionButton** control array on a form, and paste the code into the form's Declarations section. Run the example, select a **Node**, and click the form. Change the **PathSeparator** property value using the **OptionButtons**.

```
Private Sub Form_Load
   TreeView1.BorderStyle = vbFixedSingle        ' Show border.
   ' Label OptionButton controls with Style choices.
   Option1(0).Caption = "/"
   Option1(1).Caption = "-"
   Option1(2).Caption = ":"

   ' Select the last option, and set the initial Style
   Option2(1).Value = True
   Treeview1.PathSeparator = Option1(1).Caption

   Dim nodX As Node
   Dim i As Integer
   Set nodX = TreeView1.Nodes.Add(,,,CStr(1))  ' Add first node.

   For i = 1 to 5                               ' Add other nodes.
      Set nodX = TreeView1.Nodes.Add(i,tvwChild,,CStr(i + 1))
   Next i
```

```
    nodX.EnsureVisible    ' Ensure all are visible.
End Sub

Private Sub Option1_Click(Index as Integer)
    ' Change the delimiter character.
    TreeView1.PathSeparator = Option1(Index).Caption
End Sub

Private Sub TreeView1_NodeClick(ByVal Node As Node)
    ' Show path in form's caption.
    Me.Caption = Node.FullPath
End Sub
```

Previous Property (Node Object)

Returns a reference to the previous sibling of a **Node** object.

Applies To

TreeView Control, **Node** Object, **Nodes** Collection

Syntax

object. **Previous**

The *object* placeholder represents an object expression that evaluates to an object in the **Applies To** list.

Remarks

The **Child**, **FirstSibling**, **LastSibling**, **Previous**, **Parent**, **Next**, and **Root** properties all return a reference to another **Node** object. Therefore you can simultaneously reference and perform operations on a **Node**, as follows:

```
With TreeView1.Nodes(x).Previous
    .Text = "New text"
    .Key = "New key"
    .SelectedImage = 3
End With
```

You can also set an object variable to the referenced **Node**, as follows:

```
Dim NodPrevious As Node
' Get a reference to the node previouus to Node x.
Set NodChild = TreeView1.Nodes(x).Previous
' Use this reference to perform operations on the previous Node.
With nodPrevious
    .Text = "New text"        ' Change the text.
    .Key = "New key"          ' Change key.
    .SelectedImage = 3        ' Change SelectedImage.
End With
```

See Also

Child Property (TreeView Control), **FirstSibling** Property, **LastSibling** Property, **Next** Property, **Parent** Property (Node Object), **Root** Property (Node Object)

Example

This example adds several nodes to a **TreeView** control. The **Previous** property, in conjunction with the **LastSibling** property and the **FirstSibling** property, is used to navigate through a clicked **Node** object's hierarchy level. To try the example, place a **TreeView** control on a form and paste the code into the form's Declarations section. Run the example, and click the various nodes to see what is returned.

```
Private Sub Form_Load()
    Dim nodX As Node
    Set nodX = TreeView1.Nodes.Add(, , "r", "Root")
    Set nodX = TreeView1.Nodes.Add(, , "p", "parent")

    Set nodX = TreeView1.Nodes.Add("r", tvwChild, , "Child 1")
    Set nodX = TreeView1.Nodes.Add("r", tvwChild, , "Child 2")
    Set nodX = TreeView1.Nodes.Add("r", tvwChild, , "Child 3")
    nodX.EnsureVisible       ' Show all nodes.

    Set nodX = TreeView1.Nodes.Add("p", tvwChild, , "Child 4")
    Set nodX = TreeView1.Nodes.Add("p", tvwChild, , "Child 5")
    Set nodX = TreeView1.Nodes.Add("p", tvwChild, , "Child 6")
    nodX.EnsureVisible          ' Show all nodes.
End Sub

Private Sub TreeView1_NodeClick(ByVal Node As Node)
    Dim strText As String
    Dim n As Integer
    ' Set n to LastSibling's index.
    n = Node.LastSibling.Index
    ' Place LastSibling's text & linefeed in string variable.
    strText = Node.LastSibling.Text & vbLF
    While n <> Node.FirstSibling.Index
        ' While n is not the index of the FirstSibling, go to the
        ' previous sibling and place its text into the string variable.
        strText = strText & TreeView1.Nodes(n).Previous.Text & vbLF
        ' Set n to the previous node's index.
        n = TreeView1.Nodes(n).Previous.Index
    Wend
    MsgBox strText              ' Display results.
End Sub
```

Root Property (Node Object)

Returns a reference to the root **Node** object of a selected **Node**.

Applies To

TreeView Control, **Node** Object, **Nodes** Collection

Syntax

object.**Root**

The *object* placeholder represents an object expression that evaluates to an object in the **Applies To** list.

Remarks

The **Child**, **FirstSibling**, **LastSibling**, **Previous**, **Parent**, **Next**, and **Root** properties all return a reference to another **Node** object. Therefore, you can simultaneously reference and perform operations on a **Node**, as follows:

```
With TreeView1.Nodes(x).Root
    .Text = "New text"
    .Key = "New key"
    .SelectedImage = 3
End With
```

You can also set an object variable to the referenced **Node**, as follows:

```
Dim NodRoot As Node
' Get a reference to the root of Node x.
Set NodRoot = TreeView1.Nodes(x).Root
' Use this reference to perform operations on the root Node.
With nodRoot
    .Text = "New text"        ' Change the text.
    .Key = "New key"          ' Change key.
    .SelectedImage = 3        ' Change SelectedImage.
End With
```

See Also

Child Property (TreeView Control), **FirstSibling** Property, **LastSibling** Property, **Next** Property, **Parent** Property (Node Object), **Previous** Property (Node Object), **SelectedItem** Property (ActiveX Controls)

Example

This example adds several **Node** objects to a **TreeView** control. When you click a **Node**, the code navigates up the tree to the **Root** node, and displays the text of each **Parent** node. To try the example, place a **TreeView** control on a form and paste the code into the form's Declarations section. Run the example, and click a **Node**.

```
Private Sub Form_Load()
    Dim nodX As Node             ' Create a tree.
    Set nodX = TreeView1.Nodes.Add(,,"r", "Root")
    Set nodX = TreeView1.Nodes.Add(,,"p", "Parent")
    Set nodX = TreeView1.Nodes.Add("p",tvwChild,, "Child 1")
    nodX.EnsureVisible          ' Show all nodes.
    Set nodX = TreeView1.Nodes.Add("r",tvwChild,"C2", "Child 2")
    Set nodX = TreeView1.Nodes.Add("C2",tvwChild,"C3", "Child 3")
    Set nodX = TreeView1.Nodes.Add("C3",tvwChild,, "Child 4")
    Set nodX = TreeView1.Nodes.Add("C3",tvwChild,, "Child 5")
    nodX.EnsureVisible          ' Show all nodes.
End Sub

Private Sub TreeView1_NodeClick(ByVal Node As Node)
    Dim n As Integer
    Dim strParents As String    ' Variable for information.
    n = Node.Index              ' Set n to index of clicked node.
```

```
    strParents = Node.Text & vbLF
    While n <> Node.Root.Index
        strParents = strParents & _
        TreeView1.Nodes(n).Parent.Text & vbLF
        ' Set n to index of next parent Node.
        n = TreeView1.Nodes(n).Parent.Index
    Wend
    MsgBox strParents
End Sub
```

Selected Property (ActiveX Controls)

Returns or sets a value that determines if a **Node** or **Tab** object is selected. For a **ListItem** object, the **Selected** property does not set the **SelectedItem** property, and thus does not cause the object to be selected. It only returns a value indicating whether the **ListItem** object has already been selected by other means.

Applies To

ListView Control, **ListItem** Object, **ListItems** Collection, **TabStrip** Control, **Tab** Object, **TreeView** Control, **Node** Object, **Nodes** Collection

Syntax

object.**Selected** [= *boolean*]

The **Selected** property syntax has these parts:

Part	Description
object	An object expression that evaluates to an object in the **Applies To** list.
boolean	A Boolean expression that determines if an object is selected.

Remarks

Use the **Selected** property to programmatically select a specific **Node** or **Tab** object. Once you have selected an object in this manner, you can perform various operations on it, such as setting properties and invoking methods.

To select a specific **Node** object, you must refer to it by the value of either its **Index** property or its **Key** property. The following example selects a specific **Node** object in a **TreeView** control:

```
Private Sub Command1_Click()
    TreeView1.Nodes(3).Selected = True ' Selects an object.
    ' Use the SelectedItem property to get a reference to the object.
    TreeView1.SelectedItem.Text = "Changed Text"
End Sub
```

In the **ListView** control, the **SelectedItem** property always refers to the first selected item. Therefore, if multiple items are selected, you must iterate through all of the items, checking each item's **Selected** property.

Note Instead of using the **Selected** property to programmatically select a **ListItem** object, use the **Set** statement with the **SelectedItem** property, as follows:

```
Set ListView1.SelectedItem = ListView1.ListItems(1)
```

See Also

SelectedItem Property (ActiveX Controls), **Set** Statement

Examples

This example adds several **Node** objects to a **TreeView** control. When a **Node** is selected, a reference to the selected **Node** is used to display its key. To try the example, place a **TreeView** control on a form, and paste the code into the form's Declarations section. Run the example, select a **Node**, and click the form.

```
Private Sub Form_Load()
    Dim nodX As Node            ' Create a tree.
    Set nodX = TreeView1.Nodes.Add(,,"r","Root")
    Set nodX = TreeView1.Nodes.Add(,,"p","Parent")
    Set nodX = TreeView1.Nodes.Add("p",tvwChild,,"Child 1")
    nodX.EnsureVisible           ' Show all nodes.
    Set nodX = TreeView1.Nodes.Add("r",tvwChild,"C2","Child 2")
    Set nodX = TreeView1.Nodes.Add("C2",tvwChild,"C3","Child 3")
    Set nodX = TreeView1.Nodes.Add("C3",tvwChild,,"Child 4")
    Set nodX = TreeView1.Nodes.Add("C3",tvwChild,,"Child 5")
    nodX.EnsureVisible           ' Show all nodes.
End Sub

Private Sub Form_Click()
    Dim intX As Integer
    On Error Resume Next     ' If an integer isn't entered.
    intX = InputBox("Check Node",,TreeView1.SelectedItem.Index)
    If IsNumeric(intX) Then      ' Ensure an integer was entered.
        If TreeView1.Nodes(intX).Selected = True Then
            MsgBox TreeView1.Nodes(intX).Text & " is selected."
        Else
            MsgBox "Not selected"
        End If
    End If
End Sub
```

The following example adds three **ListItem** objects to a **ListView** control. When you click the form, the code uses the **Selected** property to determine if a specific **ListItem** object is selected. To try the example, place a **ListView** control on a form and paste the code into the form's Declarations section. Run the example, select a **ListItem**, and click the form.

```
Private Sub Form_Load()
    Listview1.BorderStyle = vbFixedSingle  ' Show the border.
    Dim itmX As ListViewItem
    Set itmX = ListView1.ListItems.Add(,,"Item 1")
    Set itmX = ListView1.ListItems.Add(,,"Item 2")
    Set itmX = ListView1.ListItems.Add(,,"Item 3")
End Sub
```

```
Private Sub Form_Click()
    Dim intX As Integer
    On Error Resume Next      ' If an integer isn't entered.
    intX = InputBox("Check Item", , Listview1.SelectedItem.Index)
    If IsNumeric(intX) Then    ' Ensure an integer was entered.
        If ListView1.ListItems(intX).Selected = True Then
            MsgBox ListView1.ListItems(intX).Text & " is selected."
        Else
            MsgBox "Not selected"
        End If
    End If
End Sub
```

SelectedImage Property

Returns or sets the index or key value of a **ListImage** object in an associated **ImageList** control; the **ListImage** is displayed when a **Node** object is selected.

Applies To

ImageList Control, **ListImage** Object, **ListImages** Collection, **TreeView** Control, **Node** Object, **Nodes** Collection

Syntax

object.**SelectedImage** [= *index*]

The **SelectedImage** property syntax has these parts:

Part	Description
object	An object expression that evaluates to an object in the **Applies To** list.
index	An integer or unique string that identifies a **ListImage** object in an associated **ImageList** control. The integer is the value of the **ListImage** object's **Index** property; the string is the value of the **Key** property.

Remarks

If this property is set to **Null**, the mask of the default image specified by the **Image** property is used.

See Also

Image Property (ActiveX Controls)

SelectedItem Property (ActiveX Controls)

Returns a reference to a selected **ListItem**, **Node**, or **Tab** object.

Applies To

ListView Control, **ListItem** Object, **ListItems** Collection, **TabStrip** Control, **Tab** Object, **TreeView** Control, **Node** Object, **Nodes** Collection

Syntax

object.**SelectedItem**

The *object* placeholder represents an object expression that evaluates to an object in the **Applies To** list.

Remarks

The **SelectedItem** property returns a reference to an object that can be used to set properties and invoke methods on the selected object. This property is typically used to return a reference to a **ListItem, Node**, or **Tab** or object that the user has clicked or selected. With this reference, you can validate an object before allowing any further action, as demonstrated in the following code:

```
Command1_Click()
    ' If the selected object is not the root, then remove the Node.
    If TreeView1.SelectedItem.Index <> 1 Then
       Treeview1.Nodes.Remove TreeView1.SelectedItem.Index
    End If
End Sub
```

To programmatically select a **ListItem** object, use the **Set** statement with the **SelectedItem** property, as follows:

```
Set ListView1.SelectedItem = ListView1.ListItems(1)
```

See Also

Selected Property (ActiveX Controls), **Set** Statement

Example

This example adds several **Node** objects to a **TreeView** control. After you select a **Node**, click the form to see various properties of the **Node**. To try the example, place a **TreeView** control on a form and paste the code into the form's Declarations section. Run the example, select a **Node**, and click the form.

```
Private Sub Form_Load()
    Dim nodX As Node
    Set nodX = TreeView1.Nodes.Add(, , "r", "Root")
    Set nodX = TreeView1.Nodes.Add("r", tvwChild, "c1", "Child 1")
    Set nodX = TreeView1.Nodes.Add("r", tvwChild, "c2", "Child 2")
    Set nodX = TreeView1.Nodes.Add("r", tvwChild, "c3", "Child 3")
    Set nodX = TreeView1.Nodes.Add("c3", tvwChild, "c4", "Child 4")
    Set nodX = TreeView1.Nodes.Add("c3", tvwChild, "c5", "Child 5")
    Set nodX = TreeView1.Nodes.Add("c5", tvwChild, "c6", "Child 6")
    Set nodX = TreeView1.Nodes.Add("c5", tvwChild, "c7", "Child 7")
    nodX.EnsureVisible
    TreeView1.BorderStyle = vbFixedSingle
End Sub

Private Sub Form_Click()
    Dim nodX As Node
    ' Set the variable to the SelectedItem.
    Set nodX = TreeView1.SelectedItem
    Dim strProps As String
```

```
' Retrieve properties of the node.
strProps = "Text: " & nodX.Text & vbLF
strProps = strProps & "Key: " & nodX.Key & vbLF
On Error Resume Next ' Root node doesn't have a parent.
strProps = strProps & "Parent: " & nodX.Parent.Text & vbLF
strProps = strProps & "FirstSibling: " & _
nodX.FirstSibling.Text & vbLF
strProps = strProps & "LastSibling: " & _
nodX.LastSibling.Text & vbLF
strProps = strProps & "Next: " & nodX.Next.Text & vbLF

MsgBox strProps
End Sub
```

Sorted Property (TreeView Control)

- Returns or sets a value that determines whether the child nodes of a **Node** object are sorted alphabetically.

- Returns or sets a value that determines whether the root level nodes of a **TreeView** control are sorted alphabetically.

Applies To

TreeView Control, **Node** Object, **Nodes** Collection

Syntax

object.**Sorted** [= *boolean*]

The **Sorted** property syntax has these parts:

Part	Description
object	An object expression that evaluates to an object in the **Applies To** list.
boolean	A Boolean expression specifying whether the **Node** objects are sorted, as described in **Settings**.

Settings

The settings for *boolean* are:

Setting	Description
True	The **Node** objects are sorted alphabetically by their **Text** property. **Node** objects whose **Text** property begins with a number are sorted as strings, with the first digit determining the initial position in the sort, and subsequent digits determining sub-sorting.
False	The **Node** objects are not sorted.

Remarks

The **Sorted** property can be used in two ways: first, to sort the **Node** objects at the root (top) level of a **TreeView** control and, second, to sort the immediate children of any individual **Node** object. For example, the following code sorts the root nodes of a **TreeView** control:

```
Private Sub Command1_Click()
   TreeView1.Sorted = True    ' Top level Node objects are sorted.
End Sub
```

The next example shows how to set the **Sorted** property for a **Node** object as it is created:

```
Private Sub Form_Load()
   Dim nodX As Node
   Set nodX = TreeView1.Nodes.Add(,,"Parent Node")
   nodX.Sorted = True
End Sub
```

Setting the **Sorted** property to **True** sorts the current **Nodes** collection only. When you add new **Node** objects to a **TreeView** control, you must set the **Sorted** property to **True** again to sort the added **Node** objects.

See Also

Text Property

Example

This example adds several **Node** objects to a tree. When you click a **Node**, you are asked if you want to sort the **Node**. To try the example, place a **TreeView** control on a form and paste the code into the form's Declarations section. Run the example, and click a **Node** to sort it.

```
Private Sub Form_Load()
   ' Create a tree with several unsorted Node objects.
   Dim nodX As Node
   Set nodX = TreeView1.Nodes.Add(, , , "Adam")
   Set nodX = TreeView1.Nodes.Add(1, tvwChild, "z", "Zachariah")
   Set nodX = TreeView1.Nodes.Add(1, tvwChild, , "Noah")
   Set nodX = TreeView1.Nodes.Add(1, tvwChild, , "Abraham")
   Set nodX = TreeView1.Nodes.Add("z", tvwChild, , "Stan")
   Set nodX = TreeView1.Nodes.Add("z", tvwChild, , "Paul")
   Set nodX = TreeView1.Nodes.Add("z", tvwChild, "f", "Frances")
   Set nodX = TreeView1.Nodes.Add("f", tvwChild, , "Julie")
   Set nodX = TreeView1.Nodes.Add("f", tvwChild, "c", "Carol")
   Set nodX = TreeView1.Nodes.Add("f", tvwChild, , "Barry")
   Set nodX = TreeView1.Nodes.Add("c", tvwChild, , "Yale")
   Set nodX = TreeView1.Nodes.Add("c", tvwChild, , "Harvard")
   nodX.EnsureVisible
End Sub

Private Sub TreeView1_NodeClick(ByVal Node As Node)
   Dim answer As Integer
   ' Check if there are children nodes.
```

```
      If Node.Children > 1 Then    ' There are more than one children nodes.
         answer = MsgBox("Sort this node?", vbYesNo)  ' Prompt user.
         If answer = vbYes Then    ' User wants to sort.
            Node.Sorted = True
         End If
      End If
   End Sub
```

StartLabelEdit Method

Enables a user to edit a label.

Applies To

ListView Control, **TreeView** Control

Syntax

object.**StartLabelEdit**

The *object* placeholder is an object expression that evaluates to an object in the **Applies To** list.

Remarks

The **StartLabelEdit** method must be used to initiate a label editing operation when the **LabelEdit** property is set to 1 (Manual).

When the **StartLabelEdit** method is invoked upon an object, the **BeforeLabelEdit** event is also generated.

See Also

ListItem Object**, ListItems** Collection, **Node** Object**, Nodes** Collection, **AfterLabelEdit** Event (ListView, TreeView Controls), **BeforeLabelEdit** Event (ListView, TreeView Controls), **LabelEdit** Property

Example

This example adds several **Node** objects to a **TreeView** control. After a **Node** is selected, click the form to begin editing it. To try the example, place a **TreeView** control on a form, and paste the code into the form's Declarations section. Run the example, select a **Node**, and click the form.

```
Private Sub Form_Load
   Dim nodX As Node

   Set nodX = TreeView1.Nodes.Add(,,,"Da Vinci")    ' Root
   Set nodX = TreeView1.Nodes.Add(1,tvwChild,,"Titian")
   Set nodX = TreeView1.Nodes.Add(1,tvwChild,,"Rembrandt")
   Set nodX = TreeView1.Nodes.Add(1,tvwChild,,"Goya")
   Set nodX = TreeView1.Nodes.Add(1,tvwChild,,"David")
   nodX.EnsureVisible    ' Expand tree to see all nodes.
End Sub
```

```
Private Sub Form_Click()
   ' If selected Node isn't the Root node then allow edits.
   If TreeView1.SelectedItem.Index <> 1 Then
      TreeView1.StartLabelEdit
   End If
End Sub
```

Style Property (TreeView Control)

Returns or sets the type of graphics (images, text, plus/minus, and lines) and text that appear for each **Node** object in a **TreeView** control.

Applies To

TreeView Control, **Node** Object, **Nodes** Collection

Syntax

object.**Style** [= *number*]

The **Style** property syntax has these parts:

Part	Description
object	An object expression that evaluates to an object in the **Applies To** list.
number	An integer specifying the style of the graphics, as described in **Settings**.

Settings

The settings for *number* are:

Setting	Description
0	Text only.
1	Image and text.
2	Plus/minus and text.
3	Plus/minus, image, and text.
4	Lines and text.
5	Lines, image, and text.
6	Lines, plus/minus, and text.
7	(Default) Lines, plus/minus, image, and text.

Remarks

If the **Style** property is set to a value that includes lines, the **LineStyle** property determines the appearance of the lines. If the **Style** property is set to a value that does not include lines, the **LineStyle** property will be ignored.

See Also

LineStyle Property

TreeView Control Constants

TreeLine Constants

Constant	Value	Description
tvwTreeLines	0	Treelines shown.
tvwRootLines	1	Rootlines shown with Treelines.

TreeRelationship Constants

Constant	Value	Description
tvwFirst	0	First Sibling.
tvwLast	1	Last Sibling.
tvwNext	2	Next sibling.
tvwPrevious	3	Previous sibling.
tvwChild	4	Child.

TreeStyle Constants

Constant	Value	Description
tvwTextOnly	0	Text only.
tvwPictureText	1	Picture and text.
tvwPlusMinusText	2	Plus/minus and text.
tvwPlusPictureText	3	Plus/minus, picture, and text.
tvwTreelinesText	4	Treelines and text.
tvwTreelinesPictureText	5	Treelines, Picture, and Text.
tvwTreelinesPlusMinusText	6	Treelines, Plus/Minus, and Text.
tvwTreelinesPlusMinusPictureText	7	Treelines, Plus/Minus, Picture, and Text.

LabelEdit Constants

Constant	Value	Description
tvwAutomatic	0	Label Editing is automatic.
tvwManual	1	Label Editing must be invoked.

See Also

TreeView Control, **Add** Method (Nodes Collection), **Child** Property (TreeView Control), **FirstSibling** Property, **LastSibling** Property, **LineStyle** Property, **Next** Property, **Style** Property (TreeView Control), **Visual Basic** Constants, **ActiveX** Control Constants

UpDown Control

An **UpDown** control has a pair of arrow buttons which the user can click to increment or decrement a value, such as a scroll position or a value in an associated control, known as a buddy control.

Syntax

  UpDown

Remarks

To the user, an **UpDown** control and its buddy control often look like a single control. The buddy control can be any control that can be linked to the **UpDown** control through the **BuddyControl** property, and usually displays data, such as a **TextBox** control or a **CommandButton** control.

Note Lightweight windowless controls, such as the intrinsic label control, can't be used as a buddy control.

By setting the **AutoBuddy** property, the **UpDown** control automatically uses the previous control in the tab order as its buddy control. If there is no previous control in the tab order, the **UpDown** control will use the next control in the tab order as its buddy control. Another way to set the buddy control is with the **BuddyControl** property. At design time, when either the **AutoBuddy** property or the **BuddyControl** property is set, the buddy control will automatically pair up with the **UpDown** control by sizing and positioning next to it. The **UpDown** control can be positioned to the right or left of its buddy control with the **Alignment** property.

The **Increment**, **Min**, **Max**, and **Wrap** properties specify how the **UpDown** control's **Value** property changes when the user clicks the buttons on the control. For example, if you have values that are multiples of 10, and range from 20 to 80, you can set the **Increment**, **Min**, and **Max** properties to 10, 20, and 80, respectively. The **Wrap** property allows the **Value** property to increment past the **Max** property and start again at the **Min** property, or vice versa.

An **UpDown** control without a buddy control functions as a sort of simplified scroll bar.

Note The **UpDown** control should be used in place of the Spin Button control from Visual Basic 4.0.

Distribution Note The **UpDown** control is part of a group of **ActiveX** controls that are found in the COMCT232.OCX file. To use the **UpDown** control in your application, you must add the COMCT232.OCX file to the project. When distributing your application, install the COMCT232.OCX file in the user's Microsoft Windows SYSTEM directory. For more information on how to add a custom control to a project, see the *Programmer's Guide*.

Properties

Alignment Property, **AutoBuddy** Property, **BuddyControl** Property, **BuddyProperty** Property, **Container** Property, **DragIcon** Property, **DragMode** Property, **Enabled** Property, **Height, Width** Properties**, HelpContextID** Property, **hWnd** Property, **Increment** Property, **Index** Property, **Left, Top** Properties**, Max** Property, **Min** Property, **Name** Property, **Object** Property, **OLEDropMode** Property, **Orientation** Property, **Parent** Property, **SyncBuddy** Property, **TabIndex** Property, **TabStop** Property, **Tag** Property, **ToolTipText** Property, **Value** Property, **Visible** Property, **WhatsThisHelpID** Property, **Wrap** Property

Events

Change Event, **DownClick** Event, **DragDrop** Event, **DragOver** Event, **GotFocus** Event, **LostFocus** Event, **MouseDown, MouseUp** Events**, MouseMove** Event, **OLECompleteDrag** Event, **OLEDragDrop** Event, **OLEDragOver** Event, **OLEGiveFeedback** Event, **OLESetData** Event, **OLEStartDrag** Event, **UpClick** Event

Methods

Drag Method, **Move** Method, **OLEDrag** Method, **SetFocus** Method, **ShowWhatsThis** Method, **ZOrder** Method

See Also

AutoBuddy Property, **Increment** Property, **BuddyControl** Property, **Max** Property, **Min** Property, **Value** Property (UpDown Control), **Wrap** Property, **BuddyProperty** Property, **CommandButton** Control, **TextBox** Control

Alignment Property (UpDown Control)

Returns or sets a value that determines the alignment of the **UpDown** control with its buddy control.

Applies To

UpDown Control

Syntax

*object***.Alignment** [= *value*]

The **Alignment** property syntax has these parts:

Part	Description
object	An object expression that evaluates to an object in the **Applies To** list.
value	A value that specifies the alignment of the **UpDown** control with its buddy control, as described in **Settings**.

Settings

The settings for *value* are:

Constant	Value	Description
cc2alignmentLeft	0	The **UpDown** control is aligned to the left of its buddy control.
cc2alignmentRight	1	(Default). The **UpDown** control is aligned to the right of its buddy control.

Remarks

Use the **Alignment** property to specify the positioning of the **UpDown** control next to its buddy control. By default, the **UpDown** control is displayed on the right side of the buddy control.

Setting the **Alignment** property automatically realigns the **UpDown** control with its buddy control. The buddy control's width is reduced by the width of the **UpDown** control, so that the overall width of the two controls is the same as the buddy control was alone.

Note The **Alignment** property ignores the **Orientation** property when aligning to the **UpDown** control.

See Also

BuddyControl Property, **Orientation** Property

AutoBuddy Property

Sets or returns a value that determines whether the **UpDown** control automatically uses a control as its buddy control, based on its tab order.

Applies To

UpDown Control

Syntax

object.**AutoBuddy** [= *value*]

The **AutoBuddy** property syntax has these parts:

Part	Description
object	An object expression that evaluates to an object in the **Applies To** list.
value	A Boolean expression that determines the buddy control, as described in **Settings**.

Settings

The settings for *value* are:

Setting	Description
True	The **UpDown** control uses the previous control in the tab order as its buddy control. If no controls with a previous tab index can be used as a buddy control, the **UpDown** control uses the first available control with a higher tab index as its buddy control.
False	(Default) The **UpDown** control uses the setting in the **BuddyControl** property as its buddy control.

Remarks

Setting the **AutoBuddy** property to **True** also sets the **BuddyControl** property. Setting **AutoBuddy** to **False** clears the **BuddyControl** property.

See Also

SyncBuddy Property, **BuddyControl** Property, **BuddyProperty** Property

BuddyControl Property

Sets or returns the control used as the buddy control.

Applies To

UpDown Control

Syntax

object.**BuddyControl** [= *value*]

The **BuddyControl** property syntax has these parts:

Part	Description
object	An object expression that evaluates to an object in the **Applies To** list.
value	A variant value that specifies the buddy control, as described below.

Remarks

The **BuddyControl** property can be set at design time or at run time. At run time, **BuddyControl** property in the Properties window. To set the **BuddyControl** property at run time, use the following code:

```
UpDown1.BuddyControl = Text1
```

You can also implicitly set the **BuddyControl** property by setting **AutoBuddy** to **True**. In this case, the **BuddyControl** is automatically set to the previous control in the tab order.

Setting the **BuddyControl** property to **Nothing** automatically sets the **AutoBuddy** setting to **False**.

Note Setting the **BuddyControl** property to a control that cannot be a buddy, such as the intrinsic label control, results in an error.

See Also

> **AutoBuddy** Property, **SyncBuddy** Property, **BuddyProperty** Property

---

BuddyProperty Property

> Sets or returns the property used to synchronize the **UpDown** control with its buddy control.

Applies To

> **UpDown** Control

Syntax

> *object*.**BuddyProperty** [= *value*]

> The **BuddyProperty** property syntax has these parts:

Part	Description
object	An object expression that evaluates to an object in the **Applies To** list.
value	A variant value that specifies a property of the control specified by the **BuddyControl** property. If no value is specified, the default property for the control is used.

Remarks

> If the **SyncBuddy** property is **True**, the control will synchronize its **Value** property with the property specified by the **BuddyProperty** property.

> The **BuddyProperty** can be set at design time by selecting the property out of a drop down list in the Properties window.

> The **BuddyControl** property must be set before setting the **BuddyProperty** property, or an error results.

See Also

> **AutoBuddy** Property, **SyncBuddy** Property, **BuddyControl** Property, **Value** Property (UpDown Control)

Change Event (UpDown Control)

> This event occurs when the **Value** property is changed.

Applies To

> **UpDown** Control

Syntax

> **Private Sub** *object*_**Change**([*index* as integer])

The **Change** event syntax has these parts:

Part	Description
object	An object expression that evaluates to an object in the **Applies To** list.
index	An integer that uniquely identifies a control if it's in a control array.

Remarks

The **Change** event occurs whenever the **Value** property changes. The **Value** property can change through code, by clicking the arrow buttons, or by changing the value in a buddy control when the **SyncBuddy** property is **True**.

See Also

SyncBuddy Property, **Value** Property (UpDown Control), **DownClick** Event, **UpClick** Event

DownClick Event

This event occurs when the down or left arrow button is clicked.

Applies To

UpDown Control

Syntax

Private Sub *object*_**DownClick**([*index* as integer])

The **DownClick** event syntax has these parts:

Part	Description
object	An object expression that evaluates to an object in the **Applies To** list.
index	An integer that uniquely identifies a control if it's in a control array.

Remarks

The **DownClick** event occurs after the **Change** event.

See Also

Change Event (UpDown Control), **UpClick** Event

Increment Property

Sets or returns a value that determines the amount by which the **Value** property changes when the **UpDown** control's buttons are clicked.

Applies To

UpDown Control

Syntax

object.**Increment** [= *value*]

The **Increment** property syntax has these parts:

Part	Description
object	An object expression that evaluates to an object in the **Applies To** list.
value	A long integer that determines the amount by which the **Value** property changes. The *value* cannot be a negative number. The default for *value* is 1.

Remarks

The **Increment** property determines the amount the **Value** property changes when you click the arrow buttons on the **UpDown** control. Clicking the up or right arrow, causes **Value** to approach the **Max** property by the amount specified by the **Increment** property. Clicking the down or left arrow, causes **Value** to approach the **Min** property by the amount specified by the **Increment** property.

See Also

Max Property, **Min** Property, **Value** Property (UpDown Control), **Wrap** Property, **DownClick** Event, **UpClick** Event

---

Max Property

Sets or returns the maximum value of the scroll range for the **UpDown** control.

Applies To

UpDown Control

Syntax

object.**Max** [= *value*]

The **Max** property syntax has these parts:

Part	Description
object	An object expression that evaluates to an object in the **Applies To** list.
value	A long integer value that specifies the maximum value, as described below. The setting for *value* can be a negative number.

Remarks

Pressing the up or right arrow normally causes the **UpDown** control to increase the **Value** property, however, if the **Max** property is less than the **Min** property, the **UpDown** control operates in the reverse direction.

Pressing the up or right arrow always causes the **Value** property to approach the **Max** value. Pressing the down or left arrow always causes the **Value** property to approach the **Min** value.

See Also

Increment Property, **Min** Property, **Value** Property (UpDown Control), **Wrap** Property, **DownClick** Event, **UpClick** Event

Min Property

Sets or returns the minimum value of the scroll range for the **UpDown** control.

Applies To

UpDown Control

Syntax

*object***.Min** [= *value*]

The **Min** property syntax has these parts:

Part	Description
object	An object expression that evaluates to an object in the **Applies To** list.
value	A long integer value that specifies the minimum value, as described below. The setting for *value* can be a negative number.

Remarks

Pressing the down or left arrow normally causes the **UpDown** control to decrease the **Value** property. However, if the **Min** property is greater than the **Max** property, the **UpDown** control operates in the reverse direction.

Pressing the down or left arrow always causes the **Value** property to approach the **Min** value. Pressing the up or right arrow always causes the **Value** property to approach the **Max** value.

See Also

Increment Property, **Max** Property, **Value** Property (UpDown Control), **Wrap** Property, **Change** Event (UpDown Control), **DownClick** Event, **UpClick** Event

---

Orientation Property

Sets or returns the placement of the arrow buttons on the **UpDown** control. This property is read-only at run time.

Applies To

UpDown Control

Syntax

*object***.Orientation**

The **Orientation** property syntax has these parts:

Part	Description
object	An object expression that evaluates to an object in the **Applies To** list.

Settings

The settings for the **Orientation** property are:

Constant	Value	Description
cc2orientationVertical	0	(Default). The arrow buttons are positioned vertically.
cc2orientationHorizontal	1	The arrow buttons are positioned horizontally.

Remarks

At design time, this property can be set in the Properties window or through the control's property page.

When setting the **Orientation** property, the **UpDown** control automatically repositions itself next to its buddy control.

See Also

BuddyControl Property, **BuddyProperty** Property

SyncBuddy Property

Sets or returns a value that determines whether the **UpDown** control synchronizes the **Value** property with a property in the buddy control.

Applies To

UpDown Control

Syntax

object.**SyncBuddy** [= *value*]

The **SyncBuddy** property syntax has these parts:

Part	Description
object	An object expression that evaluates to an object in the **Applies To** list.
value	A Boolean expression that determines whether the buddy control synchronizes with the **UpDown** control, as described in **Settings**.

Settings

The settings for *value* are:

Setting	Description
True	The **UpDown** control synchronizes the **Value** property with a property of the buddy control, specified by the **BuddyProperty** property. If no property is specified in the **BuddyProperty** property, then the default property for the buddy control is used.
False	(Default) The **UpDown** control doesn't synchronize the **Value** property with a property in the buddy control.

Remarks

Use the **SyncBuddy** property to automatically synchronize a property of the buddy control with the **Value** property of the **UpDown** control. For example, you can synchronize the **Value** property of the **UpDown** control with the **Text** property of a **TextBox** control. Whenever the **Value** property changes, it would update the **Text** property in the **TextBox** control and vice versa. You can also synchronize the **Value** property of the **UpDown** control with other properties of a control such as the **Top**, **Left**, **BackColor**, **ForeColor**, and others.

To see a list of the available properties you can synchronize the **Value** property with (after setting the **BuddyControl** property), select the **BuddyProperty** property in the properties window or from the Properties Page.

See Also

Increment Property, **BuddyControl** Property, **Max** Property, **Min** Property, **Value** Property (UpDown Control), **DownClick** Event, **UpClick** Event, **BuddyProperty** Property, **BackColor**, **ForeColor** Properties, **Left**, **Top** Properties, **Text** Propert, **TextBox** Control

---

UpClick Event

This event occurs when the up or right arrow button is clicked.

Applies To

UpDown Control

Syntax

Private Sub *object*_**UpClick**([*index* as integer])

The **UpClick** event syntax has these parts:

Part	Description
object	An object expression that evaluates to an object in the **Applies To** list.
index	An integer that uniquely identifies a control if it's in a control array.

Remarks

The **UpClick** event occurs after the **Change** event.

See Also

Change Event (UpDown Control), **DownClick** Event

Value Property (UpDown Control)

Sets or returns the current position of the scroll value.

Applies To

UpDown Control

Syntax

*object.***Value** [= *long*]

The **Value** property syntax has these parts:

Part	Description
object	An object expression that evaluates to an object in the **Applies To** list.
long	A long integer that specifies the current value, as described below.

Remarks

The **Value** property specifies the current value within the range of the **Min** and **Max** properties. This property is incremented or decremented when the arrow buttons are clicked. The settings of the **Min** and **Max** properties determine whether the value is incremented or decremented when the arrow buttons are clicked.

If the **SyncBuddy** property is set to **True**, the **BuddyProperty** property is synchronized when there is a change in the **Value** property or when the **BuddyProperty** property value is changed.

See Also

Increment Property, **SyncBuddy** Property, **Max** Property, **Min** Property, **BuddyProperty** Property

---

Wrap Property

Sets or returns a value that determines whether the control's **Value** property wraps around to the beginning or end once it reaches the **Max** or **Min** value.

Applies To

UpDown Control

Syntax

*object.***Wrap** [= *value*]

The **Wrap** property syntax has these parts:

Part	Description
object	An object expression that evaluates to an object in the **Applies To** list.
value	A Boolean expression that determines whether the **UpDown** control wraps its **Value** property, as described in **Settings**.

Settings

The settings for *value* are:

Setting	Description
True	The **UpDown** control wraps the **Value** property to the beginning or end when the user moves past the **Max** or **Min** properties using the arrow buttons.
False	(Default) The **UpDown** control doesn't wrap the **Value** property.

Remarks

When **Wrap** is **True**, the **Value** property wraps according to the value of the **Min**, **Max**, and **Increment** properties.

When the **Value** property wraps, its first jump is to the **Min** value. For example, if **Min** is 20, **Max** is 70, **Increment** is 10, **Value** is 70, and the user clicks the up or right arrow button, the **Value** property wraps to 20.

See Also

Increment Property, **Max** Property, **Min** Property, **Value** Property (UpDown Control)

Example

This example uses the **Wrap** property with the **UpDown** control to create a wrapping spinner control with values that range from 10 to 70 and an increment of 10. To try this example, place a **TextBox** control and an **UpDown** control on your form and add the following code:

```
Private Sub Form_Load()
    UpDown1.BuddyControl = Text1
    With UpDown1
       .Min = 10
       .Max = 70
       .Increment = 10
       .Wrap = True
       .SyncBuddy = True
    End With

    ' So the TextBox reflects the starting value
    Text1.Text = UpDown1.Value
End Sub
```

Winsock Control

The **Winsock** control, invisible to the user, provides easy access to TCP and UDP network services. It can be used by Microsoft Access, Visual Basic, Visual C++, or Visual FoxPro developers. To write client or server applications you do not need to understand the details of TCP or to call low level Winsock APIs. By setting properties and invoking methods of the control, you can easily connect to a remote machine and exchange data in both directions.

TCP Basics

The Transfer Control Protocol allows you to create and maintain a connection to a remote computer. Using the connection, both computers can stream data between themselves.

If you are creating a client application, you must know the server computer's name or IP address (**RemoteHost** property), as well as the port (**RemotePort** property) on which it will be "listening." Then invoke the **Connect** method.

If you are creating a server application, set a port (**LocalPort** property) on which to listen, and invoke the **Listen** method. When the client computer requests a connection, the **ConnectionRequest** event will occur. To complete the connection, invoke the **Accept** method within the **ConnectionRequest** event.

Once a connection has been made, either computer can send and receive data. To send data, invoke the **SendData** method. Whenever data is received, the **DataArrival** event occurs. Invoke the **GetData** method within the **DataArrival** event to retrieve the data.

UDP Basics

The User Datagram Protocol (UDP) is a connectionless protocol. Unlike TCP operations, computers do not establish a connection. Also, a UDP application can be either a client or a server.

To transmit data, first set the client computer's **LocalPort** property. The server computer then needs only to set the **RemoteHost** to the Internet address of the client computer, and the **RemotePort** property to the same port as the client computer's **LocalPort** property, and invoke the **SendData** method to begin sending messages. The client computer then uses the **GetData** method within the **DataArrival** event to retrieve the sent messages.

Properties

BytesReceived Property, **Index** Property, **LocalHostName** Property, **LocalIP** Property, **LocalPort** Property, **Name** Property, **Object** Property, **Parent** Property, **Protocol** Property, **RemoteHost** Property, **RemoteHostIP** Property, **RemotePort** Property, **SocketHandle** Property, **State** Property, **Tag** Property

Events

Close Event, **Connect** Event, **ConnectionRequest** Event, **DataArrival** Event, **Error** Event, **SendComplete** Event, **SendProgress** Event

Methods

Accept Method, **Bind** Method, **Close** Method (Winsock Control), **Listen** Method, **PeekData** Method, **SendData** Method, **GetData** Method (WinSock Control)

Accept Method

For TCP server applications only. This method is used to accept an incoming connection when handling a **ConnectionRequest** event.

Applies To

Winsock Control

Syntax

object.**Accept** *requestID*

The *object* placeholder represents an object expression that evaluates to an object in the **Applies To** list.

Return Value

Void

Remarks

The **Accept** method is used in the **ConnectionRequest** event. The **ConnectionRequest** event has a corresponding argument, the **RequestID** parameter, that should be passed to the **Accept** method. An example is shown below:

```
Private Sub Winsock1_ConnectionRequest _
(ByVal requestID As Long)
   ' Close the connection if it is currently open
   ' by testing the State property.
   If Winsock1.State <> sckClosed Then Winsock1.Close

   ' Pass the value of the requestID parameter to the
   ' Accept method.
   Winsock1.Accept requestID
End Sub
```

The **Accept** method should be used on a new control instance (other than the one that is in the listening state.)

Data Type

Long

See Also

ConnectionRequest Event

Example

The example shows the code necessary to connect a **Winsock** control using the TCP protocol. The code runs on the machine that is accepting the connection request. The **RequestID** parameter identifies the request. This is passed to the **Accept** method which accepts the particular request.

```
Private Sub WinsockTCP_ConnectionRequest _
(requestID As Long)
   If Winsock1.State <> sckClosed Then Winsock1.Close
   Winsock.Accept requestID
End Sub
```

Bind Method

Specifies the LocalPort and LocalIP to be used for TCP connections. Use this method if you have multiple protocol adapters.

Applies To

Winsock Control

Syntax

object.**Bind** *LocalPort, LocalIP*

The **Bind** method syntax has these parts

Part	Description
object	An object expression that evaluates to an object in the **Applies To** list.
LocalPort	The port used to make a connection.
LocalIP	The local Internet address used to make a connection.

Remarks

You must invoke the **Bind** method before invoking the **Listen** method.

See Also

RemoteHost Property (ActiveX Controls), **RemotePort** Property (ActiveX Controls)

BytesReceived Property

Returns the amount of data received (currently in the receive buffer). Use the **GetData** method to retrieve data.

Read-only and unavailable at design time.

Applies To

Winsock Control

Syntax

object.**BytesReceived**

The *object* placeholder represents an object expression that evaluates to an object in the **Applies To** list.

Return Value

Long

See Also

DataArrival Event

Close Event

Occurs when the remote computer closes the connection. Applications should use the **Close** method to correctly close a TCP connection.

Applies To

Winsock Control

Syntax

*object*_**Close**( )

The *object* placeholder represents an object expression that evaluates to an object in the **Applies To** list.

Arguments

None

See Also

Close Method (Winsock Control)

Close Method (Winsock Control)

Closes a TCP connection or a listening socket for both client and server applications.

Applies To

Winsock Control

Syntax

object.**Close**

The *object* placeholder represents an object expression that evaluates to an object in the **Applies To** list.

Arguments

None

Return Value

Void

See Also

Close Event

Connect Method

Requests a connection to a remote computer.

See Also

RemoteHost Property (ActiveX Controls), **RemotePort** Property (ActiveX Controls), **Accept** Method, **Connection Request** Event

Applies To

Winsock Control

Syntax

*object.***Connect** *remoteHost, remotePort*

The **Connect** method syntax has these parts:

Part	Description
object	An object expression that evaluates to an object in the **Applies To** list.
remoteHost	Required. The name of the remote computer to connect to.
remotePort	The port of the remote computer to connect to.

Return Value

None

Remarks

You must invoke the Connect method when attempting to establish a TCP connection.

ConnectionRequest Event

Occurs when a remote machine requests a connection.

- For TCP server applications only. The event is activated when there is an incoming connection request. **RemoteHostIP** and **RemotePort** properties store the information about the client after the event is activated.

Applies To

Winsock Control

Syntax

*object_***ConnectionRequest** (*requestID* **As Long**)

The ConnectionRequest event syntax has these parts:

Part	Description
object	An object expression that evaluates to an object in the **Applies To** list.
requestID	The incoming connection request identifier. This argument should be passed to the **Accept** method on the second control instance.

Remarks

The server can decide whether or not to accept the connection. If the incoming connection is not accepted, the peer (client) will get the **Close** event. Use the **Accept** method (on a new control instance) to accept an incoming connection.

See Also

Accept Method

Example

The example shows the code necessary to connect a **Winsock** control using the TCP protocol. The code runs on the machine that is accepting the connection request. The **RequestID** parameter identifies the request. This is passed to the **Accept** method which accepts the particular request.

```
Private Sub WinsockTCP_ConnectionRequest _
(requestID As Long)
   If Winsock1.State <> sckClosed Then Winsock1.Close
   Winsock.Accept requestID
End Sub
```

DataArrival Event

Occurs when new data arrives.

Applies To

Winsock Control

Syntax

*object*_**DataArrival** (*bytesTotal* **As Long**)

The **DataArrival** event syntax has these parts:

Part	Description
object	An object expression that evaluates to an object in the **Applies To** list.
bytesTotal	Long. The total amount of data that can be retrieved.

Remarks

This event will not occur if you do not retrieve all the data in one **GetData** call. It is activated only when there is new data. Use the **BytesReceived** property to check how much data is available at any time.

BytesReceived Property, **SendData** Method, **SendComplete** Event,
SendProgress Event

Example

The example uses the **GetData** method in the **DataArrival** event of a
Winsock control. When the event occurs, the code invokes the **GetData**
method to retrieve the data and store it in a string variable. The data is
then written into a **TextBox** control.

```
Private Sub Winsock1_DataArrival _
(ByVal bytesTotal As Long)
   Dim strData As String
   Winsock1.GetData strData, vbString
   Text1.Text = Text1.Text & strData
End Sub
```

Error Event

Occurs whenever an error occurs in background processing (for example,
failed to connect, or failed to send or receive in the background).

Applies To

Winsock Control

Syntax

*object*_**Error**(*number* **As Integer**, *Description* **As String**, *Scode* **As Long**,
    ↪ *Source* **As String**, *HelpFile* **as String**, *HelpContext* **As Long**,
    ↪ *CancelDisplay* **As Boolean**)

The **Error** event syntax has these parts:

Part	Description
object	An object expression that evaluates to an object in the **Applies To** list.
number	An integer that defines the error code. See **Settings** below for constants.
description	String containing error information.
Scode	The long SCODE
Source	String describing the error source.
HelpFile	String containing the help file name.
HelpContext	Help file context.
CancelDisplay	Indicates whether to cancel the display. The default is **False**, which is to display the default error message box. If you do not want to use the default message box, set CancelDisplay to **True**.

Settings

The settings for *number* are:

Constant	Value	Description
sckOutOfMemory	7	Out of memory
sckInvalidPropertyValue	380	The property value is invalid.
sckGetNotSupported	394	The property can't be read.
sckSetNotSupported	383	The property is read-only.
sckBadState	40006	Wrong protocol or connection state for the requested transaction or request.
sckInvalidArg	40014	The argument passed to a function was not in the correct format or in the specified range.
sckSuccess	40017	Successful.
sckUnsupported	40018	Unsupported variant type.
sckInvalidOp	40020	Invalid operation at current state
sckOutOfRange	40021	Argument is out of range.
sckWrongProtocol	40026	Wrong protocol for the requested transaction or request
sckOpCanceled	1004	The operation was canceled.
sckInvalidArgument	10014	The requested address is a broadcast address, but flag is not set.
sckWouldBlock	10035	Socket is non-blocking and the specified operation will block.
sckInProgress	10036	A blocking Winsock operation in progress.
sckAlreadyComplete	10037	The operation is completed. No blocking operation in progress
sckNotSocket	10038	The descriptor is not a socket.
sckMsgTooBig	10040	The datagram is too large to fit into the buffer and is truncated.
sckPortNotSupported	10043	The specified port is not supported.
sckAddressInUse	10048	Address in use.
sckAddressNotAvailable	10049	Address not available from the local machine.
sckNetworkSubsystemFailed	10050	Network subsystem failed.
sckNetworkUnreachable	10051	The network cannot be reached from this host at this time.
sckNetReset	10052	Connection has timed out when SO_KEEPALIVE is set.
sckConnectAborted	11053	Connection is aborted due to timeout or other failure.
sckConnectionReset	10054	The connection is reset by remote side.
sckNoBufferSpace	10055	No buffer space is available.

(continued)

Constant	Value	Description
sckAlreadyConnected	10056	Socket is already connected.
sckNotConnected	10057	Socket is not connected.
sckSocketShutdown	10058	Socket has been shut down.
sckTimedout	10060	Socket has been shut down.
sckConnectionRefused	10061	Connection is forcefully rejected.
sckNotInitialized	10093	WinsockInit should be called first.
sckHostNotFound	11001	Authoritative answer: Host not found.
sckHostNotFoundTryAgain	11002	Non-Authoritative answer: Host not found.
sckNonRecoverableError	11003	Non-recoverable errors.
sckNoData	11004	Valid name, no data record of requested type.

GetData Method (WinSock Control)

Retrieves the current block of data and stores it in a variable of type variant.

Applies To

Winsock Control

Return Value

Void

Syntax

object.**GetData** *data*, [*type*,] [*maxLen*]

The **GetData** method syntax has these parts:

Part	Description
object	An object expression that evaluates to an object in the **Applies To** list.
data	Where retrieved data will be stored after the method returns successfully. If there is not enough data available for requested type, *data* will be set to Empty.
type	Optional. Type of data to be retrieved, as shown in **Settings**.
maxLen	Optional. Specifies the desired size when receiving a byte array or a string. If this parameter is missing for byte array or string, all available data will be retrieved. If provided for data types other than byte array and string, this parameter is ignored.

Settings

The settings for *type* are:

Description	Constant
Byte	**vbByte**
Integer	**vbInteger**
Long	**vbLong**
Single	**vbSingle**
Double	**vbDouble**
Currency	**vbCurrency**
Date	**vbDate**
Boolean	**vbBoolean**
SCODE	**vbError**
String	**vbString**
Byte Array	**vbArray + vbByte**

Remarks

It's common to use the **GetData** method with the **DataArrival** event, which includes the *totalBytes* argument. If you specify a *maxlen* that is less than the *totalBytes* argument, you will get the warning 10040 indicating that the remaining bytes will be lost.

Example

The example uses the **GetData** method in the **DataArrival** event of a **Winsock** control. When the event occurs, the code invokes the **GetData** method to retrieve the data and store it in a string variable. The data is then written into a **TextBox** control.

```
Private Sub Winsock1_DataArrival _
(ByVal bytesTotal As Long)
   Dim strData As String
   Winsock1.GetData strData, vbString
   Text1.Text = Text1.Text & strData
End Sub
```

Listen Method

Creates a socket and sets it in listen mode. This method works only for TCP connections.

Applies To

Winsock Control

Syntax

*object.***Listen**

The *object* placeholder represents an object expression that evaluates to an object in the **Applies To** list.

Arguments

None

Return Value

Void

Remarks

The **ConnectionRequest** event occurs when there is an incoming connection. When handling **ConnectionRequest**, the application should use the **Accept** method (on a new control instance) to accept the connection.

See Also

Close Method (Winsock Control)

LocalHostName Property

Returns the local machine name. Read-only and unavailable at design time.

Applies To

Winsock Control

Syntax

object.**LocalHostName**

The *object* placeholder represents an object expression that evaluates to an object in the **Applies To** list.

Return Value

String

LocalIP Property

Returns the IP address of the local machine in the IP address dotted string format (xxx.xxx.xxx.xxx).Read-only and unavailable at design time.

Applies To

Winsock Control

Syntax

object.**LocalIP**

The *object* placeholder represents an object expression that evaluates to an object in the **Applies To** list.

Data Type

String

LocalPort Property

Returns or sets the local port to use. Read/Write and available at design time.

- For the client, this designates the local port to send data from. Specify port 0 if the application does not need a specific port. In this case, the control will select a random port. After a connection is established, this is the local port used for the TCP connection.

- For the server, this is the local port to listen on. If port 0 is specified, a random port is used. After invoking the **Listen** method, the property contains the actual port that has been selected.

Applies To

Winsock Control

Syntax

object.**LocalPort** = *long*

The *object* placeholder represents an object expression that evaluates to an object in the **Applies To** list.

Remarks

Port 0 is often used to establish connections between computers dynamically. For example, a client that wishes to be "called back" by a server can use port 0 to procure a new (random) port number, which can then be given to the remote computer for this purpose.

Data Type

Long

PeekData Method

Similar to **GetData** except **PeekData** does not remove data from the input queue. This method works only for TCP connections.

Applies To

Winsock Control

Syntax

object.**PeekData** *data*, [*type*,] [*maxLen*]

The **PeekData** method syntax has these parts

Part	Description
object	An object expression that evaluates to an object in the **Applies To** list.
data	Stores retrieved data after the method returns successfully. If there is not enough data available for requested type, *data* will be set to Empty.

(continued)

Part	Description
type	Optional. Type of data to be retrieved, as described in **Settings**. Default Value: **vbArray + vbByte**.
maxLen	Optional. Length specifies the desired size when receiving a byte array or a string. If this argument is missing for byte array or string, all available data will be retrieved. If provided for data types other than byte array and string, this argument is ignored.

Settings

The settings for *type* are:

Type	Constant
Byte	**vbByte**
Integer	**vbInteger**
Long	**vbLong**
Single	**vbSingle**
Double	**vbDouble**
Currency	**vbCurrency**
Date	**vbDate**
Boolean	**vbBoolean**
SCODE	**vbError**
String	**vbString**
Byte Array	**vbArray + vbByte**

Return Value

Void

Remarks

If the type is specified as **vbString**, string data is converted to UNICODE before returning to the user.

See Also

GetData Method (WinSock Control)

Protocol Property (Winsock Control)

Returns or sets the protocol, either TCP or UDP, used by the **Winsock** control.

Applies To

Winsock Control

Syntax

object.**Protocol** *[=protocol]*

The *object* placeholder represents an object expression that evaluates to an object in the **Applies To** list.

Settings

The settings for *protocol* are:

Constant	Value	Description
sckTCPProtocol	0	Default. TCP protocol.
sckUDPProtocol	1	UDP protocol.

Return Value

Void

Remarks

The control must be closed (using the **Close** method) before this property can be reset.

RemoteHost Property (ActiveX Controls)

Returns or sets the remote machine to which a control sends or receives data. You can either provide a host name, for example, "FTP://ftp.microsoft.com," or an IP address string in dotted format, such as "100.0.1.1".

Applies To

Microsoft Internet Transfer Control, **Winsock** Control

Syntax

object.**RemoteHost** = *string*

The **RemoteHost** property syntax has these parts:

Part	Description
object	An object expression that evaluates to an object in the **Applies To** list.
string	The name or address of the remote computer.

Remarks

When this property is specified, the **URL** property is updated to show the new value. Also, if the host portion of the URL is updated, this property is also updated to reflect the new value.

The **RemoteHost** property can also be changed when invoking the **OpenURL** or **Execute** methods.

At run time, changing this value has no effect until the next connection.

Data Type

String

See Also

Bind Method

RemoteHostIP Property

Returns the IP address of the remote machine.

- For client applications, after a connection has been established using the **Connect** method, this property contains the IP string of the remote machine.

- For server applications, after an incoming connection request (ConnectionRequest event), this property contains the IP string of the remote machine that initiated the connection.

- When using the UDP protocol, after the **DataArrival** event occurs, this property contains the IP address of the machine sending the UDP data.

Applies To

Winsock Control

Syntax

object.**RemoteHostIP**

The *object* placeholder represents an object expression that evaluates to an object in the **Applies To** list.

Data Type

String

RemotePort Property (ActiveX Controls)

Returns or sets the remote port number to connect to.

Applies To

Microsoft Internet Transfer Control, **Winsock** Control

Syntax

object.**RemotePort** = *port*

The **RemotePort** property syntax has these parts:

Part	Description
object	An object expression that evaluates to an object in the **Applies To** list.
port	The port to connect to. The default value of this property is 80.

Remarks

When you set the **Protocol** property, the **RemotePort** property is set automatically to the appropriate default port for each protocol. Default port numbers are shown in the table below:

Port	Description
80	HTTP, commonly used for World Wide Web connections.
21	FTP.

Data Type

Long

See Also

Bind Method

SendComplete Event

Occurs when a send operation is completed.

Applies To

Winsock Control

Syntax

*object*_**SendComplete**

The *object* placeholder represents an object expression that evaluates to an object in the **Applies To** list.

Arguments

None

See Also

DataArrival Event, **SendProgress** Event

SendData Method

Sends data to a remote computer.

Applies To

Winsock Control

Return Value

Void

Syntax

object.**SendData** *data*

The **SendData** method syntax has these parts

Part	Description
object	An object expression that evaluates to an object in the **Applies To** list.
data	Data to be sent. For binary data, byte array should be used.

Remarks

When a UNICODE string is passed in, it is converted to an ANSI string before being sent out on the network.

SendProgress Event

Occurs while data is being sent.

Applies To

Winsock Control

Syntax

*object*_**SendProgress** (*bytesSent* **As Long**, *bytesRemaining* **As Long**)

The **SendProgress** event syntax has these parts:

Part	Description
object	An object expression that evaluates to an object in the **Applies To** list.
bytesSent	The number of bytes that have been sent since the last time this event was activated.
bytesRemaining	The number of bytes in the send buffer waiting to be sent.

See Also

DataArrival Event, **SendComplete** Event

SocketHandle Property

Returns a value that corresponds to the socket handle the control uses to communicate with the **Winsock** layer. Read-only and unavailable at design time.

Applies To

Winsock Control

Syntax

object.**SocketHandle**

The *object* placeholder represents an object expression that evaluates to an object in the **Applies To** list.

Remarks

This property was designed to be passed to Winsock APIs.

Data Type

Long

State Property (Winsock Control)

Returns the state of the control, expressed as an enumerated type. Read-only and unavailable at design time.

Applies To

Winsock Control

Syntax

object.**State**

The *object* placeholder represents an object expression that evaluates to an object in the **Applies To** list.

Settings

The settings for the **State** property are:

Constant	Value	Description
sckClosed	0	Default. Closed
sckOpen	1	Open
sckListening	2	Listening
sckConnectionPending	3	Connection pending
sckResolvingHost	4	Resolving host
sckHostResolved	5	Host resolved
sckConnecting	6	Connecting
sckConnected	7	Connected
sckClosing	8	Peer is closing the connection
sckError	9	Error

Data Type

Integer

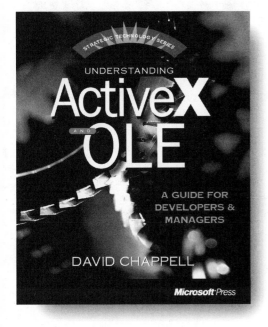

The *superfast* *way* to *get to* Java!

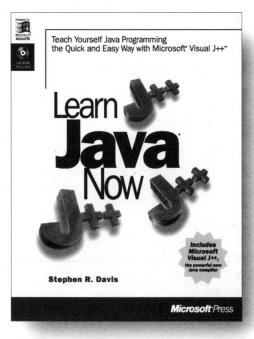

Teach Yourself Java Programming
the Quick and Easy Way with Microsoft® Visual J++™

Learn Java Now

Includes Microsoft Visual J++, the powerful new Java compiler

Stephen R. Davis

Microsoft Press

Looking for a better way to port your programming skills to the Internet? Congratulations, you just found it. Everything you need is in this unique package. The book is designed to help you quickly learn Microsoft® Visual J++™, Microsoft's powerful Java™ compiler. And on the book's enclosed CD-ROM, you'll find the Publisher's Edition of Microsoft Visual J++ version 1.0—a fully functional version of the product featuring the industry's leading integrated development environment, Microsoft Developer Studio. So why wait? Add exciting interactivity to your Internet or intranet Web sites. LEARN JAVA NOW!

U.S.A.	**$39.95**
U.K.	£37.49 [V.A.T. included]
Canada	$54.95
ISBN 1-57231-428-1	

Microsoft® Press

Register Today!

Return this
Microsoft® Visual Basic® 5.0
ActiveX™ Controls Reference
registration card for
a Microsoft Press® catalog

U.S. and Canada addresses only. Fill in information below and mail postage-free. Please mail only the bottom half of this page.

1-57231-508-3A   *MICROSOFT® VISUAL BASIC® 5.0*   *Owner Registration Card*
                         ACTIVEX™ CONTROLS REFERENCE

_____

NAME

_____

INSTITUTION OR COMPANY NAME

_____

ADDRESS

_____

CITY   STATE   ZIP

Microsoft®Press
Quality Computer Books

**For a free catalog of
Microsoft Press® products, call
1-800-MSPRESS**